NEW OXFORD HISTORY OF MUSIC
VOLUME VIII

THE 'FONTAINE DE LA RÉGÉNÉRATION' ON THE SITE OF THE BASTILLE
(1793)

On 10 August 1793 the anniversary of the storming of the Tuileries was celebrated by a festival including the first performance of Gossec's arrangement of the 'Hymne de la République' ('Hymne des Marseillais') for soloists, chorus, and band.

THE AGE OF BEETHOVEN 1790–1830

EDITED BY

GERALD ABRAHAM

LONDON

OXFORD UNIVERSITY PRESS

NEW YORK   MELBOURNE

1982

Oxford University Press, Walton Street, Oxford OX2 6DP

OXFORD LONDON GLASGOW NEW YORK
TORONTO MELBOURNE AUCKLAND CAPE TOWN
NAIROBI DAR ES SALAAM TOKYO
KUALA LUMPUR SINGAPORE HONG KONG
DELHI BOMBAY CALCUTTA MADRAS KARACHI

ISBN 0 19 316308 X

First published 1982

780 9
42298

British Library Cataloguing in Publication Data

The New Oxford history of music.
  Vol. 8: The age of Beethoven 1790–1830
    1. Music—History and criticism
    I. Abraham, Gerald
    780'.9   ML160
    ISBN 0-19-316308-X

Library of Congress Cataloging in Publication Data
Main entry under title:

The Age of Beethoven, 1790–1830.

  (New Oxford history of music; v. 8)
  Bibliography: p.
  Includes index
  1. Music—History and criticism—18th century.
  2. Music—History and criticism—19th century.
  I. Abraham, Gerald, 1904–   . II. Series.
  ML160.N44 vol. 8   780'.9s   82–6413
  ISBN 0-19-316308-X   [780'.903'3]   AACR2

Typeset by William Clowes (Beccles) Limited, Beccles and London
Printed and bound in Great Britain at the University Press, Oxford
by Eric Buckley, Printer to the University

INTRODUCTION

By GERALD ABRAHAM

THE title of no other volume of the *New Oxford History of Music* includes the name of a composer. But no other period of musical history is so completely dominated by one composer; in popular thought the years 1790 to 1830 are the Age of Beethoven. It is certainly a convenient title if not an accurate one. It is only partially accurate, for to the contemporary musical world the 1790s were dominated by Haydn whose last and greatest works of that decade are discussed in Volume VII. But when in 1803 the old Prospero ended his 'heavenly music' and broke his staff with Op. 103, the 'Eroica' was being composed. The music of the 1790s was not essentially affected by the French Revolution; it suggested some opera-subjects, some bad programme-music, and inspired a great Mass *in tempore belli* – and a number of composers took refuge in England. But the first decade and a half of the new century, the period of Beethoven's greatest creative activity, was the last, Imperial, period of French classicism – in opera with Spontini, in painting with the later David. When it was over and a badly shaken Europe emerged from the dust of universal war, a new wave of romanticism mingled with self-conscious nationalism washed over it. There had been elements of subjective pre-romanticism in the keyboard fantasias of C. P. E. Bach and Mozart, and in isolated movements by Haydn, which lived on in the early piano sonatas of Beethoven, in Clementi and Dussek. But there was nothing romantic in the music of the French Revolution, nor anything nationalistic or even revolutionary; the music of the colossal open-air festivals was equally lacking in national colour and in novelty of idiom; it was intended to be super-national and for the masses. When the same composers – Gossec, Méhul, Catel, Le Sueur, Berton, Cherubini, all professors at the Conservatoire de Musique founded by the Convention nationale in 1795 – turned to opera they produced works in the classical-heroic line of Gluck which they embellished with heroic-triadic themes. The influence of the Revolutionary upheaval was manifested mainly in the intensified cultivation of the by no means new genre of 'rescue opera', while the wars of the young Republic excited the quasi-military opening concerto movements of the violinist composers Kreutzer, Baillot, and Rode.

These men and their work were not lost on Beethoven as he entered his maturity. Asked by Cipriani Potter in 1817, 'Who is the greatest living composer, yourself excepted?', he replied 'Cherubini'. In the first years of maturity he had opened a great symphony with an heroic-triadic theme and rivalled Cherubini with a rescue opera which owes musical ideas as well as its subject to a French source and borrows its most dramatic stroke from Méhul's *Hélèna*. A few years later he opened his greatest piano concerto with a quasi-military Allegro. The artistic landmarks of the Consulate and Empire are such things as David's later paintings from 'Napoleon crossing the Great St. Bernard' (1800) onward, the operas of Spontini, *La Vestale* (1807) and *Fernand Cortez* (1809), and Méhul's *Joseph* (1807). But the spirit of the age is more comprehensively captured and preserved in Beethoven's first eight symphonies (1799–1812), his chamber music from the 'Razumovsky' quartets of 1806 to the 'Archduke' works of 1811–12, the piano sonatas from the 'Pathétique' (1799) to Op. 90 (1814).

Post-war – or post-Congress – Beethoven is strikingly different: the piano sonatas, Opp. 101–111 (1816–22), the quartets that followed them, Opp. 127–135 (1824–6), and two works fundamentally different from anything he had written before, the Ninth Symphony and *Missa solemnis* on which he worked side by side during 1818–23. It is impossible to describe these as 'classical'. And they are 'heroic' only in a personal sense; they do not absorb heroism from the ambience as the 'Eroica', *Fidelio*, the Fifth and Seventh Symphonies, the 'Emperor', the 'Waldstein', and the 'Appassionata' do. Classical forms appear liquescent from Op. 101 onward; they are latent, not obvious as in Haydn, Mozart, and his own earlier compositions. In this, but in little else, he was in harmony with the spirit of the new age exemplified by the violin concerto *in modo di scena concertante* (1816) of the 32-year-old Spohr and the 35-year-old Weber's *Concert-Stück* for piano and orchestra (1821). These younger men were also, like the still unknown Schubert of the B minor Symphony, making orchestral sound more plastic, sensuous, and colourful as John Field and others were doing with pianistic sound. Here already the musical language of mature romanticism was being formed.

In Beethoven there are plenty of premonitions of romanticism but not its full ripening. The romantic instrumental composers were more and more concerned with the expression of defined emotions, even pictorial or literary images: Beethoven during his last ten or twelve years was, except in the Mass and Ninth Symphony, almost exclusively concerned with the ineffable. He had become a more and more isolated figure, immensely respected but detached in spirit from the musical scene rather than at its centre. And not only from the musical scene. Although post-war Europe was for the rest of his life not so very different from pre-Revolution Europe, with Bourbon kings sitting once more on the throne of France and reigning again at Naples, there had been drastic territorial reshufflings and power changes in the German states; the lid was firmly placed on the cauldron of political ideas but youthful excitement found outlets in literary, artistic, and musical romanticism, in admiration for Byron and Scott, Géricault and Delacroix and Weber.

One important symptom of romanticism, consciousness of nationality, was particularly strong in Germany. Sense of German nationhood, of a common 'fatherland', had been stifled by particularism. German-speaking Austria at the head of a barely existent *Reich* but with various non-German appendages, was generally regarded as a separate entity. The new, victorious and again aggressive, Prussia was disliked for other reasons. Even the people of the smallest states ruled by their own dynasties regarded each other as foreigners. When, after the Treaty of Amiens in 1803, the remainder of the Duchy of Cleves was handed over to France and the government officials were moved to the Bishopric of Münster little more than sixty miles away, they were met there with more hostility than sympathy. On the other hand the French were far from unwelcome in Napoleon's Federation of the Rhine and he remained a hero to many Germans after the war – witness Wilhelm Hauff's *Novelle, Das Bild des Kaisers* (*c.* 1826). Hauff himself was an admirer of Napoleon, as was Goethe – who told Eckermann in 1829 that 'the hero grows in stature as more is known about him'. All through the war Goethe had remained above the battle. For ten years he and Schiller had worked away quietly at Weimar ignoring the horrors of the Revolution and the overthrow of the old Europe. When Schiller died and the French occupied Weimar after Jena, the 'enemy' officer who saved Goethe's house from pillage was the son of his old love Elisabeth von Türckheim, the Lili of *Dichtung und Wahrheit*. Later he accepted the Cross of the Legion of Honour and after 1812 told the German people to be content to rattle their chains: 'The man is too big for you; you will never break them'. He forbade his son to join the patriotic volunteers in 1813, buried himself in oriental studies during the War of Liberation, and celebrated victory in an uninspired *Festspiel*. And Napoleon was still posthumously glorified in Germany in such well-known poems as Zedlitz's 'Nächtliche Heerschau', which was to be set by Loewe, and Heine's 'Zwei Grenadiere' (composed by both Schumann and Wagner).

Admiration of Napoleon and French culture was dimmed not so

much by military humiliation – the states of the Rhine Confederation which included Bavaria, Württemberg, and Baden had not been humiliated – as by the military victory dominated by resurgent Prussia. In the dark days before the resurgence Prussian writers and thinkers – Fichte, August Schlegel, Kleist, Arndt – had proclaimed the need for a sense of nationhood. Yet the longing for a pan-German culture was felt less strongly in Prussia and Austria than, paradoxically, by elements in the Rhenish and south German states. Arnim and Brentano had given an impulse with their collection of old German folk-poems, *Des Knaben Wunderhorn* (Heidelberg, 1806–8), in the steps of Herder's *Alte Volkslieder*,[1] but it was the Saxon Theodor Körner, the Franconian Rückert, the adopted Rhinelander Arndt, who wrote the new *Vaterlandslieder*. Arndt led the way with such poems as 'Was ist des Deutschen Vaterland?', 'Der Gott, der Eisen wachsen liess', and 'Sind wir vereint zur guten Stunde', but it was Körner whose *Leyer und Schwerdt* collection inspired both Schubert and Weber.

Schubert was no doubt a patriotic Austrian but too completely Viennese to have strong pan-German feelings; most of his music was composed in the post-Congress *Biedermeier* ambience of relief and relaxation after the alarms and stresses of war. Weber worked all over Germany but it was in Dresden, another cosy home of *Biedermeier* feeling, that he contributed to the *Abendzeitung* (27 January 1817) an article pointing out that

The art-forms of all other nations have always expressed themselves more distinctly than those of the Germans. . . . The Italian and the Frenchman have formed a style of opera in which they can work satisfactorily. Not so the German. It is peculiarly characteristic of him to take to himself what is excellent in others and demand constant progressive advance: but he grasps everything *more deeply*. Whereas others aim for the most part at the voluptuousness of separate moments, *he* wants a finished work of art in which all the parts are rounded off and united.

He himself came nearest to that ideal, musically, in *Euryanthe* (1823), which he styled *Grosse heroisch-romantische Oper*, though he had composed a more thoroughly German *Romantische Oper*, *Der Freischütz*, two years earlier. With E. T. A. Hoffmann's *Undine* (1816) and Spohr's *Faust, Jessonda*, and *Berggeist* (1816–25) German romantic opera was now fairly launched and Marschner was soon to follow with *Der Vampyr* (1828) and *Der Templer und die Jüdin* (1829).

---

[1] Herder's better known international collection, *Stimmen der Völker in Liedern* was published posthumously in 1807.

Weber's free use of reminiscence themes and his handling of orchestral colours and textures were basic elements in the musical language of romanticism, yet it was probably the *Lied* rather than *romantische Oper* that most deeply penetrated the German consciousness during the 1820s: the *Lieder* of Schubert – who was then known for little else – Marschner, and Loewe. And the *Lied* composer was less liable than the opera-composer to be distracted by siren voices from Italy, Rossini's in particular. Another foreign ingredient of romanticism was beginning to be noticed by French and Italian as well as German musicians but only superficially, in the choice of subjects, not in the musical substance. This was British literary romanticism, at first represented by Scott, though Loewe published settings of translations of Byron's *Hebrew Melodies* in 1826. Schubert's *Lady of the Lake* settings appeared in the same year; Rossini's *Donna del lago* had been performed seven years before, Auber's *Leicester* in 1823 and Boieldieu's *Dame blanche* in 1825. Marschner's *Templer* appeared at the end of the decade.

Thus the musical scene of the 1820s was totally different from that of the 1790s; the Age of Beethoven was above all an age of transition. Yet Beethoven, who had played the leading role in the process for so long, now stood apart; times had changed and he had changed, but not with them. He does not belong to German romanticism. The conceptions of a political Germanic entity or a specifically German music would probably have been quite foreign to him. His admiration for Napoleon, though not constant and absolute like Goethe's, persisted. In 1809 a French officer who visited him several times recorded that 'his mind was much occupied with the greatness of Napoleon, and he often spoke to me about it . . . [He] made me think that, despite his opinions, he would have felt flattered by any mark of distinction from Napoleon',[1] and in 1810 he considered dedicating the C major Mass to him.[2] Again, in 1824, he remarked to Czerny, 'Napoleon. At one time I couldn't bear him. Now I think quite differently'.[3] He had dominated the musical world as Napoleon had the political; now Napoleon was dead and he himself was withdrawing. The great posthumous quartets of 1824–6 do not overshadow the contemporary scene; they look far beyond it. Their influence on the music of the day was nil. The influence of the last piano sonatas was at the time limited to some features of Mendelssohn's E major Sonata,

[1] See J. G. Prodhomme, 'The Baron de Trémont', *Musical Quarterly*, vi (1920), p. 374.
[2] *Die Musik in Geschichte und Gegenwart*, i, col. 1530.
[3] A. W. Thayer, *Ludwig van Beethovens Leben*, completed and edited by Hermann Deiters and Hugo Riemann (second edition, Leipzig, 1923), v, p. 135.

Op. 6 (1826), a work much less romantic than the wonderful scherzo of the Octet he had already composed and of course far surpassed by the *Midsummer Night's Dream* overture he was about to write. To include that masterpiece in the Age of Beethoven seems paradoxical; it is better considered in a different context.[1]

[1] See Vol. IX, chap. 1.

CONTENTS

VI. BEETHOVEN'S CHAMBER MUSIC. *By* GERALD ABRAHAM

Chapters III, IV, and VII have been translated by Paul Hamburger.

ILLUSTRATIONS

THE 'FONTAINE DE LA RÉGÉNÉRATION' ON THE SITE OF THE BASTILLE (1793)

On 10 August 1793 the anniversary of the storming of the Tuileries was celebrated by a festival including the first performance of Gossec's arrangement of the 'Hymne de la République' ('Hymne des Marseillais') for soloists, chorus, and band.   *Frontispiece*

I

GENERAL MUSICAL CONDITIONS

By A. HYATT KING

WAR AND THE COMPOSER

THE French Revolution and the Napoleonic Wars constituted a sequence of events which coincided with one of the grand climacterics in musical history. Beneath the strain of prolonged warfare, the theory and practice of music underwent changes as far-reaching as those which at the same time transformed the economic and social structure of the Continent. In 1815 a nominal peace did come, but the aftermath of war and long uncertainty had repercussions on all the arts. In the world of music the restoration of the balance was as slow and painful a process as that by which the classical heritage was shaped to perfection even while the ideals of romanticism were taking form.

At one time or another, the greater part of Europe was engulfed in the struggle, but the lives of musicians, artists and writers were comparatively little affected, except in so far as they had to share the general hazards of the times and the widespread material hardship caused by blockade and counterblockade. In a few cases, however, war did strike harshly on the composer. The tale of the occupation of Vienna by the French in 1805 is well known: their presence contributed not a little to the withdrawal of Beethoven's *Fidelio* after three performances. Five years earlier Michael Haydn had suffered the loss of his personal property when the French captured Salzburg, but there do not appear to have been many instances of this kind. Travel remained relatively free. The lives of Clementi, Cramer, Hummel, Paganini, Vogler, Haydn, Weber, and many other composers and virtuosi testify to the freedom of movement enjoyed by musicians. Their mobility is certainly a tribute to their fortitude, because the vile condition of the roads and the primitive state of the inns differed little from those of the early 1770s of which Burney has drawn so graphic a picture.

PUBLISHING AND POPULAR TASTE

Despite the hindrances and risks of war, trade in music and instruments flourished, and even reached an unprecedented level. Thus, in the late 1790s Longman & Broderip were importing music freely from Vienna to London, while popular works of the day were published or on sale in many countries within a year or so of their actual composition. Trade in music flowed out from England with equal freedom, even as far as Spain. Protection under copyright law being then almost non-existent, the issue of pirated editions was frequent, a reprehensible practice made all the easier by the fecundity of many composers. Between 1790 and 1809, the year of Haydn's death, his works appeared at Venice, Amsterdam, Lisbon, Berlin, Paris, Vienna, London, and elsewhere – often without his knowledge or consent – in a continuous stream which testifies to wide public interest and steady demand, war conditions notwithstanding.

On lower levels of taste, the military background of the age is not hard to discern. Every country produced large numbers of popular regimental marches, of pieces descriptive of naval and land battles, sieges and campaigns, composed chiefly for the pianoforte. Here programme music sank to a deplorably low level; some editions include engravings of martial scenes at the head of each section, and a description in words of the action portrayed by the music. Two of the most popular purveyors were Daniel Steibelt and Franz Kotzwara. Not even Beethoven's *Wellingtons Sieg, oder die Schlacht bei Vittoria* (1813) could escape the taint of mediocrity. The gulf between ephemeral, popular music and its highest, most enduring forms, has seldom yawned so widely as it did during the Napoleonic wars.

OPERA AND NEW SOCIAL IDEAS

While sonata and symphony developed along the lines marked out before 1790, in opera a fresh element appeared, by no means unknown previously, but now surprising in the rapidity of its growth. It is probable that, even without the upheaval of social ideas wrought by the Revolution, the normal swing of the pendulum of taste would have brought a general revulsion against the opera of amorous intrigue and seduction, so long popular under the *ancien régime*. Before 1789, there were signs that a different kind of plot, of loftier design, was gaining ground. In moral fervour *Die Zauberflöte* (1791) anticipates *Fidelio* (1805), and between them stretched the years of uncertainty which made men long for domestic security and universal goodwill. What nobler message could opera seek to convey than the twin ideals of married bliss and the brotherhood of man? Even in Paris, during the wildest artistic extravagances of the Revolution and the First Empire, the 'rescue' opera,[1] which broadly stood for the triumph of heroic virtue over wickedness, never lost its vogue.

But the principle *corruptio optimi pessima* has rarely been a respecter of ideals, and in this era its working resulted in the pedestrian, somewhat mawkish type of *Singspiel* popularized by Weigl, linked to the plots of Kotzebue. The former's *Die Schweizerfamilie* (1809) and its feeble successors provide as ignoble a contrast to *Fidelio* as does Kotzwara's *Battle of Prague* to the 'Waldstein' Sonata. Weigl, in fact, personified the worst side of the *Biedermeier* outlook on life and art, which was to be the bane of progressive musical life and general culture in Germany, France, and England for many years. It stood, briefly, for a devotion to sentimental lyricism and middle-class respectability; it was devoid of imagination or symbolism, and lived wholly in the present; it shrank from the vague yearnings and deep pathos of romanticism.

Another innovation in opera, partly caused by the harshness of the times, was the introduction of the elements of magic and fantasy. These too had something of their origin in the popular *Singspiel*, well before 1789, but though their treatment was often uninspired, they could never become worse than childish or silly. Having no moral implications, magic and fantasy never suffered the same debasement as the ideals of *Fidelio*, and never exercised such harmful influence on the evolution of art as did the spread of 'Biedermeier' culture. Indeed, properly used, they could be most effective. The 'natürliche Zauber-oper', beloved of Schubert and his generation, had a respectable ancestry in *Die Zauberflöte* and many another 'magic' opera. For all its whimsical nonsense, this form could inspire music of genuinely poetical qualities.[2] This popularity of the supernatural was partly due to the strong desire, which quite regularly manifests itself in time of war and material hardship, to escape from the grim realities of life. If its operatic expression needs justification, it is found in the best of the music of Spohr's *Faust*, Hoffmann's *Undine*, and Weber's *Oberon*, *Euryanthe*, and *Freischütz*. Moreover, the artistic use of these elements had an even wider significance than their use in operatic plots.

---

[1] See Vol. VII, pp. 220–1, and *infra*, pp. 31–2.
[2] Cf. the chapter on Schubert's operas by the present writer in *Schubert: A Symposium*, ed. Gerald Abraham (London, 1947).

NATIONALISM

When German composers of opera conjured up the spirits of their native woods, mountains, and rivers, they were, perhaps unwittingly, expressing something that symbolised of the wave of national feeling which was beginning to rise all over Europe. In Great Britain, this tendency appeared in musical print earlier than elsewhere, for in 1793 George Thomson in Edinburgh began the publication of a long series of editions of Scottish, Irish, and Welsh melodies, the first of which went on, with many complex accretions, up till 1841. In order to make these collections more attractive, he enlisted at various times the services of Haydn, Beethoven, Hummel, Weber, and Pleyel, to provide piano accompaniments with violin and cello *ad libitum*, though often in a totally alien style.[1] Besides William Whyte's rival volumes (Edinburgh, 1806–7) and James and William Power's famous series of *Moore's Irish Melodies* (Dublin, 1807–34), these years produced many lesser collections, which all served to foster throughout the British Isles a growth in musical self-consciousness.

In France, the fury of nationalism found vocal expression at this time less in the collection of old melodies than in the writing of new ones; of these Rouget de Lisle's 'La Marseillaise,' today by far the best known, was then but one of hundreds now mostly forgotten, though all were originally inspired by the same vibrant patriotism. In Switzerland pride in race and country was symbolized in the rich harvest of *Kuhreihen* or *Ranz des vaches* and other melodies of the hills and valleys. The earliest printed collection of these is apparently that of 1806, edited by Sigmund von Wagner: five more, published in or near Switzerland, appeared before 1830. In fact, in every German-speaking part of Europe, the collection and publication of old national melodies, whether sung by student, soldier, or peasant, soon became as sacred a duty as the composition of new ones. Inevitably, national song became the tool of political purpose. Weber's cycle, *Leyer und Schwert* (1814), set to Körner's famous lyrics, became the most famous of many similar compositions, and long proved capable of rousing intense feeling. Still more effective was the power of opera, above all if susceptible to political interpretation. Such were parts of Rossini's *Mosè*, in the Paris version of 1827. And Auber's *La Muette de Portici*, a tale of the Neapolitan rebellion of 1647, when produced at Brussels in 1830 sparked off the revolution that made Belgium independent of

---

[1] For biographical and historical details see Cecil Hopkinson and C. B. Oldman, 'Thomson's Collections of National Song. With special reference to the contributions of Haydn and Mozart', *Edinburgh Bibliographical Society Transactions* (1940) pt. 1, with 'addenda and corrigenda' in *Transactions*, iii (1954), pt. 2.

Holland. This power was to prove even greater in the next generation.

CONDITIONS IN ITALY

Italy claims first mention less for any outstanding characteristics than for the vast influence she exercised abroad. Internally, dynastic and social changes caused little shift in the balance of musical values, weighted as it was in favour of the tradition of opera. While public interest in instrumental music was shrinking to vanishing point, the composition of operas continued in an endless flood. Scarcely any other form of musical activity was of much moment. Incessant, nation-wide demand produced a gradual reduction in quality which may well have been further weakened by the steady dissipation abroad of men and ideas. For throughout the eighteenth century and during the first forty years or so of the nineteenth, Italian opera companies throve all over Europe. Even the most turbulent and depressing conditions could not sap the vitality of this hydra-headed form. Thus the nation with by far the widest musical influence developed a limitation of domestic outlook which became almost parochial. The lack of receptiveness thus fostered lasted well beyond the *Risorgimento*, and provides the background to the slow headway made by purely instrumental theory and practice.

ENGLAND

In the larger part of England, while cultural life pursued a tranquil course in elegant society, creative music sank to the nadir of triviality. John Braham's 'When the Bosom heaves the Sigh', and Bishop's 'Home, sweet Home' (inserted in his opera *Clari* in 1823) fairly represented the general level of operatic composition. Admirers of Wordsworth and Constable had to be content with Edward Griffin and J. B. Cramer as their counterparts in instrumental music. In the church, the talent of Thomas Attwood and Samuel Wesley was at least some compensation for the general mediocrity typified by the prolific John Clarke-Whitfeld.

Pianistic virtuosity both of native and visiting executants received increasing stimulus from the improved models of Broadwood, Stodart, and other makers. Orchestral music, having benefited greatly from Haydn's visits in the 1790s, was further encouraged by the foundation of the Philharmonic Society (1813) and grew in popularity despite the continued domination of Italian opera under royal patronage. Though concert-giving remained largely an upper-class affair, standards of judgement were slowly improving and interest was growing wider.

That the lute still enjoyed some popularity is shown by the tutor published by Longman & Broderip about 1800; the guitar and flute maintained and even strengthened their place in domestic accompaniment and performance, although the harp and pianoforte were rapidly gaining ground.

FRANCE

Conditions in France were in many ways unique. The leading revolutionaries quickly discovered the possibilities of music as an aid to enforcing the 'will of the people' and as a means of adding lustre to the Republic. Music became the servant of the state, the instrument of mass-suggestion, rigorously controlled and directed. Musical festivals on a gigantic scale were organized in Paris to mark every public event of note, culminating in the Fête de l'être suprème, 6–8 June 1794, in which a 'Hymn' was performed by 2,400 singers, with cannonades to accompany the refrain sung by a carefully rehearsed populace. This crude extravagance soon invaded French opera, which became ever more noisy and explosive, until Grétry was moved to observe that every opera seemed to re-enact the storming of the Bastille. Nevertheless general taste for progressive opera did improve, thanks largely to the influence of Rossini, whose cultivated elegance went far to redeem the earlier, indiscriminate enthusiasm under the Terror, when Cherubini's wife remarked to Ferdinand Hiller: 'In the morning the guillotine was kept busy and in the evening one could not get a seat in the theatre.'[1]

A few composers, among them Viotti, fled the country for ever. Pleyel left Paris for three years; one or two others suffered the fate of J. F. Edelmann who, after persecuting many victims during the Terror, was himself charged with treason and sent to the guillotine at Strasbourg. Most musicians, however, flourished under the new regime. A free school of music set up by the Paris National Guard soon became an 'Institut national de musique' and in 1795 the nucleus of the famous Paris Conservatoire which has lasted to this day. But there were some embarrassments among musicians appointed to important posts under the Republic when this was succeeded by the Empire and this in turn by the restored Monarchy. Nevertheless, Cherubini and Le Sueur were successful Vicars of Bray.

The opera house benefited from Napoleon's interest in music, although his dictatorial attitude aroused resentment. His taste tended, paradoxically, to quiet music and was carried to extremes when he

[1] Paul Henry Lang, *History of Music in Western Civilisation* (New York, 1942), p. 788.

ordered a performance of Catel's *Les Bayadères* with every instrument muted and all marks of expression cancelled. His personal treatment of musicians could be both wise and compassionate, as is shown in his dealings with Méhul and his grant of a pension to the aged Grétry. It was under Napoleon's government in 1803 that the *Grand Prix de Rome* for music was established by the reorganized Institut de France.

CENTRAL EUROPE

Any attempt to epitomize the rich and varied musical life in the German-speaking lands at this period can only become conspicuous for its omissions. By far the most important centre was Vienna, now, as for long past, the focus of conflicting influences.[1] The splendours of the Habsburg court still attracted all the multifarious talent from its outlying dominions, whence it continually derived fresh vitality. When the great Congress assembled in 1815, the musical and social life of the capital burgeoned anew. Side by side with the rise of art song among the middle class, Italian opera was all the rage, dominated by Rossini and the singular personality of Domenico Barbaja who controlled La Scala in Milan and San Carlo in Naples besides the Kärntnertor and An der Wien theatres in Vienna. Small wonder that German operas by Beethoven, Schubert, and others found little lasting favour with Viennese audiences. But even on this crowded scene, there was room for the perfecting of classical instrumental music.

Similar tendencies can be observed all over Germany, with the added difficulty for the historian that the country was still in a state of political disunity and that the enthusiastic ideals of the musicians themselves often appear muddled and bewildering. Whereas in England public music-making was concentrated in a few large towns, in Germany every city of any size or repute maintained a subsidized opera house, and provided corresponding facilities for concerts, the court being generally the centre of activity. Weber's whole life gives a cross-section of this richness and diversity, well exemplified by the success of *Der Freischütz*, which was given in twenty-two German cities within eighteen months of its first performance. But the thread which stands out brightest in the pattern of the early nineteenth century had been lacking in that of the eighteenth – namely the rapid and widespread growth of choral singing consequent on the foundation of the Berlin *Singakademie* by Carl Fasch in 1791.[2]

[1] See, for example, Marcel Brion's *Daily Life in the Vienna of Mozart and Schubert* (New York, 1962).
[2] See Georg Schünemann, *Die Singakademie zu Berlin 1791–1941* (Regensburg, 1941) and Friedrich Herzfeld, *Sing-Akademie zu Berlin* (Berlin, 1966), ed. Werner Bollert.

THE EUROPEAN PERIPHERY

In Russia, the backward state of the country favoured the prolongation of autocratic institutions, which led to curious anomalies. The court at St. Petersburg, though schooled in French manners, had early adopted Italian opera which flourished under the aegis of the tone-deaf Empress Catherine the Great.[1] (A French company did, however, enjoy a brief vogue, and one of the opera houses was actually run from 1771 to 1805 by an Englishman named Michael Maddox.)[2]

Between 1750 and 1840 nearly every Italian composer of eminence and many non-Italians visited Russia: many accepted permanent posts there but soon discovered that liberal pay could not compensate for the havoc wrought by northern winters on a non-Russian constitution. This foreign domination was serious in that it raised obstacles to Russian creative talent and the expression of national feeling, but Italomania did not touch one popular form of instrumental music, the horn bands which flourished well into the nineteenth century. Wholly characteristic of a semi-feudal society, these were formed from the retainers of the great Russian nobles who vied with each other in their maintenance. Each performer played a hunting horn which was generally capable of producing but one note. Whole bands and individual players were bought and sold like football players of the twentieth century.[3]

In Spain, the ravages of the Peninsular War effectively destroyed the tree of national musical life which had been slowly trying to outgrow the tendrils of Italian vocalism. Even after the French invasion, prolonged civil discord nullified the efforts made by Boccherini and other instrumental composers to foster creative activity. During the 1820s opera, under the stimulus of foreign musicians such as Mercadante, remained on a stereotyped Italianate level. But despite this, the native *tonadilla* took root and flourished. In Poland, torn by war and power politics, the efforts of a few native composers were submerged by the Italians. Practically all the other smaller European countries show the same picture – the struggle of the indigenous musician against the facile, all-pervading brilliance from the Mediterranean, which battened on the patronage of the royal courts. But dawn of the free expression of native musical ideals and traditions was at hand, nearer perhaps, and richer in possibilities than

[1] On 19 November 1778, she wrote to Baron Grimm: 'Je meurs d'envie d'écouter et d'aimer la musique: mais j'ai beau faire, c'est du bruit et puis c'est tout'. *Correspondence artistique de Grimm avec Catherine II*, xvii (Paris, 1932).

[2] See R.-Aloys Mooser *Annales de la musique et des musiciens en Russie au XVIIIᵉ siécle* (three vols., Geneva, 1948–51), ii, pp. 158–9.

[3] An illustration of a horn band is given in Grove, 5th ed., vi, pl. 28. The best study is by K. A. Vertkov, *Russkaya rogovaya muzïka* (Leningrad and Moscow, 1948).

any could dare to imagine during the grey, uncertain years that followed the Congress of Vienna.

AMERICA

In the United States, all round the eastern seaboard from Portland, Maine, to New Orleans, there were scattered many cities where an active musical life had grown up in the late seventeenth and early eighteenth centuries and continued to flourish after the pattern of that in such cities as Norwich, Bristol, or Dublin. New York, Boston, Charleston, for instance, had proved themselves speedily receptive to European tastes and developments. There was a continuous demand for opera. In 1794 Paisiello's *Il barbiere di Siviglia* was heard in several cities; Rossini's work of the same title reached New York in 1819, where Mozart's *Le nozze di Figaro* was given (in Bishop's perversion) in 1824. Boieldieu's *La Dame blanche* of 1825 reached New York within two years. French operatic companies regularly visited the southern states.[1] Partly because of the popularity of opera, concert life declined, but new influences arose. In 1819 the Beethoven Society of Portland was founded, and it is noteworthy that in 1815 the famous Handel and Haydn Society of Boston had asked Beethoven for a composition. Other organizations gave a steady impetus to the performance of oratorios.

One of the most influential bodies was the Musical Society of Stoughton, founded in 1786 by William Billings.[2] It became a powerful influence in popularizing the singing of hymns and psalms, and later included secular choral music.

In composition, any substantial creative effort by American-born composers still lay ahead, as did also any systematic approach to the problem of giving public instruction in music. But the sheer variety of performance, though limited in its social level, prepared the way for tremendous developments in the mid-nineteenth century.

STATUS AND OUTLOOK OF THE MUSICIAN

When Clementi, distraught after the death of his first wife, began a three-year period of wandering over Europe, he was, according to his friend William Gardiner[3] 'permitted by Bonaparte to pass through

---

[1] The first definite reference to opera in New Orleans was in 1796, with Grétry's *Sylvain*, which quite possibly had been performed there earlier. A permanent opera company was established in New Orleans in 1819 and toured the northern cities from 1827 to 1833. See Henry A. Kmen, *Music in New Orleans, the Formative Years 1791–1841* (Baton Rouge, 1966).

[2] See John Tasker Howard and George Kent Bellows, *A Short History of Music in America* (New York, 1957), p. 57.

[3] *Music and Friends* (London, 1838), i, p. 244.

the whole seat of war; and the same privilege was granted to him by the allied sovereigns'. This exceptional favour shows how highly distinguished musicians were now regarded and how changed their social status since 1781 when Mozart had been placed below the valets of the Archbishop of Salzburg's household.

For a generation before the Revolution, this change had been slowly working itself out in the lives of musicians of all degrees, but the first of the great classical composers to combine independence with security was Haydn. When his employer, Prince Nicholas Eszterházy, died, in 1790 Haydn was set free to travel and to consolidate in person his widespread fame, though he was often somewhat bewildered by the ways of a larger world which, apart from Vienna, had been virtually unknown to him until his sixtieth year. It remained for his younger contemporaries to adapt themselves more successfully to changing conditions, and to seize the chances offered by the new order.

In Beethoven's lifetime the patronage of music went through one of its most liberal stages of development. It speaks volumes for the Viennese nobility that they could tolerate his uncouth self-assertiveness and even ensure him some sort of financial security without imposing terms or obligations. The dedications of many of Beethoven's works, though still somewhat effusive, reflect a degree of appreciation more discriminating than that of the preceding era when gold rings, watches, and snuff-boxes were usually the only tangible reward of sycophantic expressions of loyalty. Beethoven was exceptionally fortunate in his independence, though perhaps he did not fully appreciate the fact.

Vogler, one of the most active musical travellers of his day, was for many years *Kapellmeister* to the King of Sweden, and presumably had to fit in his wanderings to Greece and North Africa with some attention to his official duties. Salieri, on the other hand, left Vienna only four times during the fifty years of his office (1774–1824). A composer who was also a distinguished executant need no longer fear poverty if he chose to seek freedom from court employment. In 1804 Hummel took service as *Kapellmeister* with the Prince Eszterházy and held the post until 1811. Then, returning to Vienna, he spent four years unattached; in 1816 he entered service again, this time at Stuttgart, whence he moved in 1819 to Weimar. Here, with frequent absences for lengthy tours as conductor and pianist, he stayed until his death in 1837. There are many other instances in this period of the wise tolerance shown towards the whims of musical genius by the nobility, who realized that liberal treatment paid a good dividend.

An equally humane attitude began to prevail towards orchestras, whose members would not have brooked discipline even half as rigorous as that imposed by Frederick the Great or Cannabich. The courts discerned that they would not retain good men by harshness, for this was likely to drive them to seek employment elsewhere. A growing sense of sturdy individualism sometimes led to the formation of independent orchestras. Before long, some of these co-operative bodies became influential enough themselves to assume the mantle of patronage, as in 1822 when the Philharmonic Society of London commissioned the Choral Symphony from Beethoven. But this rising individualism by no means supplanted the princely orchestras which lasted, though in declining numbers, long after the death of Schubert.

Schubert, indeed, may be taken as the example of an entirely new type of musician, whose intensely personal art had little affinity with court life but really belonged to the growing middle class. This, coupled with the fecklessness of Schubert's own character, had much to do with the origin of the popular nineteenth-century idea of the musician as a bohemian creature, vague and impractical, without deep roots even in his chosen milieu, indifferent to most of the conventions of society and utterly engrossed in the pursuit of his art. Assuredly, if singlemindedness may be taken as one of the hall-marks of the highest genius, may not diversity of interests be characteristic, perhaps even a cause, of its lesser manifestation? For in Schubert's time there lived two men very different in character from him, Weber and E. T. A. Hoffmann, whose phenomenal versatility can be briefly studied here as symbolic of the musician's new eagerness to win complete self-expression, and to assert the change in his own status.

Hoffmann was certainly the more remarkable of the two, and in himself he sums up and anticipates all the more important qualities of the later romantics. From a legal training, such as was to be the youthful lot of other musicians in the nineteenth century, he must have acquired some precision of thought which nevertheless seems curiously at variance with his later fanciful turn of mind and habits. Twice in his life he bade fair to become a successful civil servant, but such a narrow occupation would have stifled his literary and musical gifts. His critical writings on both literature and music are as important as his fantastic tales and novels. He applied himself with equal enthusiasm to painting, conducting, teaching, and the management of theatres, for which he composed eleven operas. Truly, as Carlyle wrote, 'he wasted faculties which might have seasoned the nectar of the gods'. He was, in fact, the greatest dilettante of them all.

Weber's life developed along lines less varied than those of

Hoffmann but more purposeful and quite as rich in colour. Trained from infancy to become a musician, he showed something of his versatility when in 1799 (his thirteenth year) he studied lithography with Alois Senefelder, its inventor.[1] Weber believed he could improve on its application to music printing and was so confident of his skill that on 9 December 1800 he made a business proposal for musical lithography to the Viennese publisher Artaria. Six years earlier his father had educated him in painting and drawing, to compensate for his slow musical development. Before he was 22, Weber took up the non-musical post of private secretary in Ludwig of Wurtemburg's wild establishment at Stuttgart, and here consolidated the experience of life which he had acquired in boyhood wandering with his father's theatrical company. All his life Weber remained an enthusiastic man of the theatre – composer, producer, manager, and conductor – but he also used successfully his literary gifts as novelist, librettist, and critic. He was sounder than Hoffmann, and in him the musician appears also as the confident, well-read, polished man of the world, at ease and respected in the highest social and literary circles.

Although these two musicians were unique in the degree to which they combined and used to advantage so many remarkable qualities, their versatility also serves to exemplify a widespread process. Many of their contemporaries pursued interests which, while not very striking individually, in sum show clearly how the musician had for some time been slowly developing as a practical citizen. A few older composers had managed to combine a life of varied adventure with periods of court service, but they were, on the whole, exceptional. One of them, Dittersdorf (1739–99), in his youth not only gained some experience as a soldier, but also proved his skill as forester and huntsman. Some in the next generation favoured more sedentary interests. For instance, in 1796, Reichardt, another musical man of letters, undertook the remarkable occupation of inspector of salt-mines near Halle, in an interval between two posts as *Kapellmeister*. Méhul, throughout the French Revolution, pursued with ever-increasing devotion his study of horticulture in general and of tulips in particular, on which he became a recognized authority. Such was the result of a boyhood spent in the gardens of Givet in the Ardennes. Méhul's interests were partly shared by Cherubini, who was an ardent student of botany. Not a few musicians founded businesses of one kind or another, among the more unusual being that of Viotti who in 1801 set up, though with ill success, as a wine merchant in London and

[1] On Senefelder and Weber, see Alec Hyatt King, *Four Hundred Years of Music Printing* (London, second edition, 1968), pp. 26 ff.

caused Sheridan to dub him 'Composer of wines and importer of music'.

MUSICIANS AS PUBLISHERS

Perhaps the form of business with the strongest appeal for musicians, apart from concert-promoting, was publishing, in which they played so large a part that it merits a brief outline. Composers had long been drawn to this trade. Byrd and Tallis had held a position of privileged monopoly under Queen Elizabeth and later Morley was given a licence to print. C. P. E. Bach acted, rather exceptionally, as publisher for many of his own works. In the later eighteenth century, however, the publisher-musician was more usually of the lower order of Bernhard Theodor Breitkopf (b. 1749) who set Goethe's *Jugend-Lieder* to music in 1769, but in 1777 abandoned the family business and set up his own in Russia. Among the next generation, Weber's skill in lithography has already been mentioned, and during his lifetime F. A. Hoffmeister,[1] a prolific composer of some charm but exiguous talents, built up as successful a publishing concern in Vienna as did the Andrés in Offenbach. Both Johann André and his son Johann Anton were good musicians and good publishers.[2] In Paris the First Empire saw the birth of something like a state-approved group of the most eminent 'Conservatoire' composers, which lasted from 1802 to 1811. Founded by Cherubini, it quickly expanded to include Méhul, Kreutzer, Rode, Boieldieu, and Isouard.[3] About 1795 Pleyel had established an independent business which scored an early success by issuing the first nearly complete edition of Haydn's quartets. In London, there were probably more musician-publishers than anywhere else. The names of Clementi, Cramer, Corri, Dussek, and Michael Kelly were the most famous.[4] As the century wore on their name became legion.

WIDER CULTURE OF MUSICIANS

The musician was beginning to emerge as the independent, versatile artist, sometimes linking practical knowledge of affairs with an almost

[1] See Alexander Weinmann, *Die Wiener Verlagswerke von Franz Anton Hoffmeister* (Vienna, 1964) (*Beiträge zur Geschichte des Alt-Wiener Musikverlages*, Reihe 2, Folge 8), pp. 1–14.

[2] For a study of the elder André as publisher, see Wolfgang Matthäus, *Johann André. Musikverlag zu Offenbach am Main. Verlagsgeschichte und Bibliographie 1772–1800*, i (Tutzing, 1973) (completed by Hans Schneider), pp. 15–20.

[3] See Constant Pierre, *Le Magasin de musique à l'usage des fêtes nationales et du Conservatoire* (Paris, 1895), chap. 6.

[4] Charles Humphries and William Smith, *Music Publishing in the British Isles from the Beginning until the Middle of the Nineteenth Century* (Oxford, second edition with supplement, 1970), pp. 28–37.

cosmopolitan breadth of interests. The classes of his origin were changing. From the early nineteenth-century onwards an ever-increasing number of great musicians sprang, like their contemporaries in painting and architecture, from the growing ranks of the professional classes. As a nursery of polished craftsmanship in music, the aristocracy was long to prove fertile, while the peasant and artisan classes became less productive of real genius; Haydn had few successors of the order of Dvořák. Professional musicians remained the steadiest and the most unpredictable source of all grades of genius.

Above all these material and social changes there stands out one factor, more vital and far-reaching than all the rest – the union of music and poetry, which constituted one of the earliest and most remarkable phases of the romantic movement. In 1799 Tieck issued Wackenroder's *Phantasien über die Kunst*, which he completed after Wackenroder's death; it proclaimed music to be an essential partner in real literary progress, and Jean Paul and Hölderlin echoed its sentiments.[1] This originally German idea was adopted to some extent by the romantics in other countries, but it was in Germany that it endured longest and bore most fruit. Before 1830 the only instance of this fusion of the arts is found in the mutual inspiration of Schubert's songs and the poetry of his friends and contemporaries. Hoffmann's great musical and literary gifts could not, because of his own nature, ensure their true and enduring union. Thereafter, because poets and novelists continued to hail music as the ideal art, their adulation tended to make the composer's approach to his problems ever more self-conscious. He gradually began to perceive, though dimly at first, the role that his genius was to play in the future development of the *Gesamtkunstwerk*:

> '. . . one law, one element,
> And one far-off divine event'

towards which much musical and poetic creation was beginning to move.

THE ORCHESTRA

Between 1790 and 1830 the composition of concert orchestras underwent little radical change. The forces used so resourcefully by Haydn in his twelve 'London' symphonies remained the basic norm. The actual number of string players slowly increased as the cellos won independence from the double basses. Wind and brass expanded little

[1] See Friedrich Blume, *Classic and Romantic Music, A Comprehensive Survey*, trans. M. D. Herter Norton (New York, 1970), pp. 68, 96–99, 100–1.

except for the occasional use of four horns, and the gradual introduction of three trombones. Only a few special works, such as Beethoven's Choral Symphony, called for heavy percussion, double bassoon and piccolo. Operatic scores, on the other hand, had long exceeded purely instrumental ones in their demands, a tradition which was maintained by *Die Zauberflöte* (1791), looks back to the power of Gluck at his weightiest and reaches forward through *Fidelio* to *Oberon*, to *Fierrabras* and *Guillaume Tell*. Especially did the operatic stage of Paris invite experiment and innovation. The score of Auber's *Muette de Portici* (1828), a characteristic French opera of that period, includes one ophicleide, drums, triangle, cymbals, and bass drum, but the more exotic instruments did not invade the realm of purely instrumental music in this time.

Oratorio often required as large forces as opera. A work by Johann Gottlieb Naumann given at Dresden in 1800 called for 100 players and 70 singers, fewer indeed than those employed for the Handel celebrations of 1784 in London but large enough to consolidate a tradition that went on flourishing from the time of such popular works as Haydn's masterpieces to the massive performances of the Crystal Palace era.

Precise and general statistics for the whole period are lacking, and conditions undoubtedly varied in different cities. Thus in London, both Salomon's orchestra and the Philharmonic numbered between 40 and 50 players: that of the Concerts of Ancient Music, which survived until 1848, remained static at 43, of which the wind comprised one third. Continental orchestras were rather larger. For the year 1825, figures given in the *Journals* of Sir George Smart, a precise and competent observer, who took notes in Paris and a dozen German cities, show that the very largest operatic orchestras did not exceed 75. Of the more usual total of about 65, 35 to 40 were string players. For purely symphonic music, this and other available evidence points to an average of 55 to 60 as a full complement in most European cities. When any total exceeded 60, the extra forces were nearly always in the strings.[1]

INSTRUMENTAL TECHNIQUE

The second half of this period saw a notable advance over the eighteenth century in nearly every branch of instrumental technique. It was admittedly small compared with the phenomenal strides made in the next fifty years, but those were due in no small part to the craft

[1] Adam Carse gives tabulated details in *The Orchestra from Beethoven to Berlioz* (Cambridge, 1948).

of instrument makers in responding to the demands of Berlioz, Liszt, and Wagner. The marvel is that the great players of the classical age achieved so much on what were later to seem imperfect instruments, especially in the wind and brass. From a host of virtuosi a few may be mentioned. On the flute, there were Andrew Ashe, Charles Nicholson, Louis Drouet, and Jean Louis Tulou; on the clarinet, Jean Lefèvre, Thomas Willman, Heinrich Bärmann, and Johann Simon Hermstedt (the last two specially written for by Weber and Spohr respectively); among oboists, Antoine Sallantin and Gustave Vogt, among bassoon-ists, John Mackintosh and Carl Almenräder were pre-eminent; the most outstanding horn players were Giovanni Punto, Giovanni Puzzi, and the brothers Joseph and Peter Petrides; on the trumpet Thomas Harper won wide renown. Fine string players abounded: Pierre Rode, George Bridgetower, Giovanni Battista Viotti, and Niccolò Paganini stand high among the greatest of any age. The viola was hardly developed at all as a solo instrument but the brothers Jean Pierre and Jean Louis Duport had done much for the cello. On the double bass Domenico Dragonetti, eccentric collector of dolls and snuffboxes, has had few equals. Improved construction of the pianoforte[1] increased its popularity with large numbers of peripatetic virtuosi, headed by Cramer and Clementi among the older generation, with the youthful Liszt coming to the fore as the exponent of a keyboard virtuosity comparable with Paganini's on the violin.

Yet there was some falling-off in general musicianship. A good keyboard player of Bach's day was instructed in figured-bass playing and in extemporization, and old 'methods', such as Leopold Mozart's for the violin and Quantz's for the flute, prove how broad and thorough was the general training then given. It seems fair to suppose that, *mutatis mutandis*, orchestral players of the mid-eighteenth century had a better all-round musical ability than those of the Napoleonic era. It is ironical that, with a few notable exceptions, the standard of ensemble playing was sadly imperfect during the high summer of classical instrumental music. For this, difficulties of conducting were partly responsible.

CONDUCTING

The use of a pianoforte for purposes of conducting lingered on well into the 1820s and beyond. The fact that a keyboard instrument, besides serving as a point of visual focus, continued in demand as a

---

[1] For a detailed discussion see Rosamond E. M. Harding, *The Piano-forte, Its History Traced to the Great Exhibition of 1851* (Cambridge, 1933, reprint New York, 1973), pp. 151 ff. and 177 ff.

support for the orchestra, is a signal testimony to the vitality of the tradition of the figured-bass. (In the pianoforte part of Hummel's Concerto in C, Op. 34, published in 1824, the pianist, when not playing solo, is allotted an elaborately figured part, in support of the strings.) It was still alive in 1829 when Mendelssohn, having come to London to conduct his C minor symphony for the Philharmonic Society, was led to the keyboard[1] by the pianist J. B. Cramer. Cramer's brother, François, the leader of the violins, also sometimes conducted with his bow, sharing the direction of the orchestra with the player at the keyboard, who was primarily a time-keeper. Hence it was natural that the idea of a single conductor, wielding a baton and dictatorial authority, should win only gradual acceptance. This is borne out by the varying practice of the Philharmonic Society as evinced in their programmes for more than a decade after the shock they received from Spohr's baton in 1820.[2] Here, then, was one reason for the poor standards of ensemble which may well have contributed to the lukewarm reception of many of Beethoven's works. Imagination boggles at the thought of a performance of the Choral Symphony given from the parts alone, the conductor never having seen the score, yet this actually happened at Leipzig in March 1826.[3]

CONCERTS

The rapid growth of public concerts of all kinds made it impossible for the composer to specialize in conducting his own music, as he had often done in the past, save for first performances. Thus the whole-time conductor began to come into being, exercising an influence that reached far beyond the actual place of performance. Ignaz Schuppanzigh in Vienna, though better known as a quartet leader, was noticed for his conducting as early as 1799. Often the conductor's task was not made easier by the kind of concert hall then available. Many years were to elapse before problems of resonance and the like were to be studied as a branch of acoustic science; in the early nineteenth century, old buildings, established as social or operatic centres, were pressed into service. London was fortunate in having two medium-sized halls designed for music: these were the Hanover Square Rooms (1775–1874) and the Argyll Rooms (1812–30). The Pantheon and the King's Theatre were likewise much in demand, but the latter also had

[1] Cf. Sebastian Hensel, *Die Familie Mendelssohn, 1729–1847* (Berlin, 1879), i, p. 226. A Punch cartoon showing keyboard conducting practised as late as 1844 is illustrated in Percy Scholes, *Oxford Companion to Music*, (2nd ed., London, 1939), pl. 45.
[2] See p. 186.
[3] Eduard Hanslick, *Geschichte des Concertwesens in Wien* (Vienna, 1869), i, p. 62.

a fine hall attached specially for concerts.[1] In Paris, frequent recourse was had to theatres and other halls, as also in Vienna, where the historic Redoutensaal was very popular.[2] In Leipzig the famous Gewandhaus concerts were held from 1781 in a building which, though designed as a concert-hall, rapidly became inadequate, but had to do duty until 1884.[3]

All over Europe, the length of concert programmes, which had been steadily growing before the Revolution, now reached gargantuan dimensions. Even to audiences gifted with heroic powers of endurance, the average concert must have been something of an ordeal. Blessed was the interval separating the two parts, each of which often lasted 115 minutes and seldom less than 90. A classic occasion was a concert given by Beethoven in the Theater an der Wien on 22 December 1808, entirely of his own works: the Fifth and Sixth Symphonies, the Choral Fantasia, the Fourth Piano Concerto, two movements from the Mass in C, the aria 'Ah! perfido', and an extempore fantasia on the pianoforte. The early programmes of the Philharmonic Society in London, while more varied, ran to almost as great a length. Programme-building always allowed a generous sprinkling of vocal and chamber items. Despite the wide influence of Italian opera and the popularity of domestic singing, the scales of taste were slowly but surely weighed down in favour of instrumental music. Of this tendency there is strong evidence in the heavy increase of instrumental over vocal works in publishers' catalogues.

Until after 1830, solo recitals were comparatively rare, although orchestral concerts were often planned so as to allow time for a generous number of solos besides concerted items. Public chamber music, on the other hand, was safely established in favour, with limited audiences, soon after the turn of the century, earliest of all in Paris where in 1802 the Habeneck Quartet founded a tradition that was strengthened by the Baillot Quartet from 1814 onwards. In Vienna, the Schuppanzigh Quartet (patronized by the Russian ambassador, Count Razumovsky) not only introduced Beethoven's works from 1808 onwards, but continued to build up in Vienna the repertoire of masterpieces by Mozart, Haydn, and Beethoven and to popularize them abroad with tours which lasted till Schuppanzigh's death in 1830. English records are scanty, but the frequent publications

[1] See Robert Elkin, *The Old Concert Rooms of London* (London, 1955), pp. 92–104 (on Hanover Square Rooms), 110–14 (on the King's Theatre), and 115–22 (on Argyll Rooms).
[2] On concert life in Vienna see Hanslick, op. cit.
[3] See Hermann Heyer, ed., *Festschrift zum 175 jährigen Bestehen der Gewandhauskonzerte 1780–1956* (Leipzig, 1956) and Fritz Hennenberg, *Das Leipziger Gewandhausorchester* (Leipzig, 1968).

of chamber works by Mozart, Haydn, and lesser masters tells its own tale, quite apart from the inclusion of quartets and quintets in the programmes of the Philharmonic Society. Elsewhere in Europe, save for a brief flowering in Spain under Boccherini's influence, 'the music of friends' had yet scarcely taken root in the concert hall.

SOCIETIES

The year 1813 saw the birth of the Philharmonic Society of London, hard on the heels of the Gesellschaft der Musikfreunde in Vienna (1812). Here also the Tonkünstlersocietät, founded in 1771 in imitation of the Concerts Spirituels of Paris, was expanding rapidly. Virtually every large city in England, France, and Central Europe began to develop some distinct corporative musical activity[1]. One far-reaching event was the already mentioned revival of choral singing in Germany, inaugurated by the foundation in 1791 of the Berlin *Singakademie*. Another notable event was the German collective festival, held in 1810 at Frankhausen in Thuringia, which assembled forces from several towns, perhaps inspired by the already renowned and flourishing Three Choirs Festival of England. This enterprise, which paved the way for many great festivals, was conducted by Spohr. To the *Männerchorvereine* that sprang up all over Germany, England offered an approximate parallel in her glee clubs,[2] which were never so numerous or of such high standard as during the Regency period. But England had nothing corresponding to the ubiquitous *Collegia musica* of Germany, which now took on a new lease of life, and served as a fruitful source of orchestral recruitment.

AUDIENCES

The changes that came over audiences and the wider musical public well before 1820 were not a sudden development. In 1742 C. P. E. Bach's *Sei sonate per cembalo* were dedicated to King Frederick of Prussia: in 1779 he published another of his works with the significant title: *Clavier Sonaten für Kenner und Liebhaber*. In that interval, the amateur had been steadily coming into his own, as witness a periodical that appeared weekly in 1770, *Der musikalische Dilettante*, and domestic music-making developed in good earnest. Of its enthusiasm and scope there is ample proof in the great variety of arrangements of operas, symphonies, and chamber works which were published in an endless stream. The pianoforte began its invasion of parlour and

---

[1] See Adolf Aber, *Handbuch der Musikliteratur* (Leipzig, 1922) section III, 'Pflege und Geschichte der Musik in einzelnen Ländern und Städten' (reprint, Hildesheim and Wiesbaden, 1967).
[2] See E. D. Mackerness, *A Social History of English Music* (London, 1964), p. 114.

drawing room, often in company with the flute which enjoyed an even greater vogue than in the early eighteenth century; whole operas were not uncommonly arranged for one or two flutes. The harp and Spanish guitar throve as instruments for domestic accompaniment, the guitar especially in France, England, and Austria, where the aristocracy delighted in an endless stream of solos and duets, mostly by hacks, but some by good composers such as Mauro Giuliani (1781–1829). General eagerness for musical knowledge is reflected in a remarkable increase in the publication of guides to musical theory, of primers, rudiments, and popular textbooks of all kinds. This new growth is typified by Fétis's little book *La Musique mise à la portée de tout le monde* (Paris, 1830), later translated into English, Italian, Spanish, and Russian. Enthusiasm is not necessarily a guarantee of sound taste, and audiences at operas and concerts acquiesced in practices which by modern standards seem as barbaric as bear-baiting and cock-fighting. Parodies of serious productions such as *Der Freischütz* were immensely popular and, though mostly short lived, their frequency tells its own tale. Even more regrettable were adaptations all over Europe of the kind perpetrated by Castil-Blaze in Paris and by Reeve and Bishop in London, in which the masterpieces of Gluck, Weber, and Mozart were ruthlessly mangled. Again, the custom of dividing a four-movement symphony between the two halves of a concert apparently met with little opposition. The cult of the child prodigy went hand in hand with adulation of flashy virtuosity.

MUSICAL SCHOLARSHIP

Compared with the great musical histories of the pre-Revolutionary period, those of the next half century, until 1830, are with one exception negligible. Such a book as Christian Kalkbrenner's *Kurzer Abriss der Geschichte der Tonkunst* (Berlin, 1792) is purely pedagogic, containing little new or original; Thomas Busby's *History of Music* (London, 1819) specified on the title page its debt to Burney and Hawkins, from whom, however, other compilers, like George Jones and W. C. Stafford, borrowed without acknowledgment. To Johann Nikolaus Forkel,[1] who published at Leipzig the first volume of his *Allgemeine Geschichte der Musik* in 1788 and the second in 1801, belongs the credit of expounding new ideas, although his work barely reaches 1550. In strong opposition to Burney's conception of music as 'innocent amusement', he saw it as the supreme expression of the

---

[1] See Vol. VII, p. xx; also Wilhelm Friedrich Kümmel, 'Die Anfänge der Musikgeschichte in der deutschsprachigen Universitäten', *Die Musikforschung*, xx (1967), p. 262.

emotions, parallel in growth to language, and evolving through monody and polyphony to its culmination in harmony.

During the eighteenth century musical biography was in its infancy, but Bach had received something of his due in 1802 with the publication at Leipzig of Forkel's *Über J. S. Bachs Leben, Kunst and Kunstwerke*. A number of smaller biographies continued the anecdotal tradition of the previous century, until the appearance of G. N. Nissen's copious life of Mozart (Leipzig, 1828), and Giuseppe Baini broke fresh ground with the two great volumes of *Memorie storico-critiche della vita e dell'opere di Giovanni Pierluigi da Palestrina* (Rome, 1828).

Teaching institutions such as the Conservatoire in Paris and the Royal Academy in London (founded 1822) had little or no concern with historical research or the performance of old music, nor were the universities very much more advanced. It was not until 1823 that the University of Bonn took the momentous step of appointing as lecturer in music Carl Heinrich Breidenstein (1796–1876) who became professor in 1826. In the University of Berlin Adolph Bernhard Marx (1795–1866) received a similar post in 1830. Such were the first stages in the re-birth of musical scholarship and learning which were to expand so brilliantly during the next half century. At the time, however, the significance of the appointment of two young men, not pure musicians, but both grounded in law and philosophy, was hardly realized. Indeed, in Berlin it seemed ridiculous to a diehard like Zelter to give such a post to a man who was neither composer nor virtuoso.

LEXICOGRAPHY AND BIBLIOGRAPHY

Although this period was so relatively barren of musical history and research there were compensations in bibliography and lexicography. Rousseau's *Dictionnaire de musique* (Paris, 1768),[1] a fine achievement in the age of the *Grande encyclopédie*, continued to exercise a strong influence in many countries. It can be traced even in such a very different work as the discursive but useful *Dictionnaire de musique moderne* of François Castil-Blaze (Paris, 1821). An original if somewhat diffuse compilation was César Gardeton's *Bibliographie musicale de France et de l'étrangère* (published anonymously in 1822),[2] which gives a wealth of facts about publications, publishers, performers, instrument makers, and covers almost every musical activity. The mantle of J. G. Walther's *Musikalisches Lexicon* of 1732 fell on Ernst Ludwig Gerber (1746–1819), whose *Historisch-biogra-*

---

[1] Reprinted New York and Hildesheim, 1969.
[2] Reprinted Geneva, 1978, as *Archives de l'Édition Musicale Française*, vi.

phisches Lexikon der Tonkünstler incorporated material collected by Walther for an unpublished second edition, and furnished a mine of information for contemporary French and English lexicographers. Indeed, the two editions of Gerber, the first of 1790–2, the second of 1812–14, are still indispensable to any student of the period.[1]

In Gerber, musical biography and general information are combined with bibliographical data, although before him bibliography had already been established by Forkel's *Allgemeine Litteratur der Musik* (Leipzig, 1792), a remarkably comprehensive book.[2] Soon afterwards, the first separate systematic catalogue of all music and musical literature, currently published was undertaken by Karl Friedrich Whistling, whose important *Handbuch der musikalischen Literatur* appeared anonymously at Leipzig in 1817, and included works issued since *c*. 1780. After sundry vicissitudes publication of the annual and cumulative volumes was taken over in 1829 by the Hofmeisters, father and son, with whose name the series (though with several changes of title) has been associated ever since. Comprehending from its earliest years the publications of all German-speaking countries, and many other important European centres, 'Hofmeister' has always come as near to completeness (even through two world wars) as can be expected of any work of this kind.

PERIODICALS AND JOURNALISM

Whistling would hardly have cast his net so widely had he not been fairly certain that there was a demand for such a *Handbuch*. There is further testimony to the public appetite for musical information in the rapid growth of the new musical journalism, which was an outstanding feature of this era. The periodical publication of musical works in magazines had, of course, been generally flourishing since the 1750s, while in Germany a tradition of informative criticism had begun with Johann Mattheson's *Critica Musica* (Hamburg, 1722–3) and continued up to and beyond Johann Adam Hiller's *Wöchentliche Nachrichten* (Leipzig, 1766–70). But these had catered for a restricted public. When in 1798 the Leipzig firm of Breitkopf and Härtel appointed Johann Friedrich Rochlitz as first editor of the *Allgemeine musikalische Zeitung*,[3] they relied on him to set a high standard in a journal whose

[1] Modern edition ed. Othmar Wessely, four vols. (Graz, 1966–9).
[2] Reprinted Hildesheim, 1962. Modern edition, with a new introduction by Neil Ratliff (New York, 1975).
[3] See Clemens Christoph von Gleich, *Die Bedeutung der Allgemeiner musikalischen Zeitung 1798–1848 und 1863–1882* (Amsterdam, 1969); Reinhold Schmitt-Thomas, *Die Entwicklung der deutschen Konzertkritik im Spiegel der Leipziger Allgemeinen musikalischen Zeitung (1798–1848)* (Frankfurt/Main 1969), pp. 85 ff.; Martha Bruckner-Bigenwald, *Die Anfänge der Leipziger Allgemeinen musikalischen Zeitung* (Hilversum, 1965), pp. 1–89.

policy was to record events as much as to mould opinion. This the famous 'AMZ' continued to do until 1848. Meanwhile, J. K. F. Rellstab had established between 1808 and 1813 an equally fine tradition for daily musical journalism in the Berlin *Vossische Zeitung*, which was taken up by his son Ludwig in 1826 and carried on till 1860.

Two other journals entitled *Allgemeine musikalische Zeitung* paid compliment to Breitkopf's enterprise, one in Vienna which lasted from 1817 to 1824, the other in Berlin, a faithful mirror of North German tendencies and opinion from 1824 to 1830, edited by A. B. Marx.[1] In addition to *Cäcilia*, which flourished from 1824 to 1848 and tended to be rather more concerned with past than current events, there appeared between fifty and sixty other journals. Though mainly local in interest, all these reflect the progress of musical interest in the middle-class public, which expanded all through the nineteenth century and went some way to justify the claim of the Germans to be the most musical nation in Europe.

Other countries, before 1830, had comparatively little to show, but it was often of high quality. In England *The Quarterly Musical Magazine and Review* (the first of any real substance) pursued a dignified and broadminded career from 1818 to 1828: *The Harmonicon*, justly famed for sound views, wide interests, and fine production, appeared monthly from 1823 to 1833. In France, the first periodical of any distinction or importance was *La Revue musicale*, established by Fétis in 1827, which lasted until 1880.[2]

PRINTING, PUBLISHING, AND EDITING[3]

In any era one of the most faithful mirrors of fluctuating economic conditions has been the printed page, above all when, as in music printing, the design of title-pages is closely allied to the graphic arts. Rarely have conditions been more vividly so reflected than in this epoch. In 1790, it is true, the decline from the noble standards of the 1760s and 1770s had begun, but the best work done in most countries still kept on a high plane. Printing from engraved plates enjoyed wide popularity, though the finest specimens of early lithography ran it very close. At the same time, however, much music was printed from movable type, notably by Breitkopf of Leipzig, whose best productions

---

[1] See Helmut Kirchmeyer, 'Ein Kapitel Adolf Bernhard Marx. Über Sendungsbewusstein und Bildungsstand der Berliner Musikkritik zwischen 1824 und 1830', *Beiträge zur Geschichte der Musikanschauung im 19. Jahrhundert*, ed. Walter Salmen (Regensburg, 1965), pp. 73–101.

[2] See Peter Bloom, 'François-Joseph Fétis and the *Revue musicale* (1827–1835) (Diss. Pennsylvania, 1972).

[3] For the composer as publisher and for the invention of lithography, see p. 13 above.

were well balanced and clear. Generally, before about 1800 paper remained crisp and white, margins were wide, and note-spacing good. As the general state of Europe worsened, standards declined everywhere. Seldom in all musical history have so many masterpieces been so meanly and unimaginatively printed as they were between 1800 and 1830. The paper was often very rough, of a greyish green hue, with the engraving botched and coarse, and the title-pages mostly heavy and unpleasing. Among the comparatively few exceptions were some finely illustrated title-pages of French operas, and occasional Austrian, German and English productions which were embellished with elegant vignettes.

Yet even at the height of the wars Breitkopf had shown himself a man of courage no less than of historical vision, by undertaking between 1798 and 1806 complete editions of the works of Haydn and Mozart.[1] In neither case did the series of slim *cahiers* ultimately include more than a tithe of the whole, but the venture was magnificent. Equally bold was Pleyel's work in Paris, when besides Haydn's quartets (cf. p. 13 above) he attempted the complete pianoforte works of Mozart (*c*. 1815–29).[2] Earlier, however, than all these, the importance of publishing a prolific master's works in their entirety had been realized by the English composer Samuel Arnold (1740–1802), who began in 1787 to issue Handel's music in a sumptuous edition, with artistic frontispieces by Bartolozzi and others. It needed nearly ten years for the completion of this task in 180 tall 'numbers', which actually comprise about three-quarters of Handel's huge output.[3] Although, judged by modern standards, Arnold's scholarship was faulty (but by no means so bad as Chrysander, himself far from blameless, made out), this notable English enterprise formed a landmark in the annals of musical taste and publishing.

Unlike Handel, Bach did not for very many years enjoy wide popularity, so that the publication of his music was correspondingly slower and more restricted. After the handful of editions printed in his lifetime, practically nothing appeared until the turn of the century, when *Das wohltemperirte Clavier*, *Die Kunst der Fuge*, and a few other keyboard works began to enjoy limited popularity in Germany and

---

[1] See *Die Musik in Geschichte und Gegenwart*, ii, col. 258.

[2] A useful synopsis of these and other early 'complete' editions will be found in the catalogue of the Hirsch Library (Cambridge, 1947), iv, pp. 333–409.

[3] The complexities of this edition have been studied by Paul Hirsch, 'Dr. Arnold's Handel Edition, (1787–1797)', *Music Review*, viii (1947), p. 106, and by J. M. Coopersmith in 'The First Gesammtausgabe: Dr. Arnold's edition of Handel's Works', *Notes*, iv (1947), pp. 277 and 439.

England.[1] The time was not yet ripe for a complete edition: the study of sources and the technique of editing were both in their infancy. But a great impetus, which lasted into the next generation, came from Mendelssohn's revival of the *St. Matthew Passion*; after private rehearsals, begun when he was 17, he gave a public performance in Berlin in 1829 in the face of general apathy and of professional opposition from Zelter, the head of the *Singakademie*. The musical text was a somewhat romanticized and heavily edited one of Mendelssohn's own making. Schlesinger published a score of the *Passion*, with vocal score by A. B. Marx (Berlin, 1830), and Trautwein followed with the *St. John Passion* (Berlin, 1831). Such enterprises as these were not a mere flash in the pan; they foreshadowed the large-scale publishing of classical music in which German firms were to lead Europe during the next half century.

---

[1] The earliest editions of *Das wohltemperirte Clavier* were published by Simrock (Bonn, 1801) and Nägeli (Zürich, 1801); the earliest English edition was prepared by Samuel Wesley and C. F. Horn (London, 1813).

II

FRENCH OPERA

By WINTON DEAN

THE REVOLUTIONARY DECADE

THE French Revolution of 1789 inevitably had a convulsive effect on the arts. Opera was the principal form through which it affected the history of music. This was to be expected. Not only did opera lend itself to articulate concepts; it had always been (and was long to remain) a fertile parent of new instrumental forms, among them the sonata, the concerto, the symphony, and the symphonic poem, and it was in the highest degree socially suggestible. Although aristocratic in origin and still to some extent in administration, it had by 1789 acquired a bourgeois audience; and the Revolution was a product of the bourgeois class. The two French operatic streams, the *tragédie lyrique* and the *opéra comique*, had developed on different courses from the Italianate traditions of the rest of Europe, which by 1789 were running into the sand. The *opera seria* was moribund; foreign composers with serious operatic ambitions were congregating in Paris, where the *tragédie lyrique*, thanks to Gluck's success in grafting Italian lyricism on to the rhetorical and declamatory stock inherited from Lully and Rameau, had recently touched one of its peaks. Although after the departure of Gluck it possessed no great composers, it carried the potential of growth; the 1780s were a decade of lively activity and technical experiment, encouraged, as always in Paris, by a spate of aesthetic theorising. Salieri's *Tarare* (1787), on a libretto by Beaumarchais, one of the most widely popular operas of the age, contains striking anticipations of romantic opera in its mixed genre (comedy, tragedy, satire, epic, and supernatural fantasy) and in its remarkable Prologue,[1] beginning with a stormy representation of chaos in the orchestra and introducing a chorus of souls waiting for mortal birth. The *opéra comique*, with little new blood among the composers,

---

[1] See Vol. VII, p. 244.

admitted an element of social criticism in the librettos and a few formal experiments in the music, especially in overtures and instrumental interludes. Dalayrac's *Nina ou la folle d'amour* (1786) dispensed with comic characters, and perhaps for that reason had to be tried out first in private; but its *larmoyante* temper was characteristic of the pre-Revolution form.[1]

An important effect of the Revolution was to divert the potential energy of *tragédie lyrique* into *opéra comique*. The first few years were a period of great complexity and confusion, during which many ephemeral and eccentric productions reached the stage. The stimulus of freedom led to license and then to reaction, censorship and oppression. But the revolutionary authorities saw the possibility of harnessing the arts to their own purposes. They gave particular encouragement to music and, besides exercising control over the Opéra, strove to turn the new *opéra comique* into a vehicle for popular enlightenment and patriotic stimulus. And when the revolutionary armies broke out across the frontiers of France it followed in their wake.

Thus, after nearly two centuries of Italian domination, the leading role in the development of opera passed to France. The extent and importance of this change has been obscured by the accident that the French Revolution school produced no composers of the first rank. Yet they initiated the most radical transformation in the language of music since the development of monody and major-minor tonality. The decade 1790–1800 was as influential in musical as in political history. It not only laid the foundations of romantic opera from *Fidelio* to Wagner, but (except in such matters as keyboard technique) supplied the basic musical currency of the entire romantic movement, in Germany as well as France and to some extent in Italy. French *opéra comique* was the stock on which German romanticism was grafted; the fact that the latter produced more lasting flowers is in a sense a tribute to the former. Beethoven was not alone in acknowledging Cherubini as the greatest master of the age; every prominent German composer from Spohr and Weber to Schubert and Mendelssohn explicitly or implicitly agreed, sometimes coupling his name with Mozart's.

The most spectacular impact of the Revolution on musical life in Paris (France, unlike Italy and Germany, had no alternative centres) occurred outside the theatres, in the great open-air spectacles in which all sections of the population were encouraged to take part.[2] They

[1] See ibid, p. 250, and for its important influence in Italy see pp. 392–3 below.
[2] See pp. 650 ff.

were designed to celebrate events of the revolutionary calendar, to commemorate or bury its heroes, and to honour abstract virtues (liberty, equality, the sovereignty of the people, hatred of tyrants) and useful or inevitable functions of the community (marriage, mother-hood, work, old age). All the leading composers were urged or frightened by the authorities into producing hymns and marches for these occasions. Inevitably their musical complexity was in inverse proportion to their mass. The theatres were too small to accommodate the more sensational of these activities. The Fête de la Fédération of 14 July 1790 is said to have employed 300 drums and 300 wind instruments, including 50 serpents, and as many as 2400 performers, vocal and instrumental, have been claimed for Robespierre's Fête de l'Être Suprême on 8 June 1794, not to mention 130 pieces of artillery.[1] Nevertheless their influence on opera was considerable, both in the immediate context and in the work of the next two generations. The grand operas of Spontini and the whole aesthetic of Berlioz would be unthinkable without them. They increased the size and scope of the orchestra, especially the woodwind and percussion (though the tendency to noisy scoring at the Opéra had been increasing throughout the 1780s), and modified the substance and texture of the music by their emphasis on march rhythms, massed choruses, and the full-blooded projection of simple emotions.

In 1791, under the influence of the painter David and the current taste for Roman antiquity, new brass instruments, the *buccina* or *buccin* (treble) and *tuba corva* (bass) were constructed in imitation of those depicted on Trajan's column. They were intended to make a visual as well as an aural impact (like the trombones with ferocious dragons' heads attached to their bells, with which they have sometimes been confused); they could manage very few notes, but the *tuba corva* was reported to sound like six serpents, and according to Sarrette the *buccin* made an absolutely new and terrifying sound audible at over half a mile's distance.[2] Méreaux (1745–97) wrote parts for them in the autograph of *Jocaste* (1791), but they may not have been used, as they are missing from the full score; they appeared in the theatre in Méhul's incidental music to Chénier's *Timoléon* (1794) and *Joseph* (1807), possibly to represent ancient instruments carried on stage.[3] More important in the long run was the encouragement, reinforced on the foundation of the Conservatoire in 1795, given to improved standards

[1] These were extreme cases; most of the festivals used an orchestra of about sixty.

[2] David Charlton, 'New Sounds for Old: Tam-Tam, Tuba Curva, Buccin', *Soundings*, iii (1973), pp. 39–47.

[3] Charlton, *Orchestration and Orchestral Practice in Paris, 1789–1810* (Diss. Cambridge, 1973).

in wind playing and in the instruments themselves. The tamtam, first used by Gossec in 1790, also entered the opera house by way of the open-air festivals.[1] Among their incidental effects was a marked raising of pitch, adopted to give greater brilliance and extended to the theatres, where the strings were required to adjust their tuning accordingly.

OPERA UNDER THE REPUBLIC

This mass movement soon invaded the repertory of the Opéra, renamed the Théâtre des Arts. Gossec (1734–1829), who had long before experimented with huge forces in his church music (as had Le Sueur in the 1780s), and in whom seniority and a disaffected temperament were combined with an ardent revolutionary spirit, produced his *scène réligieuse L'Offrande à la Liberté* in October 1792 and *Le Triomphe de la République, ou le Camp de Grandpré* in January 1793, both of which (like other contemporary stage pieces) introduced the Marseillaise.[2] They enjoyed enormous popularity and strong government support. For two years from the autumn of 1792 the Paris theatres poured forth a series of such ephemeral pieces, designed to inculcate the correct political and patriotic sentiments. One of the most pretentious was *La Réunion du 10 août, ou l'Inauguration de la République française* (Opéra, April 1794) by the Italian Bernardo Porta (1758–1829), described as a *sans-culottide* in five acts; two of the most eccentric, which must rank among the strangest effusions of any reputable composer, were Grétry's *La Rosière républicaine* (in which the organ first appeared on the Opéra stage,[3] and which ends with two nuns compelled by the mob to discard their habits and dance the Carmagnole) and *Denys le Tyran, maître d'école à Corinthe*, which deals with a revolt by preparatory schoolboys in the fourth century B.C. against their headmaster, the erstwhile tyrant of Syracuse. Grétry's choice of these subjects was doubtless influenced by the fact that his earlier work had made him suspect as an associate of the Ancien Régime. Although at least ten of his operas were in the repertory of the Comédie-Italienne in 1791–2, the score of *Richard Coeur de Lion* was publicly burned in 1793 in a Palais-Royal café.

Some pieces were based on contemporary events: the recapture of Toulon in 1794 and the death of the young revolutionary hero Joseph

---

[1] It made its operatic début, so far as is known, in a revival of Salieri's *Tarare* on 3 August 1790.

[2] For some years the performance of this and other patriotic songs was compulsory at every theatrical performance, whether in the substance of the piece or extraneously in the manner of a national anthem.

[3] Its part survives in manuscript (see Charlton, *Orchestration*).

Barra each inspired several operas, announced on the bills as *fait historique*. Others combined the qualities of operetta and political tract: the plot of the three-act *opéra comique Le Congrès des Rois* (February 1794) concerns a conspiracy against the kings of Europe by their mistresses, who have been won over to the ideas of the Revolution and enjoy the assistance of the adventurer Cagliostro (then in fact in prison), attending the Congress as the representative of the Pope. The opera ends with the kings dancing the Carmagnole in red bonnets. It employed the services of twelve composers, including Grétry, Dalayrac, Berton, Méhul, and Cherubini.

This midsummer madness presently gave way to a less flatulent mode of address. The classical associations of the Opéra permitted the annexation of certain heroic episodes in Greek and Roman history, designed like the contemporary pictures of David to brace the public at a time when the Revolution was beset by external as well as internal enemies. Among such *tragédies lyriques* were Méreaux's *Fabius*, the *Miltiade à Marathon* of J. B. Lemoyne (1751–96) (both 1793), and Méhul's *Horatius Coclès* (1794); the last presents the story of Rome's resistance to Lars Porsena and the Tarquins as a symbol of French defiance of Austria and Prussia.

OPÉRA COMIQUE

It soon became apparent, however, that the true vehicle of the Revolution's message must be the *opéra comique*. The fact that it employed spoken dialogue and not the stylized declamation of *tragédie lyrique* brought it closer to the broad public that both composers and authorities were anxious to woo. It had always dealt, in however limited a fashion, with the emotions of men and women whose predicaments the audience could recognize as not too remote from their own. It was inevitable that artists (as opposed to the lunatic fringe of agitators) inspired by visions of the equality and dignity of man, in whatever class of society he happened to be born, should concentrate on a form that allowed full play to the two qualities whose union gave the Revolution so tremendous an impact – its idealism and its realism.

For most of the decade Paris had two theatres devoted to *opéra comique*. The Comédie Italienne, also known as the Théâtre Favart, operated at first under its old name, then from 11 February 1793 as the Opéra Comique National. The Théâtre de Monsieur, founded in January 1789 by Marie Antoinette's hairdresser for the performance of Italian opera, moved two years later to the Salle Feydeau, whose name it took; it was directed until early summer 1792 by Viotti, and began by putting on works by Cimarosa, Paisiello, Gazzaniga, and others with insertions by Cherubini, before going over to the native product. There followed a period of intense competition between the two theatres, which lasted until the insolvency and amalgamation of the companies in 1801. All the important French operas of the decade saw the light at one or other, and on several occasions each produced an opera on the same subject within a short interval (*Lodoïska* – Cherubini and Kreutzer, both 1791; *Paul et Virginie* – Kreutzer 1791, Le Sueur 1794; *Roméo et Juliette* – Dalayrac 1792, Steibelt 1793; *La Caverne* – Le Sueur 1793, Méhul 1795[1]). Of the leading composers, Cherubini (1760–1842), Le Sueur (1760–1837), and Gaveaux (1761–1825) worked for the Théâtre Feydeau (where Gaveaux was a tenor singer), Grétry (1741–1813), Berton (1767–1844), Dalayrac (1753–1809), Méhul (1763–1817), Rodolphe Kreutzer (1766–1831), and later Boieldieu (1775–1834) chiefly for the Opéra Comique.

The spirit of 1789, as was to be expected in a nation and a movement so given to articulate utterance, appeared in the librettos before the music. Themes from post-classical history had been used before; they soon began to proliferate, especially those with liberal or patriotic overtones, such as Kreutzer's *Jeanne d'Arc à Orléans* (1790) and Grétry's *Pierre le Grand* (1790) and *Guillaume Tell* (1791), which set a fashion that spread across Europe and became a feature of romantic opera everywhere. The so-called rescue opera, in which the hero or heroine is saved at the last moment from torture, death, or worse, had its origins before the Revolution in such works as Monsigny's *Le Déserteur* (1769) and Grétry's *Richard Coeur de Lion* (1784). The idea is after all a theatrical commonplace. It was the pressure of contemporary events that gave it immediacy and established it as a genre in its own right. The villain of the earlier rescue operas is generally some representative of the pre-1789 establishment, whether court, nobility, or church. In Berton's *Les Rigueurs du cloître* (1790) the heroine is saved from being walled up in a convent, and all the nuns are sent out into the world to rear families. The threatening force was not always political; it could be some natural catastrophe, like an earthquake, a volcanic eruption, a shipwreck, or an avalanche, though human rascality was involved as well. Within a few years – so quickly did events move – the emphasis fell on the tyranny and injustice released by the Revolution itself. This is implicit in Berton's *Ponce de Léon* (1797), about the Spanish poet persecuted and imprisoned by the Inquisition, and almost explicit in two famous examples of the *fait*

---

[1] Berton's *Montano et Stéphanie* and Méhul's *Ariodant* are based on the same story, but both were produced at the Opéra Comique in 1799.

historique class, based on contemporary events in France (though for reasons of prudence the action was transferred to an earlier period): Gaveaux's *Léonore ou l'Amour conjugal* (1798), the source of later operas by Paer, Mayr, and Beethoven, and Cherubini's *Les Deux Journées* (1800). Both have librettos by J. N. Bouilly. In *Les Deux Journées* a poor family saves the lives of two fugitive aristocrats, and Bouilly stresses the moral imperative: all men should help their fellows in distress. The words of the final chorus – 'Le premier charme de la vie, C'est de servir l'humanité' – proclaim the idealized message of the Revolution, later to be taken up by Beethoven in the Choral Symphony. This upgrading of the status and dignity of the individual and his right to challenge the established institutions of society was as important in the arts as in politics; it permeates the romantic movement. So close had opera come to contemporary life that the persons whose experience Bouilly used for his plots were probably still living. It is a formidable thought that the original Leonora and Florestan could – if they survived – have seen within a few years four operas founded on their own lives.

STAGE SPECTACLE AND 'TERROR OPERA'

Two related features of the librettos were a strong element of physical violence, which has earned them in Germany the title of *Schreckensopern* (terror operas), and an emphasis on stage spectacle, described at length and in graphic detail in the scores. Neither was new in itself. Scenic transformations had always been a prominent ingredient of serious opera, and the climax of Salieri's very successful *Les Danaides* (1784) had involved 49 simultaneous murders, the signal for which was given by a three-bar crescendo from pianissimo to fortissimo on a single note, a device which had been anticipated by Lemoyne in *Electre* (1782) during Clytemnestra's dream in Act II, sc. 1.[1] What was new was the transference of these effects from classical grand opera to real-life *opéra comique*. Cherubini's *Lodoïska* (1791) combined all the features so far mentioned. It exploited the sympathy aroused by the Polish partitions (operas on Polish subjects were not uncommon) and used the hero's vote in the Polish Diet as one of the motives in the plot, which culminated in a pitched battle and the destruction of the villain's castle in a spectacular conflagration, the fainting heroine being snatched from the flames by the hero at the last moment. The libretto of Le Sueur's *La Caverne*, with its robber band, inflamed passions, fights and disguises, is wild to the point of

---

[1] For the horrors inflicted on the murderers on stage in the last act of *Les Danaides*, see Vol. VII, pp. 242–3.

incoherence. It ends with the siege and collapse of the robbers' cave, Cherubini's *Élisa* (1794), one of the first operas to exploit the romantic attractions of mountain scenery,[1] with an Alpine avalanche, the two settings of *Paul et Virginie* with a tropical storm and a shipwreck. It is no far cry to the final catastrophes, human, volcanic, or cosmic, of *Les Huguenots, Le Prophète, La Muette de Portici*, and *Götterdämmerung*. But the extravagant incidents are not primarily designed (as in Marschner or Meyerbeer) to raise a *frisson* of horror, but to multiply the obstacles in the hero's path and so to highlight the rescue when it comes. The spirit of the Revolution, like that of *opera seria* (though for different reasons), required a happy end.

The supernatural was alien to its humanistic ideals and indeed to the Latin temperament in general. Except in the later operas of Le Sueur, an eccentric in every sense, there is scarcely a trace of it in French or Italian romantic opera before 1830. When a ghost appears, as in the Semiramis operas of Catel and Rossini, it is treated in the classical manner of Gluck's oracles. Salieri's *La grotta di Trofonio* (1785) with its chorus of spirits and *Tarare* are partial exceptions; but the stirrings of romanticism are apparent in the librettos rather than the music. Salieri was however a pioneer in the use of the drums – in these supernatural episodes. In *Trofonio* he anticipated the dungeon scene in *Fidelio* by having them tuned an augmented fourth apart (C and low G flat); in the Prologue to *Tarare*, tuned a third apart, they reinforce as many different chords as possible, as if to emphasize the unstable tonality; Salieri was apparently the first composer to use three timpani, in *La secchia rapita* (1772).[2]

DALAYRAC

Another significant element in the librettos is the influence of Gothic romances, the taste for which (like that for the Ossianic poems a little later) had spread to France from England. This is perceptible in the librettos of Cherubini's *Lodoïska*, especially in the stage directions of Act II, and conspicuous in the rescue operas of Dalayrac, such as *Camille ou le Souterrain* (1791) and *Léon ou le Château de Montenéro* (1798). Léon lives a life of debauchery, cruelty, and reputed sorcery in a grim castle and kidnaps women for his pleasure; but – and this is typical of the older *opéra comique* – although he governs the plot and gives his name to the opera, he sings only a minor part in one finale. The action of *Camille* takes place in an abandoned convent, with vast corridors, cellars, and secret doors; it is dark throughout the

---

[1] Grétry had anticipated this in *Guillaume Tell*, see p. 35.
[2] Charlton, 'Salieri's Timpani', *Musical Times*, cxii (1971), p. 961.

opera. The central character is a jealous Duke who for a year has kept
his wife in an underground vault, separated from her child, on
suspicion of unfaithfulness. Yet we are expected to sympathize with
him because he genuinely loves her. She is far too virtuous to return
her rescuer's tentative advances, and is happily reunited with her
husband just after he has abandoned her and the child to starvation.
There is something here not only of the old *comédie larmoyante* but of
the later Byronic villain-hero. The link however is purely literary; we
are reminded of Heathcliff and Rochester, never of Don Giovanni.
Dalayrac continued to produce successful *opéras comiques*, often
several in a year, right through the Revolution and into the Empire.
He kept in step with his public by adopting the fashionable type of
libretto, first sentimental comedy, then rescue opera, and later, when
taste again veered, the lighter diversion popularized by Boieldieu and
Isouard. Although gifted and intelligent in his approach to drama, he
seldom managed to crystallize it in music, which explains both his
initial popularity and his posthumous decline. His operas were
immensely successful not only in France but all over Europe for a
generation after his death in 1809, and they left their mark on greater
men. The first entry of Duke Alberti in *Camille*, with three servants
carrying a desk, chair, and candles, is accompanied by a short
orchestral pantomime, *Andante un peu lent et noblement*, furnished
with full stage directions: Alberti tears up a letter, examines a portrait,
puts it away angrily and goes off without a word. The effect is naïve
and reminiscent of Burleigh's appearance in *The Critic*, but the music
is not without atmosphere and the whole scene resembles the
pantomime effects in Weber's *Silvana* and other German romantic
operas.

GRÉTRY'S *GUILLAUME TELL*

The transition to the new style can be more profitably studied in
Grétry's *Guillaume Tell*, which did attempt to bridge the gap, only to
drop straight through it. His theme, like Rossini's forty years later on
the eve of another French Revolution, was the clash between
patriotism and tyranny in a pastoral setting. It was the only opera by
Grétry to remain in the repertory throughout the Terror, though the
Swiss patriots had to be reinforced by 'les braves sans-culottes de la
nation française' in order to supply a cue for the Marseillaise; it was
banned under Napoleon. Sedaine's libretto was based on Lemierre's
tragedy of 1766 – Schiller's was first performed in 1804 – and Grétry
was not wholly unsuccessful in finding musical equivalents: the simple
popular melodies of the old *opéra comique* on the one hand, the agitated

Italian-based rhetoric of the Opéra composers, especially Piccinni and Salieri, on the other. But he could not combine them, and he had only half mastered the second; nor was his technique sufficient for the increased scale of the big scenes. Act II ends with a *levée en masse* of the Swiss people, a choral episode (combined with a storm) that ought to make an impact like the gathering of the cantons in Rossini's opera or the revolution scene in *Boris Godunov*. It was beyond Grétry's powers; the male chorus are directed to sing 'avec une fureure sourde et une rage concentrée',[1] but the music belies them. This attempt to express through the directions what ought to be in the music itself is characteristic of many composers of the period, especially Le Sueur and Spontini. By bringing the serious style of the Opéra into the *opéra comique*, however tentatively, Grétry was making an advance, but with one foot only. He was adding a piece to an old garment. Nevertheless he tried, if fitfully, to develop action through music, and his overture and entr'actes, designed to set the scene for what follows, foreshadow the romantic preoccupation with local colour, exotic orchestral detail, elaborate pantomime and genre scenes in general. He even made a special journey to Switzerland in order to prepare himself. The overture, alternating between pastoral and military moods, introduces the *Ranz des vaches* quoted by Rousseau, which may have suggested the same idea to Rossini, and employs cello harmonics, three cowhorns – and cows ('On voit passer un troupeau de boeufs dans la montagne'). The symphonic element appears again in the first finale, a turbulent C minor movement for orchestra alone, during which a soldier assaulting a dishevelled girl is driven off by Madame Tell with a table knife.[2]

INCONGRUITIES IN REPUBLICAN OPERA

A certain incongruity was a feature of the first important Revolution opera, Cherubini's *Lodoïska*, and indeed of the Revolution school in general, which adopted the serious and lofty approach hitherto reserved to grand opera but generally kept residual features of the old *opéra comique*, including comic servants. In a sense this was logical, since the new spirit demanded that all classes be treated alike; but a sense of strain developed that was relaxed only when the servants had been transformed into the peasants and countryfolk of romantic opera. Floreski's servant Varbel, whose comic resourcefulness contributes to the plot of *Lodoïska*, is, like Figaro and Papageno, a relic of the *commedia dell'arte*; it is his environment that has changed.

[1] Detailed and eccentric directions were a feature of French opera; the priests in Salieri's *Tarare* have to sing 'd'un ton dogmatique'.
[2] The battle music near the end of *Tell* is quoted in Vol. VII, pp. 221–2.

Similar characters appear in *Élisa* and Le Sueur's *La Caverne*. In *Les Deux Journées* the social levels are neatly assimilated to the plot, and that was perhaps the intention in *Paul et Virginie*; but Le Sueur's handling is less certain than Cherubini's, and his Mauritius natives, who talk pidgin French with all the verbs in the infinitive, revert to traditional low-life comedy. The one composer who broke new ground was Méhul, whose most important later operas have a medieval setting and no comic characters. This enabled him to draw from life without running into political ambushes (he said himself in relation to *Ariodant* that he found it 'easier to make paladins sing than senators and consuls'). Indeed he was too detached for the authorities, who complained of absence of lip service to the prescribed ideals in *Mélidore et Phrosine*. A few tactful insertions put that right; but the remarkable degree to which Méhul, a supporter of the Revolution and friend of Napoleon, anticipated later opera is a tribute to his vision as an artist.

A more basic contradiction underlies the music of the new school. During the 1790s all the principal operas of Cherubini, Méhul, and Le Sueur, and of lesser figures like Berton, Kreutzer, and Gaveaux, present the same singular amalgam: an energetic, basically serious, and sometimes farouche libretto, a highly impassioned and rhetorical delivery, and a musical language that, though replete with the seeds of future development, seems reluctant or unable to let them germinate. A restless urge to experiment and break new ground, to express what had never been expressed before with a total commitment to dramatic truth, meets a barrier that prevents these impulses being carried to their musical conclusion. Of Grétry's sentimentality, his tendency to reduce the tragic to the pathetic, there is little sign; even in the two *Paul et Virginie* operas, based on Bernardin de St Pierre's Rousseau-ish novel of 1787, in which the noble savages of Mauritius display a heroism that puts certain of their white masters to shame, the sentimentality lies in the libretto, not in the music. The latter drives on, eschewing titillation of the senses, but equally ignoring demands for adequate emotional expression. The energy that Gluck contributed to the French tradition can be traced; there is almost no sign of the lyrical poise, the balance between matter and subject, the penetration to the heart of a character or situation.

More than one factor is at work here. Romanticism reached articulate expression in literature at least a generation earlier than in music; to appreciate the force of this, it is only necessary to compare the early work of Goethe and Schiller in Germany, Rousseau and his followers in France, and the Gothic romances and Ossianic poems in

Britain with their musical contemporaries, Mozart excepted. Secondly, a certain restraint, especially in vocal writing, was peculiar to the French tradition, always inclined to rank a properly accented declamation of the words above the re-creation through melody of their underlying emotion. This was to persist into the nineteenth century, and is central to the style of that contradictory 'arch-romantic', Berlioz; not until Gounod did it begin to change, and then largely under German influence. Thirdly, the ideology of the Revolution was essentially virile, looking down with impatience on superfluous frippery and emotional indulgence. A strain of social and political intransigence reinforced the native resistance to sensuous Italian charm and forbade any compromise with mere ear-tickling. Fourth, a generation of young artists rushed in to tackle challenging new tasks without the technique to cope with them: a classic case of pouring heady new wine into old bottles. Last, and by no means least, was the paramount influence and example of the leading composer, Cherubini.

CHERUBINI

Cherubini was the least original of the three leaders of the school, but by far the most technically proficient. After a very thorough training under Sarti, during which he mastered the polyphonic church style, he graduated to the theatre and produced eleven full-length operas for north Italy and London between 1780 and 1788. He visited Paris in 1786 and settled there permanently two years later. He is known to have admired and studied Haydn's symphonies, from which he may have derived his economical habit of putting the first subjects of his overtures into the dominant to form the second group, and doubtless encountered Handel's oratorios in London. But the principal sources of his style were the Neapolitan *opera buffa*, which had spread all over Italy and dominated the dying *opera seria*, and the French *tragédie lyrique* as developed by Gluck, Piccinni, and Salieri. The direct influence of Gluck was slight, though the Tartars in *Lodoiska* clearly descend from the Scythians in *Iphigénie en Tauride*, and Gluck's technique for expressing Orestes' madness through *ostinato* and *sforzando* left its mark on Cherubini, as on many others. The two composers were very different in temperament. Cherubini had little of Gluck's serene simplicity or his feeling for sensuous colour. His personality was energetic, dominating, strongly antipathetic to sentimentality and excess, and thus fully in tune with the spirit of the Revolution. This did not of course inhibit deep feeling, and his operas during the 1790s are intensely passionate. But there was a strong

element of suppression as well; it is interesting that Weber, an admirer
of Cherubini almost to the point of idolatry, detected a streak of
melancholy in even his most cheerful melodies. He was a natural
classic in an age of budding romanticism, perhaps basically an
instrumental composer without the outlet in France and Italy that
Germany might have afforded, and better equipped than Boccherini
to become an Italian Haydn. (It is significant that his late work
consisted almost entirely of church music and string quartets.) He
found it difficult to unbend or adapt himself to new conditions. In later
years, when *opéra comique* reverted to triviality, he fell rapidly out of
touch.

If Cherubini, like Spontini after him, lacked the quality of melodic
invention that forms one pole of the Italian temperament – and it was
the want of this and of a certain creative warmth that kept him out of
the front rank of opera composers – he compensated by developing a
style at once rhetorical and architecturally massive. Much of his
material consists of conventional melodic formulae based on arpeggios,
scale figures (chromatic for heightened emotional situations) and tonic
and dominant progressions, all handled with the utmost energy.
Owing to the absence of coloratura (scorned as effeminate by this
manly generation with the exception of Grétry) the solo airs suggest
the skeleton of an Italian aria, firm enough but lacking the seductive
outlines of living flesh. This limitation throws great weight on the
ensembles and the orchestra. The former at their best are dramatic
and technically resourceful. In the two big duets in Act II of *Médée*,
for Medea and Creon and Medea and Jason, Cherubini develops the
psychological implications by means of harmonic tension and the
obsessive working of agitated string figures, in a manner that owes
something to *Iphigénie en Tauride* and perhaps to Méhul's *Euphrosine*,[1]
but looks forward to Beethoven and even Wagner. This symphonic
technique, which appears first in *Lodoïska* though adumbrated in
Démophoon (1788),[2] is most fully elaborated (outside the overtures) in
his finales, which are often of titanic length. Structurally they include
repetition in the tonic of long sections first heard in the dominant, and
for reasons of balance they often terminate in an extensive coda in
which the music is carried to a vehement climax. Cherubini breathes
life into the plan by bold modulations, often startling in their context
but nearly always bringing the drama into alignment with the musical
design (a technique in which only Mozart anticipated him, and which

[1] See below, p. 51.
[2] See Georg Knepler, 'Die Technik der sinfonischen Durchführung in der französischen
Revolutionsoper', *Beiträge zur Musikwissenschaft*, i (1959), p. 4.

regularly eluded Haydn and Schubert), and by a pulsating and tireless rhythmic energy. In his treatment of rhythmic accent Cherubini was the Stravinsky of his age. His scores abound in *sforzandi*, cross-rhythms, misplaced accents, and abrupt dynamic contrasts within the bar or even the beat; sometimes almost every note in every part has its own dynamic mark. Long paragraphs and entire numbers are based on one-bar accompaniment figures as in Act II of *Lodoïska*:

Ex. 1

They are admirably fitted for creating and sustaining suspense; the element of exaggeration in Cherubini's preoccupation with weak beats and subdivisions is counteracted by the forward drive of the music as a whole. This inner tension, which fell apart in the work of his imitators, was to inspire the greatest of them, Beethoven.

The ultimate source of most of these features was the Neapolitan *opera buffa*, especially its finales. The first finale of *Les Deux Journées*, the most extended movement in the opera, is an unusually solid example of a type common in Cimarosa, and the *buffo* flavour is perceptible elsewhere, for example in the military episodes in Act II, related to similar scenes in the operas of Rossini, Donizetti, and Auber. In Act II of *Lodoïska* the *sotto voce* male trio, and still more the long quintet in the finale, where Dourlinski's three emissaries are doped with the potion they have prepared for Floreski and Varbel, are brilliant extensions of the *buffo* style in structure and language. What is new is the development of a firm slow-moving harmonic framework to prolong the suspense and erect structures of great tensile strength. A fine example is the moment in Act II of *Les Deux Journées* when the fugitive Armand, safely smuggled out of Paris, is recognized by the Commandant.

Ex. 2

Commandant: What features and what foreboding! Your name! *Armand:* I am called— *Commandant:* Well?

Cherubini's skill in constructing large-scale movements from neutral and even trivial tags underlies the whole edifice of romantic opera. If he inhibited the style of his own generation – which certainly needed discipline to curb its wilder excursions – he created almost single-handed that of the next.

His characterization, like that of nearly all the Revolution composers, was at its best in daemonic figures such as Dourlinski and Medea. Dourlinski is scarcely less formidable than Pizarro, and there can be little doubt that Beethoven took him as his model.

Ex. 3

- ran - ce,   c'est sur vous seu - le dé - sor - mais,   c'est sur vous

sen - le dé - sor - mais   que

tom - be tou - te ma ven - gean - ce

(No, give up that hope. Henceforth all my vengeance will fall on you alone.)

Médée (1797), perhaps Cherubini's most potent opera, is in one sense the culmination of pre-Revolution classical tragedy; the libretto had in fact been written for the Opéra in the 1780s, but not accepted because of Framéry's (unperformed) setting of the same subject. Its violence is all the more impressive for being largely psychological and expressed in a basically classical style. Yet it derives much of its urgency from the new leaven. Between it and *Anacréon* (1803), another Greek subject, a great gulf yawns. On superficial inspection each seems to have been delivered to the wrong address: the *opéra comique* is strenuous and heroic, the grand opera seeks to divert and amuse. This dislocation is indicative of Cherubini's declining powers, and perhaps of disillusionment; Anacréon was not a character capable of carrying any political or social message. *Médée*, composed when the sap was still rising, has the immediacy of hard experience; in the ferment of agitation for the rights of man its heroine stands forth as the champion of the right of woman to be judged as an individual and not a chattel.

In orchestration, too, Cherubini was the most influential, though not the most adventurous, of the Revolution school. Apart from Mozart, he was perhaps the first important composer to exploit the sensuous possibilities of the clarinet; the little interludes that punctuate the trio in Act II of *Lodoïska* are an eloquent example. The scoring of the storm that begins Act III of *Médée* – a double storm, in the heavens and the heroine's heart (a Gluckian conception) – is more advanced in style than that of the Pastoral Symphony, for instance in the imaginative treatment of the piccolo. In general, however, Cherubini's orchestral style, with its busy string figuration, rhythmic punctuation on the wind, and contrasts between massive *tutti* and sudden hushes, often with solo woodwind left to carry on the argument, is scarcely distinguishable from Beethoven's; and it was fully evolved before Beethoven left Bonn. This is most apparent in Cherubini's overtures, especially those of *Lodoïska*, *Élisa*, *Médée*, and *Les Deux Journées* (but scarcely less in that of *Démophoon* as early as 1788), which were often played separately in Vienna and elsewhere and taken as symphonic models by the whole German school. Their thematic rhetoric, not least in the huge codas, is 'dramatic' in precisely the sense often applied to Beethoven's symphonies.

One of the most successful and still exciting features of Cherubini's operas (again echoed in *Fidelio*) is his use of *mélodrame*. The technique was not new. Conceived and partly attempted by Rousseau in *Pygmalion* (set to music in full by Coignet in 1770) and taken up in Germany, notably by Benda and Mozart, it was employed by all the Revolution school, often with considerable skill. But no one surpassed Cherubini's use of it in *Les Deux Journées*; for example in no. 12, where the refugee hero, concealed in a tree, prays for his wife's safety, and no. 13, where he leaps down to save her from molestation by soldiers, only to be recognized and arrested by the Commandant. This movement, which culminates in a powerful double chorus, illustrates an important advantage of the *opéra comique* convention, whose spoken dialogue, besides retaining the link with everyday life, offered the composer two additional grades of expression in building up concerted numbers (speech – *mélodrame* – recitative – air – ensemble). Cherubini made even more memorable use of this in the second finale of *Médée*. Jason is being married to Dirce in a temple at the back of the stage while Medea rages in the foreground. The decorous Glucklike wedding music for chorus and wind contrasts brilliantly with Medea's utterances, which break from unaccompanied speech through *mélodrame* to recitative (supported by a small group of strings) and then to full orchestral accompaniment as she works herself into an uncontrollable passion.[1] The effect is totally ruined when the dialogue

---

[1] Berlioz was surely recalling this scene in *La Prise de Troie* when the introduction of the Trojan Horse into the city coincides with the dire prophecies of Cassandra. The finale of Act III of *Médée* may likewise have suggested Berlioz's scene in the temple of Vesta.

is replaced, as it generally is today, by Franz Lachner's recitatives, composed in an alien style for a German performance in 1854.

Cherubini's antipathy to sensuous indulgence did not exclude an occasional chromaticism almost worthy of Spohr. This occurs, though rarely, at all stages of his career, in *Lodoïska* (Floreski's *Largo non tanto* in the Act I duet with Varbel[1]), *Les Deux Journées* (no. 11), *Les Abencérages* (1813, no. 15) and several times, though in a bolder, more compressed idiom, in *Ali Baba*. The example from *Les Deux Journées* occurs in the scene in Act III where the country girl Angelina waits anxiously for her bridegroom:

Ex. 4

(Antonio doesn't come!)

The alternation here of a village wedding procession, a soldiers' march and chorus, and the plaintive emotionalism of the bride is typical of romantic opera a generation later. Cherubini may have derived this harmonic wash, as Spohr certainly did, from lingering over the kaleidoscopic chromatic progressions characteristic of the mature Mozart. It is uncertain when Cherubini encountered Mozart's music. He conducted the first Paris performance of the Requiem in 1804.

---

[1] The melody is presently combined in counterpoint with Varbel's polonaise air 'Souvent près d'une belle', a device employed with relish by Berlioz in *La Damnation de Faust*, several times by Le Sueur and by Méhul in *Valentine de Milan*. In this opera an Italian march in C minor and a French march in C major at double speed are played separately and then combined.

Some pages in *Lodoïska* suggest an acquaintance with *Don Giovanni*, not given in Paris until 1805, and then in mutilated form; but Cherubini entered in his own catalogue a quartet for insertion in a projected performance at the Feydeau in 1792. Mozart symphonies had been played at the Concert Spirituel in 1786 and 1789. *Le nozze di Figaro*, in a five-act French translation with the recitatives replaced by Beaumarchais's original dialogue, was produced at the Opéra at the height of the Revolution in March 1793. It was a total failure with the public but left its mark on composers. Gaveaux's *Sophie et Moncars* contains a palpable imitation of 'Voi che sapete', and echoes of 'Non più andrai' are numerous, for instance in Act I of *Les Deux Journées*.

INFLUENCE OF *DON GIOVANNI*

In the long run the influence of *Don Giovanni* went far deeper. Since this masterpiece became a model and a shrine for almost all composers of romantic opera, it may be convenient to summarize here the features they imitated, though some of them were in general circulation: the baritone hero (a German feature, especially popular with Winter, who introduced it to Paris with *Tamerlan* in 1802); the prolongation of the overture into the first scene (often anticipated, notably by Gluck, from whom Mozart may have derived it, but also by Rameau in the unperformed *Les Boréades* of 1764);[1] the use of material from the opera in the overture (this too occurs earlier, but was systematically developed by the French school, from whom Weber borrowed it ready made);[2] thematic anticipation of an aria at the start of the previous recitative (as in 'Non mi dir'), a favourite device of Le Sueur, especially in *Ossian*; prominent stage bands (greatly extended by Mayr and Spontini, though of course found in many earlier operas, including some of Handel's); sudden modulations up or down a major third at moments of special dramatic importance, as when Giovanni addresses Elvira at her window in the Act II trio, the entry of Anna and Ottavio in the sextet, and the nodding of the statue in the churchyard scene (this became a favourite device, even a mannerism, of all early romantic composers from Cherubini to Schubert and Marschner); thematic use of chromatic scale figures (very common in the Revolution composers, especially Berton and Méhul). The particular compound of chromatic scales, diminished sevenths, syncopated string figures, solemn trombone chords, and D

---

[1] There was much discussion of the overture in Paris between Gluck and the Revolution. Berton uses the technique in *Les Rigueurs du cloître*.

[2] It also occurs in a few German operas, for example Reichardt's *Die Geisterinsel* (Berlin, 1798).

minor tonality at the climax of the supper scene was repeatedly echoed throughout the next two generations, and is still palely loitering (complete with statue) at the end of Hérold's *Zampa* (1831).

MÉHUL

This daemonic element was a cardinal feature of Méhul's operas. Although reputedly encouraged in his youth by Gluck, he had nothing temperamentally in common with his mentor. (There is no doubt about Gluck's influence on the young Méhul, but no proof of personal contact.) Méhul was an outstanding example of an artist whose restless originality and constant urge to experiment were not matched by the technical skill to exploit his ideas. Although his first opera to reach the stage, *Euphrosine* (1790),[1] contains an element of comedy, he later preferred to separate the genres while remaining within the technical ambit of *opéra comique*. His finest and most characteristic operas are intensely serious, with a strong emphasis on the darker side of human nature. The harmonic style of *Mélidore et Phrosine* (1794) is bolder than anything in Rossini, Bellini, or Donizetti, and even than early Beethoven; although it was an immediate success, Méhul withdrew it, intending to have the libretto rewritten for the Opéra, but this was never done. Much of it would scarcely be out of place in *Euryanthe* and the same is true of *Ariodant* (1799) (for example the picturesque chromaticisms suggesting the fall of darkness in the finale of Act II) and the overture to *Uthal* (1806), which is athematic, at moments almost atonal, and in no definable form. The parallel between *Euryanthe* and *Ariodant* is reinforced by the close similarity of plot: in addition to the common background of chivalry and nocturnal conspiracy, the characters of Othon and Dalinde are as palpably the forbears of Lysiart and Eglantine as the latter are of Telramund and Ortrud. Berlioz too is foreshadowed in the strange orchestral introduction to the chorus 'O nuit propice à l'amour' that begins Act II.

Cherubini criticized *Mélidore et Phrosine* for its 'brusque and incongruous harmonic transitions' and declared that Méhul's style was dominated by progressions which, 'being foreign to the principal key of the piece, frequently become incoherent and harsh'. It is easy to see what he meant. A tendency to veer through a whole range of minor keys, often scarcely related, to switch unpredictably between major and tonic minor, and to plaster melody and inner parts with

---

[1] The particulars given by Alfred Loewenberg (*Annals of Opera*, Cambridge, 1943) on this opera are inaccurate. After its production in five acts, it was reduced to three by the winter of 1792–3 and rewritten with a new third act (eliminating the comedy) in 1795. Only the second version is published; the music of the third is lost.

chronic chromaticisms is characteristic of many Revolution composers; Méhul carried it to extremes. He over-exploited certain chords
and progressions – the dominant minor ninth, the Neapolitan sixth in
a major key, the unprepared alternation of remote tonalities (D major
and A flat major in the first finale of *Mélidore et Phrosine*); but the
asperity arises as much from the abruptness with which he introduces
them, often very early in a piece, and their relationship to his general
style, which retained an element of eighteenth-century classicism. He
possessed little of Cherubini's architectural power and none of his
facility in counterpoint, which he seldom attempted in his operas.
While he used the one-bar ostinato to considerable effect in *Stratonice*
and *Mélidore et Phrosine*, his anxiety to express every shade of
dramatic nuance (no other composer applied Gluck's declared
principles – as distinct from his practice – with such fanaticism) led
him, especially in *Ariodant*, to introduce constant variations in the
basic tempo, often only for a bar or two at a time, and he was inclined
to employ temporarily superimposed sforzandi and syncopation as a
substitute for genuine rhythmic flexibility. Since his bolder strokes
nearly always spring from some verbal or dramatic stimulus without
any necessary relation to the musical design – almost as if he were
improvising – Cherubini's charge of insufficient consolidation must
be admitted. Méhul seems to have accepted it, not wholly for the
better; he was highly susceptible to criticism and took too much to
heart not only the opinion of his equals but that of the public. Some of
his later operas show all too clearly the domesticating influence of
Cherubini, who (like others since, including Wagner) ranked the
relatively insipid *Joseph* (1807) as Méhul's masterpiece.

One of Méhul's chief preoccupations was to establish the dramatic
climate and background of his operas. He introduced Spanish themes
in *Les Deux Aveugles de Tolède* (1806) and used the operatic overture
not merely to prepare the audience but to paint the scene and begin
the action. (The overture to Kreutzer's *Lodoïska*, played with the
curtain up, is a march depicting the approach of the Tartars with their
female captives.) In this Méhul was following up theories current at
the time,[1] but he did so in a decidedly original manner. Many of his
overtures are the true ancestors of the symphonic poem. Not all are
detachable as concert pieces, but they constantly aspire to the
condition of programme music and generally abandon any pretence to
sonata form. That of *Le Jeune Henri* is an imaginative recreation of a
hunting scene in a forest, and has outlived the opera. The wild overture

[1] See Basil Deane, 'The French Operatic Overture from Grétry to Berlioz', *Proceedings of the Royal Musical Association*, xcix (1972–3), p. 67.

to *Uthal* is suddenly punctuated by the cries of the heroine, who has lost her father in a nocturnal mist, a stroke possibly suggested by a similar one in Grétry's overture *Aucassin et Nicolette* (1779) ('Bruit de guerre') where a father is heard calling his son. The overture of *Le jeune sage et le vieux fou* (1793) begins with what appears to be an impressionistic portrait of the two main characters. The action of *Mélidore et Phrosine* takes place in the Straits of Messina, that of *Uthal* in the Hebrides. Méhul's music in neither case suggests the locality, but it does conjure up, sometimes with astonishing vividness, the background of nature against which the story unfolds: the contrasted moods of the sea in one opera, lowering mists and forests in the other. This musical atmosphere is extended (with varying success) throughout the operas, so that the background becomes, as the romanticism of the librettos requires, a functional part of the design. Much the same is true of the medieval courtly setting of *Ariodant*. Important scenes in all three operas (as in many others of the period, not least the four *Leonora* settings) take place in darkness, a circumstance that clearly stimulated Méhul's imagination and is reflected in the music; one is constantly aware of the time of day and the weather. Storms had long been common in French opera; at this period they became more prominent and intense as composers drew the parallel between the fury of the elements and the violence, hitherto suppressed or discreetly veiled, at the springs of human emotion. The *Mélidore* storm may owe a specific debt to that in Kreutzer's *Paul et Virginie*, which also persists for much of the third act and culminates in the hero diving into the sea; but Kreutzer's music is much milder and wholly conventional.

Beethoven, who certainly derived his treatment of the trumpet calls in *Fidelio* from Méhul's *Héléna* (1803), may have picked up a hint for his dungeon scene from Méhul's treatment of darkness. Weber was to find ready to hand the whole apparatus for the forests of *Der Freischütz*, the seascapes of *Oberon*, and the chivalry shot with dark jealousy of *Euryanthe*. The opening of the *Mélidore et Phrosine* overture seems to have suggested that of *Der Freischütz*.

Ex. 5

(answering phrase in same rhythm)

The tremendous storm that rages almost throughout Act III of the same opera and coincides with the climax of the action has an elemental force prophetic of *The Flying Dutchman*, the more so as one of the characters dives off a rocky promontory into the sea, though this occurs during one of the rare patches of spoken dialogue.

REMINISCENCE MOTIVES

These parallels with Weber and Wagner, both of whom were familiar with French opera of this period, gain increased significance from Méhul's experiments with personal motives. Ernst Bücken[1] speaks of the group whom he calls the Conservatoire composers (Grétry, Méhul, Le Sueur, Berton and Catel) adopting the motto 'Révolutionnons l'opéra!', and credits them with the invention of the personal motive that undergoes musical development in accord with the action. The first claim is true – in his preface to *Ariodant* Méhul recommended that composers of new operas should state in detail their principles and aims and the rules they have observed, with a view to moulding public taste – but the second is in some respects an over-rationalization. Cherubini, as Bücken admits, never went beyond the simple reminiscence motive, which he used very aptly in *Les Deux Journées* and several other operas, most effectively perhaps in the last, *Ali Baba*. The claims made for Catel and Berton, as well as those of Le Sueur (whom Bücken does not mention in this connection) belong to the new century and are considered below. But Méhul was indeed a pioneer, and an earlier and more radical one than Bücken suggests. There is no doubt that the flexible *Leitmotiv* in the Wagnerian sense was a product of the French school: once more the edifice was prepared for the coping stones of the next two generations.

The reminiscence motive was much in the air in the Paris of the 1780s, partly no doubt the outcome of Rousseau's theories of dramatic expression. Lemoyne in *Electre* (1782) introduced three motives associated with his heroine in the overture, one of them marked by a rising tritone, and used them later to build up her portrait. They lack individual potency and almost disappear after Act I, but their association with open-ended and interrupted forms is significant. Jean-Baptiste Rey (1734–1810) followed a similar procedure in completing Sacchini's posthumous *Arvire et Evelina* (1788).[2] In *Richard Coeur de Lion* Grétry made the reminiscence motive a central hinge of his design. Lacépède in *La Poétique de la musique* (1785) recommended the use of motives, whether in the voice parts or the orchestra, as a means of linking scenes or presaging future events; Le Sueur carried

[1] *Der heroische Stil in der Oper* (Leipzig, 1924), p. 79.
[2] Rushton, op. cit.

the same ideas into the unlikely field of church music and advocated them in a controversial pamphlet, *Exposé d'une musique une, imitative et particulière à chaque solennité* (1787), in which he remarks that the orchestra can express the thoughts and feelings of a character who himself is silent – an idea that points straight to Wagner. Le Sueur himself, who was taunted not without some reason with writing theatre music for the church and church music for the theatre, did not exploit his theories till his two grand operas under the Empire, but the whole Paris school used the reminiscence motive freely. Cherubini, with the strongest technique, was the least enterprising in his treatment of this device, perhaps because he needed it least.

Méhul made a striking advance as early as *Euphrosine* (1790), an uneven work that reveals the sources of his style (Grétry, the Neapolitans, Haydn, but not much Gluck) before the full impact of Cherubini or the Revolution. It has a brilliantly witty libretto by François Hoffman, in which the young heroine sets out to tame the surly autocrat Coradin after the manner of Anne Whitefield in *Man and Superman*. She has a rival in the Comtesse d'Arles, formerly engaged to Coradin, who has sworn to marry or punish him. True love wins in the end, and much of the music is as light-fingered as the libretto; but the emotions of jealousy and remorse released in Méhul a remarkable concentration of power and originality, as they were often to do later (for example in the characters of Othon in *Ariodant* and Siméon in *Joseph*). The repeated association of a particular group of emotions with technical experiment and music of unusual power is very striking. In the duet 'Gardez-vous de la jalousie' in Act II the Countess, while pretending to warn Coradin, works on his feelings with a hint that Euphrosine has a secret lover and drives him into a blind fury, rejoicing that she has lit in his heart a fire that will destroy him. This duet made an immediate sensation, as well it might. It was quoted at length in two contemporary works, Miller's popular ballet *Psyché* (Opéra, 14 December 1790, performed 1161 times in less than forty years) and Vandenbroeck's *mélodrame, Le Génie Asouf* (1795),[1] and singled out as a masterstroke by artists as different as the grudging Grétry and the fastidious Berlioz, who called it a worthy paraphrase of Iago's 'green-eyed monster' speech. It is largely based on a motive of a rising and falling third, heard in the bass at the outset and subjected to constant development and variation:

[1] David Charlton, 'Motive and Motif: Méhul before 1791', *Music and Letters*, lvii (1976), p. 362.

Ex. 6

(Beware of jealousy, avoid its terrible passion.)

In Act III Coradin orders his physician to poison Euphrosine. The physician gives her a harmless drink and she pretends to die, a pantomime much relished by the Countess. But Coradin is seized by bitter remorse and despair and bursts out in a highly dramatic air, 'O douleur insupportable', which is based throughout on the same motive, first in its original form and later in various transformations:

Ex. 7

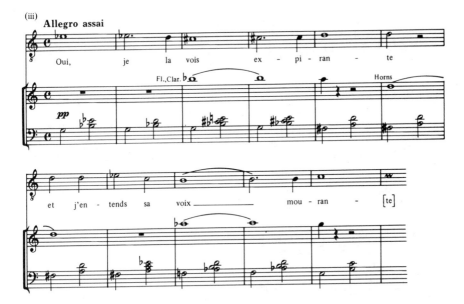

((ii) I alone committed the crime (iii) Yes, I see her expiring and hear her dying voice)

In order to leave no doubt about the matter Méhul built the introduction of the overture, *Lent tres marqué*, on the motive in octaves. The symphonic elaboration in different registers of a motive first heard in the bass was developed by Cherubini in several movements of *Médée* and (with a specific dramatic reference) by Berton in *Le Délire* and *Montano et Stéphanie* (both 1799).

The overture to *Mélidore et Phrosine* evokes the marine setting and the course of the plot, a variant of the Hero and Leander legend complicated by the incestuous love of the heroine's brother Jule, which grips him in a frenzy of jealousy throughout the opera. It consists of a stormy D minor *allegro* with a distinct anticipation of *Coriolan*, leading via a huge climax to a *grazioso* D major coda in barcarolle rhythm over a tonic pedal. Méhul uses material related to this several times in the opera to suggest a calm sea, notably at the end of the second and third acts. The finale of the latter all but anticipates the overture to *Euryanthe* and the mermaids in *Oberon* (in the same key) at one and the same time:

Ex. 8

(The sky was clearing overhead)

At the very end of the overture the horns in imitation quietly repeat another rising and falling third (very different in implication from that in *Euphrosine*). This turns out to be the phrase to which Mélidore calls Phrosine's name as she is rowed away across the strait at the end of Act II:

Ex. 9

Méhul uses it again, with other earlier motives, in the first scene of Act III, a complex of several interlinked movements, air, *mélodrame*, offstage chorus, and long sections for orchestra alone, culminating in the storm. During the introduction Mélidore lights a beacon to guide Phrosine across the strait at night. He is silent, but the orchestra reveals his thoughts: an amorous falling third from solo cello reminds the horns of Phrosine's motive, which they echo in turn, one in the pit, two more behind the scenes. The seeds of a great deal in romantic opera are implicit in these few bars:

Ex. 10

In *Ariodant* Méhul carried the whole process further and combined several features that appear separately in *Mélidore et Phrosine*. The opening of the latter had been arresting enough: Aimar, Phrosine's eldest brother, who for social reasons is violently opposed to her marrying Mélidore, answers her unheard and implied plea in the first words of the opera, which begins as it were in the middle of a duet:

Ex. 11

(No, no, abandon hope)

The opening of *Ariodant* is startling for its date. The brief irregular overture in no recognizable form, sparsely scored for very full

orchestra, ends on a dominant seventh as the curtain rises; Othon
utters a passionate outburst (spoken); and a dominant minor ninth
announces the central theme of the opera, both in the dramatic and
the musical sense:

Ex. 12

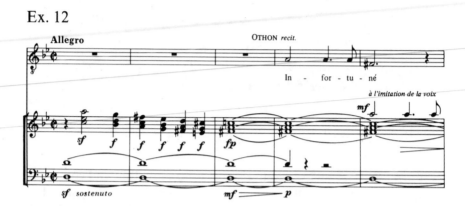

(Ill-fated, I know it myself)

Bücken calls this a revenge motive, but that is to underrate Méhul's
insight. It is associated with the unbridled passions of Othon, torn
between love for Ina and jealous hatred of the favoured Ariodant, and
occurs in various forms in at least eight of the fifteen movements of
the opera; one or two further variants cited by Bücken may be
accidental. According to him the leitmotive technique in Méhul's last
and unfinished opera *Valentine de Milan* is nearly as advanced as in
Ariodant. There is a striking anticipation of Othon's motive during the
storm in Act III of *Mélidore et Phrosine*. Five movements in *Ariodant*,
including the first three, begin with it. The continuation in each case
is very different, conforming closely to the dramatic situation but
throwing new light on the theme. The air (no. 2) in which Othon's
accomplice Dalinde, who has already deceived her mistress Ina, tries
to calm his rage begins with two bars of the motive (*allegro* 4/4),

followed by five quiet *adagio* bars in triple time accompanied by strings only ('Calmez cette colère'), and then continues *allegro* 4/4. The duet (no. 3), in which his fury returns with such violence that Dalinde fears it will deliver her to their enemies, starts as a *mélodrame* against an extended eight-bar version of the motive (fortissimo dying abruptly to pianissimo); after a short silence Othon and the full orchestra enter fortissimo with a great cry 'O démon de la jalousie!' on an augmented triad.

The same motive appears, sometimes transformed, in the middle and at the end of movements. The range of dramatic irony that Méhul evokes with it is unlike anything else in eighteenth-century opera. Ariodant's first air, a cheerful piece looking forward to reunion with his beloved, ends with a coda in sharp contrast as Ina enters for the first time; we are reminded at once of the passion she has stirred in Othon, of which Ariodant as yet knows nothing:

Ex. 13

sostenuto

(During the last four bars Ina appears.)

There is a similar passage, even more effective in its quiet irony, at the end of the long, violent and intensely dramatic finale of Act II, in which Othon's plot to expose Ina as a loose and faithless woman has apparently triumphed. In Act III Méhul introduces the motive with superb timing as the culmination of a phrase when Edgard, Ina's father, decides that he must obey his own law against transgressors and condemn her to death. It is equally prominent in the next piece, in which Ina, rejecting Othon's cajolery and threats, prefers a criminal's death to his love.

MÉHUL'S ORGANIZATION OF FORM

It is remarkable that the greatest single advance in reminiscence-motive technique outside Wagner should have occurred in an *opéra comique* with spoken dialogue. But this was not Méhul's only expedient for overcoming the structural limitations of the form. He had always sought to express dramatic evolution by musical means. The quartet in *Stratonice* (1792), a beautifully planned complex of five movements that throws new light on all four characters and brings the tangled issues to a climax, is an early example. In *Mélidore et Phrosine*, especially in Act III, which has only two short patches of dialogue, he approached through-composed form. He also began a practice, extended in *Ariodant*, of projecting a set number into the following dialogue by means of a coda in contrasted mood, often incorporating *mélodrame* or the entry of a fresh character, as in Ex. 13. This meant ending in a foreign key or on an ambiguous chord or a discord. Act II of *Mélidore et Phrosine* has a notable *coup de théâtre* of this kind. Jule asks a hermit for help in revenging himself on Mélidore for abducting his sister. But the hermit is Mélidore in disguise, and he tells Jule that the man he wants is dead. Unknown to either of them, and to the audience, Phrosine has been listening: she rushes on in the last bars of the duet, which momentarily becomes a trio, and faints, the action proceeding in dialogue:

Ex. 14

(*Mélidore:* Swallowed in the bosom of the waters Mélidore has ceased to live. *Jule:* Mélidore has ceased to live! *Phrosine:* He is dead, I die myself!)

The majority of movements in *Ariodant* conclude with some such surprise. Dalinde's first air in F ends on a first inversion of D major, Edgard's on the dominant, the duet for Ina and Ariodant in Act II (A minor-major) on a high F major chord (entry of Dalinde with a false message from Othon), Edgard's F minor air in Act III on a first inversion of E major (*mélodrame,* entry of Othon), the duet for Ina and Othon (E flat) on a first inversion of G major (*mélodrame* in which Ina, preferring death, orders her guards to escort her back to prison). In each case Méhul establishes his tonic before suddenly deviating from it. The effect of this primitive form of progressive tonality is twofold: it scores a dramatic point by means of surprise, and it makes for continuity by throwing expectation forward into the ensuing dialogue. It puts formal limitation to creative use, and must surely make an impact in the theatre. But it had no future. Later *opéra comique* composers were more concerned to satisfy expectation (in every sense) than to defy it; and the German romantics, Méhul's true heirs, presently took the next logical step and abandoned spoken dialogue for through-composition.

CHARACTERIZATION IN REPUBLICAN OPERA

Méhul's achievement undermined the *opéra comique* in another respect. One result of the Revolution's popularization of the theatre was that composers and librettists, writing for less sophisticated audiences, tended to emphasize the elementary virtues and to present their characters in black and white as morally detestable or impeccable. This sometimes led to involuntary caricature: the Tartar chief Titzikan in *Lodoiska* is a noble savage while the reckless Floreski is every inch an operatic Pole. The villains, as already noted in connection with Cherubini, are as a rule more powerfully drawn. In Méhul they are apt to run away with the composer's imagination and the opera; the atmosphere of sombre menace they instil, as of hidden powers only just held in check, assumes so pungent a flavour of tragedy that the happy end with its contrived repentance becomes aesthetically intolerable. Both *Mélidore et Phrosine* and *Ariodant*, especially the latter, collapse in resounding anticlimax, because the characters have outgrown their symbolic status and asserted their rights as individuals. (Othon is probably Méhul's most powerful character, as Medea is Cherubini's; both are the slaves of passion, and each composer dedicated his work to the other.) The romantic yeast has begun to work. The operas imply a tragic climax, which they ostentatiously proceed to shirk. It was some time before this logic was accepted, outside a few works such as *Médée* and Catel's *Sémiramis* (1802); but these were classical subjects related to the *tragédie lyrique*, and heroine and villain were one and the same. In nearly all French operas of the period the last act is by far the weakest. One of the first composers to admit the tragic conclusion was Rossini in *Tancredi*, *Otello*, and *Maometto Secondo*;[1] he was forced to bow to public opinion, but a few years later almost every serious opera ended with a death.

---

[1] See pp. 405–6.

DALAYRAC'S REMINISCENCE MOTIVES

Another composer who made interesting experiments with recurring motives was Dalayrac.[1] After his death the librettist B. J. Marsollier paid tribute to his thoughtful and stimulating approach to operatic collaboration, and thematic reminiscence was specifically built into some of his librettos. Like Méhul, Dalayrac used motives to represent moral and dramatic ideas as well as persons, and to reveal thoughts in his characters' minds, as in the second finale of *Léon* (1798), where the orchestra recalls the love duet from Act I when the lovers, unable to speak openly since the man is in disguise, are forcibly separated. Motives from all three acts, not all of them principal themes, return at the end of the opera. *Léhéman* (1801) carries the process further, bringing back as many as eight ideas and using two of them in the overture. Motives associated with hope, fear, and danger are worked into several movements, and again express sentiments which the characters dare not utter owing to the presence of enemies. Unfortunately neither the music nor the libretto is strong enough to exploit the possibilities; Dalayrac develops nothing like the concentrated power of Méhul. *Léhéman*, with its artless plot (including a man-hunt in the wilds of Silesia), its compound of violence, lofty sentiments, and earthy humour, could stand as a copybook example of rescue opera. While the music is superficial, derived from Grétry with touches of Cherubini and Mozart, Dalayrac shows no little skill in developing the action during and by means of the set numbers. For this reason it was admired by Weber, who published an article on it (as *Macdonald*) at Munich on 25 July 1811.[2]

LE SUEUR

Le Sueur's three *opéras comiques* of the 1790s – *La Caverne* (1793), *Paul et Virginie* (1794) and *Télémaque*[3] (1796) – are a strange mixture of eccentricity and dullness. *Télémaque* shows his singular preoccupation with musical archaeology; every number is assigned to its mode and *nomos* according to his theories of Greek music. The music is fussy in texture but cold and manufactured. This coldness was the last thing Le Sueur intended. As Dent remarked,[4] he was 'one of those composers who feel a great deal more than they know how to express', and he was constantly exhorting his performers in footnotes to convey

---

[1] See Charlton, 'Motif and Recollection in Four Operas of Dalayrac', *Soundings*, vii (1978), p. 38.

[2] In connection with the first performance in that form.

[3] Its first version, composed for the Opéra before the Revolution, presumably had recitatives.

[4] *The Rise of Romantic Opera* (Cambridge, 1976), p. 65.

the emotion he had omitted to supply in the music. He was addicted to such contradictory dynamic and tempo marks as *Allegro fieramente e disperato sans vitesse et largement* (Paul's air in Act III of *Paul et Virginie*). In the first finale of this opera he developed a curious technique of pauses as a substitute for modulation. The skeleton is: chorus in D major, pause, solo for new character (Allegro disperato, F minor), pause, entry of more characters and ensemble in A major. His stage directions are informative about production methods and lighting, including the method of indicating the onset of darkness by lowering the footlights. He notes with regard to a *mélodrame hypocritique* in *Paul et Virginie* that the actors must ensure that the rhythm of their movements exactly synchronizes with that of the music, and they should appear to evoke the response of the orchestra rather than the other way round.

BERTON AND RODOLPHE KREUTZER

The most influential composers of this decade were not always the most successful. Cherubini's important operas were without exception more popular in Germany than in France, which preferred Kreutzer's *Lodoiska*. Minor figures like Berton and Kreutzer were as prolific as Méhul, and not lacking in enterprise. The hero of the former's *Le Délire* (1799) is a young man driven out of his mind by dissipation; Berton endeavours to convey his insanity by a recurrent motive comprising the successive triads of C, B, and G major, which begins the overture. His more successful *Montano et Stéphanie* (1799) was famous for a mammoth crescendo in the second finale; it was supposedly imitated from Giuseppe Moscà (1772–1839), but could just as well have come from Cimarosa or any other Neapolitan. This opera, on the same subject as *Ariodant* but with a weaker libretto (which also suffered from police intervention owing to the central scene being laid in a chapel with a sympathetic priest), shows Berton experimenting in much the same way as Méhul, whom he resembled in approach but not in skill or originality. The modulating links with the dialogue are more tentative; the recurring motives, though sometimes effective, are apt to be clichés – so much so that it is sometimes hard to determine if they are used deliberately or by accident. Berton is at his best in the Glucklike wedding music, where he uses the serpent to suggest an organ, and the Cherubinian first finale with its happy treatment of ostinato and canon. There are interesting textural details, such as the use of muted drums as a true bass when Montano rages at Stéphanie's supposed infidelity and a wedding chorus in which the voices go below the orchestra; but the score is uncertain in style and direction, with a great deal of strenuous thrashing about to little purpose.

GAVEAUX AND STEIBELT

   Gaveaux, the original Floreski in Cherubini's *Lodoiska* and Steibelt's Roméo, earned the distinction of leaving his mark on the music as well as the libretto of *Fidelio*.[1] His *Sophie et Moncars ou l'Intrigue portugaise* (1798) has a charming quartet accompanied by horn and cello soli and a substantial and well-constructed entr'acte in the form of variations with each solo woodwind coming to the front in turn, an idea doubtless borrowed from Grétry's *La Rosière de Salency* and echoed in the overture to Boieldieu's *Un Tour de soubrette* (1806). An interesting curiosity among Revolution operas is Steibelt's *Roméo et Juliette* (1793).[2] The libretto with its happy end and the replacement of Friar Laurence for political reasons by a secular Greek named Cébas, might not pass muster today; but the music, profoundly influenced by Mozart (whom Steibelt may have encountered before he left Germany for Paris in 1790) and not at all by Gluck, has a melodic and harmonic warmth and a flexibility in the management of ensembles uncommon in French opera of this period. (It was criticized at the time as too German.) The orchestration is rich, and many episodes have a distinct romantic flavour, notably the Act I love duet, which ends as a trio as Juliet's nurse warns them that dawn is near, the almost Weberian scena in Act II when Juliet is terrified by the ghost of Théobald (Tybalt), the long mourning sequence at Juliet's tomb that opens Act III (four-part female chorus, with muted drums and 'beffroi'[3]), Romeo's air introduced by solo cello and horn over pizzicato basses, joined later by upper strings and obbligato clarinet, and the beautifully contrived enharmonic modulation (E flat to E via C flat) at Juliet's awakening. Steibelt might have supplied the German warmth required to balance French thrust and inventiveness before romantic opera could break free (a task presently achieved by Weber); he was a composer of great talent but, according to Felix Clément, 'd'une immoralité rébutante', and he left Paris under a cloud in 1796. He returned later, but made no contribution to opera.

[1] See pp. 467 and 472.
[2] Shakespeare was entering his first period of great popularity as an operatic source. Dalayrac's opera on the same subject, *Tout pour l'amour* (1792), was damned, libretto and music, by Berlioz in *À travers Chants*, as 'une oeuvre composée par deux imbéciles qui ne connaissent ni la passion, ni le sentiment, ni le bon sens, ni le français, ni la musique'.
[3] This is often quoted as the first appearance of the tamtam in opera; it was probably a tuned bell. Steibelt had composed the score for the Opéra, which at that time possessed large bells sounding C and G, notes that would fit the C minor tonality of the passage. (Charlton, *Soundings* (1973) op. cit.)

INNOVATIONS IN ORCHESTRATION

The orchestration of French *opéra comique* at this period had interesting and peculiar features. At the start of the decade the Opéra orchestra still retained traces of the old concertino-ripieno grouping, and a keyboard continuo player was employed as late as 1810. The *opéra comique* theatres, which had smaller orchestras but a higher reputation for ensemble (at least until the Opéra was reorganized in 1797–8), took over the noisy scoring for which the Opéra was notorious but not its conservatism (the obbligato for solo bassoon in Neris's air in *Médée* was a rare reversion to baroque practice). A number of instruments, especially the clarinet, cello, and horn, were employed in new ways; but the most important feature was the development of the orchestra as a composite unit for picturesque scene-painting and an elemental force in competition with the voices. This prepared the way for the grand opera of the Empire and, even more strikingly, for the German romantics, especially Weber. While Cherubini deployed his forces in the formidably massive style soon to be associated with Beethoven, Méhul was more adventurous if less accomplished, notably in his treatment of the horns. He used them more melodically than Mozart and Beethoven, both in solos and in inner parts. The first finale of *Mélidore et Phrosine* contains a remarkable passage of stopped notes for four horns, in D, G, and F, when Aimar, struck down by Mélidore in the darkness, calls on his brother Jule to avenge him. Phrosine's air earlier in the scene has a solo horn part stopped on almost every note of the scale. This was a special effect (though Méhul and Berton continued to emphasize stopped notes when their juniors treated the instrument more conventionally), but it reflects a conspicuous enlargement in the range of expression available to the horn, to which the enterprise of composers, the skill of the players and the simultaneous use of different crooks all contributed.[1] A complete chromatic scale over four octaves up to g‴ was theoretically available by 1807, but doubtless only a few virtuosos could manage this. Elaborate horn solos in romantic contexts became common, as in Boieldieu's *La Famille suisse* (1797) and Spontini's *Milton* (1804). A favourite device was the raising of the bells at climaxes (for example in the explosive coda of the *Euphrosine* duet and at the height of the storm in *Mélidore et Phrosine*, where the whole orchestra makes a Weberish sound), and *cuivré* effects could be obtained by loud stopped notes. In the dungeon scene of *Léonore* Gaveaux instructs the horns to play with their bells opposite each other to produce a cavernous effect. Berlioz in *À travers Chants* attributes this innovation to Gluck in

[1] Charlton, *Orchestration.*

Alceste, but seems to be commenting on later practice. Gaveaux's idea was copied by Catel in *Sémiramis* (at the appearance of Ninus' ghost) and Le Sueur in *La Mort d'Adam* (the trumpets of chaos).

The horns were used much more frequently than the trumpets: Le Sueur's 'four religious trumpets' in Act III of *Ossian* are horns with raised bells. Many opera scores contain four horns, and a number – *Stratonice*, *Mélidore et Phrosine*, Dalayrac's *Adèle et Dorsan* (1795), *Médée*, *Les Deux Journées*, Boieldieu's *Béniowski* (first version, 1800[1]), and *Uthal* – dispense with trumpets altogether. Even if this reflects a shortage of brass players (the instruments were probably doubled), it represents a clear preference. Méhul was addicted to selective scoring for purposes of colour: *Stratonice* has no oboes and *Uthal* no violins (but divided violas). Gaveaux's *L'Amour filial* (1792) and Dalayrac in *Gulistan* (1805) also omitted the oboes, and the latter reserved his trumpets for the finale of Act III. Clarinet parts were generally notated in C but not always played on C instruments, the players making their choice of transposition. Whereas seven types of clarinet were current before the Revolution, only those in B flat, A, and C were in common use after 1800.[2] A single trombone was used until 1800, when *Béniowski* added a second (the presence of three in Steibelt's *Roméo et Juliette* and Le Sueur's *Télémaque* was probably due to the fact that these works were originally composed for the Opéra). The harp is prominent in *Ariodant* and *Uthal*, associated with bards, and became common in both theatres after the turn of the century. The emancipation of the cello, like that of the horn, was associated with Méhul, who often gave it expressive solos. The opening bars of the *Ariodant* overture are scored for three obbligato cellos and string basses,[3] and a similar division into three groups (two to a part) occurs in the ritornello of Edgard's Act III air. This sombre sonority was copied by Catel in *Sémiramis* (march, *Lent et réligieux*, for the entry of priests and sages in Act I), Cherubini in *Faniska*, Mayr in more than one opera, and – most memorably – Rossini in the opening bars of the overture to *Guillaume Tell*.

The use of mutes on many instruments increased greatly after the Revolution, and according to *Le Courrier des Spectacles* of 12 April 1801 was particularly associated with mystery, darkness, fear, and doubt – situations in which Revolution *opéra comique* was particularly rich. Grétry, often wrongly regarded as an unenterprising orchestrator,

[1] For the revival in 1824 Boieldieu added one natural and one slide trumpet and extra percussion.
[2] Charlton, *Orchestration*.
[3] Not three cellos and trombone, a misreading of the score originated by Gustave Chouquet in *Histoire de la musique dramatique en France* (1873) and repeated by Henri Lavoix in *Histoire de l'instrumentation* (1878) and in the first five editions of Grove.

had violins, horns, trumpets, and drums simultaneously muted in *Richard Coeur de Lion* to suggest a frowning fortress; he had many followers. Boieldieu in *Béniowski* used muted horns and trumpets answering one another as signals, on and off stage. The muting of drums by means of cloth (*voilées* or *couvertes*) became very common after 1798; later the muffled sound was probably achieved by means of softer or covered sticks, asked for by Dalayrac in *Lina* (1807) and Spontini in *Fernand Cortez* (1809).[1] The earliest example of drum chords occurs in Jean Paul Martini's *Sapho* (1794), where one player rolled in fourths at the heroine's suicide; the idea was copied by Le Sueur in *La Mort d'Adam* (two players rolling in thirds for the Seven Thunders of the Apocalypse), whence it was borrowed and refined by Berlioz. The object of all these devices was as much pictorial as dramatic. The enlarged range of orchestral imagery initiated by the linking of certain timbres and combinations of instruments with specific emotions may be seen as a necessary prerequisite to the romantic movement.

The exaggerations of that movement had their birth in the Revolution composers' love of contrast, whether in plot, scoring, or dynamics. They felt not only entitled but encouraged to go to extremes. This did not only mean extremes of noise, though there was plenty of that – as there had been in some of the grand operas of the 1780s (for example Lemoyne's *Electra* and *Phèdre*), when the braying of the trombones, released from oracular duties, threatened to get out of hand. Composers took a fancy to ending an act, or even an opera, very quietly, especially after a major climax. This may have originated in the need to get the chorus off stage, but it became an effect in its own right; there is an early instance in Act I of Grétry's *La Caravane du Caire* (1783). Cherubini's *Lodoiska*, after the prolonged uproar of the conflagration scene with its spectacular battle and last-minute rescue, closes with a sudden diminuendo to bare minim octaves for violins and string basses. Act II of Le Sueur's *Paul et Virginie* ends *pppp* with an empty stage, and the same multiple marking closes the corresponding act of his *La Mort d'Adam*. Méhul produced similar effects in *Mélidore et Phrosine* (Act II) and *Ariodant* (Acts I and II), Cherubini in Act I of *Lodoiska*, Steibelt in *Roméo et Juliette* (Act II), Berton in *Montano et Stéphanie* (Act II) and Boieldieu in *Béniowski* (Act I), on each occasion after a scene of noise or violence. They set the fashion for many later operas, for example the second acts of *Fernand Cortez* and Catel's *Wallace*, Act I of Weber's *Silvana*, and the long diminuendo orchestral codas of Rossini's *Moïse* and *Le Siège de Corinthe*.

[1] See Charlton, *Orchestration*, 335 ff. for a full discussion of this question.

VOCAL WRITING

The fuller orchestration must have imposed formidable demands on the singers. The pre-Revolution *opéra comique*, with its strophic song forms, simple ensembles, and avoidance of any suggestion of learning or spiritual profundity (which the meagre musical training of the composers was in any case unfitted to supply), depended on singing actors, chiefly light tenors and soubrettes. A delivery of the utmost fervour and intensity would be required to realize the powerful effects demanded in the 1790s. The virile element was strongly emphasized, and with rare exceptions, such as *Médée*, the operas were built round male voices. A few, such as *Horatius Coclès* and *Joseph*, had no female characters at all, though the part of Benjamin in *Joseph* was sung by a woman. The female contralto was ignored and some operas had only a single soprano, who was thrown into the sharpest possible relief by the other voices. This is a prominent feature of *Mélidore et Phrosine* and Dalayrac's *Léhéman*, and still more of Cherubini's *Lodoiska*, where no female voice at all is heard before the first finale. Then the imprisoned heroine makes her entry, not on stage but as an unseen voice from a cell in a high tower, a brilliant stroke communicating a true romantic thrill.

France had always abjured the castrato; the heroic male roles were taken by the peculiar type of high tenor known as *haute-contre*. The music, with a very high tessitura, was notated in the alto clef. They were not heroic tenors in the manner of Verdi's *tenore di forza* or Wagner's *Heldentenor*, but much closer to the lyrical *tenore di grazia*, and their method and training presumably included falsetto. They played sympathetic and sensitive characters, contrasted with a dark baritone (*Lodoiska*), a second and more vitriolic tenor in his traditional clef (*Ariodant*), or both (*Mélidore et Phrosine*).

The chorus assumed growing importance, especially in its dramatic role. Male choruses, usually in three parts, are prominent, and often we find two such groups in opposition: for example the Tartars and Poles in *Lodoiska* and the retainers of Aimar and Mélidore in *Mélidore et Phrosine*. Musically they derive from Gluck, down to a besetting squareness of rhythm (Act II finale of *Ariodant*); there are no massive choruses in eight or more parts, as in Spontini and Rossini's French operas (composed for the Opéra), perhaps because of insufficiency of trained singers. Méhul anticipated, and probably influenced, the vogue for 'characteristic' choruses of sailors, soldiers, peasants, bridesmaids, etc. that became popular in the next generation and possibly also owes something to Dalayrac's immensely popular *Les deux petits Savoyards* (1789). Act II of *Mélidore et Phrosine* contains choruses of sailors and villagers; the latter with their mincing 2/4 time carry a hint of the *Freischütz* bridesmaids.

There was however little sign of local or exotic colour in the music, no doubt because composers were concerned to emphasize the realism rather than the remoteness of their subjects. Indeed the fashion for oriental and magic settings that had flourished under the Ancien Régime and reappeared around 1800, to last throughout the nineteenth century, almost disappeared during the revolutionary decade apart from minor works like Dalayrac's *Gulnare*. Cherubini's vocal polonaise in *Lodoiska* – apparently its first appearance in opera – adds the faintest flavour of local colour. But it set a fashion that spread rapidly; there are countless examples in the operas of Mayr, Paer, Rossini, Donizetti, Spohr, Weber, and many others. The initial impetus may have been partly political (sympathy with partitioned Poland), but the catchy rhythm soon lost its national associations, assuming a military, patriotic, or even flirtatious aspect (as in Ännchen's air in Act II of *Der Freischütz*) or becoming a vehicle for mere display. Romantic opera is full of vocal polonaises not so called because the scene is laid in India or Central America or some other place remote from Poland, and the same is true of other dance forms, including the waltz (said to have been introduced at the Opéra by Méhul in the ballet *La Dansomanie* in 1800). Cherubini gave a slightly stronger tint to the Savoyard choruses in *Élisa* and later included a bolero in *Les Abencérages*, set in Spain at the time of the Moorish wars. The bard's song in *Ariodant* is perhaps the first sign of French opera's brief mania for Ossian. Kreutzer and Le Sueur each produced a mild musical equivalent for the natives of Mauritius in their *Paul et Virginie* operas. But even in later works with non-European settings, such as *Sémiramis*, *Gulistan*, *Fernand Cortez*, and *Les Bayadères*, the musical exoticism is wholly superficial and shows no advance on Gluck's Scythians in *Iphigénie en Tauride* or the naïve but curiously effective pseudo-medievalism of Blondel's melody in *Richard Coeur de Lion*. Indeed Grétry went further in this direction in *Guillaume Tell* than the composers of the next generation.

OPERA UNDER THE CONSULATE AND EMPIRE

The new century saw a sharp break in the history of *opéra comique*. With *Les Deux Journées*, produced in January 1800, Cherubini said farewell to the form, and to success in the theatre. Le Sueur had already embarked on grand opera. Boieldieu's two productions in 1800 might have been designed to symbolize the change of direction. *Béniowski* is a rescue opera to end all rescue operas: the action takes

place in a penal settlement in Kamchatka and ends with the rescue of
the entire cast, the camp commandant as well as the convicts, from
the horrors of the Siberian climate. *Le Calife de Bagdad* is a pseudo-
oriental light comedy of a type that was to retain its popularity and
supply the theatre's staple diet for the next 75 years. In fact the
traditional *opéra comique* – the *comédie mêlée d'ariettes* – had never
quite disappeared; two of the most popular works of the Revolution
decade had been *Les Visitandines* (1792) by François Devienne (1759–
1803) and Jean-Pierre Solié's *Le Secret* (1796), and Boieldieu and
Pierre Della Maria (1769–1800) had their first major successes in
1798. (Boieldieu's career had begun the previous year with *La Famille
suisse*, dedicated to Gaveaux, who both sang in it – very badly
according to the press – and published it.) This turning away from the
problems of life towards artificial light entertainment was a natural
reaction after a decade of civil strife, denunciation, and shrill
propaganda. The speed with which it occurred may be illustrated by
the fate of *Fanny Morna ou l'Écossaise*, by Louis Persuis (1769–1819).
A great success at the Favart in 1799, it failed completely when
revived in 1802, and the critic of *La Semaine ou le Souvenir
hebdomadaire* remarked on 3 December: 'Cette pièce, d'un ton
lugubre, n'a produit qu'un effet médiocre. On commence à croire que
l'opéra-comique n'est pas fait pour pleurer.' The change coincided
with a revival in the fortunes of Grétry and a fresh vogue for the
Neapolitan *opera buffa* of Paisiello and Cimarosa. Napoleon, besides
arranging for a production of *Zémire et Azor* at Fontainebleau, paid
many attentions to Grétry, who found it easy to adopt the role of the
Vicar of Bray but could not breathe life into his last compositions.
Nevertheless he was on friendly terms with Dalayrac, Berton, and
Boieldieu (who dedicated *Jean de Paris* to him) and served as artistic
godfather to the new movement. Dalayrac moved away from the
rescue opera after *Léhéman*; the best of his later works, *Gulistan* (1805),
has an Arabian Nights background, and Isouard in *Cendrillon* and
Boieldieu in *Le Petit Chaperon rouge* turned to fairy stories. However,
as late as 1817 Catel tried to revive the Revolutionary form of rescue
opera in *Wallace*, described as *opéra héroïque* though produced with
dialogue at the Comique. It is a frigid work without dramatic or
musical tension; the mixture of Cherubini and mild romanticism
anticipates the less inspired productions of Mendelssohn.

Napoleon's campaigns in Italy may have given his armies a taste
for Italian opera. Certainly Napoleon's tastes lay in this direction, and
French composers were swift to note the fact. Méhul's *L'Irato* (1801),
a one-act burlesque complete with crescendos, was produced pseud-

onymously and won a striking success. It took in Napoleon, who asked to be deceived again and accepted the dedication. Méhul endeavoured to oblige with two further comedies in 1802, *Une Folie* (which was even more successful) and *Le Trésor supposé*, a slight work closer to Grétry than to Cimarosa; but his serious temper drew him back towards his earlier manner in *Héléna*, *Uthal*, and *Joseph*. He was the only composer in France still writing in this style.

ASCENDANCY OF SERIOUS OPERA

Napoleon's musical tastes are of more than academic importance; they were scarcely elevated, but it was expedient to obey them. They also took a practical turn. Among his favourite operas were Zingarelli's *Giulietta e Romeo*, Paer's *Achille*, and anything he heard by Paisiello; he contrived to bring all three composers to Paris, using force on Zingarelli, who had sampled Paris in 1790 and disliked it. Paisiello was appointed *Maître de Chapelle* in 1802 and produced a French grand opera, *Proserpine*, in 1803, but retired two years later owing to the hostility of the public and native musicians. Paer accompanied Napoleon to Poland in 1806, took up residence in Paris in 1807, composed the bridal march for the Emperor's second marriage in 1810, and was made director of the Théâtre-Italien in 1812. Here he succeeded Spontini, who had already established himself as the Imperial composer *par excellence*. This invasion of Italians, several of whom, especially Paisiello and Paer, were notorious intriguers, was naturally unpopular with French composers – and, despite his Italian blood, with Cherubini. The latter antagonized Napoleon, who could no more abide contradiction on music than on any other subject, by disputing his opinion of Paisiello and Zingarelli, and the dislike was mutual and hearty. Although Cherubini did not abandon the stage, and even wrote a one-act Italian opera, *Pimmalione* (1809), for Napoleon's private theatre, he became progressively isolated and embittered, devoting himself principally to teaching and church music.

With the rise of Napoleon the Opéra regained its former status, especially when he took to subsidizing it and (in 1807) closed all the smaller theatres except the Ambigu-Comique. The balance of power swung back from the people to the court – a new court, but one equally despotic and jealous of its rights. During the 1790s the Opéra had become a backwater. Méhul, like Cherubini, had never enjoyed success there. His *Cora* (1791), originally composed in 1786 and revised before performance, was remembered only for a spectacular volcanic eruption (the scene is Mexico). *Adrien*, based on Metastasio's *Adriano in Siria*, was banned in 1792 and taken off by order of the

Directory after four performances in 1799 (though again revised later to include a ballet); it was too soon to project a sympathetic emperor in the theatre. The only successful novelty of the decade was Grétry's *Anacréon chez Polycrate* (1797), a wholly reactionary work in which a surly tyrant is charmed out of his brutal inclinations by the poetic and musical talent of the middle-aged epicene artist. The latter's philosophy

> L'indulgence est ma loi sévère . . .
> Le plaisir est mon souverain,
> La nature est le dieu qu'Anacréon adore

with its echoes of Rousseau and the Ancien Régime deliberately turns its back on the strenuous message of the Revolution. The music, too light-boned in construction to fill its large frame, has a picturesque charm. The first grand operas of the new century were also recessive. Catel's *Sémiramis* and Peter von Winter's *Tamerlan*, both based on tragedies by Voltaire and produced in 1802, were attempts to continue the pre-Revolution *tragédie lyrique*, one by an academic composer under the influence of Cherubini, the other by a foreigner who never came to grips with the French style. In 1803 Cherubini himself returned to the Opéra with *Anacréon*, ironically choosing for his hero the same bland voluptuary as Grétry. All three ventures failed, and *Anacréon* established a precedent by being hissed. The Opéra made up for its operatic failures with some very popular ballets.

OPERA UNDER THE EMPIRE

The new regime found its first spokesman in an unlikely quarter. Besides Italian music of the lighter sort Napoleon had a predilection for the works of Ossian, whose mystique of bardic aggression and a warriors' Valhalla made a predictable appeal to a dictator. The Opéra opened under its new title of Académie Imperiale on 10 July 1804 with the first performance of Le Sueur's *Ossian ou les Bardes*, an early version of which had been rehearsed at the Feydeau in 1796, the year of the first Ossianic play on the Paris stage. The identification of Fingal's victorious warriors with the expanding armies of France is scarcely less explicit than in Girodet's picture of 1802, which inspired the dream scene in Act IV.[1] The opera, dedicated to the Emperor, was very successful and earned the composer high rewards; Paisiello nominated him as his successor as Napoleon's *Maître de Chapelle*. Le Sueur also had a hand in the Opéra's next major production, *Le Triomphe de Trajan* (October 1807), most of which was composed by

[1] Charlton, *Orchestration*.

the influential and worldly but artistically negligible Persuis. Designed to celebrate Napoleon's Prussian campaign, it was a political gesture, but sufficiently popular to be revived under the restored monarchy as late as 1827. Le Sueur, however, was too much of an introvert to make a court musician, and his only subsequently produced opera, *La Mort d'Adam et son Apothéose* (1809), though one of the most interesting works of its age, was a total failure. The disillusioned composer withdrew from the theatre, and his place was taken by Spontini.

Spontini's arrival in 1803 had been inspired by hope and ambition, but he soon gained a valuable patron in the Empress Joséphine and within a few years held a position in French musical life unrivalled since the days of Gluck. After three one-act pieces at the Opéra-Comique,[1] the first of which, *La Petite Maison* (May 1804), an attack on the morals of the Ancien Régime, caused a scandal and a riot, he entered the imperial arena with *La Vestale* (December 1807), substituting the clear light of ancient Rome for the misty archipelago of the Hebrides. Only the background, an elaborate eulogy of the authority of the state, had a contemporary application; the story of the Vestal Virgin sentenced to death for neglecting her vows (but in this instance granted a Metastasian reprieve) appealed to public taste and was repeatedly imitated in the next half century. *Fernand Cortez* (1809) on the other hand presented Napoleon under the most transparent disguise as the liberator of a new world; Amazily's reference to Cortez as the greatest man alive was a direct compliment to the Emperor. The production was timed to coincide with his invasion of Spain; when this miscarried, there were not wanting voices to point out that the opera emphasized the courage and resolution of the Spaniards, and it was hastily removed from the boards. Its success dates from the revival, after extensive revision, in 1817. Spontini's third grand opera *Olympie* was not produced till 1819, when the social and artistic climate had once more changed, and only won the popular vote, again after extensive revision, at Berlin in 1821. Spontini had few rivals at the Opéra. Cherubini's *Les Abencérages* (1813) was a failure, and only Kreutzer's *Aristippe* (1808) and Catel's *Les Bayadères* (1810) enjoyed a measure of success. *Aristippe*, another Anacreon opera, was designed as a vehicle for the influential but aging tenor Laïs, who liked to play the part of the elderly voluptuary surrounded by pretty girls and crowned with roses.

The climate of these years was not conducive to artistic integrity. The idealism of Méhul yielded to a worship of national pomp and circumstance and the pursuit of the tangible rewards of success. The

[1] See Dennis Libby, 'Spontini's Early French Operas', *Musical Times*, cxvii (1976), p. 23.

hero as individual retired behind the symbol of imperial expansion. After the years of militant atheism spectacles with a religious flavour became popular, generally combining the portentous with the pastiche. The first was a version by Steibelt of Haydn's *Creation* (December 1800), enlivened by an attempt on Napoleon's life; both enterprises failed. Ludwig Lachnith's notorious arrangement of *Die Zauberflöte*, interspersed with excerpts from other Mozart operas and Haydn's symphonies, followed in August 1801 under the title *Les Mystères d'Isis*; this travesty, which excited the indignation of Spohr and many others, remained in the repertory till 1827. The first Paris production of *Don Giovanni* (17 September 1805) was a similar mutilation by Christian Kalkbrenner: *Le Journal de l'Empire* opined that Mozart had 'nothing in the class of *opéra comique* that one could rank above or equal to' certain works of Piccinni, Paisiello, Sacchini, 'and some of the masterpieces of Grétry'; he clearly thought less of theatrical situations than of harmonic richness 'scattered everywhere with extreme profusion' and noisy orchestration. One important result, however, was to make Mozart's music widely known, and it left its mark; the trio of priestesses in Act II of *Sémiramis* owes a palpable debt to that of the three boys in the first finale of *Die Zauberflöte*, and is in the same key.

These ungainly pasticcios with their manipulation of religion to factititous ends undoubtedly contributed to the grand opera of Scribe and Meyerbeer, whose origins lie in this period. Étienne de Jouy, the voluminous librettist of *Milton, La Vestale, Fernand Cortez, Les Bayadères, Les Abencérages*, and Rossini's *Guillaume Tell*, imitated Metastasio's weaknesses (but not his strength) and anticipated those of Scribe. The cross-hatching of dynastic and amorous motives, the unmotivated outbreaks of quixotic magnanimity (as in Act III of the 1817 *Cortez*) and the contrived happy end (particularly ludicrous in *Tamerlan* and *Les Bayadères*) are Metastasian features; the subordination of character to incident and the use of religion, sex, and politics as gambits on which to hang a tergiversation of the plot are Napoleonic legacies to Scribe. The most depressing feature is not the elevation of spectacle and ballet out of alignment with the plot (this had always been a feature of *tragédie lyrique*) or such unlikely developments as the conversion to Christianity of the Mexican princess Amazily and the idealized portrait of Montezuma as a noble savage after Rousseau, but the cynical attitude of librettists towards their own work. The 1817 *Cortez* is admittedly a rehash; but Jouy does not bother to make Amazily's movements in Act III even credible and never tells us what becomes of her brother Telasco and the Mexican priests who dominate the first act. The librettist of Catel's *Sémiramis*, one Philippe Desriaux, wrecked a potentially fine subject, a variant of the Agamemnon story, through fear of its implications; he obscures the central situation (including the royal adultery), leaves the conspiracy of the Queen's paramour Assur in the air, and fails to make clear whether the Queen's death at the hands of her son is murder or accident.

SPONTINI'S FRENCH OPERAS

Of Spontini's three creative periods (Italian 1796–1801, French 1804–19, German 1820–41) only the second is historically important. Brought up in the tradition of *opera buffa* as practised by Piccinni, Paisiello, and Cimarosa, he began by adopting the same manner in Paris. His one-act *Milton* (1804), is a curious cross between Cherubinian *opéra comique* (it was announced as *fait historique*) and later romantic developments. It was one of the first operas[1] to adopt the idea of the creative artist as hero (Ossian is more warrior than poet or harpist); Spontini's Milton is the forerunner of Benvenuto Cellini and Hans Sachs. There is a conventional love affair between Milton's daughter and his secretary, the disguised son of Sir William Davenant who has saved Milton's life in return for Milton saving his father's, and a comic subplot contributed by a Quaker Justice of the Peace and his elderly niece, a 'fille surannée et demi-caricature' in search of a husband. The strands are unravelled in a big quintet during which Milton dictates part of the Garden of Eden scene in *Paradise Lost*, introduced by his daughter playing the harp on stage. This and Milton's hymn to the sun, with an elaborate harp obbligato, are interesting for their scoring and their common use of E flat, a key associated with nocturnes, religious ceremonies, and *Die Zauberflöte*. In the quintet the whole orchestra, woodwind as well as strings, is divided into muted and unmuted groups, and the cellos play in four parts. Spontini was fascinated by Milton. In Berlin from 1822 on he made repeated plans to revise and expand his early *opéra comique*. In 1830 Raupach wrote him a full-length German libretto on the subject, and he spent many years, including a period of research in England, at work on it. The title was changed to *Das verlorene Paradies*, but the opera was never finished.

Spontini's assumption of the mantle of grand opera was an act of calculated policy foreshadowed by nothing in his early work. He was doing violence to his own nature, and the strain shows. A fertile composer in his youth (*La Vestale* was his seventeenth opera), he

---

[1] Isouard's *Michel-Ange* preceded it by two years. The Swiss poet and painter Salomon Gessner is a character in Grétry's *Lisbeth* (1797).

found increasing difficulty in settling the form of his later works and left many of them unfinished. Three different versions of *Cortez* and *Olimpie* and at least two of *Agnes von Hohenstaufen* reached the stage. The constant retouching and even wholesale revision to which his mature operas were subjected, both during rehearsal and after production, indicate (as with Meyerbeer) an exceptional degree of self-doubt. With this was linked a progressive alienation of artistic cause and effect. He must share with Jouy the responsibility for shirking the tragic end of *La Vestale* (which the subject demands as peremptorily as that of *Norma* on virtually the same story); the final scene in the temple of Vesta is a feeble anticlimax, for which the preface to the libretto makes a shamefaced apology. When the first version of *Olimpie* failed, he not only rewrote the last act, substituting a conventional reconciliation for Statira's suicide and falsifying all that had gone before, but did his best to destroy the original. He constantly interfered in the production of his operas, insisting on accurate scenery and costumes, the engagement of singers of the correct physical type, and a rehearsal schedule regardless of expense and convenience. Where Le Sueur in *La Mort d'Adam* sought authenticity by clothing his characters in the skins of animals (ermine and lamb for Eve's daughters, bears, lions, tigers, leopards, and other savage creatures for the children of Cain), Spontini called in not only the taxidermist but the stables and the zoo. The historical Cortez invaded Mexico with a force of seventeen cavalry, so seventeen horsemen cantered and manoeuvred on the Opéra stage – until they upset the rhythm of the music and were returned to barracks. The cast of *Olimpie* in Berlin included three elephants.

It would be unfair to attribute this craze for authenticity wholly to opportunism. Both Spontini and Le Sueur consciously aimed at a *Gesamtkunstwerk* to which all the arts should contribute. It was left to Wagner, whose ideas were deeply influenced by French grand opera (his zoological demands in *The Ring* were one of its legacies), to demonstrate that the aim could be realized on the highest artistic level. But Spontini's urge to pad out basically simple plots with all manner of extravagances may have been propelled by an instinctive knowledge that his musical creativity was limited. He was lucky with the libretto of *La Vestale*, a variant of the rescue theme which had been written for Boieldieu and rejected by Méhul and Cherubini. It was a manageable design and it made his reputation. After that he chose ambitious themes on a titanic scale: the Spanish conquest of the New World, the disintegration of Alexander the Great's empire, the convulsive quarrels of the Hohenstaufen dynasty in the twelfth century, subjects more suited to a doctoral thesis than an opera of even several hours' duration. He put as much as he could on the stage. *Cortez* in 1817[1] offered a thunderstorm in which the statue of a Mexican god is destroyed by lightning (Act I), a mutiny of the Spanish army, a large bi-national ballet and the scuttling of the whole Spanish fleet (Act II), two hot military engagements, a siege and a tattoo culminating in an 'Évolution d'Infanterie et de Cavalerie' (Act III). In the 1809 version Amazily was not in love with Cortez (she committed suicide by diving into a lake), Montezuma did not appear at all, and the eventual Act I appeared as Act III; the entire plot was subverted with surprisingly little effect on the music. The notorious tendency of French grand opera to dissolve into fragments, so that acts and scenes could be transferred or left out, as in Meyerbeer (*passim*), Auber's *La Muette de Portici*, and Rossini's *Guillaume Tell*, began with Spontini. He was the initial purveyor of 'effects without causes'.

His musical language was based, like Cherubini's, on *opera buffa* and the *tragédie lyrique* of Gluck and Piccinni. The composer Spontini most admired was Mozart; he was the first to revive *Don Giovanni* in Paris in its original form, and his performances of what he called 'l'immortel chef d'oeuvre' were famous there and in Berlin. But although Mozart's influence is apparent, for example in the D minor storm music in Act III of *La Vestale* and the *Marche réligieuse* in Act I of *Olimpie* with its strong aura of *Die Zauberflöte*, the difference in temperament between the two composers inhibited any genuinely fertile contact. Spontini's mind lacked the nimbleness, the insight into the multiple complexities of character and situation, and the sheer power of invention, whether melodic, rhythmic, or harmonic, to keep his huge structures airborne. Like Cherubini, he was weak in melody and endeavoured to compensate by cross-accents, heavy sforzandi on weak beats, and a rhetorical violence that becomes offensive in the absence of a strong forward impulse. He outdid Méhul in superimposing extreme dynamic effects on basically square and static ideas. In the short chorus of demoralized soldiers, 'Nous redoutons le plus funeste sort', in Act II of *Cortez*, the exaggerated dynamics (*ff* to *ppp*) and multiplicity of accents on different beats in different parts cannot conceal a basic lack of drive. The effect is quite different from Cherubini's use of similar devices (see Ex. 1):

[1] References below are to this version.

Ex. 15

(The cruel Mexicans are closing all the passages)

Spontini's harmony seldom advances beyond heavily accented appoggiaturas and the sprinkling of occasional chromaticism over the regular tonal procedures of his day. When he wishes to suggest the exotic or barbaric, as in the music for Cortez's Indian allies the Tlascaltètes in the grand march at the beginning of Act III, he relies not on harmonic colour but on hollow octaves in the minor mode and rude and aggressive scoring. His recitative, though it incorporates rare patches of free arioso reflected in Marschner and early Wagner, is generally stiff in gesture, rhetorical rather than expressive and over-dependent on the diminished seventh and a mannered use of interrupted cadences. In the airs and duets he rejected coloratura but retained the honeyed thirds and sixths of the Italian style and other clichés, including piled-up sequences and a surfeit of feminine endings. The melodies seldom possess a personal imprint; they rise and fall with the model Spontini happens to be following. They are emptiest when he inflates the Neapolitan idiom, as in the Presto assai agitato of the *Vestale* overture, best when he is closest to Gluck, as in the beautiful morning hymn in the same opera.

Spontini's strength lay in his manipulation of big scenes of dramatic confrontation and in his enriched treatment of chorus and orchestra. The best of his ensembles do convey a sense of monumental grandeur, of mighty events afoot. The huge tableau in Act I of *Olimpie* at the heroine's marriage to Cassander in the temple of Diana at Ephesus, during which the rival King Antigonus breaks in with his army to demand vengeance, is impressive in its deployment of musical forces (five soloists and double chorus) and in suggesting the clash of violently opposed dramatic motives. In *La Vestale* Spontini gains weight by dividing the chorus into nine parts. These movements depend less on the themes, which may suggest Cimarosa, Mozart, or even (in his late work) Rossini, than on the accompaniment figures, especially when they are developed at length as rhythmic ostinatos. The creeping G minor dotted figure as Licinius contemplates the tomb prepared for Julia, the big chorus and funeral march in F minor, and the duet for Julia and the Grand Vestal with its plangent oboe solo, all in Act III of *La Vestale*, are successful examples of this technique. So is the duet in Act II of *Cortez* in which Amazily and Cortez pray for the success of a peace embassy against a threatening 'Marche des Méxicains dans le lointain'; the odd choice of slow triple time for a march strengthens the impact.

Some of Spontini's most powerful strokes of dramatic irony are reinforced by the spatial possibilities of the large Opéra stage. In Act III of *Cortez* a party of Spanish soldiers accompanied by a stage band approach gradually from the distance rejoicing at the release of their companions, unaware that the Mexicans have recaptured them and will only release them if Amazily is delivered to the priests for execution. On stage Cortez, Amazily, and Moralez (who know this) sing a trio expressing different emotional reactions, while Amazily's female attendants (who do not) dance with the Spaniards as they arrive in groups. The scene is handled with great skill; at its climax Amazily, ready to die for Cortez, brings back the melody of her preceding air against the other voices, and the military band reaches the middle of the stage before Cortez breaks the news. The following love duet for him and Amazily is redeemed from rhythmic squareness by intermittent fanfares for trumpets, horns, and drums, muted and unmuted, variously disposed about the theatre as the Spaniards muster their forces to renew the fight. The elaborate intertwining of personal and political themes in a historical setting, characteristic of so much nineteenth-century opera and carried to its highest point in Verdi's *Don Carlos*, was largely a legacy of Spontini.

He made less frequent use of recurrent motives than Le Sueur or Méhul, and generally for structural rather than dramatic purposes. He modified the design of set pieces by camouflaging the links with recitative (in this he was following up the open-ended experiments of Gluck's successors in the 1780s), adding subsidiary sections of varying length, and employing a freer tonality. The big duet for Julia and Licinius in Act II of *La Vestale* consists of three sections, in A flat, C, and B flat. Amazily's Act I air in *Cortez*, though riddled with melodic clichés, expresses violent emotion by modulating very early from A to B flat and then to C. In this opera, besides the shifts of a third characteristic of the period, Spontini employed keys a semitone apart as symbols of dramatic conflict. The central scene of Act II in which Cortez single-handed quells the mutiny of his army (*Entrée de la cavalerie et de l'infanterie de Cortez en révolte* – the orchestra imitates the rhythm of horses' hooves) has a bold tonal scheme. The chorus sing their earlier music (Allegro prestissimo con furore) in E flat, modulating to E (F♭), whereupon Cortez interrupts them in C. The next ensemble section is in B major; again Cortez recalls them to duty in C. When he has finally shamed them into renewed allegiance he joins them in B, the key associated in Act I with the Spaniards' love of their country. The trio and chorus with military band in Act III, mentioned above, is in E flat with a central section in D (when the band resumes playing much nearer). Abrupt tonal shifts and enharmonic modulations, if sometimes crudely executed, are characteristic of Spontini and part of his legacy to romantic opera.

SPONTINI AND THE ORCHESTRA

Still more influential was his treatment of the orchestra. His early operas owe a good deal to Simon Mayr,[1] a pioneer in the use of novel instrumental combinations and an elaborate network of solos, especially for woodwind. The prominent viola solos and divided violas and cellos in Spontini's *opéra comique Julie* (1805) are in part a reflection of Mayr's practice, as is the treatment of the quintet in *Milton*. *La Vestale*, which was considered intolerably noisy, links the outdoor ceremonies of the Revolution with the large romantic orchestra; the Opéra could accommodate far more instruments than

[1] See pp. 401–3.

the Opéra-Comique, although military manoeuvres had been executed on the Comédie-Italienne stage, accompanied by gunfire as well as a substantial windband, in Martini's *Henri IV*[1] as early as 1774. *Cortez* requires at least six trumpets, quadruple woodwind, three trombones, and very heavy percussion, *Olimpie* an even more formidable brass contingent: the huge stage band (four trumpets, two horns – 'tous les pavillons en l'air' – bass trombone, ophicleide, triangle, cymbals, and bass drum) for the triumphal march in Act III competes against a more than ample orchestra, with full brass (two trumpets, four horns, three trombones), in the pit. The score of *Cortez* is almost a sequence of military marches and parades, reflecting the tramp and jingle of the armies of Austerlitz and Jena; the percussion seems continuously in action for scenes on end. It was the first opera to use four clarinets; the 1809 autograph, copy score and manuscript parts (but not the printed score) contain parts for two high military instruments in F. The stage march in Act III is scored for two each of flutes, oboes, and clarinets, all the bassoons, four horns, timpani, triangle, cymbals, and bass drum (side-drum and tam-tam appear elsewhere in the opera). At first all except flutes, bassoons, triangle, and bass drum are muted ('dans le lointain, ou à l'orchestre avec sourdines'), the oboes and clarinets 'en renfermant le bas de l'instrument dans une bourse de peau'[2] – an innovation often ascribed to Berlioz, who imitated it in *Lélio* but bagged a complete clarinet. When the band reaches the centre of the stage the mutes are removed and the full orchestra, including trombones, joins in *fortissimo* from the pit.

SPONTINI'S INFLUENCE

Spontini told Wagner in 1845 that everything new since *La Vestale* had been stolen from his scores. This is the exaggeration of a disappointed man, but it is not quite so preposterous as the modern reader, who scarcely ever hears a Spontini opera, might suppose. His influence throughout Europe was enormous and can be traced in the grand operas of Schubert (who heard *La Vestale* at the impressionable age of fifteen), Weber, Marschner, Berlioz, Meyerbeer, early Wagner (especially *Rienzi* and *The Flying Dutchman*), the Verdi of *Don Carlos*, and even Pfitzner's *Palestrina*. The violent enharmonic modulations of *Euryanthe*, the rhythmic ostinatos in the ensembles of Rossini's *Mosè*, and the brassy bounce, halfway between the ballroom and the parade-ground, of Meyerbeer's ballets all owe something to Spontini.

[1] See Vol. VII, p. 221.
[2] According to Charlton, *Orchestration*, the bags may not have been used in performance; they are not mentioned in the autograph or copy score.

Berlioz and Wagner imitated features of his orchestration. His German opera *Alcindor* (1825) begins with a chorus of gnomes accompanied by tuned anvils.[1] Several passages in *Olympie* strikingly anticipate Wagner, especially Statira's furious outburst (based on tremolando strings) towards the end of Act I when she hears the name of Cassandre, the supposed murderer of her son. Spontini's last opera, *Agnes von Hohenstaufen* (1829), on a German libretto by Raupach, which contains traces of Spohr and Weber, foreshadows very closely the manner of *Rienzi* and in places, such as the chorus of knights and troubadours in the first scene of Act III, *Tannhäuser* and *Lohengrin*. Occasionally one can be more specific. The famous two-step in the *Guillaume Tell* overture is surely an echo of the second finale of *Cortez*. The Allegretto of Amazily's air earlier in Act II underlies melody, rhythm, and accompaniment of 'Durch die Wälder' in *Der Freischütz*.

Ex. 16

(I have only one desire left, to please you)

Most striking of all, because it reaches so far into the future, is the phrase with which Licinius greets Julia at their secret meeting in Act II of *La Vestale* (i), and which reappears to the words 'Julia va mourir!' in Act III (ii); it is almost identical with the death motive in *Die Walküre*.

---

[1] The untuned anvil made its operatic début in Kreutzer's *Abel* (Opéra, 1810); it accompanies a dominant minor ninth when demons forge the club with which history's first murder is committed (Charlton, op. cit.).

Ex. 17

(Julia will die!)

LE SUEUR

Le Sueur's grand operas (both are said to have been composed by 1800) are a backwater that might be left undisturbed but for their vital influence on his pupil Berlioz and the fascinating light they throw on one aspect of this period. They are quite as grandiloquent as Spontini's, which undoubtedly owed something to *Ossian*, but very different in flavour, both in the librettos and in the music. Unlike any of his contemporaries, Le Sueur had a feeling for the supernatural and seems to have been more excited by visionary experiences than by ordinary human behaviour. He can use the direction *andante religioso* without absurdity, whereas Spontini's *religiosamente e espressivo* at once suggests grease-paint. The dream sequence in *Ossian*, in which the condemned hero sees a vision of the bardic heaven replete with the spirits of his ancestors, has a force of imagination absent from the rest of the score.[1] There is about the whole conception of *La Mort d'Adam*, based on Klopstock, *Paradise Lost*, Genesis, and the Book of Revelations (the librettist was N. F. Guillard, who had furnished Gluck with *Iphigénie en Tauride* and Sacchini with *Oedipe à Colone*),

[1] For an account of the opera, its sources, and the Ossianic movement in France, see Charlton, 'Ossian, Le Sueur and Opera', *Studies in Music*, xi (1977), p. 37.

an apocalyptic quality whose nearest artistic parallel is perhaps the visionary paintings and prophetic books of William Blake. Here is the same mixture of the naïve and the titanic, the esoteric and the sublime. In spirit Le Sueur's operas have more affinity with the pictorial arts and literature than with other music (that of Berlioz excepted). The dark Caledonian forests and lakes of *Ossian* belong to the same world as the romantic landscapes of John Martin and James Ward, who would have found a perfect subject in the setting of Act IV, a vast cavern cut in the rock where the Scandinavians keep prisoners destined for sacrifice to Odin, a sequel to the basic set of *La Caverne*. There are parallels too with the strenuous gestures superimposed on a classical pose characteristic of Le Sueur's French contemporaries David, Delacroix, and Géricault, and with the early novels of Chateaubriand.

Ossian himself is presented as an artist hero, insuperable as warrior, lover, and harpist; the portrait may have been designed to flatter Napoleon, but seems equally appropriate to Nero. The language of the libretto has a distinctly romantic flavour; the chorus in praise of forest solitude at the end of Act II (to be sung *avec une exaltation intérieure*) suggests a mixture of Rousseau and Wordsworth:

> C'est là que le feu du génie
> Sait animer tous les objets d'une douce mélancolie;
> On y sent son âme attendrie,
>   Seul avec la nature,
>   D'une volupté pure
> On sent son coeur ému.

In sheer scale *La Mort d'Adam* eclipses even Spontini. It attempts to transmute all the sources mentioned above. The characters comprise the entire human race (all are on stage together at one point in Act III, occupying hills, forests and both banks of the Euphrates) and the total complement of heaven and hell. The plot embraces the sum of history up to the death of Adam, together with a military assault on heaven by Satan and his rebel legions and a prolonged apotheosis in which God too appears (represented by a triangle – a symbol in the sky, not an instrument in the orchestra).

The performance of Le Sueur's operas would present immense difficulties. They require enormous forces, including several choruses and regiments of dancers and supers, and their demands on stage machinery have seldom been exceeded before or since. He was quite aware of what he was doing, and gave practical and elaborate instructions for the realization of his effects, from the use of gauzes to indicate eclipses of heavenly bodies to minute details of costume appropriate to the inhabitants of heaven and hell. He went further, prescribing not only what the singers, dancers, machinists, and instrumental players must do, but the exact impressions and nuances they must convey to the audience. The rhythm of the orchestral passage leading to Adam's first entry must mark

la marche lente et grave du patriarche des hommes qui s'avance derrière la montagne. Quoiqu'il ne soit encore vu de loin par Sélime et Seth, c'est à la verité et à la gradation de l'exécution à faire que les spectateurs comptent déjà ses pas en entendant le Rhythme musical qui semble les compter lui-même : c'est à cette exécution à joindre ainsi la scène imaginaire . . . à la scene réelle . . . Enfin c'est à l'orchestre . . . à étendre, pour ainsi dire, la scène, en l'agrandissant à l'oreille au delà de ce que l'on voit, et en rendant présent a l'ouie ce qui est encore absent et hors du Théâtre. L'exécution doit faire ici que la musique instrumentale semble appartenir seule à Adam . . . et la musique vocale à Seth et Sélime.

All this for a few bars in ♩ ♩♩ rhythm! Adam's first words must suggest 'la grande ricordanza della creazione'. When he contemplates the prospect of death, the performance should indicate 'per il sentimento e l'accento la rimembranza grande e sventurata della prima caduta, del primo disastro'. When he shows Cain the tomb prepared for him, the orchestra must paint for the benefit of the audience (i) the site of the tomb, (ii) how it appears in Adam's eyes, (iii) the sinister impression it makes on Cain and Seth, although it is not visible on the stage. The singers receive similar instructions. Cain's first air is marked 'Allegro fieramente, sans vitesse et largement, sotto voce, d'une voix sourde et concentrée. Tout l'air, avec une action agitée. Jusqu'à la fin, d'un accent rude, sauvage et tragique. Colla verità e l'energia d'esecuzione musicale, ch'avevano i primitivi canti delle passioni; e colla franchigia ch'aveva l'armonia antica. Anche eseguito col sentimento de la ritmopoeia ebraica.' This is all on the first bar; during the course of the air Cain has to sing 'coll'accento che conviene alla terribile Ricordanza della prima morte, e col sentimento de quest'imago dell'innocente sangue d'Abel che s'eleva al ciel e grida vendetta.' Yet the voice part (though not that of the orchestra) is wholly devoid of character.

It would be easy – and true – to conclude that Le Sueur is putting into words what the inadequacy of his invention and technique is unable to express in the music. But his grappling with the problem led him to experiments that are of great interest and some importance. He uses the 'personal motive' more extensively, if less pithily, than Méhul, both as dramatic reminiscence and as symbol. He is particularly fond of anticipating important scenes in advance, so that the motives seem to grow in significance. *Ossian* has about ten recurring motives, some of them, especially in the last two acts, employed with considerable subtlety. An accompaniment figure in Rosmala's Act II air where she recalls Ossian's harp-playing ('Au souvenir de tes accords touchants, le même amour, le même élan me presse') appears in the orchestra in the minor when Hydala and the bards search for her in the forest in Act III, becomes the main theme of the 'Chant de Selma' in which Hydala summons her back (presently combined with another motive from Act II in contrasted rhythm), and returns very movingly towards the end of Ossian's *Air chevaleresque* in Act IV: imprisoned and condemned to death, he thinks of his beloved.

Ex. 18

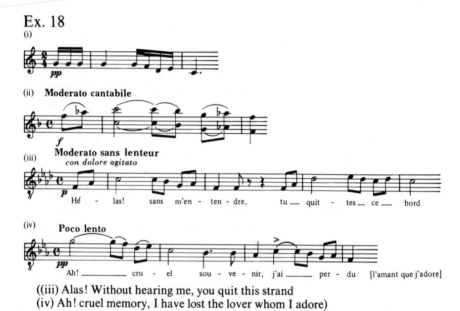

((iii) Alas! Without hearing me, you quit this strand
(iv) Ah! cruel memory, I have lost the lover whom I adore)

In *La Mort d'Adam* Le Sueur goes much further. All the principal characters have their personal motives; Cain's two and Seth's with its prominent falling fourth are particularly striking. Others symbolize ideas and emotions, such as Adam's presentiment of death. His words in Act I, viii, 'O mort! je sens que je succombe' are thus introduced in the orchestra:

Ex. 19

This returns several times; in Act III, v, when Adam enters immediately after Seth has told Eve of the Angel of Death's warning, it appears in the augmented form:

Ex. 20

In the death scene itself Le Sueur brings back at least twelve motives, often contrapuntally combined. Several of them have labels of religious significance, such as 'Chant d'Action de Grace', 'Chant filial', 'Chant de prière', 'Chant de Bénédiction d'Adam', etc. This is still a long way from the comprehensive technique of *The Ring*, but the elaboration of the scheme, combined with Le Sueur's compulsive urge to embrace all things visible and invisible in a mammoth compound of drama, symbol, vocal and instrumental music, dancing, mime, painting, and scenic spectacle inevitably points towards Wagner. Beaumarchais had pleaded for such a union of the arts in the preface to *Tarare*, and it was the logical climax of French grand opera, especially when infused with the spirit of the Revolution. Le Sueur, who chose a subject of universal validity fully worthy of it, posed the problem that Wagner's infinitely greater musical genius was to solve. Wagner could not have heard *La Mort d'Adam*, though he might have seen the published score in his Paris days. It is possible that both composers developed their motive technique under the double stimulus of an apocalyptic vision and limited melodic invention, in the endeavour to unify a structure that threatened to sprawl. Perhaps Le Sueur's nearest approach to Wagner's music occurs at a few moments of solemn grandeur, such as the *pppp* brass and woodwind chords, following a recitative over string tremolo, when the Angel tells Adam he must die:

Ex. 21

- non - ce - ra ma pré - sen - ce   et   ta   mort.

(A sound like thunder will announce my presence – and thy death.)

LE SUEUR'S INFLUENCE ON BERLIOZ

The composer Le Sueur most strikingly prefigures is Berlioz (whom he accepted as a pupil soon after publishing the full score of *La Mort d'Adam* in 1822), and here there can be no question of anything but direct influence; indeed certain elements in Berlioz's style can be explained only by reference to Le Sueur. The contrast between epic grandiosity of conception and classical restraint of utterance is common to both. The tone of *Ossian*, with its remote subject, violent passions, supernatural visitations, and the mixture of jaggedness and marble in its surface, is extraordinarily like that of *Les Troyens*. Berlioz's peculiar habit of presenting dramatic episodes, whether in his operas or other works, in the form of set tableaux with the intervening links omitted or at best implied, and of appealing directly to the knowledge and experience of the audience, comes straight from Le Sueur. So do innumerable other idiosyncracies. There is a *symphonie funèbre* and more than one *symphonie fantastique* in Act III of *La Mort d'Adam*. *Ossian* begins with a *Marche nocturne* (compare *L'Enfance du Christ*), followed by a hymn in which the ensemble drops suddenly into pianissimo octaves, a favourite device of both composers. Later in the Act a Druid, like Mercury in *Les Troyens*, 'frappe avec une lance un énorme bouclier suspendu' (tamtam, supported by trombones and timpani). Several times Le Sueur doubles solo voices in ensembles with two chiefs from the chorus, as Berlioz does in the *Troyens* septet. The trick of presenting two contrasted themes in their entirety and then superimposing them was used by Cherubini and Méhul, but Berlioz is more likely to have picked it up from Le Sueur – perhaps from the finale of *Ossian*, an elaborate ballet for Scandinavians and Caledonians, where both themes have a Berliozian strangeness of shape and colour.

Ex. 22

(i) LES SCANDINAVES

(ii) LES CALÉDONIENS ET LES BARDES

Above all, Le Sueur accounts for Berlioz's harmonic peculiarities. He was convinced that he was composing in the style of the ancients, whether Hebrews, Chaldeans, Greeks, or Caledonians, a style that would have been comprehensible to Adam himself. His view of musical antiquity was wholly subjective, based partly on controversial statements by ancient writers, partly on the ecclesiastical modes, and partly on Gluck. He justified it in a voluminous series of notes in French and Italian, amounting in the score of *La Mort d'Adam* to a built-in treatise on 'antique harmony', which all interpreters of the music were expected to master. Many of these dissertations on 'ritmopoeia' and 'melopoeia' offer an antique 'explanation' of a perfectly ordinary harmonic procedure; Le Sueur's so-called 'enharmonic' metamorphoses often amount to little more than the substitution of one chord for another, for instance the relative minor for the major. Elsewhere they justify a mingling of tonal and modal processes, a texture that continually pretends to modulate but never actually does so, or a long string of 6/3 or root-position chords (this is described as the purest form of religious music among Hebrews, Egyptians, and Chaldeans). Most of the deviants are modal in origin, but they sometimes appear startlingly inconsequent through their attachment

to eighteenth-century clichés and dominant-tonic codas. Le Sueur's
style is seldom consistent for long. The dance of demons in Act III of
La Mort d'Adam reverts to the baroque idiom of the Bach-Handel
period, ending with a peroration in which the three principal themes
are presented simultaneously. Elsewhere dominant-subdominant
modal progressions and a tonality in which the line between major
and minor is constantly blurred alternate with a flavour of the early
romantics, foreshadowing Mendelssohn and Weber. The dying
Adam's prophecy of future world history with its wars and rumours of
wars, its parricide and fratricide, opens with an outburst of 'Puccini
octaves'. The Scandinavian march in Act V of *Ossian* has rhythmic
and harmonic peculiarities to be expected rather in Grieg.

The appeal of this mélange to Berlioz can be detected again and
again, for example in the mysterious prelude to *La Mort d'Adam* with
its hesitant tonality

Ex. 23

which returns in Act III when the sun is eclipsed at Adam's death.
The pastoral scenes, generally marked *col locale carattere* or *collo stile
locale*, have a suggestion of archaic remoteness, of primitive innocence
and melancholy, extraordinarily like *L'Enfance du Christ*; Le Sueur's
direction *d'una malincolia felice ch'avevan' i primi canti nuziali* exactly
hits a characteristic Berlioz mood. A few short extracts – quirky
cadence figures, spare in texture – illustrate some of the things Berlioz

found in Le Sueur. Whether he believed in the theoretical explanations is immaterial; he certainly justified the procedure, sometimes baffling posterity in the process.

Ex. 24

The manner of *La Damnation de Faust* is strikingly foreshadowed in the long apotheosis at the end of *La Mort d'Adam*, for example in the introductory *Symphonie aérienne et fantastique*, very barely harmonized, with the melody on solo flute and bassoon two octaves apart, and the final chorus with its spare texture, irregular phrase-lengths, long pedals, and passages of motionless harmony, which may be compared with the 'chorus of shades, young virgins and bards of second rank' in the vision scene of *Ossian*. The best of Le Sueur's big tableaux, such as the splendid ensemble and double chorus towards the end of Act II, where the race of Cain defy Adam's children and the patriarchs as Adam lies unconscious, have a lapidary quality almost worthy of his pupil. Here again Le Sueur combines themes previously sung by the two parties separately; and the piece ends with a *Ritournelle hypocritique* based on one of Cain's motives. The death scene, culminating in a blow on the tamtam, a total eclipse with black mists rising from the Euphrates, a long pause ('Pendant ce silence profond et terrible on entend quelquefois des gemissements vagues et lointains') and the return of the bleak prelude on bassoons and muted strings, is distinctly impressive. If Le Sueur's melodic powers could have sustained the level of such noble inspirations as the chorus 'O du ciel bienfait adoré!' at the end of Act II (which bears a strong resemblance to the Rosmala motive in *Ossian*, Ex. 18), his operas might not be forgotten. *La Mort d'Adam*, despite its fumblings and inadequacies, does from time to time express a vision unique in dramatic music outside the work of his most famous pupil.

LE SUEUR AND THE ORCHESTRA

Le Sueur was an eccentric orchestrator. In *Ossian* he uses the tamtam[1] consistently as a bardic property (the 'Bouclier aux sept voix' in Act III and the 'Bouclier de la mort' in Act V) and a massed body of twelve harps to suggest the hundred harps of Selma. He never divides them into more than two groups, but allows them to saturate the texture by doubling other instruments. Yet in *La Mort d'Adam*, where stage directions and dramatic situations make constant and sometimes specific demands for trumpets and harps, he uses the former very little and the latter not at all. The trumpets of chaos are horns with their bells placed against each other; the harps, despite their field day in *Ossian*, are represented by muted violins and pizzicato lower strings. Although he was capable of such novelties as pairs of timpanists rolling in thirds and strings accompanied only by triangles, cymbals, and tambourine in the sinister Scandinavian march in *Ossian*, and was particularly fond of subdivided strings, he had little feeling for the individuality of wind instruments and often wrote the same parts for oboes and clarinets and for horns and trumpets.

OTHER GRAND OPERAS OF THE PERIOD

Of the other grand operas of this period, Winter's *Tamerlan* (1802)

[1] He had introduced the tamtam in *Télémaque* and seems to have been responsible for its acclimatization in the opera orchestra. He was followed by Méhul in *Uthal*, Spontini in *La Vestale* and *Cortez*, Kreutzer in *Abel*, and later by Bellini in *Norma*.

and Paisello's *Proserpine* (1803) are incurably demure. The one interesting point about the former is that hero and heroine, a married couple as in *La Caverne, Les Deux Journées, Faniska*, and the Leonora operas, are taken by low voices, baritone and mezzo-soprano. Paisiello's attempt to inflate his mildly *galant* style to suit French taste produces an interminably tedious opera. Act II contains a friendly eruption of Etna and a chorus of nymphs in which twelve solo sopranos echo each other.

Cherubini's *Anacréon* (1803) is an old-fashioned opera-ballet whose slight story, little more than a celebration of wine, women, dance, and song, is no match for the amplitude of the composer's apparatus with its profusion of canonic and contrapuntal detail. The score contains some charming music, a formidable orchestral storm, and a masterly overture based on motives from the opera, three of which are heard simultaneously towards the end. A curiosity is a parody of the scene between Orpheus and the shades in Act II of Gluck's opera; in *Anacréon* it is the truant Cupid who pleads with the company not to send him back to his mother. There is something incongruous in the composer of *Médée* attempting such frivolities; indeed he seems to have become quite disorientated at this period. *Pimmalione* (1809) follows the same relaxed manner as *Anacréon*, except that (presumably to please Napoleon) Cherubini reverted to a castrato hero and abjured his contrapuntal dexterity – until the finale, which contains a splendid canonic trio. The scoring is full of exquisite detail, especially in the treatment of lower strings, but there is little plot and the melodic impulse is weak. Much the same applies to *Le Crescendo* (1810), in which Cherubini sits heavily on the story of Jonson's *Silent Woman*; the central figure is a Prussian major. *Les Abencérages* (1813) has a heroic plot, set in Spain during the Moorish wars, packed with knightly pageantry, military demonstrations, patriotism betrayed and desperately defended. Both libretto and music are much indebted to Spontini's *Cortez*. The apparatus is massive, with triple choruses and frequent marching and counter-marching, but despite one or two impressive ensembles – notably the G minor funeral march and chorus in Act III – the music is basically cold. The workmanship has an almost German solidity, if not stolidity, with occasional harmonic touches worthy of Spohr. It remained for Weber, with half Cherubini's technique, to apply his genius for melody and atmosphere to precisely this style; whereupon it burst instantly into flower. Cherubini's last opera, *Ali Baba* (1833), was condemned as 'learned', a judgement to be expected from an age given over to the surface glitter of Boieldieu, Auber, and Meyerbeer. Nevertheless it has greater vitality than his middle-period operas, especially in the numerous ensembles, which amount to a series of witty scherzos. The epigrammatic and elliptical style, and a harmonic idiom that (as in the contemporary string quartets) often takes unexpected turns, show a virility creditable in a septuagenarian. The score is said to be based on the suppressed *Koukourgi* of 1793; this may be true of the themes, but it is difficult to believe that they were not completely reworked.

CATEL

Catel wrote for both opera houses, but his serious temperament, which had much in common with Cherubini's, unfitted him for the lighter types of *opéra comique* popular after 1800; he might have done better in the 1790s, when he wrote nothing for the theatre at all. He was a professor at the Conservatoire and published a treatise on harmony in the same year as *Sémiramis* (1802); in the state of French taste then and for most of the nineteenth century this was enough to damn him as a pedant. His grand operas have solidity, energy, and classical strength, but lack a personal flavour; like Cherubini he was weak in lyrical invention. The tragic end of *Sémiramis*, a very short finale in E flat minor, is the more effective for the almost complete avoidance of the minor mode before Act III. Even so the mood of the opera is remarkably sombre, due partly to the scoring, in which horns, trombones, and divided lower strings are prominent, and partly to Catel's constant avoidance of the tonic chord early in a movement. The whole conception of the tormented queen owes much to *Médée*, for example in the short rhythmic phrases with cross-accents tossed between violins and basses throughout her first air. *Sémiramis* was popular in Vienna from 1806; the impressive overture has a strong foretaste of *Egmont*. Its introduction, which returns in place of a development and again in the opera as a motive for the queen, illustrates Catel's power of harmonic suggestion.

Ex. 25

Les Bayadères (1810) shows no change in style; Etienne de Jouy's libretto, which combines the spectacular, exotic, amorous, and bellicose with a synthetically contrived climax, is another attempt to repeat the pattern of *Cortez*. The obscurantist priests of that opera reappear in Brahmin dress, and the appeal to anticlerical feeling is so blatant as to suggest a hint to Napoleon to throw over the Concordat. The score has any amount of dignity, but could do with a touch of impudence. The harem scenes are ponderous and totally lacking in voluptuousness; the appeal of a trio of Bayadères in Act I to Dourga 'féconde déesse' produces a mixture of limp rhythm and chromatic harmony exactly in the manner of Spohr, and once or twice Catel anticipates the more succulent properties of Gounod's *Faust*.

Ex. 26

The only clear trace of Spontini is the elaborate use of fanfares, in the pit and behind the scenes, to depict military operations during the finale of Act II.

Some German writers[1] have credited *Les Bayadères* with an elaborate *Leitmotiv* system, postulating a basic motive that recurs in many interrelated forms directly and indirectly associated with the idea of warfare. Had Catel intended any such thing, he would surely have established its character firmly, as music and symbol, on its first appearance at Démaly's words 'Olcar ce guerrier témeraire' (Act I, 3). The motive consists of little more than a written-out turn; its later appearances are never identical and sometimes remote; many of the

[1] Bücken, op. cit. pp. 84–5; Karl Wörner, 'Beiträge zur Geschichte des Leitmotivs in der Oper', *Zeitschrift für Musikwissenschaft*, xiv (1931–2), pp. 164–5.

contexts, which include the trio of favourites and Laméa's air of self-sacrifice in Act III, have no reference to warfare (unless any link with sex is automatically placed under that head). Moreover Catel uses the phrase with equal freedom in other operas, especially *Sémiramis*. It is a superficial mannerism with no structural or dramatic significance. A similar claim on behalf of Berton's *Virginie ou les Decemvirs* (1823)[1] rests on even less stable foundations. The motives cited – an arpeggio of the chord of C major which becomes a diminished seventh when related to the Decemvirs, rising chromatic scales, and syncopated string accompaniments – are all commonplaces of the period.

BALLET AND THE EXOTIC

Most of these operas contain ballets with oriental, African, Spanish, Mexican, or Scottish settings and a bellicose or bloodthirsty content. Only Le Sueur gave them any harmonic colour; elsewhere a very mild exoticism emerges mouse-like from a welter of brass and percussion. The Mahratta choruses and the ballet finale of *Les Bayadères* suggest Germany rather than India. Any extra tints are supplied by the scoring. Berlioz gave Spontini credit for introducing the bass drum in *La Vestale*, but Catel had done so in *Sémiramis* and it was a regular component of eighteenth-century 'Turkish' orchestration. Cherubini wrote for a cor anglais in *Anacréon* (though the part seems to have been taken by a clarinet), as did Catel in his ballet *Alexandre chez Appelles* (1808) and in *Les Bayadères*, and a guitar, played on stage by a dancer, in *Les Abencérages*. The harp became increasingly popular, not merely to represent instruments mentioned in the text. It appears frequently in *Proserpine* and has a long obbligato just before the rape. Catel used it constantly, as did Boieldieu (e.g. in *Les Voitures versées*). Berlioz, thinking no doubt of *Ossian*, approved the use of massed harps and remarked that the timbre blended particularly well with the brass. For Catel in *Wallace* it had military as well as bardic associations; the hero refers in ringing tones to his 'harpe belliqueuse'. Elaborate double obbligatos for harp and horn became suddenly popular at both theatres (especially the Opéra) after 1800, when Méhul set the fashion in his *Chant National*; they were undoubtedly composed for particular virtuosos, such as the harpist F. J. Naderman and Frédéric Duvernoy, first horn at the Opéra from 1799 to 1816. (On the bills of the first performance of *La Vestale* Duvernoy's name appeared in larger type than that of any other artist.) Examples of such double obbligatos occur in *Sémiramis*, *Anacréon*, *Proserpine*, *La Vestale*, Catel's *Les Artistes par occasion* (1807) and *Les Bayadères*, the overture

[1] Bücken, pp. 86–8; Wörner, p. 165.

to Isouard's *Cendrillon* (1810), and an undated and unpublished
Spontini air marked *Obbligazione di Corno e Arpa.* Charlton[1] cites
further instances from ballets by Steibelt, Méhul, Cherubini, and
Catel (1802–8) and Paisiello's Mass for Napoleon's Coronation. Two
of them include two harps. There appears to be an association with
pastoral innocence and natural religion, and with the key of C major,
which is used in eleven of the fourteen examples (the others are in F,
B flat, and E flat).

OPÉRA COMIQUE UNDER THE EMPIRE

Méhul's later *opéras comiques* cannot compare with the works of the
nineties. *Uthal* (1806), based on the Ossianic poem *Berrathon,* and
Joseph (1807) both suffer from weak librettoo inculcating a rather
insipid nobility. The former, though in a single act with spoken
dialogue, was obviously modelled on *Ossian* (which Méhul probably
knew from the score) no doubt for the further edification of Napoleon.
It shares the same highly romantic subject, the same Celtic twilight,
the same bardic orchestral effects. Both operas begin at night in a
forest by the sea and contain an important recognition scene for a
father and daughter long separated; the hero of each invokes the spirit
of his ancestors. Méhul's music on the other hand may have influenced
Spontini, especially in its spatial use of choral and instrumental forces,
sometimes unusually constituted, on and behind the stage. The chorus
'Rejouis-toi, Morven', a *Marche triomphale derrière la scène* beginning
with a crescendo from *pp* to *ff* as the warriors approach, and with
abrupt modulations from D to B flat and C (twice), looks straight to
Cortez. The combination of *mélodrame,* recitative, and ensemble in
the movement describing the arrival of Fingal's army (with wind and
harp backstage), though indebted to Cherubini, is origina! in its
context. Nevertheless, despite the startling impact of the overture,
Méhul's conception is stronger than his execution; he overdrives his
ideas. This impression of failing invention is even more conspicuous
in *Joseph,* which consists of a long and lachrymose recognition scene
in three acts without subplot of any kind. All the dramatic incidents
of the Bible story have been ruthlessly pruned. The best music occurs
in the ensembles, which are skilfully worked;[2] only Siméon's guilty
conscience allows Méhul's fiery gifts any play. The *comédie larmoyante*
is back in control.

The most popular *opéra comique* composers during the Empire were
Boieldieu and the Maltese Nicolò Isouard (often known simply as

---

[1] *Orchestration.*

[2] See the excerpts from 'Non! Non! l'Eternel que j'offense' in Act I, in *The History of Music in Sound,* viii (London, 1958), p. 15.

Nicolò), both born in 1775. Each gained a striking success early in the century, Boieldieu with *Le Calife de Bagdad* (1800) and *Ma Tante Aurore* (1803), Isouard with *Michel-Ange* (1802); but Boieldieu's career was split by eight years in St. Petersburg (1803–11), during which time the facile and prolific Isouard led the field. Boieldieu's return initiated a period of intense rivalry, personal and artistic, lasting until Isouard's death in 1818. As well as new works Boieldieu brought out revised versions of several of his St. Petersburg operas, notably *Les Voitures versées* (1808; Paris 1820), and he continued to exploit the same vein in *Jean de Paris* (1812), *Le Nouveau Seigneur du village* (1813), *La Fête du village voisin* (1816), *Le Petit Chaperon rouge* (1818) and *La Dame blanche* (1825). His later career was one of almost uninterrupted success; he managed to keep his finger on the public pulse, and many of his operas remained in the repertory for decades. He owed much to his refusal to aim too high. He avoided politics and, after one or two early experiments like *Béniowski* (1800) and *Télémaque* (a setting of Le Sueur's old libretto, produced at St. Petersburg in 1806), the more serious type of *opéra comique*. (He did, much later, plan an *opéra comique* on *Faust*, in which the scenes with Mephistopheles masquerading as a pretty woman were expected to supply openings for mirth; this was abandoned because Scribe was brooding over the subject for Meyerbeer.) The innate conservatism – Philistinism might be a better term – of Paris bourgeois taste had quickly reasserted itself; as in the eighteenth-century *comédie mélée d'ariettes*[1] the product was judged by literary considerations as a play with musical interludes, criticism being directed primarily – sometimes almost exclusively – on the libretto. Even *Le Petit Chaperon rouge* was condemned as learned music, the press complaining that the composer had been absorbed in the member of the Institut, to which Boieldieu had just been elected. Moreover France during this period was a police state, and it must have been difficult for artists, especially in the years 1814–15 when the regime changed three times, to do other than play the Vicar of Bray. The numerous operatic collaborations in which all the leading composers took part were mostly occasional pieces written at the express demand of the authorities.

BOIELDIEU

It is scarcely surprising that Boieldieu, whose character, both personal and musical, inclined towards pliancy and charm – the exact antithesis of the Cherubini school – should have gone out of his way, like Grétry, Spontini, and later Meyerbeer, to placate his critics and

[1] See Vol. VII, p. 204.

the public. Whenever one of his operas met with a stern reception he hastened to make cuts and alterations. He completely reshaped *Ma Tante Aurore* after the first night – the libretto's title page described it as 'sifflé en trois actes le 23 nivôse, applaudis en deux le 25 du même mois' – and made similar adjustments to *Les Voitures versées*. Both these operas are partly satirical, the former at the expense of the English Gothic novel, the latter of provincial snobbery, but on a safe social level. It would be wrong to condemn Boieldieu for time-serving. He knew his limitations and (unlike Isouard) was generous to his rivals. Something of this easy-going nature comes out in his music.

His style was founded on Grétry and the Neapolitans. The story that he took a three-year course of instruction under Cherubini after the latter had criticized *Le Calife de Bagdad* is almost certainly untrue, but he was on friendly terms with the older man, who was a witness at his second marriage and composed an 'O salutaris' for the occasion.[1] The best of his early operas, such as *Les Voitures versées* (on a libretto set in contemporary France), display fluent melody, deft scoring, neatly fashioned ensembles and a light touch that embraces wit and humour but generally avoids the sentimentality of the *semiseria* convention popularized by Paer. He retains many Italian features, for example tripping melodies in the orchestra during ensembles (also popular with Dalayrac, as in Nos. 3 and 10 of *Gulistan*), and Cimarosa's favourite device of making individual instruments answer a cue in the text (Dorneuil's air in Act I of *Les Voitures versées*). He developed a pleasant gift for parody and burlesque. Késie's air in *Le Calife de Bagdad* asks for parodies of the French, Italian, Spanish, Scottish, German, and English styles; the young Boieldieu scarcely brings this off, though he introduces a few vocal extravagances for the Italian stanza, and in the Spanish the strings imitate the guitar by playing with the back of the bow, an idea promptly imitated by Isouard and Dalayrac. The parodies in *Les Voitures versées* are on a much higher level; they include an operatic love scene in Madame de Melval's air with a compass of more than two octaves, a set of vocal variations on the old tune 'Au clair de la lune', and a burlesque music-lesson in which the master's dictation of a theme opens the way to canons, first on each half of the melody, then on the whole of it, with a final stretto. Act I begins with an admirably sustained sextet and ends with a most entertaining finale. A coach accident, deliberately engineered by the provincial hostess bored by absence from Paris, brings in three stranded Gascons and a professional tenor who fears

---

[1] The influence of Cherubini on *Béniowski* is undeniable. See Georges Favre, 'L'Amitié de deux musiciens, Boieldieu et Cherubini', *Revue musicale*, cci (1946), pp. 217–25.

that his voice has been damaged by the impact, insists on trying it out, and fails lamentably to reach his top G. After several attempts he is stranded on F sharp and collapses into speech ('Oh mon Dieu! J'ai perdu mon *sol*'), whereupon the rest of the party sing a lament ('O perte irréparable!') beginning with delightfully comic effect in E flat. The finale ends with a quick movement about food and drink in which the main theme of the overture is treated canonically by the voices. Boieldieu handles this with something of Offenbach's wit and more than Offenbach's technical skill. The famous auction scene in *La Dame blanche*, much admired by Rossini, was only one of the novel pretexts for an operatic ensemble devised by Boieldieu.

It is not true that his style remained static. His later operas with their larger orchestra, more florid vocal writing, and less perfunctory attempts at local colour show acquaintance with Rossini and Weber. He was not overwhelmed; although he could not appreciate Spontini ('My cat would not write music like that', he said of *La Vestale*), his earlier Italian contacts had inoculated him against the inflammatory virus of Rossini, whom he admired without idolatry. The orchestra at the Opéra-Comique had to be augmented for *Les Voitures versées* in 1820, and still more for the 1824 revival of *Béniowski*. For this he composed a new overture less dependent for exotic detail on the conventional Turkish battery of *Le Calife de Bagdad* (he had acquired personal knowledge of the Russian climate). The chromatic runs on the clarinet and chords marked 'faites trembler le son' and 'faites vibrer' are mild enough, nor are the Scotticisms of *La Dame Blanche* (based on genuine folk-songs; the libretto derives from a conflation of Scott's *The Monastery* and *Guy Mannering*) bold by later standards. But they are telling in their context, and the tune of 'Robin Adair' is put to genuine dramatic use in Act III: Brown hears it, recognizes it as a faint memory of childhood, and takes it up, first tentatively and then with growing confidence. Although Boieldieu might have learned this from *Richard Coeur de Lion*, *La Dame blanche* is the first French opera (along with Auber's *Le Maçon*, produced earlier the same year) to reflect the influence of Weber and repay some of the debt that for years had been accumulating in the opposite balance. This is not merely the plot, with its haunted castles, lost heirs, unjust stewards, and faithful retainers – not to mention its ghost (quick rather than dead): these ingredients of early romanticism had in any case been pounded down into the conventional pemmican by Scribe. It is present in the music, for example, the main theme of Brown's Act II cavatina and the ballad of the White Lady itself, which in key (B flat minor), harmony, and scoring hints at the mysterious world of *Der Freischütz*.

Boieldieu's music, like Massenet's, seems to enshrine something of the quintessential French spirit. It offers a light vein of poetry and sentiment, amorous rather than passionate, a technique sufficient but never pedantic, and a gift of graceful entertainment not to be taken too seriously. Paul Landormy[1] calls him 'one of the most charming musicians France has ever produced, and one of those whose works come nearest to perfection'. He and Jules Combarieu[2] both speak of him as a French Mozart. This is to ignore his limitations. His harmonic idiom and his emotional range are severely restricted; he himself confessed that he could compose only on cheerful ideas. While it is true that his operas show a perfect fusion of words, drama, and music, they are unambitious and stereotyped in subject and, however polished the expression, the tone is essentially *petit-bourgeois*, the Paris equivalent of the Viennese *Biedermeier*.

NICOLÒ ISOUARD

Isouard reached Paris in 1801 after a busy career of several years in Malta and Italy. He had great facility, producing thirty French *opéras comiques* at the rate of two a year, and was as successful as Boieldieu at hitting public taste. He too was most at home in light domestic subjects, as his titles (*Les Confidences, L'Intrigue aux fenêtres, Le Déjeuner de garçons, Les Rendez-vous bourgeois, Le Billet de loterie*, etc) sufficiently indicate. *Michel-Ange* is only superficially an exception; the *Décade philosophique* of 21 December 1802 reproached him for treating the hero 'comme un Colin d'opéra comique'. His *Cendrillon* (1810) held the stage all over Europe till its eclipse by Rossini's opera on the same subject. He is at his best in *Joconde* (1814), a mixture of Grétry pastoral and social comedy. The plot resembles that of *Così fan tutte* with a cosy egalitarian moral. There are two pairs of lovers; men and girls plot independently to test each other's fidelity while the bass, though he initiates nothing, is in the confidence of both parties. After the usual play with transparent disguises, the philandering aristocrats are outwitted not only by their mistresses but by the peasant girl they both woo on the side, and the pompous *bailli* is satisfactorily deflated. The setting is Provençal, and Isouard's local colour, with piccolo and tambourine, faintly anticipates that of Gounod's *Mireille*; but he characteristically does not bother to write a proper part for the tambourine. The music is an agreeable soufflé of gay tunes and lively rhythms, without surprises, and becomes insipid in bulk. While the sources of his style are the same as Boieldieu's, his scoring is thinner

[1] *La Musique française* (Paris, 1943).
[2] *Histoire de la musique*, ii (Paris, 1913).

and his technique more slipshod. He evidently believed in sparing himself effort; the copious return of earlier material in Act III, though not unsuited to the context, gives the impression of being inspired by laziness rather than dramatic design. On the other hand the overture is soundly constructed on four themes from the opera, two of which appear in modified form.

OPERA UNDER THE RESTORED BOURBONS

The restoration of the Bourbons produced less change than might have been expected in the repertory of the Opéra. Several successes of the Empire held their place; the revised *Fernand Cortez* of 1817 was considerably more popular than the original, but *Olympie* (1819) had to wait for its triumph till the Berlin revival of 1821, after Friedrich Wilhelm III of Prussia (having failed to obtain his first choice, Cherubini) had translated Spontini to his capital. Even then the stage elephants failed to stamp out the young German school exemplified by the première of *Der Freischütz* five weeks later. The later operas of Catel and Berton made little mark. Among the curiosities were Liszt's juvenile and unsuccessful *Don Sanche* (1825) and Chélard's *Macbeth* (1827) which enjoyed considerable success in Germany. This eclectic compound of the styles of Spontini, Rossini, Weber, and Spohr has an extraordinary libretto by Rouget de Lisle, which crosses Shakespeare with Ossian and bestows the name Elsie on the First Witch; the score includes a ballet on 'Auld Lang Syne'.[1] The two successes of the decade 1815–25 were both trivialities, reflecting the taste of an age of tired reaction. Lebrun's one-act *Le Rossignol* (1816) offered a spectacular contest between a soprano and a flute; a later performance in 1820 witnessed the assassination of the Duc de Berri. Isouard's posthumous *Aladin, ou la lampe merveilleuse* (1822, completed by Angelo Benincori) had 53 performances in its first season, thanks largely to its ballet and spectacular production, but is remembered (if at all) by the simultaneous première of the ophicleide in the pit (it had appeared on stage in *Olympie*) and gas-lighting on the stage.

INFLUX OF FOREIGNERS

Paris was ripe for a new wave of foreigners; and it came. Rossini, Weber, and Meyerbeer in turn left permanent marks on French opera. Rossini's influence, which transformed the repertory of both theatres, arrived some time before his person. The first of his operas heard in Paris, *L'Italiana in Algeri* in February 1817, was a failure, but

[1] For further particulars, see *Shakespeare in Music*, ed. Phyllis Hartnoll (London, 1964), pp. 157–8.

L'Inganno felice and *Il Barbiere di Siviglia* created a furore in 1819, and the arrival in the next three years of eight more Rossini operas inspired one of those pitched battles, like the Querelle des Bouffons in 1752 and the Gluck-Piccinni controversy in 1778, that periodically excite the Paris public to gaseous controversy. On the one hand Rossini was acclaimed as the advocate of freedom, the musical counterpart of political liberalism and literary romanticism; Stendhal and others found him at once classical and popular, gratifying the most delicate connoisseurs and the vulgar palate of the masses, and compared him with Voltaire. On the other hand he was damned for cynical opportunism, neglect of dramatic truth, and every imaginable sin against prosody. In October 1819 *La Renommée* found *Il barbiere* feeble, incoherent, without character or unity; *Le Moniteur Universel* condemned it as sterile, laboured and 'dénuée de chant'; and ended its notice with 'Bravo, Paisiello'.[1] French literary taste, always touchy about the 'poem', accused Rossini of giving the voices clarinet and bassoon parts and reducing them to the level of mere mechanics. Many writers censured his fondness for the noisiest instruments, especially brass and percussion, a charge that could as easily have been brought against Spontini. Berton exploded in a vitriolic pamphlet, *De la musique mécanique et de la musique philosophique* (1826), denouncing the 'immeasurable profusion of semiquavers' and declaring that 'dans la roulade est tout le sublime de la nouvelle école', and kept up the fight for several years. As late as 1829 Joseph D'Ortigue ridiculed 'these shocking contradictions between the expression and the subject, which are as far removed from nature as they are condemned by taste'. Apart from the matter of declamation, it was the animal rhythms and crescendos, the violent contrasts and sudden thumps and pauses, that upset French ears and soon, to the consternation of journalists, began to infect the French school as well. The production of *La Dame blanche* in 1825 was taken as a symbol of retaliation and its success as a national triumph. Virtually the entire Paris press hailed Boieldieu's opera as a mortal blow to the false doctrine of Rossini's 'absurd system': 'Boieldieu is a painter, Rossini only a decorator', 'Farewell *le rossinisme*! The score of *La Dame blanche* has given it its passport' – without the aid of auxiliary trombones or supplementary cymbals.

Rossini himself first visited Paris in November 1823. The following year he was made director of the Théâtre-Italien, where he revived more of his earlier operas, and from 1825 till 1830 he held an appointment under the French crown, with the understanding that he

[1] Quoted by Combarieu, op. cit.

should settle in Paris and compose for the Opéra. Weber's only visit took place early in 1826 on his journey to London, but the production of *Der Freischütz* in December 1824, even in Castil-Blaze's emasculated version under the title *Robin des bois* (with the scene laid 'dans le Yorkshire' during the reign of Charles I), had been an immense and influential success. It was followed in the next few years by *Preciosa*, *Oberon*, and *Euryanthe*, and in 1829 by *Fidelio*. Meyerbeer was invited to compose for the Opéra as early as 1823. His long letter of reply to the bass Nicolas Levasseur (5 July) shows a characteristic circumspection: he welcomes the invitation, complains about the taste of Italian librettos, agrees that Paris is the only place for the composer who wishes to write genuinely dramatic music, but hesitates because French opera has the reputation of presenting immense difficulties and years of delay before performance. He went to Paris for the first time in September 1825 for the production of *Il Crociato in Egitto* (under Rossini), and presently began to compose *Robert le Diable*. Though it appeared at the Opéra in 1831, this was planned as an *opéra comique* with spoken dialogue on the model of *Der Freischütz*, whose blend of religion and black magic Meyerbeer sought to imitate and excel.

ROSSINI'S FRENCH OPERAS

Strictly speaking, Rossini composed only one new work for the Paris Opéra, *Guillaume Tell* (1829). His first three productions there were adaptations: *Le Siège de Corinthe* (1826) and *Moïse* (1827) from operas of his Italian period (*Maometto Secondo*, 1820, and *Mosè in Egitto*, 1818[1]), *Le Comte Ory* (1828) from an occasional piece in Italian given three times at the Théâtre-Italien in honour of the coronation of Charles X in 1825. Nevertheless all four works take a high rank in the history of French opera. The common notion of Rossini as a lazy and casual composer who always took the shortest distance between two points, misleading for his Italian period, does no justice to his French operas, which show a scrupulous care for the niceties of French prosody (Saint-Saëns compared him very favourably with Meyerbeer in this respect)[2] and for the vocal and dramatic style to which the French were accustomed. In his choice and treatment of subject he went some way towards reviving the more generous ideals of the Revolution. It is easy to point disparagingly to his shrewdness in selecting the title *Le Siège de Corinthe* and changing the besieged heroes from Venetians to Greeks just when the Turkish siege of

[1] See pp. 417 ff.

[2] But the autograph of *Guillaume Tell* shows that he had some outside assistance: cf. Philip Gossett, *The Operas of Rossini* (Diss. Princeton, 1970), pp. 35 ff.

Missolonghi was filling the newspapers; but it is the rousing vitality of the new music he composed for the patriotic scenes that made the success of the opera. This is equally true of *Tell*, a subject he chose himself. In all three of his French grand operas (*Le Comte Ory* belongs to a different convention) the political aspect is far more important than the love story, which, like the ballet, remains secondary and conventional. It would be interesting to know how he proposed to treat the opera he considered on Joan of Arc.

Rossini combined three vital elements that had never cohered before: the liberal impulses released by the Revolution, the historical pageantry of Spontini's operas under the Empire, and the rich lyrical heritage of Italian vocal writing of which he was the living embodiment. The characters, as in earlier grand opera, are types rather than individuals and drawn larger than life; but they stand for forces projected, often with great brilliance, in the choruses and ensembles. All three are operas of rebellion against oppression: Moses and the Jews against the Egyptians, the Greeks against the Turks, the Swiss against the Austrians. In the 1820s this was gunpowder; it is no wonder that a rehearsal of *Tell* on 29 July 1830 contributed to the 'July Revolution'. (Tell's cry 'Ou l'indépendence ou la mort' in the Act III trio was taken up by everyone in the theatre, musicians, stage hands, and soldiers on guard, and all rushed into the streets.) The opera was constantly mutilated by the censorship, especially in Italy and Russia; the hero being variously metamorphosed into Andreas Hofer, Charles the Bold, 'Guglielmo Vallace', and 'Rodolfo di Sterlinga'.

The similarity between the three operas is far more striking than the differences, both in the drama and the music, even though two of them were new only in part. The nature and purpose of Rossini's changes for Paris have seldom been understood. It is not true that all or even most of the best music dates from the revision, that the patriotic element was weak in the original, or that the rich choral, orchestral, and ensemble writing in *Tell* was a new development in Rossini's style. Both versions of both operas are stronger in their choruses, ensembles, and orchestration than in their solos and duets; that is to say, Rossini was approaching the French balance of forces before he set foot in France, influenced in part by Cherubini and Mayr but also by Mozart. Many episodes in the Italian *Mosè*, such as the Andante quintet and nearly the whole First Act (the first two numbers were transferred to Act II in Paris), show the *Tell* style in full bloom, though it was far from consistently applied throughout. Both operas in their Italian dress begin with striking scenes in which the patriotic note is firmly and eloquently struck. It is true that the Paris changes are mostly improvements (not always: the female chorus that begins Act II of *Maometto* is far superior to the poor ballade, lifted from *Ermione*, that replaced it[1]), and that many weak spots in drama and music were expunged; but the transformations are more interesting than this.

Rossini's object seems to have been threefold. First, and most obviously, to come to terms with the French style of declamation and marry it to Italian lyrical flexibility; one of the terms of his engagement was that he should raise the standard of French singing. He managed this very successfully in the newly written pieces. Most of the recitatives were of course recomposed. In *Le Siège de Corinthe* some of the voices were changed, the hero (originally a coloratura contralto) becoming a tenor and the heroine losing her mezzo tessitura; in both operas the characters were renamed, producing considerable confusion, especially in *Moïse*. In the set numbers Rossini sought to substitute expression for flamboyance. The original music for the Sultan Maometto often suggests not so much a tyrant as the *buffo* pasha of *L'Italiana in Algeri*. Rossini toned down the voice part, but did not always get rid of the military jauntiness of the accompaniment, for example in the cabaletta of his Act I aria. This example illustrates his method:

Ex. 27

MAOMETTO SECONDO (1820)
Allegro marziale

Du - ce __ di tan - ti, __ di tan - ti __ E - ro - i   crol -

LE SIÈGE DU CORINTH (1826)
Allegro

Chef   d'un   peu - ple, d'un peu - ple in-domp - ta - ble   et gui-

---

[1] Rossini had previously inserted the ballade in Act I of *Maometto* for the Venice revival of 1823. This Venice score incorporates a number of changes usually attributed to the Paris version, which was partly modelled on it: see Gossett, op. cit. pp. 455 ff.

(Leader of so many heroes / Chief of an unconquerable people and guide of their valour)

That he was aware of the danger and not lacking in self-criticism is evident from his second aim, which was to raise the dignity of the music by modifying its heavy impregnation with the buffo style. He introduced a gradual process of refinement, but did not always go far enough. All the rejected movements in *Mosè*, especially the bass arias for Moses and Pharaoh, are better away, but one or two weak pieces in the same manner remained; for example the duet in which Pharaoh, with the best intentions, urges a diplomatic marriage on his son, who unknown to him loves someone else. (A duet of rather similar design in *Maometto*, no. 12, did lose its cabaletta.) Occasionally Rossini adapts old material to a new situation without passing it afresh through his imagination. In no. 5 of *Le Siège de Corinthe*, an air for Pamira, he conflates solos composed for two different characters, separating them with new material. The strangest instance is the second finale of *Moïse*, when not only is the protagonist changed but the dramatic situation is utterly remote from the original. In the Italian score, Moses's daughter proclaims her love for Pharaoh's son, who assaults Moses but is killed by a thunderbolt (modulation from E to A flat); whereupon (cabaletta) she bids the furies rend her while all lament the day of horror and disaster for Egypt. In the French version the air is given to Pharaoh's wife, who begs her son to listen to a mother's prayer. He demands vengeance on Moses; but the modulation to A flat occurs when an offstage chorus summons him to the temple of Isis and he agrees to go, abandoning his vengeance. The cabaletta is his mother's exclamation of joy that he has returned to the path of honour. Yet the music is basically unchanged, and the phrase conceived for the words 'Oh istante orribile!' is now sung to 'O gloire, O douce ivresse!' Needless to say, the original is much the more convincing.

The third point concerns the patriotic content. As well as emphasizing it, Rossini gave it an explicit contemporary reference, especially in *Le Siège de Corinthe*, where, apart from turning the Venetians into Greeks, he restored the tragic end. (The original end, in which the heroine stabs herself to deprive Maometto of his vengeance after revealing his plans to the Venetians, was one of the causes of the opera's failure in Naples. Rossini was persuaded to alter it for Venice.) But the restored end was far more spectacular and emphasized a specific moral inconceivable in an earlier age: that the public interest must override even a solemn oath. This perhaps could only have been said at that time in France; it became the hub of the Paris libretto. The new music for the patriotic scenes in Act III, inspired by the desperate resistance of the Greeks who perish to the last man, woman, and child, is of superb quality. The opera ends with an elaborate tone-poem depicting the sack of Corinth by the Turks during a storm. The voices sing only a few broken phrases at the beginning, the rest being left to the orchestra. The Berliozian final tableau, in which the Turks break into the tombs while the Greek women kill themselves or are killed and the city burns in the background, is a link between *Médée* and *La Prise de Troie*.

The orchestral finale, a stroke of genius, has no parallel in *Maometto*; but Rossini had anticipated it in the Italian *Mosè*, where it represents a similar catastrophe, the overwhelming of the Egyptian army by the Red Sea after the Israelites have passed safely across. Here too the first half of the movement is in the minor, the second half in the major. Rossini greatly strengthened this in the French *Moïse*, giving the music a sharper rhythmic vitality and significantly altering the dynamics. In 1818, after a short pianissimo, the opera ends with nine fortissimo bars; in 1827 the whole major-key episode is a long diminuendo from forte down to pianissimo (fifteen bars) as the storm dies away to a calm seascape, a beautiful effect reminiscent of *Mélidore et Phrosine*.[1] The final scene of *Tell*, though not confined to the orchestra, is closely related to this: it has the same minor-major gradation, the same key (C), and the same dramatic sequence of a prayer-ensemble (with strong melodic appoggiaturas in the theme) followed by a storm and the return of calm. It ends, however, not with a diminuendo but with a long crescendo, perhaps the noblest and grandest (as it is the last) of Rossini's extensive series. It is symbolic rather than dramatic, as is the whole dénouement of *Tell*, which Dent suggested must have been in Wagner's mind when he composed the closing scene of *Das Rheingold*.[2] But the symbolism (sun after storm: freedom after tyranny) is implicit in both the earlier operas.

The romanticism of Rossini's late operas emerges less in the substance of the musical language than from his manipulation of dramatic motives: the social-political climate, the tragic end, the prayer, and the treatment of nature. When he revised *Maometto Secondo* he turned it into one long sequence of prayers. It already contained three movements of this type: he gave a similar slant, by alteration of the words, in whole or part to no fewer than five old pieces and added others as well. This superabundance of praying does not, and was not intended to, increase the religious content of the story. Prayer is treated as an adjunct to patriotism, as it was later in Verdi's *Nabucco* and countless other romantic operas. Likewise the background of Alpine scenery, lakes, and mountains in *Tell* makes a direct contribution to the national content of the drama, as it does in Schiller's epic play on which the libretto is based. We are constantly aware not only of the locality but of the weather and even the time of day; the difference from *Mélidore et Phrosine* is not that Rossini is more romantic than Méhul, but that he is more accomplished.

GUILLAUME TELL

Some of the local colour in *Tell* is traditional, for example the pastoral episodes in Act I, the fisherman's song with harp accompaniment, and the chorus of shepherds with drone and triangle. The backstage horn fanfares representing Gessler and the Austrians, though they make their point, are less evocative than similar passages

---

[1] The brief (and ineffective) final *cantique* was very soon dropped, probably during the 1827 run. It is marked as cut in the manuscript score used at the Opéra in 1827–32 (Gossett, op. cit., p. 420).

[2] *The Rise of Romantic Opera*, p. 124.

in Weber and Donizetti, or even Méhul. But the hidden menace of the forest suggested by the drums in Matilda's Act II air and the combination of picturesque scoring (clarinets, horns, cellos, and basses) and march rhythms to convey mystery and expectancy as the men of the cantons assemble in the darkness, culminating in the blazing brass fanfares of the oath, show Rossini exploiting the new expressive resources of the French orchestral style, to which he added one new colour in the cornets. He doubtless picked up hints from Weber, Méhul, and others; he had heard the Vienna première of *Der Freischütz* in March 1822; and he had a gift for assimilating just as much as he needed from his predecessors and contemporaries. Each section of the *Tell* overture has a model in some earlier French opera. The divided cellos of the introduction derive from *Ariodant*; the storm has countless predecessors, including several Méhul overtures (*Mélidore et Phrosine, Uthal*); the *Ranz des vaches* is modelled on the corresponding episode in Grétry's *Tell* – which Berton had re-scored for a revival at the Opéra Comique in 1828, designed to take the wind out of Rossini's sails – and the march echoes *Fernand Cortez*. Each section, of course, represents an important strand in the opera – the aspirations and the rising of the patriots in the first and fourth, the scenic setting in the second and third; and the whole overture is projected with that incisiveness and certainty of aim that native French opera had generally lacked.

The librettos of these operas are loose in design and awkwardly put together. This was to be expected in the two reshaped works, though both are improvements on the originals, especially *Le Siège de Corinthe*; here a powerful conflict of loyalties is developed, and the first finale is much tighter as a result. The *Tell* libretto has been much abused; certainly Act I contains too much extraneous matter and Act IV provides a perfunctory wind-up to the plot; but it is less muddled than most of Jouy's work and less false to its emotional premises than Scribe's. The male trio in Act II conspicuously advances the action, since Arnold learns of and reacts to his father's murder in the course of it; the music must therefore express a wide variety of response. Rossini fills the ample design of this act, and indeed of the whole opera, without adding significantly to the technical resource of his Italian operas. Perhaps the most original movement is the arioso with solo cello 'Sois immobile' (which won the admiration of Wagner), addressed by Tell to his son before his toxophilic feat with the apple. The slightly extended use of recurring motives in the Paris operas is less impressive than the increased flexibility and more remote tonal contrasts in the new Introduction to *Moïse*, which includes a supernatural touch in a mysterious voice from heaven. But the happy extension of the ostinato figure of the original Introduzione to *Mosè* (no. 7 of the Paris score) through the following recitative was present in 1818.

ROSSINI'S INFLUENCE

If Rossini's French operas were largely a consolidation of earlier trends, their influence was deep and widespread. Tell is a Risorgimento figure, the heroic baritone conspirator whom we meet again in Verdi's *La battaglia di Legnano*. His duet with Arnold is the model for many of Verdi's tenor-baritone scenes, and Arnold's air in Act IV follows a plan – romantically scored cavatina, summons to action from male chorus, fiery cabaletta – that Verdi carried to almost grotesque lengths in *I Masnadieri*. Anticipations of Verdi in *Moïse* (apart from the prayer, the obvious model for that in *Nabucco*) include the electric rhythm of the Act III finale and the E minor section of Anaï's Act IV air, especially its semiquaver accompaniment figure; and in *Le Siège de Corinthe* Neoclès's passionate air in Act III, which wholly transcends the buffo style. The superb scene of the blessing of the flags in the same opera clearly suggested that of the blessing of the daggers in *Les Huguenots*; and it may not be fanciful to see in the F minor section with its creeping ostinato figure and long trills a foretaste of the funeral march in *Götterdämmerung*. The true heirs of *Guillaume Tell* were not Meyerbeer's operas, which broke up the grand design into segments for immediate and often meretricious effect, but the Paris works of Donizetti and Verdi, especially *Don Carlos*, which took another Schiller play with a noble political theme and alone surpassed the model.

LE COMTE ORY

Le Comte Ory is a unique phenomenon in the history of the French Opéra. Whereas at all periods the repertory of that institution has aimed at a dignified if not heroic utterance, this brilliant work set out to ridicule those very qualities. It is a kind of anti-opera, fully equipped with recitatives and set in the 'heroic' period of the Crusades, which it handles with the sustained flippancy of Offenbach. Its influence on the latter, and on the whole school of French operetta, both in temper and in substance, was overwhelming; the tearaway galop tune of the first finale is one obvious exemplar. Scribe, always safer with comic than with serious subjects, for once avoids bourgeois complacency and adds a touch of spice by introducing the Count and his friends (male chorus) disguised as nuns, to the castle of his beloved, during the absence of her husband and the rest of the male population in the Holy Land. He gives exceptional interest to the role of the chorus, whether as superstitious countryfolk consulting the 'hermit' in Act I or as tenor and bass nuns and timorous females in Act II. The slightness of the plot, which exploits the same situation (albeit an amusing one) in both acts, throws all the greater responsibility on the music. Rossini easily sustains it. This was his first comedy for ten years, and it remains his subtlest. It is hilariously funny, but not wholly farcical in the manner of his Italian *opere buffe*. If a little of their animal energy has gone, the loss is more than counterbalanced by an extra dimension in Gallic wit, greater harmonic refinement, and an occasional hint of profundity behind the trivial and absurd. The characters, especially the slightly absurd Countess and the page Isolier, are neatly characterized in music that employs vocal ornament as a dramatic means and not an end. The Count and Raimbaud, though clearly related to their counterparts in *Il barbiere di Siviglia*, are very much alive; Raimbaud's Act II patter song, with the orchestral tune entering repeatedly in unexpected keys, is perhaps Rossini's highest achievement in this kind. What is new is his use of a highly artificial convention to reveal an unsuspected insight into human nature, very much as Mozart does in *Così fan tutte*. This is glimpsed in the Act I duet for Isolier and the Count, the Countess's entrance music and first air, and most of all in the trio towards the end of the opera, where a grotesque situation ripe with sexual ambiguity yields music of exquisite tenderness and delicacy. The lingering woodwind cadences that so delighted Berlioz have a poetical quality rare in Rossini but characteristic of Mozart, from whom they may be derived.

AUBER'S *MUETTE*

The only important native grand opera of these years, the *Muette de Portici* of Daniel Auber (1782–1871)[1] was produced in 1828 before *Guillaume Tell*, but now seems so faded that its sensational success is difficult to account for. The rabble-rousing vengeance duet in Act I sparked off the Brussels revolution of 1830. A potentially fine subject, the Neapolitan revolution of 1647 (coupled by dramatic licence with the 1631 eruption of Vesuvius), is wrecked by the frivolous approach of both librettist and composer. By making no attempt to deal seriously with the political angle, which should be paramount, and by

[1] The *Masaniello* by Michele Carafa (1787–1873) on the same subject, produced two months earlier, had pre-empted Auber's title. This and *Le Solitaire* (1822), both at the Opéra-Comique, were Carafa's most successful stage works. He was little more than an imitator of Rossini, whom he revered.

the cynical inconsistency of his attitude to character and drama, Scribe reduced the whole thing to a sentimental charade. Auber was not equipped to tackle grand opera. His eclectic style owes something to Spontini and a little to Weber and Spohr, for example the soulful diminished sevenths of the Act I wedding chorus; the prayer in the Act III finale, with its square rhythms and scarcely less sugary harmony, is said to have been taken from a Mass of 1812. But the overwhelming influence comes from Rossini's earlier operas. Auber constantly approaches pathetic situations with the jaunty gait of Figaro; his music, here and elsewhere, teems with echoes of the first finale of *Il barbiere*, which crop up in the most unsuitable places. The fidgetiness of his manner, with its reliance on dotted rhythms, agitated figuration, and a superfluity of triplets, excludes any tempo slower than *andante* (and even that is generally hustled along by the accompaniment); indeed one has to search hard for a genuinely slow tempo in any of his operas. The melodies themselves, for all their limited scope, are often charming, but they proceed by repetition (generally louder), and the big ensembles and finales are aggregates, not articulated or organic wholes. Hence the prominence of the chorus as a dramatic agent is largely wasted.

The opera's most unusual features, to which it doubtless owed much of its success, are the choice of a dancer for the heroine Fenella (anticipated by Weber in *Silvana*) and the finale, at once fatal and spectacular: Fenella jumps from the Viceroy's palace in Naples into lava from the erupting volcano, a remarkable feat even for a French ballerina. Unfortunately this follows an act so ludicrous (in which the gratuitous poisoning of Masaniello induces hallucinations, a mad scene, and pathetic reminiscences of earlier music, all abruptly switched off to make way for a 'heroic' battle scene) that the sense of genuine tragedy is absent. The *mélodrames* in which the dumb heroine, with the assistance of the orchestra, has to mime all manner of sentiments, nuances, and even narratives (some of them calculated to expose her to a charge of public indecency) are often effective in their unexpected modulations and recall of earlier motives, and so is the use of barcarolle rhythm as a symbol of revolt and, to a limited degree, a structural agent; but a more adept composer would have given them a stronger impact. The best of the barcarolles, sung by the fisherman Pietro at the beginning of the last act, has a suitably sinister touch. Auber makes full use of other characteristic devices of early romantic opera: prayers, solo and choral, Spanish and Italian dance rhythms (including the tarantella that soon became almost obligatory in such contexts), and sumptuous orchestration, for which he was praised by

Wagner. A few scenes have a genuinely romantic tinge in the music, for example Elvira's air 'Arbitre d'une vie' in Act III, which suggests a compromise between Weber and Donizetti. The whole opera, with its tinkling tunes, glittering dances, icing-sugar vocal flourishes, square rhythms, and accumulation of small-scale ideas to interpret grandiose dramatic situations became – much more than *Guillaume Tell* – the model for Meyerbeer.

AUBER'S *OPÉRAS COMIQUES*

Auber's true home was the Opéra-Comique, where he produced some 33 works between 1813 and 1869, 28 of them in collaboration with Scribe. Although Boieldieu was still active for some years, Auber's principal rival was Ferdinand Hérold (1791–1833), who from 1817 brought fifteen operas (excluding collaborations) to the same stage. The style of both rested on the same foundations, the *comédie mêlée d'ariettes* of Grétry as transmitted by Boieldieu, the irrepressible bounce of Rossini's youthful farces, and (more particularly in Hérold) a German strain from Mozart and Weber. The artificial librettos avoided deep feeling and complex emotions; if they happened to raise a point of psychological subtlety, they took care to evade its implications. The music employed simple forms, strophic *couplets*, ternary structures, and rondos; ensembles and finales, if sometimes extensive, consisted of little more than a mosaic of fairly short movements in contrasted keys. There was almost no large-scale architecture. Both composers exploited the new devices of romantic opera: 'characteristic' choruses of peasants, soldiers, sailors, fishermen, and other professions, with a faint exotic seasoning supplied by popular dance rhythms (especially the polonaise, polka, waltz, and barcarolle – the old courtly forms of minuet, gavotte, and sarabande were reserved to Ancien Régime contexts), discreet use of religion (prayers, Easter choruses, and the like), and a wholly conventional treatment of the basic emotions of love, jealousy, and revenge, never pushed to extremes. A common ingredient was the narrative ballad, often sung by the heroine to explain the background of the story and brought back at the end when everything has been solved. There are examples in Auber's *Le Maçon* and *Fra Diavolo* and Hérold's *Zampa*; the original model was probably *Les Deux Journées*. The use of recurring motives seldom went deeper than this.

In temperament Auber and Hérold were very different. Auber's style scarcely developed at all. Nearly all its characteristic features are present in the one-act *Le Testament et les billets-doux* (1819), the scene of which is the lounge of a Paris hotel – the spiritual home of Auber's

smart sophisticated art even when the characters tell us we are in
Portugal, England, or North Africa. It has no feeling for nature or the
open air and preserves its dapper spruceness regardless of geography.
Here already is the neat craftsmanship, the polished scoring, the
bubble and squeak of early Rossini without its animal gusto and
occasional surprises. Auber could turn out a clever imitation of
Rossini, as in the Act II quartet of *Leicester* (1823), but he never risked
the bolder strokes of Rossini's serious operas. His love music contains
no passion (characteristically an amorous duet in *Leicester* is marked
Nocturne and Allegro moderato); his quick pieces are incorrigibly
chirpy; he avoided minor keys almost as consistently as slow tempos.
Light irony served as a substitute for sentiment, which he distrusted.
He treated all subjects alike, with the result that the quality of his
operas depends to a considerable extent on Scribe's contribution. In
Leicester Scribe contrived to drain all romanticism out of Scott's
Kenilworth, which he reduced to a formula; neither he nor Auber
attempted to dissolve the drama in the music. The part of Queen
Elizabeth, a coloratura mezzo with a huge compass and much frothy
coloratura, is anything but regal; the music for her first entrance

Ex. 28

is of exactly the same calibre as that devised by Auber, much more
suitably, for a bronze horse in his opera of 1835.

Le Maçon (1825) reflects the influence of *Der Freischütz* in the music
of the more serious characters; they are contrasted with peasants who
speak in clipped dialect and sing in the manner of Grétry seasoned
with Rossini (and a little Mozart: the first ensemble begins with a
near-quotation from the *Figaro* overture). When however in Act III
the peasant Roger has a prayer, Auber throws consistency to the
winds. The opening of the overture on a diminished seventh, a gambit
repeated in *La Muette de Portici*, may have been suggested by Weber's
C major piano sonata; but Auber, unlike Hérold, does not allow
German influence to go to his head. In *Fra Diavolo* (1830) he and
Scribe are at their best. The plot is amusing and mildly naughty; the
air in which Zerlina undresses on stage penetrated Mendelssohn's
prudish defences. The music, over which Auber seems to have taken
more trouble than usual, is a neat compound of irony, sentiment, and

sophisticated wit. He does not (again unlike Hérold) take his bandit-hero-villain too seriously; he even makes fun of the fashionable barcarolle by putting a sterling specimen in Diavolo's mouth as he palms an English peeress's locket. The ballad in which Zerlina describes his fearsome reputation nicely blends comedy with a faint romantic *frisson*, and the whole score, which might be described as two parts Rossini to one part Boieldieu, never becomes dull or insipid.

PLATE I. DESIGN FOR ACT III (SCENES 2 AND 3) OF AUBER'S *FRA DIAVOLO*

Performed at the Opéra-Comique, Paris, on 28 January 1830. Lithograph by Godefroy Engelmann.

HÉROLD

Hérold was a potentially more interesting composer who never adjusted his aims to his capacity or managed to reconcile contradictory influences. A great admirer of Méhul, one of his teachers, he tried to raise *opéra comique* to a more serious level without making certain that it had something more serious to express. He was a poor judge of a libretto, and repeatedly saddled himself with ramshackle plots and incredible characters, into whom he could not breathe life, although he possessed a stronger feeling for the dramatic use of harmony than Boieldieu or Auber and with it the means for penetrating below the surface. He fell more deeply under German influence than his rivals, not always for the better; but Henri's cavatina in the first scene of *Marie* (1826), which owes a good deal in melody and harmony to *Der*

Freischütz, even reproduces something of the quality of the model. This opera has considerable freshness of invention, and in the second finale Hérold handles the climax of the action with real imagination; the dramatic treatment of storm music and a barcarolle (heard earlier) antedates similar scenes in *La Muette de Portici* and *Guillaume Tell*, and derives perhaps from Rossini's *Donna del lago*.

In *Zampa* (1831) Hérold overreached himself. The libretto, which reads like a cross between *Don Giovanni* and *The Pirates of Penzance* with elements borrowed from *Der Freischütz*, *La Muette de Portici*, *Fra Diavolo*, and *Robert le Diable*, could only work as a parody of high romantic melodrama, but Hérold tried (in part at least) to take it seriously. A. H. J. Mélesville, an imitator of Scribe, stuffed in everything – lost heirs, a pirate hero, sexually irresistible villainy, the statue of a violated maiden, a marriage service with organ voluntary, an eruption of Etna, and the removal of the pirate to hell in the iron grip of the statue. He did not bother about sense, common or uncommon; the reprieve of Zampa in the second finale is even more gratuitous than the coincidence that makes him and Alphonse brothers. While the use of a basically *buffo* idiom for serious as well as comic situations is characteristic of the period, Hérold's breathless leaps from one end of the spectrum to the other are disconcertingly abrupt. The score has a flavour of Meyerbeer; as chorus master at the Opéra Hérold had assisted at the production of *Robert le Diable*. Traits of German, Italian, and French origin are alike inflated, with the aid of a substantial chorus and a huge orchestra equipped with copious percussion, which accompanies nearly all Zampa's own music. This pirate, a baritone with an upward tenor extension to D flat, who ranges impartially over both clefs, is the Byronic demon hero carried *à l'outrance*. He expounds his philosophy of rape in a rondo in polka rhythm adorned with extreme bravura and leaps of up to two octaves less a semitone, and is clearly intended to give off the fascinating ambivalent aroma of a Don Giovanni. Hérold uses the full Wolf's Glen panoply – incidentally echoing 'Und ob die Wolke' in Camille's first air and Pietro's barcarolle in Act V of *La Muette de Portici* in the first finale – and lays a Teutonic stress on the supernatural. The statue motive, a chord sequence scored mostly for brass, heard first in the overture, breaks into all three finales:

Ex. 29

When Hérold mimics the German *Volkslied* type of melody, as in Camille's ballad ('Complainte'), he supplies a foretaste of the Gounod of *Faust*, especially in its sanctimonious return at the end of the opera. The liveliness of his basses and the characteristically sudden modulations to the flattened submediant, major or minor, give some of the bigger ensembles more thrust than Auber's. But much of it is dissipated in a constant straining after maximum dramatic emphasis, for example in violent, if not perverse, sforzando effects on the last semiquaver of a bar:

Ex. 30

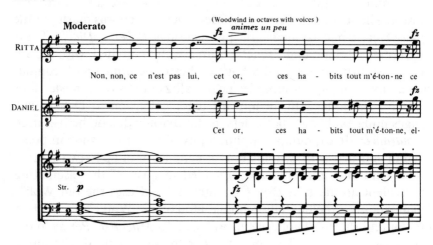

(*Ritta*: No, no, it is not him, this gold, these clothes astonish me. *Daniel*: This gold, these clothes astonish me, she is troubled, thanks be to God)

In the final resort this overloaded score recalls the *opéra comique* of the Revolution without the saving grace of a revolutionary or any other deeply felt impulse.

Hérold's last completed opera, *Le Pré aux clercs* (1833), on a complex and obscurely handled historical subject, again has a serious (though not a supernatural) content; the last Act revolves round a duel in which the hero kills a rival lover. The music is full of hectic ensembles and bustling activity, with even more polkas and florid coloratura than *Zampa*, but the melodic freshness of the best parts of that opera has vanished. Hérold seems to be imitating the animated puppetry of Auber to the extent of excluding slow music. It makes a disappointing end to a career that promised greater things. The next work to attempt a serious view of *opéra comique* was *Carmen* in 1875.

III

BEETHOVEN'S ORCHESTRAL WORKS

By PAUL MIES

THE table on pp. 122–3, based on the Kinsky-Halm catalogue,[1] shows the most important data in the history of Beethoven's symphonies. It also conveys some more intrinsic information and prompts questions that lead far into matters of Beethoven's musical style and methods of work.

It was not until he was thirty that Beethoven appeared before the public with his First Symphony. For the eighteenth century this was a late beginning; Haydn wrote his first symphony in his twenty-seventh year, Mozart as early as his eighth. In the next century Brahms waited to the age of forty-three, Bruckner to thirty-nine. Thus, reluctance to put such demanding works before the public had grown in the intervening time. Just as Haydn's and Mozart's symphonies impelled Beethoven to severe self-criticism, his own works had the same effect on his successors.

Sketches for earlier symphonies by Beethoven are extant. Nottebohm[2] tells of sketches for a symphony in C major whose first movement shows affinities with the finale of the First; Schiedermair[3] prints a draft of 111 bars showing similarities with the first movement of the early Piano Quartet in E flat (Kinsky-Halm, WoQ 36 I).[4] From his earliest works on, Beethoven's rhythms are sharply profiled, often irregular, with a predilection for syncopations and accents. The powerful rhythms of the first movement of the 'Eroica' are a

---

[1] *Thematisch-bibliographisches Verzeichnis aller vollendeten Werke L. van Beethovens* by Georg Kinsky, completed and edited by Hans Halm (Munich, 1955). An updating of the information in Kinsky-Halm is given in *Beiträge zur Beethoven-Bibliographie: Studien und Materialien zum Werkverzeichnis von Kinsky-Halm*, ed. Kurt Dorfmüller (Munich, 1978), pp. 281–440.

[2] *Zweite Beethoveniana*, ed. Eusebius Mandyczewski (Leipzig, 1887), p. 228.

[3] Ludwig Schiedermair, *Der junge Beethoven* (Leipzig, 1925), p. 394.

[4] For a transcription of Beethoven's earliest symphonic sketches and commentary on it, see Joseph Kerman's edition of the 'Kafka' sketchbook (*Ludwig van Beethoven: Autograph Miscellany from circa 1786 to 1799*; London, 1970), ii, pp. 166–77 and 290–1.

culmination of these tendencies. The continuous syncopations after bar 93 in the first movement of no. 4 produce two complementary phenomena: the normal course of the hitherto predominating smooth rhythm is disturbed and, owing to the relatively long duration of the disturbance, a new sense of equilibrium establishes itself during bars 92–102.

For the listener, the bar-line has moved, only to be jolted back to its place in bar 112. Cross-rhythms and syncopations are remarkably effective and invigorating in Beethoven, whereas the syncopations of romantic composers are often designed to make the rhythm unclear or obliterate it. Another example that may be quoted in this context is the first subject of the Ninth with its ties and broken rhythms from bar 16 on; it is instructive here that trumpets and drums follow only the rhythmic pattern of the orchestra in a kind of tonic-dominant double-pedal, without fundamentally disturbing the effect of unison.

'TWIN' SYMPHONIES

Preparatory work on the Ninth Symphony occupied Beethoven for a long time. A sketchbook page from 1818 bears the remark 'Vielleicht auf diese Weise die ganze 2te Symphonie charakterisirt'.[1] Beethoven's factotum Schindler indicates that his master had projected a tenth symphony,[2] and Rochlitz reports Beethoven as saying in 1822 that he had 'two great symphonies in mind, each different from all the others'. This refutes the view taken by the romantic age, and particularly by Wagner, that Beethoven had employed a chorus in the Ninth because the instruments of the orchestra were no longer sufficient for his purposes. The fact is that in the Ninth two at first unrelated plans converged: the general scheme of a symphony, and the intention, ever recurring since his Bonn days, of setting to music Schiller's ode 'To Joy'. The table on pp. 122–3 shows that there were other twins in Beethoven's symphonic output: the Fourth and Fifth, and Seventh and Eighth Symphonies. It is a phenomenon also encountered in other composers, as with Brahms in his Piano Quartets Op. 25 and Op. 26, the Overtures Op. 80 and Op. 81, the Violin Sonatas Op. 100 and

---

[1] *Zweite Beethoveniana*, p. 163.
[2] Ibid., p. 12. Questions about the extent of Beethoven's actual work on a tenth symphony were proposed by Ludwig Misch ('Wo sind Beethovens Skizzen zur X. Symphonie?', *Neue Zeitschrift für Musik*, cxvi (1955), pp. 132–4; reprinted in Misch, *Neue Beethoven-Studien und andere themen* (Bonn and Munich, 1967). See also – and in English – Robert Winter 'Noch einmal: Wo sind Beethovens Skizzen zur Zehnten Symphonie?', *Beethoven–Jahrbuch*, ix (1977), pp. 531–52.

Title, opus number, and key	Dates of composition and 1st perf.	First Movement	Second Movement	Third Movement	Fourth Movement	Instrumentation	Dedication
First Symphony Op. 21 C major	1799–1800 2 April 1800	Adagio molto (12 bars) Allegro con brio (286 bars)	Andante cantabile con moto (195 bars)	Menuetto. Allegro molto e vivace (137 bars)	Adagio (6 bars) Allegro molto e vivace (298 bars)	N.* Andante without second flute	Baron Gottfried van Swieten
Second Symphony Op. 36 D major	1801–2 5 April 1803	Adagio molto (33 bars) Allegro con brio (327 bars)	Larghetto (276 bars)	Scherzo. Allegro (130 bars)	Allegro molto (442 bars)	N, Larghetto without trumpets or timpani	Prince Carl von Lichnowsky
Third Symphony Op. 55 E flat major	1803–4 7 April 1805	Allegro con brio (691 bars)	Marcia funebre. Adagio assai (247 bars)	Scherzo. Allegro vivace (397 bars)	Finale. Allegro molto (473 bars)	N, plus third horn	Prince F. J. von Lobkowitz
Fourth Symphony Op. 60 B flat major	1806 March 1807	Adagio (38 bars) Allegro vivace (460 bars)	Adagio (104 bars)	Allegro vivace (397 bars)	Allegro ma non troppo (355 bars)	N, but only one flute	Count von Oppersdorf
Fifth Symphony Op. 67 C minor	1804–8 22 December 1808	Allegro con brio (502 bars)	Andante con moto (247 bars)	Allegro (373 bars)	Allegro (444 bars)	N, plus 3 trombones, piccolo, and double bassoon in the finale	Prince von Lobkowitz and Count Razumovsky
Sixth Symphony (Pastoral) Op. 68 F major	1807–8 22 December 1808	Allegro ma non troppo (512 bars) (Awakening of cheerful feelings on arrival in the	Andante molto (139 bars) (Scene by the brook)	Allegro (264 bars) (Merry gathering of country people)	Allegro (155 bars) (Storm). Allegretto (264 bars) (Shepherd's song. Glad and	N. Trumpets only in the last 3 movements. Trombones only in the storm and finale. Piccolo only in the storm. In the	As the Fifth Symphony

	Date					Orchestration	Dedication
		country)			thankful feelings after the storm)	Andante, two solo cellos	
'Wellingtons Sieg oder die Schlacht bei Vittoria' Op. 91.	1813 / 8 and 12 December 1813	First section: Battle. Signal, Marcia, Rule Britannia (30 bars). Signal, Marcia, Marlborough (43 bars) Battle (289 bars)			Second section: Victory symphony Intrada, Allegro ma non troppo (8 bars) Allegro con brio (328 bars)	N, plus piccolo, triangle, cymbals, bass drum, 3 trombones. Outside the orchestra: 2 great drums, 2 rattles, 4 trumpets, military drums	Prince Regent of England
Seventh Symphony Op. 92 A major	1811–12 / 8 December 1813	Poco sostenuto (62 bars) Vivace (388 bars)	Allegretto (278 bars)	Presto (653 bars)	Allegro con brio (465 bars)	N.	Count Moritz von Fries
Eighth Symphony Op. 93 F major	1811–12 / 27 February 1814	Allegro vivace e con brio (373 bars)	Allegretto scherzando (81 bars)	Tempo di menuetto (78 bars)	Allegro vivace (503 bars)	N. 2nd movement without timpani and trumpets.	
Ninth Symphony Op. 125 D minor	1822–4 / Earliest drafts and sketches 1817–18 / Earliest sketches for the Ode to Joy 1797. / 7 May 1824	Allegro ma non troppo, un poco maestoso (547 bars)	Molto vivace (559 bars)	Adagio molto e cantabile (157 bars)	Presto. Allegro assai. Rezitativo. Allegro assai (940 bars) Text from Schiller's 'Ode an die Freude'	N, plus 2 horns. 3 trombones in the 2nd and 4th movements. In the 4th movement: double bassoon, piccolo, triangle, cymbals, bass drum, four solo voices, and mixed chorus.	Friedrich Wilhelm III of Prussia

* N = String quintet, plus two each of flutes, oboes, clarinets, bassoons, trumpets, horns and timpani.

Op. 108. It may well be that with some composers simultaneous work on two pieces of different character heightens the unity of each. For Schubert, matters were different; work on his Fifth Symphony was interrupted in favour of the Fourth and resumed after its completion. (No external reasons for this are known.) When these symphonies were first performed at the same concert, their numbers were interchanged. Could Beethoven, when establishing the definitive order of his symphonies, have been following a principle of contrast, an impassioned heroic powerful work succeeded by a calm-contemplative-cheerful one? This resulted, particularly in the nineteenth century, in under-estimation of the even-numbered symphonies; Beethoven was seen much too one-sidedly, as the man of the 'Eroica' and the 'Appassionata'. But the even-numbered symphonies are just as truly Beethovenian, reflect his personality as faithfully and significantly as the others.

PATRONS AND PUBLIC

Further thought is prompted by the names of the dedicatees: they are all of the nobility. Thus Beethoven stands, at least superficially, still in the eighteenth-century relationship of the composer to his patron. His patrons were, to begin with, the Electoral Court at Bonn; Count Waldstein for his journey to Vienna; and subsequently the noble families of that city, in whose houses he gave concerts and lessons and also found friends. Mozart had gained his freedom from princely commissions only at the cost of his livelihood – not to the detriment of his genius but to that of his personal existence. The aging Haydn owed his social equality to the benevolence of Prince Eszterházy. But Beethoven attained his by force – not only for himself but for the whole profession. He was convinced that the artist was the equal of the most eminent, and he gained his point. (Here the character of the Rhinelander, which always includes a strong democratic streak, played a part.) Grove[1] was not entirely wrong when he connected this change in social position with the 'abrupt and dynamic changes of key and tone' in Beethoven's work, unnatural to 'the domestic servants of archbishops and princes'. But there was another factor. Public concerts began to flourish after Paris, in 1725, had given the lead with the Concerts Spirituels; the Bach–Abel concerts in London (1764), the Gewandhaus concerts at Leipzig (1781), and others brought into being a large new public. If the artist managed to establish a relationship with this public and convince it of

---

[1] *Beethoven and his Nine Symphonies* (London, 1896), p. 35.

the value of his work, he could then create freely and express what he had to say in any manner he liked. And in spite of many difficulties with public and critics, Beethoven did that – perhaps uniquely.

CONTEMPORARY OPINIONS

It is appropriate to cite here some contemporary critical opinions. How high Beethoven's reputation stood already at the time of the Second Symphony is shown by an episode at the final rehearsal, reported by Ferdinand Ries.[1] Owing to the overlong programme customary in those days – it consisted of the First and Second Symphonies, the C minor Piano Concerto, and the oratorio *Christus am Ölberg* – the rehearsal had gone on long past the lunch hour, whereupon Prince Lichnowsky had bread and butter, meat and wine brought in, and asked that the programme be rehearsed once again 'in order that the evening should go well and that the first work of its kind by Beethoven should be brought before the public in a worthy manner'. A critic of the first performance of the First Symphony says: 'The concert ended with a symphony of his composition displaying great art, novelty and wealth of ideas; there was, however, too much use of wind instruments so that it seemed more like a piece for wind-band than for full orchestra.'[2] The Leipzig critic Spazier called the Second Symphony 'a gross enormity, an immense wounded snake, unwilling to die'.[3] But another Leipzig critic, F. J. Rochlitz, despite a number of objections to length and excessive use of wind instruments, wrote: 'But all this is outweighed by the powerful fiery spirit that blows through this colossal production, by the wealth of new ideas and their almost completely original treatment, as well as by the composer's profound musical science, so that one may predict that the work will live and be heard with ever renewed pleasure when a thousand pieces now fashionable and acclaimed will have long gone to the grave.'[4] It was not only for this symphony that Rochlitz's prophecy proved right. That a work of such novelty as the Third Symphony should not be understood at once goes without saying. At its first Leipzig performance, in 1807, brief notes indicating the character of each movement were provided in the programme, with the result that this

[1] F. G. Wegeler and F. Ries, *Biographische Notizen über Ludwig van Beethoven* (Koblenz, 1838; suppl. Bonn, 1845; both reprinted in 1972), p. 76.
[2] A. W. Thayer, *Ludwig van Beethovens Leben*, ii (second edition by Hugo Riemann) (Leipzig, 1910), p. 172. The most recent edition of this biography, *Thayer's Life of Beethoven* revised and edited by Elliot Forbes (Princeton, 1964), quotes in English at length from this concert review on pp. 255–6.
[3] Grove, op. cit., p. 44.
[4] *Allgemeine musikalische Zeitung*, vii (1804), p. 215.

new, unprecedented work could be played three times in ten months. The two substantial and impressive essays by the poet and composer E. T. A. Hoffmann on the Fifth Symphony and the *Coriolan* Overture[1] are too well-known to need more than a mention here. Even the Fourth Symphony did not win universal approval. Here again the treatment of the instruments was criticized, and Weber wrote an amusing account of the complaints of the orchestral instruments.[2] With the Fifth Symphony and with *Wellingtons Sieg*, however, the approving voices predominate more and more. In spite of many mishaps, due to bad preparation, the Fifth was enthusiastically received. In 1816 it reached London, and in 1828 Paris, where it was at once put on the programmes of the next three concerts. And Beethoven's reputation later stood so high that the first performance of even the Ninth Symphony, a work that was to give trouble even to some great nineteenth-century artists, met with quite unexpected success. Beethoven stood facing the orchestra, and as he could not hear the applause, one of the solo singers had to turn him round. He bowed – and this was the signal for an almost unending storm of applause, though we may be sure that the public had not understood everything. Another sign of Beethoven's popularity was the repeated performance of the cantata Op.136, *Der glorreiche Augenblick* (composed in celebration of the Vienna Congress), very beautifully produced copies of which were presented to the allied monarchs. Yet other signs were the various commissions for festival overtures (cf. the table on p. 150) and other occasional works. In the eyes of his contemporaries Beethoven was the most distinguished composer of his time, even though not all of his works met with full understanding.

TREATMENT OF THE ORCHESTRA

As we have seen, Beethoven's treatment of the orchestra was often criticized. Yet the table on pp. 122–3 shows that, up to the Ninth Symphony, Beethoven made no essential changes in the constitution of the Mozart–Haydn orchestra. Maurice Cauchie,[3] using contemporary sources, has investigated the numerical strength of orchestras in 1770 (concert under the direction of Haydn), 1813 (Beethoven's demands regarding the Seventh Symphony), 1813 (the Prague Opera orchestra under Weber) arriving at an instrumental force of four first violins, four second, two violas, two cellos, and two double basses, with pairs of flutes, oboes, clarinets, bassoons, horns, trumpets, and

[1] Reprinted in his *Musikalische Schriften*, ed. H. vom Ende (Cologne and Leipzig, n.d.).
[2] Translated in Grove, op. cit., pp. 101–2.
[3] *La pratique de la musique* (Paris, 1948), p. 14.

timpani. It is obvious that such a relation between strings and wind produced a very different sound from what we are used to today.[1] Beethoven often adds single instruments to the normal orchestra. His use of the third horn in the 'Eroica' and of the four horns in the Ninth Symphony had been anticipated by Haydn in his symphony 'Auf dem Anstand' of 1765.[2] The score of the 'Eroica' contains the direction 'la parte del corno terzo e aggiustata della sorte, che possa eserguirsi ugualmente sull Corno primario ossia secundario'. For the rest, it should be noted that Beethoven employs these additional instruments only in single movements or in few passages – remarkable artistic economy. Beethoven saves up the instrument for some special effect or expression. A good example is the 'Turkish music' (cymbals, triangle, bass drum) so popular in Beethoven's day. He uses it in marches, in the incidental music to Kotzebue's *Die Ruinen von Athen*, Op. 113, and the Battle Symphony, Op. 91, for its special colour, and hardly goes beyond the fashionable convention. In the *Alla marcia* in the finale of the Ninth, at the words 'Froh wie seine Sonnen liefen dieses Himmels prächtgen Plan, laufet Brüder eure Bahn, freudig wie ein Held zum Siegen', the employment of triangle, cymbals, and bass drum, restricted to this one passage, helps to suggest a unique vision of the hero's triumphal progress attended by stars and suns. It is not the introduction of new instruments but their novel, purposeful, and sparing use that characterizes Beethoven's orchestration. Some instruments have a special expressive meaning for Beethoven. Generally speaking, he prefers deep, dark colours; his orchestra sounds more opaque than Mozart's or Haydn's. The oboe is for him a bright, gay instrument. It must give way to the clarinet wherever its gay sound might be out of place.[3] The sharp sound of the piccolo suits the 'victory symphony' at the end of the music to *Egmont* and the concluding section of the overture, as well as the finale of the Fifth Symphony. Karl Nef[4] has pointed out the novelty of Beethoven's procedure in giving the first theme of no. 2 first to cellos and basses and only later to the violins. And the double-bass passage in the trio of no. 5 represents a revolutionary step in developing the mobility of this seemingly ponderous instrument.

[1] This point is emphasized by Josef Mertin, 'Zur Klangbalance im symphonischen Werk Beethovens', *Beethoven-Kolloquium 1977: Dokumentation und Aufführungspraxis*, ed. Rudolf Klein (Kassel, 1978), pp. 52–6. But see also Otto Biba, 'Beethoven und die "Liebhaber Concerte" in Wien im Winter 1807/08', ibid., pp. 82–93.
[2] *Kritische Gesamtausgabe*, series 1, No. 31.
[3] See Hans Wlach 'Die Oboe bei Beethoven', *Wiener Studien zur Musikwissenschaft*, xiv (1927), p. 107.
[4] *Die neun Sinfonien Beethovens* (Leipzig, 1928).

It is this participation of all the instruments in every kind of musical happening that fundamentally constitutes the novelty of Beethoven's orchestration, often apparently unjustified in the ears of his contemporaries. This may be demonstrated in the case of the timpani. Originally they supplied a vigorous bass to the bright blare of trumpets; tuned to tonic and dominant, they usually entered with them. But even in this form, Beethoven uses them not only dynamically but also thematically. A significant example occurs in the Allegretto of the Seventh, from bar 174 onward. The rhythm ♩ ♫ | ♩ characteristic of the movement, is stated alternately by cellos and basses, and drums and trumpets, being in this interchange reduced first to ♫ | ♪ and then to ♫. In the slow movement of no. 1, the dotted motive from the first theme (bar 3) enters, at bar 53, on the drum as a pedal-point, and in this form becomes of great importance when taken up by the strings in the development; it becomes thematic. One other point is of interest in this movement. It is written in F and the drums would normally have been tuned to F and C. But whereas in other symphonies, e.g. the Third and Ninth, the drums are re-tuned according to the key of the movement, in no. 1 the tuning of the first movement is retained in the Andante since Beethoven wants to use the dominant of the dominant, G, for the important drum-rhythm. The note is sounded only in that one passage, but it determines Beethoven's planning. A similar case is the A flat Andante of no. 5, where the drums retain their C–G tuning in order to provide the bass of the triumphant fortissimo passages in C major. In the Presto of no. 7, the drums are re-tuned to F–A, so that they can join in the tutti octaves before the trio; the tuning is adjusted solely for the sake of this motive; the drums take part in the melodic line. A further step is taken in the finale of no. 8, where the tuning is tonic-octave. This lessens the drums' ability to give harmonic support, but enables them to participate in, and augment, the important characteristic octave motive from bar 150 on and to introduce the coda with it alone pianissimo. (This latter passage might even suggest that the octave motive was in the first place invented with the timpani in mind.) The drums in the scherzo of the Ninth Symphony, tuned to the octave F (minor third of the tonic chord) are the virtual carriers of the entire motivic development. Nottebohm[1] cites sketches for this movement from the years 1815 and 1817, most of which begin with the characteristic octave leap. As these sketches date from not long after the first performance of the Eighth Symphony, it was perhaps the

[1] Op. cit., pp. 157 ff.

finale of the latter that prompted the idea of making the drum octave leap the basic motive of the scherzo of the Ninth, in which the drum at last becomes a solo instrument. In the middle part of the movement, the drum even enforces an abrupt modulation; at the passage marked *ritmo di tre battute* (bar 177) the theme is stated by the woodwind for nine bars in E minor, then nine bars in A minor, ending on the dominant seventh of A minor, all piano. After the forte drum octaves on F, the wind turn abruptly to D minor, still piano – a passage of the utmost harmonic, motivic, and dynamic boldness. Mention must also be made of the vital importance of the drum motive in the first movement of the Violin Concerto. It is in Beethoven's original cadenza to the pianoforte version of this work that the kettle-drum celebrates its greatest triumph; alone of all the orchestral instruments, it interrupts significantly at important junctures.[1]

In order to demonstrate the novelty of Beethoven's orchestration, so startling to the ears of his contemporaries, I have deliberately chosen the extreme case of the timpani, instruments seemingly capable only of providing harmonic support to cadences and supplying dynamic and rhythmic background. Much the same could be shown in the cases of the other instruments. Basically, this opening up was a consequence of what we call Beethoven's 'thematic-motivic work', 'open-work texture', or 'obbligato accompaniment'. After all, he did maintain that he had come into the world 'mit einem obligaten Akkompagnement'.[2] For the wind instruments this entailed the disappearance of the last vestige of their function as substitutes for the *basso continuo*, which they still fulfilled in the early symphonies of Haydn and Mozart.

INTRODUCTION OF THE CHORUS

Something may be said here on the introduction of the chorus in the Ninth Symphony. I have already said that it was not Beethoven's intention by this act to declare the bankruptcy of instrumental music. Nor was it his first venture in this direction; the Fantasia for piano, chorus, and orchestra, Op. 80, of 1808, is really a piano concerto, in the final variations of which the chorus participates. Even in the finale of the Sixth Symphony Beethoven may have contemplated a sung prayer of thanksgiving.[3] The difficulties and quandaries

---

[1] See Mies, *Die Krise der Konzertkadenz bei Beethoven* (Bonn, 1970), pp. 30–1.

[2] Letter of 15 December 1800, to the publisher Hofmeister. See *The Letters of Beethoven*, ed., Emily Anderson (London, 1961), p. 42: 'I cannot compose anything that is not obbligato, seeing that, as a matter of fact, I came into the world with an obbligato accompaniment.'

[3] See Willi Kahl 'Zu Beethovens Naturauffassung', in *Beethoven und die Gegenwart* (*Festschrift Ludwig Schiedermair zum 60. Geburtstag*) (Berlin and Bonn, 1937).

Beethoven had to contend with in introducing the 'Ode to Joy' have often been described and need not detain us here.[1] Incidentally the 'Freude' melody illustrates how closely Beethoven's expressive formulas were connected, throughout his whole life, with certain harmonic, melodic, and rhythmic elements. Consider the theme of the setting of Bürger's 'Gegenliebe' of 1794–5 (Kinsky-Halm WoO 118) at its textual climax (i):

Ex. 31

The same melody appears in the Choral Fantasia, Op. 80, of 1808, to the concluding words 'Wenn sich Lieb und Kraft vermählen, lohnt dem Menschen Göttergunst' ('When love and strength are united, the gods smile upon man'). Ex. 31(ii) is an unused sketch for the chorus 'Wer ein holdes Weib errungen', dating from 1804;[2] Ex. 31(iii) is the theme of the 'Ode to Joy' as it appears in a sketch-book of 1824.[3] In each case the joyful mood of the text is musically reflected in a rising and falling diatonic line of slight rhythmic differentiation, on a simple harmonic basis. Considering how many years separate these examples, their similarity is astounding. To the same expressive sphere belong transformations such as we find in the fugato of the 'victory symphony' of Op. 91, derived from 'God save the King', Ex. 31(iv). The joyous mood leads to similar rhythmic and melodic formations.[4]

[1] Mies, *Die Bedeutung der Skizzen Beethovens zur Erkenntnis seines Stiles* (Leipzig, 1925), p. 131; English edition (London, 1929, reprinted 1969 and 1974), p. 145.
[2] Nottebohm, op. cit., p. 445.
[3] Ibid., p. 165.
[4] Mies, 'Stilkundliche Bemerkungen zu Beethovens Op. 91', *Neue Musik-Zeitung*, xlviii (September 1927).

BEETHOVEN AND HIS PRECURSORS

Even a genius such as Beethoven builds on the achievements of his predecessors. Contemporary criticism pointed out often enough – and reproachfully – his deviations from the masterpieces of Mozart and Hadyn. Yet it is pertinent to investigate Beethoven's relation to his precursors. This has often been done, mainly in connection with two circles: first and foremost, the Vienna circle of Mozart (who but for his death would have become Beethoven's teacher) and Haydn under whose instruction he was to receive 'Mozart's spirit from Haydn's hands'.[1] To the same ambit belonged the distinguished opera composer Antonio Salieri (1750–1825) and the theorist and composer J. R. Albrechtsberger (1736–1809), both of whom were teachers of Beethoven. Grove suggests[2] that the imitations in the first movement of no. 1 'would have pleased Albrechtsberger'. That may well be. But in reality these contrapuntal formations are a manifestation of what is called Beethoven's 'obbligato accompaniment'; the homophonic texture is loosened up and every group of instruments gets its thematic share. It was not until later that Beethoven fashioned for himself, particularly in his piano sonatas and string quartets, a distinctly individual contrapuntal style. Grove's comment on the Second Symphony[3] is wide of the mark: 'The historical place of the symphony is that ... it is "pure music". No one ... has ever suggested a programme or image for any of its movements.' This remark springs from the nineteenth-century attitude that regarded programme music as progressive and thus, as already mentioned, was an obstacle to true appreciation of the even-numbered symphonies. To be sure, the early symphonies differ from the later ones; but the difference has nothing to do with 'programmes'.

Other writers, in particular Arnold Schmitz,[4] have drawn attention to another basis of Beethoven's work: the French music of the Revolutionary age, the music of Grétry, Méhul, Cherubini, Gossec, Rodolphe Kreutzer. Some of this had already come to Beethoven's notice in Bonn; the messengers of the Revolution had early penetrated into the Rhineland. We know that Beethoven highly esteemed Cherubini; and Kreutzer, violinist and opera composer, was to be the dedicatee of his Violin Sonata, Op. 47. Schmitz quotes numerous passages from the works of these French composers, whose style has

---

[1] Count Waldstein's valediction in Beethoven's Bonn album (29 October 1792), quoted in Thayer, op. cit., i, p. 290.
[2] Op. cit., p. 7.
[3] Ibid., p. 24.
[4] *Das romantische Beethovenbild* (Berlin and Bonn, 1927).

been called 'heroic',[1] and similar ones in Beethoven. He draws particular attention to the 'signal' motives of French opera which re-appear in many works of Beethoven, from the first Allegro theme of the First Symphony, the 'Eroica', the *Leonore* overtures, the Battle Symphony, to the recitatives of the Ninth. It is true that the heroic came naturally to Beethoven, though not in the external but in the ethical sense. (This is rather like his use of Turkish music, which is symbolically transmuted in the Ninth Symphony.) Who, knowing Beethoven's deeply moving representation of marital fidelity in the figure of Leonore, remembers that the subject was one of the many 'rescue-dramas' of the French theatre? When in no. 8 of the *Egmont* music, a melodrama, the trumpet breaks in with a signal, Beethoven's written comment makes clear what this signal meant to him: 'Der Eintritt der Trompete deutet auf die für das Vaterland gewonnene Freiheit' ('The entry of the trumpet signifies the freedom won for the fatherland'). The opening theme of the First Symphony already shows the symphonic spirit Beethoven was able to draw from signal-like motives. The bars at the start of the finale of the Ninth, which recur before the entry of the recitative, are often called the 'terror fanfare'; they are certainly derived from fanfare-like sounds, and show once again how Beethoven expands the traditional. The link with tradition does not in the least detract from Beethoven's originality; on the contrary, it proves his independence in turning to account given material, which he was effortlessly able to incorporate and further develop in the mighty edifices of his symphonies.

EXTENDED DIMENSIONS

The bar-numbers in the table on pp. 122–3 show that, with the exception of the Eighth Symphony, there is a steady increase in length. This was often taken amiss by Beethoven's contemporaries, although Mozart had preceded him in such works as the 'Jupiter' Symphony. Length in music has its reasons; it is not by chance that the monothematic movements of baroque music are usually short. So it is with the symphonic writing of the eighteenth century. A long work must draw on different, in some respects also ampler, resources in order to avoid boredom and longwindedness. Mozart and Haydn had developed the means suitable to build their immortal masterpieces; Beethoven's stylistic and artistic progress consisted in the expansion and enrichment of these resources and their combination with his own spirit. This step by step expansion of old resources and the employment

---

[1] Ernst Bücken *Der heroische Stil in der Oper* (Leipzig, 1924), p. vii.

of new ones set the seal on Beethoven's unique development, the origins of which are apparent even in his early works. Expansion of resources necessarily led to expansion of forms, though he left their essentials untouched.

BEETHOVEN'S HARMONY

In considering the separate elements of Beethoven's musical individuality, it is harmony that first claims attention. Its abruptness, roughness, strangeness were again and again censured by his contemporaries. And even today, after the enormous development of harmonic procedures in the nineteenth century, Beethoven's harmony still affects us deeply. A work employing only the simplest forms of cadence, slight modulations and harmonic alterations, must needs be short, however significant its ideas. Tonality is always firmly established with Beethoven, but his range of modulation and harmonic connection exceeds that of his predecessors. A few instances from his symphonies must suffice. The very first chord of the First Symphony earned the composer the personal enmity of several critics: a piece had to begin with the tonic, leaving the listener in no doubt of its key. But Beethoven had started with the dominant seventh of F major; the full close in G major at bars 3–4 seems to affirm *that* key as the tonic, and it is only in the further course of the slow introduction that C major is established. The C major minuet of the same symphony also introduces an unprecedented audacity: in bar 33 D flat is reached, after which a few chromatic side-slips, during which basses, bassoons, and oboes toss motivic fragments to and fro, lead back through E flat minor to C major. A similar juxtaposition of remote keys occurs in the coda of the first movement of the 'Eroica', after bar 555, by the step-wise, dynamically sharply contrasted succession of E flat major, D flat major, and C major. From bar 33 of the introduction to no. 7 – a work particularly rich in surprising changes – Beethoven modulates in the shortest possible way from C major through E major, F sharp major, to F major, and subsequently to the main key, A major. Thus very remote keys are given significant value. The peculiar, mysterious effect of the introduction to the B flat Symphony is partly due to its harmonic scheme. Certainly the opening octave B flat affirms the key, but already in the second bar this note becomes the fifth of E flat minor. The G flat entering here plays an important role in the subsequent bars and is eventually changed to F sharp; rich modulation then leads through G, C, A, B flat, A, and F major to the main key: B flat. The fullest use is made here of the ambiguity of chromatic scales within a basic key. Sometimes there are sudden insertions. The trio of the Second Symphony begins with an eight-bar wind paragraph, *p*, in pure D major; the second paragraph is a string unison, *f*, in F sharp major. It dies down to *pp* on an F sharp, after which a *ff* octave (A) leads back to the D major paragraph. This passage remains as surprising today as it must have been at its first performance. The march-like and fanfare-like elements in the first movement of the E flat Piano Concerto lead, toward its close, to a powerful affirmation of the tonic key; the B major opening of the muted, hymn-like music of the strings in B major comes in singular contrast. The development of the finale of the Fourth Symphony begins with a semiquaver figure derived from the main subject, modulating away from F major; after 18 bars this is brought to a halt by a unison *ff* B natural of the whole orchestra, whereupon the strings leisurely resume the theme in F major, *p*. In the first movement of no. 8 the first subject modulates to B flat, but there is no transition to the expected E flat; instead, after a general pause of one bar, there appears a dominant seventh in D – in which key the new theme enters; it is repeated in C, thus reaching the dominant. The ebullient F major theme of the finale of the same symphony is brusquely stopped short in bar 17 by a syncopated *ff* C sharp of the whole orchestra, which is followed by the theme, back in F major, but now *ff*. The sustained E flat of flutes, oboes, and bassoons after bar 97 in the Andante of no. 5 worried some distinguished nineteenth-century musicians. According to Berlioz,[1] Fétis changed it to F, with the comment 'This E flat must be an F. Beethoven could not possibly have made so gross a blunder'. The passage is still exciting today, though in another sense. Finally there is the 'terror fanfare' in the finale of no. 9; whether one explains it in harmony textbook terms as some altered form of the dominant seventh, or whether with Berlioz one rejects it since it simultaneously contains almost all the notes of the minor scale,[2] it remains a unique harmonic intuition of undiminished power. Fétis's 'correction' reminds one of various nineteenth-century attempts to mollify the asperity of the introduction of Mozart's so-called 'Dissonance Quartet' (K. 465). Certainly, harmonic audacities and surprises occur at all periods, in Bach and Handel as well as in Mozart and Haydn. But the extent of their occurrence, their employment not as isolated effects but as significant events in the total symphonic argument, makes them an important trait of Beethoven's character. The introduction of remote keys, while preserving tonality, makes possible – indeed compels – a widening of external range through internal forces.

[1] *Memoirs* (trs. David Cairns) (London and New York, 1969), p. 217.
[2] *À travers chants* (Paris, 1862), p. 55, from which translated excerpts relating to Beethoven are given in *Beethoven by Berlioz*, ed. R. DeSola (Boston, Mass., 1975).

ATTITUDE TO FORM

Equally important for this widening is Beethoven's attitude to form, in small as in great. He made no essential changes in the overall symphonic form of his predecessors, in contrast to the manifold forms of his piano sonatas. Except in the Ninth Symphony, the slow movement always comes before the quick middle movement, whatever it may be called. In the case of the Ninth, the reversal of the middle movements may have been due to the length and exceptional seriousness of the first movement. The Sixth Symphony is really a four-movement work like all the others; the 'storm' is an intermezzo, suggested by the general idea of the work, between scherzo and finale.

So-called 'sonata form' is standard for most of the first and last movements of Beethoven's symphonies: the first, second, and fourth movements of both nos. 1 and 2, the first of the 'Eroica', first and fourth of nos. 4, 5, and 8, and the first movements of nos. 6 and 9. Slow introductions are prefixed to the first movements of nos. 1, 2, 4, and 7, and in very brief form to the finale of no. 1. In this, Beethoven followed Haydn. It should be noted that the systematic textbook description of sonata form, with definitions of first and second subject, exposition, development, and so on, did not yet exist; except for a few vague remarks about contrast of themes, scarcely anything is to be found in contemporary literature. Sonata form was not yet a 'teaching subject'. When later on it became one, it was largely Beethoven's work that provided the norm for present-day concepts. The *Lehrfächer* of the age were fugue and counterpoint.

A few distinctive examples will serve to illustrate Beethoven's attitude to sonata form in his symphonic movements. In his expositions, there is always strong contrast between the first and second subjects. With Mozart the wealth of thematic invention in the exposition at times makes it difficult to distinguish them; with Haydn the only criterion may be the appearance of the dominant key, since first and second subjects are often similar or identical. Beethoven usually widens the exposition by repetition of the first subject and organizes it by contrasts, thus ensuring the over-all intelligibility of even greatly expanded structures. Contrasts in the course of the exposition were already a stylistic feature of the second half of the eighteenth century, but it was first in Beethoven's total output that they emerged in sharp definition. Beethoven's method is often to derive the second subject from the first, but so that their relationship is much less obvious than their contrast. Arnold Schmitz[1] coined the term *kontrastierende Ableitung* ('derivation by contrast') for this.

[1] *Beethovens 'Zwei Prinzipe'* (Berlin and Bonn, 1923).

Occasionally the relationship is more apparent in the sketches than in the final version; there it becomes suppressed in favour of contrast, development, variation, yet remains a latent force.[1] A sketch for the first subject of the Second Symphony introduces the dotted rhythm as early as the repeat of the theme on the descending triad; the final version reserves it for the ascending triad of the second subject (bar 40), thus pointing the contrast.[2] It sometimes happens that the themes of several movements of a work derive from one sketch. Ex. 32 shows two early ideas for the first movement of no. 7.[3]

Ex. 32

(i)

(ii)

Comparison with the final version shows that (i) was to supply the melodic material of the third movement. The dactylic rhythm of (ii) was 'sharpened' and found its ultimate value in the first movement. The triadic thematicism of bars 3–4 of (ii), which also dominates (i), in the symphony begins to predominate a little later at about bar 12. Thus the sketches show a distinct connection between the first and third movements, which become less recognizable and more contrasted in the final forms. In the Fifth Symphony Beethoven made such relationships more obvious: the opening motive appears in the bass at the entry of the second subject and is significantly woven into the transition from the third to the fourth movement and into the development of the latter. Fundamentally, however, rhythms such as ♫ | ♩ from bar 23 on and at many other points in the slow movement,

---

[1] For a similar but greatly expanded view of the relation between sketches and final version, see Philip Gossett, 'Beethoven's Sixth Symphony: Sketches for the First Movement', *Journal of the American Musicological Society*, xxvii (1974), p. 248.

[2] Mies, *Die Bedeutung*, p. 106 (Eng. ed., p. 117).

[3] Nottebohm, op. cit., pp. 102–3.

or in the last movement the triplet-group ♩♩♩ | ♩ from bar 143 or the ♩ ♩ ♩ | ♩ of the deep basses from bar 365, are all emanations of the same motive, which thus dominates the whole symphony. In the case of other symphonies, too, attempts have been made to find such unifying ideas. Many years ago Grove[1] drew attention to 'the prominent occurrence in every movement [of the Second Symphony] of a *tremolo* figure in the fiddles'. Erich Schenk[2] actually attempted to prove that the First Symphony has the B–A–C–H motive as a leading element. All such attempts – they are not always equally convincing – spring from a definite feeling that every work of Beethoven forms a consistent, unified, inseparable whole.

One consequence of a connexion between the two themes in the exposition is that Beethoven frequently makes little or no use of the second one in the development. The second subject's function of contrast, which must be re-established in the recapitulation for the sake of structural comprehensibility, might in certain circumstances be endangered. Another means of securing unity is Beethoven's device of deriving bridge-passages (e.g. between first and second subjects, or between second subject and end of exposition) from the themes themselves, whereas Haydn and Mozart often had recourse to new material in these sections. From the Third Symphony on, Beethoven's derivation of bridging passages from the thematic material and resumption of the first theme or its components at the end of the exposition, is always clearly in evidence. It is therefore hardly accidental that just this kind of transition gave Beethoven difficulties, as appears in his sketches for the finale of the 'Eroica'.[3]

All this is a by-product of Beethoven's 'motivic-thematic work'. Adolf Sandberger[4] has shown that the discovery of this principle, in its classical form, was due to Haydn. But here, too, Beethoven progressed virtually to the limits of the possible. His thematic developments and motivic transformations are unprecedented, and new in every work and movement. A few examples will suffice to show what it is that again and again strikes and captivates the listener. Thus the first movement of no. 5 lives solely by the rhythmic motive ♫♫ | ♩, in every new melodic shape, contrapuntal application, structural grouping, yet never giving an impression of continuous repetition. In the corresponding movement of no. 7 almost every bar

[1] Op. cit., p. 41.
[2] 'Beethovens "Erste" – eine B–A–C–H Symphonie', *Neues Beethoven-Jahrbuch*, viii (1938), p. 162.
[3] See Mies, 'Ludwig van Beethovens Werke über seinen Kontretanz in Es-dur', *Beethoven-Jahrbuch* (1953–4), p. 80.
[4] 'Zur Geschichte des Haydnschen Streichquartetts', *Ausgewählte Aufsätze zur Musikgeschichte* (Munich, 1921), p. 224.

brings the rhythm ♩ ♪♪ on one instrument or another without inducing a sense of monotony. It has often been remarked that the opening bars of the 'Eroica' really have nothing inherently heroic about them; the melodic parallel is always drawn with the beginning of Mozart's overture to *Bastien und Bastienne*. But what becomes of this simple triadic motive in Beethoven can be best shown by comparing a few passages which by no means exhaust the numerous forms developed from it:[1]

Ex. 33

Beethoven's capacity for transforming and developing motives is inexhaustible, so that he is able to fill even the most extended forms with a few motives. Hence also the intensive work on motives and themes in his sketches.

We see this already in the First Symphony. Ex. 34(i) shows how in the theme of the slow movement the fourth of the initial upbeat is contracted to a third in the second bar, to a second in the third bar, bringing life to the whole theme. Subsequently the interval is expanded – for instance, in the instrumental dialogue shortly after the start of the development (Ex. 34(ii)).

[1] cf. Alfred Lorenz 'Betrachtungen über Beethovens Eroica-Skizzen', *Zeitschrift für Musikwissenschaft*, vii (1925), p. 409, and 'Worauf beruht die bekannte Wirkung der Durchführung im I. Eroicasatze?', *Neues Beethoven-Jahrbuch*, i (1924), p. 159.

Ex. 34

Commentators on the development in the first movement of the 'Eroica' make much of the introduction of an entirely new theme, the so-called episode', in the development. If, however, one examines the passage from bar 43 on (Ex. 35(i)) in the exposition – first the quaver figure, then from bar 88 (ex. 35(ii)) the violin part derived from the second subject, next the cello counterpoint to the wind theme of the 'episode', which is its inversion (Ex. 35(iii)) – Beethoven's train of thought becomes clearly recognizable. Circling about a central point is common to all these forms.

Ex. 35

This is not to say that Beethoven always consciously followed such lines – but his spirit did. Finally I may draw attention to my analysis of the motivic development in the storm movement of the Sixth Symphony,[1] since this movement is too frequently considered from the point of view of programmatic realism rather than that of musical structure.

[1] Mies 'Über die Tonmalerei', *Zeitschrift für Aesthetik und allgemeine Kunstwissenschaft*, vii (1912), pp. 397 and 578.

These examples of Beethoven's motivic work illustrate other points. In Ex. 33, bars 17 ff. and bars 132–133, Ex. 34, and Ex. 35(i) the melodic line is not given to a single instrument but divided between several. This is another aspect of Beethoven's 'open-work texture', his 'obbligato accompaniment'. The already noted participation of the drums in the total musical argument is paralleled in the case of every instrument. All get relief from exclusive employment as bass or filling-in parts or melody-carriers, and are used singly or in groups for all purposes; the scherzo of the Seventh Symphony is full of obvious examples. It is no wonder that the critics noticed – and often condemned – this as one of the most distinctive features of Beethoven's style. Moreover the relative proportions of the orchestra in Beethoven's time gave the wind more prominence than they have in today's orchestra with its preponderance of strings.

Beethoven's treatment of other important features of sonata form is no less striking. One important point is the beginning of the development. Beethoven usually ends the exposition with a distinct coda and nearly always repeats the exposition. Omission of these repeats is a serious fault, upsetting the structural plan of the movement with its double presentation of the main material. An equally important point is the transition from the development to the recapitulation. The enlarged scope of movements made it necessary to give this point special emphasis. Haydn liked to disguise the entry of the recapitulation; he often restates the theme first in a 'false reprise', before the orthodox resumption of the exposition. Beethoven, on the other hand, thoroughly prepares the recapitulation, drawing the listener's attention to it. The start of the recapitulation in the first movement of the 'Eroica' has long been famous. It shows that Beethoven spared no pains in preparing it. The sketches show[1] that Beethoven had from the first intended a particularly characteristic, somewhat 'brutal' solution. In the final version the *pp* entry of the horn theme cuts across the *ppp* tremolo of the violins on B flat and A flat; tonic triad and parts of the dominant seventh are thus sounded simultaneously. As is well known, at the rehearsal of the symphony this passage so upset Beethoven's pupil Ries that he exclaimed 'That damned horn-player! Can't he count?' and almost got his ears boxed by Beethoven, but even Wagner is alleged to have changed the violins' A flat to G. For us the passage has lost it 'terror' but not its effect. As if from far off, the theme mingles with the hazy tremoli of the end of the development, and makes it a beginning to the recapitulation that

---

[1] Alfred Heuss, 'Rund um die Dominante-Tonika-Stelle der Eroica herum', *Zeitschrift für Musik*, xciv (1927), p. 504.

is as emotive as it is structurally assured. Not so exciting harmonically but equally surprising is what happens in the B flat Symphony. Of the theme, only the two-note motive D flat–B flat remains, changed enharmonically to C sharp–A sharp; over the sustained F sharp major triad, the rising semiquaver motive of the beginning of the Allegro creeps in on the first violins; a scale passing through all the strings – it too derives from the first subject – effects the change of the F sharp to G flat, and its descent to F. Above a 26-bar drum-roll on B flat, beginning *pp* and after 18 bars quickly rising to *ff*, the first theme breaks through to the recapitulation. In the finale of the Fifth Symphony Beethoven prepares the entry of the recapitulation with the same motives that have effected the transition from the third movement to the fourth.

NOVEL TREATMENT OF RECAPITULATION

Beethoven's stress on the transition from development to recapitulation had a further reason. In most of his works he gave the recapitulation a new function. With his predecessors the recapitulation was essentially only a repeat of the exposition; the transposition of the second subject to the tonic had the function of strengthening the main key. In Beethoven's case, the strong contrast of the second subject, the interpenetration of bridge-passages by motivic work, the powerful motivic-thematic evolutions of the development, all forced upon him a different concept of the recapitulation. It was no longer a recapitulatory confirmation of the exposition – for that, too much had happened in the development – but a restatement of the exposition in a fresh form. In the process the recapitulation often becomes shorter than the exposition; this is particularly the case with the first-subject group, whose importance has been stressed by repetition in the exposition. The second subject and its complex themes are retained in the recapitulation; the contrast inherent in these must make its full effect once again. Modulations, too, are more far-reaching. On occasion, the second subject appears in the subdominant in the recapitulation, necessitating a broadening of the final cadence. This occurs in the finale of no. 1, where the recapitulation brings the second subject in F major instead of C. The recapitulation of the finale of no. 5 frequently goes to the subdominant. In the first movement of the Ninth, the second subject is in B flat in the exposition; in the recapitulation it begins in F sharp minor. Harmonic phenomena of this sort, occurring in almost every movement, help to fill the enormous spaces of Beethoven's symphonic writing. Next to modulation and structural devices it is the orchestration that enriches Beethoven's recapitulations – points like the insertion of the oboe cadenza in the first movement of the C minor and the violin passage at bar 280 in the 'Erwachen heiterer Gefühle' of the 'Pastoral'. These are not extraneous additions but developments within the recapitulation based on previous musical happenings. As a further example, the start of the recapitulation in no. 9 may be instanced. At the beginning of the symphony, the theme evolves from its motive, above the mysterious string tremoli, until in bar 17 it fully emerges in the *ff* unison of the whole orchestra; after the working-out of the development, this would not have made sense as a start to the recapitulation, so – prepared by a strongly accented unison passage of the whole orchestra – the introduction now enters *ff* to thunderous drum rolls, and supported by wind chords. The theme no longer appears mysteriously and gradually but undisguised in its full, terrible power.

CODAS

The last part of the sonata form, the coda, also gained in significance with Beethoven. The repeat of the second section of sonata-form (development and recapitulation), preserved by Mozart in the finale of the 'Jupiter' Symphony, was abandoned by Beethoven in his symphonies though not elsewhere. After the vast expansion of development and recapitulation, a return to the middle of the movement was no longer possible; instead there had to be a new, convincing, and powerful conclusion. Thus Beethoven became the first, and thereafter unsurpassed, master of the great coda. There is the closest interrelationship between the growth of the coda on the one hand and, on the other, the growth of the development, the enhancement of the recapitulation as compared with the exposition, and the pervasion of all sections with thematic-motivic work. A few examples will give an idea of the size of the separate sections:

		Exposition	Develop-ment	Recapitu-lation	Coda
no. 2 (finale)		106 bars	78 bars	106 bars	152 bars
no. 3 (first movement)		‖:152:‖	245	159	135
no. 4 (finale)		‖:103:‖	85	89	78
no. 5 (first movement)		‖:124:‖	123	126	129
no. 7	,,	62+ ‖:114:‖	101	110	63
no. 8	,,	‖:103:‖	95	103	72
no. 9	,,	159	141	126	121

The increase in the length of Beethoven's codas, when compared with those of his predecessors, is shown not only in these, but in nearly all his symphonic movements. One can often speak of a four-sectional sonata form. Since the recapitulation is not merely a repetition but a further development, a section preparing the end becomes necessary – using no new material but displaying earlier material in new form. This kind of coda has sometimes been spoken of as a second development, rightly so far as its motivic-thematic structure is concerned. It has, however, another function: it must lead to the final tonic. In the first movement of the C minor Symphony, the four sections have almost the same number of bars. But one must remember that the impact of a section is determined not only by its number of bars; content and structure are also important. The coda of the first movement of no. 9 beginning at bar 513, on an ostinato bass motive which gradually rises to fortissimo, is quite as important as the other sections. It is significant that the coda of the parallel movement of no. 8 was – perhaps even at the first performance – originally shorter by 34 bars;[1] obviously Beethoven became conscious of a lack of balance. The coda of the finale of no. 4 is particularly striking. The movement is a mixture of rondo and sonata form; the coda is marked by striking modulations, dynamic developments, and two *fermate* – giving the impression that Beethoven intended a conclusion that would give special weight to the finale as a whole. This is even more pronounced in the Eighth Symphony where the last section consists of 229 bars, as against the 283 of the rest, a very unusual proportion for Beethoven. But perhaps he was thinking in terms of a sonata form extended by varied repetition of the entire second part:

Exposition	*Development 1*	*Recap. 1*	*Develop. 2*	*Recap. 2*	*Coda*
97	64	112	82	83	64

yet another example of Beethoven's multifarious compoundings of sonata with rondo form particularly in his finales.

METRICAL PLANNING

Contrast between first and second subjects, repeat of exposition, emphasis on the important beginnings of development and recapitulation, extension of the coda: these were Beethoven's means for ensuring clear perception of the whole despite its growing dimensions. Study of the coda has shown his sense of proportion. Sometimes this is strikingly evident. Lorenz[2] has drawn attention to bars 65–82 in the Allegro con brio of the 'Eroica'. For this there exist three sketches and the final version, in some respects differing widely in content; they are

[1] Nottebohm, *Beethoveniana* (Leipzig and Winterthur, 1872), p. 25.
[2] 'Betrachtungen'.

all of 18 or 17 bars – evidence of large-scale metrical planning preceding and over-riding musical content. At bars 45–56 of the same movement Beethoven notes down the bar-numbers in the sketches without filling them in; the extent of the passage was clear to him before its actual substance. Such large-scale metrical design is found in all his work. I have shown elsewhere[1] how regular the metrical structure of his themes eventually becomes, even though the original sketch may have been asymmetrical. Such movements as the first of no. 5 and no. 6 can be divided almost throughout into regular four-bar groups. The modulations and bar-groupings in the development of no. 5 show this sort of regularity: bar 130 F minor, 146 C minor, 154 G minor, 178 D major, 180 G minor, 188 C minor, 196 F minor, i.e. groups of 16, 8, 24, 2, 8, 16 bars. The insertion of the two-bar group has the effect of a special event.[2] There is a controversial passage at the end of the exposition in the 'Eroica'.[3] In the scherzo of the Ninth Beethoven himself indicated the bar-groupings by the words *Ritmo di tre battute* and *Ritmo di quattro battute*. Such large-scale metrical designs make it easy to grasp as wholes movements consisting of groups balanced against each other. What is thus effected on the grand scale is similarly achieved within individual sections by largely symmetrical bar-groupings. Thus even the most expansive movements become intelligible. It is interesting that in the sketches of Brahms and Bruckner, both of whom took over, even expanded, Beethoven's extension of form, we also find such metrically predetermined passages.

THE SCHERZI

Only twice in his symphonies did Beethoven adopt the designation 'Menuetto' for a middle movement. In no. 1 the tempo is Allegro molto e vivace, and the piece is far from dance-like. The slowest of these movements is the Tempo di menuetto of no. 8, with a trio-theme somewhat similar to the Minuetto quasi Allegretto of a flute duet of 1792 (Kinsky-Halm WoO 26). Its tempo is probably due to the fact that the preceding Allegretto scherzando is not a true slow movement, and also proceeds at a moderate pace. The first movement to be entitled Scherzo is in no. 2, a true Beethovenian scherzo with all its surprises – including humorous ones – its fast tempo and its typical

---

[1] *Die Bedeutung der Skizzen.*
[2] The problem of large-scale metric organization in the first movement of the Fifth Symphony is discussed at length by Andrew Imbrie, '"Extra" Measures and Metrical Ambiguity in Beethoven', *Beethoven Studies*, ed. Alan Tyson (New York, 1973; London, 1974), p. 45.
[3] See Mies, *Bedeutung*, p. 76; English edition, p. 84.

orchestration. Of the others, only that of the 'Eroica' is actually so called – although it originated in the sketch for a minuet.[1] All the other fast middle movements merely bear tempo indications: Allegro, Allegro con brio, etc. (The designation 'scherzo' is much more frequent in Beethoven's chamber music than in his symphonies.) Gustav Becking[2] attempted to determine the musical elements which for Beethoven defined the word 'scherzo', and to prove that its application or non-application is not arbitrary or accidental, but corresponds to the content and structure of the movements. In any case, Beethoven completely abandoned the original dance character of the fast middle movements. However, he retained the ubiquitous 3/4 time, deviating from it only once, in the central section of the Ninth. This had first been sketched in 2/4 time and so entered in the score; subsequently, pairs of bars were brought together in single bars of 4/4. In this and in other examples from Beethoven, I have shown[3] how the change transforms the thrusting pulsation of 2/4 time into the longer-breathed arcs of the final version. Beethoven also retained the overall ternary form of fast middle movements, with a central trio not always so named. In the Fourth and Seventh Symphonies he extended the form to A–B–A–B–A-coda by repeating the first two sections.[4] This, too, is one of his ways of extending the scope of his works. The material was so significant that he was not content to state it once only. But it is noteworthy that there are no scherzos with two different trios in his symphonies such as occur in Mozart's divertimenti where the aim is diversity within narrow limits. The romantics, particularly Schumann, were fond of this extension of form and Brahms sometimes combined it with variation. But in the Ninth Symphony the individual sections were already so extensive that repetition would have spoiled the proportions of the work; the trio is merely alluded to in the coda.

Beethoven not only deprived the fast middle movement of the symphony of its dance character, but gave it greater weight within the framework of the symphony than it had previously had. The Allegretto scherzando of the Eighth Symphony, which stands in place of a slow movement, was the forerunner of the intermezzo-like middle movements which Brahms and other later composers provided for their symphonies.

[1] Nottebohm, *Ein Skizzenbuch von Beethoven aus dem Jahre 1803* (Leipzig, 1880); new edition by Paul Mies (Leipzig, 1924), p. 44; English translation by Jonathan Katz in *Two Beethoven Sketchbooks* (London, 1979), p. 89.

[2] *Studien zu Beethovens Personalstil. Das Scherzothema* (Leipzig, 1921).

[3] 'Stilkundliche Bemerkungen zu Beethovenschen Werken', *Neues Beethoven-Jahrbuch*, vii (1937), p. 91.

[4] Also in the scherzo of no. 5 as originally conceived. See Peter Gülke, *Zur Neuausgabe der Sinfonie No. 5 von Ludwig van Beethoven* (Leipzig, 1978).

THE PROBLEM OF THE FINALE

Besides sonata form, ternary form, and the various kinds of rondo, Beethoven made significant use of variation in his symphonies. Its somewhat free employment in the C minor follows the example of Haydn's 'double variation'. But symphonic variation played a further role in the solution of what may be called 'the problem of the finale'. In early symphonic writing, and still in Haydn and Mozart, the centre of aesthetic gravity lies in the first movement. This is not a value-judgement: the first movement was cast in the large-scale sonata form, still relatively unfamiliar, and therefore demanded alert listening. The last movement was a rondo or simple variations, thematically and formally easier to grasp. Mozart already had tried to give the last movement equal weight with the first; the 'Jupiter' Symphony is the clearest example. And this aim became more obvious in Beethoven. The great coda to the Allegro con brio of the Second Symphony and the unique form of the finale of the Eighth were prompted by it. The conclusion of the symphony thus assumed a monumental character. With the recurrence of the basic rhythm of the first movement at an important juncture in the finale of the Fifth, Beethoven established a simple precedent for Bruckner's striving to create an overtowering synthesis in his finales by combining the themes of earlier movements.[1] Beethoven employed variation form twice in symphonic finales: in the 'Eroica' and the Ninth. Both were special cases. The Eroica theme – originally a contredanse – was also used in the finale of the ballet *Die Geschöpfe des Prometheus*, Op. 43, and in the Variations for Piano, Op. 35. Detailed study (see p. 137 n. 3) shows that the same formal elements – rondo, variation, polyphony – play a part in all three. In Op. 43 rondo form takes the first place; in Op. 35 variation form; in the 'Eroica' rondo form with variation treatment and polyphonic writing in the most important passages. The frequent splitting-off of theme-heads is again characteristic of Beethoven's thematic work. Once this is grasped, the ordering of the sections and their relationships are easily perceptible.

The finale of the Choral Symphony is also a variation movement, though in a form which long made understanding difficult. That Beethoven early had variations in mind is apparent from his sketches.[2] Indeed, the stanzas of Schiller's 'Ode to Joy', from which Beethoven selected his text, begin with varied repetitions of the same thought:

---

[1] Alfred Orel, *Anton Bruckner* (Leipzig, 1925), pp. 93 ff.
[2] Nottebohm, *Zweite Beethoveniana*, p. 167.

'Freude schöner Götterfunken',
'Freude trinken alle Wesen',
'Freude heisst die starke Feder', etc.

Beethoven adopted this poetic suggestion and form, and theme and variations are represented by the following sections:

Baritone solo, 'Freude schöner Götterfunken';
Solo quartet, 'Wem der grosse Wurf gelungen';
The movement 'Freude trinken alle Wesen';
Allegro assai vivace, Alla marcia;
Fugal instrumental interlude;
Choral setting of 'Freude schöner Götterfunken';
Andante maestoso on 'Seid umschlungen', to a theme subsequently
    used as a counterpoint to the 'Joy' melody;
Allegro energico with the 'Joy' melody and its counterpoint;
Allegro ma non tanto.

Interspersed among these variations are a number of sublime visions inspired by the text: 'Und der Cherub steht vor Gott', 'Ihr stürzt nieder', 'Wo ihr sanfter Flügel weilt'. If the forms and substance of poem and music are considered from this angle, the finale of the Ninth Symphony is no longer difficult to grasp. The two arts are most perfectly balanced and complementary. Beethoven found what was virtually the only possible way to set Schiller's text.

BOGUS 'PROGRAMMES'

Everything said so far has been concerned with historical facts or based on objective textual reality. Yet something must be said about the attempts at subjective interpretation of their 'meanings'. This started in Beethoven's lifetime; angered by importunate questioners, he often gave them the answer they deserved, thus creating further confusion. The nineteenth century invented numerous fanciful 'programmes' for the symphonies and a *ne plus ultra* was reached in the twentieth when Arnold Schering[1] asserted that almost all Beethoven's works were based on poetic models. According to him, the Third Symphony is based on the *Iliad*, the Fourth on four poems of Schiller, the Fifth is a revolutionary symphony. To the Sixth he underlaid Thomson's *The Seasons*, to the Seventh Goethe's *Wilhelm Meister*. Despite Schering's arguments, his theory has been generally rejected. Speaking of his ideas and their evolution, Beethoven himself is said to have told a young musician:[2] 'I change much, reject and try

[1] *Beethoven und die Dichtung* (Berlin, 1936), *Beethoven in neuer Deutung* (Leipzig, 1934), *Zur Erkenntnis Beethovens* (Würzburg, 1938).
[2] Thayer, op. cit., iv, p. 420.

again until I am satisfied; but then the working-out begins to grow in my head in breadth and detail, height and depth, and since I know what I want, the underlying idea never leaves me; it rises and grows apace; I hear and see the image in its full extent, standing before my mind's eye as if in one cast'. He says nothing about these ideas being any but musical ones. In some cases, it is true, he pointed out extra-musical ideas that were in his mind during the composition of a work, but there were only a few works in his entire output where this seemed to him important and necessary. Schering's thesis was wrong in that he made general inferences from these exceptions and did not hesitate to twist Beethoven's own comments on the Third and Sixth Symphonies. Anyone who has studied Beethoven's sketches knows that he put on paper anything that moved him at the time, but he set down nothing that can be adduced to support Schering.

GENUINE EXTRA-MUSICAL CONTEXTS

The three symphonic works in connection with which Beethoven himself mentioned extra-musical contexts are the Third and Sixth Symphonies and Op. 91. The history of the Third Symphony has often been described with varying degrees of accuracy. The title-page of a non-autograph copy still shows the words 'intitulata Bonaparte' nearly erased, but this was a title, not a dedication. The heroic was very close to Beethoven's personality; it was also a concern of his time; he wished to express the idea of 'the heroic' in terms of music and for a time he connected this idea with Bonaparte. Actually the later title 'Sinfonia eroica' is much clearer and unambiguous.[1]

Beethoven's feeling for nature was uncommonly strong (see p. 129 n. 3 above); all his life he sought the open air and expressed his enthusiasm in conversations and sketches. It is not surprising that nature gave him the underlying idea of a symphonic work. Adolf Sandberger[2] has shown how long the ancestral line of this work is, but only one composition need be singled out here for comparison: Vivaldi's four *concerti grossi* entitled *Le stagione* (The Seasons), Op. 8, nos. 1–4. Vivaldi maintains the form of the *concerto grosso*, but the titles and 'explanatory sonnets' engraved at the head of the principal violin part of each[3] announce detailed programme-music. There is, for instance, a passage in 'Spring' where a solo violin is marked 'The

[1] See also Maynard Solomon, 'Beethoven and Bonaparte', *Music Review*, xxix (1968), pp. 96 ff.) revised as chapter 13 of *Beethoven* (New York, 1977; London, 1978).
[2] 'Zu den geschichtlichen Voraussetzungen der Pastoralsinfonie', *Ausgewählte Aufsätze*, ii (Munich, 1924), p. 154.
[3] The sonnets are printed in full in Marc Pincherle, *Antonio Vivaldi et la musique instrumentale* (Paris, 1948), i, pp. 290–1.

goatherd who sleeps', while at the same time the violin imitates 'The dog that barks'. There is hardly anything of this in Beethoven. Each movement, including the thunderstorm, is devised and developed according to the laws of music. The only gloss concerns the bird-calls; Beethoven probably felt it unfair to omit the voices he had so often enjoyed. He was aware of the danger of being misunderstood: hence the inscription 'Mehr Ausdruck der Empfindung als Malerei' (More expression of emotion than painting). In the Pastoral Symphony there can be no question of a realistic programme and its translation into music; characteristic emotions are expressed in purely musical form.

Beethoven's farthest excursion into the realm of programme music is his Op. 91. This is due largely to the subject-matter, as well as to the fact that the work was originally designed for the 'Panharmonikon' of the inventor Johann Nepomuk Mälzel. In the first section, the advance of the armies with their signals and hymns, and the actual battle, are described very realistically with the aid of rattles and very large drums. But the work does not deserve the negative criticism of which the Beethoven literature is full (see p. 130, n. 4 above). Beethoven himself took it very seriously, as is shown by his comprehensive instructions for performance; it had great success; and it contains its full share of Beethoven's individual traits. When at the end of the first section the march of the beaten army disintegrates, this is the same device with which Beethoven ends the funeral march of the 'Eroica', similar to that used in the Allegretto of no. 7 and to that symbolizing the death of Coriolanus in Op. 62. And the second section, the 'victory-symphony', again strikes one as genuine Beethoven. Ex. 31(iv) on p. 130 gives some idea of it. This is not programme-music, not realistic music descriptive of victory, but the idea of victory in a purely musical form.

Perhaps the last word on the relationship between music and meaning in Beethoven was said by Stravinsky: 'What difference does it make whether the Third Symphony was inspired by the figure of Bonaparte as republican or as emperor! What matters is the music alone. But to speak about music – that's a risky business, entailing responsibilities, so people prefer to stick to harmless inessentials. That is easy and may pass for profundity. . . . It's high time that this should be realized. One must rescue Beethoven from the unjustified domination of the "intellectuals". One must hand him over to those who seek nothing in music but music.'[1]

---

[1] *Melos*, March, 1947.

THE OVERTURES

Title, Opus number and key	Dates of composition and 1st perf.	Tempo indications and number of bars	Purpose
Die Geschöpfe des Prometheus, Op. 43, C major	1800–1 28 March 1801	Adagio–Allegro molto con brio (283)	For a ballet by S. Viganó, at the Imperial Theatre, Vienna
Coriolan, Op. 62 C minor	1807 1807	Allegro con brio (314)	For a tragedy by H. J. Collin
Leonore II, C major	1805 20 November 1805	Adagio–Allegro (530)	For the first performance of the opera
Leonore III, C major	1806 29 March 1806	Adagio–Allegro (638)	For the second, shortened version of *Leonore*
Leonore I, Op. 138, C major	1806–7 1828	Andante con moto–Allegro con brio (365)	For a projected production of the opera in Prague
Fidelio, E major	May 1814 26 May 1814	Allegro (308)	For the third version, *Fidelio*, of the opera *Leonore*
Egmont, Op. 84 F minor	1809–10 15 June 1811	Sostenuto ma non troppo–Allegro (347)	For the performance of Goethe's tragedy at the Imperial Theatre, Vienna
Die Ruinen von Athen, Op. 113 G major	1811 9 December 1812	Andante con moto–Allegro ma non troppo (175)	For the inauguration of the theatre at Pest
Zur Namensfeier, Op. 115, C major	1814–15; sketches 1809, 1811–12 25 December 1815	Maestoso–Allegro assai vivace (335)	
König Stephan, Op. 117, E flat major	1811 9 December 1812	Andante con moto–Presto (501)	as Op. 113
Die Weihe des Hauses, Op. 124, C major	1822 3 October 1822	Maestoso e sostenuto–Allegro con brio	For the opening of the Theater in der Josephstadt, Vienna

This table of Beethoven's overtures shows that they were to a large extent commissioned for special occasions; their number indicates the esteem in which he was held by his contemporaries. One can divide them into those for dramatic works (*Egmont, Coriolan, Leonore*) and those for non-dramatic occasions (ballets, festivities). Even super-ficially they show some interesting differences from Beethoven's symphonies. Almost all of them employ four horns; several need trombones, which occur in only five movements of the symphonies. Most of them have slow introductions and in their further course there are many more changes of tempo and time than in the symphonic movements. Dynamics, too, have a wider range: *ppp* and *fff* occur more frequently than in the symphonies. The festive purpose and the content of the play naturally influenced the overture. Quotations may be included in the overture, but the significance of a quotation depends on the manner of its employment.

The normal overture plan of Beethoven's period was sonata form, as in the symphony, but with no repeat of the exposition. The slow introduction plays a greater role and the development is much shortened or even omitted and replaced by a contrasting middle section. This was the common form, for instance in Dittersdorf, Cherubini, and also in Mozart. Beethoven follows it in the *Prometheus* overture (without middle section), in *Leonore* No. 1 (with a short, slow middle section), in the festival overture *König Stephan* (where instead of a development the slow introduction is repeated). These are admittedly not among Beethoven's strongest works. But from the theatrical point of view, this form has the advantage of homogeneity; it may easily be adapted to reflect the general content of the action. Mozart's overture to *Figaro* is a superb example of this type; in substance it is connected with the opera, but by virtue of its self-contained form it may be detached and performed by itself. This, after all, is how most of Beethoven's overtures are performed nowadays. The first *Leonore* was neither printed nor played in Beethoven's lifetime. Beethoven's remark on an old copy, *charakteristische Ouvertüre*, shows that he was conscious of the peculiarity of this form. The same quality appears in Hungarian guise in *König Stephan*, written for Pest.

Fully developed sonata form and fairly extended slow introductions distinguish the second and third *Leonore* and Op. 115, known as *Zur Namensfeier*. The last has a special position among Beethoven's overtures for it is the only one that does not introduce a drama, ballet, or celebration. It has had various titles in the course of time: *La chasse, Zum Namensfest unseres Kaisers, Zur Namensfeier*. Its history proceeds from sketches of the year 1809 through others of 1811 and 1812, to its completion in 1814. Its key was changed several times, and for a while it was to be connected with Schiller's 'Ode to Joy'. The first drafts have the title *Ouvertüre bei jeder Gelegenheit oder zum Gebrauch im Konzert* (Overture for any occasion or for concert use). It was published in 1825 simply as 'Ouvertüre für Orchester'.

The *Fidelio* overture in E major was written in 1814. It includes no quotation from the opera; a long introduction is succeeded by a sonata form with little contrast between first and second subjects. This, too, is a 'characteristic' rather than a 'dramatic' overture. (*Leonore* No. 3 will be discussed below.) The overture to *Die Ruinen von Athen* is Beethoven's shortest work of this kind; all sections are brief and the recapitulation has no second subject. The overture *König Stephan* was composed in 1811 for the same occasion – the opening of a new theatre at Pest. A play by a Hungarian author was preceded and followed by a prologue (*Stephan*) and epilogue (*Die Ruinen*) by Kotzebue, for both of which Beethoven contributed overtures and incidental music.

In 1822 Kotzebue's *Ruinen von Athen* was drastically adapted as *Die Weihe des Hauses* for the inauguration of a theatre in Vienna. The old overture, Op. 113, was too insignificant for the purpose, so Op. 124 was substituted. It shows no relation to the *Festspiel* and probably the commission converged with a plan Beethoven had long had in mind. Polyphonic elements appeared more and more in his late works; Handel was one of the masters he held in high esteem; and when his London friend Johann Andreas Stumpff presented him on his sick-bed with Arnold's collected edition of Handel, he is reported to have said 'This I have long wished for; for Handel is the greatest, the most masterly composer; from him I can still learn'.[1] Thus in 1822 he had wanted to write an overture in strict 'Handelian style', which seemed to him especially festive and suitable for the occasion. Hence the old 'French overture' form; hence the fugato; hence too the immediate entry of the counterpoint to the fugato subject in the manner of Handel's double fugues. The festive character is reflected in the key of C major, the instrumentation with four horns, two trumpets, three trombones, and in the heroic, joyous signal motive of the transition. Op. 124 also is really an overture 'for any festive occasion', a concert overture in a form unusual for the period. It should be noted that during the composition of the Ninth Symphony in the years 1822–24 Beethoven was also planning to write a B–A–C–H overture. This did not get beyond scanty sketches and some remarks may be quoted in order to show what Beethoven meant when he used the word 'ideas':[2] 'This overture with the new symphony: will make an academy [i.e. concert] at the Kärntnertorth [eatre].' 'Also instead of a

[1] Gerhard von Breuning, *Aus dem Schwarzspanierhaus* (Vienna, 1874; reprinted Berlin and Leipzig, 1907), p. 94.
[2] Nottebohm, *Zweite Beethoveniana*, pp. 12 and 167.

new symphony a new overture on Bach [i.e. B–A–C–H], much fugued, with 3 [trombones].'[1] (Nottebohm wondered whether Beethoven meant three themes or three trombones.)

These overtures are quite different from those which can be called 'dramatic': *Egmont, Coriolan*, and *Leonore* No. 2, for in these the purely musical sonata form is adapted to the content of the drama. These works show how Beethoven proceeded when he wished to impose extra-musical modifications on an instrumental work. Nothing like it is found in his symphonies: an important reason for rejecting the validity of extra-musical associations in them. Various attempts have been made to relate the themes of the *Egmont* overture to the characters of the drama – Egmont, Clärchen, Alba – but no general agreement has been reached. The piece as a whole is sombre, only intermittently brighter. At first we have a normal sonata form with the motive of the slow introduction playing an important role in the second-subject group. The most striking feature is the great appendix in the tonic major, unparalleled in any other sonata movement by Beethoven; it is identical with the last number of Beethoven's incidental music to *Egmont*, the 'victory-symphony' introducing the piccolo. Similar figures appear in the first of Clärchen's songs, imitating fifes, and as an ostinato motive in the postlude of her song. The end of the overture anticipates the end of Goethe's drama, the catastrophe and its transfiguration into a symbol of victory.

A similar anticipation also occurs in the *Coriolan* overture; its end, where the theme gradually disintegrates, has been referred to above in comparison with Op. 91, with the funeral march of the 'Eroica', and the Allegretto of no. 7. Here it symbolizes the death of Coriolanus. The sonata form undergoes a number of structural modifications and it is peculiar that in the extensive coda the second subject plays an unusually large role. All these peculiarities may be connected with the developments in Collin's tragedy,[2] yet the work remains remarkably self-contained, musically and formally. Its effect as a whole is independent of the drama. A general title such as 'tragic overture' would describe it quite as appropriately.

There remains the second *Leonore* overture.[3] In this, the structure of sonata form is significantly transformed, and the operatic quotations

[1] Nottebohm, op. cit., p. 474.
[2] See Mies, 'Beethoven – Collin – Shakespeare; zur Coriolan-Ouvertüre', *Zeitschrift für Musik*, cv (1938), p. 156.
[3] For a detailed study of *Leonore* overtures cf. Josef Braunstein, *Beethovens Leonore-Ouvertüren* (Leipzig, 1927), and Alan Tyson, 'The Problem of Beethoven's "First" Leonore Overture', *Journal of the American Musicological Society*, xxviii (1975), p. 292. On the basis of manuscript studies, Tyson demonstrates that the overture known as 'Leonore no. 1' was written in 1806–7 for a projected performance of the opera in Prague. See also Tyson, 'Yet another "Leonore" Overture?', *Music and Letters*, lviii (1977), p. 192.

appear at important junctures. Whereas in *Leonore* no. 1 the Florestan aria appears only in the introduction, here it enters the second-subject group and the development, thus occupying a central position. It begins with a descending unison scale, symbolizing the descent into the dungeon. The twice-stated 'liberation fanfare' is heard at the end of the development and is followed by a passage whose faltering *pp* pulsation must be related to the fainting Leonora, and by Florestan's aria. But this is the dénouement of the drama. By a unique stroke of genius Beethoven now omits the recapitulation and goes at once into the brief, joyous conclusion based on the first subject – confirmation that this overture is a musical description of the dramatic action of the last act, closely corresponding to its catastrophe and peripeteia. It thus anticipates the symphonic poem of the later nineteenth century. Though the starting-point is traditional form, this is inflected and transformed to suit a given content. As in the *Egmont* and *Coriolan* overtures, the *Leonore* no. 2 musically anticipates the catastrophe and solution of the drama.

It is characteristic of Beethoven's attitude to instrumental music that he was not satisfied with this freer form. He transformed the work into the third, the so-called 'great', *Leonore* overture. Details apart, this transformation is easily described: he restores normal sonata form by including an exact recapitulation and curtailing the other sections to avoid undue length. Thus, the fanfare moves to the centre of the overture. To formulate it precisely: the dramatically conceived form of the second *Leonore* was superseded in the third by a form conceived in terms of absolute music.

Posterity, even during the nineteenth-century vogue of the symphonic poem, has endorsed Beethoven's decision. It is not the dramatic second *Leonore*, but the formally perfect third that has become the favourite of the concert-hall. Beethoven's overtures for the theatre, also, have today become almost wholly detached from the dramas that occasioned them. They perhaps unduly anticipate the course of the drama, its catastrophe and solution; they are no longer merely 'characteristic', the form perhaps most suitable for an opera overture. And yet their structure is musically so strong that they remain intelligible in spite of deviations from the norm. While the more balanced third *Leonore* has replaced the second, the fourth (*Fidelio*) as well as the first belong rather to the 'characteristic' type.

MARCHES AND DANCES

In considering the symphonies we have seen how the quick middle movement gains in speed and loses its original dance character. This is the place to refer again to the transformation of a minuet sketch for the scherzo of the 'Eroica', which still shows a relationship to the first movement (see p. 145), and to mention the exclusion of a slow appendage to a trio for the same movement. The scherzo of the First Symphony is foreshadowed in a collection of *12 deutsche Tänze* (Kinsky-Halm, WoO13, no. 2). The use of a *contre danse* in the finale of the 'Eroica' has been mentioned. Our musical age is all too prone to forget that men like Mozart, Haydn, and Beethoven wrote true *Gebrauchsmusik* for all sorts of festive occasions. We have a great number of marches, polonaises, and écossaises for military band (WoO 18-24) by Beethoven. A march in D major, written for Archduke Anton as commander of the *Hoch- und Deutschmeister* regiment, was entitled by Beethoven 'Marsch für die böhmische Landwehr'; during the War of Liberation it became extremely popular under the name of 'Yorkscher Marsch' (after the Prussian general Yorck). We have seen how the heroic element, symbolized in signal and march motives, connects Beethoven with the music of the French Revolution;[1] sketches for the 'Yorkscher Marsch' are found together with those for the Piano Concerto, Op. 73. This, too, is a 'heroic work' with a number of march motives. Sketched concurrently, the march and concerto share the same elements.

Besides these marches Beethoven left well over a hundred minuets, Deutsche, Ländler, Kontretänze (WoO 3, 7-17). They were intended for balls, name-day celebrations, and festivities of the 'Pensionsgesellschaft der bildenden Künstler'. Some are extant in their original form for orchestra, some in the then popular form of trio arrangement for two violins and bass, some again in the composer's own piano-reductions. The charming *6 Ecossaisen* (WoO 83), of which we only have a copy in an unknown hand, are probably also piano transcriptions. More use should be made of all these small forms in private music-making and popular concerts. They prove that Beethoven was not all the time the 'hero', the 'titan', the 'heaven-stormer', as which he is commonly represented. That this was not so is shown by the circumstances attending the composition of his finest set of dances, the so-called *Mödlinger Tänze* (WoO 17) for seven string and wind instruments (composed in the summer of 1819, published in 1907). At the time Beethoven lived at Mödling, occupied with the composition of the Missa solemnis. A band of musicians playing at the inn 'Zu den drei Raben' urgently begged him for a set of waltzes. He obliged with these dances, himself writing out the instrumental parts.

[1] See also Frida Knight, *Beethoven and the Age of Revolution* (London, 1973).

From the Missa solemnis to the dances for a *Heurige* band; from the *contre danse* to the finale of the Third Symphony; from the grandiose vision of the Alla marcia, 'Froh wie seine Sonnen fliegen', in the Ninth Symphony to the 'Yorkscher Marsch' – such was the vast expanse of Beethoven's music for the orchestra.

IV

THE ORCHESTRAL MUSIC OF BEETHOVEN'S CONTEMPORARIES

By PAUL MIES

Two terms need definition here: 'contemporaries' and 'orchestral music'. 'Contemporaries' may be understood as 'composers living at the same time as Beethoven' or it may be limited to those actually belonging to the same generation.[1] The present chapter is generally limited to orchestral music composed between 1790 and 1830 though a few older works are taken into account and Haydn's last symphonies are discussed in Vol. VII. Alfred Lorenz[2] wrote that Pinder very rightly emphasized that 'the historical process does not go on in a direct line but rather "quasi multidimensionally". Styles did not march "in single file" behind each other but often existed for a long time side by side in representatives of different ages.' So we shall not be surprised that the works treated in this chapter show numerous differences. Contemporaries are life-associates rather than stylistic associates.

A second limitation is needed for the term 'orchestral music'. This chapter is principally concerned with the symphony, treating overtures and dances only marginally, and leaving concertos to Chapter V. The antecedents of the symphony were the Italian opera symphony and the symphonies of the Mannheimers and the Viennese School.[3] The facts that the symphony was originally prefaced to an opera and slowly freed itself, that the same piece might be played in an opera-house and on its own in a concert-hall, effaced differences of type; the same work appears under the title of symphony and of overture. The concert overture of the Romantics had an early forerunner, as we have seen in the previous chapter, in Beethoven's *Ouvertüre zur Namensfeier*. And since the miniature form of the dance is represented in the minuets of the symphonies, there is no need to discuss actual dance-music here.

---

[1] On this conception see Alfred Lorenz, *Abendländische Musikgeschichte im Rhythmus der Generationen* (Berlin, 1928).

[2] Ibid, p. 27.

[3] See Vol. VII, chap. VI.

How the Mannheim and Viennese styles left their mark will be shown in detail. Perhaps the Berlin symphonic style should also be taken into account; both Mozart and Haydn admitted the significance of C. P. E. Bach. The Berlin style made itself felt above all in the employment of polyphonic methods. The influence of the finale of Mozart's 'Jupiter' symphony and Haydn's canonic minuets is also considerable.

BEETHOVEN'S UNIQUENESS

It is remarkable that even the names of the symphony composers of Beethoven's time are hardly remembered today and that their works have almost disappeared. To a greater extent than at any other time one composer – Beethoven – overshadowed all his contemporaries. Beside Palestrina there were Lassus, Victoria, and others; beside Bach, Handel; beside Haydn, Mozart; in the later nineteenth century, beside Wagner, Brahms. But the period we are considering is represented by one name alone. To a certain extent this was true even in Beethoven's own day. When a critic, writing of the performance of the Fourth Symphony at the Niederrheinisches Musikfest in 1828, declared that 'nothing more magnificent of this kind has probably ever been written, nor ever will be written',[1] that was not an isolated judgement but one constantly reaffirmed by Beethoven's contemporaries. If not all his works were fully valued at once, if contemporaries were for a while placed by his side, he was in his own day already regarded as the greatest living composer. Hermann Kretschmar was correct when he said:[2]

The reconstruction of the symphony from a simple occasional music to a tone-poem in the grandest style was completed in the comparatively short space of sixty years. The musical public adapted itself remarkably easily to the change and it is absolutely astounding how quickly and correctly the relationship to Beethoven was established. We hear and read a great deal nowadays about the non-understood Beethoven. But this depends on shorter or longer ill-humours of the composer himself, on bitter and heated judgements of rivals and adversaries. . . . But in relation to the novelty and boldness of his works, these were only few – and they were not decisive. Beethoven's symphonies were the first and for a long time the only ones to be printed in score during the composer's lifetime.

The parts of Beethoven's First Symphony appeared in 1801; in 1809 his first three symphonies together with 18 by Haydn and six of

[1] Eugen Brümmer, *Beethoven im Spiegel der zeitgenössischen rheinischen Presse* (Würzburg, 1933), p. 73.
[2] *Führer durch den Konzertsaal. I: Sinfonie und Suite* (Leipzig, sixth edition, 1921), p. 251.

Mozart's works were published in London in score.[1] From *Wellingtons Sieg*, Op. 91, onward, score and parts appeared together.

CONDITIONS OF PUBLICATION

Lack of scores makes the study of this period particularly difficult; beside the editions of parts one can only fall back on later editions and piano arrangements. Yet the number of symphonies composed during these years must run into many hundreds. There was a great demand. The 'periodical' publications that came from the Parisian presses about the middle of the eighteenth century were followed by those of Goetz at Mannheim and Munich, André at Offenbach, and Schott at Mainz. Yet nothing of these has survived in our repertory. They were forgotten already during the nineteenth century. The reasons for this oblivion must be examined – and it is undeniable that here and there a notable work or particularly successful movement stands out. But none has achieved that which is common to the late symphonies of Mozart and Haydn, and Beethoven's above all: an easily recognizable individuality, its own physiognomy. None has earned a name, a title, like so many works of the great masters. Such name-giving is often the sign of a wish to designate a particularly loved work. But there is one exception to all this: Franz Schubert. As regards time and location he was quite particularly Beethoven's contemporary; he will be considered at the end of this chapter.

The sources are the hitherto not very extensive literature of the subject, together with numerous works in old editions, in *Denkmäler* publications, and in new 'practical' editions from which, despite a great deal of editorial manipulation, it is possible to extract essentials.[2]

INSTRUMENTATION

To begin with some general points: the instrumentation is usually specified as 'à deux Violons, Alto et Basse, Cors et Hautbois etc. ad libitum'. Particularly during the first half of the period there are no separate parts for cello and bassoon, though occasionally in the general part the cello is given a separate stave or is marked *solo*; the same is true of the bassoon. The slow movements are essentially string music as in early Haydn, though a solo flute is often employed. Clarinets appear only later. Except for a few, seldom extended, solo passages, the wind serve only as harmonic supports or double the strings in

[1] Georg Kinsky and Hans Halm, *Thematisch-bibliographisches Verzeichnis aller vollendeten Werke Ludwig van Beethovens* (Munich, 1955), p. 54.
[2] This area is now being increasedly covered, notably in such publications as *The Symphony 1720–1840, A Comprehensive Collection of approximately Six-Hundred Full Scores in Sixty Volumes*, ed. Barry S. Brook (New York, 1979–   ).

octaves or support them in thirds. Sometimes the solo passages of other instruments are inserted as cues in the first violin part. Actually the works could be conducted from that alone; a score was hardly necessary. Here was the first difference with Beethoven, in whose First Symphony all the instruments participated freely. Most of his contemporaries held to the traditional treatment of the wind; there is only a little evidence of Haydn's influence in thematic/motivic work; they were hardly aware of Beethoven's 'open work' and 'obbligato accompaniment' (see p. 129), both of which are for us inseparable from the conception of symphonic style.

The instrumentation specified above is one of the indications that first and foremost the German composers came from the milieu of domestic and chamber music, the music of the small courts. W. H. Riehl says in his essay, 'Die göttlichen Philister':[1]

There was a time when the so-called 'little' symphony was domestic music, the music of wealthy and aristocratic houses. When the symphony became ever bigger, i.e. more many-voiced, this came to an end and even many a princely house no longer had room for a full orchestra. And yet the owners were unwilling to forego symphonic music on festive evenings. . . . So purely symphonic works were written for strings alone or wind alone.

Kretzschmar[2] mentions a series of 'easy' symphonies by Johann Anton André (1775–1842), son of the *Singspiel* composer Johann André, in one of which

the minuet consists of a waltz as principal section with a trio in the form of an embellished chorale. But in spite of André and in spite of the difficulties, Beethoven's symphonies remained at the head of the repertory, even above Haydn and Mozart . . . although usually incompletely played, and the orchestra was . . . for their sake gradually transformed at great expense.

It is interesting that the works of French composers like Méhul and Cherubini, and of the later Clementi, are more symphonic even in our sense. The earlier cultivation of the public concert in France may have contributed to this.

STRUCTURAL PROBLEMS OF LESSER MASTERS

With a little exaggeration one might say that the contemporaries had difficulties with structure, particularly in the evolution of the existing sonata-style and the thematic material suited to it. Despite the splendid models provided by Haydn and Mozart they were still stuck in the rudimentary stage of motivic-thematic treatment.

[1] *Musikalische Charakterköpfe*, i (Stuttgart and Augsburg, seventh edition, 1886), p. 178.
[2] Op. cit., p. 262.

Sometimes clear-cut themes harm development more than they help it. It is not by chance that the slow movements and rondo-type finales appeal to us most today, while the often stiff and commonplace minuet-movements are far from the types of Haydn and Mozart. With Beethoven there are no difficulties with form, only – as the sketches show – with the details, with the theme, the basic motives, the transitions. Hence the magnificent first movements and finales which in turn affect the structure and shaping of the middle movements; hence his concentratedness. Already in the First Symphony he had far outgrown the chamber-music element. For the early romantics, for Schubert above all, after Beethoven's example things were – as we shall see later – quite different. We have become accustomed to speak of Mozart, Haydn, and Beethoven as the triple constellation of the classics; in doing so, we are not nearly conscious enough that we are grouping together great stylistic differences, often incompatibilities. The real style of these decades can best be grasped from the works of the lesser men; the distinctiveness of the great masters lies in their growth above and beyond a period style.

The first movements of the symphonies of Beethoven's time are usually in so-called sonata-form, often with a slow introduction which seldom has any connection with the fast movement which follows. The opening bars of a Symphony in C,[1] by Ignaz Pleyel (1757–1831), a pupil of Haydn, may serve as an example:

Ex. 36

The traditional dotted rhythms of the French overture, the short sequences, the chromatic shifts, the dynamic contrasts in the Mannheim manner, are clear; the first bars are played by unison strings. Triadically built themes after the manner of the Italian overture were long favoured; noisy tremolos and schematic passage-work heightened the sound-effect and lent symphonic character. Beside the short sequences one is struck by the constant repetition of groups of bars. What above all in Mozart's cadences can be so charming, here becomes mechanically schematic. The second theme

[1] *Symphonie périodique*, No. 9, Schott (Mainz), published in 1791. See Rita Benton, *Ignace Pleyel: A Thematic Catalogue of his Compositions* (New York, 1977), p. 38.

tries to be cantabile, often without much success. Transitional passages between themes and final groups are seldom based on thematic-motivic work, but introduce new patterns without achieving that sense of unity with which Mozart so incomparably invests them. Larger coda formations are rare; the endings of exposition and recapitulation are materially the same. The developments consist more of sequential stringings together of quotations, particularly from the first subject, rather than of thematic evolution and working-out. A favourite device is to put the main theme in the bass and shift it chromatically against the runs and tremolos of the remaining strings. The imperfectly mastered formal structure is supported by numerous fermatas, dividing the separate sections and interfering with the flow of the whole. The slow movements are mostly in ternary form with repeat of the first section at the end, sometimes in variation form. Development of the minuet in the sense of Mozart and Beethoven is hardly ever attempted. The finales are rondo forms, pleasant in their lively way though one misses any deeper note. Mozart and Haydn had done it all more perfectly, and what Haydn and Mozart had not yet supplanted now fell a sacrifice to Beethoven's works. Even such notable symphonies as those of Johann Stamitz were completely lost. While the Germans found it difficult to evolve from the sphere of domestic music into the genuinely symphonic, the symphony in France at this time was a scholastic exercise rather than a master-work, more a proof of talent than an area of artistic accomplishment.[1] Kretzschmar sums up the position in Germany thus:[2]

There came a time when the critics were quite at sea, when those composers who attempted Beethoven's pathos were sharply reprimanded as 'bombastic' and Haydn's followers as 'childish', when the symphonic form was said to be exhausted and when almost every criticism of a new work began with the depressing phrase, 'So-and-so who now comes forward with yet another symphony, which etc.'

The men who in these difficult circumstances managed to assert their position as symphonists, who penetrated the repertory beside the classics and won a place after Beethoven, do not deserve to be totally forgotten. Without a look at the nature of these numerous secondary figures one can hardly understand fully the golden age of the Viennese School and the individuality of its classics.

---

[1] According to Barry S. Brook, *La Symphonie française dans la seconde moitié du XVIIIe siècle*, i (Paris, 1962), pp. 43–4, the Revolution 'delivered an almost fatal blow to the French classical symphony, which already had resisted with difficulty the Haydnesque inundation . . . and with only a few exceptions, the symphony served essentially as an exercise for students at the Conservatoire'.

[2] Op. cit., pp. 261–3.

THE DISCIPLES OF HAYDN AND MOZART

Kretzschmar and Karl Nef[1] in dealing with this period distinguish two principal schools, that of Mozart and that of Haydn. To the latter Nef assigns Karl Ditters von Dittersdorf (1739–99), at any rate as regards the essential part of his output, František Antonín Rössler (Francesco Antonio Rosetti) (1746–92), Johann Baptist Wanhal (Jan Křtitel Vaňhal) (1739–1813), Josef Mysliweczek (Mysliveček) (1737–81), Sigismund von Neukomm (1778–1858), Ignaz Pleyel (1757–1831), Paul Wranitzky (Pavel Vranický) (1756–1808), Johannes Sperger (1750–1812), Adalbert Gyrowetz (Vojtěch Matyáš Jírovec) (1763–1850), Franz (František) Krommer (1759–1831), Franz Hoffmeister (1754–1812), and also Luigi Boccherini (1743–1805). Pleyel and Neukomm were actual pupils of Haydn. To the Mozart school belong Friedrich Kunzen (1761–1817), Muzio Clementi (1752–1832), Johann Franz Xaver Sterkel (1750–1817), Friedrich Witt (1770–1836), Johann Anton André (1775–1842), Franz Xaver Blyma (1770–1822), Joseph Woelfl (1773–1812), and Anton Eberl (1765–1807). Kretzschmar agrees on the whole with Nef except that he places Dittersdorf with the Mozart school – to which he adds Michael Haydn (1737–1806). Carl Czerny (1791–1857) and Ferdinand Ries (1784–1838) were Beethoven pupils. From France we must add such men as Louis-Joseph-Ferdinand Hérold (1791–1833), Étienne Nicolas Méhul (1763–1817), and Luigi Cherubini (1760–1842), and among the early Romantics Georg Joseph ('Abt') Vogler (1749–1814), Carl Maria von Weber (1786–1826), Louis Spohr (1784–1859), and above all Franz Schubert (1797–1828). All these were active in Beethoven's lifetime.[2]

In view of the great number of composers and works – some wrote symphonies by the dozen – individual treatment or anything like a complete survey is impossible; one can only discuss some of the more important works and trends. Before examining typical examples, we may note some critical judgements from the earlier twentieth-century literature which first attempted a conspectus. According to Kretzschmar, Witt was 'a little Berlioz, distinguished by experiments and tricks of instrumentation: whole adagios with pizzicato, in the allegros bass drum and Turkish music'; this is a rash generalization from Witt's Symphony in A minor ('Turque'). But Witt's best known work is a Symphony in C, closely modelled on Haydn's nos. 93 and 97 and long believed to be an early work of Beethoven's.[3] On the other hand, the most Austrian is the Salzburger Woelfl, described by Kretzschmar

[1] Nef, *Geschichte der Sinfonie und Suite* (Leipzig, 1921).
[2] Brook's *Comprehensive Collection* includes works by most of these composers.
[3] Ed. Fritz Stein as *Ludwig van Beethoven: Jenaer Symphonie* (Leipzig, 1911).

as 'pleasant, amiable, sometimes intimate – but careless and unoriginal'.[1] In 1818 – at Rio de Janeiro – Neukomm composed a symphony 'Héroïque' dedicated to Spontini, into the finale of which he worked Handel's 'See the conqu'ring hero comes'; according to Nef, it is *militärisch pathetisch*.

The first notable representatives of the North German School were Andreas Romberg (1767–1821) and his cousin Bernhard Romberg (1767–1841),[2] both of whom had played in the Electoral orchestra at Bonn with the young Beethoven. Andreas produced his First Symphony (E flat, Op. 6) in 1794, his last (D major, Op. 22) in 1806, although two others and several unpublished ones bear later numbers and opus-numbers; Bernhard began symphonic composition only in 1810 with a *Trauer-Sinfonie*, Op. 23, for Queen Luise of Prussia. Andreas's D major Symphony is marked by such romantic traits as chromatic appoggiaturas and passing-notes:

Ex. 37

Bernhard's *Trauer-Sinfonie* is in two movements divided into sections: Andante lento maestoso-Allegro and Adagio non troppo-Allegro non troppo-Con più moto-Andante-Andante grazioso. The final section, for wind and drums only, is touching in its classical simplicity:

[1] Op. cit., p. 283. Heinz Wolfgang Hamann considers the G minor (1803) the more significant of his two symphonies and says its minuet shows his mastery of the strict style, *Die Musik in Geschichte und Gegenwart*, xiv, cols. 760–1.
[2] See Elmar Wulf, 'Andreas Jakob Romberg, Bernhard Heinrich Romberg', in *Rheinische Musiker*, i, ed. Karl G. Fellerer (Cologne, 1960), which contains complete lists of their works.

Ex. 38

With the Rombergs may be grouped the Saxon composer (Johann Christian) Friedrich Schneider (1786–1853) who produced the earliest of his 23 symphonies and 20 overtures in 1803; he deliberately took Beethoven as his model, most successfully in his scherzos, but in the large-scale forms he 'lacked long breath and the motor energy of an idea'.[1]

Another conscious imitator of Beethoven was his direct pupil Ries,[2] whose work in general is marked by effects of dynamic surprise. Most Beethovenian in style – but in nothing else – is his Fifth Symphony (1835), presumably the one referred to by Beethoven in his letter of 5 February 1823. His Second, in C minor, has a vigorous opening:

Ex. 39

but the anaemic Andante is all too characteristic of the slow movements of the secondary composers of the period.[3]

[1] Martin Wehnert, *Die Musik in Geschichte und Gegenwart*, xi, col. 1902. Helmut Lomnitzer, *Das musikalische Werk Friedrich Schneiders (1786–1853)* (Diss., Marburg, 1961), pp. 42–5, cites Haydn as Schneider's early model (through Symphony no. 7), in his use of slow introductions (only nos. 17 and 19 lack such a beginning), and in the 'fiery scherzo movements'. He finds the influence of the older North German tradition of strict contrapuntalism is also prominent.

[2] A. W. Thayer, *Ludwig van Beethovens Leben*, iv (second edition by Hugo Riemann) (Leipzig, 1910), p. 383.

[3] See Cecil Hill, *The Music of Ferdinand Ries: A Thematic Catalogue* (Armidale, New South Wales, 1977).

DITTERSDORF

The earlier symphonies of the enormously prolific Dittersdorf,[1] including the famous set 'exprimant les Métamorphoses d'Ovide' are discussed in Vol. VII (pp. 402–3). A slightly later symphony, in C (Krebs 93),[2] dating from 1788, deserves more detailed examination. The first theme, Ex. 40(i):

Ex. 40

(i)

(ii)

consists of four motives, and the second theme also begins with the repeated notes of bars 1 and 3. The semiquaver motive constantly reappears but its stretto at the beginning of the reprise (ii) comes as a surprise. Despite the addition of pairs of oboes, bassoons, horns, trumpets, and drums, they rarely strengthen the strings melodically; otherwise they are limited to giving harmonic support, thus making the keyboard continuo superfluous – though no doubt it was played. The Larghetto consists of a theme with three very simple variations. The theme itself with its eightfold motive repetition:

Ex. 41

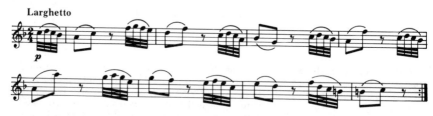

[1] Carl Krebs's thematic catalogue, *Dittersdorfiana* (Berlin, 1900) (reprint New York, 1972) included 127. Margaret Graves, *The New Grove* (New York, 1980; London, 1981), v, pp. 500 ff., ascribes about 120 symphonies to Dittersdorf.
[2] Ed. Kretzschmar (Leipzig, 1895).

lacks tension and development despite the variety of the quaver leaps. It is, however, a typical variation-theme of the time. After a short Menuetto I a second minuet follows with a flute solo as its middle section, then a repeat of the first minuet, and finally a coda derived from the flute passage. The finale is a Prestissimo full of pseudo-polyphonic work on a theme consisting of three motives, *a*, *b*, *c*, running in sequence from instrument to instrument thus:

Number of bars	7	7	7	7	8	7
Vn. I	*a* *b*	*c*	–	*a*	*c*	
Vn. II	–	*a*	*b*	*c*	*a*	*a*
Va.	–	–	*a* *b*	*c*	*b*	
Cello	–	–	–	*a*	*b*	*a*

Similar thinking underlies the finale of Mozart's 'Jupiter' Symphony, written in the same year; such writing was not uncommon at the time. The ensuing repeat of the minuet with a new coda is certainly a surprise but it is not, as Kretzschmar suggested, an anticipation of the scherzo repetition in Beethoven's Fifth; Dittersdorf simply aims at the shock of the unexpected – Haydn had done something similar in his no. 46 – whereas Beethoven's is an organic development already prepared by the significance of the 'knock' motive throughout the first movement.

The structure of the opening of the A minor Symphony (Krebs 95),[1] with its sequences and group-repetitions, may be shown by a diagram. × indicates sequence; ‖: :‖ repetition; *a*, *a′*, *b*, *b′* motives with their variants; the numbers, bars:

$$2 \times 2 + \|{:}2{:}\| + \|{:}2{:}\| + 4^\frown + 3 \times 2 + 2 \times 2 + \|{:}3{:}\|$$
$$a \qquad b \qquad b' \qquad\qquad a \qquad a' \qquad c$$

Obviously such a structure must in the long run become boring, especially since the principal motive *a* is predominant in all the transitions and in the development. This shows striving for unity but the treatment is not plastic enough – as Dittersdorf himself seems to have felt when he decided on drastic shortening of the first subject in the recapitulation. The Larghetto begins with a cantabile melody on the first violins which is followed first by a short-breathed motive and then by a 'horn fifths' theme on oboes and horns; all this constitutes the first subject of a movement in sonata form, with a melodious, richly decorated theme for solo cello as second. The development is full of sequences and repetitions. In the recapitulation the cello solo is

[1] Ed. Victor Luithlen, *Denkmäler der Tonkunst in Österreich*, Jg. xliii(2), vol. 81 (Vienna, 1936), p. 35. The volume also contains two of his earlier symphonies.

not only transposed but reshaped to introduce an element of tension which would otherwise be lacking. The Prestissimo finale is notable for some piquant transitions.

What distinguishes Dittersdorf is his sense of humour, his surprise in form or in transitions. He is unable to play off the diversified thematic elements against each other and interlace them. But the striving for unity, shown in the relationship of the themes and the employment of the principal motives in transitions, is noteworthy. It was certainly important for its time but is so heightened in Beethoven's work that we scarcely notice it in his early contemporaries.

RÖSSLER

Oskar Kaul's thematic catalogue of Rössler's symphonies[1] lists 34, which Kaul divides into three groups: up to 1780, to *c.* 1782, and to 1792. He was thus a predecessor of Beethoven not a contemporary. 23 are in four movements with minuet; twelve begin with slow introductions which are sometimes connected with the following Allegro. Ex. 42(i) shows the triadic opening of a C major Symphony dating from about 1781, (ii) the inversion of the triad in the Allegro molto:

Ex. 42

It is instructive to compare the Allegro theme with that of Beethoven's First Symphony; build and use of the 'Mannheim rocket' are similar but how feeble is Rössler's sequence by comparison with the tension of the Beethoven! In a Symphony 'in Dis' (=E flat) of 1784 the slow introduction anticipates the theme of the Allegro assai. Here we have a contrapuntal combination of two motives:

[1] *Denkmäler der Tonkunst in Bayern*, xii (1), which contains five examples.

Ex. 43

At the beginning of the Allegro the triadic motive enters in the violins, the counterpoint in the bass. This counterpoint also accompanies the second subject; note repetition, treated as a motive, plays a part in the conclusions of both first and second sections. (We may ascribe all this to Haydn's influence.) The development of a D major Symphony (1784) connects first and second themes in various ways; the coda, more extended than usual, combines two motives of the first subject with their inversion over a pedal, and dies away *pp* pizzicato. In the rondo-like Allegro scherzato last movement of the G minor Symphony of 1787 the opening motive permeates the entire movement and influences the later themes; the minor key of this finale is unusual for that period – but the movement ends *ff* in G major. (Rössler ends many movements with a dying away *p* or *pp*.) He is not particularly rich in thematic invention; his best work is probably this G minor Symphony, the opening of which:

Ex. 44

with its restlessness and immediate imitation, actually reminds one a little of Mozart's G minor. The second subject is insignificant; its second section begins with the inversion of the first theme. But the development is very lively, the upbeat fourth-motive widened as much as an octave and in this form playing an important role as an ostinato bass. The harmony is rich and varied; Rössler is fond of occasional bold turns; for instance, the exposition of the first movement of the D major Symphony ends in A and the development then begins in F sharp major. Frequent chromaticisms suggest Mozart. The motley of thematic forms disappears more and more from the later works in favour of greater unity. All Rössler's symphonies demand two violins, viola, bass, two oboes, and two horns; one of his peculiarities is the frequent divisi of violas; cello, bass, and bassoon are unisono; flutes are required in 17 symphonies, clarinets in three, trumpets and drums in 15.

PLEYEL

Pleyel's C major *Symphonie périodique*, no. 9, has already been mentioned. He was one of the most popular composers of the day and wrote symphonies by the dozen.[1] (He was Haydn's pupil and the two men were forced into factitious rivalry in London in 1792.) While the minuet is not particularly developed in any of his symphonies, he does try to strengthen the balance of the movements as a whole. For instance, in the C major Symphony the Andantino allegretto is of very considerable length; it includes an extensive flute solo written into the oboe part. Contrasting middle sections of A–B–A forms appear in Op. 30, no. 2 – Adagio amoroso (A major); Allegro assai (A minor); Tempo I (A major) – and Op. 33, no. 1: Adagio (G minor); Presto (G minor); Tempo I. These are noteworthy since the pattern was then unusual.

Thematic contrast is the principal aim in Pleyel's sonata-forms. Group repetitions, long chains of sequences, the marking off of sections by numerous fermatas are typical of his method. In the recapitulation the first theme is often shortened, even left out altogether – in which case it returns to end the movement, a practice not uncommon in Mozart also. One can hardly speak of thematic-motivic treatment in the transitions and developments; transpositions, sequences and thematic quotations play the main part. In the development of the first movement of Op. 27, no. 1, a motive from the slow introduction appears; this section is also distinguished by a new oboe melody (cued into the first violin part) which, however, merely marks the end of the development and is not to be compared either structurally or in effect with the 'episode' in the first movement of Beethoven's 'Eroica'. It is just part of the motley of thematic forms, intended to conceal the want of formal security. The frequent over-expansion of movements – three or four hundred bars are not uncommon – is unfortunate. Ex. 45 shows two transitions to the repeat of a theme in the final rondo of Op. 3, no. 1; one is involuntarily reminded of the first movement of Beethoven's Fifth – but also obliged to notice the fundamental difference:

[1] In her thematic catalogue (see p. 161, n. 1), Rita Benton lists about 40 works as real symphonies. In 'À la recherche de Pleyel perdu', *Fontes Artis Musicae* (1970), p. 11, she notes that Brook, *La Symphonie*, ii, pp. 543–8, lists 58 symphonies by Pleyel but argues that several are arrangements of other kinds of works. On Pleyel's symphonies see also Vol. VII, pp. 425–6.

Ex. 45

There is a nice abbreviation of a sequence in the development of the first movement of Op. 27, no. 1:

Ex. 46

though the effect is weakened by the constant repetition. The development of a thematic motive, as in Ex. 47 from the first movement of Op. 30, no. 2, is among the rarities:

Ex. 47

but such experiments are commoner in the middle and rondo movements than in sonata-form where it is precisely the moulding that presents difficulties; hence the increased use of the already mentioned 'syncopated attack' and empty but noisy runs and tremolos.

In his use of instruments Pleyel differs little from his contemporaries. Occasionally he adds further instruments to the normal strings and pairs of oboes and horns. Cello and bass parts are always combined though separation of roles is sometimes indicated. The above mentioned oboe melody in the development of Op. 27, no. 1, is exceptional; for the most part the wind supply harmonic support or strengthen the string melody, but when the first theme in the first movement of the C major Symphony already referred to is repeated on the oboe it is altered – a rare instance of the nature of an instrument being taken into account:

Ex. 48

The slow section of the second movement of Op. 30, no. 2, brings the theme on divisi violas but here, as in so many cases, the parallel thirds and sixths – a stereotype stylistic element of the time – become boring.

Contrapuntal formations like Rössler's are practically non-existent in Pleyel.

Nor is his harmony very varied. The reprise in the finale of the C major Symphony begins with the first theme in the subdominant; it is not until the coda that it reappears in the main key. Here too the recapitulation is shortened and inverted, thus certainly strengthening the conclusion. The development in the first movement of Op. 30, no. 2, brings lively harmonic movement, with dynamic effects; Ex. 49 shows the first violin part:

Ex. 49

This is superficially somewhat Beethovenian, but only superficially; ideas, thematic growth, instrumental interdependence are wanting. In the G major Symphony, Op. 33, no. 2, there are plenty of divagations to the minor. The development of the first movement brings in the G major theme in E minor and the second subject also appears in the minor. The above mentioned middle movement is in G minor. The main theme of the final rondo turns to G minor when it is repeated and a developing section sequences through various keys, closing to G minor, before the repeat begins in G major.

This account shows how many good beginnings one finds in these symphonies, but rarely – least of all in the sonata-form movements – do they lead to really noteworthy working out. The light-weight content, modest instrumentation, and sheer delight in sound make it easy to understand why such works dominated domestic and concert music for some time; but their inner poverty marked their inferiority to Haydn and Mozart while Beethoven's works cut the ground from under them.

FERDINAND WALDSTEIN

The only symphony by Beethoven's benefactor Count Waldstein (1762–1823) is available in a modern edition.[1] Composed between

[1] Ed. Ludwig Schiedermair, *Denkmäler rheinischer Musik*, i (Düsseldorf, 1951). Josef Heer has

1788 and 1794, it employs a large orchestra without clarinets or trombones. More than other composers Waldstein indulges in three-part writing, e.g. for two violins and viola, sometimes in unison with two wind, i.e. lacking the wind bass, as in the second subject of the first movement and the beginning of the development. The two themes of this movement show sharp contrast but there is not much working out, though Heer finds more here than in the short development proper; but it is not genuine thematic evolution – the opening theme is repeated in the bass against string syncopations and tremolo, another persistent style-mark of the time. One uncommon feature, however, particularly with the minor masters, is the interesting structure of the slow-movement theme with the grouping 5 5 2 2 4 3 2. Threefold beginning of a minor episode in the rondo:

Ex. 50

was later to become an important feature of Beethoven's style.[1]

GYROWETZ

Of the forty or more symphonies of Adalbert Gyrowetz (Vojtěch Jírovec),[2] most of them written before 1804, about half survive and there are a number of misattributions. He confessedly took Haydn's symphonies as his models and one of his works was published in Paris as Haydn's; conversely he has been credited with one of Wranitzky's and there has been confusion of his works with J. A. André's and Pleyel's. A few bars from the first movement of a Symphony in D, Op. 13, no. 1 (c. 1792) will illustrate the superficiality of his technique:

Ex. 51

discussed it in detail and shown its stylistic connections with Mozart, *Der Graf von Waldstein und sein Verhältnis zu Beethoven (Veröffentlichungen des Beethoven-Hauses in Bonn*, ix*)* (Leipzig, 1933).
[1] Paul Mies, *Die Bedeutung der Skizzen Beethovens zur Erkenntnis seines Stiles* (Leipzig, 1925), pp. 42 ff.; English translation by Doris L. Mackinnon (London, 1929), pp. 46 ff.
[2] Autobiography ed. Alfred Einstein in *Lebensläufe deutscher Musiker von ihnen selbst erzählt*, iii–iv (Leipzig, 1915).

Reprise

At first glance that looks like genuine motivic-thematic work although the material is admittedly trivial; in reality it is merely empty play with the five-quaver upbeat and the note-repetitions. And when one looks at the first movement of Op. 23, no. 1 in G (Paris, 1796) one finds the same: again sequences and repetitions, the five-quaver upbeat, note-repetitions, bits of triads and scales. It is routine, not serious work. Yet the movements are often extensive; the first movement of Op. 13, no. 1 is 314 bars long. The opening of the slow movement of the same symphony:

Ex. 52

Andante moderato

shows how in bar 5 the innocent theme is suddenly smothered in superficial ornamentation. After a restless, modulating middle section the theme is taken up again – but, strangely enough, undecorated; the ornamentation in the example had been introduced in the beginning not as an enhancement but merely for the effect of its insertion. If the 59-bar main part of the minuet is rather longer than the norm for the symphony of the period, Gyrowetz does not attempt any development. The final rondo has a lively theme over a 'bagpipe bass', common enough in symphonies of the period (e.g. Haydn's no. 82 ('L'ours')). The accumulation of the most diverse themes, the filling out of transitional passages with empty figuration, the by no means outstanding instrumentation despite the ample forces employed (with flutes, horns, and trumpets) all contributed to the oblivion that overtook Gyrowetz's symphonies – after their extraordinary early success – during the last forty years of his life despite his official position as *Hofkapellmeister* and conductor of the Court opera at Vienna until 1831.

EBERL

Anton Eberl is to this day mentioned in connection with Beethoven, thanks to the circumstance that his E flat Symphony was played at the concert in which the 'Eroica' was heard for the first time. (At least one critic preferred Eberl's.) His five symphonies – three youthful works (1783–5), the E flat (1804) and one in D minor (1805) – have been examined in detail by Franz Josef Ewens,[1] who again and again draws attention to the marks of traditional style and the influences of Haydn and, above all, of Mozart whose pupil he was. All the points already illustrated in my musical examples again show up; the slow unison openings of the Viennese School, the frequent triadic themes, the note-repetitions of the melody (not unrelated to the *parlando* of *opera buffa*), the numerous sequence-like formations, the beginning of the reprise with the second subject or a shortened form of the first, heavy leaning on melodic and rhythmic models. The fugal section in the finale of the D minor Symphony derives from Mozart's 'Jupiter'. But Ewens also draws attention to noteworthy new features. On the development of the first movement of the E flat Symphony he writes: 'Just 50 bars long, it is based essentially on the existing material and the chief theme is meaningfully simplified. Here we have a development in Beethoven's sense, the themes worked with and against each other, and apparently insignificant secondary ideas play an important role'. The minuet, despite its name, is more a scherzo in Beethoven's manner 'which goes considerably beyond the limits of the ordinary dance'. In order to give the movemant greater independence a second trio is added, something unknown to Beethoven. Here is a nice example of theme-transformation from the finale:

Ex. 53

(i) is the theme, strongly reminiscent of early classicism in its dual nature, (ii) the diminution, which in the *ff* unison of the orchestra leads to the end. It is interesting that contemporary criticism censured

[1] *Anton Eberl: Ein Beitrag zur Musikgeschichte in Wien um 1800* (Dresden, 1927), which contains a thematic catalogue. See also Robert Haas, 'Anton Eberl', *Mozart-Jahrbuch 1951* (Salzburg, 1953), p. 123, and H. C. Robbins Landon, 'Two Orchestral Works wrongly attributed to Mozart', *The Music Review*, xvii (1956), p. 29, which discusses Eberl's Symphony in C major (1785).

the orchestration, the over-use of the wind, for which Beethoven and Schubert were blamed even more. Basically it was a consequence of the increased *durchbrochene Arbeit* already spoken of (see p. 160). Eberl's harmony is particularly newfangled; he is fonder even than Mozart of chromaticism and third-relationship of keys; Ewens derives this from his acquaintance with French opera. Ex. 54 shows the opening bars of the Andante maestoso e sostenuto of the first movement of the D minor Symphony with their unisons and tutti chords, a bold juxtaposition.

Ex. 54

Ex. 55 is the corresponding introduction of the E flat Symphony, its delicate, sentimental suspensions and passing-notes anticipatory of a good deal of Spohr's chromaticism.

Ex. 55

Eberl's last two symphonies are undoubtedly significant works, which attracted both attention and praise in their day, but the incompatibility of the strong traditional elements challenging comparisons with Mozart and Haydn with the new ones foreshadowing romanticism militated against their survival.

CLEMENTI

In Italy the number of composers concerned with the development of the symphony was small. At their head stands Luigi Boccherini whose works are discussed in Vol. VII (pp. 379–81). The life-span of his younger contemporary Muzio Clementi (1752–1832), famous all over Europe as composer, piano virtuoso, conductor, and publisher, completely overlapped Beethoven's.[1] Most of his twenty or more symphonies remained unpublished during his lifetime, though two appeared as Op. 18 in London in 1787 and as Op. 44 at Offenbach (in 1800) and Paris.[2] They are scored for the 'Haydn orchestra' and are obviously modelled on his style. Very different are two of the five symphonies performed by the London Philharmonic Society, of which he was one of the founders, between 1816 and 1824 and directed by himself.[3] Contemporary criticism was divided, which is perhaps the reason why Clementi continued to revise them and finally decided against publication.[4] He was clearly aiming at a 'grand' symphonic style and added clarinets, trumpets, trombones, and drums to the normal forces. (He too was censured for over-use of the wind.) The dimensions were large; the first movement of the D major Symphony consists of 434 bars plus a 22-bar introduction. Haydn's influence shows, for instance in the finale theme with its two-part violins and vigorous syncopations:

Ex. 56

Both second and last movements, as well as the first, are in sonata-form although the finale lacks a true development. Beside simple harmony one finds very rich chromaticism, rather like Spohr's, as in the introduction:

Ex. 57

[1] See Leon Plantinga, *Clementi: His Life and Music* (London, 1977), pp. 252–6, and Alan Tyson, *Thematic Catalogue of the Works of Muzio Clementi* (Tutzing, 1967).
[2] Ed. Renato Fasano (Milan, 1961 and 1959).
[3] These two have been reconstructed, the C major rather freely, and published by Alfredo Casella from autographs and sketches, the D major in 1936, the C major in 1938 (both Milan). See Casella, 'Muzio Clementi et ses symphonies', *La Revue musicale*, xvii (1936), p. 161. More recently Pietro Spada has similarly reconstructed four other symphonies (Milan. 1978).
[4] Clive Bennett, 'Clementi as Symphonist', *Musical Times* cxx (1979), p. 207, says Clementi's non-publication of these works may be ascribed to commercial considerations – scores were difficult to sell at that time – rather than to 'any intrinsic musical doubts' he might have had.

Sometimes, as in the finale of the C major Symphony, the chromatic slides are still greater in extent. In the development of the first movement of the D major the *fausse reprise* is very effective; it brings in the D major theme on first violins and bassoon after vigorous chromatic shifts in F minor. Sequences, short-breathed successions, trivial figuration and transitions often spoil the effect; moreover the formal structure is often better than the themes. Ex. 58 is the first subject of the D major; rhythmically not unskilful, it stays in the tonic key too long to be interesting:

Ex. 58

especially as it is immediately repeated by the wind. (The wind are employed independently and treated contrapuntally, as in the minuet of the C major.)

Genuine *durchbrochene Arbeit* occurs rarely and motivic transformation is not extensive though sometimes happily conceived – as in the *sempre più animato* of the coda:

Ex. 59

A special feature of both symphonies is the incorporation of canons in all the movements. The D major has them in the first movement in the transition between the subjects (two-part), in the second part of the second subject (three-part for viola, cello, and flute, with a free contrapuntal part for violin), in the transition to the codetta, in the development (four-part), in the Larghetto cantabile (three-part) also with shorter entries, in the coda of the finale. It is similar in the C major Symphony – and in the Op. 50 piano sonatas (see pp. 330–1). Haydn's free counterpoint, developed by Beethoven by way of *durchbrochene Arbeit* and 'obbligato accompaniment', was transformed by Clementi into firm polyphonic forms, but these firm forms impede the real symphonic flow. These late symphonies are notable achievements of an artist of whom it has been rightly said that he was no genius but a talent of the first order.

GOSSEC AND MÉHUL

Despite his long life and his early popularity as a symphonic composer in Paris[1] François-Joseph Gossec was of little significance in the later development of the symphony. Most of his production was over by *c.* 1777 but in 1809 he produced a remarkable *Symphonie en dix-sept parties* in F said to show 'the assimilation of Haydn's symphonies';[2] it remains unpublished. Much more important were the two published by Etienne Henri Méhul (1763–1817) in the same year;[3] indeed 1809 may be said to be the birthdate of the revival of the French symphony. Schumann in 1838 wrote of no. 1 in G minor that it was 'solid and clever, yet not without mannerisms'[4] and went on to point out similarities between Méhul's finale and the first movement of Beethoven's Fifth Symphony – which Méhul could not then have known[5] – and between the Beethoven and Méhul scherzos. There are other stylistic connections with Beethoven. The slow introduction to the first movement of no. 2 in D:

Ex. 60

[1] On the earlier symphonies see Vol. VII, pp. 421–2.
[2] Frédéric Hellouin, *Gossec et la musique française à la fin du dix-huitième siècle* (Paris, 1903), p. 95.
[3] For a detailed study of these two works, with numerous musical examples, see Alexander L. Ringer, 'A French Symphonist at the Time of Beethoven', *Musical Quarterly*, xvii (1951), p. 543.
[4] *Gesammelte Schriften*, ed. Martin Kreisig (Leipzig, 1914), i, p. 376.
[5] See Ringer, p. 552.

reminds one of similar things in Beethoven. The themes, particularly the second subjects of the sonata movements, are often weak; but Méhul employs them and part of them, especially those of no. 1, as material for transitions. And passages like Ex. 61:

Ex. 61

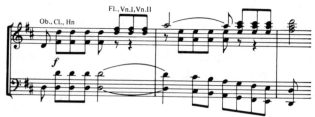

show strong leanings toward *durchbrochene Arbeit*. Here again the already mentioned note-repetitions of the Viennese School, with their rhythmic pattern, show an affinity with Beethoven's Fifth. The second theme (ii) is basically derived from the first (i), the note-repetitions being replaced by held notes:

Ex. 62

interchanged between the instruments. The development begins with the first theme in F, briefly reached from A major. The thematic work takes many shapes; themes are disintegrated; sequences are, as in Beethoven, shortened in the course of working out. The Andante is in B minor and begins with a long-held F sharp on horn and bassoon; then the theme enters with the rhythm ♩ ♫, reminding one of Beethoven's Seventh and Schubert's 'personal rhythm'.[1] Méhul's harmonic shifts:

[1] Cf. Paul Mies, *Franz Schubert* (Leipzig, 1954), p. 105.

Ex. 63

also have parallels in Schubert, and there are episodic imitations and canonic leanings. The Minuet begins with a 'curtain'-like repetition of the octave D, is as a whole not protracted, but demands a quick tempo. The finale begins with a stroke of genius; over an ostinato motive for double bass and drum a D major chord is built up and joined by the first theme, the basic motive of which is derived by augmentation from the ostinato motive:

Ex. 64

The ostinato motive plays a part in all important passages of the movement down to the *ff* ending. Here again all the episodes are developmental. The development itself is on a grand scale with fairly extensive 'pattern groups'.[1]

Much the same may be said of Méhul's G minor Symphony. The

[1] This concept of *Modellgruppen* was first advanced by Wilhelm Broehl, 'Die Durchführungs-gestaltung in Beethovens Sonatensätzen', *Neues Beethoven-Jahrbuch*, vii (1937), p. 37, but particularly pp. 43 ff.

Andante is a free variation movement on the lines of Haydn and Beethoven with contrapuntal passages and sharp dotted rhythms. The main part of the minuet is a pizzicato piece, more scherzo than minuet, while the trio is what, if it were German, one would call a *Ländler*. The Allegro agitato, like the finale of the D major Symphony, is held together by motivic permeation, e.g. Méhul's favourite anacrusic, often chromatic, strongly accented motives (Ex. 65, and also Exs. 60 and 64):

Ex. 65

CHERUBINI

The single symphony, in D,[1] of Luigi Cherubini (1760–1842) is the only one of this period that can stand beside Beethoven and Schubert. 'Terminato il 24 aprile 1815', it was performed a week later by the Philharmonic Society of London which shortly afterwards elected him a member. It employs the normal 'Haydn orchestra', plus flutes, clarinets, trumpets, and drums. The first movement begins with a Largo introduction slightly related to the ensuing Allegro. The second subject is noteworthy for a beautiful canonic section in the minor, to which a free bass line is added later after a return to the major, producing genuine three-part polyphony. The movement is marked by contrapuntal skill, motivic development, climaxes with sequence-foreshortenings, strong leanings toward *durchbrochene Arbeit*, and full use of the wind. The Larghetto cantabile is fine in workmanship and rich in variety. The Allegro assai scherzo breathes Beethoven's spirit, also in its changing rhythms, while the trio is peculiar – foreign-sounding in mood and scoring. A symphonically developed finale, beginning over an ostinato bass motive, concludes the work. The

[1] Ed. J. S. Winter (Leipzig and Vienna, 1935). In 1829 Cherubini reworked it as a string quartet in C, with a fresh slow movement.

whole – in sound, structure, and technique – often reminds one of Beethoven.

ABT VOGLER

The composers discussed up to now have been either older or only slightly younger than Beethoven. Besides these, a few composers generally reckoned among the Romantics also composed symphonies during Beethoven's lifetime. Although Vogler really belongs to the earlier group, he is mentioned at this point on account of his romantic connections. James Simon[1] detected both classic and romantic traits in his so-called 'Paris symphony' of 1782. He describes the contemplative Andante with its cheerful Haydnish melodies as classical; likewise the 'pedantic' minuet and the employment of motives from Mozart's Violin Sonata, K.304, in the first movement. But the key-schemes are romantic. The passionate, impetuous theme of the first movement is in D minor, the second subject in C major, while the exposition closes in A minor. And in the recapitulation the second subject appears in F major instead of D major. The second theme of the D minor finale turns into E major. A certain celebrity was enjoyed by a C major symphony of 1799, particularly after it was converted into a partly choral 'Bayerische Nationalsinfonie' in 1806. A brief description will suffice to show why it failed to achieve lasting success. The opening theme is one of those which are immediately repeated a tone higher, but unlike Beethoven's First it is made to sound short-winded by fermatas:

Ex. 66

Throughout the movement the chorus sing:

[1] *Abt Voglers kompositorisches Wirken mit besonderer Berücksichtung der romantischen Momente* (Berlin, 1904).

Ex. 67

Ich bin ein Bay - er, ein — Bay - er bin ich!

(I'm a Bavarian, a Bavarian am I)

a striking innovation, for Peter von Winter's 'Battle Symphony' was still to come. There are many interesting contrapuntal and harmonic details but the material is too commonplace. The second movement, an Andante in 6/4 time, consists of variations on the fifteenth-century Christmas song 'Joseph, lieber Joseph mein', perhaps an allusion in rather bad taste to the name of the new Bavarian king, Maximilian Joseph. But the accompanying and variation figures are mostly trivial and empty; the opening of the *minore* variation may serve as an example of Vogler's harmony:

Ex. 68

He endeavours to give the repeat of Minuet II heightened significance by varying it slightly, but to little effect. The *fugierte Final: die Skala* – a polyphonic treatment of the C major scale, with inversion, stretto, augmentation, dismemberment, and combination with a second theme – was no doubt suggested by Mozart's 'Jupiter'. But the astonishing thing in that is not so much the combination of the four themes but the fact that Mozart was able to build such a diversified masterpiece on such simple bases. And this is what Vogler could not do; his polyphony remains superficial and unvaried. However, Vogler's symphony well illustrates the interweaving of a number of period tendencies.

WEBER

In 1807 Vogler's pupil Weber wrote two symphonies in C major for the orchestra of Prince Eugen of Wurtemberg at Karlsruhe.[1] The constitution of the orchestra accounts for the absence of clarinets and the preference for oboe and horn for solos. Weber had studied Haydn and Beethoven to good purpose. The Presto scherzo of the First

[1] Miniature scores ed. Fritz Oeser (London, n.d.) and Hans Schönzeler (London, n.d.).

Symphony has some genuinely Beethovenian surprise effects, among them the *ff* trills of the unison beginning and the many changes of rhythm. The trio is given mostly to the wind; in the middle it makes a sudden movement to E major. The short minuet of the Second Symphony is in C minor; its C major trio has curious general pauses which serve to break up the eight-bar pattern but are not convincingly motivated. Weber had not yet really mastered sonata form. He wrote of the First Symphony in 1815:

God knows I would now write a good deal of my First Symphony differently; I'm really not quite satisfied with any of it except the minuet and perhaps the Adagio. The first Allegro is a wild fantasy movement and the last could be better worked out.[1]

The Second Symphony contains a superabundance of thematic material which is not properly welded; there are certainly not so many group repetitions and sequences as in the First, but many fermate which disturb the flow. Characteristic for the future composer of *Freischütz* are the numerous effective instrumental entries; the scherzo of no. 1 has already been mentioned; the Andante begins with brass chords. The viola solo of the Adagio of no. 2 is heralded by sustained horn-octaves. In the finale of no. 1 Weber employs the double tone-colour of the open and stopped *d* on the violins. The numerous dotted rhythms – in the first movement of no. 1 and the first and last of no. 2 – are characteristic of a master of the polonaise. It is interesting how the cello theme of the Andante of the First Symphony reminds one of bars 5ff of the first theme of the first movement. The second theme of this 'wild fantasy' movement is in B minor and has something exotic in melody, rhythm, and harmony, but its entry is over-prepared by the preceding fermata and two bars of accompaniment; the motives of the first theme are well worked out. A few bars from the finale of the symphony will show how Weber's use of the wind produces a texture suggesting *durchbrochene Arbeit*:

Ex. 69

[1] Friedrich Wilhelm Jähns, *Carl Maria von Weber* (Berlin, 1871), p. 65.

Altogether these two symphonies of 1807 include much that was new and forward-looking, though as wholes their structure is insecure. Weber never essayed the symphony again.

SPOHR'S EARLY SYMPHONIES

Two of Spohr's symphonies were composed during Beethoven's lifetime – no. 1 in E flat (1811) and no. 2 in D minor (1820) – and the Third, in C minor (1828), soon after his death. After that, Spohr turned more and more to the 'programme symphony'.[1] The D minor Symphony was written for the London Philharmonic Society and the rehearsal and first performance on 10 April 1820 were historic occasions, for Spohr, instead of conducting from the piano as expected, took the score from Ries who was at the piano, placed a desk in front of the orchestra, 'drew from his pocket a baton, and started to direct proceedings in the way to which he had been accustomed in Germany.'[2] This was more than an outward change. Symphonies like Dittersdorf's, Pleyel's, and the rest could be conducted from the keyboard and the first violin part, even when no written scores were available; this was also true of many of Haydn's and Mozart's symphonies, the scores of which were soon printed. (On the printing of Beethoven's scores see above, pp. 158–9.) But Beethoven's works – and Weber's and Spohr's – owing to their structure could no longer be satisfactorily directed from piano and violin; they needed a single responsible conductor although even Spohr's early works did not appear in score.

The D minor Symphony is scored for the normal orchestra with clarinets, trumpets, and drums. The influence of Beethoven is most apparent in the Presto scherzo third movement; after the repeat of the scherzo, Trio I is repeated with heavier scoring as Trio II; the

[1] See Vol. IX, and H. Heussner, *Die Symphonien Ludwig Spohrs* (Diss., Marburg, 1956).
[2] Percy A. Scholes, *The Mirror of Music 1844–1944* (London, 1947), i, p. 373. Spohr was wrong, however, in claiming that 'the victory of the baton was decided and from then on no one sat at the piano for symphonies and overtures' (*Selbstbiographie*, ii (Kassel and Göttingen, 1861), p. 88). The practice lingered on for some years.

movement is rounded off by a shortened version of the main part by way of coda (see Ex. 71 below). Distinct codas appear in all the movements. The tendency to thematic unity points to Beethoven's Fifth. Thus the first movement begins with a sort of fanfare and a rising scale as 'curtain', which is followed by the true first subject. Both, separated or simultaneously, play the leading role in what follows. The short cantabile second theme appears only once in the exposition; it is marked by the picturesque rhythm of the accompaniment and by the key of A flat; in the development it is counterpointed with fragments of the first theme, but since the themes are not particularly fertile and the rhythms, as so often with Spohr, rather flaccid, 'thematic unity' has disadvantages. The finale also has a short introduction in quick tempo, which is referred to at the outset of the development. Chromaticism and harmony achieve great richness – though occasionally weakness – as at the beginning of the slow movement:

Ex. 70

The Beethovenian threefold start of the theme and the sharp dotted rhythms are notable. And the way in which the originally diatonic scherzo theme becomes more and more chromatic in the course of development is characteristic:

Ex. 71

In the exposition of the first movement the themes are in D minor and, as already mentioned, in A flat major, in the recapitulation in D major and F major; the movement ends in the minor. Development and development-like episodes modulate strongly and chromatically. The wind are much employed soloistically, less in the sense of 'thematic work'. As a whole the symphony is a respectable composition but the material is sometimes insignificant and not developed enough for the length.

COMPOSERS IN THE PERIPHERAL LANDS

Beside the craftsmen of the symphony discussed above, one should perhaps mention the Saxon Friedrich Schneider (1786–1853) who produced 23 symphonies and the Czech Leopold Kozeluch (Koželuh) (1752–1818) who left about thirty; the very quantity of their output indicates that it belonged to an earlier type. Another Czech, Antonìn Reicha (1770–1836), settled in Paris and there composed four symphonies during 1808–11, thus contributing to the already mentioned rebirth of the symphony in France. But the most remarkable Czech symphony of the period was the D major (1823) of Jan Hugo Vořišek (Worzischek) (1791–1825).[1] The first movement of this virile, well constructed work is held together by the opening motive (i) which is inverted to provide the bass for the first tutti, woven into the accompaniment of the second subject (ii), and (inverted again) opens the development (iii):

[1] Ed. Jan Racek and František Bartoš, *Musica Antiqua Bohemica*, xxxiv (Prague, 1957).

Ex. 72

In the slow movement occur passages of genuine *durchbrochene Arbeit*:

Ex. 73

Indeed the influence of Beethoven is perceptible on many pages of the Symphony, though passages of the scherzo have a distinctly Czech flavour.[1] Homespun symphonies with occasional traces of national flavour had been composed in Poland during the latter half of the eighteenth century,[2] but the earliest Polish symphonist to attract attention outside his own country was the Silesian-born Józef Elsner (1769–1854). In the last two of his eight symphonies – C major, Op. 11 (Offenbach, 1805), and B flat, Op. 17 (Leipzig, c. 1818) – Elsner 'tried to combine the rhythm of the minuet with the rhythm of the mazurka',[3] as in the trio of the minuet of the C major Symphony (i), and employed the krakowiak for the finale of the same work (ii):

Ex. 74

---

[1] Vořišek never moved farther than Vienna, but a fellow-townsman of an earlier generation – both were born at Vamberk in north-eastern Bohemia – Arnošt Vančura (Ernest Wanzura) (c. 1750–1802) went to Russia and concocted extremely amateurish 'Russian', 'Ukrainian', 'Polish', and other national symphonies from folk-tunes during the 1790s.

[2] See Gerald Abraham, 'Some Eighteenth-Century Polish Symphonies' in *Studies in Eighteenth-Century Music*, ed. H. C. Robbins Landon and Roger E. Chapman (London, 1970), p. 13.

[3] Alina Nowak-Romanowicz, *Józef Elsner* (Cracow, 1957), p. 49.

Composers in the peripheral countries – Pehr Frigel (1750–1842) in Sweden, whose B flat Symphony dates from 1805, and Juan de Arriaga (1806–26) in Spain – usually failed to find publishers. The Portuguese João Domingos Bomtempo (1775–1842) was more fortunate, for the first of his six symphonies[1] was published by Clementi in a piano-duet arrangement in London on his arrival there in 1810. But neither Clementi nor any other publisher printed the five symphonies of Samuel Wesley (1766–1837); two in D, one in E flat and one in A (1781–4) and a later one in B flat (1802). The earlier ones, pleasant lightweight works in the manner of J. C. Bach, are scored for strings and horns only;[2] the B flat adds pairs of flutes and oboes, and a bassoon, and has a more individual finale.

ORCHESTRAL FANTASIAS AND PROGRAMME MUSIC

Among the symphonies of Beethoven's contemporaries only the works of one master, Franz Schubert (1797–1828), have survived although Schubert's two masterpieces remained unknown for years after his death. But before turning to these, two subordinate forms of classical symphonism must be considered briefly. In the early part of the century the orchestral fantasia made its appearance. Karl Emil Franz von Schafhäutl[3] in his catalogue of Vogler's works includes a D minor *Phantasie* as no. 118a, and Haydn's pupil Neukomm published three (Leipzig, 1809, *c*. 1810, and 1821).[4] Kretzschmar[5] describes Neukomm's D major *Phantasie* as 'a two-movement composition in which the concertante element is well to the fore' and adds that it was still popular in the 1830s. Beethoven's *Chorphantasie*, Op. 80, belongs to this category.

Programme music played a modest role in the classical period; the difference from the romantic age lay not so much in the number of works as in the fact that they were considered to belong to an inferior category whereas the later nineteenth century tended to take the opposite view. Dittersdorf's programme symphonies have been described in Vol. VII, p. 402, and Adolf Sandberger[6] has discussed the historical antecedents of Beethoven's 'Pastoral' Symphony,

---

[1] Ed. Filipe de Sousa, *Portugaliae Musica*, Série B, viii (Lisbon, 1963).

[2] Nos. 2 in D and 5 in A, ed. Richard Platt (London, 1976 and 1974).

[3] *Abt Vogler: Sein Leben, Charakter und Musikalisches System* (Augsburg, 1888).

[4] See Rudolph Angermüller, *Sigismund Neukomm: Werkverzeichnis, Autobiographie, Beziehungen zu seiner Zeitgenossen* (Munich, 1977).

[5] Op. cit., p. 285. In 1818 – at Rio de Janeiro – Neukomm composed a symphony 'Héroïque' dedicated to Spontini, into the finale of which he worked Handel's 'See the conqu'ring hero comes'.

[6] *Ausgewählte Aufsätze zur Musikgeschichte*, ii (Munich, 1924), p. 154, particularly pp. 190 ff. on Knecht.

particularly the *Portrait musical de la Nature ou Grande Simphonie* (Speyer, 1784) of Justin Heinrich Knecht (1752–1817) which Beethoven may have known. Two even less known works may be mentioned since they help to put in the right perspective Beethoven's *Schlacht von Vittoria*, Op. 91. One is *La Bataille*, a symphony for strings, pairs of flutes, oboes and horns, trumpet, and drums, Op. 11 (Offenbach, 1794), by Franz Neubauer (1760–95).[1] This 'Bataille de Martinesti à la gloire de S. A. Msgr. de Saxe Cobourg' was so popular that it appeared in several editions. It is in seven movements, the first of which depicts the morning; semiquaver and demisemiquaver figures in the wood-wind suggest the morning breeze, flute trills bird-calls. The reveille is a rather paltry trumpet fanfare. The third movement brings the 'Address to the warriors', in which the bass part includes a stave marked 'bassoon solo' while the basses play pizzicato. This is no doubt the 'Address' of the programme; it may be suited to the bassoon but two brief quotations:

Ex. 75

will show that the effect is comic rather than an incitement to battle. Next comes an Allegretto as the troops draw up in battle-order, a hopelessly trivial march in which two alternating combinations suggest the opposing armies. The fifth movement, a two-part form, depicts the battle with runs, tremolos, accents; the trumpet plays a D major chord, and the drum breaks in from time to time with rolls and offbeat strokes; there is nothing of symphonic development. The sixth movement is the return to camp, naturally in march form, and the last is the victory celebration. There is no suggestion of solemnity and grandeur; march-like melody predominates and the constantly recurring ♫ ♫ or occasional ♩♩♩ ♩♩♩ rhythm has no effect of development but only makes the music more monotonous.

[1] See Richard Dale Sjoerdsma, *The Instrumental Works of Franz Christoph Neubauer (1760–95)* (Diss, Ohio State, 1970), which includes a thematic catalogue.

Wranitzky's[1] *Grande Sinfonie caractéristique pour la paix avec la République françoise*, Op. 31 (Augsburg, 1797) is not much better. Again there is a detailed programme. The first movement depicts the Revolution in sonata-form, with an 'English march' on the woodwind after the first theme of the exposition and a 'March of the Allies' for strings, oboes, and bassoons; there is no thematic development but an abundance of runs, excited syncopations, and so on. The second movement presents 'The fate and death of Louis XVI' in a sigh-filled Adagio affettuoso played by muted strings and a funeral march without violins; there is a constant striving to use the instruments characteristically; a clarinet melody in the first part certainly has a programmatic significance that we can no longer recognize. The next movement juxtaposes the two marches and represents the 'Tumult of a battle' with many syncopations, rolls, runs, and tremolos. This is followed by 'The Peace negotiations', an Andante grazioso in 6/8:

Ex. 76

The change of barring in bar 5 is a rarity for the period. The melody is played first in thirds, from bar 2 in triple octaves on flutes, strings, and bassoon. The last movement, 'Rejoicing on the Conclusion of Peace', is again a sonata-movement with interpolated fanfares. The themes are insignificant; the development at least juxtaposes them and introduces some modulations. One has only to compare Beethoven's Op. 91 with its clear shape, the varying of the marches, the off-beat strokes of the bass drum, with such pieces as Wranitzky's, Neubauer's, Peter von Winter's (with five orchestras and final chorus) to recognize how high he towers above all his contemporaries even in this type of composition.

It remains to consider Schubert's works – or, as he put it himself in his letter of 31 March, 1824, to Leopold Kupelwieser, his 'way to the great symphony'. Schubert was certainly a contemporary of Beethoven; equally certainly he did not belong to the same generation; the peculiar connection of the two masters has often been falsely represented. The following table gives a general view:

[1] See Milan Poštolka, 'Thematisches Verzeichnis der Sinfonien Pavel Vranickýs', *Miscellanea Musicologica*, xx (Prague, 1967), p. 101.

Number and key	Composition, 1st Perf. and 1st Ed.	First Movement Tempo and no. of bars	Second Movement
1. D major	1813 1813?, 1881 1884	Adagio (20) Allegro vivace (535)	Andante (126)
2. B flat major	1814–15 1815?, 1877 1884	Largo (10) Allegro vivace (608)	Andante (122)
3. D major	1815 1815?, 1860 (last movt.) 1881 (1st full perf.) 1884	Adagio maestoso (18) Allegro con brio (204)	Allegretto (124)
4. Tragic† C minor	1816 1816?, 1849 1884	Adagio molto (29) Allegro vivace (267)	Andante (271)
5. B flat major	1816 1816?, 1841 1885	Allegro (299)	Andante con moto (141)
6. 'little' C major	1817–18 1818?, 1828 1895	Adagio (30) Allegro (361)	Andante (134)
7. E major	1821 unpublished‡	Adagio (39) Allegro (367)	Andante (116)
8. 'Unfinished' B minor	1822 1865 1866	Allegro moderato (348)	Andante con moto (312)
9. 'Great' C major	1825? 1839 shortened 1840 parts 1849 score	Andante (77) Allegro ma non troppo (607)	Andante con moto (380)

* N = Strings plus pairs of flutes, oboes, clarinets, bassoons, horns, trumpets, and timpani.
† So called by the composer.

SCHUBERT'S SYMPHONIES

Schubert's symphonies, in fact almost all his instrumental compositions, had to overcome two kinds of difficulties: external with regard
to the impression they made and their dissemination; internal with
evolution and composition. The external are shown in the table.[1] Only

[1] Otto Erich Deutsch and Donald R. Wakeling. *Schubert: Thematic Catalogue of All His works
in Chronological Order* (London, 1951), revised and expanded as *Franz Schubert. Thematisches
Verzeichnis seiner Werke in Chronologischer Folge*, ed. Walter Dürr, Arnold Feil, and Christa
Landon (Kassel, 1978). The latter re-numbers Schubert's last symphonies, so that the sketched
Symphony in E has no number, the 'Unfinished' is now no. 7, and the 'Great' is no. 8.

Third Movement	Fourth Movement	Instrumentation*
Allegro (62) Trio (33)	Allegro vivace (366)	N less 1 flute
Allegro vivace (44) Trio (24)	Presto (727)	N
Menuetto: Vivace (56) Trio (28)	Presto. Vivace (420)	N
Menuetto: Allegro vivace (54) Trio (32)	Allegro (434)	N
Menuetto: Allegro molto (88) Trio (40)	Allegro vivace (394)	N less 1 flute; no trumpets or drums
Scherzo: Presto (178) Più lento (180)	Allegro moderato (575)	N
Scherzo: Allegro (122) Trio (70)	Allegro giusto (620)	N + 3 trombones
Allegro (112)§ Trio (16, not completed)	—	N + 3 trombones
Scherzo: Allegro vivace (238) Trio (166)	Allegro vivace (1155)	N + 3 trombones

‡ Sketch of the whole symphony.
§ Third movement only in sketch.

one of them, the Sixth was – in the year of Schubert's death – given in a real public concert, though Otto Biba[1] has shown that contemporary performance materials for nos. 1, 2, 3, 5, and 6 are preserved in the archives of the Gesellschaft der Musikfreunde and 'we are quite safe in assuming that Schubert heard' the great C major 'in an orchestral rehearsal'. The question-marks in the table indicate performances either at the Imperial choir-school, the *Konvikt*, or by his father's enlarged domestic orchestra. None was published during his lifetime; most of them appeared first toward the end of the century in the

[1] 'Schubert's Position in Viennese Musical Life', *19th Century Music*, iii (1979), p. 108.

Kritische Gesamtausgabe.[1] Schubert himself did not wish the earlier ones to be performed, for in a letter dating presumably from early 1823 he wrote:

Since I really have nothing for full orchestra which I could send out into the world with a clear conscience ... I must ask you to forgive my inability to oblige you, since it would be detrimental for me to appear with anything mediocre.

This shows clearly that he regarded the early symphonies as studies, trials, sketches; he did not, like Beethoven, sketch the details but used for the same purpose whole works which he left in very different stages of completion when they had served their purpose. Insufficient attention to this fact has led to many false conclusions in the Schubert literature. Parallels have been drawn between his early symphonies and Beethoven's, regardless of the fact that he wrote them as a youth and student – the 'Unfinished' at the age of twenty-five and the great C major at the age when Beethoven composed his first two. Comparing the youthful symphonies with the works of the minor masters discussed earlier in this chapter, one recognizes how much is further developed or new in Schubert. Beethoven's influence on Schubert is clear and perfectly natural. To whom else should he turn – particularly in Vienna? As a boy he had confided to his friend Spaun, 'Secretly I hope I may be able to make something of myself, but who can do anything more after Beethoven?',[2] evidence of his awareness of Beethoven's uniqueness and proof of his own self-criticism. He studied Beethoven's works closely, sometimes transcribing. The title 'Tragic' given to his Fourth Symphony was no doubt suggested by Beethoven's C minor; Ex. 77 shows the relationship of the first theme of the Allegro vivace to that of Beethoven's C minor Quartet, Op. 18, no. 4.

Ex. 77

(i) SCHUBERT

(ii) BEETHOVEN

[1] Ed. Eusebius Mandyczewski *et al.* (Leipzig, 1884–97).
[2] Otto Erich Deutsch, *Schubert: die Erinnerungen seiner Freunde* (Leipzig, 1957), p. 109; trans. Rosamund Ley and John Nowell as *Schubert: Memoirs by his Friends* (London, 1958).

But there were also very different influences; the tarantella-like passage beginning at bar 128 of the finale of the Sixth Symphony is only one of a number of evidences of Schubert's infection by the Viennese Rossini-mania of the period.

SCHUBERT AND BEETHOVEN

This is not the place to trace Schubert's path in detail;[1] one might call it 'the path right through Beethoven'. But a few points may be made. If one compares the number of bars in the first movements one finds the first two symphonies are the most extensive; there is a marked retrogression in the following ones and a return to the earlier proportions only in the great C major. I have shown in the previous chapter on Beethoven's symphonies that bar-reckoning is not merely something superficial but has stylistic significance, and I hope to show why a certain breadth – what Schumann called 'heavenly length' in the case of the C major Symphony – was necessary for Schubert's style. The youth of the First and Second Symphonies wrote untroubled. What he could learn at first from Beethoven, such things as *durchbrochen* and thematic work, 'obbligato accompaniment', he learned quickly; other things, like thematic invention, harmonic expansion, the treatment of instruments, feeling for tone-colour, rhythm, came to him by nature; he needed only to cultivate them systematically. The compression of Beethoven's utterance, its density, manner of development and shaping, must have seemed to him worthy of imitation; yet in many ways they ran counter to his individuality and his thematic invention. So he forced his themes into Beethovenian forms, as the symphonies from the Third to the 'Unfinished' clearly show. The inward coming to grips with Beethoven benefited him but also obstructed him. He was well aware of this: hence the letter of 1823 quoted above; hence his remark of 1824 that through the composition of a couple of quartets and the Octet he wanted to get on the right 'way to the great symphony'.

Ex. 77 not only shows a relationship between Beethoven and Schubert but at the same time gives an idea of the difference in their ways of shaping a theme, and it is this which conditions the whole form – unless one regards 'form' as mere mould or scaffolding. Key, metre, dynamics, tempo, the threefold attack, even the individual

[1] So far as the first movements of the symphonies are concerned, this has been done by Hans Joachim Therstappen in *Die Entwicklung der Form bei Schubert* (Leipzig, 1931).

motives, are common to both. But how different is their sense! Beethoven's theme unfolds itself quickly and never returns to its beginning but goes on to the transition. Schubert's is extended and returns firmly to the note C. It is, like most of Schubert's themes, rounded off, self-contained. All parts of the movement show the same tendency; everything therefore is spacious. Consider the great groups of 20 and 16 bars, again articulated in themselves, which begin the development in the finale of the Second Symphony. Great harmonic spaces are thus covered by the simple throb of the personal rhythm

. Schubert's themes and fashioning run counter in some ways to the concept of thematic working; they do not lend themselves to fragmentation as readily as Haydn's and Beethoven's. In Schubert's conception the groups occasionally stretch out beyond the audible part; thus the finale of No. 6 ends with three silent bars. All these spacious themes and sections have to be dovetailed and made to flow into a whole. That was the difficulty of form for Schubert. Thus the slow introduction became for him the determinative constituent part of the whole movement. Already in the first movement of the First Symphony it is employed in the Allegro vivace – in the necessary augmentation – to end the development, i.e. as introduction to the recapitulation. Only in the first movements of No. 5 and the 'Unfinished' does it seem to be missing, merely a curtain. In No. 5 it is merely four bars long yet it plays an important role in the development; in the B minor it is the 'solo' of the basses. Hence all the intermediate parts take on developmental character; hence also the extended sections of the form are separated by pauses or 'suspense bars' which may be purely rhythmic, chordal, or accompanimental anticipations before themes. The difficulties mostly concern the first movements. The table on pp. 194–5 shows how the dimensions of the final movements remain rather more stable, while the third movements grow. With Beethoven too the fine motivic-thematic work in connection with his dramatic sonata-form is more pronounced in the first movements than in the finales. It is wrong to judge Schubert's works by Beethoven's forms when he had not yet clearly distinguished his own form principles, when themes and forms are often at variance. Outwardly Schubert was no revolutionary; all his symphonies are in four movements with the fast middle movement placed third. He soon turned from the slow minuet, even when, as in the Third, Fourth, and Fifth Symphonies, he retains the title; the *menuetto* of no. 5 is marked 'Allegro molto'; this type of scherzo reaches its culmination in the great C major. For the trios he had no prototype, hence nothing to surpass.

SCHUBERT'S FIFTH SYMPHONY

Considering Schubert's symphonic output as a whole, it is obvious that in three works – the Fifth, the 'Unfinished', and the C major – he achieved heights not only among his own compositions but in the whole symphonic literature. The Fifth shows by its instrumentation (without drums and trumpets) and purpose (performance by his father's orchestra) that even in his symphonies he did not eschew domestic music. And there is hardly any work since Haydn's days that so perfectly answers to the conditions of this kind of domestic music. In this respect it must be compared with the works of Pleyel, Gyrowetz, and their contemporaries, whereas from the first Beethoven's symphonies are concert music – though mainly for the orchestras of the nobility. All the movements of the Fifth are short yet show Schubert's peculiarities. The four-bar 'curtain' consists of two elements: the woodwind cadence and the sparkling run of the violins down into the theme. Parts of this quaver run mix into the theme itself and when the theme is repeated the flute takes it up to fill out the pauses – a light-handed application of *durchbrochene Arbeit*. The development begins with a four times repeated 'block' consisting of the quaver run and the rhythmically altered first motive of the first subject; the key sequence D flat–B flat minor–G flat–E flat minor exploits third-relationship boldly but gracefully. In almost every bar one could demonstrate the agreement of form and content. As so often with Schubert, the recapitulation begins in the subdominant instead of the tonic, allegedly a device to avoid the composition of new transitions though this is a strange charge to bring against perhaps the mostly richly inventive composer of all time. Actually the emergence from the subdominant expresses a different sound-purpose, a different sound-feeling. Each key corresponds to a new sound, hence the juxtaposition of so many groups in different keys in the developments and transitions, in which Schubert sometimes almost approaches impressionistic sound-concepts. The other movements of the Fifth Symphony also contain many beauties. Thus in the Andante the immediate following of E flat major by F flat major in bar 24, and the ensuing interplay of violins with oboe and bassoon, and again the dying fall of the end of the movement. The opening motive of the Menuetto has something of Haydn's minuets but is widely differentiated by the fast tempo; the trio is a lively waltz. The development section of the last movement has particularly charming interchanges between strings and wind. The freshness and simplicity of the Symphony, despite all the art concealed in it, have understandably made it a favourite.

THE 'UNFINISHED'

Yet it is understandable that of all Schubert's symphonies the most loved and most performed is the 'Unfinished'. One might put it that here Schubert's peculiar idiom is most perfectly compatible with Beethoven's formal dimensions, which were accepted as the norm. The classical slow introduction has here become a mysterious solo for the basses; the first theme is brought in with its accompaniment. Just as the 'curtain' corresponds to the sound of the basses, so does the first subject to that of oboe and clarinet, the second to that of the cellos; each theme is an individual, born out of the sound of the instrument. 'Curtain' and second theme are rounded off in the way already described (p. 198); they return to the opening note. The development splits up the themes but not in such small particles as Haydn and Beethoven do; that would be foreign to their character. But the working out is nevertheless stronger, more dramatic than is usual with him; it is remarkable what becomes of the original unison bass and how the syncopated accompaniment of the second subject comes into its own between the plunging *ff dim.* tuttis in C sharp minor, D minor, and E minor. The end brings back the theme of the introduction, thus closing the ring.

One passage in the Andante shows how consciously Schubert proceeded with harmonic turns which afterwards have such a surprising and convincing effect. The B minor Symphony is the only one for which we have an extant piano sketch.[1] This piano sketch shows the motive over the harmonic change D flat–A flat before C sharp minor only once:

Ex. 78

whereas in the finished score it occurs three times, interchanged between oboe and flute. The re-interpretation of D flat as C sharp is of course one of the numerous enharmonic changes which stamp Schubert as one of the boldest harmonists of classicism and romanticism. As a result of the repetition the predominant key is

[1] Published with the facsimile of the full score (Munich, 1924). A newer facsimile edition, which includes the first 11 bars of the abandoned scherzo (discovered by Christa Landon in Vienna in 1969), was issued as vol. iii (Munich–Salzburg, 1978) of the *Publikation der Sammlung der Gesellschaft der Musikfreunde in Wien*. A series of sketches for three incomplete symphonies (D.615, D.708A, D.936A), ed. Ernst Hilmar, has been issued in facsimile of the autographs (Kassel, 1978). On Schubert's use of sketches see L. Michael Griffel, 'A Reappraisal of Schubert's Methods of Composition', *The Musical Quarterly*, lxiii (1977), p. 186, and John Reed, 'How the "Great" C Major was Written', *Music & Letters*, lvi (1975), p. 18.

clearly underlined, the enharmonic effect strengthened. One thus gets the impression that latent in the frequent repetition of phrases in Schubert's instrumental music is the significance of harmonic intensification. Shortly before the end of the movement, G sharp in the falling E major chord-line is re-interpreted as A flat, and the key of A flat duly enters. But originally Schubert had, after four bars, made the reverse re-interpretation. To lessen the harmonic disturbance he inserted in the margin of the piano sketch the bars bracketed here:

Ex. 79

By substituting C flat for C natural, he made possible the double re-interpretation

A flat/G sharp
C flat/B.

Schubert's careful consideration is obvious and also the fact that the harmonic boldness, which in his songs is often motivated by the text, is here born out of the spirit of instrumental music. Examination of Schubert's harmony cannot be taken further here but it should be noted that, despite its boldness, chromaticism and use of enharmonic devices it never quite approaches Méhul's block-shifts (e.g. Ex. 63) or the insipid chromaticism noticeable in Clementi which becomes mannerism in Spohr.

The two-movement condition of the Symphony has given rise to much debate. T. C. L. Pritchard suggested in 1942[1] that Schubert had actually completed a four-movement work and that part of it had been lost by the notoriously careless – and seemingly not altogether honest – Hüttenbrenner brothers to whom he had entrusted the manuscript. The piano sketch includes the first part of the third movement complete and the opening of the trio, and it has been argued[2] that the first entr'acte of the incidental music to *Rosamunde* may have been

[1] 'The Unfinished Symphony', *The Music Review*, iii (1942), p. 10.
[2] Gerald Abraham, preface to *Scherzo in B minor for the 'Unfinished' Symphony* (London, 1971).

originally conceived as the last movement. The identity of key and certain stylistic similarities with the first movement could point to this. Schubert had to prepare the incidental music in a great hurry; he took as overture the one already written for *Alfonso und Estrella* (see p. 518) and could have taken the finale of the B minor Symphony as an entr'acte.

Here we must glance briefly at Schubert's numerous overtures. Some do not belong to dramatic works, e.g. the two 'Im italienischen Stil' of 1817 and the E minor of 1819. The first two are said to have been his reaction to friends' over-praise of Rossini's overtures, which provoked him to declare he could 'do that sort of thing with the greatest ease' at any time. One of them – it is not certain which – was the first major work of Schubert to be given a public performance in Vienna (1 March 1818). But Schubert's overtures show quite a different style from that of the first and last movements of his symphonies; for instance all the symphonic first movements and most of the finales repeat the exposition whereas the overtures never do. A number of features of the *Rosamunde* entr'acte – the many unisons, the strong dynamic contrasts, the non-repeat of the exposition – suggest the overture style. The relatively slow tempo marking, Allegro molto moderato, differentiates it from the other symphonic finales. Schubert may have originally thought of using it as the overture to *Rosamunde*, whence the relationship to the overture style. But something of the B minor key remained in his mind so that certain stylistic relationships with the Symphony crept into it.

Why, then, did he not complete the Symphony? For the answer we may turn to the sketch of the E major Symphony of 1821. This stood, at any rate in Schubert's mind, complete. 165 pages contain all the requisites for a complete score, though only twenty are fully orchestrated. For the most part only the most obviously important musical happenings are notated in one line, directly for the requisite instrument in the right position in the score with all directions for dynamics and phrasing. And this from first to last bar of an extensive work. From it we can judge the unusual concentration of the act of composition. The whole work was completed; Schubert only needed to fill it out as it stood in his mind. This is something basically different from Beethoven's joining and interlacing of sketches. But Mozart, too, wrote first only the main parts including the bass and filled out later.[1] It is this concentrated, uninterruptedly progressing work which explains the unusual unity of a Schubert composition as a whole. When this sense of unity was disturbed, e.g. through interruption of

[1] Walter Gerstenberg, 'Zum Autograph des Klavierkonzerts KV.503 (C-dur)', *Mozart–Jahrbuch 1953*, p. 38.

work, Schubert had difficulty in recapturing it – another difference from Beethoven who could work on several compositions at the same time. Only Schubert's A flat Mass was begun in 1819 and not finished till 1822. Otherwise he would leave compositions on one side when they had served the purpose he had in mind, rather than finish them; there are plenty of such torsos. For some reason he lost the sense of unity while composing the B minor Symphony and for a hundred years now we have seen the fragment as a consummate masterpiece equal to the finest works of our great masters. But Schubert did not see it so. In 1823 he described his earlier orchestral works as 'mediocre'; in 1824 he talked of making his 'way to the great symphony'. The B minor was not that; he had learned from it what he wanted to learn, so the labour of completing it was unnecessary.[1]

THE GREAT C MAJOR

He reached his ideal in the symphony which we must now date to 1825 or 1826;[2] at any rate he dedicated it to the Gesellschaft der Musikfreunde in October 1826. But it was not understood, thanks to its new fashion and – for the time – very great difficulty. The peculiar elements of Schubert's style in melody, harmony, rhythm, and form are here united. In the first movement the first theme has again become slow introduction. It begins with the note C and, after touching it several times, returns to it. The same may be said of the first theme of the Allegro ma non troppo, bars 1–17, of the recurrence of the note E in the theme of the slow movement, of the trio of the scherzo. One might say that the primal element of music, the note, is intensified in an entirely new way. Note-repetition, often schematic with his contemporaries, gains life in ever new forms; it vibrates in the dreaded woodwind triplets of the first movement; it hovers in the line-drawing of the second theme; it forms the lower stratum of the accompaniment of the slow-movement theme; it begins the main theme of the scherzo; it swings bar after bar into the trio and plays a dominating role in the wide arches of the movement; sharply dotted, it opens the last movement and in long portamento notes begins its second theme. And all these details are joined seamlessly in a broad stream. The theme of the slow introduction forms the heart of the development of the first movement and rounds the movement off at the end. The development begins, after the G major close of the exposition, in

[1] Martin Chusid, 'Beethoven and the Unfinished', in *Franz Schubert: Symphony in B Minor ('Unfinished')* (New York, 1971), pp. 109–10, suggests that Schubert's growing awareness of the similarity of the 'Unfinished' to Beethoven's Symphony No. 2, and the fact that he could not remove the similarities without destroying the unity of his own symphony, prevented him from completing the work.
[2] See John Reed, 'The "Gastein" Symphony Reconsidered', *Music & Letters*, xl (1959), p. 341.

Schubert's favourite lower-third key – here A flat – with the G up-beat. This A flat is a new sound-plane. In the second group it becomes A and swings back to A flat before falling through the dominant G into the reprise. If one takes into account the exposition-ending on the dominant, a surprising outline emerges:

Ex. 80

again an orbit about G, in small degrees each of which is treated as a new sound-plane. The effect of such a comprehension of the whole is demonstrated by an interesting alteration. The main theme of the first movement took the form of Ex. 81(i); Schubert later altered it in every place in the movement to (ii):

Ex. 81

The alteration was made, as Ernst Laaff has shown,[1] after the completion of the whole symphony. Had the constant repetition of the fourth motive struck him as too abrupt? Was the decision the result of the fact that the new interval suggested accord with the theme of the introduction? Or was it that the note C was, as it were, illuminated on two sides by the alternating approach from the G below and the D above? This is one of the sound-phenomena characteristic of Schubert. Every composer stands on the ground of his predecessors, Beethoven on Mozart's and Haydn's, Schubert on Beethoven's. But in this symphony everything that one can call influence and tradition is recast as something peculiar to Schubert. With it he created his 'great symphony'.

THE AGE OF BEETHOVEN

To sum up: Beethoven's 'contemporaries', the composers who for a number of years lived at the same time as himself, may be classified in several groups. The first, really belonging to the previous generation, may be described as pre-classicists. Some were so little able to overcome tradition that they faded out even in their lifetime, as was the case with Gossec. Some effected a perfect combination of personal style and period style which earned them great popularity but has not

[1] *Franz Schuberts Sinfonien* (Wiesbaden, 1933).

saved them from oblivion. At their head stands Boccherini. Most of them lacked the perseverance to create works of lasting value.

A second group includes Beethoven's closer contemporaries: Eberl, Méhul, Cherubini, Clementi. They have a good deal in common with Beethoven but they were unable to preserve the unity and greatness of the style of a Haydn or Mozart, and Beethoven's development was beyond them. Their works contain much that is noteworthy, yet not enough to keep them in the repertory.

Finally we have the younger generation of romantics. They had Beethoven as a model but, with one exception, were unable to go beyond him. Weber soon turned away from the symphony altogether. Spohr became more and more involved in programme-composition. Only Schubert managed at last to break free from the model and create something of his own, equal in value. Neither his influence nor Beethoven's had much effect on the romantic symphony of the immediate future. Despite the many beauties of the symphonies of Mendelssohn – who had written a competent if unoriginal Symphony in C minor in 1824, at the age of fifteen – Schumann, and Berlioz, real symphonism reappeared much later with the Schubert–worshipper Brahms, who nevertheless aimed rather at Beethovenian concentration, and Bruckner who expanded still further Schubert's swinging orbits.

V

THE CONCERTO

By JOHN A. MEYER

THE INFLUENCE OF FASHION AND TASTE

THROUGHOUT its history the solo concerto has been dependent on
and shaped by particular social and cultural forces, probably to a
greater degree than any other of the major instrumental forms. This is
particularly true of the concerto in the years between 1790 and 1830,
that period of revolution and war in Europe which saw a gradual (but
not total) collapse of the *ancien régime* and its system of patronage, the
burgeoning influence of the professional and commercial classes, the
rapid proliferation of public concerts, and the rise of the instrumental
virtuoso to a position of eminence previously reserved almost
exclusively for the operatic singer. This was an age which abounded
in brilliant performers, and many of the concerto's most characteristic
features were determined by current fashions and taste, as well as by
the structure of concert life. Of course the element of display had
never been absent from the instrumental concerto, but it now tended
to take greater priority over purely musical considerations than
hitherto; that Beethoven's Violin Concerto was scarcely a popular
success during its composer's lifetime may be attributed to its almost
complete lack of virtuosic brilliance, at least in its first two movements.
Today the concerto repertory of this period has largely disappeared
from view; from the nearly forty years separating the last of Mozart's
piano concertos (1791) and the F minor Concerto by Chopin (1829),
for example, only one concerto for piano – other than those by
Beethoven – appears with any frequency in modern concert programmes, and that is Weber's *Konzertstück*, a work which departs
radically from the conventional concerto form of the time. Such a gap
in our knowledge is somewhat surprising when it is considered that
this period, represented by such composers as Clementi, Dussek,
Field, Cramer, Hummel, Moscheles, Weber, and, of course, Beethoven
and Schubert, forms a highly significant stage in the development of
piano music, culminating in the great flowering of romantic piano

music in the work of Chopin, Schumann, Mendelssohn, and Liszt. The same is true, although perhaps to a lesser extent, of the music for other instruments – the clarinet, for instance. So although many of the concertos that were written and performed in the early nineteenth century have little lasting value in a purely artistic sense, the form was a vital medium for the development of instrumental technique. In addition, a closer examination of this corpus of music helps not only to place the great concertos of Beethoven in a new perspective, but also to trace the gradual emergence of the more familiar romantic concerto style from its source in the virtuoso concerto of the early nineteenth century.

MOZART'S LEGACY

Any account of the concerto in the age of Beethoven must inevitably take Mozart as its point of departure, for not only should the concertos of this period be examined in the light of those by the composer whose achievement in the genre is equal to that of any other, but by far the greater proportion of them adhere to the form and conventions of the classical concerto, the greatest examples of which are those by Mozart.[1] Of all the instrumental forms that flourished in the late eighteenth century, the concerto is unique in that it had already become thoroughly established during the baroque period. It is due to this earlier evolution that the form of the classical concerto is essentially different from that of the symphony, solo sonata and string quartet, all of which use sonata form in their first movements. The principles of sonata form became so pervasive in the late eighteenth century that the concerto could hardly resist absorbing them, but never at the expense of its own peculiar structure which arises from the opposition not of contrasting themes or key centres, but of contrasting sonorities. By its very nature, the ritornello structure of the baroque concerto had proved to be an excellent vehicle for expressing this essential feature of the concerto idea, and instead of dispensing with it, the composers of the classical period simply modified the ritornello pattern by combining with it the main principles of sonata form. As seen in the concertos of Mozart and his contemporaries, therefore, the classical form consists of a basic alternation of four ritornellos and three solo sections, the latter normally corresponding to the exposition, development, and recapitulation of sonata form.[2] This structure is apparent in most concertos

[1] On Mozart's concertos see Vol. VII, pp. 487 ff.

[2] For a discussion of contemporary descriptions of concerto form, see Jane R. Stevens, 'An 18th-Century Description of Concerto First-Movement Form', *Journal of the American Musicological Society*, xxiv (1971), p. 85, and 'Theme, Harmony and Texture in Classic-Romantic Descriptions of Concerto First-Movement Form', ibid, xxvii (1974), p. 25.

until at least the 1830s, even though within the basic plan there is often considerable variety of detail (but never so much as in the concertos of Mozart himself).

Despite the outward structural complexity of Mozart's concertos, they possess a marked degree of flexibility and freedom, exemplified by such fantasy-like development sections as those of K.414 and K.453, which help to create an illusion of improvisation by the performer. The concertos of this period are also, of course, vehicles for actual improvisation, the most significant opportunity being the cadenza at the end of the first movement – and often at the end of the other two movements as well. There are also numerous occasions, such as at the later appearances of the main theme in rondo finales, where a pause is indicated in the score, giving the soloist a chance to improvise a brief flourish or parenthesis before continuing with the music as written. Further opportunities for soloistic licence occur in the slow movements, as it was the custom for the soloist to add his own embellishments to the printed melody.[1]

PREDOMINANCE OF THE PIANO CONCERTO

Mozart wrote more concertos for the piano than for any other instrument because he was a pianist; almost all his concertos for other instruments resulted from commissions or were specifically designed for a particular performer. The emergence of the piano as a principal solo instrument is a feature of the concerto in the last two decades of the eighteenth century; by 1800 it was firmly challenging the supremacy of the violin, a supremacy which had not previously been challenged since the rise of the solo concerto nearly a century earlier. The tone of the early pianos was relatively weak and this explains why in many keyboard concertos of the late eighteenth century (including Mozart's early examples) the soloist completely dominates the solo sections – the orchestra had to remain in the background, otherwise the soloist would hardly have been heard. By comparison with those of the Romantic era, these concertos are still essentially chamber music, with usually the strings accompanying the piano and the full orchestral complement used only in the tutti passages. But gradually

---

[1] The art of embellishment continued to be practised in the concerto of the early nineteenth century, as is indicated by the autograph first movement of Hummel's Piano Concerto in A minor, Op. 85 (British Library, Add. 32219) in which the first and second subjects appear in bare melodic outline; the additional ornamentation in the printed edition is no doubt a written record of what Hummel added during performance. Various editions of Mozart concertos by Hummel and others, include lavish ornamentation in slow movements. When he heard Cramer playing in London in 1821, Moscheles resented the way he introduced 'his own and frequently trivial embellishments' into a Mozart Andante; this seems to indicate a changing attitude towards the practice of adding ornamentation (Charlotte Moscheles, ed., *Aus Moscheles' Leben*, Leipzig, 1872), i, p. 53).

Mozart increased both the size and the importance of the orchestra, and from K.450 onwards the wind instruments have the same independence and significance that they have in his operas.

THE VIENNESE CONCERTO AFTER MOZART

We now regard Mozart's concertos as the *ne plus ultra* of the classical form, and those of his contemporaries are all but unknown; but this was not the situation at the end of the eighteenth century, despite the admiration of such individuals as Beethoven, Cramer, and Spohr for Mozart's concertos. In Vienna itself the Bohemian pianist Leopold Anton Kozeluch (Koželuh) (1752–1818) was, according to Gerber,[1] the most popular living composer, and his concertos[2] were probably more widely disseminated than Mozart's, since about half of them were published during his lifetime whereas only a handful of Mozart's appeared in print before his death. Kozeluch, Jan Křtitel Vaňhal (1739–1813), Franz Anton Hoffmeister (1754–1812), and Franz Krommer (Kramář) (1759–1831) had one decided advantage over Mozart: although they were his contemporaries, they all outlived him by many years, and so were able to consolidate their position as the chief representatives of the Viennese concerto during the period immediately following his death. The *galant* character of their concertos indicates that they were designed for largely aristocratic audiences (both Kozeluch and Krommer enjoyed appointments as court composers); hence their formal clarity, and relatively simple melodic and harmonic language. Compared with Mozart's concertos, the first movements lack melodic variety; indeed, in some of Kozeluch's keyboard concertos, the opening Allegro is virtually monothematic. Usually, however, the two main themes of the ritornello are duplicated with a minimum of alteration in the solo exposition. These concertos are thus more conventional, more predictable than those of Mozart, and so gained ready acceptance among audiences in Vienna and elsewhere.

In the piano concertos of Kozeluch and Vaňhal, the solo writing is fluent but not quite as florid as that of another contemporary, Jan Ladislav Dussek (Dusík) (1760–1812), a much more significant figure in the early history of piano music. Vaňhal, in fact, confines his figuration almost exclusively to the right hand. But Kozeluch's slow movements exhibit an extremely decorative style of keyboard writing that is derived from Wagenseil and Leopold Hofmann[3] and is later

---

[1] Ernst Gerber, *Historisch-biographisches Lexikon der Tonkünstler* (Leipzig, 1790–2).

[2] See catalogue of Kozeluch's concertos in Milan Poštolka, *Leopold Koželuh: Život a dílo* (Prague, 1964).

[3] See Vol. VII, pp. 466 and 468.

evident in the concertos of Hummel and other early nineteenth-century composers.

Unlike the emerging itinerant virtuoso performers, these court-centred composers did not write concertos exclusively for their own particular instrument. Krommer, for example, was a violinist, but he wrote concertos for flute, oboe, and clarinet as well as for the violin. In fact, Krommer's Clarinet Concerto in E major, Op. 36, is one of the best of the early compositions for that instrument, while his Oboe Concerto in F major, Op. 52, is another attractive work, with an unusually chromatic, expressive Adagio. Both Krommer and Anton Hoffmeister, who alone wrote more than twenty concertos for the flute, made the most distinctive contribution to the Viennese wind concerto, giving those instruments a prominence that they generally lacked as members of the supporting orchestra in works for strings and keyboard. For despite Mozart's example, in such cases the wind instruments were still only rarely heard during the solo sections of the first movements, although they occasionally had a more prominent role in the later movements: for example, the third variation in the finale of Kozeluch's Piano Concerto in D major[1] is given to the woodwind group of two oboes, two horns, and bassoon.

THE FRENCH VIOLIN CONCERTO

It would hardly be an exaggeration to claim that Giovanni Battista Viotti (1755–1824) played as significant a role in the development of the classical violin concerto as did Mozart in the realm of the piano concerto. Within a year of his Parisian début, at the Concert Spirituel in March 1782 (at which he played his Concerto no. 1 in C major), Viotti had established a reputation as the greatest violinist of the day, at least as far as the French capital was concerned. Although he limited his public appearances in Paris, and then from 1792 onwards spent most of the remainder of his life in London, he became recognized as the leading figure of the so-called French violin school, which also included his pupil Pierre Rode (1774–1830) as well as Rodolphe Kreutzer (1766–1831) and Pierre Baillot (1771–1842). These four composers were all prolific in the field of the violin concerto: Viotti wrote twenty-nine, Rode thirteen, Kreutzer nineteen, and Baillot nine. Viotti's first nineteen concertos were published before his move to England, and it was probably these works that had the greatest immediate influence on his French disciples, because the concertos he composed while in London were not published in Paris until some years later. The London concertos are the more mature

[1] No. 7 in Poštolka's catalogue.

works, as Viotti responded to the discerning taste of English audiences and was also influenced both by the larger dimensions of the London orchestras and by personal contact with Haydn and his symphonies. Among the best of these later concertos are no. 22 in A minor, no. 23 in G major (nicknamed 'John Bull', presumably on account of the Handelian style of its slow movement), and no. 26 in B flat. As a composer, Viotti naturally cannot be put in the same class as Mozart, but the best of his concertos deserve a worthier fate than to be regarded as teaching fodder.

Paradoxical though it may seem, the French violin concerto was essentially Italian in origin. Viotti, of course, was an Italian and he was a pupil of Pugnani, who had successfully preserved the tradition of Corelli, Tartini, and Vivaldi. The Italian element is especially apparent in Viotti's predominantly cantabile style, and in this respect he has much in common with J. C. Bach and Mozart. The particular French elements of his concertos are the martial nature of many of his themes and ritornellos, the use of the *romance* for the slow movement – with a melodic style bordering on the popular – and the characteristic *rondeau* finale. Viotti's dotted-rhythm themes (which are paralleled in a number of Mozart's piano concertos written at about the same time) may owe something to the French overture, and indeed the slow introduction of no. 16 in E minor[1] could be taken as a clear manifestation of this link, although on the other hand it is perhaps closer stylistically to Haydn's symphonic introductions. Not all of Viotti's main themes have a military flavour, however; in fact the limpid opening theme of no. 22 and the flowing second subject of no. 24 in B major, are more characteristic of his melodic style. The melodic invention of Viotti's successors is on a somewhat lower level, and in their hands the martial theme becomes more of a convention.

In some of their formal characteristics, the first movements of Viotti's concertos differ from Mozart's. Three of them (nos 16, 25, and 27) have slow introductions, in each case the introduction having a different relationship with the main body of the movement. Although other composers, such as Dussek, Rode, and Spohr, occasionally followed Viotti's example, the slow introduction remained a rarity in the concerto of this period. Much more typical is the presentation of the second theme of the ritornello in the dominant or relative major (of the last sixteen concertos, nine are in a minor key), with further references to the first subject associated with the ensuing return to the tonic. The development sections usually contain new material, with alternation between melodic and figurative passages, but often the

[1] To which Mozart added trumpets and timpani for a performance in Vienna (K. 470a).

second subject, or some other important theme from the first part of the movement, appears in full towards the end of the development in a remote key. In no. 22, for example, the second subject in C sharp minor leads into the transition theme, already in A major and preparing for the recapitulation that follows almost immediately. This particular recapitulation is typical of Viotti in consisting of the first subject and solo episode only, the omission of the second subject thus contradicting one of the chief conventions of sonata form. Such a movement as this, in fact, has little of the dynamic quality of the sonata style, its episodic character being emphasized by the many full closes and opportunities for miniature cadenzas. Brahms was no doubt referring to this air of spontaneity when he said of the work that 'it sounds as if [Viotti] were improvising, and yet everything is masterfully conceived and carried out.[1]

One result of this free approach to the form of the first movement may be seen in the development of what has just been referred to as the 'solo episode'. This is the passage that occurs after the second subject in the exposition, and again in the recapitulation; in the classical concerto it already provided an opportunity for bravura solo writing and for generating tension and excitement in the approach to the cadenza and the return of the ritornello. Mozart's embryonic solo episodes normally flow directly out of the second subject, whereas with Viotti this part of the structure becomes more clearly articulated, as well as being free of any direct thematic references.

Similar episodes are found in the last movements too, for the finale of the French violin concerto was designed to provide a brilliant and diverting conclusion to the proceedings. For this purpose the flexible *rondeau* form was eminently suitable. There is considerable variety of effect and invention in Viotti's finales; they range from the formality of Concerto no. 13 in A major (later arranged as a vocal polacca and probably the model for the popular polonaise finales of Viotti's followers) through the sparkling tunefulness of no. 24 (whose refrain is cleverly varied at each appearance) to the deliberate rusticity of no. 23.

In April 1792 a series of concerts was given in the Théâtre Feydeau; they featured the leading Parisian singers and instrumentalists, including the violinists Kreutzer, Rode and Paul Alday, who played not only their own concertos but also some by Viotti. According to Fétis the concerts were a particular triumph for Rode as a virtuoso and for Viotti as a composer. With the latter's flight to London in the

[1] Letter to Clara Schumann, June 1878, in Berthold Litzmann, ed., *Clara Schumann – Johannes Brahms: Briefe aus den Jahren 1853–1896* (Leipzig, 1927), ii, p. 145.

same year, Rode and Kreutzer became the leading exponents of the French violin style, and their concertos are closely modelled on Viotti's. Kreutzer's Concerto no. 3 in E major provides a good example of the typical French form, with a martial ritornello in the first movement, a short romance as the second movement, and a polonaise finale.

By the first decade of the nineteenth century the French style had penetrated the string concerto in all parts of Europe. Both Spohr and Paganini were strongly influenced by Rode: the 'French' characteristics of Spohr's Violin Concerto no. 2 in D minor (1804) include a lyrical solo entry immediately repeated two octaves lower, a condensed recapitulation in the first movement, and an *alla polacca* finale. But the influence of the French school was not confined to the string concerto. A number of Viotti's violin concertos were transcribed for piano by Dussek, Steibelt, Cramer and others, and their own keyboard concertos display many of the same structural features and popular effects. Even Beethoven, with his genuine admiration for French music, did not wholly escape this influence. In many ways it was Viotti rather than Mozart who provided the model for most of the concertos written in the early part of the nineteenth century.

THE FASHIONABLE CONCERTO

At the end of the eighteenth century a new type of concerto was beginning to emerge in certain European centres, responding to changing fashions and attitudes and becoming eventually the forerunner of the virtuosic or early romantic concerto. Social conditions in England and France differed from those in the Austro–German region, where, despite occasional upheavals and the ravages of the Napoleonic wars, the old aristocratic order remained until well into the nineteenth century. The rapid growth of a more bourgeois audience in revolutionary France and democratic England, on the other hand, together with their longer established tradition of public concerts, encouraged the independent musician who was no longer in the service of a noble patron but who established his reputation and earned his living from concert performances and from becoming a fashionable teacher of his particular instrument.

Among this new generation of virtuosos the most notable were the pianists, who flourished especially in such cities as London, Paris, and St. Petersburg. Their prominence in the musical life of the first two cities at the turn of the century was complemented by a rapid development in piano manufacture and the growth of a large domestic market for new piano music. Almost all of them were expatriates,

attracted to Paris (in the post-Revolutionary period) and London by
the opportunities for earning fame and money that arose from the
prevailing social and economic conditions. The most popular of these
pianists included the Bohemian Jan Ladislav Dussek, the Austrian
Joseph Woelfl (1773–1812) and the Prussian Daniel Steibelt (1765–
1823). Of these Dussek forms the most important link between Mozart
and the early romantic piano concerto of Field, Hummel, and
Moscheles; his first concertos were published in 1782, before Mozart
had begun his great series of Viennese concertos, while his last was
composed at about the same time as Beethoven's 'Emperor'.
Associated with these three are the composers of the so-called London
piano school, including the Italian Muzio Clementi (1752–1832), only
one of whose concertos has survived, Johann Baptist Cramer (1771–
1858), born in Germany and the most indebted to Mozart of this
group, and the Irishman John Field (1782–1837), who, like Cramer,
was a pupil of Clementi, but whose seven piano concertos really
belong stylistically to a slightly later period.

The popularity of the concertos by the most fashionable composers
was due not so much to their intrinsic merit as to their meeting the
desire of audiences for novel and brilliant effects, both in the technical
sense and in the application of descriptive titles or programmes, the
latter a phenomenon more readily apparent in the shorter solo pieces
of the period but by no means absent from the concerto. That Woelfl's
Piano Concerto no. 4 in G major was such a great success when it first
appeared in London in 1806 was undoubtedly due to its having a slow
movement entitled 'The Calm' (its main theme being obviously
modelled on the slow movement of Beethoven's 'Pathétique' Sonata)
and a polonaise finale. But an even greater sensation was created by
Steibelt's Storm Concerto (his no. 3 in E major), the third movement
of which was played incessantly throughout Europe in all sorts of
instrumental arrangements. Its popularity rivalled that of the solo
battle pieces which were then in vogue, such as Vaňhal's *Die Schlacht
bei Würzburg*, which was far more famous than any of his concertos.
The fashion for battle pieces is reflected in the number of military
concertos that were composed at this time; Dussek, Woelfl, and
Steibelt each wrote a 'Grand Military Concerto', and in Steibelt's
work an additional orchestra is used in the second of the two
movements. This second orchestra is virtually a military band and
includes, besides the expected trumpets, trombones, and timpani, a
serpent (then commonly used in military bands) and a large array of
percussion – side-drum, tambourine, cymbals, and triangle.

Although the piano was the best instrument for depicting battles, such works were not confined to it alone, because of course much of the military flavour was actually conveyed by the orchestra.[1] Military concertos for other solo instruments include the Violin Concerto no. 2 in D, Op. 21, by Karol Lipiński (1790–1861), the Violoncello Concerto no. 6 in F major, Op. 31, by Bernhard Romberg (1767–1841), and even one for harp by Robert Bochsa (1789–1856). But the content of some military concertos seems to have only tenuous links with their titles. Dussek's Piano Concerto in B flat major, Op. 40, has an elegant, fluent rondo typical of its composer, but despite its title (Rondo militaire) it is completely devoid of dotted rhythms, trumpet fanfares, or other features that are normally characteristic of a military style. Nor does the orchestra include the obligatory military instruments, trumpets and drums. One suspects that Dussek's title was simply a concession to the fashionable taste for battle pieces. The work was extremely popular when it first appeared during the 1798 London season; Dussek played it in six oratorio concerts within five weeks.[2] Of course, martial themes characterized by dotted rhythms are typical of the period, not only in the concerto but in all instrumental music. While this may be seen as a reflection of the prevailing atmosphere of revolution and war, in the concerto the march-like opening theme can be traced back to both Mozart and Viotti and became something of a convention for at least half a century.

The pastoral element is also much in evidence in the concertos of this period, just as it had been during the early history of the Italian *concerto grosso*. The final movement of the piano concerto (1795) by François Adrien Boieldieu (1775–1834), for example, is a 'Pastorale con variazioni' in F major with a folk-like theme in a lilting 6/8, played by the piano and repeated with the melody doubled by an oboe, above a sustained pedal note giving the effect of a drone bass. The siciliano also appears in several violin concertos by Viotti and Spohr, as well as the Piano Concerto no. 4 in E flat major by Field. Other pastoral images make their appearance in Steibelt's concertos, the chase in the 'Rondo à la chasse' of his Fifth Concerto in E flat major – predictably dominated by a hunting fanfare for horns – and the storm in the finale of his Third Concerto. This latter movement is the previously mentioned 'Storm Rondo' or, to give it its full title, 'Rondo Pastoral, in which is introduced an imitation of a Storm'. The recurring main theme, with its 6/8 rhythm and folk-like character, represents a shepherds' dance:

---

[1] On purely orchestral military pieces see the previous chapter, pp. 192–3.
[2] See H. A. Craw, *A Biography and Thematic Catalogue of the works of J. L. Dussek (1760–1812)* (Diss. University of Southern California, 1964), p. 92.

Ex. 82

This is interrupted in the second couplet by the storm, heralded by the distant thunder of tremolos in the piano's bass. At the height of the storm the piano has a descending triadic figure in octaves over tremolo chords, followed by arpeggios up and down the keyboard, and all this is supported by loud orchestral chords and tremolos:

Ex. 83

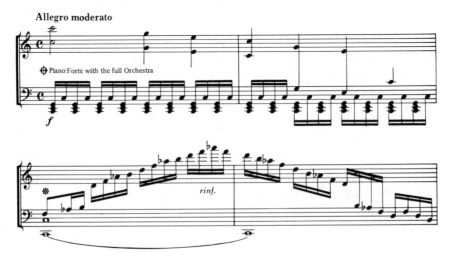

Another storm concerto is Field's Fifth, in C major, entitled *L'Incendie par l'Orage* (1817); this work was no doubt inspired by the extraordinary success of Steibelt's Third Concerto and of a solo piano piece by the same composer, *The Conflagration of Moscow*, but Field's storm differs from Steibelt's in several ways. It occurs as an episode within the development section of the first movement, not in the finale, and whereas Steibelt's storm is in C major, Field's is in C minor. He also uses a second piano to reinforce the solo part, while the much greater length of the episode, as well as the use of a tam-tam and a series of recurring B naturals on a bell, suggests a more complex as well as a more ominous programme than Steibelt's.[1]

INTRODUCTION OF POPULAR MELODIES

Another favourite method of courting popularity for concertos was the inclusion of folk or popular melodies, a natural parallel to the vast output of instrumental variations, improvisations or fantasies on the popular melodies of the day. In the autobiography of Ignaz Moscheles we read many accounts of concerts where his concerto was well received but his 'Anticipations of Scotland', or an improvisation on 'Rule Britannia' or on a duet from Spohr's *Jessonda* created the greatest sensation. It is hardly surprising then that Moscheles was one of many who used popular melodies in their concertos. Indeed, his

[1] Field may have been trying to suggest some catastrophe resulting from the storm, perhaps a fire caused by lightning, or even the burning of Moscow in 1812. See Patrick Piggott, *The Life and Music of John Field* (London, 1973), p. 167.

initial public success was gained through the performance in Vienna
in 1815 of his 'Alexander' Variations for piano and orchestra, the
theme he used being supposedly the favourite march tune of the Tsar
Alexander. Moscheles's Fourth Piano Concerto, composed in 1823
during his sojourn in England, uses another march melody, 'The
British Grenadiers', as the main theme of its rondo. This had the
desired effect, judging by a report of the first performance:

M. Moscheles played a new concerto, in which deep musical knowledge and
fancy were happily blended; in his finale he introduced the well-known
English tune, the Grenadier's March, and put every head, and almost as
many hearts, into motion.[1]

Some thirty years earlier, Dussek had scored a similar success by using
'The Plough Boy' from William Shield's popular comic opera, *The
Farmer*, for the rondo theme of his Piano Concerto in E flat, Op. 15.[2]

Ex. 84

The use of these particular themes was undoubtedly designed to
appeal to audiences of the nation concerned, but foreign melodies
proved to be just as acceptable, particularly those from Scotland and
Russia.[3] Slow movements of piano concertos by Steibelt and Field are

[1] *Harmonicon* (July 1823), p. 103.
[2] On the late eighteenth-century vogue in Britain for popular tunes as concerto material, see Vol.
VII, pp. 485–7.
[3] The vogue for Scottish airs may have been stimulated by the arrangements of folk-songs by
such composers as Haydn, Beethoven, Pleyel, and Kozeluch, commissioned by the Edinburgh
publisher George Thomson.

based on Scottish melodies and take the form of sets of free variations; in the Adagio of Field's Concerto no. 1 in E flat, for example, several statements of 'Within a mile of Edinboro' Town' are both interrupted and separated by brief cadenza-like passages of *fioriture*.[1] But ironically the melody used by Field is not a genuine folk tune; it was composed by the Englishman James Hook (1746–1827), himself a successful practitioner of a pseudo-Scottish idiom which he employed especially in the finales of concertos designed for performance in the London pleasure gardens. Distinction between the genuine article and its imitation hardly mattered to audiences of that period. Indeed, in many concertos the composers deliberately cultivated a stylized representation of a particular folk idiom, whether or not genuine folk melodies were borrowed: for example, the 'Rondo à l'hongroise' of Cramer's Fifth Piano Concerto in C minor, with its gypsy themes and bagpipe episodes, and the 'Rondo alla Spagnuola' of Hummel's Piano Concerto in A flat, Op. 113, with its dominating bolero rhythm. Both slow movement and finale of Lipiński's above mentioned 'Concerto militaire' introduce Ukrainian folk-tunes and the slow movement of Bochsa's Military Concerto is based on the Scottish tune, 'Auld Robin Gray', whereas the Rondo Russo of the Flute Concerto in E minor (1819) by Saverio Mercadante (1795–1870) conjures up the more formal atmosphere of an aristocratic ballroom.

SLOW MOVEMENTS

The slow movements of the fashionable concertos around the turn of the century are invariably short, as well as less complex or expressive than Mozart's. Dussek's slow movements are usually larghettos or romances of the type found in many of Viotti's violin concertos, in ternary form and with a *galant* flavour. Sometimes a slow movement serves as little more than an introduction to the finale, as in the Military Concerto by Woelfl or Field's Fifth. In the light of Field's importance in the development of the nocturne, it is not surprising to find nocturnes in his piano concertos. Although not entitled a nocturne, the brief Adagio of his Second Concerto is an early example, while in his Sixth Concerto Field inserted a transposed version of his sixth Nocturne, virtually unchanged except for the addition of an orchestral accompaniment that is confined almost entirely to pizzicato strings. Although Field's Third Concerto was published with only two

---

[1] Piggott, op. cit., p. 147, suggests that Field may have been influenced by the success of Steibelt and the young English composer George Griffin (1781–1863), both of whom introduced piano concertos with slow movements based on Scottish airs to London audiences in the two years prior to Field's. Griffin's no. 1 in A major, Op. 1, includes a set of variations on 'The Blue Bells of Scotland', and its structure is an exact model for Field's movement.

movements, he occasionally performed the rondo preceded by a nocturne – probably a version for piano and orchestra of his well known one, No. 5 in B flat.[1] It is not unusual, however, for concertos of this period to be without a slow movement; several by composers such as Dussek, Steibelt, Field, Boieldieu, and Pleyel have only two movements and there is evidence to suggest that some of Viotti's concertos originally lacked slow movements. This procedure recalls the majority of J. C. Bach's keyboard concertos as well as the French *symphonie concertante*, but it also reflects the relatively superficial approach of the early virtuoso concerto composers as well as the taste of their audiences, who desired to be charmed and dazzled rather than moved. An illuminating comment on the limitations of the average virtuoso composer is provided by a report in the English journal *Harmonicon* of a performance in Milan by the flautist Louis Drouet (1792–1873):

... he delighted the audience with two concertos. His execution is truly surprising, and in his shake he has no equal; but he afforded us no opportunity of judging of his powers in an adagio movement.

to which is added a forthright editorial footnote:

And most likely never will. To play an adagio requires more knowledge, taste, strong feeling and judgment, than such giddy galloping performers, – such ephemeral favourites – usually possess.[2]

FIRST-MOVEMENT STRUCTURE

For the first movements of these concertos the classical form provided a conveniently conventional framework which the fashionable virtuoso, while never attempting to imitate the structural subtleties of Mozart's concertos, was able to use primarily as a vehicle for solo display, with the orchestral ritornellos becoming relatively formal pillars framing the extended solo sections. Some of the first movements by the less conventional composers, like Steibelt and Field, are extremely episodic, often with long lyrical paragraphs and separate transition-themes divided by more energetic bravura passages, expanded to an inordinate length in the case of such movements as the 885-bar Allegro of Steibelt's Sixth Concerto. Field's discursive

---

[1] At a concert in Geneva in 1833, Field played 'Nocturne et rondo du troisième concerto ... avec accompagnement d'orchestre', according to the advertisement in the *Journal de Genève* (28 September 1833), reproduced in Heinrich Dessauer, *John Field, sein Leben und seine Werke* (Langensalza, 1912), pp. 71–2. There is an unpublished score of an orchestral accompaniment to the nocturne in a version entitled 'Serenade' which was published as a solo piece by Senff in 1863 (Piggott, op. cit., pp. 125 and 157–8).
[2] *Harmonicon* (November 1823), p. 177.

style is particularly apparent in his development sections, which almost always introduce completely new material; examples are the recitative passage in the Second Concerto, the storm episode in the Fifth, and the several self-contained episodes in the Seventh Concerto, the first of which exists independently as the Nocturne no. 12 in G major. It is their discursive, almost improvisatory first movements that help to distinguish these concertos from those of Beethoven, and in this and other ways they foreshadow the breakdown of the classical structure and the emergence of the freer forms of the romantic concerto.

BEETHOVEN AND THE SYMPHONIC CONCERTO

Beethoven's interest in the concerto extended from the period of his adolescence in Bonn until at least 1815, when he sketched the greater part of an opening movement for a piano concerto in D major. Besides eight completed concertos – six for piano, one for violin, and the *Grand concerto concertant* for piano, violin, violoncello, and orchestra (the 'triple concerto') – and several shorter concerted works, such as the two Romances for violin and orchestra, and the Choral Fantasia[1] there exist sketches for, or fragments of, a number of works that were either unfinished or have been lost. It appears that Beethoven composed at least three concertos before he left Bonn for Vienna in 1792, but only the Piano Concerto in E flat major has survived in anything like its completed form.[2] An oboe concerto has been completely lost,[3] while of the Violin Concerto in C major only a substantial part of the first movement has been preserved.[4] It may be assumed that these two latter works were designed for members of the Elector's orchestra in Bonn, but the piano concerto was obviously intended as a vehicle for displaying the young Beethoven's own prowess as a pianist, and his later concentration in Vienna on concertos for his own use brought him directly into the orbit of the virtuoso performer-composer.

Beethoven's completed concertos may be divided into two groups, the first consisting of the early piano concertos – in E flat (1784), B flat (1794), and C major (1796) – and the second of the Violin Concerto (1806) and the last two piano concertos – in G major (1806) and E flat

---

[1] See p. 600.

[2] From a copy of the solo part, Willy Hess reconstructed a full score (revised edition, Kassel, 1961; miniature score, London, 1969).

[3] A sheet with the opening themes of the three movements is preserved in the Beethovenhaus, Bonn, and the themes are reproduced in A. W. Thayer, *Life of Beethoven*, rev. and ed. Elliott Forbes (Princeton, 1964), i, p. 126.

[4] Library of the Gesellschaft der Musikfreunde, Vienna; reproduced in Ludwig Schiedermair, *Der junge Beethoven* (Leipzig, 1925), pp. 427–78.

major (1809) – with the C minor Piano Concerto (1800) and the Triple Concerto (1804) occupying a transitional position.

BEETHOVEN'S EARLY WORKS

Beethoven probably did not know any of Mozart's concertos when he wrote his juvenile E flat Concerto, but in it and in the next two concertos he followed Mozart's usual practice of drawing a clear distinction between the first ritornello and the solo exposition. In all three works the soloist enters with new material, and only in the Concerto in B flat does the piano part make any reference at all during the exposition to the first subject. In the C major Concerto the piano's opening idea is not used again throughout the movement, a circumstance that recalls among others Mozart's in the same key, K.503. Like the latter work, too, the solo entry is followed by orchestral statements of the first subject separated by descending piano arpeggios, and in both cases an apparently insignificant solo entry follows a ritornello of the utmost power and grandeur.

The first movement of the B flat provides the most striking instance in Beethoven's concertos of an exposition that owes almost nothing to the first ritornello. The ritornello itself does not contain anything that could be called a second subject or second theme, and in this respect it is unique in Beethoven's concertos and is certainly at variance with the practice of the period, although there are at least two such instances in Mozart (K.459 and K.491). At the point where one would normally expect the second subject, the orchestra suddenly modulates to D flat and begins to develop a phrase from the first subject. This unexpected modulation has a parallel in the exposition: after the second subject has at last been introduced, the piano turns from F major into D flat major and inserts another new theme before moving into the solo episode. But the parallel is harmonic, not thematic. The opposing ideas of the ritornello and the exposition are brought together in the recapitulation in the same way that Mozart usually achieves such a reconciliation – the first-subject section is taken from the ritornello, with the presence of the soloist now adding an extra dimension, while the second subject and solo episode are taken from the exposition.

In Beethoven's other two early concertos, the second subject is introduced in an incomplete form in the ritornello, enabling the piano to have the first definitive statement of the theme during the exposition. In the first movement of the C major, the second subject appears in the ritornello in the remote key of E flat and consists of a four-bar phrase (i) played three times sequentially, the modulations being effected by a twice interpolated four-bar phrase for strings and woodwind. But in the exposition the orchestra introduces the second subject in the expected dominant key as a complete eight-bar melody (ii), which is then expanded by a further four bars when repeated by the piano.

Ex. 85

Beethoven also uses an incomplete, sequential suggestion of a second subject during the ritornello of the G major Concerto. The question of modulation during the ritornello, to be discussed below, obviously has some bearing on the manner in which Beethoven treats his second subject.

The piano writing in Beethoven's first three concertos is extremely brilliant; in the E flat Concerto it is already surprisingly assured and difficult enough for a thirteen-year-old even with Beethoven's ability. The themes lack individuality, however, and undue attention is consequently directed to the extended sections of figuration, whereas the next two concertos strike a much more satisfactory balance between thematic content and technical display. In both these works the first-movement solo episode is expanded into a powerful bravura passage, the soloist either playing alone or with light orchestral accompaniment. In each case there is a temporary relaxation before solo and orchestra build up together to the climactic trill cadence. These early solo episodes are thematically independent of the rest of the movement, as in the virtuoso concerto but unlike those of Beethoven's later concertos (and some of Mozart's) in which some reference is normally made to material from the first ritornello.

The most immediately striking movements in Beethoven's early concertos are the rondos, in which the composer's peculiar energy and

verve are combined with wit and virtuosic brilliance. The finale of the
E flat is an Allegretto with a rather naive bourrée-like refrain and four
contrasting couplets that provide almost endless opportunities for solo
display – the sort of rondo favoured by Dussek and the other early
virtuoso composers. The rondos of all three concertos have the
customary central *minore*, which in the E flat major comprises the
third of the four episodes and is in the tonic minor, while in the other
two works the relative minor is used for the central episode of a
sonata-rondo structure. The rondo of the C major is an early example
of the type of virtuoso finale to be found in the concertos of such
composers as Hummel, Moscheles, and Ries. Whereas the rondo of
the earlier B flat major work is still close to the style of Mozart and
Haydn (particularly Haydn), this movement clearly bears Beethoven's
individual stamp, and nowhere is that individuality more obvious
than in the rhythmically exciting refrain, and in the final sudden
outburst that shatters the calm of a coda which has been brought to an
almost complete halt.

STRUCTURAL INNOVATIONS IN THE MATURE CONCERTOS

Attention has been drawn many times to what appear to be
structural innovations in Beethoven's later concertos, such as the
presentation of the soloist at the beginning of the G major and E flat
major concertos, the written-out cadenza in the latter, the so-called
'Emperor', the linking of the second and third movements in the same
work as well as in the Triple Concerto and the Violin Concerto, and
the use of the soloist in the coda of the first movement in all from the
C minor onwards. However, precedents for each of these apparent
innovations may be found in earlier works. The use of the piano at the
beginning of the work (as a separate entity and not as part of the
continuo), is a feature of Mozart's Concerto in E flat major, K.271
(1777), while there are written-out cadenzas in several of the six
keyboard concertos (Wq. 43) published in 1772 by C. P. E. Bach. In
each of these Bach concertos all the movements are connected, while
linking of the second and third movements also occurs in piano
concertos by Kozeluch, Dussek, and Woelfl, all composed before 1800.
Finally, the soloist continues to play after the cadenza in two concertos
by Mozart (K.271 and K.491), in each case the final ritornello being
expanded into a short coda.

Although Beethoven was not the originator of any of these novelties,
his manner of using them is significant; in no case did he merely copy
the previous example; instead he imparted an individual stamp to the
particular idea. For instance, in its appearance at the beginning of

Mozart's Concerto in E flat, the piano merely shares with the orchestra in the presentation of the first subject. In the fifth of his Wq. 43 set, C. P. E. Bach had already allowed the soloist to play the main theme of the first movement without assistance, but only after an introductory adagio for the orchestra. Beethoven's method in his G major Concerto differs from both these examples; instead of taking part in a dialogue with the orchestra, as in the Mozart, or following an orchestral introduction with the main theme, as in the Bach, the piano is here the first instrument to be heard, completely alone and with a full statement of the first subject. Thus the piano asserts a position of pre-eminence in a twofold sense, both as the first individual instrument to be heard and as the bearer of the chief thematic material, and this is achieved without recourse to either power or brilliance on the part of the soloist. Neither here nor in the Concerto in E flat is the opening ritornello discarded, but although in this respect the classical form is not violated, the relationship between solo and orchestra inevitably takes on a new aspect. The soloist's assumption of primacy is asserted much more aggressively in the E flat major, where Beethoven constructs an introductory section of unprecedented grandeur by expanding the simple chord progression I–IV–V–I into what is virtually an opening cadenza, before the orchestra continues with the ritornello in the normal manner. A further variant on the use of the soloist at the beginning of a work may be seen in the sketch for the unfinished Concerto in D, in which an initial orchestral statement of the first subject is followed by a brief cadenza-like elaboration of the theme by the piano. This introductory section returns in a modified form at the outset of the recapitulation, just as the corresponding section of the E flat major recurs at the same point in that work.

Although the written-out cadenza in the E flat major appears in the orthodox position towards the end of the movement and is preceded by the customary six-four chord and fermata, it is actually less a self-contained section designed for solo display than the beginning of the coda, as after only a few bars of keyboard brilliance the soloist settles into a statement of the second subject, echoed immediately by the horns who recall their own version of the same theme from the first ritornello. Beethoven himself appears to cast doubt on the interpretation of this passage as a cadenza, to judge from his direction to the performer: 'Non si fa una Cadenza, ma s'attacca subito il seguente'. But it is hardly right to assert, as several writers have done,[1] that he had 'for the first time, forbidden extemporization', for there are

[1] Donald F. Tovey, *Essays in Musical Analysis*, iii, 'Concertos' (London, 1936), p. 86; Marion M. Scott, *Beethoven* (London, 1934), p. 184; Ernest Walker, *Beethoven* (London, 3rd edn., 1920).

numerous concertos from this period that appear to have no provision at all for a cadenza.

It was also a common practice of the period to link the last two movements, not only in the concerto, but in other instrumental forms as well. Beethoven follows this procedure in the Triple Concerto, the Violin Concerto, and the last piano concerto, and as has already been mentioned they are by no means the first such examples in the literature of the concerto. It is doubtful, however, whether any previous composer had created such a magical transition between slow movement and finale as Beethoven did in the E flat with its sustained octave on the bassoons sinking a semitone from the tonic of the Adagio (B natural) to the dominant of the Rondo (B flat), to be followed by the quiet anticipation of the finale's refrain by the piano. The transition in the Violin Concerto is no less effective, with its sudden fortissimo modulation to the dominant of D major at the end of a subdued movement that remains in G major throughout. In this work, and even more in the Triple Concerto, the slow movement acts as an extended introduction to the finale, and this is characteristic both of the period generally and of other works composed by Beethoven around the same time, such as the 'Waldstein' Sonata.

Some of Beethoven's innovations are less obvious than those that have just been discussed, but they are no less significant in their departure from the established concerto pattern. Compared with the concertos of his contemporaries, Beethoven's are not as sectional, but display an integration of material that is more characteristic of the symphony of the period. The thematic and formal freedom of Mozart and Viotti – their sense of 'planned improvisation' – is now replaced by a more tightly-knit structure that unfolds in a less static or disjointed manner. Both the elimination of the self-contained cadenza and the linking of movements may be viewed as attempts to impose greater continuity, but such continuity is also achieved by other means, especially in the first movements. In the concerto of the late eighteenth century it was customary for both first and second ritornellos to come to a full close before the entry of the soloist, and Beethoven follows this procedure up to and including the C minor Concerto. But in his later concertos the solo entries overlap orchestral cadences, in most cases producing not only a greater sense of continuity but also an extraordinarily beautiful effect. In the G major Concerto, for example, the piano's re-entry after the first ritornello consists of a continuation of the orchestra's cadential theme, but as the latter is a variant of the first subject the solo is really regaining its own material, which it then expands in a new quasi-improvisatory manner. The piano returns after the second ritornello in exactly the same way, except that now its entry occurs slightly earlier, after only two phrases of the cadential theme and with a dramatic, though understated, change from major to minor. In this movement even the transitions from exposition and recapitulation to the following ritornellos are achieved almost imperceptibly, while in the rondo the conventional distinction between the solo refrain, tutti, refrain, and episode is almost completely disguised by a constant dialogue between solo and orchestra.

One of the reasons why composers brought the orchestra to a complete halt at the end of the opening ritornello was no doubt to heighten the effect of the solo entry, and such a method of focussing attention on the soloist was fully exploited by the performer-composers with loud, bravura entries – of which there is only one example in Beethoven: the C minor. But already in some of Mozart's concertos there are examples of solo entries overlapping the end of the ritornello, and of course with the soloist already having been in action at the beginning of Beethoven's last two piano concertos, there was no need for the orchestra to be completely silenced before the re-introduction of the piano. In the 'Emperor' the orchestra is still stressing the dominant chord as the piano steals in with its quiet ascending chromatic scale, while the corresponding passage in the Violin Concerto, in which a similar overlapping of the cadence by the soloist occurs, is expanded to such an extent by the cadenza-like solo entry that the dominant remains unresolved for thirteen bars. The first subject follows immediately in both these cases, and in addition both entries are repeated after the second ritornello (with new continuations), although not at the beginning of the recapitulation.

BEETHOVEN'S TREATMENT OF KEY

Beethoven's dynamic approach to tonality also ensures that his concertos are never static. Despite his inclination in the early concertos to modulate during the first ritornello, these primary sections never depart from the classical principle of closing in the tonic. But Beethoven did depart from a convention that was almost as strongly maintained, namely that the second ritornello closed in the dominant or relative major key. This convention was merely a continuation of the baroque procedure whereby each ritornello confirmed the key to which the preceding solo section had modulated. In concertos of the early nineteenth century in which this practice is continued the secondary-key area is often extended well into the development, usually with a transposition of the solo entry section of the exposition.

This can be seen in the Triple Concerto, where the first subject, now in A major (which Beethoven here uses for his secondary key in preference to the dominant) is played again by each of the three soloists in turn, a passage comprising a literal repetition that lasts for more than one-third of the development section. In the Violin Concerto and the 'Emperor', on the other hand, the second ritornello modulates and in both cases a literal restatement of material from the latter part of the opening ritornello is modified only minimally in order to effect the modulation.

Beethoven's creation of a more organic structure may also be seen in his reduction of the number of purely bravura passages, although he certainly continued to exploit both the solo episode and the cadenza. But in his solo episodes as well as in his cadenzas, he gradually introduces more thematic references than do most of his predecessors and contemporaries. The solo episodes in the early B flat and C major concertos are already more brilliant than any of Mozart's but their function is largely restricted to providing an opportunity for display and an extended harmonic preparation for the exposition's cadence. For much of the time the orchestra is silent, but its participation increases considerably in the solo episodes of the later concertos. In the C minor, for instance, the piano passage-work is accompanied by orchestral references to the rhythmic figure of the third bar, then the first subject itself is played by clarinets and horns under the piano's cadential trill.

THEMATIC DERIVATION OF SOLO EPISODES

The most spectacular of Beethoven's solo episodes is that of his last piano concerto, the E flat, yet by this stage the episode has become almost completely thematic. The piano develops the opening figure of the first subject, then plays the third theme in C flat major, which is immediately repeated by woodwind in the movement's dominant key (this C flat–B flat relationship having previously been exploited in the second subject) and is followed by the second part of the same theme on the piano.

Beethoven's most revolutionary treatment of the solo episode is seen in the G major Concerto and the Violin Concerto, and it is no coincidence that they happen to be the most lyrical and least showy of his concertos. In both cases, the latter part of the ritornello is essentially repeated in the exposition by the orchestra, with the soloist providing an obbligato decoration. But whereas there are some bars of passage-work and a prolonged cadence in the Violin Concerto, following a lengthy expansion of the ritornello's cadential theme, the element of display in the G major Concerto is subordinated to such an extent that the solo episode is virtually non-existent. The conventional trill resolves not into the second ritornello, but into an expressive statement by the piano of the movement's third theme. All the ritornello themes in this movement feature some sort of threefold repetition, and this one consists of three varied statements of a two-bar phrase, the last extended to form a complete eight-bar period. In this instance the full orchestra takes over the third statement and continues as the second ritornello. So not only has the solo episode virtually disappeared, but the transition between the end of the exposition and the following ritornello is handled in a highly original manner illustrating Beethoven's readiness to depart from the conventional trill for the conclusion of his solo sections. It is true that the trill is found in his earlier concertos and is even extended to cover seven bars, combined with ascending scales, in the Triple Concerto. But in the later works, the trill is either followed by solo scale passages (the Violin Concerto) or omitted altogether – as in the 'Emperor' where the powerful climax is attained through ascending broken chords followed by chromatic scales in contrary motion.

THE QUASI-SYMPHONIC ELEMENT

For many of Beethoven's contemporaries the latter part of the development section provided a further opportunity for a solo episode, and in their concertos the third ritornello is not so much the point of recapitulation as a culmination of the second solo section. As in his works in other forms, however, Beethoven's recapitulations are usually strongly articulated and there are several examples of first subjects that are not simply repeated but transformed completely in mood while remaining the same in substance. Such a transformation occurs in its simplest form in the Violin Concerto, where the full orchestra has a *fortissimo* statement of a first subject that had initially consisted of quiet timpani strokes answered almost as softly by the woodwinds. A somewhat different transformation is found in the 'Emperor' where the introduction is brought back before the recapitulation proper. Here the first two piano passages are shorter and more brilliant and convey a far greater sense of urgency than at the beginning, while the third passage begins as an exact repeat but then is extended so as to culminate in the ascending chromatic scale derived from the solo entry. Once again, however, Beethoven is at his most original in the G major Concerto; as in the Violin Concerto, a quietly lyrical first subject is completely altered in character by a *fortissimo* statement, in this case by the soloist, with much fuller harmony than it had at the opening of the work and with elaborate melodic flourishes driving it more urgently to the cadence. Then the orchestral reply is beautifully decorated by piano figuration in the treble register, although 'decoration' hardly seems the right word to describe such a process whereby the solo instrument adds a completely new dimension to previously used material.

When such features as those that have been discussed are placed in their proper perspective, they may all be seen as part of the process through which Beethoven brought the concerto far more definitely into the realm of the symphony by modifying its previously close relationship to opera. The ritornello, solo episode, and cadenza are features of the concerto that all have an operatic origin, while in the concertos of Mozart and others of his generation, much of the melodic material, the aria-like slow movements, and the ornamental writing emphasise the concerto's role as an expression in purely instrumental terms of operatic values and conventions. There is a gradual modification of almost all these elements in Beethoven's concertos and a corresponding increase in significance of those elements that may be described as symphonic. In his early concertos the first ritornello already begins to sound remarkably like the exposition of a symphony, an impression that is conveyed by the typically symphonic sound of the orchestral writing, the pervasive use of motivic development, and the irresistible tendency to move away from the tonic.

In these works the new keys are simply interpolations, but in the C minor there is a carefully planned modulation to E flat major for the second subject. Beethoven was by no means the first to modulate during the opening ritornello, but his development of ideas from the first subject as material for the transition as well as his long and careful preparation of the new key makes the ritornello much more symphonic in character than most parallel examples. He may have been influenced in this respect by Viotti, but since it was such a widespread practice even before Beethoven's time, Tovey's claim that the C minor Concerto set the pattern for composers like Spohr, Hummel, and Chopin, is open to question.[1] Less arguable is his contention that Beethoven's conversion of the ritornello into a symphonic exposition reduced its effectiveness as a preparation for the solo entry and that it left nothing essential for the piano to add. Indeed, the exposition follows the course of the ritornello very closely in this work, and although the practice is continued in Beethoven's later concertos, he is able to achieve harmonic variety in the ritornello

[1] Tovey, op. cit., p. 71.

by such means as alternation between the major and minor of the same tonic rather than by modulating to a completely new key.

The fact that first ritornello and exposition are so alike in Beethoven's later concertos is indicative of the equal status he accorded to both soloist and orchestra, in contrast to the virtually unchallenged dominance enjoyed by the former in the other concertos of the period. The greater proportion of the solo sections in the Violin Concerto actually consist of thematic statements by the orchestra with the violin providing an obbligato; there is virtually no new material in the exposition, which provides an excellent example of a soloist embellishing a repetition of ritornello themes. The orchestra also plays a significant role in most of Beethoven's development sections, where the soloist usually has passages of figuration while the actual thematic development is carried out by the orchestra. Even in the development section of the early Concerto in B flat major there is a long passage of dialogue (bars 246 ff.), signifying the equal status of the two protagonists as well as departing from the normal practice of the period of having the soloist playing more or less continuously throughout the solo sections.

The symphonic orientation of Beethoven's concertos is evident in many details and not only in the first movements; the finales of his later concertos, for example, exhibit a gravity of musical thought that is far removed from the gay or ostentatious finales of the virtuoso concerto. There is extensive thematic development in the central sonata-rondo couplet of both the C minor and E flat major concertos, while the codas are expanded even further than in the first movements. In all the later concertos there is generally a quickening of the tempo and a transformation of the main themes in the coda that – together with brilliant solo passage-work – helps to bring each work to both a musically satisfying and a crowd-pleasing conclusion.

While it cannot be denied that the element of virtuosity is still present in Beethoven's later concertos, it may also be observed that as the technical demands on the soloist increase, so paradoxically the significance of the concerto as a vehicle for display seems to decrease. Beethoven's changing attitude to virtuosity is reflected in his handling of the cadenza and the solo episode. This may partly have resulted from his gradual withdrawal from the concert platform following the onset of his deafness, but the same apparent paradox may be observed in the later sonatas and quartets and is indicative of his unceasing search for the means whereby he might adequately express his unique musical thought.

CONCERT AND CONCERTO IN THE EARLY NINETEENTH CENTURY

No concertos of the same period can be equated with Beethoven's, yet in many ways his concertos are not at all typical of their age. The majority of concertos composed in the early decades of the nineteenth century were written by men whose talent as performers far exceeded their talent for composition. Naturally there were exceptions, especially among the pianists; as a rule the concertos for piano, and to a lesser extent for violin, have the most value, but concertos for those two instruments do not form as large a proportion of the total number as might be imagined.[1] Concertos were written for virtually every orchestral instrument, as well as for instruments not then normally found in an orchestra; for instance, Dussek's Concerto in C major, Op. 30, is 'for the Pedal Harp or Piano-Forte' and his E flat work, Op. 15, was originally a harp concerto,[2] while Hummel's Piano Concerto in G, Op. 73, is actually a transcription of a work originally written for mandoline and orchestra. Then too there were concertos for even more exotic instruments, purveyed by such entertainers as a certain Mr Koch who, according to a report from Prague, 'performed a concerto on – the Jewsharp! and will it be believed when it is asserted, that it was as rapturously applauded as a concerto of a Hummel or a Pixis'.[3] Contemporary accounts also mention concertos for such novelties as the *physharmonika, chitarra coll'arco* and *flûte d'amour* among others, but such works were rarely published since they doubtless had no more than curiosity value, and their creators were usually more accomplished as showmen than as musicians. But they were welcomed by a public that thirsted for novelty and also acclaimed the new generation of performers on more conventional instruments. The virtuoso's audience was a more varied one than it had been in the pre-Revolutionary era, and the changing tastes of such audiences as well as the rapid expansion of concert life[4] determined to a large extent the nature of the early nineteenth-century concerto.

All concerts had mixed programmes, comprising both vocal and instrumental items, but almost always a concerto was included[5] and in many cases there was more than one concerto, not necessarily involving the same instrument or performer. In general the music

---

[1] See Eduard Hanslick, *Geschichte des Konzertwesens in Wien* (Vienna, 1869–70), i, p. 154. Concertos for violin and piano form together about half the number of concertos reviewed or announced in the *Allgemeine musikalische Zeitung* from its inception in 1798 until 1830.

[2] See Craw, op. cit., p. 238.

[3] *Harmonicon* (April 1824), p. 72.

[4] See chap. I, p. 17.

[5] Concertos were originally excluded from the London Philharmonic concerts, but began to appear in the programmes from 1819 onward.

performed in the subscription concerts of the more important societies, such as those of London, Leipzig, and Vienna, was of a higher quality than that performed in the average benefit concert, where success depended almost entirely on the approval of what was hardly a discriminating public to whose taste the programmes were directed. In these circumstances the concerto was actually regarded as a serious form of music, and even though its principal function was the display of the performer's talents, it remained in a different class from the potpourris, fantasias, variations, storm and battle pieces that comprised the main part of the virtuoso's repertory.[1] It was no doubt because of the form's comparative severity and adherence to specific structural principles, as well as to its greatly expanded dimensions, that it was not uncommon for single movements to be performed separately. When Leopoldine Blahetka played Beethoven's B flat Concerto in Vienna in 1820, for example, she was praised for her boldness in 'playing a complete concerto by a classical master in our age of polonaises and potpourris', while in 1827 the violinist Leopold Maurer was commended by one reviewer for playing a complete concerto because 'we would normally expect to hear only one of its movements'.[2] Often the second and third movements only were performed – a practice which persisted in the London Philharmonic concerts as late as the 1880s, though only occasionally; the combination of a short adagio with a loosely organized and crowd-pleasing finale demanded less concentration from the audience and ensured for the soloist a more easily gained ovation than a more formal first movement.[3] Hence the function of the slow movement in many virtuoso concertos is not so much to provide a contrast in tempo and mood after an extended opening allegro, as to form an introduction to the finale, into which it often leads directly.

Another common practice which today seems even more obnoxious than the performance of separate movements of the same work was the linking of movements from different works, sometimes by entirely different composers. For example, Weber first performed the finale of his Second Piano Concerto together with the first and second movements of his First Concerto, while at a London Philharmonic

[1] The distinction was well recognized by Schumann who, in the *Neue Zeitschrift für Musik*, often advised composers to turn from smaller forms to the 'higher forms: the sonata or concerto'. See Leon B. Plantinga, *Schumann as Critic* (New Haven and London, 1967), p. 181.

[2] Hanslick, op. cit. i, p. 92 (see also pp. 156–9). In a review of Ludwig Böhner's *Concert en fantaisie*, Op. 13, the *Allgemeine musikalische Zeitung* remarked, 'It is seldom that one hears a whole concerto or symphony instead of merely one or two movements' (August 1815, col. 535).

[3] Some concerted works of the period use this two-movement form, e.g. Hummel's 'Rondo brillant', Op. 56, Weber's 'Andante e rondo ongarese' for bassoon (originally viola), and Chopin's 'Andante spianato' and Grand Polonaise in E flat (originally separate pieces but published in this way).

concert conducted by Weber in 1826, the German pianist Ludwig Schuncke played a composite concerto consisting of movements by Hummel, Beethoven, and Pixis. Cramer's admiration for Mozart extended to his playing the first two movements of his own Concerto in C minor with the finale from Mozart's great concerto in the same key, while there are many examples of performances of violin concertos consisting of movements by two different composers.

FORMAL CHARACTERISTICS OF THE VIRTUOSO CONCERTO

Although it was now the practice to publish most concertos so that they were played by others beside the composer, each was still essentially designed to display the particular qualities of the composer's talents as a performer. With a still relatively novel and developing instrument such as the piano, for instance, the concerto proved to be an apt vehicle for the exploration of technical and expressive possibilities, and in this respect the solo parts of such works are full of interest and variety. By contrast, the approach of most of the virtuoso composers to the structure of the concerto was far from adventurous, no matter for which solo instrument they were writing. They were content merely to utilize the conventions of the classical form, often without appreciating their implications for the relationship between solo and orchestra, and if such conventions were modified at all it was almost always for the one purpose of drawing greater attention to the solo performer. Although the ritornello structure of the first movement remains in the virtuoso concerto, it does not have quite the same function as it has in the concertos of Mozart and Beethoven. The first part of the opening ritornello has now become almost indistinguishable from a sonata exposition, with the second subject invariably appearing in the dominant or relative major and the modulation to the secondary key being thoroughly prepared in a long transition from the first subject. As the return to the tonic is often marked by a restatement of the first subject and one or more cadential themes may be added after that, the first ritornello has now been expanded far beyond its previous length, so that its effectiveness in preparing for the soloist's entry is diminished. As it expands, so the later ritornellos are shortened and often (as in Chopin's concertos) are not thematically linked to the first. Sometimes the third ritornello is omitted altogether, while the final one becomes a perfunctory, cadential tutti, without any of the beauties of the codas in the first movements of Beethoven's later concertos.[1]

---

[1] The brief final ritornello in Beethoven's early concerto in B flat exemplifies this typical feature of the virtuoso concerto.

SOLO ENTRIES

The truncated final ritornello is but one feature of the concerto's first-movement form which may be seen as a direct outcome of the early nineteenth-century emphasis on virtuosity. Other aspects of the form that were similarly affected include the initial solo entry, the solo statement of the second subject and its preparation, the solo episode, and the cadenza – all structural elements with obvious opportunities for solo display. The most typical solo entries in the virtuoso concerto are loud, pompous, and rhetorical, sometimes constituting a transformation of the first subject but often consisting of completely new material. Such entries often consist of two separate but complementary and balanced phrases, usually beginning on tonic and dominant respectively, followed by a more melodic continuation and a passage of figuration that either culminates in a full close or leads directly into the transition. Typical of this kind of solo entry is Hummel's Concerto in E major, Op. 110 (1814), where the piano has loud octave chords separated by scale flourishes:

Ex. 86

A similar example is Chopin's Concerto in E minor (1830), where the second part of the first subject is used for the melodic continuation and is immediately developed into an extended lyrical episode.

With the expansion of the opening ritornello and the consequent delay of the solo entry, the treatment of the latter point in the structure assumes particular significance if the composer is to avoid making the introduction of the soloist appear to be an anti-climax. The ways in which Beethoven created interesting entries have already been examined, and there are parallels in the works of some of his contemporaries and immediate successors. In Hummel's Piano Concerto in A minor, Op. 85 (c. 1816), for instance, the soloist steals in with a quasi-improvisatory decoration of the orchestral cadence (as in Beethoven's Violin Concerto), and although it might be thought that after the extended ritornello its appearance is long overdue, the entry of the solo at that precise moment is both unexpected and striking in its impact.

Ex. 87

The cadence is followed by some new material, organized in the two balanced phrases of the typical bravura entry, then the solo continues with the second part of the first subject. It is only after a short bravura passage that the soloist at last presents a now highly embellished version of the first subject proper. Chopin probably had this work in mind when in his F minor Concerto (1829) he likewise allowed the solo to enter before the completion of the ritornello; but whereas Hummel's entry is unobtrusive, Chopin's descending flourish in loud octaves is '[an] impatient dramatic entry of the pianoforte [which] needs all the delay Chopin has given it'.[1]

The solo entry in Hummel's Piano Concerto in B minor, Op. 89 (1819), is even more impressive. After an extremely long ritornello lasting 153 bars, the piano again enters quietly, with a broken-chord accompaniment figure for the left hand in the tonic *major*; after four bars B minor is restored for a new declamatory solo theme that gradually flowers into a passage of considerable eloquence. The piano is not for some time diverted from its path, despite the gentle hints at the first subject by the orchestra, and in fact it is not until the development section that it makes its first direct reference to the main theme of the movement.

Sometimes the first subject is used in a modified form for the solo entry and sometimes it is totally ignored in the exposition, but in most virtuoso concertos the second subject is taken directly from the ritornello. It may either be an embellished version of what has already appeared in full, or an expansion of an incomplete second subject into a long lyrical paragraph, with embellishments and *fioriture* gradually increasing in complexity. In most cases the second subject is preceded by a free passage for the soloist, usually unaccompanied and often restricted to a single melodic line, even when the piano is the solo

[1] Tovey, op. cit., p. 104.

instrument; although such a passage is written out in full and is contained within the metrical framework, it is obviously a direct descendant of the improvised *Eingang* in the classical concerto.

SOLO EPISODES

In the same way it is possible to trace the evolution of the solo episode from the passages of bravura at the end of the solo sections in earlier concertos. In the virtuoso concerto these solo episodes are almost always self-contained, thematically independent sections which have as their main purpose the display of the soloist's technique. Hans Engel's term *Spielepisode* is not easily translated, but with its connotations of technical display it conveys very well the basic character of these sections. Just as the lyrical passages of the virtuoso piano concerto often exhibit those characteristics of what may be described as an emerging 'nocturne' style, so the solo episodes are naturally closely related to the étude in their concentration on technical brilliance. In many concertos these episodes simply belong to the 'school of velocity', consisting of a series of technical exercises and having little musical value, but some of them have melodic or rhythmic interest; Hummel's episodes usually have a distinctive dance-like character, for example, while other composers introduce temporary modulations to distant keys such as the flattened sixth (such interpolations already occur in some of Dussek's concertos). The self-contained nature of the solo episode is illustrated by the fact that in many concertos the recapitulation has a completely new episode.

With composers like Moscheles, Kalkbrenner, and Herz, the solo episode becomes so important that it often comprises more than half the length of the exposition or recapitulation and is itself almost as long as the opening ritornello. Such expansion is also a feature of the cadences, especially in the piano concerto, in which the simple trill formula of the classical concerto is extended into a lengthy passage where the trill is combined with scale or melodic figures, or filled out chordally to form double-note trills or tremolos. Hummel's B minor Concerto provides an example of such an exaggerated cadence; at the end of the recapitulation there are twenty-two bars of trills, interspersed with several scale-like flourishes and culminating in a brilliant dominant-seventh arpeggio. The following brief cadential tutti would no doubt have been smothered by the loud bursts of applause from an audience suitably impressed by the soloist's virtuosity. Writing about the première of his *Scena cantante* in Milan in 1816, Spohr reported that the noisy applause after the solo sections disturbed the continuity of the work as his carefully worked-out tuttis went unnoticed and the audience heard the soloist return in a new key without realizing that the orchestra had modulated to it.[1]

In a sense the solo episode had become something of a cadenza *in tempo*; indeed most virtuoso concertos as originally published have no provision for a formal cadenza either in its normal position at the end of the first movement or anywhere else. This is true of the concertos of Hummel, Chopin, and all but one by Moscheles (the G minor, which, like Beethoven's E flat major, has a short written-out cadenza). A general absence of extemporized cadenzas seems to be implied by a remark made by Spohr about a violinist performing a concerto in St. Petersburg in 1802: 'In all three movements he interpolated improvised cadenzas according to the old custom.'[2] On the other hand, some contemporary reports mention cadenzas in concertos which do not appear to have them in the published scores. It may be that the tendency to have extended solo episodes at the end of each of the three solo sections rendered superfluous the inclusion of a 'set-piece' cadenza.

THE VIRTUOSO PIANO CONCERTO AND CHOPIN

Among the most prominent pianists of the early nineteenth century who contributed to the development of the virtuoso piano concerto, Johann Nepomuk Hummel (1778–1837), Ignaz Moscheles (1794–1870), Ferdinand Ries (1784–1838), and Carl Czerny (1791–1857) all had a close association with Vienna, spending at least the formative part of their careers in that city. Hummel and Moscheles were the two foremost pianists of the period, but whereas Hummel – generally regarded at that time as Mozart's musical heir – was essentially a traditionalist with an elegant, decorative style, Moscheles was a more brilliant, spectacular virtuoso who later moved towards formal experimentation and the expression of a romantic feeling somewhat akin to Mendelssohn's and Schumann's. Friedrich Kalkbrenner (1785–1849), Henri Herz (1803–88), and Johann Peter Pixis (1788–1874) represent the group of German pianists living in Paris who were so mercilessly criticized by Schumann on account of their showy but empty piano pieces, while both Sigismond Thalberg (1812–71) and

---

[1] Spohr, *Lebenserinnerungen*, ed. Folker Göthel (Tutzing, 1968), i, p. 252. See also the reviews of Paganini's début in Berlin in 1829: e.g. 'he stamps his feet and the orchestra rushes in and fades away in the thunder of the unparalleled enthusiasm of the audience' (A. B. Marx, in the *Berliner musikalische Zeitung*).

[2] Spohr, ibid., p. 43. The comment is ambiguous, however; Spohr may have meant that the earlier custom was to improvise cadenzas in all three movements.

Frédéric François Chopin (1809–47) belong to the younger generation that was coming into prominence around 1830.

Chopin's two piano concertos are early works, the F minor dating from 1829 and the E minor from the following year, and although they cannot be regarded as the greatest of his works, the criticisms frequently levelled at them have usually resulted from unfair historical comparison. It is almost certain that Chopin knew none of Beethoven's concertos at the time his own were written, before he left Warsaw for Paris. The concertos he did know and admire were above all Hummel's A minor and B minor, Moscheles's G minor and Field's Second, and it is as the culmination of this early period of the virtuoso piano concerto that Chopin's concertos should be judged. Thus the often heard criticism that his development sections show little evidence of actual thematic development ignores the fact that in this they hardly differ from the episodic middle solos characteristic of almost all virtuoso concertos. Considering the previous history of the concerto, and remembering that its evolution occurred independently of the symphony and the solo sonata, it is not surprising that such works lack truly symphonic development sections. The most typical pattern is of two virtually separate sections, the first being either a transposed repetition of the solo entry, or a lyrical episode based on new or used material. This first part is followed by an extended section of solo figuration, sometimes with thematic references in the orchestra but only rarely in the solo part. Both of Chopin's first-movement development sections conform to this scheme. They begin with a rhapsodic section based on first-subject themes, followed by the longer section of solo figuration. In the E minor this latter section is really a spectacular solo episode which gradually increases in brilliance and excitement and reaches a splendid climax in the recapitulation of the first subject by the orchestra.

Tovey has rightly said of Chopin's F minor Concerto that 'its style is the perfection of ornament'.[1] Without discounting the unique individuality and poetry of Chopin's piano writing, the fact is that much of the lyrical, ornamental style that characterizes his two concertos – admittedly early works, composed before his genius had fully flowered – is foreshadowed in the concertos not only of Field and Hummel but of such other composers as Ries, Kalkbrenner, and Moscheles. Its two main sources were Viennese keyboard music, represented especially by Wagenseil and Mozart, and Italian opera, which continued to be immensely popular not only in Austria but in such widely separated centres as London and St. Petersburg. In a

[1] Tovey, op. cit., p. 103.

movement such as the Larghetto of Hummel's A minor Concerto, both the orchestral introduction and the heavily decorated piano cantilena have an operatic character. It has been pointed out that the essential difference between the ornamental writing of Mozart and that of Hummel and his generation is that in the former case the decoration is usually applied to melodic repetitions and the original melody still emerges strongly, while in the latter the melodic line is almost completely smothered by the embellishments.[1] With Chopin, however, the embellishments somehow seem to be a necessary and integral part of the melody, and when one compares the Larghetto theme of the F minor Concerto as it stands with the plain, unornamented version shown by Tovey,[2] it will be readily apparent how much the appeal of this movement is due to its ornamental melody. Chopin's slow movements are both accompanied nocturnes, although not so entitled, and a similar lyrical style pervades his first movements, but without quite the same florid ornamentation. Field, Hummel, and Chopin strike a balance between lyricism and bravura in their concertos, whereas Ries, Kalkbrenner, and Moscheles tend to place greater emphasis on the bravura and the brilliant. But Chopin far surpasses all of them in his ability to impart melodic beauty to even transition passages (Ex. 88) and solo episodes (Ex. 89).

Ex. 88

(i) CHOPIN: E minor Concerto

[1] Eva and Paul Badura-Skoda, *Interpreting Mozart on the Keyboard* (London, 1962), p. 182.
[2] Op. cit., p. 105.

(ii) HUMMEL: A minor Concerto

Ex. 89

(i) CHOPIN: F minor Concerto

(ii) KALKBRENNER: E minor Concerto

FINALES

Chopin's finales, however, are real showpieces for the soloist, with exceptional keyboard virtuosity in the tradition of such spectacular finales as the G minor and E flat major concertos of Moscheles (1820 and 1825), Hummel's Op. 89, and the C sharp minor concerto of Ries (1812). The finale of Moscheles's Concerto in E flat is a polonaise, composed and often performed before the other two movements had been written, and is indicative of the widespread popularity of concerto finales in dance style. The polonaise was especially popular and may be found in concertos by Beethoven (Triple Concerto), Field (Third Piano Concerto), Weber (Clarinet Concerto in E flat), Spohr (several of his violin concertos), and many lesser composers. The *tempo di menuetto* finale had been similarly popular in the late eighteenth-century concerto, and the contrast in the way these two dances are used is a reflection of the change from an age of elegance to an age of virtuosity. Just as such finales use the polonaise in a stylized form, so Chopin's two finales are stylizations of other Polish dances, the mazurka and the krakowiak.

The finale of Chopin's E minor Concerto exhibits a modification of rondo form that is characteristic of the virtuoso concerto. In this modification the sonata-rondo pattern is followed exactly to the second appearance of the rondo theme and the second episode usually begins with some development which may be combined with, or even replaced by, new material, but this section then leads directly to a return of the second theme in the tonic, followed not by the rondo theme again but by a coda. Occasionally the coda is in a faster tempo and sometimes includes a transformation of the rondo theme; an example of this occurs in the finale of Moscheles's G minor.

THE ROLE OF THE ORCHESTRA

In the virtuoso piano concerto the composer's concentration on the solo part meant that it was normally given a full texture; Chopin's

highly embellished slow movements and his propensity for developing
inner voices left little room for use of the orchestra in any other way
than as accompaniment. But the secondary role of the orchestra is
apparent not only in piano concertos of the period. In Weber's clarinet
concertos, for example, the clarinet is generally accompanied only by
the strings, often with simple accompaniment patterns typical of
Italian opera:

Ex. 90

WEBER: Clarinet Concerto in F minor (second subject of first movement)

In defending Chopin's orchestral writing, Tovey has remarked that
his orchestration is exactly right for the nature of his solo parts,[1] while
Abraham suggests that it should be regarded in the light of the delicate
water-colour orchestration of Hummel and Field rather than the
brilliant oil-painting of Berlioz, Mendelssohn, and Glinka.[2] In
addition the standard of orchestras in the early nineteenth century
varied widely, as did their exact constitution, so it is natural that the

[1] Ibid., p. 104. As Tovey says, the 'improvements' of Klindworth and others simply reinforce
   this impression.
[2] Gerald Abraham, *Slavonic and Romantic Music* (London, 1968), p. 23 – a more sympathetic
   view of Chopin's orchestration than in his *Chopin's Musical Style* (London, 1939), pp. 29–30.

orchestral writing tends to be homogeneous in character and not very enterprising. Moscheles's visit to Edinburgh in 1828 clashed with performances by an Italian opera company, so for his concerts he had to make do with a 'third-rate orchestra, got together anyhow from regimental bandsmen',[1] while as late as 1835 he complained about the poor orchestra in Amsterdam, and commented that he often omitted an Adagio because of the orchestra's inability to play softly.[2] Spohr, too, for his Italian tour in 1816–17 decided to write some new violin works 'with very simple and easy accompaniments ... as from all accounts the orchestras there are worse than those of the provincial towns in France',[3] and this accounts for the dominance of the solo in such pieces as his A minor Concerto '*In Form einer Gesangsszene*', which was composed for that tour. Sometimes piano concertos were actually played without accompaniment and they were normally published in such a way that the piano part could be played as a solo piece. The general acceptance of the secondary role of the orchestra is illustrated by the customary titles (such as 'Concerto for ... with the accompaniment of an orchestra') as well as by comments like the following on one of Moscheles's concertos: 'The instrumental parts are so blended with it [the piano] and so essential to its effect, that, like the concertos of Mozart and Beethoven, it ought to be considered as an orchestral piece.'[4]

It is therefore not suprising that the orchestra has a minor role in Chopin's concertos, but in fact it is not ignored as completely as is sometimes supposed. The combination of solo horn with the piano during the second subject of the E minor Concerto is a good example of a single instrument engaging in an effective duet with the piano, in a way that was later copied by Schumann and Liszt:

[1] Moscheles, op. cit., i, pp. 185–6.
[2] Ibid., p. 314.
[3] Spohr, op. cit., i, pp. 226–7. See also Spohr's comments on the French and Swiss orchestras of the period, pp. 217–26.
[4] *Harmonicon* (May 1828), p. 116.

Ex. 91

CHOPIN: Piano Concerto in E minor
Hn.(actual sound)

Chopin also gives thematic references to the orchestra in his development sections; but these certainly tend to be overshadowed by the brilliant solo writing, and it must also be conceded that apart from the ritornellos there is virtually no dialogue between piano and orchestra or examples of the solo accompanying the orchestra (although one example of the latter is to be found in the coda of the Larghetto of the E minor). We can now accept, however, that this was in accordance with the custom of the day, and that Beethoven was almost alone in his consistent involvement of the orchestra as an equal partner with the soloist.

PAGANINI

Because the individual concertos of the virtuoso period were so clearly identified with the musical personality of a particular performer, it is almost impossible to create in modern conditions the effect they made on the audiences of the time. This is particularly true of the violin concertos of Niccolò Paganini (1782–1840), who was without doubt the most sensational virtuoso of the early nineteenth century. Although Paganini did not play outside Italy until 1828, he had during the previous decade – thanks to the reports from the Italian correspondents of musical journals as well as from foreign travellers in Italy – established a reputation as the most brilliant violinist in all Europe.

He is said to have written as many as eight concertos, but so far only six have come to light in one form or another.[1] None was published in his lifetime – the set of Caprices was his only substantial work in print before his death – as he guarded the scores jealously and not even the orchestral parts were in general circulation. This did not mean that the concertos were not widely known – at least after Paganini had played them in Vienna, Berlin, Paris, and London – for their themes were quoted in fantasies for the piano as *Souvenirs des Concerts de Paganini*, or in theatrical farces like *Der falsche Virtuose, oder Das Concert auf der G Saite*, which had a successful run in Vienna during Paganini's 1828 visit. By refusing to publish them, however, Paganini reserved the right of performance to himself alone, and there is little doubt that his concertos were virtually created anew each time that he, a master of improvisation, played them. Such involvement in the actual process of creation is inevitably absent from modern performances of Paganini's concertos, and this affects our judgement of them when they are examined in the light of today's quite different sensibilities and more exacting criteria.

Paganini is known to have played concertos by Rode and Kreutzer, but in his own style and sometimes with the insertion of new material.[2] The influence of the French violin school on his own concertos may be seen in the disjointed, episodic nature of the first movements, their condensed recapitulations – usually consisting of only the second subject and the solo episode, with the third ritornello omitted – and the fashionable appeal of the finales. His most popular concerto movement was the *Rondo à la campanella* of the Concerto in B minor (later transcribed for piano by Liszt), while two of the concertos have polonaise finales. But Paganini's concertos are far more theatrical, even melodramatic at times, than those of his French models, and this must be attributed to the strong influence of Italian opera. Italy was the birthplace of the concerto, but now it was primarily a land of opera; all accounts by foreign visitors comment on the lamentable

[1] Two were published in 1851. Autographs of five concertos (in E flat major, B minor, E major, D minor, and A minor) are in the Biblioteca Casanatense, Rome. Of the fifth concerto, Paganini completed only the solo part. A sixth concerto in E minor, recently discovered in an arrangement for violin and guitar and containing indications of tutti and solo, has been orchestrated by Federico Mompellio (who also orchestrated the A minor Concerto) and published by the Istituto di Studi Paganiniani in 1973. This is thought to be the earliest of Paganini's surviving concertos.

[2] In Vienna, for example, he played an Adagio religioso to a concerto by Rode. Wilhelm Speyer, in a letter to Spohr (17 September 1829), described a private performance of Beethoven's Sonata in F, in which Paganini played the rondo theme in harmonics, and also lavishly embellished the Adagio.

standard of instrumental music, and the concert as it existed in the rest of Europe was a rarity in Italy. Many of Paganani's recitals in the earlier part of his career were actually 'intermezzo concerts' during the intervals of theatrical performances;[1] hence the operatic style of his concertos, with their abrupt changes in key or dynamics, their passionate solo melodies, and their abundance of dazzling technical tricks. Paganini's opening ritornellos usually sound like a Rossini overture, with their noisy orchestration, *bel canto* second subjects, and concluding fanfares; the Concerto in E flat, no. 1 provides a good example. The second subject of the B minor, no. 2, is particularly reminiscent of Rossini's melodic style, and such expressive cantilena is typical of Paganini's lyrical themes in the first and second movements, themes often accompanied by no more than pizzicato strings. Like most of the virtuoso composers, Paganini alternates constantly between the lyrical and the bravura, and often with dramatic effect, as in the declamatory fantasia that opens the second solo of the Concerto in E flat. But he was often criticized for spoiling the effect of a beautiful cantabile passage by suddenly indulging in spectacular tricks. His concertos are indeed strange mixtures; side by side with the passages of double stops, harmonics, and trills are such deeply felt movements as the Andante of the A minor Concerto no. 5, or the touching simplicity of the rondo's second episode in the E flat (a passage that is often omitted in modern performances). With them we stand on the threshold of the romantic concerto, even though they retain all the structural features of the classical form.

FORERUNNERS OF THE ROMANTIC CONCERTO

The influence of Beethoven is occasionally perceptible in concertos by those who studied with him, such as Moscheles, Ries, and Czerny, although it is usually confined to melodic or textural details. The arioso and recitative in the slow movement of Moscheles's Second Piano Concerto in E flat, for example, is obviously indebted to the Sonata in A flat, Op. 110,[2] and there are thematic similarities between Beethoven's G major and the first movement of the Piano Concerto in C sharp minor by Ries (1812). But Beethoven's influence may also be seen in the generally thematic nature of Moscheles's development

---

[1] Even during religious services; at Lucca, in 1801, he played a concerto at the conclusion of the Kyrie which not only lasted nearly half-an-hour but also included imitations of birds, the flute, trombone, and horn. See Geraldine de Courcy, *Paganini the Genoese* (Norman, Oklahoma, 1957), i, p. 67.
[2] This slow movement was completed in 1822, shortly after Moscheles had first studied and performed Beethoven's Op. 109 and Op. 110. Moscheles, op. cit., p. 63.

sections, in the short written-out cadenza in the G minor Concerto, and in the anticipation of the rondo theme during the slow movement of the same work. Moscheles belongs to a small group of early nineteenth-century composers in whose concertos there is more than mere virtuosity; others in this category include Carl Maria von Weber (1786–1826), Louis Spohr (1784–1851), and Felix Mendelssohn-Bartholdy (1809–47).

Because the virtuoso composers were concerned primarily with projecting the solo instrument against the background of an orchestral accompaniment, their works show little evidence of contrapuntal writing, but counterpoint at a fairly rudimentary level is apparent in the first movement of Moscheles's Concerto in G minor, where the second subject is accompanied by the first in both its orchestral and solo statements. There are several passages in Weber's piano concertos where the solo combines with the orchestra in presenting a similar synchronization of themes. In the recapitulation of the First Concerto in C major, for instance, the theme of the solo episode is played by the piano simultaneously with the second subject for flute and bassoon:

Ex. 92

In the finale of the same work the last appearance of the rondo theme for the piano is combined with an important woodwind melody from the second episode. Contrapuntal writing is also a feature of Mendelssohn's youthful concertos, especially in the double concertos composed in 1823–24 – two for two pianos, in E major and A flat major, and the Concerto in D minor for violin, piano, and strings.

The concertos of Weber, whether written for himself as pianist in 1810 or for the clarinettist Heinrich Bärmann in 1813, are cast in the virtuoso mould, especially as far as their brilliant and generally effective finales are concerned. But they also foreshadow the romantic concerto in their shorter or melodic solo episodes and their greater emphasis on an expressive cantabile rather than the profuse ornamentation of the virtuoso style. In his slow movements Weber created a new romantic atmosphere, which is heightened by his use of particular orchestral instruments, e.g. the solo cello in the C major Piano Concerto, or the three horns that play a chorale in the Adagio of the F minor Clarinet Concerto.

In contrast to the expansion evident everywhere in the virtuoso concerto, Weber maintained the modest dimensions of the eighteenth-century concerto without, however, being constrained by its formal conventions. Both piano concertos have condensed recapitulations in their first movements, with the first part drastically reduced by comparison with the exposition even though the second part is actually expanded. In the F minor Clarinet Concerto, the recapitulation is little more than a coda. Weber's opening ritornellos are also comparatively short, and in the same work the first ritornello consists only of the first subject and a bridge leading not to the second subject but to a cadential theme based on the first. Weber's formal freedom is, however, most apparent in the Clarinet Concertino (1811) and the *Concert-Stück* (1821) for piano and orchestra, which both renounce completely the structural principles of the classical concerto.

NEW FORMS

In this phase of the concerto's history a number of attempts were made to depart from established formal conventions. The three movements of the Piano Concerto no. 2, in C minor (1824) by Konradin Kreutzer (1780–1849) are played without a break; the first movement is in neither sonata nor ritornello form, while the main theme of the finale is derived from that of the slow movement. Cramer's Concerto no. 8 in D minor (1825) has an abbreviated first movement, extending only to the end of the first solo and then leading directly into the slow movement. There are also examples of single-movement works, such as the three concertinos for piano by Czerny, published as his Op. 78, and the *Concert en Fantaisie* in A major, Op. 14 (1815), by Johann Ludwig Böhner (1787–1860). The latter is a true one-movement work with most of the features of the classical concerto form, but it is expanded through a series of independent episodes and also contains new material during the recapitulation. Böhner's first *Concert en Fantaisie*, in D minor, Op. 13 (also 1815), is even more unorthodox, beginning with a recitative and consisting of several linked sections that could almost be regarded as separate movements.

Some of the newer forms were derived from operatic models. Just as the ritornello aria had earlier been paralleled by the baroque concerto, so now the dramatic scena provided the impetus for a fresh structural basis. In works like the Oboe Concerto in E flat by Vincenzo Bellini (1801–35) and the Concertino for cor anglais (1817) by Gaetano Donizetti (1797–1848), a slow movement linked to an Allegro correspond to the cavatina and cabaletta of the Italian operatic scena. Both works begin with short orchestral introductions, and in Spohr's Violin Concerto no. 12 in A major (also known as his First Concertino – the term 'concerto' was often avoided in these formally experimental works) the introduction is expanded into a longer section of accompanied recitative.

The most famous example of a concerto explicitly modelled on the operatic scena is Spohr's Concerto no. 8 in A minor, *in modo di scena cantante*, written expressly for his visit to Italy in 1816. It too has an introductory section with a vigorous orchestral opening and a solo recitative that gradually becomes more dramatic and florid, an Adagio with a tender cantilena and a more declamatory middle section, followed by an extended Allegro moderato that is an unusual combination of the concerto-sonata and rondo forms. The solo part is basically vocal in origin but the violin is obviously able to transcend the limitations of the voice through its much wider range and through the employment of double stops, which are featured in the recitative that links the Adagio and the Allegro, as well as in the cadenza at the end of the work.

WEBER'S *CONCERT-STÜCK*

Spohr's concerto may well have influenced the single-movement structure of Weber's *Concert-Stück* of 1821 but it was probably not the only model for what proved to be a significant landmark in the development of concerto form. Weber doubtless knew Böhner's fantasy-concertos, and his own already mentioned Concertino for clarinet and orchestra, with its succession of Adagio, Andante, and rondo, also provided a precedent for a work consisting of a series of sections in varying tempo and character. However the order of the sections is different in the *Concert-Stück* from any of these apparent models. The opening Larghetto affettuoso is essentially an introductory fantasia that provides an extended dominant preparation for the following Allegro passionato in F minor, while the march in C major has a similar role with regard to the second of the two fast sections in the brilliant style, the final Presto giocoso. The novel form of the *Concert-Stück* is partly an outcome of its programme, which was not printed by Weber but was recounted to his pupil Julius Benedict, who published it with what he claimed to be the composer's approval.[1] The story of a noble lady, who has a terrifying vision of her knight lying dead on a battlefield in the Holy Land, only to be suddenly reunited with him as the Crusaders return triumphant, is in fact a detailed development of the more generalized programme that Weber already had in mind when he first planned an F minor concerto in 1815. The work was originally designed in the conventional three movements, and Weber felt that 'as concertos in the minor without definite evocative ideas seldom work with the public, I have instinctively inserted into the whole thing a kind of story whose thread will connect and define its character.'[2] The basic outline of Weber's 'story' – separation, lament, and jubilant reunion – may have been

---

[1] Julius Benedict, *Carl Maria von Weber* (London, 1881), p. 65.
[2] Letter to Friedrich Rochlitz, 14 March 1815, in Max Maria von Weber, *Carl Maria von Weber: Ein Lebensbild* (Leipzig, 1864), i, p. 479.

suggested by Beethoven's Op. 81a, which had been published in 1811.[1]
But extra-musical ideas do not determine the structure of the
'Lebewohl' sonata in the same way as they do in the *Concert-Stück*,
and in this respect the latter also differs significantly from most of the
concertos of the same period that have programmatic associations.
The storms of Field and Steibelt, for example, form self-contained
episodes within a development section and a rondo respectively. Of
course few of these works have a programme anywhere near as
detailed as Weber's, and even in Steibelt's *Voyage sur le Mont Bernard*
(Concerto no. 6 in G minor) (before 1816) – which has a preface
detailing the composer's intention to describe the wild mountain
scene, along with the hospice and the monks' chants and resounding
bell beckoning the lost traveller to this hospitable haven[2] – the directly
evocative ideas are confined almost completely to the first ritornello.
Weber's *Concert-Stück* is thus a truly romantic work in that its form
is dictated by other than purely musical considerations, yet its
significance for the concerto can be seen not so much in its
programmatic successors, for these are relatively few,[3] but in its
complete abandonment of ritornello form and of the sequence of three
separate movements.

MENDELSSOHN

It was Mendelssohn who finally broke away altogether from the
classical form. Although his Piano Concerto in G minor (1831) was
written at almost the same time as Chopin's piano concertos and
Paganini's last violin concertos, it really belongs to an entirely new
era. The first movement is in sonata form, without any trace of a
ritornello – in fact, the only two extended tuttis occur after the
statement of the first subject by the piano, and at the end of the
movement, this latter being extended into a transition to the slow
movement. Like Weber's *Concert-Stück* and Spohr's *Scena cantante*,
the work is played without a break, although it still consists of the
conventional three movements. But a greater sense of unity is achieved
by the use of the same linking fanfare in the two transitional passages,
and by a recollection of the first movement's second subject
immediately before the coda of the finale. The brilliance and élan of

---

[1] Other 'farewell' piano concertos are Hummel's in E major, Op. 110 (*Les Adieux de Paris*),
played in Paris in 1825 but probably composed as early as 1814, and Ries's in A, Op. 132
(*Abschieds-Concert von England*), first played at Ries's farewell London concert in 1824.

[2] Steibelt was accused of borrowing this programme from Cherubini's opera *Élisa ou le Voyage
au Mont Bernard*. See p. 33, and *Allgemeine musikalische Zeitung* (August 1816), col. 548.

[3] Moscheles's No. 8 in D (*Pastorale*), composed in 1838, has a detailed programme which the
composer revealed in a letter to Mendelssohn, but in his two previous concertos, the *Fantastique*
and the *Pathetique*, there is no such elaboration.

Mendelssohn's piano writing is derived from Moscheles and Weber, while the latter's influence is also felt in the Andante, where the cellos have an important role. The final appearances of the main theme – the first for lower strings with elaborate piano decoration, and the second for the piano in octaves, accompanied by *divisi* string tremolos – effectively combine solo and orchestra in a manner already foreshadowed by Weber in his slow movements. Mendelssohn clearly built on the foundations laid by the virtuosos of the early nineteenth century, but with this particular work he also inaugurated a new chapter in the history of the concerto.

VI

BEETHOVEN'S
CHAMBER MUSIC

By GERALD ABRAHAM

BEETHOVEN'S chamber music displays not only his genius but the full extent of his creative career more completely than any other single field of his activity. The piano quartets of 1785 were preceded only by the three piano sonatas of 1783, the E flat Concerto of 1784, and a few minor works; the last great string quartets came after the *Missa Solemnis*, the last Piano Sonata, the 'Diabelli' Variations and the Ninth Symphony. And the chamber works constitute not only an event of the first magnitude in musical history but the central feature of a long and most notable period in history. They are not – like Bach's keyboard music, for example – one of those great mountains of artistic achievement which interrupt the historian's course and give him dominating views over a surrounding plain but whose crossing does not advance him very far on his journey; they are, rather, a great plateau in traversing which it is all too easy for him to forget the country on either side. Indeed when he comes to the end of it and looks out over the cliff of the last quartets he finds that he has to retrace his steps. It took the rest of music, conveniently personified in this case by Wagner, a quarter of a century to grow to comprehension of those quartets. Beethoven had compressed nearly seventy years of musical evolution into just over forty. But if the end of the chapter takes us up to a group of works astonishingly different from any other music that was being written in the eighteen-twenties, the beginning is firmly planted in contemporaneity.

JUVENILIA

The fifteen-to-sixteen-year-old boy who wrote the *Trois quatuors pour le clavecin, Violino, Viola e Basso* (WoO 36)[1] in 1785 and the *Trio concertant a clavicembalo, flauto, fagotto* (WoO 37) probably during the next year or so seems to have known little or nothing of Haydn, and

[1] WoO numbers refer to Georg Kinsky and Hans Halm, *Das Werk Beethovens, thematisch-bibliographisches Verzeichnis* (Munich, 1955).

though he manifestly idolized Mozart he was unable to take the latter's piano quartets as models for his own: the G minor, K.478, was written only the same year, the E flat, K.493, not till the following one. He was content for the most part to follow the contemporary fashion for chamber music in which the centre of gravity was placed in the keyboard instrument while the strings 'accompanied'. The cello part seldom has a genuinely independent existence, the one markedly exceptional passage being the fourth variation in the E flat Quartet where it takes the lead; the bassoon in the Trio enjoys much more independence. Only in occasional rudimentary antiphony between piano and strings, e.g. in the first movement of the D major Quartet,[1] does the boy appear more venturesome than his older contemporaries in the use of the medium. Structurally, too, these first chamber compositions are typical of their period – and only slightly more mature than Beethoven's own three piano sonatas of 1783. The development sections of the sonata-form Allegros begin to be more interesting, however; that of the E flat Quartet is based on the chromatic figure of the codetta – B flat, C flat, B flat, A natural – which seems to have caught the composer's fancy, for he uses it again in the parallel passages of the C minor Trio, Op. 1, no. 3; that of the C major is still more striking, beginning with a plunge into a remote key and working over the material of the exposition at considerable length (43 bars); the development section of the piano, flute, and bassoon Trio, opening in typically Mozartean fashion in octaves, is based on an entirely new theme. The slow movements, as in the earlier sonatas, are nearly always in 2/4 time; they are almost completely overgrown with ornamentation – Mozartean singing fioriture, turns, the form of appoggiatura that has come to be known as the 'Mannheim sigh'. Sometimes one can put one's finger on a specific Mozartean model. Thus 'Thayer' – a convenient collective name for Thayer himself and his posthumous German collaborators Deiters and Riemann – pointed out that the obvious model for the E flat Quartet was Mozart's violin Sonata in G (K.379) 'with its slow introductory movement, the Allegro in the minor, the final variations', and similar parallels between other quartets and other Mozart violin sonatas have been observed by later scholars.[2] (The rather rambling E flat major Adagio assai of the E flat Quartet, leading without a break into the E flat minor Allegro con spirito, has a parallel in the rather rambling G minor Adagio, leading without a break into the G major variations –

---

[1] For an earlier version of the opening of the D major Quartet, see Ludwig Schiedermair, *Der junge Beethoven* (Leipzig, 1925), pp. 297–8.
[2] Notably Maynard Solomon, *Beethoven* (New York, 1977; London, 1978), p. 47.

again final variations – of the early Trio; and both sets of variations end in the same way, for which there was a Mozartean precedent in the Divertimento in F (K.253), with a return of the theme in quicker tempo. But the workmanship of the Trio is in every respect superior.) Both the second phrase of the Adagio of the E flat Quartet and the principal theme of the rondo-finale of the C major call to mind Mozart's Rondo in D (K.485), written the following year. Yet here and there already one detects in the smooth boyish face traits of the man he is to become. Even the E flat Adagio opens with a suggestion of the emotional depths to be revealed by Beethoven's mature slow movements (though the fifths between treble and bass in its antepenultimate bar remind us that he is still only fifteen), while the Allegro to which it leads is quite astonishingly passionate. The opening theme:

Ex. 93

starts with one of those 'Mannheim rocket' ideas that open so many 'allegro' movements of this period (cf. the Trio for piano, flute, and bassoon) but not only has the principal theme the power and urgency common to other 'rocket' themes in the minor, such as those of the finale of Mozart's great G minor Symphony and the first movement of Beethoven's own, later Piano Sonata in F minor, Op. 2, no. 1, and a seven-bar length that proclaims its contempt for routine; its continuation, the bridge-passages, the second subject in the dominant *minor* throughout, all sustain its fire and confident energy. It is not surprising to learn from Nottebohm[1] that Beethoven thought of using a modified form of Ex. 93 in C minor[2] as a theme for a symphony.

Nothing came of this very early Symphony in C minor but other material from the piano quartets, never published in Beethoven's lifetime, was later embodied in two of the Sonatas, Op. 2, dedicated to Haydn, which the composer considered worthy of publication

[1] *Zweite Beethoveniana* (Leipzig, 1887), p. 567.
[2] Quoted in Grove, *Beethoven and his Nine Symphonies* (London, 1896), p.181; the whole 111-bar sketch is reproduced in Joseph Kerman, *Ludwig van Beethoven: Autograph Miscellany from c. 1786 to 1789* (Brit. Lib. Add. MSS 29801) (London, 1970), sketch, i, fo. 70r and v; transcription, ii, p. 175.

eleven years after the quartets were written. The opening of the
Adagio con espressione of the C major Quartet:

Ex. 94

was polished into the Adagio of Op. 2, no. 1, and comparison of the
two versions – revealing the virtual identity of the first four bars, the
elimination of the curious dynamic effect in bar 4, and the later
transfiguration of bars 6 and 7 – is as illuminating as most comparisons
of Beethoven's final thoughts with their embryonic forms. The second
strain of the sonata movement begins with the suggestion that it too
is going to repeat the quartet music but diverges at once; the two
movements have nothing more in common except a wealth of – quite
different – florid ornamentation. A more odd proceeding was

Beethoven's dovetailing of two passages from the first movement of the same quartet into the first movement of the sonata in the same key, Op. 2, no. 3; so insignificant are the string parts that he was able to transfer the piano part almost unmodified. The first passage, bars 21–26 of the sonata, springs naturally from the sparkling context of the quartet movement with its suggestion of *opera buffa* overture, but the transition to the G minor theme common to both – again the dominant minor emphasized in a second subject – is not abrupt as in the sonata; in the quartet the bars equivalent to 26 and 27 of the sonata are separated by fourteen bars in which the new key is duly approached through its own dominant.

THE BONN INSTRUMENTALISTS

The quartets were presumably written with members of the Bonn Hofkapelle in mind. We know from a report of 1784 that the Elector's orchestra had one excellent violinist – Franz Ries (father of the composer Ferdinand Ries) – as well as one described as 'very good', two as 'good', and four as 'mediocre'; both the 'Braccists' are listed as 'mediocre', but the young composer may have played the viola himself instead of the harpsichord; the sole cellist was 'good' – but was given only one passage in the whole of the three quartets where he could show himself as such. Whether the Trio was also written for the Electoral orchestra is more doubtful. One of the three bassoonists, Kicheler, was 'very good' and moreover had 'two boys, of whom one plays the *Fagott Solo* well, the other tolerably on the *Flaute*'. But more probably the piece was composed for the bassoon-playing Freiherr von Westerholt, his son Count Wilhelm, who is said to have been a master of the flute, and one of his daughters, four years younger than Beethoven, his pupil and boyish idol, and a brilliant harpsichordist. Beethoven wrote his Trio for good players, therefore more probably for the Westerholts than for the young Kichelers. The elder Westerholt is known to have had a good domestic orchestra 'particularly of wind instruments', formed by his servants, and the Elector himself maintained an excellent *Tafelmusik* consisting of two oboes, two clarinets, two bassoons, and two horns. According to Carl Ludwig Junker, an amateur composer who heard the latter in 1791 and published a long and enthusiastic account of them in Bossler's *Musikalische Korrespondenz*,[1] these eight players were 'masters in their art'. It is not surprising therefore to find the young Beethoven writing a good deal of wind chamber music during his Bonn period.

[1] Reprinted in Thayer, *Ludwig van Beethovens Leben* (Leipzig, third ed. 1917), i, p. 268; translated in Elliot Forbes's edition of Thayer (Princeton, 1964), pp. 104–5.

EARLY WORKS RECAST

Some of these early compositions are of little interest. We need not concern ourselves with the three Duos for clarinet and bassoon (WoO 27), which are probably not by Beethoven, the Allegro and Minuetto for two flutes (WoO 26) which Beethoven wrote 'for friend Degenharth' on '23 August 1792. 12 at night', or the doubtfully authentic Sonata in B flat for flute which anyhow was published in a badly garbled form.[1] But two works composed for the full combination of the Electoral *Tafelmusik* deserve a brief examination; they are an Octet – or, as Beethoven himself called it, 'Parthia' – in E flat, posthumously published as Op. 103, and a Rondino (WoO 25) in the same key. Both are attractive specimens of late-eighteenth-century wind chamber music, though the 'Parthia', it should be noted, is not a 'serenade': it keeps to the four movements of symphony and sonata. Although written for the same combination, the actual parts of the Octet and Rondino differ so markedly that it is hard to believe they were intended for the same players; the horns in the Octet have nothing like the melodic importance they enjoy in the Rondino, and the clarinets in the Rondino have parts not inferior in interest to those of the oboes, while in the Octet the oboes, particularly the first, have the more important roles. Documentary evidence[2] dates the Octet 1782, at the very end of the Bonn period; internal evidence suggests that the Rondino was written earlier.

At some time before February 1791, probably when he was composing the C major Piano Sonata, Op. 2, no. 3, with its closely related opening theme, Beethoven re-cast the Octet as a String Quintet, Op. 4, and comparison of the two versions shows considerable light on his development as an instrumental composer during those four important formative years. (The theory sometimes advanced, that the Quintet is the earlier version, is preposterous; Beethoven never altered a work structurally for the worse.) The Quintet is by no means an arrangement of the Octet; unlike Mozart's parallel re-casting of his Octet for the same combination of instruments (K.388) as a String Quintet (K.406), it is in many respects a new work. Everything has become more plastic; stiff formulae are softened; the texture is lightened in weight but enriched by polyphony and the devices of 'obbligato accompaniment'. The harmony, too, has become richer:

---

[1] Cf. Thayer, op. cit., i, p. 321; Thayer-Forbes, p. 130; and Willy Hess, 'Der Erstdruck von Beethovens Flötensonate', *Neues Beethoven-Jahrbuch*, vi (Brunswick, 1935), p. 141.
[2] See Nottebohm, op. cit., p. 517, and Thayer, i, p. 310 (Thayer-Forbes, p. 121).

Ex. 95(i) and (ii)

(ii)

there is a wider and bolder handling of key in transitional passages, still more in the development section of the first movement with its opening plunge into a far remoter region:

Ex. 96(i) and (ii)

The only passage common to the two first-movement developments is a fifteen-bar episode which in the Octet traverses A flat major, E flat major, and C minor, in the Quintet D flat, E flat minor, and F minor – even in that detail taking a less obvious path. In the Octet it is simply a non-thematic episode, though it is referred to in the coda; in the Quintet, as Hans Gál points out,[1] Beethoven contrives that it shall arise naturally from a thematic context and the opening theme is later interwoven with it. Structurally everything is worked out in the Quintet on lines that are at the same time broader and subtler: the exposition of the first movement of the Quintet is 88 bars long as compared with the 69 of the Octet, the development 77 as compared with 56. The sixteen-bar periods that open minuet and trio of the Octet are expanded to 22 and 24 bars respectively in the Quintet, and the structure becomes much clearer, less fussy. (The theme of the minuet, particularly in the second paragraph of both works, is elder brother of the scherzo-theme of the Ninth Symphony.) In the rondo finale the principal subject runs to 28 instead of 12 bars, the entirely new first episode is nearly twice the length of the one it replaces, and the principal subject returns three times instead of only twice. All in all, it is hardly an exaggeration to say that the difference between Octet and Quintet represents the whole difference between the *al fresco*, serenade music that was just going out of fashion and the new

---

[1] 'Die Stileigentümlichkeiten des jungen Beethoven', *Studien zur Musikwissenschaft*, iv (Leipzig and Vienna, 1916), particularly p. 112.

finely wrought quartet style of late Haydn with its 'openwork texture', its so-called *durchbrochene Arbeit*.[1]

There is actually a story that the Quintet version was begun as a quartet. According to Wegeler[2] Beethoven was in 1795 commissioned by Count Apponyi to compose a string quartet: 'Beethoven twice set to work but the result of his first attempt was a great Violin Trio (Op. 3), of the second a Violin Quintet (Op. 4).' It is quite true that much of the Quintet could be played on four instruments; in fact the second trio of the minuet, for which there was no original in the Octet, is scored for quartet only. But one's confidence in Wegeler is shaken by the knowledge that the String Trio in E flat, Op. 3, a divertimento-like work in six movements clearly inspired by Mozart's Divertimento, K.563, existed as early as 1792 though Beethoven may well have revised it before he published it in 1797.[3]

FIRST VIENNESE WORKS

Beethoven's removal from Bonn was more than a merely external change. It brought him under the immediate influence of Haydn and it brought him on to a much wider, more public stage where he naturally wished to revise earlier works before he published them. One composition, however, seems to have been rushed out – the Variations for piano and violin on Mozart's 'Se vuol ballare' which were published as early as July 1793 – the reason, as appears from Beethoven's letter of 2 November to Eleonore von Breuning, being his discovery that Viennese pianists were listening to his improvisations and copying his mannerisms. To 'copyright' his style, as it were, he hurried into print these Variations, which thus give some idea of his keyboard improvising – for, as Josef Müller-Blattau had little difficulty in showing,[4] the Variations were originally conceived for piano solo, the violin part having been added, partly as an 'accompaniment' in the earlier eighteenth-century manner (particularly in variations 1, 2, 3, 11, and 12), partly to relieve the difficulties of the piano part (as in the coda). The rather earlier set of fourteen Variations in E flat for

---

[1] On the relationship between Octet and Quintet see also Thayer op. cit., ii, p. 33 (Thayer-Forbes, p. 678); Alfred Orel, 'Beethovens Oktett Op. 103 und seine Bearbeitung als Quintett Op. 4', *Zeitschrift für Musikwissenschaft*, iii (1920), p. 154, Friedrich Munter, 'Beethovens Bearbeitungen eigener Werke', *Neues Beethoven-Jahrbuch*, vi, p. 159; 'Ein Skizzenblatt Beethovens aus den Jahren 1796–7', by Benedikt Szabolcsi, *Zeitschrift für Musikwissenschaft*, xvii (1935), p. 545; Hubert Unverricht, 'Original und Bearbeitung: ein Beitrag zu Beethovens eigenen Bearbeitungen seiner Kammermusikwerke', *Beethoven-Kolloquium 1977: Dokumentation und Aufführungspraxis*, ed. Rudolf Klein (Kassel, 1978), p. 190.

[2] *Biographische Notizen über Ludwig van Beethoven* (Koblenz, 1838).

[3] For Beethoven's later attempt to re-cast Op. 3 as a piano trio see Wilhelm Altmann's article and reproduction, *Zeitschrift für Musikwissenschaft*, iii (1920–1), p. 129.

[4] 'Beethoven und die Variation', *Neues Beethoven-Jahrbuch*, v (Brunswick, 1933), p. 101.

piano, violin, and cello, published in 1804 as Op. 44, belongs to the same category; the string parts in most of the variations are either superfluous or could easily be made so, and a piano cadenza evidently for the coda, printed by Nottebohm in his first collection of *Beethoveniana*, heightens one's suspicion that these variations, too, originated as piano improvisation. Their chief interest lies in the theme – detached quavers played by all three instruments in bare octaves, essentially only a bass and harmonic skeleton rather like the theme of the later and far more famous *Prometheus* and 'Eroica' variations, and itself very like no. 4 of the *Prometheus* music, Op. 43 – but they are also characteristic both of Beethoven's curious mania for the key of E flat at this period and of his interest in the piano trio combination.

In addition to these Variations, four full-length piano trios, two of them also in E flat, date from the early 1790s. According to Franz Gräffer, who compiled a manuscript catalogue of Beethoven's works, the posthumously published Trio in E flat (WoO 38) was 'composed *anno* 1791 and originally intended to be one of the 3 Trios Op. 1, but omitted by Beethoven as too weak'. 1791 is quite probable, for the Trio while certainly not later than the Bonn period is considerably more accomplished than the piano quartets; and if Gräffer is right he helps us to establish when Beethoven first began to think of writing a set of trios. The three that he eventually published in 1795 as his Op. 1 cannot be dated precisely; we know that they were performed soon after his arrival in Vienna, in 1793 or early January 1794, at Prince Lichnowsky's in the presence of Haydn, but the sketch-books show[1] that Beethoven was working on them later in 1794; probably, like the String Trio, Op. 3, they are compositions of the Bonn period revised, perhaps even new movements substituted, in 1794. The sketches show that the final movements of both the G major and the C minor bring together themes not originally conceived in such relationship. But if these three Trios were originally conceived at about the same time as the wind Octet, their revision in 1794 reveals no such craftsmanship as the re-writing of the Octet for five strings in 1796–7.

The material of the Trios is oddly diverse. We find the old Mannheim rocket (opening of Op. 1, no. 1, opening of the Adagio introduction to no. 2 – answered by an anticipation of the first theme of the Allegro vivace, opening of the finale of no. 3), Mozartean cantilena (the Largo con espressione of no. 2), the unmistakable new

[1] Nottebohm, *Zweite Beethoveniana*, pp. 21–8 and Kerman, ii, pp. 1–7.

influence of Haydn (scherzo and finale of no.1, finale of no. 2, Minuet of no. 3); in the first sixteen-bar period of the Allegro vivace of no. 2 Haydn seems to be answered by Mozart – the sketches show that at one period of gestation Haydn was answered by Haydn. The string parts have won much more independence than in the piano quartets but are not yet completely emancipated; there is documentary evidence that the scherzo of no. 2 and the principal subject of the finale of no. 3 began their existence as piano-pieces, the latter being also transmogrified, like the opening subject of Schumann's G minor Piano Sonata, from 'andante' to 'prestissimo'.

The earlier E flat Trio is in only three movements; these are all four-movement compositions. But it is worth noting that the middle movement of the early E flat is called 'scherzo' ('allegro ma non troppo'): apparently the first occasion on which Beethoven used the word. The E flat and G major Trios of Op. 1 have 'scherzi', the former marked 'allegro assai', the C minor a 'Menuetto'. But Beethoven seems to have attached little importance to the distinction; the sketch of the scherzo of no. 2 is headed 'Menuetto' and in the oldest edition two of the parts are marked 'Menuetto', the third 'Scherzo'. The important point is the appearance of the new Haydnish scherzo-feeling; the scherzo of Op. 1, no. 1, opens with nearly the same rhythmic pattern as the 'Menuetto' of the Octet but is as unmistakably a scherzo as the other is a minuet.

Not only in the material but in the structure of the Op. 1 Trios one observes those Haydnish features which came to be characteristic of Beethoven too: for instance, the long and important codas – practically second development sections – of the first movements of nos. 1 and 2 in particular. There are considerable changes in the first-movement recapitulation of no. 2: poetic touches like the alteration of the piano's 'Mozartean reply' and the addition of the cello imitation a dozen bars later, more important changes in the transition. The changes in the recapitulation of the Allegro con brio of the C minor Trio are absolutely Beethovenian. But then practically the whole Trio is Beethovenian. The semitone higher echo in bars 5–6 of the striking unison opening theme, very different from the formal opening of its companions, is highly characteristic; the subsidiary idea beginning at bar 19, with the sforzando on the second beat, is a foretaste of the parallel passage in the 'Eroica'; the E flat minor transition recalls the passionate vehemence of the early Piano Quartet movement in the same key, while the codetta literally recalls the parallel passage in that movement. The boldness of the modulations at the beginning of the development is easily surpassed by the boldness of the beginning of the reprise, which steps almost immediately into C *major* and then into the 'Neapolitan' key, D flat major. Again in the second movement, not only is the theme Beethovenian in feeling: the variations are on the whole genuine trio variations. Nor would many composers in 1794 have thought of ending a work with 87 bars of almost unrelieved *pianissimo*, the last 11 of them a *tierce de Picardie* 'composed out' in piano scales. It is hardly surprising that Haydn, who admired the other two trios, according to Ries, advised Beethoven not to publish the C minor; or that Beethoven was correspondingly annoyed by the older man's disapproval of his own favourite of the three. He must have continued to think highly of the C minor Trio in later years when he had come to dislike other of his first-period works such as the Septet, for in 1817 – incited by some bungler's attempt to do the same thing – he transcribed it for string quintet, in which form it was published in February 1819, as Op. 104.[1] Moreover he did not find it necessary in recasting the Trio after more than twenty years to carry out anything like the drastic reconstruction of the Wind Octet after four or five; the texture is completely recast in terms of five strings and sometimes enriched by a new part (e.g. trio of the minuet, coda of the finale), pianistic passages are rewritten, but there is no real structural change. The only passage he completely rejected was the jejune chromatic scale for piano which heralds the recapitulation in the last movement; this he replaced by eight thematic bars; even so, part of the chromatic scale remains in the first violin part. In the first movement he removed the piano turn on the first note of the opening theme wherever it occurs, but no other ornaments. The sole lesson in composition – as distinct from transcription – one can draw from comparison of the two versions is (what one already knew) that Beethoven grew to dislike non-thematic texture. In several places (e.g. bars 18 and 22 of the development of the Allegro con brio, bars 6–7 of the recapitulation, the passage in the finale just mentioned) an 'empty' passage is strengthened or a caesura bridged by a fragment of theme.

MUSIC FOR VIENNESE WIND-PLAYERS

With these early trios we may group the rather later Trio in B flat for piano, clarinet, and cello, Op. 11, of 1798. It is an amiable but, despite its striking opening, an undistinguished work, interesting only for the facts that the Adagio is known to have sprung from the same sketches as the minuets of the earlier Piano Sonata, Op. 49, no. 2

[1] See Unverricht, op. cit., and Alan Tyson, 'The Authors of the Op. 104 String Quintet', *Beethoven Studies (1)*, ed. Tyson (New York, 1973; London, 1974), p. 158.

(1796) and the later Septet (1800) and that the theme of the final variations – the Trio is in three movements – is a terzetto from Weigl's opera *L'Amor marinaro*, produced the year before. The theme was apparently not his own choice; the publisher Artaria claimed that it was his; according to Czerny, 'it was at the wish of the clarinet-player, for whom B. wrote this Trio, that he employed the above theme by Weigl (which was then very popular) as the finale. At a later period he frequently contemplated writing another concluding movement for this Trio and letting the variations stand as a separate work'. We must take this 'occasional' element, this willingness to oblige an individual player – in this case possibly the clarinettist Josef Beer or Pär – into account in considering Beethoven's wind and partly wind chamber music of the early Viennese as of the Bonn period. (He even wrote two short pieces for mandoline and piano to please his friend, the mandoline virtuoso Wenzel Krumpholz.)

Two of these compositions, both in E flat, the three-movement Sextet for strings and two horns, Op. 81b (1794–5) and the four-movement Sextet for two clarinets, two bassoons, and two horns, Op. 71 (probably 1796), are frankly serenade- or divertimento-like in character; Hans Gál[1] surmises that they may originally have had additional movements, omitted on publication. Both are somewhat Mozartean; both, as one expects of divertimenti, are *al fresco* in style, charming in sound but without the finer polish of true chamber music. Op. 71, the better of the two, has two points of special interest: a second-subject theme in the first movement rhythmically resembling the already mentioned 'Eroica'-like theme in Op. 1, no. 3, and, like it, stressed on the second beat, and a *Choral*-like episode in even minims in the finale almost identical in melody and harmony with the passage just before the violin cadenza in the finale of the Septet, Op. 20, in the same key – A flat – and with nearly the same scoring (clarinet and two horns – clarinet, bassoon, and horn). Equally Mozartean, but in the more intimate chamber-music style, is the Quintet in E flat for piano, oboe, clarinet, horn, and bassoon, Op. 16, which may have been written in Vienna at any time before 1797; in this case Beethoven even took a specific Mozartean model, the Quintet (K.452) in the same key, for the same combination, and laid out in the same general form. Op. 16 was published also in a version for piano, violin, viola, and cello, the only instance of Beethoven's return to the combination with which he had begun his career as a composer of chamber music. Comparison of the two versions is in this case of little interest; the piano part is the same in both and although the strings sometimes play

[1] Op. cit., p. 111.

where the wind had been left silent, the only instance worth drawing
attention to is near the end of the finale where the violin four times
plays a snatch of the rondo theme to bridge the caesurae in the piano
part (cf. the similar additions in the Quintet version of the C minor
Piano Trio). Yet it is perhaps worth while to show how Beethoven
recast for the viola a florid melody in the Andante cantabile originally
given to the horn, if only for the sake of drawing attention to the
Mozartean nature of the *fioriture* and chromatic appoggiaturas in
both:

Ex. 97

The name of the already mentioned clarinettist Josef Beer figures in
contemporary accounts of performances of both this Quintet and the
Sextet, Op. 71. Whether Beethoven was specially interested in any
particular oboe-player it is difficult to say. We know the names of
several oboists with whom he was acquainted; he had an intimate
understanding of the instrument's mechanism and limitations[1] and
seems to have preferred it to the clarinet. He chooses it, for instance,
in an E flat Quintet for oboe, three horns, and bassoon which survives
only in a fragment of which the beautiful Adagio alone is complete.
Two compositions for the curious combination of two oboes and cor
anglais – a full-length four-movement Trio (or, as Beethoven himself
called it, a Terzetto) in C major, Op. 87, and a set of variations on
Mozart's 'La ci darem' – were almost certainly suggested by a Serenade
in C major for the same three instruments by the oboist, composer and
arranger of music for wind ensemble Johann Went, performed at a
meeting of the Viennese Tonkünstlergesellschaft on 23 December
1793 by the brothers Johann, Franz, and Philipp Teimer. (Hence we

[1] Cf. Hans Wlach, 'Die Oboe bei Beethoven', *Beethoven-Festschrift* (Vienna, 1927), p. 107.

are fairly safe in dating the two Beethoven works 1794.) Wlach[1] found Went's composition in the Library of the Gesellschaft der Musik-freunde[2] where it is erroneously described, by a later hand, as 'Serenade per due flauti e corno inglese' and the oboe parts altered for the sake of the substituted flutes; the fact that, in place of the missing second oboe part, Wlach found the second part of Beethoven's Op. 87 (inscribed 'Flauto secondo') confirms the connection between the two works. According to Wlach, Went's composition is in six movements: Allegro, Andante più tosto allegretto, Menuetto con Trio, Andante, Menuetto con Trio, Rondo; 'most of the melodies and their pitiful workings-out dissolve into passage-work and broken chords'. Beethoven's Op. 87, on the other hand, is notable not only for its skilful handling of the instruments and the three-part texture of limited total compass but for its firm, clear form; indeed, while no masterpiece, it is an excellent specimen of early Beethoven and more individual than a number of the works written at about the same period. Equally attractive and in some places, e.g. the first oboe's chromatic runs in the fifth variation, equally difficult considering the mechanism of the instrument in Beethoven's day, are the 'Variationen für zwei Oboen und Englisch-Horn über ein Thema aus Mozarts *Don Juan*' (WoO 28), though they were omitted from the *Gesamtausgabe* and had to wait till 1914 before Breitkopf published them. Like Went's Serenade and the Trio, Op. 87, they are in C major.

WORKS WITH CELLO

Themes from a Mozart opera – 'Ein Mädchen oder Weibchen' (Op. 66) and 'Bei Männern, welche Liebe fühlen' (WoO 46) from *Die Zauberflöte* – are also the bases of two out of three sets of variations for cello and piano which date from 1798 and 1801 respectively. *Don Giovanni* and *Zauberflöte* must have been much in Beethoven's mind at this period for reminiscence-hunters have found echoes of both in the Quintet, Op. 16. The third set of cello variations, on 'See the conqu'ring hero comes' (WoO 45), is earlier (1796), and marked by more stiff and conventional writing for both instruments and unenterprising harmony; there is a certain amount of tentative canon and imitation but the whole set belongs to the same world as Beethoven's more perfunctory piano variations of the same period, with penultimate slow variation and lively finale in triple time. The two 'Mozart' sets are more interesting. To take only one point of comparison: they too have slow penultimate variations and lively

[1] Op. cit., p. 113.
[2] VIII 1229.

finales in triple time, but the slow variations – in the cases of the 'Mädchen oder Weibchen' set, *two* slow variations in the minor – though still marked by the general floridity of Beethoven's slow music of this period, sound a note of deeper feeling and reveal a more interesting musical texture than the corresponding 'Handel' variation. The finale on 'Ein Mädchen oder Weibchen' plunges into a subsidiary variation in polacca rhythm, almost identical in key and opening motive with the Allegretto alla polacca in the Trio Serenade, Op. 8, and diverges attractively to the submediant key; that on the other *Zauberflöte* theme introduces an entirely fresh idea in the minor as a highly effective foil.

But these cello variations are naturally overshadowed in interest by the two Sonatas for cello and piano, Op. 5. We can date these more precisely. In the summer of 1796 Beethoven visited Berlin and performed at the court of the cello-playing King Friedrich Wilhelm II, patron of Boccherini and instigator of Mozart's 'Prussian' quartets; as Friedrich Wilhelm admired both Handel's oratorios and Mozart's operas – *Die Zauberflöte* had reached Berlin two years before – we should probably be not far wrong in connecting the variations also with this visit, but there is no doubt whatever about the sonatas; they were written for, and played with, the King's principal cellist, Jean Louis Duport,[1] and dedicated to the King himself. The celebrated Duet in E flat for viola and cello, *mit zwei obligaten Augengläsern* (WoO 32),[2] probably dates from the same period; Beethoven himself played the viola and his friend the excellent amateur cellist Zmeskall von Domanovecz, with whom he loved to joke, is known to have had weak eyes.

The Op. 5 Sonatas are historically important in more than one respect. They are not only Beethoven's earliest duet sonatas[3] but the earliest known attempts to write true duet sonatas for cello and piano: that is, in which neither instrument is treated as a mere accompaniment to the other. In both of them Beethoven oddly reverts to the form he had employed in his very earliest chamber work, the E flat Piano Quartet of 1795: a long and florid introductory Adagio leading without a break into an Allegro, and a final rondo (instead of variations as in

---

[1] Not, as commonly assumed, by his brother Jean Pierre. See Lewis Lockwood, 'Beethoven's Early Works for Violoncello and Contemporary Violoncello Technique', *Beethoven-Kolloquium 1977*, p. 175.

[2] Sketches in Kerman, ii, pp. 73–9. First movement published by Fritz Stein (Leipzig, 1912), minuet by Karl Haas (London, 1952); see Willy Hess, 'Beethovens "Augengläserduett" – ein Torso', *Musica*, vii (1953), p. 535.

[3] Sketches in Kerman, ii, pp. 8–11. For further information on their genesis see Andreas Holschneider, 'Unbekannte Beethoven-Skizzen in Bergamo', *Analecta Musicologica*, ix (1977), p. 130.

the Quartet); strangely enough he returned to it, or to something very like it, in his last Piano Sonata, Op. 111. Having no 'inside' movement, it sets a problem – of avoiding key-monotony – which Beethoven solves in the second sonata in G minor, by change of mode in the finale, in the first, in F major, by a touch of chromatic harmony in the opening bar of the principal rondo subject which serves to veil for a second the tonic key. As usual the minor key seems to release Beethovenian characteristics more easily than the major, and in the vigorous Allegro molto of no. 2 occurs another instance of the 'Eroica'-like theme we observed in precisely the equivalent place in the C minor Trio, Op. 1, no. 3. But on the whole the Sonatas are more showy than individual, like the C major Piano Sonata, Op. 2, no. 3.

EARLY VIOLIN SONATAS

Brilliance, particularly brilliance of piano-writing, is also the chief characteristic of the third of the three Violin Sonatas, Op. 12, though a new note of what one can only call 'romanticism' is sounded just before the recapitulation of the first movement (combination of remote key – C flat major – with dark, unusual scoring and chromatic movement of melody) and the middle section of the Adagio (again an unexpected key – the minor subdominant – and piano in a low register). There are romantic traits also in the Andante, più tosto Allegretto in A minor of the second Sonata, which after a somewhat Mozartean opening makes a good deal of play with a rhythm ♩ ♫ that inevitably calls to mind a much later and greater Beethoven Allegretto in the same key and time, though the key of emotional release is not in this case A major, as in the Seventh Symphony, but F major as in the closely related movement of Schubert's great C major Symphony. Romantic, too, is the fourfold dwelling on a single tiny melodic-harmonic idea in bars 18–20 and 26–28 of this movement. But, considered as a set, these three Sonatas of Op. 12 are charming rather than outstanding specimens of early Beethoven. They are true duet sonatas and highly polished technically, but the material is generally of the kinds we call Haydnish (last movement of the E flat Sonata) or Mozartean and the handling of form is unenterprising. Only the finale of the second Sonata, in A, which is a minuet-and-trio not only with all the repeats written out in full but with a key-scheme that has taken a hint from sonata, or sonata-rondo, improves on convention. The sonatas were probably composed in 1798, yet several similarities of style suggest that no. 1 was conceived at the same period as the Piano Sonata, Op. 7, begun two years earlier. One of the similarities – the *sfz* on the second quaver of a 6/8 theme (rondo of Op.

12, no. 1, bars 2 and 6; first movement of Op. 7, bars 41, 43 and still more markedly 51 and 53) – is also common to the rondo finale of the B flat Piano Concerto and also to one appearance of the principal theme of the Rondo in B flat for piano and orchestra (WoO 6) which was the original finale of the Concerto. The other principal link between Op. 7 and Op. 12, no. 1 is the final, coda appearance of both their rondo themes in a key a semitone too high.

THE STRING TRIOS, OP. 9

As a group the Op. 12 Sonatas are less representative of the Beethoven of 1795–8 than the three fine String Trios that constitute Op.9 – or the three Piano Sonatas, Op.10. But before considering Op.9 we must glance at the previous opus-number: the Serenade in D for the same combination. Op. 8 makes no great pretensions, though one notices at once not only the more skilful handling of the three instruments as compared with Op. 3, but the finer treatment of design. (Compare the recapitulation of the sonata-form Adagio of Op. 8 with that of the Allegro con brio of Op. 3; yet the second subject of the Op. 8 movement is unashamedly a Mozartean formula.) The horn-imitations in the coda of the minuetto are genuine Beethoven and the 'allegro molto' scherzo in 2/4 time which twice interrupts the second, the D minor, Adagio faintly foreshadows the passages in the same time and key in the finales of the Piano Sonata, Op. 10, no. 2, and the 'Eroica' Symphony. More definite relationships are those between the Allegretto alla polacca and the finale of the 'Mädchen oder Weibchen' Variations, already mentioned, and between the Serenade variations and those in the same key and time of the Quartet, Op. 18, no. 5; not only the themes but some of the variations have a family likeness, and there is a parallel divagation to B flat – more dramatically contrived in the Quartet – near the end of each. The variations in the Serenade end on a dominant seventh which is resolved by a repeat of the march that begins the work and whose opening – a nice point – now sounds like one more variation:

Ex. 98

(i)   Thema. Andante quasi allegretto

dolce

(ii)   Marcia. Allegro

sf

A set of similar variations on a not dissimilar 'andante' theme in 2/4 time is the central movement of the Serenade in the same key for flute, violin, and viola, Op. 25, which must have been written at about the same time. It is often delicious in sound but a very uneven work. The scoring of the entrata is delightful, while the workmanship of the two trios of the 'Tempo ordinario d'un Menuetto' does not rise above journeyman's level, hardly above apprentice's. The finale, again, is Mozartean. This Serenade and the pleasant but unimportant Horn Sonata of 1800 were Beethoven's last essays in the use of wind in chamber-music – with the single exception of the great Septet and possibly a flute quintet in his very last years.[1] With the same important exception, Opp. 8 and 25 were his last compositions in the form of the five- or six-movement serenade or divertimento. Not only was the day of those essentially eighteenth-century forms over; they were forms never particularly congenial to Beethoven. He could joke but it was not natural to him to write 'light music'. The Septet, when it came, was more like a chamber symphony with additional movements; and he never repeated the experiment. For the rest of his life, during the whole of his full artistic maturity, he conceived his chamber compositions entirely for strings with or without piano and in the overwhelming majority of cases in the sanctified four-movement form.

To turn from Op. 8 to Op. 9, as with the Octet, Op. 103, and the Quintet, Op. 4, is to hear at once the difference between the serenade style and the more finely wrought chamber style with its *durchbrochene Arbeit*. In style and in aesthetic value the trios of Op. 9 stand on the same level as the quartets of Op. 18 and it is strange that, because they give the second violin a rest, they are so much less known. Technically Beethoven now had nothing more to learn from any master of the past: form and texture are handled superbly; the part-writing is masterly – it is worth remembering that Beethoven continued his contrapuntal studies with Albrechtsberger till 1796 or 1797 – and one never feels the lack of a fourth instrument – though Beethoven must have done so, for he never wrote for string trio again; the balance between homophony, solid or broken up, and polyphony is perfectly kept. Beethoven's remark to the composer-publisher Hoffmeister in 1800 – '*Tutti obbligati*. I cannot write anything not obbligato' – is as true of these Trios as of the Septet which called it forth. The returns to the recapitulation in the three first movements, always such a vital point in Beethoven, provide a little study in themselves. One would say that the return is effected skilfully in the G major, no. 1, where it

[1] See p. 286.

drops so naturally and unexpectedly on the tail of a little passage based on a figure from the Adagio introduction, but there is finer craftsmanship at the same point in the second Trio, in D major, with its totally different scoring, its syncopation of the melody, and its division of it between violin and cello. And this, in turn, is thrown into the shade by the parallel passage in the C minor (which as a whole is as indisputably the finest of these three Trios as its brother in the same key is of Op. 1); here the opening:

Ex. 99

is, after a passage of wonderful tension and a cadential passage in which two of its elements are heard simultaneously:

Ex. 100

at last brought back with tremendous power, all its elements recombined:

Ex. 101

(Even the figure *x* has been heard in bars 12-16 of the exposition.)

The Adagio of Op. 9, no. 3, is often florid, but the floridity is of a new kind, more expressive, less ornamental; the movement as a whole is as profoundly felt as the Largo, con grand' espressione, also in C major, of the Piano Sonata, Op. 7. On the other hand, the 6/8 D minor Andante quasi allegretto of no. 2 hardly bears comparison with the Largo e mesto of Op. 10, no. 3. The beautifully euphonious Adagio of Op. 9, no. 1, without suggesting any particular parallel, takes a high place among Beethoven's earlier slow movements. Of the third movements of Op.9, that of no. 2 is a charming Menuetto, 'allegro' but still a minuet, that of no. 3 a wild, truly Beethovenian scherzo in 6/8 time, while that of no. 1 is of the intermediate type, an unmistakable scherzo and actually so-called but one that does not deny its minuet ancestry as its companion in C minor does. A sheet of paper once in the possession of Clara Schumann and given by her daughter Marie to the Beethoven House at Bonn[1] shows that at a date soon after the publication of Op. 9 in 1798 Beethoven composed a second trio, also in C major, for the scherzo of no. 1:

[1] Reproduced in facsimile and transcription, with critical commentary by Arnold Schmitz, *Beethoven: Unbekannte Skizzen und Entwürfe* (*Veröffentlichungen des Beethovenhauses*) (Bonn, 1924).

Ex. 102

with a fresh lead back to the scherzo proper. It will be recalled that when Beethoven recast his 'Parthia' in E flat as the String Quintet, Op. 4, he added a second trio to the minuet there, too.

The final movements of Op. 9 are equally diverse: that of no. 2 a typical early Beethoven rondo finale, that of no. 1 gay as the overture to some comic opera but with a second subject presaging the first movement of the C major Symphony and a strange intruder – strange in key and in gait – who mysteriously crosses the stage during both exposition and recapitulation. But again it is the C minor that is the most unmistakably Beethovenian, with its passionate energy, the romantic beginning of the second subject in E flat *minor* (G minor in the recapitulation):

Ex. 103

and the treatment of an apparently insignificant passage (bars 5-8) in the first subject: unfolded at the beginning of the development but warmed to full expansion in the major only in the recapitulation.

THE OP. 18 QUARTETS

The fact that the first six string quartets were published three years later than the trios, in 1801, and with the opus-number 18, should not blind us to the fact that they were begun soon after, one of them perhaps even earlier than, the reported Apponyi commission of 1795. Riemann has demonstrated conclusively[1] the close thematic connection of no. 4 in C minor with the Duet for viola and cello *mit zwei obligaten Augengläsern*, which seems to date from about 1796, though we need not follow him in supposing the Duet to be *later* than the first movement of the Quartet. Czerny and Ries agree that no. 3 in D was the first that Beethoven 'wrote' or 'composed' (which we may take to mean 'completed'); Nottebohm[2] confirms from the evidence of the note-books that the D major was the first on which Beethoven worked continuously and shows that the sketches for its first movement were well advanced by 1798. Next in the same book come the sketches for the first two movements of the F major, of which the original form[3] completed by June 1799 is actually inscribed 'Quartetto II'. Another sketch-book shows the continuation of work on the F major and seems by the inscription over the original end of the Adagio:

Ex. 104

---

[1] See his long footnote in Thayer, op. cit., ii, pp. 188–90.

[2] *Zweite Beethoveniana*, pp. 476 ff.

[3] Published, with an introduction by Hans Josef Wedig, as no. 2 of the *Veröffentlichungen des Beethovenhauses* (Bonn, 1922).

to confirm Karl Amenda's story that Beethoven here had in his mind the tomb-scene from *Romeo and Juliet*. Next in order come sketches for the G major Quartet, the A major, and the second, third, and fourth movements of the Septet; the counter-theme introduced in the coda of the variations of no. 5 appears in a jotting that Nottebohm dates as early as 1794 or 1795 – rather slender ground for the often repeated statement that 'a part of the variations appears to have been sketched' in those years. The sketches for the last movements of the G major and the B flat are on separate sheets and give no indication of chronology; another from 1800,[1] embedded in those for the Violin Sonatas, Opp. 23 and 24, gives us an interesting glimpse of Beethoven in the act of remodelling a passage in the already completed F major Quartet, the version which he asks Amenda to withhold (letter of 1 July 1801) 'because I have altered it a great deal, as I now for the first time know how to write quartets properly'. It almost goes without saying that the revision tends to make the parts more 'obbligato'; it also brings about a characteristic diversion into the 'Neapolitan' key a great deal more skilfully. In the first completed version Beethoven had written:

Ex. 105 (i)

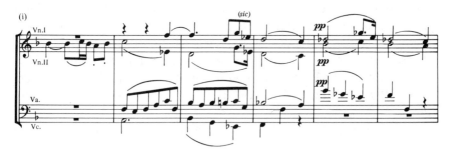

just after the beginning of the recapitulation. In the sketch:

Ex. 105 (ii)

we see him feeling towards the definitive form:

[1] Nottebohm, *Zweite Beethoveniana*, p.231.

Ex. 106

'More obbligato' does not necessarily imply 'more thematic' though it often does. But the revision shows several points at which fussy, over-frequent repetitions of the opening theme – a typical early-Beethoven cliché (cf. first movement of Op. 3, second subject; Op. 9, no. 1, first movement, latter part of second subject) – have been replaced by figuration derived from the theme; we feel such apparently conventional figuration to be organically right without quite knowing why it is. Even so, the movement remains the most closely thematic of the whole set. Another feature of the earlier form which disappeared in the revised one is the repeat of development and recapitulation, a feature that is, however, retained in the A major and B flat Quartets as in Op. 9, nos. 1 and 3. And the sonority is improved in many places.[1]

The most finely wrought first movements of Op. 18 are those of the G major, no. 2, and the A major, no. 5 (for we must adopt the published, not the chronological numbering), the most obviously Beethovenian that of the C minor, no. 4 – though the derivation of second-subject material from first is more Haydnish than Beethovenian. The first movement of no. 6 is the weakest, its opening theme old-fashioned, its second subject beginning rather like that of Op. 9, no. 1, its structure conventional. Of the slow movements the D minor Adagio of no. 1 is almost indisputably the finest; Wedig, in his

[1] For further discussion of the genesis of Op. 18, see Douglas Johnson, 'Beethoven's Sketches for the Scherzo of the Quartet Op. 18, No. 6', *Journal of the American Musicological Society*, xxiii (1970), p. 385; Sieghard Brandenburg, 'The First Version of Beethoven's G major String Quartet, Op. 18, No. 2,' *Music and Letters*, lviii (1977), p. 127. See also *Beethoven: Ein Skizzenbuch zu Streichquartetten aus Op. 18* (the Beethoven manuscript known as Grasnick 2 in the Staatsbibliothek Preussischer Kulturbesitz), facsimile and transcription, ed. Wilhelm Virneisel, 2 volumes (Bonn, 1972–4).

introduction to the score of the original version, detects in it the influence of the Adagio of E. A. Förster's Quartet, Op. 7, no. 5, published in 1793, and it is generally agreed that the Op. 18 set show a certain debt to the Op. 7 of the older man whom he sometimes spoke of as his 'old master' and whom in later years he recommended to Count Razumovsky as a teacher of quartet composition – a debt possibly repaid to some extent in Förster's Op. 16 (published in 1798).[1] The general modelling of Op. 18, no. 5, perhaps reflects Mozart's Quartet, K.464, in the same key. Op. 18, no. 2, has another of the 'deeply felt' C major Adagios, with a curious 'allegro' middle section based on its cadential motive. The likeness of the Haydnish Andante scherzoso of no. 4 to the slow movement of the First Symphony has often been remarked upon.

Nos. 1, 2, 3, and 6 all have 'true' scherzi, though that of no. 3 is not actually so-called; no. 5 has a curiously old-fashioned Menuetto, placed second – before the variations; but the Menuetto of no. 4 surpasses them all in interest. Though styled a minuet and marked 'allegretto', its surging chromatic restlessness, its third beat sforzandi and, above all, the 'più allegro' repeat after the trio bring it near to the scherzo type. The final movements of Op. 18 are in either sonata or sonata-rondo form, except no. 6 where Beethoven makes one of his earliest experiments in breaking the classical moulds. He prefaces the main part of the movement, a sort of 'Deutsche' in *moto perpetuo* semiquavers, with an Adagio entitled 'La Malincolia' which throws up a cloud of modulation, that returns in the middle of the *Deutsche* thus:

Adagio
First 'allegretto' subject in B flat
Second subject in F
First subject in B flat
Second subject in B flat
First subject (B flat – A minor – G major – B flat) twice interrupted
    by Adagio, and rounded off by coda.

The finales are particularly rich in relationships with other works of the same period: no. 1 with the first movement of Op. 9, no. 2 (second subject), no. 5 (opening) with the first movement of the Septet and (second subject) with both the first movement of Op. 10, no. 3, and the finale of Op. 13.[2]

[1] On Förster, see pp. 305–6.
[2] On the relationship of the finale of no. 4 to that of Mozart's C minor Quintet (K.406), see Reinhard Oppel, 'Über Beziehungen Beethovens zu Mozart und zu Ph. Em. Bach', *Zeitschrift für Musikwissenschaft*, v (1922–3), p. 30.

According to Thayer[1] only nos. 2 and 4 at first appealed to the public, a fact which moved Beethoven to unprintable language. A correspondent of the *Allgemeine musikalische Zeitung* in August 1800 said of the first three that, while giving 'a complete demonstration' of Beethoven's art, they 'must be played often and very well, as they are very difficult to perform and not at all popular'.

THE SEPTET AND SOME TRANSCRIPTIONS

On the other hand, the same correspondent heard the first public performance of the Septet, Op. 20, on 2 April 1800, and found it 'written with very much taste and feeling'; it quickly became popular and Beethoven grew to dislike it. Put side by side, those judgements are illuminating. The Septet is close in material to the quartets; but its spirit is different. Its six movements, its inclusion of wind instruments, and such features as the violin cadenza in the finale relate it to the past; even its key, E flat, recalls the earlier wind-music; the quartets look to the future. Despite Beethoven's already quoted assertion to his publisher, the texture is not so noticeably 'obbligato' as that of the quartets; and in the same letter he shows his indifference to the wind-colours which give the Septet much of its charm to our ears by suggesting that 'the 3 wind instruments, namely bassoon, clarinet, and horn might for common use be replaced by an additional violin, an additional viola and an additional cello'. Similarly he allowed the Horn Sonata to appear in versions for cello or *violin*. More surprisingly, he allowed and approved the publication of a transcription of the Septet, transposed to G major, for flute and string quartet, just as a little later he allowed Hoffmeister to publish arrangements of Op. 25 and Op. 8, supervised and improved by himself, as Op. 41 (piano and flute) and Op. 42 (piano and viola) respectively.

It would be easy to quote, from Beethoven's letters and reported sayings, outbursts against the fashionable practice of transcription for other media but his general practice seems to have been to shrug his shoulders and accept the fashion. In 1803 he even published, as Op. 38, an arrangement by himself of the Septet for piano, clarinet, and cello; it is beautifully done, a real re-casting in terms of the new medium, with practically no alteration of material – a striking demonstration of how little Beethoven depended on instrumental colour, though one does miss the horn. His general principle was to transfer the original string parts to the piano, to retain the original clarinet part – though in compliment to the violin-playing doctor to whom the transcription is dedicated, it may be replaced by the violin

[1] Op. cit., ii, pp. 183 and 200.

– and allow the cello to be by turns its original self or double-bass or horn or bassoon, usually the last. This, perhaps, is the place to mention his still more surprising arrangement in 1806 of the Second Symphony as a piano trio (without separate opus-number); the principle is the same as in the Septet transcription – the piano takes over the original string parts, violin and cello sketch in the original wind, thus preserving the original contrast of weights and colours – but although most skilfully done the result is less successful than the Septet arrangement.[1] Far more interesting and more valuable than these is Beethoven's transcription in 1802 of the Piano Sonata in E, Op. 14, no. 1, as a String Quartet in F,[2] a work almost worthy to stand beside Op. 18. The substance of the music is unchanged, except that in the equivalent of the G major episode of the finale of the Sonata there is a wonderful clothing of a mere harmonic skeleton with flesh, but the texture is completely transmuted. All the same, one observes how easily much of Beethoven's first-period piano-writing – not only in this Sonata – does transcribe for quartet and Nottebohm[3] significantly remarks that it is 'questionable' whether the sketches for the Sonata are 'for piano or for several instruments'. We know that the first movement of the Piano Sonata, Op. 31, no. 1, was first conceived as a quartet movement;[4] the sketches suggest that the rondo of Op. 13 was originally thought of for violin and piano;[5] and it is more than probable that the piano sonatas embody other fragments of unsuccessful ensemble composition.

THE MATURE MASTER

From this point onward, the history of Beethoven's chamber music unfolds much more simply. There is no more experimentation with media. They were settled: strings only, almost invariably a quartet of them, or piano with violin or cello or both. There is no more wind-music; there are no more piano quartets. There is, indeed, only one original full-length String Quintet, the fine C major, Op. 29, of 1801, which belongs to the sphere of the Op. 18 Quartets and even parallels in its final Presto the formal experiment of the finale of Op. 18, no. 6:

[1] On these two transcriptions, see also Wilhelm Fischer, 'Die Klavier-Trio Fassungen des Septetts und der Zweiten Symphonie', *Österreichische Musikzeitschrift*, vii (1952), Heft 3.
[2] Republished by Nottebohm in 1875 (Simrock) and by Altmann in 1911. On these transcriptions in general, see Friedrich Munter, 'Beethovens Bearbeitungen eigener Werke', *Neues Beethoven-Jahrbuch*, vi, p. 159, and Altmann, 'Ein vergessenes Streichquartett Beethovens', *Die Musik*, v (1905), 4, and his preface to the miniature score (Leipzig, 1911).
[3] *Zweite Beethoveniana*, p. 47.
[4] See Nottebohm, *Ein Skizzenbüch von Beethoven* (Leipzig, 1865; reprinted in *Zwei Skizzenbücher von Beethoven*, ed. Paul Mies, 1924), p. 33.
[5] *Zweite Beethoveniana*, p. 42.

First subject in C
Second in A flat and G
First subject beginning in C but modulating and, first in D minor,
        combined with a theme that provides the missing link
        between the opening of Haydn's last symphony and that of
        Beethoven's last
Andant con moto e scherzoso, in A major
First Subject in C
Second subject in D flat and C
Andante con moto, in C
Coda (on first subject)

But although Beethoven takes due advantage of the second viola, its
presence did not inspire him as it did Mozart. Except the already
mentioned transcription of Op. 1, no. 3, and a couple of fugues written
in 1817 when he was studying Bach – one, a beautiful piece of
craftsmanship in D major, published posthumously as Op. 137, the
other in D minor, unfinished but absorbed into work on the Ninth
Symphony – Beethoven never returned to the string quintet; the
quintet on which he was working at the time of his death[1] seems to
have been for flute and strings.

VIOLIN SONATAS, OPP. 23–47

The period in Beethoven's chamber music between the Op. 18
Quartets and the 'Razumovskys', Op. 59, is covered mainly by a series
of violin sonatas: in A minor and F major, Op. 23 and 24 (both 1801),
in A major, C minor, and G major, Op. 30 (1801–2), and in A major,
Op. 47, the so-called 'Kreutzer' (1803) of which the finale was
originally the last movement of Op. 30, no. 1 – that is to say, by all
Beethoven's violin sonatas except the three of Op. 12 and the last in
G major, Op. 96.[2] Already in Opp. 23 and 24, which were originally
intended for publication as a pair, with one opus-number, fresh traits
appear. The rather grim rondo-finale of Op. 23 is very different from
the type of rondo-finale to which contemporary musicians were
accustomed, but a more delightful surprise must have been the
opening of Op. 24. One is tempted to call the beautiful, plastic violin
melody, its wide, gracious curves given spring by the chromatic
appoggiaturas, a prototype of German romantic lyrical melody: the
melody of Weber, Schumann, Brahms, and Wagner. In the F major
Sonata Beethoven introduces for the first time in his violin sonatas –

[1] Nottebohm, *Beethoveniana*, p. 79, and *Zweite Beethoveniana*, p. 522.
[2] For an extensive discussion of Op. 30 and other chamber works written between the early and
    middle quartets, see Richard Kramer, *The Sketches for Beethoven's Violin Sonatas, Opus 30*
    (Diss. Princeton, 1974). See also Sieghard Brandenburg's new edition, in facsimile and
    transcription, of the 'Kessler' sketchbook of 1801–2 (Bonn, 1976–8), and the facsimile of no.
    3, with an introduction by Alan Tyson, *British Library Music Facsimiles*, iii (1980).

and he does it only twice later, in Op. 30, no. 2 and Op. 96 (and is said to have had doubts about it) – a fourth movement: a scherzo with a typically Beethovenian joke in the delayed violin part of bars 10–12 and the parallel passages. There is a certain affinity between this Allegro molto – originally conceived as a sober minuetto[1] – and the opening theme of the Andante scherzoso, più allegretto of the companion sonata. In the Op. 30 set, while one must admire the beautiful three-part writing of the opening of no. 1, the violin cantilena of its slow movement, the pleasant Allegretto con variazioni which replaced its original finale, and the Schubertian (by anticipation) middle movement of no. 3, it is the second sonata that dominates the group. One grows used to finding that the C minor work in a group is the outstanding piece. Its first movement is one of the greatest things Beethoven had written so far: thematically related at several points to the first movement of the Second Symphony, written at the same time, but a finer piece of work. The return of the first subject and the coda of the sonata, to take only two passages, touch decidedly greater heights than the parallel places in the symphony or in the two other sonatas. The A flat Adagio of Op. 30, no. 2, originally conceived in G major, again anticipates Schubert.

If the C minor Sonata suggests the beginning of s symphonic tendency in Beethoven's chamber music, the Sonata of the following year written in a few days for the mulatto violinist George Bridgetower and later dedicated to Rodolphe Kreutzer[2] shows a parallel tendency to concerto-style, as the composer himself recognized in a proposed title:[3] '*Sonata scritta in un stilo* (*brillante* crossed through) *molto concertante quasi come d'un concerto*'. The parallel in the piano sonatas is the 'Waldstein', Op. 53, written not long afterward. Nothing else in the 'Kreutzer' is quite as memorable as its opening, with its unaccompanied double- and triple-stops and the piano's reply. The first Presto is very fine in its showy way, with its curious piano cadenza (which Bridgetower imitated at bar 9[4] apparently to Beethoven's delight), but the beautiful theme of the second movement is decorated with merely ornamental variations and the final Presto seems hardly more in place here than it would have been in its original context in Op. 30, no. 1.

---

[1] *Zweite Beethoveniana*, p. 235.
[2] See pp. 210–3.
[3] Nottebohm, *Ein Skizzenbuch von Beethoven aus dem Jahre 1803* (Leipzig, 1880; reprinted 1924), p. 74.
[4] Bridgetower's cadenzas are given in Thayer, ii, p. 396; Thayer-Forbes, p. 333.

THE 'RAZUMOVSKY' QUARTETS

This quasi-symphonic tendency is still more strongly marked in Beethoven's next chamber works: the famous set of three Quartets, in F major, E minor, and C major, Op. 59, composed in 1806 and dedicated to the quartet-playing and quartet-composing Russian Ambassador in Vienna, Count Razumovsky. The date is worthy of note for two reasons. Razumovsky may have had a political, or at least patriotic, motive for commissioning 'some quartets with Russian melodies' soon after the Austro-Russian military catastrophe at Austerlitz. And there is a noticeable gap between the date of the 'Kreutzer' Sonata and 1806. Whereas up to 1800–1 Beethoven had composed chamber music prolifically, the stream runs thinner through the violin sonatas and then dries up for two or three years altogether. Then, beginning with the 'Razumovskys', we have a series of masterpieces spaced out at an average of one a year till 1815; after that, almost complete silence in this direction for eight or nine years before the last great crop of 'posthumous' quartets. The explanation is, of course, that Beethoven's main interests were otherwise directed: towards opera and symphony and concerto, then toward a new kind of piano sonata. And those interests are reflected in the chamber music of his early 'middle period': the 'Kreutzer' Sonata, the 'Razumovsky' Quartets, and the A major Cello Sonata. The Triple Concerto of 1804, for piano, violin, cello, and orchestra, shows Beethoven actually experimenting with a fusion of chamber music and concerto, and it is perhaps not insignificant that the trio arrangement of the Second Symphony dates from the year of the 'Razumovsky' Quartets.

The 'Razumovskys' mark the opening of a new period in the history of the string quartet; they are the spiritual parents of all the quasi-orchestral string quartets of the later nineteenth century. Not that they themselves are orchestral, though they sometimes come near to overstepping the boundary-line of true chamber-style (as in the last movement of no. 3); their 'symphonic' character lies in their less intimate nature – they are emphatically chamber music for a hall and an audience – in their dimensions, and in the inner organization that expanded them to such dimensions.[1] No quartets of such length can ever have been written before. In no. 1 all four movements are in full sonata-form;[2] in no. 2 the first two are, while the third has a second

[1] Joseph Kerman has argued that it was the composition of the *Eroica* which enabled Beethoven to write quartets on this scale (*The Beethoven Quartets*, London, 1967, pp. 100–1).

[2] Beethoven originally intended a repeat of the entire 'second part' (i.e. the section comprising the development and recapitulation) of each of the first two movements. See *Beethoven: String Quartet Opus 59 No. 1*, facsimile of the autograph, with an introduction by Alan Tyson (London, 1980).

repeat of the trio (on the familiar Russian theme 'Glory to God in Heaven') and a third of the main section, as in the B flat Symphony of the same year, and the finale is a huge sonata-rondo; the extraordinary fugal finale of no. 3 is, again, in sonata-form. The working out of two Adagio molto movements in full sonata-form with development, as in nos. 1 and 2, was bound to produce very long movements, though such is their beauty of sound that no one can ever have wished them shorter; and in the first movement of no. 2 Beethoven again indicates a repeat of development as well as exposition. The first movements of both the F major and E minor are both, in their different ways, masterpieces of musical logic; the flowering of the first fourteen bars of no. 2 entirely from the seed of the two opening chords is typical of their closely, but never pedantically, knit tissue. In no. 3 – which contemporary musicians found the most attractive of the 'Razumov-skys' and modern ones perhaps the least – Beethoven for the first time provides a slow introduction to a string quartet, a procedure for which he had only one precedent in Haydn (Op. 71, no. 2) and two in Mozart (K.171 and K.465); indeed Beethoven very clearly took K.465 as his model – in both cases a tonal fog, very dense in Beethoven's case, precedes a brilliantly clear, rather formal Allegro in C major – and even quotes one of its prominent figures. The second movement of no. 3, an Andante con moto quasi allegretto played almost entirely *piano*, identical in key and close related in mood to the Allegretto of the Seventh Symphony, sketched at the same time, is in its very different way as great as the 'profounder' Adagios of its companions: the 'weeping willow or acacia-tree on my brother's grave' of the F major, the *Harmonie der Sphären* of the E minor. (The one remark is reported by Czerny, the other cryptic utterance was found in a note-book.)[1] Beethoven certainly reached new heights in the beauty of the harmonic polyphony of the opening of the Adagio of no. 1, the beauty of the scoring of the same passage at the beginning of the recapitulation, and the extraordinary loveliness of the D flat passage just before.

In no. 1 the Adagio is the third movement, being preceded by that long Allegretto vivace, compounded of wit and tenderness, whose cello opening on a repeated B flat was considered by contemporaries to be a joke in very bad taste. Neither the hiccoughing Allegretto of no. 2, which Beethoven remembered eight years later when writing the first movement of the Piano Sonata in the same key, Op. 90, nor the rather square-cut Minuetto grazioso of no. 3 can compare with that wonderful movement. The minuet of no. 3 leads through a

[1] *Zweite Beethoveniana*, p. 83.

romantically modulating coda into the finale without a break, as does
the Adagio of no. 1 through a first-violin cadenza and trill. (Again the
concerto feeling is noticeable.) And the finales of all three 'Razumovskys' are remarkable in their different ways. Beethoven obviously
spent a great deal of time pondering over the problem of instrumental
finales and it must be said that while he often found happier solutions
than in the Ninth Symphony he has left us some doubtful successes.
In the third 'Razumovsky' he begins his exploration of one favourite
line of solution: the fugal or semi-fugal finale that we shall meet again
in the Cello Sonata, Op. 102, no. 2, the original finale of the B flat
Quartet, Op. 130 (published as the *Grosse Fuge*, Op. 133), and in three
of the late piano sonatas. Here the fugal theme whose exposition
constitutes most of the sonata 'first subject' consists of ten bars of
incessant quavers, 'allegro molto', from which by contrapuntal friction
Beethoven contrives to generate heat rather than life. In no. 2, as in
the Cello Sonata, Op. 5, no. 1, but now with ten years more mastery,
Beethoven solves the problem of avoiding monotony of key – the
preceding movements are all in E minor or major – by veiling the
tonic key at the beginning of the rondo subject; indeed the subject is
almost entirely in C major, except for a touch of E minor in the eighth
bar – the one common element in the otherwise very different sketches
for this theme.[1] There is a tonal problem also in the first theme of the
finale of no. 1, arising from the – really modal – nature of the Russian
folk-lament which Beethoven borrowed and successfully turned into
a lively dance-tune.[2]

CHAMBER MUSIC OF 1808–9

The A major Sonata for cello and piano, Op. 69 (1808), is in some
respects a counterpart, a much finer counterpart, of the 'Kreutzer' in
the same key: in points of detail, both open with the stringed
instrument *solo* and the piano has a brilliant cadenza-like passage at
nearly the same point in each work. But the real parallel is in the
broad, symphonic or concerto-like feeling and there is a noticeable
affinity between the beautiful opening melody and the thematic world
of the Violin Concerto (1806). The Sonata has one feature, and hardly
more than one, in common with the early Cello Sonatas, Op. 5: the
avoidance of a slow movement proper, though here the short Adagio
introduces the finale instead of the first movement. The central

[1] *Zweite Beethoveniana*, pp. 84–5.
[2] The Russian melodies in Op. 59, nos. 1 and 2, were taken from the collection of Russian folk-
songs published in 1790 by the Russified Czech, Jan Práč ('Iwan Pratsch'). For Práč's versions
see *Zweite Beethoveniana*, p. 90, or Thayer, ii, p. 532.

movement of the Sonata is one of Beethoven's most characteristic middle-period scherzos, but the most remarkable feature of the work is the relation between the two instruments – over which Beethoven took considerable pains – and the perfect balance between them, achieved here for the first time in an 'accompanied' sonata.[1] The two Piano Trios, in D and E flat, Op. 70, written the same year have a number of affinities with this great Cello Sonata; among others, beautiful plastic themes that tend to flow or run in even crotchets (opening themes of first and last movements of the Sonata, their parallels in the finale of Op. 70, no. 1, the first and third movements of Op. 70, no. 2) and final movements in sonata-form. But the quasi-symphonic tendency begins to abate, although it is still perceptible in the celebrated Largo assai of the D major Trio which has earned the work its nickname of 'Geister-Trio' from the fact that its theme was first noted in connection with the opening chorus of witches in a projected *Macbeth* opera; but this long and powerful movement, sounding rather like an orchestral sketch, seems to have little connection with the two on either side of it.

These two Trios are indeed chiefly remarkable otherwise for the superb handling of this somewhat difficult medium. The cello is, of course, completely emancipated from its bass-doubling thraldom and the balance between piano and strings is beautifully kept in a generally transparent texture of two or three 'real' parts with never more than light harmonic filling-out; the play of parts and their constantly varied scoring is a continual delight to the ear. The opening of the Allegro non troppo of no. 2 was quoted both by Stanford in his *Musical Composition* and by Dunhill in his *Chamber music* as 'a model piece of trio-construction' and it would be easy to find many similar felicities in these two scores. Nor must we leave them without mention of the most prophetically Schubertian movement in the whole of Beethoven's chamber music, the Allegretto ma non troppo in A flat (originally conceived as a minuet): anticipating Schubert alike in melody, harmony, and figuration, and at the same time giving a backward glance (bars 26-7) at his own younger self (first movement of Op. 10, no. 1).

The same intimacy and lyricism and fine workmanship mark the E flat String Quartet, Op. 74, of the following year – foolishly nicknamed the 'Harp' from the not very harplike pizzicato passages in its first movement. That movement has two other striking features; its Poco adagio introduction, a polyphonic conception evolved from a motive

---

[1] See Lewis Lockwood, 'The Autograph of the First Movement of Beethoven's Sonata for Violoncello and Pianoforte, Opus 69', *The Music Forum*, ii (1970), p. 1.

that must have been one of the parents of the 'day' theme in *Tristan*, which not only establishes the 'wrong' key of A flat but casts the shadow of that subdominant key over the first subject of the Allegro; and the long coda, serenely joyous, in which that shadow is at last lifted and the tonic key emerges in all its purity. It is followed by one of Beethoven's most beautiful A flat Adagios and one of his finest C minor scherzos (on the extended ABABA plan of the Allegretto of the second 'Razumovsky'), which leads without a break into the final variations – on a theme whose original form[1] was remarkably like the variation-theme in the Septet. Only this scherzo, with the incessant fortissimo crotchets of its trio, has any symphonic character; the Adagio is quite different in feeling and style from the Adagios of Op. 59, nos. 1 and 2.

FINAL MASTERPIECES OF THE MIDDLE PERIOD

The next year, 1810, saw the production of another isolated Quartet, Op. 95 in F minor. The original manuscript is rather curiously marked *Quartetto serioso* and the same adjective recurs in the tempo-marking of the third movement, Allegro assai vivace, ma serioso; the word may have had a special meaning for the friend to whom the Quartet is dedicated, the already mentioned amateur cellist Zmeskall von Domanowecz, who seems to have been Beethoven's confidant at this time in his unfortunate love-affair with Therese Malfatti. It is perhaps more to the point that it immediately followed the *Egmont* music and that there are certain affinities, parallels rather than relationships, between it and the *Egmont* music: the key of overture and Quartet, certain points in the *Siegessymphonie* and the coda of the finale of the Quartet, the passage near the end of Entr'acte III and bars 6–17 of the Quartet, and others even fainter but still perceptible. The F minor Quartet is a strange work, its first movement violent and wilful, the others enigmatic and restless, till suddenly at the end of the finale comes light – even dazzling light – in the brilliant, shimmering coda: a passage quite different thematically and in mood from anything else in the Quartet. The first movement is intensely romantic in the sense of recording a personal experience, yet with all its energy and passion there is nothing in the least symphonic about it. Everything is condensed and elliptical; the modulations are sudden and to unexpected keys; there are constant changes of mood and musical idea; the themes are scrappy. Yet the whole movement is melted and cast in a whole by the heat of Beethoven's creative fire, and stamped all over with the fierce little semiquaver figure with which it opens.

[1] *Zweite Beethoveniana*, p. 94.

Here, in short, is an isolated and very premature foretaste of Beethoven's 'third period'. Both here and in the Allegretto ma non troppo, the familiar outlines of textbook form are blurred by the baulking of cadences and the close organic texture. The Allegretto, with its deliberate avoidance of the nominal key (D major) now on the dominant, now on the subdominant side, and its tortuous fugatos, comes to a pause on a diminished seventh which then springs to rhythmic life in the first bar of the Allegro assai vivace, an extended scherzo like those in the second 'Razumovsky' and Op. 74. The final Allegretto agitato, a movement with some affinity with the second movement of Op. 59, no. 3 (though its form is that of the finale of Op. 59, no. 2: a sonata-rondo with the second subject returning immediately after the central episode) is introduced by a short but poignant Larghetto, the transition from which is effected by the same means as the parallel transition in the *Egmont* Overture, the quickened repetition of its final motive.

Even earlier than the F minor Quartet, at the same time as the *Egmont* Overture, Beethoven had made sketches for the first three movements of a Piano Trio in B flat, completed in 1811 and afterwards published as Op. 97. The opus-number between the quartet and the trio was given to the last violin sonata, the G major written in 1812, but revised for publication in 1815,[1] and both trio and sonata were dedicated to the Archduke Rudolph – though only the trio has been nicknamed after him. The two works have a great deal in common and both belong to a totally different world from Op. 95. (As, for that matter, does another Trio in B flat (WoO 39) that he wrote in 1812 for his child-friend Maximiliane Brentano 'to encourage her in piano-playing': a totally unimportant single movement in sonata-form.) Here once more, as in the A major Cello Sonata and even much more than there, everything is clear, serene and spacious, diatonic and euphonious. Both first movements are more lyrical than most of Beethoven's first movements but very masculinely lyrical; both are marked 'allegro moderato' and in both the 'moderato' is more important than the 'allegro'. If the first movement of the Trio (in particular) moves on Olympian heights, both slow movements sound untroubled depths and that of the Trio, as Ernest Walker so finely said, ends with 'a coda of an unearthly purity hardly matched elsewhere even in Beethoven'. Both scherzos give an impression of great power at play and if the final rondo of the Trio sounds disappointing – as the final variations of the Sonata do not – it is only

[1] See Sieghard Brandenburg, 'Bemerkungen zu Beethovens Op. 96', *Beethoven-Jahrbuch*, ix (1977), p. 11.

because of the impossibility of finding *any* music that could follow that Andante cantabile. The relationship between these two master-pieces is noticeable even in points of general structure:

Sonata	Trio
I. Allegro moderato	I. Allegro moderato
II. Adagio, leading without a break into	II. Scherzo
III. Scherzo	III. Andante cantabile (variations) leading without a break into
IV. Poco allegretto (variations)[1]	IV. Allegro moderato

as well as in such details as the key-divagations in both finales. There is a spiritual, if much less tangible, affinity also with the Symphonies of 1812, nos. 7 and 8. Indeed, the Trio, superb as it is, is open to the charge of being too symphonic for its medium; it is unthinkable in any other but it is not a model of trio-writing like its predecessors of Op. 70.

In 1815 Beethoven returned for the last time to the problems of the sonata for cello and piano, for this combination seems to have set him problems of form as well as of balance. The two Sonatas in C and D, Op. 102, written for Joseph Linke, the cellist of the Schuppanzigh Quartet, are curious works. The C major, which like Op. 69 and the last two violin sonatas begins with the stringed instrument unaccompanied, has a strange form – Beethoven himself called it a '*Freye Sonate*' – which one hardly knows whether to connect with the formal experiments of the earliest Cello Sonatas, Op. 5, or with those of the 'third period' (last piano sonatas and last quartets) generally. It opens with a longish Andante (including a cadenza-like passage for piano, like the first movement of Op. 69) which leads into an Allegro vivace in sonata-form but *in A minor*; then a short improvisatory Adagio leads, through a seven-bar reference to the opening Andante, to the final rondo which begins innocently enough but takes some unmistak-ably third-period bypaths. The D major, no. 2, is a more normal work, its first movement belonging to the virile, diatonic world of Opp. 96 and 97 though inferior to them in quality. And now at last Beethoven writes a full-length slow movement in a cello sonata: an Adagio con molto sentimento d'affetto whose first strain is a worthy companion to the slow movements of Op. 96 and Op. 97 and whose second looks back to the Largo of Op. 70, no. 1, in the same key and dedicated to the same Countess Marie von Erdödy. The Adagio comes to a pause

---

[1] The Malherbe collection in the Library of the Paris Conservatoire contains a variant sketch for the finale: see facsimile in *Die Musik*, xxxv (1942–3), facing p. 49.

on a dominant seventh which is resolved by the theme of the fugal finale, where Beethoven seems almost perversely to have added an unnecessary complication to the problem of writing for cello and piano and with which we know he was afterwards not completely satisfied. A sketch four years after the publication shows him planning a stricter fugal answer ('*in den Violonschellsonaten zu verbessern*').[1]

After 1815 Beethoven wrote no more chamber music for eight or nine years, except the already mentioned Quintet Fugue and the quintet arrangement (Op. 104) of Op. 1, no. 3 (both 1817), although he sometimes began sketches of chamber compositions: for instance a Trio in F minor in 1815. Among the sketches for this Trio occurs a marginal note which may throw some light on that rather mysterious work, the Trio Variations on 'Ich bin der Schneider Kakadu' from Wenzel Müller's opera *Die Schwestern von Prag*. Beethoven published them in 1824 as Op. 121a and they are supposed – on the flimsiest evidence[2] – to have been composed the year before. But the marginal note of 1815 – 'Variations of my youthful years' – suggests that Beethoven had thought of furbishing up some old trio variations[3] for this work. Müller's opera dates from 1795; its revival in Vienna in 1814 may well have reminded Beethoven of some early variations; and the 'Kakadu' Variations present an odd mixture of styles: a remarkable long introduction in G minor, Adagio assai, in which the theme gradually emerges in the most masterly way, and a set of variations decidedly varied in quality. (One curious point is that the strings are both silent in Variation I, the cello in Variation II, the violin in Variation III, and the piano in Variation VII.) As they stand, in G major, the 'Kakadu' Variations would hardly fit into a Trio in F minor, but G major may have been their original key. It would not be difficult to connect the 6/8 theme in C minor from the sketch of the 1815 finale with the C minor passage in the 6/8 portion of the 'Kakadu' finale.

THE LAST QUARTETS

To turn from the 'Kakadu' Variations to the last string quartets is to retrace a familiar step – from the sometimes very nearly ridiculous to the sublime. These five works carry not merely the string quartet but the art of music into new regions. Studies of them and commentaries on them are innumerable; like *Hamlet* they will never

[1] *Zweite Beethoveniana*, p. 345. *Beethoveniana*, p. 33.
[2] See Thayer, iv, pp. 458–9.
[3] Alan Tyson has suggested that a publishable version of these may have been ready by 1803. See *Musical Times*, cxi (1970), p. 1001.

yield up their last secrets or admit of a 'final' solution. They are inexhaustible and all that can be done here is to indicate in what ways they advance the frontiers of the art of music. The first to be completed (in 1824), and the only one published during Beethoven's lifetime, was the E flat, Op. 127. Then came the A minor, Op. 132, and the B flat, Op. 130 (but with the afterwards separated Grosse Fuge, Op. 133, as its finale) (both 1825), the C sharp minor, Op. 131, the F major, Op. 135, and the present finale of Op. 130 (all in 1826). The immediate impulse to their composition may have been given by a commission from another quartet-playing Russian nobleman, the Prince 'von Galitzin' (more accurately 'Golitsïn') to whom Opp. 127, 130, and 132 are dedicated, but Beethoven speaks of a forthcoming quartet in a letter to Peters of Leipzig written five months before Golitsïn's enquiry.

Beethoven's deafness and consequent spiritual isolation combined with certain specifically musical factors to make many things in the last quartets incomprehensible to contemporaries and not easily comprehensible to later generations. The difficulties of Beethoven's final style are of several kinds though all are inter-related. Of sound: his inner ear came to accept as tolerable a degree of dissonance painful to most physical ears for more than half a century after his death. Of texture: the true essence of the music often lies less in 'themes' or 'melodies' with sharp profiles, though these are not lacking, than in the total web of sound woven from the thematic particles of *durchbrochene Arbeit* brought to its highest development and from fragments of harmonic polyphony. Of form: both in the structural innovations and in the combination of factors which often obscure, obviously because Beethoven wished to obscure, the familiar outlines of orthodox forms – closely woven, highly organic texture with frequent concealment of cadences and ends of sections; variation of themes sometimes not highly striking in themselves and of the 'total web'; tonality that is often less than classically clear; changes of tempo within a movement, often at unexpected points, sometimes bringing a complete and sudden change of texture – seemingly conditioned by a secret 'programme' – sometimes misleading a careless listener on points of structure. Thus in the first movement of Op. 127 the 'maestoso' idea which opens both exposition and development returns some thirty bars before the beginning of the recapitulation and, being followed as before by the first 'allegro' theme, suggests that the reprise is already starting – in the wrong key.

Apart from this, and the changes of rhythm and tempo in the scherzo (not actually so called), the E flat Quartet is perfectly orthodox in structure with a most beautiful set of variations (also not so described) for slow movement and a sonata-form finale in which the only novel feature is the long coda, 'allegro commodo', which appears to be as independent of the rest of the movement as the corresponding passage in Op. 95 but is really a transformation of the first theme, after the four-bar 'curtain', of the finale. The sketches for the slow movement, published by Nottebohm[1] who for once seems not to have fully understood their purport, suggest that to Beethoven this coda represented the fulfilment not merely of the finale but of the whole Quartet. They seem to show that he played with the ideas (i) of interpolating in the A flat variations an 'allegro' variation in C major, (ii) perhaps of preceding the Adagio with an Allegro grazioso on the same C major theme, which he here entitles 'La gaieté'. One violin counterpoint in this 'La gaieté' sketch certainly seems to be connected with the C major opening of the coda of the finale:

Ex. 107

The complete domination of this coda by unbroken semiquaver triplets, like the tendency to flows of even crotchets in first movement and trio and finale, and the ostinato rhythm of the scherzo, are typical of the last quartets.

The other two Golitsïn Quartets, Op. 132 and Op. 130, present more difficult problems. Both begin with slow passages that return to interrupt the normal course of the following Allegro. Their function differs, however, in each work. In the A minor the angular Assai sostenuto theme, evolved from the same sketches as the theme of the Grosse Fuge,[2] is an essential part of the first subject and its notation, like the one-bar 'adagio' a little later, represents a sort of written-out *rubato*. On the other hand, the longer Adagio, ma non troppo at the beginning of the B flat Quartet has all the appearance of being a

---

[1] *Zweite Beethoveniana*, p. 210. For a fuller discussion of these sketches see Viktor Zuckerkandl, *Man the Musician* (Princeton, 1973), p. 312.

[2] In addition to those published by Nottebohm, sketches for Op. 130, Op. 132, and the finale of Op. 127 are contained in note-books described in De Roda's article, 'Un quaderno di autografi di Beethoven (1825)', *Rivista musicale italiana*, iii (1905), pp. 63, 592, and 734, and in M. Ivanov-Boretsky, 'Ein Moskauer Skizzenbuch von Beethoven', *Muzïkalnoe obrazovanie*, i–ii (Moscow, 1927) (facsimile, with German translation of editor's text, p. 75).

normal slow introduction; its return after five bars of the Allegro, which it thus dislocates and pushes into the dominant for five bars, seems to be indeed an interruption; yet all these happenings are oddly included in an otherwise conventional repeat of the exposition. The interruption recurs at the beginning of the development, is avoided in the recapitulation, but occurs again and is overcome only with a sense of struggle in the coda. Yet otherwise the first movement of the B flat is quite normal, unless the appearance of the second subject in G flat in the exposition and D flat as well as B flat in the recapitulation be accounted a real abnormality. (The two-key return of the second subject is paralleled in the finale of Op. 131.) The first movement of the A minor is more experimental. There is no repeat of the exposition, and after a quite short development of some thirty-eight bars comes what one can only call a 'false recapitulation' in E minor and C major – the original key of the second subject being F major – which in due course is followed by a normal recapitulation in the tonic minor and major, in which the whole material of the movement is set in a clearer light.

The second movements of both these quartets are the equivalents of normal scherzos with trios, though that of the B flat – one of Beethoven's most fascinating – is in 2/2 time with a 6/4 trio. The Allegro non tanto of the A minor has two points of interest: the practical identity of its three-note opening motive and its later inversion with the opening motive and inversion of the Scherzando vivace in Op. 127, and the melodic and harmonic quotation of the first part of an A major Allemande for piano (WoO 81) dating from 1800,[1] bars 9–16 of the Allemande melody being first divided between viola and first violin, bars 1 ff. then appearing on the viola and later on the first violin. Apparently the main part of the middle section of the Allegro ma non tanto was originally to have been an Allemande in A major which later became the Alla danza tedesca of Op. 130; the passage that replaced it has a companion-piece (high register and musette-like drone effect) in the A flat trio of a little Waltz for piano written in 1824 (cf. *Gesamtausgabe*, Series XXV, no. 303).

After this point the general structures of the two quartets begin to differ fundamentally. The 'inside' movements of Op. 130 are no fewer

[1] Published in *Beethoven: Unbekannte Skizzen und Entwürfe* (Bonn, 1924); a later version of the Allemande is published in the *Gesamtausgabe*, Series XXV, no. 307. See also Arnold Schmitz, 'Eine Skizze zum zweiten Satz von Beethovens Streichquartett, Op. 132?', *Zeitschrift für Musikwissenschaft*, vi (1923–4), p. 659. The second part of the Allemande melody occurs also in no. 11 of a set of '12 Deutsche' written in the 1790s (cf. Thayer, v, pp. 265–6) and, in part, in the Largo of the Trio, Op. 1, no. 2, and the third of the *Ländlerische Tänze* published in the *Gesamtausgabe* as Series XVIII, no. 197, and Series XXV, no. 291.

than four in number, equivalents of two scherzi alternating with two slow movements as in the early Septet:

Presto (B flat minor)
Andante con moto (D flat)
Alla danza tedesca (G major)
Cavatina (Adagio molto espressivo) (E flat)

Each is a masterpiece of its kind: the Presto of pianissimo sound, the Andante of finest jeweller's work (*durchbrochene Arbeit* of the subtlest and most highly finished kind), the 'German dance' of quiet humour (particularly the fantastic theme-dissection of the coda), while the Cavatina achieves the impossible by showing that even the slow movements of Op. 96 and Op. 97 can be surpassed in their own kind. All these movements are, relatively, short; Beethoven intended to rest people's ears before confronting them with the Grosse Fuge which he conceived as the original finale.

That finale, regardless as it was of the demands of the human ear in 1826 and still is of the limitations of the quartet medium, both sketchy in texture and harsh in sound, does make a far more satisfying finale to the quartet than the pleasant but not very distinguished movement with which Beethoven decided to replace it. The architectural plan of the Grosse Fuge is not difficult to grasp, especially when one takes into account Beethoven's love of varied recapitulation (cf. bars 139 *et seq.* with bars 31 *et seq.*). Here again study of the sketches is a real help to the understanding of the music, for one sketch in particular shows that Beethoven regarded the counter-subject in the Meno mosso sections and the counter-subject in the main sections as related; they are indeed variations of the same basic idea:

Ex. 108

It may be only a coincidence that the second subject of the substituted finale has also some affinity with Ex. 108. But it is certainly not mere coincidence that the substituted movement begins like the 'Overtura' of the Grosse Fuge with a simple octave G and reaches the tonic key by an unusual path. (When the Grosse Fuge is played as a separate piece, its opening can hardly be said to make sense; it was conceived as the transition from the E flat of the Cavatina.)

One of the sketches for the Fugue[1] shows a combination of the fugue-subject with one of the variations of the 'joy' theme of the Ninth Symphony:

Ex. 109

The whole outline of Op. 132 closely parallels that of the Symphony. The slow movement, like that of the Symphony (which dates from the autumn of 1823), consists of variations on a Molto adagio in common time (in this case the famous 'Convalescent's devout song of thanksgiving to the Deity, in the Lydian mode', one of Beethoven's supreme achievements) alternating with an Andante in triple time and in D major (here entitled 'Feeling new strength'). The autobiographical revelation of the headings, a reference to the composer's illness of April 1825, though interesting as a 'romantic' trait, have attracted too much attention from commentators; six or seven years earlier, in 1818, Beethoven had been contemplating in connection with a choral symphony an 'Adagio Cantique – Pious song in a symphony in the old modes – We praise thee, Lord God – alleluja – either for itself alone or as introduction to a fugue . . . . in the Adagio text of Greek *Mithos* Cantique Eclesiastique – in the Allegro Bacchic festival'. It, or a companion, was to be a 'Sinfonie allemand' with a movement 'alla autrichien'[2] and the earliest sketches – first in A major – for the Andante of the slow movement of the Ninth Symphony, which was conceived before the Adagio which it interrupts, show a continuation with an arpeggio figure[3] which one might connect on the one hand with the A major Allemande of 1800 (WoO 81) and on the other with the arpeggios in the under parts of the middle section of the Allegro ma non tanto in Op. 132. The initial conceptions of the D minor Symphony and the A minor Quartet are completely entwined and the inscriptions on the Quartet Adagio might, one suspects, stand with equal justice at the head of the two sections of its counterpart in the Symphony. But the symphonic movement, great as it is, never attains the Palestrinian otherworldliness of the last section of the Quartet movement. The mood of that extraordinary passage is roughly dispelled by a brisk and rather

[1] De Roda, op. cit., p. 735.
[2] *Zweite Beethoveniana*, pp. 163, 166–7.
[3] Ibid., pp. 174–6.

commonplace march in A major; but the march soon breaks off, a violin recitative says as plainly as the baritone in the Ninth Symphony 'O friends, not these sounds!', and then begins the finale proper: a sonata-rondo whose principal theme had actually been conceived in the first place as the theme of the finale of the Ninth Symphony.

The C sharp minor Quartet, Op. 131, shows traces of relationship to the opening of the A minor and the subject of the Grosse Fuge (cf. bars 16-19 of the Allegro molto vivace) but does not otherwise belong to the same world of ideas. It builds its own, and in a curious form:

> Adagio (fugue in C sharp minor)
> Allegro molto vivace (sonata-rondo in D major)
> Allegro moderato and Adagio (eleven bars of modulating recitative)
> Andante (with six variations and coda, in A major)
> Presto (scherzo and trio in 2/2 time, E major)
> Adagio quasi un poco andante (essentially an introduction in G
>   sharp to
> Allegro (sonata form, C sharp minor)

But the seven movements are soon seen to be the usual four, with a fugal prologue and two interludes, though one does not expect to find a sonata-rondo near the beginning of a work. The difficulties of Op. 131 are those common to all the late quartets, not special ones arising from its unusual structure.[1]

The F major, Op. 135, presents no problems, except that of the autobiographical trivialities that are put forward[2] as the explanation of the title of the last movement, 'The difficult resolution: Must it be? It must be'. It was conceived as a light-weight work originally in only three movements and it was natural that Beethoven should follow it with the present finale of Op. 130. But it has its own subtleties. In the first movement Beethoven refines upon a favourite device of Haydn's: the 'false reprise' soon after the beginning of the development. The real recapitulation, beginning 22 bars later, is one of the most beautifully disguised in the whole of Beethoven. Beautiful, too, is the return of the scherzo proper after a trio (neither is actually so named) in which the use of an ostinato is carried to a point that must have seemed lunatic to most of Beethoven's contemporaries. The lovely D flat Lento assai will appear to the inattentive hearer to be in simple ABA form, but is really a theme with four variations. And in the last

---

[1] For a discussion of Beethoven's early ideas on movement and key sequence in this work, see Robert Winter, 'Plans for the Structure of the String Quartet in C sharp minor, Op. 131', *Beethoven Studies 2*, ed. Tyson (London, 1977), p. 106.

[2] Thayer, op. cit., v, pp. 301–3; Thayer-Forbes, pp. 976–7; and Altmann's preface to the Eulenburg score.

movement Beethoven springs a final surprise by suggesting an old-fashioned repeat of development and recapitulation – *al suo piacere* – before the coda.

VII

THE CHAMBER MUSIC OF
BEETHOVEN'S CONTEMPORARIES

By HANS MERSMANN *and* GERALD ABRAHAM

STYLISTICALLY the four decades 1790–1830 comprise two fairly distinct periods. The earlier stands mainly under the shadow of Beethoven's overwhelming personality and development and could be called classic; the latter represents the first generation of German musical romanticism. In both, chamber music played a decisive role.

From the evolution of two centuries, the concept of 'chamber music' had emerged with ever-increasing clarity. At first identical with instrumental music *per se* in distinction from church music and theatre-music, its frontiers ill defined and, until well into the eighteenth century, open toward the genres of symphony, orchestral trio, and concerto, chamber music proper and its forms were established mainly by Haydn and Mozart. It was Haydn who detached the string quartet from the welter of suite-type music, and stylistically carried it to the point where it could become Beethoven's most personal instrument. With Beethoven, the development reached its peak. Not only was the string quartet sharply delimited in idiom and content from symphonic and pianistic writing, but also the individual provinces of chamber music became clearly separated; string quartets and works for strings with piano were now fundamentally different in expressive means and artistic aims. In retrospect one recognizes here the impact of Beethoven's personal stylistic development.

DITTERSDORF AND HIS CONTEMPORARIES

Most of the composers who stood on the periphery of that development were contemporaries of Beethoven in the exact sense. Only one among them belonged to the immediate neighbourhood of Haydn: Carl Ditters von Dittersdorf (1739–99) who has become known chiefly by his comic operas and orchestral music. His instrumental works comprise more than a hundred symphonies, divertimenti, concertos, two sets of string quintets (1782 and 1789), and six string quartets. These quartets appeared only in 1788,[1] at a time, that is, when many of the most important works of Haydn and Mozart had already been written; the string quartets which Haydn described as being 'set in a new manner' had appeared in 1784. Dittersdorf had published trio sonatas at the start of his career (Paris, 1767), and it was probably due to Haydn's influence that he proceeded to the string quartet.

Dittersdorf's works are important in the history of the string quartet not so much for originality of invention as for the clarity and richness of their textures. Influenced by Haydn – whose greatest quartets from Op. 64 onward were still to come in the course of the 1790s – and also by Mozart, Dittersdorf's chamber music is typical of Viennese instrumental music in the last decades of the eighteenth century. To his generation, overshadowed by the two great masters, belong Johann Georg Albrechtsberger (1736–1809), Emanuel Alois Förster (1748–1823), Ignaz Pleyel (1757–1831), and Paul Wranitzky (1756–1808), all prolific composers of chamber music.

PLEYEL AND FÖRSTER

Mozart in 1784 had found Pleyel's quartets 'very well written and very pleasant'[2] and, according to Josef Klingenbeck,[3] Boccherini particularly admired his quartets in F minor, Op. 34, no. 6, and Op. 67, no. 3,[4] for the quality of their workmanship. It is well exemplified in this passage from the first movement of Op. 34, no. 6:

Ex. 110

[1] See Vol. VII, p. 563. On his chamber music generally, see Gertrude Rigler, 'Die Kammermusk Dittersdorfs', *Studien zur Musikwissenschaft*, xiv (1927), p. 179.
[2] Letter to his father, 24 April 1784, *Mozart: Briefe und Aufzeichnungen*, ed. Wilhelm A. Bauer and Otto Erich Deutsch (Kassel, 1963), iii, p. 311.
[3] 'Ignaz Pleyel, sein Streichquartett im Rahmen der Wiener Klassik', *Studien zur Musikwissenschaft*, xxv (1962), p. 276.
[4] These are the opus numbers of the edition by André of Offenbach. His Op. 34 was published by Longman and Broderip (London, 1791) as Op. 23, by Imbault of Paris as 8. *livre*. André's Op. 67 was issued by Franz Reinhard (Strasbourg, 1803), as Op. 9.

But if we set Haydn aside as *hors ligne*, the most notable Viennese quartet composer before Beethoven entered the field was his friend Förster. Beethoven's counterpoint tutor had been Albrechtsberger, who left numerous quartets, including six early *Quatuors en fugues*, double quartets, and other chamber music,[1] but Beethoven put Förster beside Albrechtsberger as a contrapuntist and far above him as a composer of string quartets, calling him 'mein alter Meister' and recommending him to Razumovsky as a teacher of quartet composition. There is something of Beethoven's own power and passion in Förster's Op. 16, no. 5 (1798) (i) and his C minor Quintet, Op. 19 (ii):[2]

[1] See Vol. VII, p. 560.
[2] *Denkmäler der Tonkunst in Österreich*, Jg. xxxv (1) (vol. 67), pp. 17 and 36.

Ex. 111

Besides his string quartets Förster also published three pairs of quartets for piano and strings, Op. 8 (1794), Op. 10, and Op. 11 (1796), less remarkable than those for strings alone yet historically interesting as the most important link between Mozart and Beethoven in this medium. They look both ways, the cello, for instance, sometimes tamely doubling the pianist's left hand, sometimes making it quite independent and taking it up into its highest register.

NEW INSTRUMENTAL COMBINATIONS

It is strange that a pianist like Pleyel should never have attempted the piano quartet – those attributed to him are arrangements of works for other combinations – though he is credited with a number of piano trios. It was his almost exact contemporary, another pianist, Jan Ladislav Dussek (1760–1812), and Dussek's friend and pupil Prince Louis Ferdinand of Prussia (1772–1806), who first after Förster notably followed Mozart's lead. Dussek's preferred chamber music combination, like Pleyel's, was the piano trio in which the cello was still struggling to emancipate itself from a mere strengthening of the piano's bass. His F major Trio, Op. 65 (1807), is one of his finest chamber works.

Dussek's first piano quartet (F minor, Op. 41, *c.* 1802) is always described as a quintet but the double bass part is *ad libitum*; his second (E flat, Op. 56) followed in 1804 when he had already met the soldier-prince. Louis Ferdinand had already published a true piano quintet (C minor, Op. 1) in Paris in 1801; two piano quartets (E flat and F minor, Opp. 5 and 6) date from 1804, and an Andante with variations for the same combination, Op. 4, from 1806. It must be said that the amateur pupil far surpassed the professional master, both in the handling of the medium and in the quality of invention; the instruments are 'emancipated', nuances are freely indicated. Louis Ferdinand seems to look forward to Schubert and Mendelssohn, and Schumann justly called him 'der Romantiker der klassischen Periode'. The opening of the development of the first movement of his F minor Quartet is typical:

Ex. 112

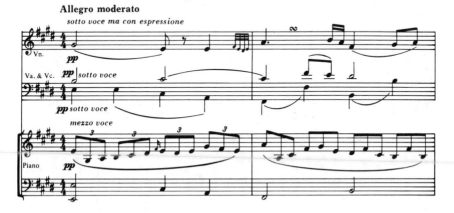

His piano-writing links him with the florid, ornamental style of Dussek and the two *Divertissements* (1810) of John Field (1782–1837) in which the string quartet does little more than accompany, though in the later *Andante con espressione* in A flat (*c.* 1814), which Field actually styled 'quintet' the interest is more evenly divided between strings and piano. The influence of Louis Ferdinand's style in general is marked in the Piano Quartet (1809) of Carl Maria von Weber (1786–1826).

New instrumental combinations became popular during the early decades of the century. The flute could be substituted for the violin in duet sonatas or the harp for the piano as in the Quintet (*c.* 1807)[1] by E. T. A. Hoffmann (1776–1822), composer as well as novelist and writer on music. Hoffmann also left a conventional Piano Trio in E major (1809)[2] in which effective climaxes arise from the opposition of piano and strings; the opening of the first movement suggests a sketch for a fugal exposition which collapses altogether in the unison of bar 7:

Ex. 113

---

[1] Ed. Gustav Becking, *E.Th.A. Hoffmann: Musikalische Werke*, ii, no. 1 (Leipzig, 1922).
[2] Scherzo printed as supplement to Georg Jensch, 'Ein verschollenes Klaviertrio von E.T.A. Hoffman', *Zeitschrift für Musikwissenschaft*, ii (1919–20), p. 23.

SCHUBERT'S EARLY QUARTETS

The 'romanticism' foreshadowed by these composers is more clearly apparent in a far greater than any of them: Franz Schubert (1797–1828).[1] Romanticism implies a certain loosening of form. The structure of a movement is no longer based on the development of germinal motives but on free, almost improvisatory lines. Overflowing imagination dissolves form into a succession of episodes. The clear distinction between symphonic and quartet styles established by Beethoven is lost and the chamber music of Schubert, Mendelssohn, and their successors is less specifically chamber music than 'instrumental music for a small ensemble'. The general thematicism of romatic instrumental music was penetrated by the influence of song, which even draws attention to itself when the themes of Schubert's songs surface in his chamber compositions. Other of his instrumental themes suggest the beginning of a song, a characteristic that goes to the heart of the problem of romantic instrumental music; the developmental power of a theme is exhausted with its appearance, thus necessarily leading to a multiplicity of ideas and episodes.

As with Beethoven, the string quartet took the first place with Schubert; he wrote fourteen.[2] In addition there are two string trios and the C major String Quintet. His chamber music with piano comprises two trios and a Quintet with double bass ('The Trout'). More nearly orchestral is the Octet, the only work employing wind. Opus numbers indicate neither chronological order nor development. All, except the A minor Quartet, Op. 29, appeared only posthumously.

Even the youthful quartets are characteristic in several aspects. With them the fifteen-year-old Schubert began to take his work seriously. While the early vocal music often shows the first signs of maturity, there were more serious obstacles to be overcome in quartet writing. Stimulated by his father's domestic quartet, which offered him opportunities for hearing what he had written, Schubert began to struggle with the development of the medium's expressive possibilities. The string quartet was his natural starting-point. Most of his quartets were written during 1812–15. His development proceeded at an unheard-of pace. While the quartets of 1812 and 1813 show all the marks of first attempts, those of the next year already manifest rapid growth, and a secure grasp of the means of expression, particularly in harmony. They impress one as an integrated corpus of work.

[1] See Walter Riezler, *Schuberts Instrumentalmusik, Werkanalysen* (Zürich, 1967), and Jack Westrup, *Schubert's Chamber Music* (London, 1969).
[2] See Hans-Martin Sachse, *Franz Schuberts Streichquartette* (Münster, 1959) and Richard A. Coolidge, 'Form in the String Quartets of Franz Schubert', *The Music Review*, xxxii (1971), p. 309.

Stylistically the works of the first two years find the true limits of chamber music only gradually. The idiom shows orchestral traits; *tutti* passages in the manner of the classical orchestra alternate with more subtly written sections. The thematic style is closer to the symphony than to the string quartet; the ideas are primitive and ponderous. The young Schubert instinctively avoids points of repose. Fast tempi are preferred, slow movements being either of no great consequence or omitted altogether, but the minuet movement has to remain. First and last movements are usually worked up to presto. The assurance in maintaining consistency of invention in these early works is surprising.

Among the early quartets, the D major of 1814 (D.94)[1] represents a turning point that coincides with the great decision of his life: his leaving the Konvikt and becoming his father's school assistant. While the themes of earlier works had been impersonal, the very first one of this quartet presents a melodic line of a peculiar cast. It is a first symbol of the romantic theme: lacking genuine strength or inner tension, it enters four times on the 'floating' third of the chord, and glides from there in various directions. Its growth is governed harmonically, not as a matter of tensions but as change of colour:

Ex. 114

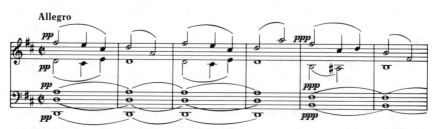

In this early quartet one clearly sees the salient features of the romantic sonata type handled with great certainty. It is no longer drama, conflict of forces, broken up development, but a cycle, swinging between the thematic poles and eventually completing itself, in the unity of which all oppositions have merely relative significance. This is particularly the case in the development section which is no longer an arena of conflict, and in which harmonic tension reaches its ultimate limit.

---

[1] D. numbers refer to Otto Erich Deutsch (with Donald Wakeling), *Schubert: Thematic Catalogue of All his Works in Chronological Order* (London, 1951); revised and expanded as *Franz Schubert. Thematisches Verzeichnis seiner Werke in chronologischer Folge*, ed. Walter Dürr, Arnold Feil, and Christa Landon (Kassel, 1978).

The Quartet in B flat (D. 112) Op. posth. 168, was also written in 1814. In it Schubert maintains his new level throughout all the movements. Here, too, it is the theme that determines the whole development; rooted in sonority and colour it does not build, it oscillates. Instead of growth we find new, specifically romantic processes: harmonic reinterpretation, concealed variation, colour changes. The preponderance of musical substance over thematic definition and structural planning is noticeable in the other movements as well, particulary in the finale which by virtue of its athematic form and its essentially colouristic expansion represents a new type of movement.

This first period of quartet composition concludes with the Quartet in G minor (D.173, Op. posth.) of 1815. It stands under the shadow of Beethoven, particularly in its first movement; not only as regards its direct relation to Op. 18, no. 2, but in the plasticity of its motives and the rhythmic and formal decision of the writing. The Quartet in E (D.353), composed in 1816 and posthumously published as Op. 125, no. 2, is concise in structure, its themes strongly defined. Unable as yet to escape from the influence of Beethoven, Schubert was still fighting against himself. It is only in the later works, where he no longer checks the flow of his ideas but gives them free vent, that his creative power is fully revealed. The first theme of the E major Quartet marks the critical point of his development: the contrast between the dotted octave-leaps and the smooth, legato melodic lines has the force of a true antithesis on which Beethoven would have built an entire work. But Schubert opts for the gentler aspect of the theme and evades the potential conflict.

OTHER TYPES OF CHAMBER MUSIC

From the time of these quartets we also have some works which, though they do not belong to the mainstream of Schubert's chamber music, afford an opportunity to consider peripheral varieties of chamber music which are characteristic of early romanticism. For romantic chamber music underwent the same transformations as romantic piano music, dissolving into concertante, rhapsodic, or programmatic forms.

Schubert himself temporarily turned his back on the string quartet. It had become the medium of a personal line of development and in it he had tested the thematicism, part-writing, and sound-textures that gradually were to carry him from the Beethovenian ideal to the establishment of his own idiom and form. Now, however, he began to branch out: in 1816 he wrote an (unfinished) string trio (D.471) and an

Adagio and Rondo concertante (D.487) for piano and strings. There is an intrinsic connection between these and such later works as the Variations for piano and flute on a theme from 'Die schöne Müllerin' (D.802) of 1824 and the Fantasia in C for piano and violin (D.934) of 1827.

This whole body of chamber music has become almost forgotten. Schubert's indebtedness to his own age is most apparent in these works where no formal law constricted his wandering fancy. The participation of the piano was a new and, as we have seen, fashionable factor. Schubert's next large-scale work was a piano quintet.

Of special interest is the place of the violin sonata in Schubert's output. In his hands it shed its remaining links with the sonata proper. The new type appeared as a development in two directions, one diminishing, the other extending; ease of performance led to utilitarian sonatina-like works, while compositions called 'duo' or 'fantasia' were enlarged by the absorption of rhapsodic and concertante elements. Both species are represented in Schubert. To the latter type belongs the 1817 Duo in A major, Op. 162 (D.574) whose four-movement lay-out and structural plan are taken over from the sonata, while its thematicism and piano-writing are relaxed and improvisatory, at times also *concertante* in character. The other works of this species all centre on the *Lied*. The already mentioned C major Fantasia (D.934) and Flute Variations (D. 802), are built around paraphrases of *Lieder*, even though the variations of the Fantasia are preceded by an independent main movement. The so-called 'notturno', Op. 148 (D.897) for piano trio belongs to the same species.

'Utility music' is represented by the three violin sonatas, Op. 137 (D.384–5 and 408) (D major, A minor, G minor) of 1816. They are deliberately simple in thought and idiom and their facility of execution, which has made them indispensable as teaching material, is reflected by their straightforward, clear-cut themes. The D major work is reminiscent of Mozart; Schubert significantly called it 'Sonata for pianoforte with violin accompaniment' as if it were an eighteenth-century composition.

THE WORKS OF SCHUBERT'S MATURITY

These transitional works, most of them dating from 1816 and 1817, mark a natural division in Schubert's life. He was now twenty years of age, and while still slightly overawed in his chamber music by the image of Beethoven, he had probed all possibilities and extended his horizon. He now entered the final decade of his life in which he was to produce a limited number of master-works, each perfect and self-contained, free from all the dross of immaturity but embracing the strongest contrasts. There are nine of these works (if the isolated *Quartettsatz* in C minor is included). The series begins with the Piano Quintet and ends with the String Quintet; between these are the three string quartets, the Octet, and the two piano trios.

The earliest of these is the Piano Quintet of 1819, nicknamed 'The Trout' from the song on which the third movement is based; it has to this day remained one of the most popular of Schubert's instrumental compositions. Like the Octet and the Beethoven Septet, it belongs to the permanent stock of popular chamber music concerts. Its well-deserved popularity is by no means founded on the song-variations alone, but on the inner simplicity, strength, and freshness of all the themes of this unproblematic and highly inventive work. The piano carries into the circle of stringed instruments sonorities that seem to stem from Schubert's transition period of free and easy improvisation. Inserted between scherzo and finale, the fourth movement brings the 'Trout' variations; the theme consists of the song-melody played by the four strings; the piano enters with the first variation, playing the theme in bare octaves. The variations continue by surrounding the melody with loose garlands of figuration, and after radical transformations the theme is restated in its original form.

Although separated from the Quintet by a space of five years, the Octet (1824) is closely related to it. In this work, the string quartet is again joined by a double bass, as well as by clarinet, horn, and bassoon. The instrumentation reminds one of Beethoven's Septet; for Schubert, too, the combination of wind and strings in a chamber work was to remain an isolated experiment. The enlarged body of instruments is significant not for the work's structure, but for its sound. The eight movements form a suite-like succession; an Andante with variations, standing between scherzo and minuet, is reminiscent of the old serenade form and occasional colour contrasts suggest the opposition of tutti and soli.

These transitional works mark the way to the heights of Schubert's chamber music, which begin with the Quartet Movement in C minor of December 1820, followed in the autograph by 41 bars of an Andante in A flat. Although only three years had elapsed since the Quartet in E major, Schubert, in returning to the genre, faced it with a new assurance. His inner development was completed. Classical form, the model of Beethoven, no longer hung over him. He now renounced tradition, offering his own riches, giving himself up to his own wealth of inspiration, and seeking his own ways of transmuting it.

One notices at once the decisive breakthrough of harmonic forces.

Harmony stands in a new, more independent relationship to the other elements; it participates decisively in all developments. Breaking out of the limitations of the older musical 'logic', it could move freely within the circle of fifths; tonal space could now be traversed easily in all directions. Already with Beethoven, the relationship of keys a third apart had been acknowledged, and Schubert now added to this his own consistently planned chromaticism. Any chromatic degree in the scale could now be harmonized as a leading-note. Song-writing had given Schubert confidence in this respect; he had already written entire songs in which all the essential connections depend on chromaticism alone.

The unfinished C minor Quartet became the basis for the last three great string quartets of Schubert, which form the summit of his development. Unlike his former works, these quartets are not inflections of one underlying type, but three self-contained contrasting individualities which, at the same time, reflect three contrasting zones of Schubert's mind. If we include the String Quintet, the creative space of Schubert's chamber music appears to be fully plumbed and defined in all directions by these works.

THE LAST THREE QUARTETS

The first of the three quartets, the A minor, was composed and published as Op. 29 in 1824. Its opening theme is one of Schubert's most perfect ideas. The basic shape descends a fifth (i). How this shape is transformed without developing, and how on its third occurrence it briefly lights up in the tonic major key of A, immediately reminds one of Mozart:

Ex. 115

This melodic growth, extending over three curves, is of perfect plasticity and at the same time of the utmost freedom. One is conscious of no shaping hand, no act of will; all the transformations have the simplicity of a natural event. The development of the movement is not really rooted in the theme but, as often with Schubert, in new elements which directly grow out of the musical substance. As in the theme itself, major and minor are not opposing poles but are simply changes of illumination.

All the movements of this work are of the same immediacy; they are, as it were, permeated by the original theme which, indeed, seems to have suggested the material for that of the second movement; the fifth e-a continues to be an important interval. Common to the movements is their reticence, their delicate sweetness:

Ex. 116

While in the first two movements melody is the prime element, the minuet and finale bring a new development. The way from A minor to A major, foreshadowed in Ex. 115, is now extended into a vast curve ending in the dance-like theme of the finale which releases all the light and strength that had still been withheld in the gentle, allusive minuet.

In its idiom, though not in its content, the G major Quartet is one of Schubert's most subjective works. Whereas in the A minor the centre of gravity lies almost exclusively in the thematic material itself, to which evolution and development are subordinated, the reverse is the case in this work. The themes are characterized by harmonic and rhythmic tensions rather than by melodic purpose. Their development avoids all definite thematic or motivic connections. From the very first theme of the first movement, the alternations of major and minor seem not so much changes in illumination as almost a cerebral game. As John Reed has put it, 'the assertion that major implies minor and vice versa recurs like a point of reference before the recapitulation and again at the end, so that the movement has a logical coherence and tautness which seems a little uncharacteristic.'[1]

The contrasts of these two works are summed up in the great D minor Quartet, Op. posth.[2] Its centre of gravity does not really lie in the variations of the middle movement, which plumb the ultimate depth of Schubert's song 'Der Tod und das Mädchen'; actually all the movements are equally powerful and important. Strong, always

[1] *Schubert: The Final Years* (London, 1972), p. 51.
[2] On this work see Harold Truscott, 'Schubert's D minor Quartet', *The Music Review*, xix (1958), p. 27.

inspired themes are combined with structures, clear yet strained at times almost to breaking-point, and with a creative power that surpasses even the two previous quartets. The various kinds of expressiveness coalesce: the flowing cantabile melodies of the counter-themes combines effortlessly with the dark, massive energy of the principal ideas. The unification of those very contrasts which had sealed the fate of the Unfinished Symphony, is here achieved with quiet, irresistible self-confidence. Behind the almost uncontrollable flood of ideas one detects that desire for strength and unity, the highest realization of which Schubert saw in Beethoven. Thus, the basic motive of the first theme, distantly reminiscent of the opening of the Fifth Symphony, is a unification of these contrasts in which the rhythmic strength of the triplet motive, augmented to crotchets, at once effects the development of the theme:

Ex. 117

The rhythmic play of the triplets, which gradually loses in tension, leads to a complex of counter-themes characterized by buoyancy of rhythm and looseness of texture:

Ex. 118

It is characteristic of romantic sonata-form that both themes undergo retrograde developments: while the main theme becomes increasingly relaxed, the counter-theme grows in emotional stature.

In his song 'Der Tod und das Mädchen' Schubert, by a stroke of genius, converted the binary dialogue of the protagonists into a ternary form by prefacing the maiden's plea with an instrumental introduction anticipating the voice of Death. Thus, in the quartet movement, it is not a song-melody that is varied, as in the Trout Quintet, but an independent instrumental passage which is further developed. We must understand Schubert's intention in placing this movement in this context. The dark, fateful theme of the first statement resolves itself here in a manner similar to the funeral march of the 'Eroica'. But Schubert's concept of death is different from Beethoven's. It is romantic death as conceived by Hölderlin, resolved in longing and transfiguration, and not to be related to the classical funeral march. The expressive device of veiled sound-forms beneath a sustained upper part, had often been used in opera and song as a symbol of the supersensual: J. F. Reichardt had already employed it in his setting of 'Erlkönig'. Schubert, however, exploits this effect of colour to create a ternary form in which each section is subtly differentiated: eight bars of passive diatonic chords, eight of larger, more sonorous intervals, and eight more in which the harmony becomes more colourful and cadences in the major. Owing to the contrasts of its themes, the first movement had ended in a quaternary coda on somewhat similar lines.

The 'hammering' theme of the scherzo recalls the opening of the first Allegro. The movement leads the sombre mood of the variations into the headlong Presto of the finale. This is at first propelled by motoric force, but new motives enter later and impede the forward rush. The clash of these elements repeatedly results in harmonic tensions that sometimes crystallize into tangible shapes like the clenched *sforzandi* of this passage just before the end:

Ex. 119

PIANO TRIOS AND STRING QUINTET

Once more the piano became important in Schubert's chamber music. In 1827, the penultimate year of his life, he wrote the two Piano Trios, Op. 99 in B flat and Op. 100 in E flat. Both are of the strongest possible directness; the B flat, impelled by its urgent opening theme, especially in the realm of pure sound; the E flat in its broad fresco-like thematicism and a melodic simplification that derives from the *Lied*. These piano trios belong to an area of chamber music already opened up by Beethoven; in it the string quartet and the piano trio which, with Haydn and Mozart, were still closely related (and which were to approach each other again with Brahms), were at this juncture the opposite poles of chamber music. The association of the piano evokes an atmosphere of elegant social music, while music for strings alone becomes an area of concentrated thought and workmanship.

This area was traversed once more by Schubert in a work that seems his last bequest to us: the C major Quintet, Op. 163. The string quartet is augmented by a second cello, which makes possible a contrast of two trio textures, the viola combining either with the cellos or the violins. The String Quintet is a synthesis. Contrasts that had earlier essentially determined the character of a work are here reconciled. Warmth, radiance of sound, directness of melodic utterance do not lie on the obvious surface of this work but seem woven into the fabric of the independent parts. The opening of the first movement is symbolic: it is only after the tonic chord has dissolved into the four notes of a diminished seventh, that the theme breaks out melodically, ascends, loosens, and swings free:

Ex. 120

Allegro ma non troppo

It is only in the gradual growth of the work that the forces pressing toward the surface of these bars are fully liberated and made clear. The rhythms of the second subject appear not so much as a contrasting idea as a new refraction of the same medium; the last vestiges of dramatic tension are eliminated and the movement proceeds into a spacious development, of strong inner dynamism, whose climax is reached in the codetta idea – which to a great extent also dominates the development section. One might put it that, no longer threatened by the structural tensions of Beethoven, no longer endangered by its own dark conflicts, the work shines forth in pure perfection. The masterly five-part writing remains unparalleled even in Schubert.

The slow movement seems an unbroken continuation of the first. It is based on an 8-bar period which at first attracts the ear less than the little embellishing counterpoints of the outer parts. This displacement of emphasis is an essentially romantic effect. (One thinks of those landscapes by Caspar David Friedrich which depict foreground figures gazing out to sea or at the moon; the figures themselves are much less important than the melancholy landscape which is the actual theme of the painting;)[1] The middle part of the ternary movement is sharply antithetical in F minor, after which the Adagio returns to its original realm of pure light.

The clear, bright colours, the simple melodies, and strong, determined rhythms of both scherzo and finale would make them seem an indissoluble unit, were it not for the intervention of the strange, wholly unexpected trio. With an independence unique in both Beethoven's and Schubert's scherzo forms, this Andante sostenuto in common time plunges into a sombre *espressivo* that is maintained throughout without much change or development; it constitutes a shattering breakthrough of subjectivity, all the more impressive by contrast with the scherzo proper.

Schubert was never to hear this, perhaps his most significant chamber work. Rather as in Mozart's case, one asks oneself whether it is possible to conceive of a development for which such music as this might have been a stepping-stone. In unsurpassable perfection, the Quintet shines forth from the tragically early end of its creator's life.

[1] Cf. Fritz Novotny, *Painting and Sculpture in Europe 1780–1880* (Harmondsworth, 1960), pp. 54–5.

SCHUBERT'S CONTEMPORARIES

Schubert was the last composer of chamber music whose work was conditioned by Beethoven's. It was only considerably later that the inner development of the genre was to continue. For the time being the concept of chamber music lost clear definition. The works of the first generation of romantic composers removed chamber music from the central position given it by Beethoven. Although most of them wrote it, its specific values declined. What they said in a trio might have been expressed just as well, if not better, by the piano alone. For this once more plays an essential role and, as it had to some extent in the eighteenth century, makes chamber music a province of piano music.

An exception was Ludwig Spohr who, although Schubert's senior by ten years, definitely belongs to the romantic era, the span of which approximately coincides with his long lifetime (1787–1859). Spohr's roots were still in Beethoven. His operas are historical monuments, his thirty odd concertos[1] are still given occasional performances; but his chamber music is forgotten. It comprises a great number of works, the centre of which always lies in the strings. The increase in the external apparatus of music, so characteristic of romanticism, is fully revealed for the first time by Spohr. The first violin is given exceptional prominence in all his thirty or more quartets, not only those, such as the D minor, Op. 11 (1807), which are actually styled 'brillants' where the violin writing is frankly *concertante*. In 1823 Spohr published the first of his four double-quartets in which the combining and contrasting of two ensembles frequently leads to interesting effects but also to over-fullness of sound and a superficially effective style in which, however, the subtleties of part-writing are necessarily obscured. Spohr's themes are often fresh and plastic, though lacking in depth and power of development. In some works he combined strings and wind,[2] notably an Octet (1813) and Nonet (1814)[3] which show both his romantic vein and his thematic workmanship at their best, as in the second subject of the first movement of the Octet:

[1] See Chap. V, pp. 251–2.
[2] Johann Nepomuk Hummel (1778–1837) had been almost unique in including the piano with strings and wind in his Septet (1816).
[3] Clementi's Nonet in E flat, scored for the same unusual combination of instruments as the Spohr, 'was probably written in response to it'; see Leon Plantinga, *Clementi, His Life and Works* (London, 1977), p. 251.

Ex. 121

Carl Maria von Weber (1786–1826) also belongs to the first generation of German romanticists. His instrumental music in general is dominated by the piano, but chamber music takes a subordinate place in his total output. It comprises the already mentioned Piano Quartet, a Quintet for clarinet and strings (1815) and a Trio for flute, cello, and piano (1819). Of these the early Piano Quartet in B flat, Op. 8, is most characteristic of Weber's individuality. The themes stand close to Mozart; the structure is loosened to the point of extemporization by a succession of independent episodes and by the *concertante* role of the piano. Though in the slow movements the melodic flow is relaxed almost to the simplicity of folksong, at other points it sometimes oversteps the proper limits of chamber music. In the E flat Adagio of the Piano Quartet – finished in 1806, three years before the other movements – the tonic is suddenly transformed at the second bar into a *forte* dominant seventh chord in A flat; a playful piano figure detaches itself from the flowing part-writing of bar 3, but breaks off abruptly and, after a bar's rest, is concluded by pizzicato chords:

Ex. 122

This process is an expression not only of a personal, but also of a contemporary attitude which constantly recurs with other, lesser composers. Weber also wrote six *Sonates progressives pour le Pianoforte avec Violon obligé* (1810) which, like Schubert's, are cast in small forms. In these, too, the piano dominates, occasionally leading toward free improvisation. Much more important, though as problematic as the Piano Quartet, is the G minor Trio for piano, flute, cello (1819). Like the Quartet, it has a strongly dramatic element; for instance, the third movement, entitled 'Schäfers Klage' and obviously based on a setting of Goethe's poem, has a passionate piano interruption:

Ex. 123

corresponding to Goethe's fourth stanza ('Die Türe dort bleibet verschlossen').

There is a certain amount of pianistic exuberance in the early chamber music of Mendelssohn (1809–47), notably his Sextet in D for piano, string quartet, and double bass (1824). It includes three piano quartets, four string quartets, a String Quintet, and a String Octet, all written in the period 1822–9, already a much larger corpus of work than Weber's and practically all true chamber music. Two compositions of 1825, the B minor Piano Quartet and the Octet, remained unsurpassed in Mendelssohn's later years; the Octet in particular – not a 'double quartet' like Spohr's – is masterly not only in its Allegro leggerissimo, *sempre pp e staccato*, scherzo. The string quartets already reflect the influence of Beethoven, even late Beethoven, as in this *fugato* in the Adagio non lento of Op. 13 in A minor (1827):

Ex. 124

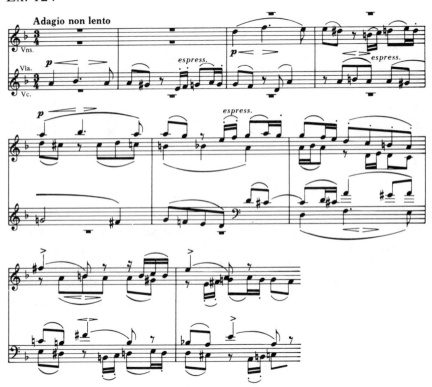

CHERUBINI

Little chamber music of lasting value was composed at this time outside the German-speaking lands, though the work of three foreigners settled in France deserves notice: the Italian Luigi Cherubini (1760–1842), the Czech Antonin Reicha (1770–1836), and the Englishman George Onslow (1783–1852). Reicha and his pupil Onslow were prolific, and Reicha's two dozen wind quintets are

specially noteworthy.[1] But Cherubini's small output of chamber music
– six string quartets and a quintet – makes up in quality for its limited
quantity.[2] Three of the quartets were printed during his lifetime; the
later three became known only after his death. He liked to preface his
quartets with slow introductions and was fond of the play of contrasts
within a narrow space. But such contrasts are with him not mere
gestures, but a true interplay of forces. Thematic development
becomes all-pervading and sometimes even relates themes in different
movements; thus in his first quartet (in E flat, 1814) the forceful
opening of the first movement (i) is transformed in the unison
beginning of the finale (ii):

Ex. 125

In Cherubini's chamber music, the stronger outlines of symphony
and occasionally the pathos of grand opera, conflict with true quartet
style; in fact his C major Quartet of 1829 is a transcription of a
symphony composed in 1815.[3] During the rest of the nineteenth
century chamber music was to become increasingly quasi-orchestral
in style.

[1] See Udo Sirker, *Die Entwicklung des Bläserquintetts in der ersten Hälfte des 19. Jahrhunderts* (Regensburg, 1968), pp. 25 ff. on Reicha, pp. 35–6 on Onslow.
[2] See Basil Deane, *Cherubini* (London, 1965), pp. 43–5, and Siegfried Saak, *Studien zur Instrumentalmusik Luigi Cherubinis* (Göttingen, 1979), pp. 106 ff.
[3] See p. 182, n. 1.

VIII

PIANO MUSIC

By PHILIP RADCLIFFE

By 1790 Mozart had written practically all his music for piano solo. Haydn's last three sonatas date from 1794,[1] and in the following year Beethoven published his Op. 2. The piano sonatas of both Haydn and Mozart are in many ways more varied in size and treatment than their symphonies; Beethoven at once accepted the four-movement design that Haydn used only twice in very early works, and no other composer has handled the piano sonata with such versatility. Haydn's sonatas are also surprisingly varied in size, and it is significant that his latest, in E flat, though only in three movements, is one of the broadest and most massive of all his works. Towards the end of the eighteenth century the piano sonata was increasing its general scope and emotional range; even the amiable, if unadventurous, works of the Bohemian composer Leopold Kozeluch show a certain spaciousness of design. But of far greater importance is the piano music of the Italian Muzio Clementi.

CLEMENTI

Born in 1752, Clementi spent a considerable portion of his life in England, making for himself a wide reputation as a piano virtuoso and becoming in 1798 a partner in a publishing and piano-building firm, Longman, Clementi and Co.[2] After their celebrated contest before the Emperor Joseph II in Austria, Mozart wrote disparagingly of Clementi's virtuosity which seemed to him to be inspired by too exclusive a preoccupation with pianistic effects. The sonatas, Op. 2[3] 'with an Accompaniment for a German Flute or Violin' (1779), are certainly the work of a virtuoso. They are full of brilliant passages in

[1] See Vol. VII, pp. 600-1.
[2] The name of the firm underwent various changes.
[3] The opus-numbers of Clementi's works are in considerable confusion. See William S. Newman, *The Sonata in the Classic Era* (Chapel Hill, 1963), pp. 742-5. The numbers in this chapter are the original opus-numbers: see Alan Tyson, *Thematic Catalogue of the Works of Muzio Clementi* (Tutzing, 1967) and Leon Plantinga, *Clementi: His Life and Music* (London, 1977).

thirds and octaves, but the thematic invention is undistinguished and the general manner grandiose and self-assured but with little individuality or imagination. But his style soon began to develop in different directions, and Op. 7 (1782) shows entirely new features, though the second sonata, in C, is in much the same style as Op. 2, with a barren outburst of rapid octaves in the final movement. But the others, though smaller and less pretentious, have far more character. In the first, in E flat, the slow movement has remarkable warmth and richness of colour, and sonata-form is handled with far more continuity and concentration than in the earlier works. The third, in G minor, is finer still and shows the peculiar intensity to be found in all Clementi's sonatas in minor keys. It is felt at once in the opening theme:

Ex. 126

and when, during the development, this is presented in augmentation in a major key it produces a kind of spaciousness strongly prophetic of Beethoven. The third movement is remarkable both for its resourceful thematic treatment, and for its wide range of modulation. Another sonata in the same key, Op. 8, no. 1 (1782), 'with an Accompanyment for a Violin or German Flute', is similar in character, with a first movement notable for its very free recapitulation. Clementi soon, in Op. 10, no. 3 (1783), hit on the idea of giving his first movements greater unity by deriving the second subject from the first:

Ex 127

(i) Op.10, no.3 (first subject)

(ii) Op.13, no.4 (first subject)

The Sonatas in F minor, Op. 13, no. 6 (1785), and F sharp minor, Op. 25, no. 5 (1790), are rather larger but remarkably unified in mood, both having the unusual feature of a slow movement in a minor key. The C minor Largo e sostenuto of the F minor is particularly striking with its grinding dissonances:

Ex. 128

It is preceded by a powerful and impassioned Allegro agitato. All these works composed before 1790 are completely free from excessive virtuosity; their texture is for the most spare, but they often show surprising emotional power, and in the longer movements it is not uncommon to find a single theme treated with imagination and resource. The decorative ornamentation of the Maestoso e cantabile opening movement of Op. 25, no. 4 (1790), is a foretaste of a style developed by others a quarter of a century later.

Other sonatas, less striking in character, are neatly and attractively written, sometimes with a pleasantly Italian melodiousness. But Clementi was not always able to resist the temptations of virtuosity, and when this happens the results are diffuse and straggling, the themes being interspersed with passages of padding. For instance the Sonata in C, Op. 32, no. 3, published as late as 1794, does not differ greatly in essential qualities from those of Op. 2. The first movement contains an otiose cadenza and the whole work, though broadly planned, is hollow in style, and it is hard to believe that it, and other works of the same kind, were written by the composer of such music as Op. 13, no. 6. By a coincidence two of Clementi's sonatas include sets of variations on themes similarly treated by Mozart. Those on 'Je suis Lindor' that conclude Clementi's Sonata in B flat, Op. 12, no. 1 (1784), are in his emptiest manner, and Mozart's set (1778), though by no means one of his best, is far superior. But of the two sets on 'Lison dormait', Clementi's, which comes in the Sonata in F (1790), published in Vienna as 'Oeuvre 21', is on the whole the more interesting; it contains a foretaste of the canonic writing so characteristic of his later works. The variety of these earlier sonatas is very remarkable; sometimes the music is ornate to a fault, sometimes surprisingly bare and ascetic. The moods range from the intensity of the works in minor keys to the grace of such delightful miniatures as the minuet and trio from the Sonata in A, Op. 10, no. 1 (1783). The best of the slow movements are warm and expressive, melody of a flowing, Italian type being presented against a remarkably rich harmonic background. On the other hand the contrapuntal writing so frequent in the later works is not yet so much in evidence, as can be seen if the first

movement of the B flat, Op. 41, no. 2, which he played in the presence
of Mozart in 1792, is compared with the overture to *Die Zauberflöte*
in which Mozart, consciously or otherwise, used the same theme,
treating it with far greater contrapuntal resource.

CLEMENTI'S LAST PERIOD

The two Sonatas, Op. 34, which appeared in 1795, are the first that
may be described as belonging to Clementi's final period. The first, in
C major, is said to be an arrangement of a piano concerto,[1] and, like
most of the sonatas in that key, is brilliant and showy in character. But
it is not solely a virtuoso piece, as can be seen at once if it is compared
with some of the more pretentious earlier works, or with Op. 3, no. 3.[2]
In the first movement of Op. 34, no. 1, a rather Beethoven-like phrase
is several times introduced with remarkable effect in unexpected
places, and the theme of the second movement is varied delightfully
at each of its reappearances. The second sonata, in G minor, is one of
Clementi's finest. The slow introduction, an unusual feature in piano
sonatas of this period, at once anticipates the main theme of the first
movement and reappears in a grandiose quasi-operatic version in the
development. The long canonic passage in the development of the
finale is very characteristic of Clementi's later style. The sonata as a
whole has all the striking qualities of the earlier works in the same
key, presented on a far larger and broader scale. It has been stated that
some of Clementi's sonatas, including this, are transcriptions of
symphonies,[3] but their general texture is no more orchestral than that
of many of Beethoven's sonatas, and often markedly less so. The
remaining sonatas of this period are not all of equal value, but several
are of very great interest. The third sonata of Op. 32 has already been
mentioned as an unfortunate throwback, but its two companions are
of much higher quality. The delightful canonic opening of the finale
of the Sonata in A, Op. 32, no. 1, is worth quoting.

Ex. 129

Presto

---

[1] According to his pupil Ludwig Berger; see Plantinga, op. cit., p. 163.
[2] This also originated in a concerto, a manuscript copy of which is preserved in the library of the
Gesellschaft der Musikfreunde, Vienna; see Riccardo Allorto, *Le Sonate per pianoforte di
Muzio Clementi* (Florence, 1959), p. 120.
[3] The authority in the case of Op. 34, no. 2, is again Berger.

and the Sonata in F, no. 2, is notable for the very ingenious treatment
of the single theme on which the first movement is built, and also for
the large number of three-bar phrases to be found in both movements.
Op. 40, no. 1, which appeared in 1802, is the only sonata in four
movements, the minuet being in canon and the trio in canon by
contrary motion. Both are ingenious and fluent. But the finest sonata
in this set is undoubtedly the second, in B minor. This consists of two
movements, each of which is preceded by a slow introduction. The
contrast of colour between these slow sections is remarkable, the first
being very dark and rich, and the second, which anticipates the theme
of the finale, mostly in a bare two-part texture. Despite the uniformity
of key there is no danger of monotony; the development of the first
movement is particularly varied in its modulations, and the galloping
energy of the finale suggests Domenico Scarlatti, a composer with
whose work Clementi must have been familiar. The sustained tension
of this sonata is most striking; it is one of the most individual that
Clementi wrote. The work in B flat, Op. 46 (dedicated to Kalkbrenner
'as a mark of esteem for his eminent talents' and published in 1820),
is, apart from the slow movement, slighter in content, but it is
admirably planned and would make a thoroughly effective concert
piece.

Clementi's last three Sonatas, Op. 50 (dedicated to Cherubini and
published in 1821),[1] give comprehensive expression to the curiously
varied aspects of his personality. Virtuosity and counterpoint,
luxuriance and austerity are blended with remarkable success; like
others of his later works they are strewn with very elaborate Italian
directions, and they probably sound more statuesque and less intense
to us now than to contemporary audiences, but they are works of great
interest. The leisurely and opulent first movement of the first sonata,
in A, looks back in mood to that of an earlier work in the same key,
Op. 25, no. 4, but there the music, though of considerable charm,
tends to stagnate, and here the interest never flags. The slow
movement, like that of Haydn's well-known Sonata in D, no. 37,[2] has
something of the solemnity of a Bach sarabande,[3] and strong contrast
is provided by the canonic central section, which is developed
ingeniously from a seemingly insignificant phrase. The D minor
Sonata, no. 2, has a short slow movement of great delicacy and
tenderness, with a chromatic colouring that looks at the same time

---

[1] Plantinga, op. cit., pp. 216-7, gives reasons for believing them to have been composed much
   earlier, c. 1804-5
[2] Quoted in Vol. VII, p. 599.
[3] Clementi knew and published a number of Bach pieces; Plantinga, op. cit., pp. 165, 188, 207,
   273.

back to Mozart's Rondo in A minor, and forward to things of Chopin. The third sonata, in G minor, is entitled 'Didone Abandonnata; scena tragica'. The Largo introduction is marked 'patetico' and the ensuing Allegro 'diliberando, e meditando', but the general form of the work is not noticeably affected by the title, except for the unusually rhapsodic character of the slow movement, Adagio dolente, which leads without a break into the finale. It is one of the longest of the sonatas and here, more than in the more concentrated work in B minor, there is a danger lest the prevalence of the minor key in all the movements may lead to monotony. But the sonata has great vigour and pathos; again the colouring of the slow movement suggests very late Mozart, and the finale, Allegro agitato e con disperazione, with its insistent rhythm and startling opening dissonance:

Ex. 130

has remarkable impetus. In all these late works Clementi shows himself an assured master of sonata-form on a large scale; his developments are often long but seldom flag, and landmarks such as the return of the main theme for the recapitulation are presented with real dramatic significance. His thematic invention seldom has the inevitable quality of that of the greatest masters, but it is often extremely attractive, sometimes with strong suggestions of Italian opera.

MISCELLANEOUS WORKS

Similar in quality to the later sonatas are the two Capricci, Op. 47 (1821), of which the second, in C major, has the unusual feature of a slow introduction in quintuple time. The sonatas for two pianos and for piano duet are unassuming but pleasant. The celebrated *Gradus ad Parnassum* inevitably contains much that is mainly of pedagogic importance, but a certain number of the studies have real musical interest. The best of the fugues are far from being sham antiques, and there are several pieces of surprisingly romantic character. No. 5, in B flat, is full of charmingly flowing counterpoint; the 'Scena patetica', no. 39, is richly expressive but overlong; no. 42, in F minor, is a vigorous movement in sonata-form. No. 91, in B major, is an almost Schumannesque lyric, but perhaps the most striking of all is the short Adagio in D minor, no. 51, one of Clementi's finest pages. His thorough mastery of the piano, and the great variety of colour he could produce when writing for it, give him a place of outstanding importance in the history of keyboard music. But there are other considerations; he was also thoroughly versed in the art of composition, and his skill in the handling of large designs may well have influenced Beethoven, who knew and highly esteemed his work. His increasing devotion to counterpoint, in particular, is remarkable in view of the fact that it was becoming less and less fashionable during his later years, and it is the combination of this severe, ascetic strain with his more luxuriant and showmanlike qualities that gives his music its peculiar attractiveness.

DUSSEK

The increasing resources of the piano, which developed with particular rapidity in England, led to the production of a vast amount of keyboard music, good, bad, and indifferent, during the last decades of the eighteenth century, by composers who spoke in the musical idiom of their day with unending fluency but little distinction. Of greater importance is Jan Ladislav (Johann Wenceslaus) Dussek (1760–1812), an erratic but interesting figure. Born in Bohemia, he became a pupil of Carl Philipp Emanuel Bach at Hamburg, and came in 1790 to England, where he enjoyed great popularity as a pianist and received warm encouragement from Haydn and Clementi (whose firm published some of his compositions). In 1800 he returned to Germany and soon found a benefactor in Prince Louis Ferdinand of Prussia. His output of piano music was large and extremely varied in quality. There are innumerable drawing-room pieces built on popular tunes, and several essays in programme music of the kind that was very popular in England at that time: a so-called sonata depicting 'The Naval Battle and Total Defeat of the Dutch Fleet by Admiral Duncan, 11 Oct. 1797' and pieces dealing with such dissimilar subjects as 'The Sufferings of the Queen of France' and 'A complete Delineation of the Ceremony from St. James's to St. Paul's, 19 Dec. 1797' (the thanksgiving for Duncan's victory at Camperdown). His keyboard variations include an unusually serious and sombre set on 'Vive Henri Quatre', but Dussek's sonatas for the piano, though not all of equal value, contain much music of great interest, often curiously prophetic in quality. His two earliest sets, Opp. 9 and 10, were published c. 1789[1] with optional violin parts like so many of Clementi's. Comparison with Clementi at once shows the difference of the two personalities.

---

[1] Ed. Jan Racek, *Musica Antiqua Bohemica*, 46 (Prague, 1960).

The attractive bareness of texture and concentration so characteristic of the best of Clementi's earlier sonatas does not appear in Dussek's, but Dussek has more lyrical warmth and a greater variety of mood. The contrasts may seem in themselves rather obvious but there is a wealth of flowing melody and the colour is often rich, with occasional unexpected modulations. Op. 10 is considerably more individual than Op. 9 and, as often happens at this period, the music is notably more intense when in a minor key. The melancholy opening movement of the Sonata in G minor, Op. 10, no. 2, leads to a virile Vivace con spirito, and in the Sonata in E, Op. 10, no. 3, a rather diffuse and flowery Andante maestoso is followed by a very lively Presto con fuoco which foreshadows both Beethoven and Mendelssohn. There are sometimes original features in the treatment of form, such as a tendency to curtail the recapitulation, and in the later works this freedom increases noticeably. But the most personal characteristic of Dussek's style is its concern not so much with design as with detail, suggesting the nineteenth rather than the eighteenth century. Many of his quick movements have some qualifying direction such as *maestoso* or *moderato* or *con espressione*, and they contain much that fails to make its effect if the music is taken too fast.

By 1790 Dussek's style was completely mature and can be seen, not at its most distinguished but in a thoroughly characteristic vein, in the Sonata in B flat, Op. 24 (1793).[1] The ideas of the first movement are commonplace but there are unexpected harmonic digressions. Dussek's finales are nearly always in rondo form, but they are very varied in mood; some of them are surprisingly subdued and reflective, moving at quite a slow pace. On the other hand some of the livelier specimens, e.g. the finale of Op. 45, no. 3 (*c.* 1800):[2]

Ex. 131

are among the numerous pieces of evidence that the rhythms of the Czech polka were known decades before the dance suddenly won

[1] Ibid., 53.
[2] Ibid., 59.

enormous popularity under that name. Of the sonatas written between
1790 and 1800, there are two of outstanding interest. The earlier of
these is Op. 35, no. 3, in C minor (1797),[1] the first movement of which
is one of his finest. It has remarkable continuity and concentration,
with less of the usual contrasts of mood; Eric Blom pointed out its
resemblance to Beethoven's 'Pathétique' Sonata,[2] which it preceded
by several years, but indeed there are passages such as

Ex. 132

that look even further into the future. The rest of the work does not
reach quite so high a level, but it is interesting that Dussek evidently
felt the contrast between the florid expressiveness of the Adagio and
the defiant frivolity of the finale was excessive, and therefore separated
them by a short intermezzo anticipating in a minor key the cheerful,
rather vulgar theme of the finale. Finer still is the Sonata in E flat, Op.
44,[3] dedicated to Clementi and composed shortly before Dussek's
departure from England in 1800. It is written on an unusually massive
scale, with hardly a trace of Dussek's lighter moods. The elaborately
developed first movement is preceded by a sombre and very impressive
slow introduction which anticipates a prominent feature of its main
theme. The Adagio is one of Dussek's richest and has a development
section in which a single figure is taken with a strange, almost feverish
persistence through a variety of keys and with rapidly changing
dynamics. The third movement, a rather peppery minuet, has a
remarkable coda in which its angry mood gradually subsides. The
finale, with its frequent syncopations and square-cut phraseology, is
a thoughtful and finely sustained movement, expressive in its harmonic
colouring. It is interesting to put it beside Beethoven's Op. 7, in the
same key, composed a few years before. They have points in common,
but Beethoven shows already an intellectual power and an ability to
get the maximum of effect from the slenderest means. Dussek's Sonata
seems by contrast to be the work of a romantic dreamer, full of ideas
but not in complete control of them.

[1] Ibid., 53.
[2] Grove's Dictionary of Music and Musicians (fifth ed., London, 1954), ii, p. 827.
[3] Musica Antiqua Bohemica, 59.

The Sonatas, Op. 45,[1] that follow this remarkable work are of slighter character, though often attractive. The fine Adagio of no. 1, in B flat, and the lively contrapuntal Allegro of no. 2, in G, are both admirable, but the next work of outstanding interest is the two-movement Sonata in F sharp minor, Op. 61 (1807),[2] sub-titled 'Elégie harmonique' and written in memory of Prince Louis Ferdinand, who was killed at Saalfeld in 1806. The first movement has a slow introduction of improvisatory character and surprising modulations, and in the finale syncopation is continued from beginning to end with almost excessive persistence. The sonata as a whole has remarkable intensity and here again there is a very vivid foretaste of romanticism.

Early in the nineteenth century Joseph Woelfl (1773–1812), a fluent but undistinguished composer of piano music, had published a sonata which he entitled 'Non plus ultra' suggesting that it represented the last word in pyrotechnics. Dussek retaliated in 1807 with his Op. 70, in A flat[3] which has the alternative sub-titles of 'Plus ultra' or 'Le retour à Paris'. Whether or not it excels Woelfl's sonata in technical difficulty it certainly has far greater musical interest. The opening theme, with the unexpected colouring of its fourth bar, is very noteworthy:

Ex. 133

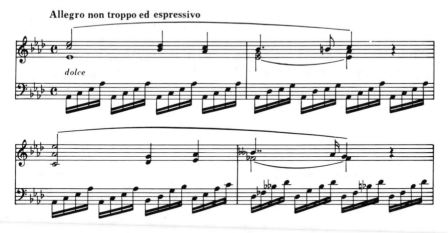

and the powerful and passionate second subject is still more restless harmonically. The Molto adagio is richly emotional (*dolcissimo, con anima ed espressione*) and the return of the main theme, which in some

[1] Ibid., 59.
[2] Ibid., 63
[3] Ibid., 63.

of Dussek's longer movements is somewhat lame, is here beautifully contrived, as a result of the unexpected behaviour of a cadential trill. This movement – described by a contemporary critic as 'one of the most beautiful adagios in existence' (*eins der schönsten Adagios, die es gibt*) (*Allgemeine musikalische Zeitung* (3 October 1810)) – is in E major and the minuet that follows – it was borrowed from Dussek's string quartet, Op. 60, no. 1 – though ostensibly in A flat, opens with highly original effect in the remote key of F sharp minor. The long and delightful finale is marked *Scherzo*, and throughout the sonata the brilliant passage-work has far more character than in the earlier works.

Of Dussek's last two sonatas, Op. 75, in E flat (1811),[1] is pleasant but comparatively slight. Such passages as

Ex. 134

show a naïve enjoyment of the increasingly rich tone-colour obtainable from the piano. On the other hand Op. 77, in F minor, known as 'L'Invocation' (1812),[2] is spaciously built in four movements, for the most part in a sombre mood; the final rondo ends *smorzando*. The opening Allegro, like that of Op. 70, is remarkably rich in themes, the first remarkably powerful:

Ex. 135

[1] Ibid., 63.
[2] Ibid., 63.

The main part of the second movement, Tempo di minuetto, is in canon throughout, an unusual feature. Dussek was far from incompetent as a contrapuntist; there is some admirable fugal writing in the finale of the Sonata in B flat, Op. 35, no. 1,[1] and the three *Fugues da camera* for piano duet, though diffuse, are of considerable interest, but counterpoint does not play so prominent a part in his music as in the later works of Clementi. In the minuet of 'L'Invocation' the bare texture provides a striking contrast to its luxuriant surroundings. The Adagio rivals that of Op. 70 in solemn beauty, and the final rondo, though somewhat diffuse, has a central episode of great charm, and a very sombre and impressive close. This serious and darkly coloured work, Dussek's last, ends in a surprising way the creative output of a musician whose career as a composer had undoubtedly suffered to some extent from his great popularity as a virtuoso. He was unable to resist the temptation of turning out a large quantity of the kind of music that would inevitably win the applause of the fashionable public, but in a handful of sonatas he produced work of a remarkably imaginative and prophetic nature, and it is fascinating to turn from the blandly self-satisfied 'Rondo à la militaire' in Op. 47, no. 1[2] to the finale of 'L'Invocation' and see how both movements are clearly the work of the same composer, yet in astonishingly dissimilar guises.

EARLY BEETHOVEN

The three sonatas by the boy Beethoven published at Speyer in 1783 are too often dismissed as mere juvenilia, yet the lion-cub already shows his claws on the first page of the F minor Sonata and in this passage in the development of the first movement of the D major:

[1] Ibid., 53.
[2] Ibid., 59.

Ex. 136

but it was only in 1796 that he published another set of three, Op. 2.
By that time he could have known all the keyboard compositions of
Haydn and Mozart and Clementi's sonatas up to Op. 32 (issued by his
own publisher two years before). In Op. 2, the first, in F minor, owes
most to Haydn and Mozart, and is the least adventurous in its
keyboard writing. In the first three movements the individuality is to
be found not so much in the general idiom as in such touches as the
very effective outburst at the end of the first movement; the finale is
by far the most prophetic section of the work. The Adagio, adapted
from an early piano quartet,[1] also shows the influence of Mozart, but
the first movement and minuet owe much more to Haydn. The
admirably prolonged feeling of suspense towards the end of the
development of the first movement is a feature that Beethoven derived
more from Haydn than from Mozart, and later expressed on a far
larger scale. The second sonata, in A, is not very much bigger in actual
size, but far richer and maturer in content. The exposition of the first
movement is astonishingly eventful, and the modulations in the
second subject are new, not in themselves, but in the speed and
intensity with which they move. Equally characteristic of Beethoven
are the beautiful cadential passage that rounds off both halves of the

[1] See chap. VI, p. 258.

movement, and the ease and conviction with which the different moods succeed each other. On the other hand the rather Mozartean rondo of the A major has a more aggressive central episode which never seems quite to suit the mood of its surroundings, though Beethoven does his best to justify it by referring to it in the coda. But the most strikingly new part of this sonata is the Largo, with its vivid suggestions of orchestral colouring. The mood is not unlike that of some of Haydn's later slow movements, but comparison with the Adagio of Haydn's last piano sonata[1] shows at once how different in texture are the two movements; Haydn's is hardly less solemn than Beethoven's, but the solemnity is expressed with far more elaborate ornamentation; he would never have written for the keyboard a melody as simple as that of Beethoven's Largo. Beethoven is here not concerned with keyboard effects, but shows how very successfully the piano can suggest the textures of the string quartet or even the orchestra. The third sonata, in C, is more of a concert piece; the rather diffuse and showy first movement, with its borrowings from an early piano quartet and its florid cadenza, has points in common with Clementi's as yet unpublished Op. 36, no. 3, but its themes have more individuality, and the sforzandi so characteristic of Beethoven appear. The contrapuntal writing in the scherzo also suggests Clementi in his more restrained moods, but the richly coloured Adagio particularly the central section, is more like Dussek. The finale is in a lighter vein than those of the other two sonatas, but it makes a more satisfactory whole, the gentler episode in F falling admirably into line with the rest.

These first three sonatas seem to point in various directions. The A major led the way to the Sonata in E flat, Op. 7 (1797).[2] This is larger in scale, particularly in the flowing and broadly designed first movement, with its very imaginative coda. The slow movements and finales of the two sonatas are alike in mood, but the Largo of Op. 7 is even richer in orchestral suggestions, and the charming E flat rondo is a decided improvement on its predecessor. Pianistically the most striking feature of the work is the central section of the third movement with its slowly moving harmonies and a melody that is implied rather than actually sung through a veil of arpeggios. Of the three sonatas, Op. 10 (1798), the first, in C minor, is a pleasant but not outstanding work, individual in isolated details, such as the coda of the finale, rather than in general manner. On the other hand the fresh and delightful little work in F, for which Beethoven had a special affection,

[1] See Vol. VII, p. 601.
[2] Dates are those of publication.

has been unduly neglected; the central Allegretto, like the Allegro of
Op. 7, replaces the scherzo, and the finale achieves the difficult task of
combining fugal texture with sonata form. The first movement of the
third sonata, in D major, is intensely characteristic of Beethoven in
every way; never before had he developed a short phrase so fully and
with so much imagination or shown so powerfully the sense of
spaciousness that lies behind so many of his most vigorous utterances.
The tragic mood of the Largo has precedents in Haydn, particularly
the central movement of the piano Sonata in D, no. 37,[1] but there it
is usually brushed aside after a short time, while here Beethoven
sustains it throughout a movement of extraordinary power and beauty.
The finale is a lighter, more whimsical counterpart of the first
movement, with a wonderful touch of harmonic poetry shortly before
the end.

The significance of the title 'Pathétique', given by Beethoven
himself to the Sonata in C minor, Op. 13 (1799), is most clearly
understood if we remember that *pathétique* is best translated as
'emotional'. Even so it is only to the first movement that the word now
seems particularly applicable. The very effective return of the
introduction during the later stages of the movement had been
anticipated by Clementi in his already mentioned Sonata in G minor,
Op. 34, no. 2, and also, in a tentative way, by Beethoven himself in the
first movement of his F minor Sonata of 1783. The passionate first
movement of Op. 13 is intensely dramatic and the first phrase of the
touching Adagio must have sunk deeply into Beethoven's consciousness as variants of it occur in the first movements of two more or less
contemporary works, the Quartet in G major, Op. 18, no. 2. and the
Septet, and was to recur many years later, in a far broader form, in the
slow movement of the Ninth Symphony. The central episode of the
rondo of the 'Pathétique' also introduces an idea already used in the
first movement of Op. 10, no. 3, which reappears in the finale of the A
major Quartet, Op. 18, no. 5: the opening of Op. 14, no. 1, is cast in the
same mould. The two sonatas, Op. 14 (1799), lack the more heroic,
spectacular qualities of their predecessors and have therefore
sometimes been unjustly dismissed as minor works, but Beethoven set
such store by the E major Sonata, no. 1, that in 1802 he made a string
quartet version of it in F major.[2] The first movement of the Sonata in
B flat, Op. 22 (1802), returns to the brilliance of Op. 2, no. 3, but with
considerably more subtlety. It also contains a striking piece of
thematic metamorphosis: a short phrase that appears near the end of

[1] See Vol. VII, p. 598-9.
[2] See p. 285.

the exposition, stalking aggressively up and down the scale, reappears
at the end of the development creeping smoothly, with slowly moving
harmonies in an atmosphere of suspense. The very attractive Adagio
con molt' espressione is full of melody of the flowing Italianate kind
that plays a more important part in Beethoven's music than German
critics have always been willing to admit; it is however surrounded
with a romantic haze that is essentially Teutonic. The minuet and
rondo both interrupt graceful lyricism with occasional bursts of
irritation; the results are subtle and highly individual.

In these first eleven sonatas the traditional form is treated with
considerably variety, but there is no inclination to modify its general
scheme; the next three, however, Op. 26 and Op. 27, nos. 1 and 2
(1801), contain between them only one movement in full sonata-form.
The variations with which Op. 26 opens have, like the Adagio of the
'Pathétique', a broadly flowing lyricism which reappears, on a higher
plane, in the slow movement of the Quartet in E flat, Op. 74; it is
perhaps significant that all three pieces are in the key of A flat. The
scherzo and finale are both full of lively keyboard counterpoint which
had not appeared in the sonatas since the finale of Op. 10, no. 2. The
funeral march that separates them has something of the grandiose
manner of the opening of the 'Pathétique', but is more advanced
harmonically, particularly in the impressive coda. In spite of much
fine music, the work as a whole, like Mozart's Sonata in A, K.331,
gives the impression of a suite rather than a sonata. Beethoven might
well have called it, as he did its companions of Op. 27, 'Sonata quasi
una fantasia'. In Op. 27, no. 1, in E flat, the scheme, though equally
free, is actually more highly organized, but the movements are directed
to be played without a break. An Andante of haunting and childlike
beauty is interrupted by a lively Allegro in C major, after which it
returns in a shortened and modified form. The scherzo has something
in common with that of the Fifth Symphony, the mysteriously
foreboding main section being contrasted with a rather grotesque trio.
A short Adagio in A flat then leads straight into the finale, but makes
a brief reappearance shortly before the end. Despite the variety of
mood, the work is a convincing and unified whole, and the finale,
though in rondo form, is firmly and solidly built, and provides a fine
climax. The Sonata in C sharp minor – which the poet Ludwig
Rellstab many years later associated with moonlight – is more direct
in its appeal and more orthodox in structure, though it lacks a normal
first movement. Beethoven is known to have been a wonderful
extemporizer, and the quiet opening Adagio, with its single theme
and slow, deliberate harmonic motion, may have been the result of an

inspired improvisation; the modulations and, especially, the frequent use of the Neapolitan sixth, give the movement a 'romantic' flavour that is not dissipated by the central Allegretto which follows without a break. The finale, in full sonata form, is a powerful piece of rhetoric, less subtle than the rest of the work, but remarkably exciting.

In Op. 28, in D (1801), Beethoven returned to the usual four movements, and it is worth for a moment comparing the opening Allegro with the finale of the C sharp minor Sonata. They are totally different in atmosphere, the one stormy, the other serene, but both show how effectively Beethoven could sustain a single mood throughout a fully developed sonata movement without monotony. In the first movement of Op. 28, as in that of Op. 22, the concluding stages of the development are particularly imaginative, owing to the skilfully prolonged harmonic suspense. The Andante is less striking as a whole but there is a remarkable moment in the coda when the light-hearted theme of the central section reappears in an unexpectedly sombre mood. The epigrammatic humour of the scherzo is not unlike that of some of Haydn's latest minuets, such as that of the Quartet in F, Op. 77, no. 2. The final rondo, like that of Op. 10, no. 3, is the perfect counterpart of the first movement, lighter in mood, but with the same spaciousness.

MIDDLE-PERIOD BEETHOVEN

The three sonatas, Op. 31, of which the first two were published in 1803 and the third in 1804, struck out on what Beethoven himself regarded as 'a new way'.[1] This 'new way' is apparent in the abrupt and whimsical first movement of no. 1 in G, less so in the long Adagio grazioso which Czerny astutely described as 'a *Romanze* or *notturno*'.[2] The sonatas in D minor and E flat were among the most striking works that Beethoven had yet written, far more so even than the slightly later Second Symphony. Both begin on an unusual harmony. The darkly coloured first movement of the D minor Sonata is far less rhetorical than the finale of the C sharp minor or the first movement of the 'Pathétique'; it is astonishingly terse, but every appearance of the opening arpeggio phrase, whether in slow or in quick tempo, produces an effect of great breadth. The use of recitative in a sonata movement was not new; there is an instance in the first of the six sonatas dedicated by Emanuel Bach to the King of Prussia.[3] But the

---

[1] His remark 'Ich bin mit meinen bisherigen Arbeiten nicht zufrieden; von nun an will ich einen neuen Weg betreten' was reported by Czerny. See Willibald Nagel, *Beethoven und seine Klaviersonaten* (Langensalza, revised edition 1924), ii, p. 1.

[2] Nagel, op. cit., ii, p. 18.

[3] See Vol. VII, p. 584.

two passages are very different in character; Bach's recitative heightens the tension of a slow movement while Beethoven's provides one of the few moments of reflection in a quick and agitated one. It is all the more effective for coming at the opening of the recapitulation, which is the last place at which anything so unusual would be likely to occur; Beethoven was to employ a similar procedure a few years later in the first movement of the Fifth Symphony. The rather Haydnesque quality of the Adagio is particularly effective in its context, and the frequently recurring drum-like figure in the bass gives a feeling of tension. Both these movements have a strong suggestion of orchestral colour but the final Allegretto is pure keyboard music from start to finish. All three movements are remarkable for their codas; the tragedy of the Allegro is summed up perfectly in ten quiet bars of the chord of D minor, in the Adagio a new melody enters just before the end and fades into the distance, and the Allegretto, after a brief climax, ends with great simplicity. The delightful comedy in E flat, Op. 31, no. 3, is an equally perfect work, the general scheme of which foreshadows the Eighth Symphony, the second movement having the spirit, though not the usual form of a scherzo, and the third being a slow minuet. The tarantella finale is notable for the powerful and imaginative handling of almost comically trivial material.

The Sonata in C, Op. 53, dedicated to Count Waldstein (1805), is a work that may seem at first sight to break more new ground than is actually the case. The unusual harmonic scheme of the first movement had been, as Tovey pointed out,[1] anticipated by Beethoven in a far more abrupt manner in Op. 31, no. 1, and the brilliance of the piano writing is in a line of succession from Op. 2, no. 1, the first movement of Op. 22, and the Adagio of Op. 31, no. 1, to say nothing of the first three concertos. What is entirely new is the extremely spacious scale on which everything is planned. Particularly characteristic of Beethoven is the opening of the first movement, with the combined effect of the rhythmic energy produced by the repeated chords and the feeling of immense breadth resulting from the slow harmonic motion. The strong contrast between the first and second subjects is a feature considerably less common in Beethoven's music than is often imagined. The very simple melody of the second subject is followed by a decorative variation of itself, but it is not allowed to luxuriate. The dramatic suspense before the return of the main theme after the development is prolonged to an extent only possible in a movement designed on a very broad scale. It was at a quite late stage in the composition of the sonata that its original slow movement was

[1] *A Companion to Beethoven's Pianoforte Sonatas* (London, 1931), p. 157.

removed in favour of a short Adagio introduction to the finale. The original Andante in F,[1] though beautiful, would have seemed over formal beside the drama of the first movement and the gigantic and leisurely simplicity of the finale; the Adagio, without incongruity, increases immeasurably the emotional range and depth of the whole work. It is very characteristic of Beethoven that the 'Waldstein' Sonata, one of the most expansive of his works, should have been followed immediately by one of his most reticent, the Sonata in F, Op. 54 (1806). Of its two movements the first is a compromise between minuet and rondo, with two almost grotesquely contrasted themes. The second movement has a superficial similarity to the finale of Op. 26 but moves at a more leisurely pace and is far more subtle and reflective, wandering with quiet persistence through innumerable keys in an almost hypnotic manner and eventually ending with something of the forceful abruptness of the first movement of Op. 10, no. 3. The whole sonata is unlike any of the others.

The Sonata in F minor, Op. 57 (1807), from which the publisher Cranz's description 'Appassionata' is now inseparable, might be regarded as a kind of intensification and expansion of Op. 31, no. 2. The first movement opens in the same mood of foreboding and is similarly dark and stormy in colour. But, being on a far larger scale, it has more room for contrast, provided by the magnificent opening of the second subject, which has an obvious thematic connection with the first theme. The side-slip from F minor to G flat was an effect Beethoven was to employ again in similar places in the Quartets Op. 59, no. 2, and Op. 95. After its many violent climaxes the first movement of the 'Appassionata' ends in the same mood of exhaustion as that of the D minor sonata, and the openings of the two slow movements are not dissimilar in emotional effect. But the longer and stormier first movement needs to be followed by a simpler and more serene slow movement, in fact a very simple set of variations on a solemn theme that never leaves its key. The finale, which brushes aside the Andante with a sudden dramatic stroke, has a semiquaver movement almost as persistent as that of the finale of the D minor Sonata and far more vehement, ending in a whirlwind. The idea of a *moto perpetuo* finale seems to have interested Beethoven particularly at this time; shortly after this powerfully tragic specimen he wrote another, vastly different in mood, for the Fourth Symphony. Three times in Op. 57 the chord of the diminished seventh makes a particularly prolonged and emphatic appearance, but with completely dissimilar results. At the end of the development of the first movement

[1] Published separately in 1806 and later known as 'Andante favori'.

it comes as the climax of a gradually gathering storm, at the end of the slow movement as an unexpected shock leading into the finale, and at the end of the development of the finale as the one reflective moment in a feverishly restless movement.

The next piano sonata, a special favourite of Beethoven's, did not appear till 1810 – it was the earliest to be first published in London by Clementi – and during the interval he had written the Fourth, Fifth, and Sixth Symphonies, the G major Piano Concerto, the Violin Concerto, *Fidelio*, and a quantity of chamber music. The contrast between the 'Appassionata' and the Sonata in F sharp, Op. 78, could hardly be greater. In the former there is a certain amount that could only be played on the piano, but there are also strong suggestions of the orchestra, and sometimes the music seems completely to burst its medium; the two movements of Op. 78 are both exquisitely pianistic. Indeed the whole sonata is exquisite in workmanship: 'subjectively profound, elegant in its line-drawing, delicate in its harmonic colouring' as Nagel says.[1] There is infinite charm in the main themes of both movements and they end with delightful informality. Op. 79 in G (1810) is far inferior; Beethoven marked the first sketch 'Sonata facile';[2] but it has freshness and individuality, and in the first movement the combination of sonata-form and *tedesca* rhythm is surprisingly successful. The next sonata, in E flat, Op. 81, 'Les Adieux, l'Absence et le Retour', was written on the occasion of the Archduke Rudolph's temporary absence from Vienna in 1809, when the city was occupied by the French, and (like Opp. 78 and 79) published by Clementi (1811). Though on a comparatively large scale, much of the music, especially in the first two movements, is very subtle and intimate in character. The opening phrase of the slow introduction, which is also used as the second subject of the Allegro, is intended to suggest the German word *Lebewohl* – Beethoven preferred the German title to the French version given by Clementi – and the coda, with its curious clashes of tonic and dominant conveys vividly the impression of a prolonged and affectionate leave-taking, but on the whole the character of the work is not greatly affected by the programme. The first movement is in fact a remarkably fine terse and imaginative handling of sonata-form, with a poetical development and coda. After the restless 'L'Absence', the finale seems rather conventionally brilliant, but its main theme recurs with charming effect in a slower tempo just before the end.

A glance at the sonatas of the first decade of the century shows how

[1] Op. cit., ii, p. 143.
[2] Gustav Nottebohm, *Zweite Beethoveniana* (Leipzig, 1887), p. 269.

much more gradual was the development of Beethoven's style in this field than in any other branch of his music. There is no parallel to the marked difference of idiom between the quartets of Op. 18 and Op. 59, or between the Second and Third Symphonies. The larger sonatas of the middle period develop on a bigger scale features that had already appeared to some extent in the more progressive of the earlier works; on the other hand, in some of the smaller sonatas, particularly Op. 78, there are things that foreshadow the 'third period'; the landmarks stand out less obviously and the cadences are less emphatic. Op. 81 seems to be in some ways a compromise; the brilliance of the finale is of the kind that looks backward rather than forward, but even here there are such things as the apparently casual return after the development that are very characteristic of Bethoven's latest manner, and the development of the first movement also has a prophetic quality. Beethoven was not the self-conscious type of revolutionary whose aim is to break with the past; even in his latest works it is possible to find individual phrases and figures which in themselves might fit quite happily into the music of an earlier generation.

The two-movement Sonata in E minor, Op. 90, which appeared in 1815, the first in which Beethoven uses German as well as Italian tempo indications, is already in certain respects markedly different from Op. 54 and Op. 78. In the Sonata in F the half-thoughtful, half-ironic atmosphere pervades the whole work; in the F sharp major there is more difference between the melodious lyricism of the first and the capricious gaiety of the second movement, but in general feeling the work is strongly unified. Between the two movements of Op. 90, one in the minor, the other in the major, there is far more marked contrast. The intensity of the first movement is due largely to its great rhythmic variety, which gives an impression of alternating fierceness and exhaustion; this is particularly noticeable in the strange passage which leads to the recapitulation.

THE FINAL MASTERPIECES

In Op. 90 the contrast between Beethoven's fiercer and more lyrical moods is expressed with the greatest clarity; in Op. 101, in A major (1817), both emotional and structural schemes are considerably more complicated. The Allegretto first movement combines sonata-form with the continuity of a lyric, since the second subject emerges naturally from the first instead of contrasting with it; it is the shortest section of the work, indeed the shortest of all Beethoven's sonata first-movements. In the Vivace alla marcia second movement (in F major)

Beethoven employs in a half-aggressive, half-jocular mood the *durchbrochen*, semi-contrapuntal texture characteristic of his last five sonatas, and the middle section is mostly two-part canon. A very short but profound Adagio in A minor then leads through a *non presto* cadenza and a brief reminiscence of the opening Allegretto, again in A major, which passes into the huge, sonata-form finale. This is by far the most elaborately developed part of the work, rich in ideas, but for the most part dominated by the opening theme which appears at first in quasi-canonic double counterpoint and is used for a long and exciting fugal development.[1] The counterpoint is rough and uncompromising, with bold and exhilarating clashes. The low murmuring trill that occurs in the bass during the coda is very characteristic of Beethoven's latest keyboard style.

The *Grosse Sonate für das Hammerklavier* in B flat, Op. 106 (1819), was composed in 1818 after receiving Broadwood's present of a magnificent piano. The first movement has points in common with the finale of Op. 101, notably a long fugal episode in the development and in the final bars a gradual diminuendo which is suddenly brushed aside. But it is on a larger scale, majestic in style and more varied in mood, with an astonishing wealth of ideas. Three themes, very different in character, are given out in rapid succession and three more constitute the second subject. As might be expected of Beethoven, the opening phrase, which has the strongest rhythmic force, receives the fullest treatment, including the fugal development. Next in importance is the third theme of the G major second subject, which is the most serene and sustained. The long internal trill by which this is frequently accompanied is a device that had already appeared in the finale of the 'Waldstein' and recurs in several of the later sonatas. Perhaps because of the vast scale of this first movement, Beethoven had curious doubts about the over-all construction of the rest of the sonata, his longest. In March 1819 he wrote to Ferdinand Ries in London, where his disciple was arranging the publication of an edition that appeared within a few weeks of Artaria's in Vienna:

Should the sonata not be right for London, I could send you another, or you can leave out the Largo and begin the last movement straightaway with the fugue, or take the first movement, Adagio and for the 3rd the scherzo and the Largo and Allo. risoluto. Or you could take the first movement and scherzo, and let them form the whole sonata. I leave this to you, to do as you think best.

---

[1] See the detailed analysis in John V. Cockshoot, *The Fugue in Beethoven's Piano Music* (London, 1959), pp. 31-7.

A month later Ries was startled to receive an instruction to insert the magical A–C sharp octaves at the beginning of the Adagio. And in the event he thought best to issue the work in two parts: 'Grand Sonata' (Allegro, Adagio, and scherzo in that order) and 'Introduction & Fugue'.[1] The main theme of the scherzo is notable for its frequent use of seven-bar phrases that give it a peculiar capriciousness with which the very broad harmonic movement of the trio contrasts strikingly. After its wilful and inconsequent end the first bar of the Adagio has an effect of extraordinary solemnity, besides bridging the wide harmonic gulf between the keys of B flat and F sharp minor. No sonata since Op. 10, no. 3 had had a slow movement of so tragic a character as this and a comparison between the two is illuminating. Both are in slow sextuple time and are similar in mood, but the later movement is not only far larger but, not unnaturally, mellower in tone; there are fewer *sforzandi* and cries of protest and it ends in a comparatively resigned mood. Sonata-form is here used with enormous breadth; the magnificent stream of floridly beautiful melody that leads from the first to the second subject is one of the most pianistic passages Beethoven ever wrote. The final fugue, which is preceded by a strange improvisatory Largo, puts a heavy strain on instrument, player, and listener alike, a strain intensified by the fact that until the last page it is almost entirely in three parts only. Apart from its initial trill the subject is not easy to grasp, even when it is not presented in augmentation, inversion, or cancrizans. As in the fugal development in the finale of Op. 101, the counterpoint sometimes leads to harshness – relieved by the lovely episode in D major towards the end. Long and patient study is necessary in order to grasp as a whole the immensely powerful structure of the movement, with its varied tonal scheme and frequently changing moods.[2]

The Sonata in E, Op. 109 (1821), has none of the monumental character of its predecessor, but is equally unconventional. The 'first subject' of the first movement consists of 7½ flashing *vivace, ma non troppo* bars already modulating to the dominant, the 'second' of 7 bars of *adagio espressivo*; the contrasts in style and texture as well as tempo could hardly be more extreme. The middle section – continuation rather than development – resumes the *vivace* pattern so that the recapitulated first subject passes almost unnoticed. And the recapitulation of the *adagio* is varied by an astonishing two-bar C major parenthesis. The coda returns to the *vivace*, likewise with a parenthesis, so that the innocent ear may easily take the whole movement for a

[1] See Alan Tyson, *The Authentic English Editions of Beethoven* (London, 1963), p. 102.
[2] See Cockshoot, op. cit., pp. 70-94.

quasi-Bachian 'pattern' piece with two emotional *adagio* interruptions. The Prestissimo second movement is in sonata-form, though with minimal contrast of subjects, but in the most important movement – here the finale – Beethoven discards sonata-form altogether in favour of variations. They are longer and cover a wider range of mood than any other set in the sonatas, but they have a clearly organized scheme. After the extremely beautiful theme, the first variation is concerned entirely with presenting an equally lovely and mostly new melody over a very simple accompaniment. In the second there are hints of polyphony and of the *vivace* figuration of the first movement, and the third consists entirely of simple invertible counterpoint. The fourth opens in a more elaborately contrapuntal style which grows more harmonic as the variation proceeds; the fifth on the other hand maintains a fugal texture throughout. After this, counterpoint is abandoned and the last variation begins with the original theme at the original pace but proceeds to dissolve it in a shower of continuously diminishing note-values and internal trills until it re-emerges in its original form at the end.

For the A flat Sonata, Op. 110 (1821), Beethoven returned to the general scheme of Op. 101: a fairly short and intimate first movement, a fast movement in duple time, and a short Adagio ma non troppo leading straight into a great fugal finale. But the first movements of the two works are very dissimilar. That of Op. 101 is one of the most forward-looking pieces of music Beethoven ever wrote, while the Moderato of Op. 110 looks backward as well as forward; bars 5-8 are a quotation from the Tempo di minuetto of the Violin Sonata, Op. 30, no. 3. The detached chords at the end of the short and abrupt second movement prepare the opening of the Adagio in which Beethoven feels his way through recitative to an Arioso dolente. From this point onwards the Sonata employs the most diverse resources with complete success. The long-drawn melody of the Arioso dolente, supported by a simple accompaniment of repeated chords, is followed by the final fugue without any sense of incongruity, and when this in its turn is interrupted by a varied return of the Arioso in an unexpected key (G minor), the result is intensely dramatic. The counterpoint in the fugue[1] is smoother and more euphonious than that of the three previous sonatas; its subject is related in outline to the theme of the first movement and is sufficiently melodious in character to form the basis of a magnificent, non-contrapuntal peroration which sums up the whole sonata with an air of complete inevitability.

After this complex and varied scheme, the last sonata, in C minor,

[1] On the structure of the fugue and the finale generally, see Cockshoot op. cit., pp. 95-120.

Op. 111 (1822), employs a simpler plan of two movements only, one in sonata-form and the other a set of variations. Here again are glimpses of the past though the defiant opening bars of the introduction far surpass the 'Pathétique'. The Allegro, like the first movements of Opp. 101, 109, and 110, is very compressed but the final bars of the development and the whole of the coda have a feeling of infinite spaciousness. The texture is fugal at times, indeed the earliest sketch of the opening, marked '3tes Stück' (third movement), shows a fugal treatment of what became unison.[1] The arietta with variations is completely different in character from the finale of Op. 109: more continuous, less varied in texture, and simpler in essence. The harmony of the arietta of Op. 111, wonderfully prepared by the superb coda of the first movement, could hardly be simpler and the subtle harmonic changes introduced in the different variations, particularly towards the cadences, are all concerned with detail rather than outline, and therefore make all the more effective the mysterious modulating interlude that separates the fourth variation from the final return of the theme. Despite the variety of the figuration, the outline of the melody is usually preserved, and the coda is built entirely on phrases from it – here lifted to the empyrean amid trills and shimmering demisemiquavers.

BEETHOVEN'S VARIATIONS

Many of Beethoven's separate sets of variations are of early date and some are quite negligible. But he soon began to take note of the possibilities of the coda, for which there had been notable precedents in Mozart's two best sets for piano solo, on Gluck's 'Unser dummer Pöbel' and on 'Ein Weib ist das herrlichste Ding' and still more in Haydn's magnificent Andante and Variations in F minor. Beethoven is not at first always successful in this; in the set on 'Une fièvre brûlante' (c. 1797) (from Grétry's *Richard Coeur-de-Lion*) the modulation in the final page is a little too consciously impressive, and the return from it is lame. But several not particularly distinguished sets come to life in their codas, notably those on 'Tändeln und Scherzen' (1799) (from Süssmayr's *Soliman)* and on 'Rule, Britannia' (1804). Better than either of these are the very pleasant sets on 'La stessa, la stessissima' (1798) (from Salieri's *Falstaff*), 'Kind, willst du' (1798) (from Winter's *Das unterbrochene Opferfest*), and the Russian dance from Wranitzky's ballet *Das Waldmädchen* (c. 1796), a tune that was also treated, in a far more superficial way, by Dussek. In the Russian dance the five-bar phrases of the theme give it a particular charm, and

[1] See Nottebohm, *Zweite Beethoveniana*, pp. 467-8.

the poetry in the modulations of the coda foreshadows Schubert. With the exception of the variations on 'Rule, Britannia', these sets all date from between 1790 and 1800; earlier and in many ways more striking than any of them is the set on 'Vieni amore' from Vincenzo Righini's *Dodici Ariette*, written in 1790. Here a theme of great simplicity, both melodic and harmonic, is treated with extraordinary resource and imaginativeness. Such things as the trills in the fourth variation and the changing moods of the fourteenth look towards far later works, and the final page, in which the movement becomes steadily slower and eventually disappears completely, is remarkably original. Here the pianistic brilliance is entirely free from superficiality.

Two important but very dissimilar sets appeared in 1803, Opp. 34 and 35. Op. 34, in F major, on an original theme, is unusual in design, the variations being different, not only in tempo, but also in key, the tonality falling by a major or minor third after each one. The piano writing is often of a luxuriance typical of the concertos rather than the sonatas, the nearest approach in the latter being the Adagio from Op. 31, no. 1. For Op. 35 Beethoven took as his theme the melody from his own *Prometheus* ballet music which he later used for the finale of the 'Eroica' Symphony. It is pianistically one of the most varied works of this period, the colour ranging from the hilarious brilliance of var. 3 (i) to the delicacy of var. 5 (ii):

Ex. 137 (i) (ii)

As in the finale of the 'Eroica', the bass of the theme is at first treated independently before the theme itself appears. Eventually there is a fugue on the bass of the theme, in which the contrapuntal writing is full of character. Apart from the likeness in general plan, certain individual features of the finale of the symphony are strongly anticipated here, but always in pianistic, not orchestral terms. The thirty-two Variations in C minor, without opus-number, published in 1807, are on a theme of eight bars only, and in general scheme are not unlike Bach's Chaconne in D minor for violin solo, over-long but containing some fine and imaginative music.

The last and most remarkable of Beethoven's separate sets of variations was published in 1823, a year after his last sonata. Anton Diabelli, publisher and composer, had sent a theme of his own composition to thirty-two musicians, inviting each of them to contribute a variation on it; Beethoven, after expressing a strong dislike for the theme, wrote not one but thirty-three variations, which were published as Op. 120. The theme is prosaic; its very clear and obvious structure make it eminently suited for variations and the opening phrases have points in common with the beginning of the arietta in Op. 111. But in writing variations on that, Beethoven had been concerned to produce a broad and continuous slow movement, in which startling changes of mood would not be necessary; here he writes an enormous set probably more varied in content than any since Bach's 'Goldberg' variations. The exquisitely subtle chromatic details with which Beethoven varied the broadly diatonic structure of the arietta have already been mentioned; in the Diabelli variations the same process appears but with greater boldness, sometimes altering the harmonic scheme of the theme, though never departing from the main features. In a few variations even the rhythmic scheme is altered. Some of the variations are marked by capricious humour; particularly the thirteenth with its absurd silences, the twenty-first with its odd changes of mood, and the twenty-second with its quotation from Leporello's 'Notte e giorno faticar' in *Don Giovanni*. On the other hand the sixth variation is marked *serioso*. After the announcement of the theme the very dignified first variation is electrifying and its mood reappears in the equally impressive fourteenth. A considerable number are delightfully lyrical; the twentieth is remarkable for its mysterious chromatic colouring, and is astonishingly effective in its surroundings. After three minor variations, during which there is a gradual increase of intensity, the key changes for the fugue.[1] Counterpoint of a quietly flowing kind had already appeared in the twenty-fourth, the fughetta; here it is more harsh, though less

[1] Dismissed by Tovey in a few perfunctory lines, *Beethoven* (London, 1944), pp. 127 and 129, treated more seriously by Joseph Müller-Blattau, *Neues Beethoven-Jahrbuch*, v (1933), pp. 132-4, and analysed microscopically by Cockshoot, op. cit., pp. 121-44.

so than in the finale of Op. 106. Eventually it leads to the surprisingly gentle last variation through what is one of the strangest passages Beethoven ever wrote:

Ex. 138

BEETHOVEN'S MISCELLANEOUS PIECES

One of the more interesting of the remaining piano works is the Fantasia, Op. 77 (1809). After a restless start, in which theme after theme is announced and abandoned, it settles down to a series of continuous variations in B major, the second of which employs a formula later exploited in the Sonata, Op. 109. The scheme looks back to the Choral Fantasia written during the previous year, and on to the finale of the Ninth Symphony, but is not wholly successful in this work. An attractive little *Klavierstück* in B flat, dated 14 August 1818, treats in an improvisatory style a theme that makes a very fleeting appearance four years later at the beginning of the sixth Bagatelle of Op. 119. Of the three sets of Bagatelles, the first, Op. 33, was published in 1803; nos. 6 and 7 had been recently composed, but the rest were probably earlier though the date '1782' on the *Stichvorlage* of no. 1 is highly improbable. The pieces seem sketchy when compared with the best lyrical movements in the early sonatas, though the coda of the sixth, in D, has an impressive breadth. Nos. 7–11 of the second set, Op. 119, appeared 1821, the complete set in Paris in 1823. Nos. 4, 8, and 11 are among the most perfect miniatures Beethoven ever wrote; the quick pieces are attractively epigrammatic, the tenth consisting of only twelve bars, while the seventh in C major, with its long trills, is a wild outburst rising to an exciting climax. The six Bagatelles, Op. 126 (composed in 1823 and published two years later) are similar in general style but on a larger scale; the second and fourth are in a capricious vein, but the slower pieces speak the language of the slow movements of the last sonatas, though in a simpler manner.

As the compass of the keyboard of the piano extended, Beethoven made use of all possible variety of colour, sometimes concentrating on its extreme registers. The result is often less euphonious than the later works of Clementi and Dussek, but has a strongly individual character. At the same time an increasing interest in counterpoint leads to more and more subtlety of detail.

SOME LESSER MASTERS

It is not suprising that, as the capacities of the piano increased, a vast number of studies should be written for it; the term seems to have been originated by Johann Baptist Cramer (1771–1858), one of the finest pianists of the day, who produced an enormous amount of piano music of all kinds.[1] The work of Daniel Steibelt (1765–1823) and Friedrich Kalkbrenner (1785–1849) has fluency and showmanship, and both cultivated a style of florid, genuinely pianistic cantilena exemplified in these passages from Steibelt's 'Grande Sonate', Op. 64 (*c.* 1806) (i) and Kalkbrenner's F minor *Sonate dédiée aux manes de Haydn* (ii):[2]

Ex. 139

(i) STEIBELT

Cantabile

p con espressione

(ii) KALKBRENNER

Moderato e sostenuto

[1] See infra, p. 357.
[2] Both quoted here from William S. Newman, *The Sonata since Beethoven* (Chapel Hill, 1969), pp. 470 and 475.

The same kind of cantilena was cultivated by Beethoven's already mentioned disciple, Carl Czerny (1791–1857). Czerny's best sonatas – A flat, Op. 7 (1820), F minor, Op. 57 (1824), and Op. 76 in E (also 1824) – are marked by occasional 'romantic' harmony as in this passage from Op. 76:

Ex. 140

The work of Ignaz Moscheles (1794–1870) is, at its best, more solid; the 'Sonate mélancolique', Op. 49 in F sharp minor, in one 247-bar movement (1814), is of considerable interest, though its effect is sometimes spoiled by rather empty passage-work. But a *Sonate caractéristique* in B flat, Op. 27, also dating from 1814, attempts to express 'Vienna's emotions on the return of His Majesty Francis the First, Emperor of Austria, etc. etc. in the year 1814'; the first movement is entitled 'Expression of heartfelt sense of delight at His Majesty's glorious return'; the second is an Andantino espressivo 'On the theme "Freut Euch des Lebens"', and the final waltz-rondo is filled with the 'Jubilation of happy Austria'. Most of these composers wrote concertos, and this undoubtedly affected the style of their works for piano solo, not only in the showiness of the keyboard writing but also in the treatment of sonata-form, the themes standing out in rather obvious contrast against their surroundings.

HUMMEL

There is considerably more character and solidity in the work of Johann Nepomuk Hummel (1778–1837) who was for two years a piano pupil of Mozart. For a considerable time he lived with Mozart and it is not surprising that his mind was steeped in Mozart's phraseology. In the finale of his Sonata in F minor Op. 20 (*c*. 1807), the coda introduces the first theme of the finale of the 'Jupiter' Symphony in a manner so obvious that it is hard to believe it is not a deliberate quotation, and the second subject of the first movement of the Sonata in C, Op. 38 (1808), has a strong resemblance to the main theme of the finale of Mozart's Sonata in C, K.330. Thematic invention was Hummel's weakest point, and this quite often diminishes the effect of what might otherwise be music of considerable interest. In the Fantasia, Op. 18, for instance, there is some striking and adventurous writing but the ideas themselves are conventional in character; in a later work, the polacca *La Bella Capricciosa*, the melody of the central episode is introduced in an unexpected key but the tune itself is uninteresting.

Hummel's treatment of sonata-form is by no means mechanical; the first movements of the sonatas in F minor and F sharp minor both vary their recapitulations freely, and in the latter case with strikingly dramatic effect. The Sonata in F sharp minor, Op. 81 (1819), is Hummel's most interesting; the outer movements are both vigorous and powerful, and the Largo, very florid like all his slow movements, has a romantically emotional quality. A quotation (ii) from it may be put beside another (i) from a sonata (K.280) by the seventeen-year-old Mozart to show the two composers going through the same harmonic process, but with very different textures:

Ex. 141

(ii) **Largo con molt' espressione**

Hummel's last and most ambitious sonata, *Grande Sonate brillante* in D, Op. 106 (1824), is more of a bravura work and as its title indicates, very brilliantly written; the second movement, curiously described as 'Scherzo all'antico' is very effective and the long contrapuntal coda of the finale is admirably done though old-fashioned by comparison with the kind of counterpoint Beethoven was writing at that time in his last sonatas.

PUPILS OF CLEMENTI

Two or three pupils of Clementi are interesting in different ways. The curious blend of virtuosity and counterpoint in Clementi's own work has already been mentioned; both of these elements can be found in the music of his pupil August Klengel (1783–1852), though the virtuosity is more subdued. The love of counterpoint finds its fullest expression in a collection of forty-eight canons and fugues, in all the major and minor keys, published posthumously. It cannot be said that these pieces have the individuality of the best of Clementi's contrapuntal work, but some of the fugues have strong and attractive subjects. The element of brilliant virtuosity is still more subdued in the music of Ludwig Berger (1777–1839), who put his best work into his *Études*, Op. 12 (1820). Berger's *Grande Sonate pathétique* (comp. 1804; pub. 1815 as Op. 7) and Klengel's in E, Op. 9 (*c.* 1805) are both notable compositions.

Yet another Clementi pupil, older than Berger or Klengel, was the already mentioned Cramer. He is remembered mostly for his studies: *Étude pour le Pianoforte en 42 exercices dans les différents tons* (1804), the *Suite de l'Étude en 42 exercices* (1810), and various later sets including *25 Études charactéristiques*, Op. 70, *12 nouvelles Études en forme de Nocturnes à 4 mains*, op. 98, and *12 Pièces caractéristiques en forme d'études*, Op. 111, which – particularly the first eighty-four – had enormous influence on pianistic techniques throughout the nineteenth century. But Cramer was also a very prolific composer of sonatas, the finest of which, in A minor, Op. 53 (1815), he styled 'L'Ultima' though it was followed by many others, notably 'Le Retour à Londres' (1818). Many of his sonata-movements tend to be *étude*-like in texture and passage-work but the middle section of the beautiful Adagio of Op. 8, no. 2 (*c.* 1793) shows pre-romantic traits:

Ex. 142

JOHN FIELD

Very different in his approach to music and in his general development was the Irish-born John Field (1782–1837), who was employed by Clementi to display the tone quality of the pianos at his warehouse in London and, like Klengel and Berger, was taken by Clementi to Russia. The others returned to the West but Field settled there permanently. Among his earlier publications for piano solo was a set of three sonatas, Op. 1, dedicated to Clementi (1801). These all consist of only two movements and show little of the dreaming lyricism that is the most attractive feature of his more mature work. Some of the melodies have an Italian air not surprising in the work of a pupil of Clementi, but the most individual trait is a robust gaiety, expressed with much gusto in the Allegretto scherzando rondo of the first sonata. The most remarkable of the three is the third, in C minor; the first movement shows the influences of Beethoven and Clementi, but has considerable power and is remarkably free in its treatment of sonata-form, with a long and varied development; the finale opens in a mood of bucolic good humour, but later on there are some surprising and quite dramatic incidents. These sonatas seem to forecast developments that never actually occurred, and they are certainly free from the diffuseness that is so apt to spoil Field's concertos.

But it is in his nocturnes, the earliest of which appeared at St. Petersburg in 1812, that Field produced his most distinguished and prophetic work, and a glance at the opening bars of the first nocturne shows at once that, in its unassuming way, it was saying something new:

Ex. 143

The simple but beautifully spaced accompaniment, sustained of course by the pedal, provides just the right kind of support for the equally simple melody; with a few possible exceptions, such as the opening Adagio of Beethoven's Sonata in C sharp minor, no earlier keyboard music depended so much for its effect on the use of the pedal. The second nocturne, in C minor, is similar in texture but far more emotional; the third, in A flat, has a subtler and more highly organized accompaniment, and the fourth, in A, in a kind of free binary form, is broader in general style, with moments of surprising harmonic freedom. No. 5, in B flat, may well have suggested Chopin's Nocturne in A flat, Op. 32, no. 2, but it is significant that, though both the themes in Chopin's are like Field's, their harmonies move at exactly twice the pace; Field still belonged in many ways to the more leisurely eighteenth century. There are other anticipations of Chopin. The theme of the so-called Rêverie-Nocturne in C, no. 7:

Ex. 144

may have suggested Chopin's Étude in E flat, but it is given to the left
hand throughout, accompanied by a persistent 'curling' figure. No. 14,
also in C, a charming but rather diffuse piece, very operatic in style,
has a coda remarkably anticipatory of that of Chopin's Impromptu in
F sharp. Despite its simple texture and gentle manner, Field's music
is by no means lacking in harmonic interest; sometimes surprisingly
expressive clashes occur, often arising from at least a suggestion of
counterpoint. The long dominant pedal at the beginning of the
beautifully serene Nocturne no. 11, in E flat, gives it a highly
individual character. The forms of these pieces vary considerably in
character. In no. 11 everything grows from the opening phrase of the
melody; on the other hand in several, such as no. 9, in E flat, and no.
12, in G, there is nothing that can be classified under any formal
headline, but a continuous flow of melody with a minimum of
repetition of any kind. The seventeenth, in E, exists in two versions,
in one of which the melody is preceded by an introductory passage
and followed by an equally rambling coda; the result is rather diffuse
but these additions have more harmonic interest than the rest.

Composers frequently amused themselves at this period by writing
fantasias and variations on national airs; one of the most popular was
'Within a mile of Edinboro' Town', which Field himself used in the
slow movement of his first Concerto.[1] There is a reminiscence of this
in the A major Nocturne, and the inverted dotted note or 'Scotch
snap' is liable to appear elsewhere, sometimes rather unexpectedly.
Field's technique when writing long and extended movements was
erratic, but he had the power of continuing a melodic line and
sustaining a mood. It is not certain whether the description 'nocturne'
was intended by him for all the pieces to which it has been applied in
later editions; there seems to be no doubt about the first twelve, but
some are adaptations by himself or other hands of movements from
concerted works. Field's remaining piano music includes several
rondos, sets of variations mostly on Russian airs, and other pieces, but
little that approaches the best of the nocturnes.

WEBER

Carl Maria von Weber (1786–1826), four years younger than Field,
was equally successful as a public pianist, and in his piano works
virtuosity and the atmosphere of romantic opera blend attractively.
His sonatas should not be judged by the standards of Beethoven's; his
aims were too different. He was not consciously concerned with
elaborating or varying sonata form, and while Beethoven tended more

[1] See chap. V, p. 219.

and more to avoid, or at any rate modify, the conventional harmonic formulae of the times, Weber obviously derived great enjoyment from presenting them with as much gusto and brilliance as possible. And while in Beethoven's later works the themes tend to be woven with increasing closeness into the texture of the music, Weber, primarily a composer for the stage, tends to make his themes stand out more vividly against an effectively contrasted background. In the first movement of his first Sonata, in C, Op. 21 (1812), the showmanship is a little too obvious; the rather commonplace character of the first theme is emphasized by the heroic flourish that precedes it. The brilliance of the *moto perpetuo* finale for which this sonata was long famous seems now somewhat faded, but the Adagio shows real dramatic power in the passage where a persistent rhythmic figure, appearing at first in the background, becomes gradually more prominent and eventually takes the stage at a grandiose climax. The so-called minuet is equally good. The second Sonata, in A flat, composed partly in 1814, the rest in 1816, is the richest in operatic atmosphere. The opening bars of the first movement, with their suggestion of distant horns sounding against a quietly rustling background, anticipate the mood of the opening of *Der Freischütz*, and there are a number of passages which, though essentially instrumental in texture, suggest an operatic duet. A charming instance occurs early in the first movement, and in the opening of the Andante a plaintive heroine, or oboe, is eventually consoled by a sympathetic hero, or cello. The whole movement may have been suggested by some kind of programme, particularly the last appearance of the main theme after the rather blatant but effective outburst in C major. In the trio of the *minuetto capriccioso* there is a vivid operatic scene, suggesting a soprano singing passionately against a background of conspirators. The finale reveals the influence of Beethoven's Op. 22, a work that must have made a special appeal to Weber. The Sonata in D minor. Op. 49, composed in November 1816 immediately after the A flat, is more of a bravura piece. The first movement is powerful and effective, and the moment when the main theme returns unexpectedly in a major key, combined contrapuntally with one of the others, is remarkably dramatic. The Andante, though pleasant, is over-long for its material; the finale opens in a mood similar to that of the *moto perpetuo* of the C major Sonata, but has more variety, with a sentimental love-duet as second subject. The Sonata in E minor, Op. 70, was written during 1819–20 and 1822, partly before and partly after the composition of *Der Freischütz*, and in several places the sonata reveals a relationship to the opera. The trio of the minuet has points of resemblance to the peasants' dance in the First Act, and the opening theme of the Andante:

Ex. 145

is a more wistful relative of the melody of the bridesmaids' chorus. Equally characteristic is the more Italianate melody that appears later in the same movement:

Ex. 146

The quiet, melancholy first movement is the most subtly organized in the sonatas; the minuet is in a wild and violent mood that contrasts effectively with the placidly flowing trio. The finale is a tarantella in which the temporary triumph in the major key shortly before the end and the subsequent collapse are very effective.

Of the shorter piano works the most successful is the celebrated 'Aufforderung zum Tanz' (1819). The two polonaises and the 'Rondeau brillante' are effective but the early 'Momento capriccioso' has considerably more character. Of the sets of variations the most interesting is on the Ukrainian folk-tune 'A Cossack went beyond the Don', known in Germany as 'Schöne Minka' (1815); it has an introduction which anticipates ingeniously the main features of most of the variations, and a finale that begins surprisingly *alla spagnuola* with a new bolero theme that is eventually driven out by the Russian tune. In these works the brilliance of the piano writing is tempered by the warmth resulting from Weber's love of orchestral colour and his sense of the dramatic. Weber was conscious of his nationality, and his tunes are sometimes related to the German *Volkslied*, but, as Ex. 146 illustrates, he derived much from Italy – more, possibly, than he would have been willing to admit.

SCHUBERT

Schubert's piano music, like Weber's, has suffered from irrelevant comparisons with Beethoven's but it is far more varied in character and constitutes a much more important section of his total output than

Weber's does in his. He differs from Beethoven as a lyric poet does from a dramatist. Beethoven possessed a great fund of melody, but he was less indulgent to his melodies than Schubert. One of Beethoven's most luxuriant movements is the Adagio of Op. 106, but even here there is a sense of firm control; beside it the even more luxuriant slow movement of Schubert's Sonata in D, Op. 53, has the air of an improvisation. But Schubert did not find his lyric gift at once, and it took longer in instrumental work than in his songs. The earliest works for keyboard are three Fantasias for piano duet (D.1, 9, and 48),[1] of which the first two, written in 1812, are rambling compositions of little interest. The third, dating from the following year, has more character, with some striking chromatic fugal writing, but none of them is Schubertian. The next keyboard works were not written till 1815; there are two Sonatas, in E and C (D.157 and 279), both without final movements. The former is the more interesting, particularly its minuet and trio, but a set of ten variations on an original theme in F (D.156) (1815), despite one or two lapses and a perfunctory final flourish, comes nearer than any previous piano work to Schubert's intimate lyricism. In 1816 came a set of five pieces (D.459) which may well have been intended as a sonata in E, the slow movement coming between two strongly contrasted scherzos. This has something of the tunefulness of the Fifth Symphony, which dates from the same year, but is more reflective and more mature, particularly the first scherzo, which is in full sonata-form with no trio. The following passage, from the Adagio, is already characteristic:

Ex. 147

The first movement is marked by an early instance of the alternating major and minor so characteristic of Schubert.

---

[1] D. numbers refer to O.E. Deutsch, *Schubert: Thematic Catalogue* (London, 1951). Schubert's opus-numbers are given only when authentic.

THE SONATAS OF 1817

1817 saw the production of five piano Sonatas,[1] the best of which show a marked increase of individuality. The Sonatas in A flat and E minor (D.557 and 566), of which the one ends out of its key and the other has been conjecturally reassembled, are of minor interest, but the others are works of considerable beauty. D.568, in E flat, of which there is a slightly earlier and incomplete version in D flat (D.567), is the least adventurous but thoroughly characteristic in its flow of melody and the spontaneous ease of its modulations, particularly in the elegiac Andante, and the delightful development section of the finale. The other two are the most enterprising instrumental works Schubert had yet written. The first movement of D.575, in B major, modulates in a striking but rather breathless manner through a number of remote keys before reaching the dominant in the exposition; if this passage is compared with a similar process in the much later posthumous Sonata in B flat (D.960) it will be seen that a certain amount of leisure was necessary for Schubert's mature harmonic schemes, and the later passage, though far less direct, is also far more beautiful. The finale of D.575 has some of the same restlessness, but the two central movements, though not particularly pianistic, are admirable. In D.537, in A minor, the central Allegretto is built on a theme used much later in the posthumous A major Sonata (D.959); its unusual key scheme, E, C, F, D minor, and back to E, is particularly successful. In these three works Schubert's treatment of sonata-form is unconventional; with the exception of the first movement of D.575, the developments of all the movements in sonata-form are built entirely on new material. The rhythms are becoming increasingly free; the five-bar phrases in the trio of the minuet of D.568, and at the opening of D.537, are extremely effective.

The influences of Haydn and Mozart can still be felt; Beethoven inevitably affected Schubert greatly, though not necessarily through the works that seem to us now to be the most obviously bold or prophetic. Certain lyrical movements among Beethoven's earlier sonatas – the Allegretto of the Sonata in F, Op. 10, no. 2, or that of the Sonata in E, Op. 14, no. 1 – must have made a strong appeal to him. But a glance at Beethoven's Op. 10, no. 3, will show that Schubert was influenced far more by the melodiousness of the minuet than by the drama and passion of the first two movements. It is noteworthy that when, at the beginning of the finale of D.537, Schubert moves quietly for a moment into the key of the flattened supertonic, as Beethoven had done in the opening theme of the 'Appassionata', the result is

[1] Six if one reckons the fragmentary F sharp minor (D. 570-1).

wistful and pathetic, with none of Beethoven's breathless suspense. The only remaining piano work dating from 1817 is a set of variations (D.576) on a theme from Anselm Hüttenbrenner's String Quartet, Op. 3; this is a decided advance on the earlier set of 1815, and the theme may have attracted Schubert by its resemblance to the Allegretto of Beethoven's Seventh Symphony, a movement by which, particularly in his later works, he was deeply influenced.

The year 1818 produced little keyboard music except for the piano duet Sonata in B flat, Op. 30 (D.617), a pleasant but undistinguished work, a set of variations, also for piano duet, on a French song in E minor, Op. 10 (D.624), and an unfinished Sonata in F minor (D.625). On the other hand the solo Sonata in A (D.664), composed in 1819, is a work of peculiar intimacy and charm, combining a completely mature style with a conciseness remarkable for Schubert; the transition from the lyrical first subject to the second is effected by a simple one-bar scale. It is an idyllic work, growing rather more animated in the finale; in the Andante an effect of tenderness is produced by the subtle blending of phrases of two and three bars.

WORKS OF 1822–5

Apart from the small dance movements which Schubert composed in profusion at all periods, there is no more keyboard music till 1822, when he wrote the most obviously experimental of all his piano works, the Fantasia in C major, Op. 15 (D.760), consisting of four sections, following each other without a break and thematically connected, but with no suggestion of sonata-form. In the first section the aggressive dactylic rhythm of the opening soon reappears in a gentler version:

Ex. 148

The second bar of this eventually grows into the second main theme of the movement:

Ex. 149

The theme of the Adagio, taken from the song 'Der Wanderer', shares the dactylic rhythm; the scherzo has one new theme but is built mainly on material from the first section; its opening, in A flat, after the E major close of the Adagio, being remarkably dramatic. The final section opens with free fugal treatment of the opening theme of the work and its later stages, without any note-for-note repetition, give the effect of a kind of recapitulation of the first section. Towards the end the piano writing becomes ungrateful, but the work is of particular interest for its demonstration that Schubert was capable of carrying out a formal experiment with great power and conviction.

By this time he was producing orchestral and chamber music that was fully on a level with his songs, though so far none of the piano works had reached quite the same heights. In 1823 Schubert wrote the Sonata in A minor (D.784), one of his most original conceptions. The sombre and dramatic first movement has a concentrated power worthy of Beethoven; it is magnificent music, which almost needs an orchestra for its full realization. The equally fine short Andante is built on a single theme of great breadth and beauty. In the final rondo the second theme appears three times, in different keys; it does not quite reach the level of the other two movements but the sonata as a whole is remarkably imaginative and powerful. Finer still, however, is the so-called Grand Duo in C, for piano duet (D.812). Here, as in D.784, there is much that is orchestral in feeling. The first movements of both have points in common; in both the first theme is announced quietly in octaves and returns shortly in a blaze of light, but that of the Grand Duo is planned on a larger scale and contains some particularly characteristic features; for instance, the tonality of the second subject, which begins in a remote key and moves gradually to the dominant, the alternating moods of the development, and the coda which rises to a climax only to die away in the final bars. The slow movement recalls the mood of the Larghetto of Beethoven's Second Symphony, and one theme has a strong likeness to a prominent phrase in the Beethoven movement. But Schubert's individuality is always manifest, particularly in the modulations. He uses quietly and lyrically the kind of modulation that Beethoven, except in his latest works, would reserve for a specially dramatic climax. The scherzo has a Beethovenish boisterousness, but the strong contrast of mood between it and its trio is eminently characteristic of Schubert who in almost all his later works tends to attach a particular emotional significance to the trio. The finale of the Grand Duo is a fine instance of serious and imaginative treatment of seemingly flippant ideas.

Two other large works for piano duet appeared during the same

year, the 'Divertissement à l'hongroise', Op. 54 (D.818), and the
Theme and Variations in A flat, Op. 35 (D.813). Of these the former
consists of three sections, the second a short march. The other two are
enormous rondos, both with two episodes, each of which forms a kind
of ABA design of its own. This inevitably results in a large amount of
repetition, and the work as a whole, though interesting as a stylistic
essay, has an air of self-conscious picturesqueness. Op. 35 on the other
hand is a wholly delightful work, the best of Schubert's separate sets
of variations. Here the influence of Beethoven extends beyond that of
his earlier works and there are reminiscences of the Seventh
Symphony, particularly in the fifth variation:

Ex. 150

and the finale, which recalls the dotted-note rhythm – but not the
Olympian energy – of Beethoven's first movement. The third variation,
with two voices singing quietly against a background of repeated
chords, is the purest Schubert, and the seventh is harmonically very
striking. Three pieces for piano duet, built partly on French themes,
were intended as a sonata (D.823) but divided by the publisher Weigl
as Op. 63, no. 1, and Op. 84, nos. 1 and 2; the best is the charming
little set of variations in B minor.

The year 1825 was rich in sonatas on a larger scale than their
predecessors. Op. 42, in A minor (D.845), is one of the most
imaginative, and, like D. 784 and D.664, is strongly unified in mood.
Its first movement is remarkable for its original treatment of the form.
The first subject has two contrasting elements, one wistful, the other
aggressively rhythmic; these both reappear, in the opposite order, for
the second subject, the second in C major and the first, which would
obviously lose its individuality in a major key, in C minor. At the end
of the exposition comes a new idea, derived to some extent from the
first. This is never allowed its own way for long, until the coda, when
it gradually asserts itself in a long crescendo and, sweeping aside
opposition from both the others, takes the stage in the final bars. No
other first movement of Schubert's ends with so powerfully organized
a climax, except that of the C major Symphony, and it is not surprising
that of the two passages the sonata should be tragic and the symphony
triumphant. The second movement of Op. 42 is a set of variations,

from which a few bars may be quoted as an example of Schubert's magically effective use of modulation:

Ex. 151

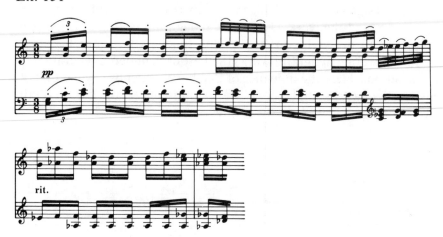

The scherzo and finale are full of restless energy deriving largely from unusual and unexpected phrase-lengths; the finale anticipates strikingly the four repeated minims of the finale of the C major Symphony. In the Sonata in D, Op. 53 (D.850), the first movement is remarkable for its sustained bustle and energy though it is thematically less attractive. The Con moto second movement is in a form of which Schubert was particularly fond, a rondo in which the second episode is a recapitulation of the first; here again are reminiscences of the Larghetto of Beethoven's Second Symphony. After this long movement the rhythmic energy of the scherzo is most effective with its alternations of the mock-heroic and the playful; in the magnificent trio occurs one of Schubert's grandest chains of modulations. The final rondo, cheerful, even playful in its opening, covers a surprising variety of mood; there are two spacious episodes, of which the second, as so often with Schubert, is in a complete ABA design of its own, and the main theme is resourcefully varied at each appearance, the opening phrase being delightfully recalled in its original form in the final bars.

The third sonata of this year, in C major (D.840), was completed only in its first two movements, which are both of splendid quality.[1] The first has much in common with that of the Grand Duo: the simplicity of its opening, the unexpectedly quiet end, and the generally

---

[1] The earliest of a number of attempts to complete the minuetto and rondo finale is Křenek's (Vienna, 1923).

PLATE II. ANDANTE OF SCHUBERT'S SONATA IN G. OP. 78 (1826)

Above: The deleted first page of the autograph; *Below*: the final version. (Brit. Lib., Add. 36738, ff. 6v–7r).

broad and spacious style. The introduction of the second subject in a remote key is one of Schubert's most dramatic touches and the return to the recapitulation one of his most subtle. The Andante is similar in form to the second movement of Op. 53, but considerably more sombre, with moments of fierce energy that look ahead to several later slow movements. The minuet is promising, and the trio, which was completed, very fine, but the finale, though thematically pleasant, shows signs of diffuseness. The Sonata in G, Op. 78 (D.894), returns to the idyllic mood of D.664, but with increased depth and serenity. The first movement, with its finely sustained development, is one of Schubert's loveliest and the contrast between its contemplative first and gently waltzing second subject is delightful. The Andante is in the same form as those of Op. 53 and the unfinished C major Sonata, but here the recapitulated episode is itself in a terse binary design, resulting in much repetition. Yet the movement – 'half lyrical, half defiant' as Einstein called it[1] – is so delightful that one accepts 'repetition' as 'heavenly length'; like the first movement it ends *ppp*. The minuet and trio handle Viennese *Ländler* rhythms with even more than Schubert's usual imaginativeness. The finale, like that of the D major Sonata, is a rondo with two episodes; it has however no strong contrasts, being for the most part a light-hearted march with Slavonic or perhaps Hungarian undertones. The last four bars unexpectedly recall the opening but *pp un poco più lento*.

IMPROMPTUS AND *MOMENTS MUSICAUX*

To the year 1827 belong the two sets of Impromptus (D.899 and 935); some of the six *Moments musicaux*, Op. 94 (D.780), were written at this time and some as early as 1823. In these can be seen the influence of the more lyrical Beethoven, and also of the Czech composers Václav Jan Tomášek (1774–1850), and Jan Voříšek (1791–1825). Tomášek's seven sets of Eclogues for piano (1807–23) are pleasant, flowing pieces, all in ABA form, in a tuneful and unpretentious style which may well have appealed to Schubert, and the same may be said of Voříšek's six Impromptus, Op. 7 (Vienna, 1822). The following quotations show some similarities:

[1] Alfred Einstein, *Schubert* (London, 1951), p. 287.

Ex. 152

(i) VOŘÍŠEK: Impromptu, Op.7, No.4 (1822)

Allegretto

(ii) SCHUBERT: Impromptu, Op.90, No.4 (1827)

Allegretto

(iii) TOMÁŠEK: Eclogue, Op.66, No.2 (1819)

Allegro risoluto

(iv) SCHUBERT: Impromptu, Op.posth., Op.142, No. 1

Allegro moderato

Schubert's two sets of Impromptus both contain fine music, particularly Op. 90, with the nocturne-like no. 3, in G flat, and the magnificently broad central sections of the second and fourth pieces. But of all the smaller piano works the most perfect are the six *Moments musicaux* especially, perhaps, the second, fourth, and sixth. The opening of the fourth is curiously similar in outline to the great central tune of the A flat Impromptu, Op. 90, no. 4. The three *Clavierstücke* (D.946) – so-called by Brahms, who edited the first publication in 1868 – were composed in 1828. They are on a larger scale than any of the Impromptus but less immediately attractive; nevertheless they contain some interesting music, especially in the second piece. Of the innumerable sets of dances composed by Schubert at all periods of his life, a special word may be said for the twelve *Ländler* (D.790), written in 1823, nearly all of which are exquisite.

SCHUBERT'S LATER FOUR-HAND WORKS

The marches and polonaises for piano duet are less subtle, but delightfully vivacious, the marches being surprisingly varied. Two larger works for piano duet, both composed in 1828, are interesting for the closeness with which each follows the plan of a work by an older composer. The Fantasia in F minor, Op. 103 (D.940), is very similar in its general scheme to Mozart's fine work in the same key for mechanical organ, K.608, the material of the opening section returning with more elaborate contrapuntal treatment at the end. Instead of Mozart's central Andante, however, Schubert has two contrasted sections, a Largo and a scherzo, both in the remote key of F sharp minor, to which Mozart also makes a brief but very striking modulation during the course of his work. Schubert's Op. 103 is a more sombre and intimate work than his C major Fantasia, Op. 13 (the 'Wanderer'), and the contrapuntal writing is far more effective. The Rondo in A (D.951) follows even more closely the plan of the finale of Beethoven's Sonata in E minor, Op. 90; the themes of the two movements are very similar in shape and key system, in both the second episode is a development of the last strain of the first, and in both the main melody appears near the end in the tenor register. But in both of these instances Schubert's music is intensely individual; on the other hand, the separate Allegro in A minor (D.947) (called 'Lebensstürme' by the publisher), also for piano duet, without suggesting any particular work, is strongly Beethoven-like in general atmosphere, though there are things, such as the modulation that introduces the second subject, that could only have come from Schubert.

THE LAST THREE SONATAS

The last three sonatas, composed six weeks before Schubert's death in 1828, are the longest and most introspective of them all, and rise in their finest pages to a kind of brooding ecstasy for which there are few parallels in his music. The first movement of the Sonata in C minor (D.958) is filled with foreboding, but the second subject, followed by some variations of itself, is beautifully serene. The Adagio, broad and simple in outline, varies delightfully the setting of the main theme on its reappearances. Instead of a scherzo there is a short minuet with a trio in *Ländler* rhythm. The restlessly galloping finale recalls those of Schubert's last two string quartets; its unflagging energy and fascinating tonal schemes fully justify its enormous length. The first movement of the Sonata in A (D.959) opens in Schubert's grandest manner, and has a second subject of extraordinary charm; the development is of an unusual type, a cadential phrase of two bars from the second subject being taken through a series of keys against a background of repeated chords, with exciting effect; the coda, in which the opening bars return in a gentler mood, is deeply impressive. The Andantino is notable for the almost startling contrast between the broad and simple main theme and the wild central section; the passage leading to the return of the former is of great beauty. The gay scherzo is interrupted for a moment by reminiscences first of the central section and then of the main theme of the Andantino with dramatic effect. The theme of the rich and luxuriant rondo looks back to the Allegretto of D.537, and the whole movement is built on a plan very similar to that of the rondo of Beethoven's Op. 31, no. 1. Features common to both movements are a repetition of the first theme by the left hand under a counterpoint of triplets, a passage of alternately rising and falling arpeggios in the first episode, and a more rapid coda preceded by a broken version of the theme. But the two movements end differently, Beethoven's disappearing quietly and humorously while Schubert's grandiose final bars look back very effectively to the opening of the first movement.

Fine though both these sonatas are, the last, in B flat (D.960), reaches a still higher level. The first movement, with its solemn opening, is one of the longest and quietest that Schubert ever wrote; the later stages of the development and the final coda are of overwhelming beauty. The theme of the Andante is a more solemn relative of the song 'Ständchen' written a few months earlier; when it returns, with a new accompaniment after the rich, warm central section, the sudden modulation from C sharp minor to C major is thrilling:

Ex. 153

The delicate scherzo and its sombre trio are equally fine, and the finale opens in a foreign key to which it constantly returns with cheerful defiance.

Schubert's piano writing, even at its best, is less varied in texture than Beethoven's and he accepted the sonata form with far less intellectual curiosity. He handles it in his own inimitable way and often, as in the first movement of the B flat Sonata, shows wonderful imagination in presenting a theme against a completely new harmonic background. But his general effects are usually less cumulative than Beethoven's, and it is the individual beauties rather than the whole design that remain in the memory. Schubert made no attempt to curb his exuberant lyricism and frequently allowed single episodes to form themselves into complete designs of their own, regardless of the effect on the general plan of the work. Such preoccupation with details rather than outlines is a familiar symptom of the Romantic movement.

THE RISING GENERATION

As we have seen, this is even more true of Weber. And Field's almost complete neglect of the sonata after his Op. 1 – he published only one more, in 1812 – is another symptom of Romanticism. Voříšek also composed a fine sonata, in B flat minor (1820), but following in the wake of Tomášek's eclogues and rhapsodies and dithyrambs, he preferred to write rhapsodies, rondos, variations, and impromptus. The short piece was generally preferred to the sonata by the rising generation. In Poland the young Fryderyk Chopin (1810–49) composed rondos, polonaises, valses, and mazurkas for which he had models in the works of Michal Ogiński (1765–1835), Jósef Elsner (1769–1854), and Maria Szymanowska (1789–1831), models which he quickly excelled. He waited until 1828 before attempting his first, quite uncharacteristic, sonata.

Chopin's almost exact contemporary, Felix Mendelssohn-Bartholdy (1809–47), who as a boy studied the piano with Berger, was a more precocious sonata-composer. His earliest, in G minor, was written at the age of eleven; it is an accomplished if unoriginal work with traces of Haydn's influence in the first movement. The E major Sonata, Op. 6, of 1826 is much more Mendelssohnian; the movements are to be played without a break, except for a *piccola pausa* at the end of the first, and some passages reflect his knowledge of Beethoven's last sonatas – then very new. His third sonata, in B flat (1827), is decidedly disappointing and Mendelssohn never returned to the sonata for piano. Much more individual are the shorter works: the Andante and Rondo capriccioso, Op. 14 (1824), the Capriccio, Op. 5 (1825), and the seven *Charakterstücke*, Op.7 (comp. 1825–7). There is influence from Weber in the Andante of Op. 14 but also from Domenico Scarlatti in Op. 5 and Op. 7, nos. 2 and 6, but the Rondo capriccioso itself, the Capriccio, and the seventh of the *Charakterstücke* all exemplify that delicate fairylike quality which was uniquely Mendelssohnian. And before long he was to embark on the earliest of those *Lieder ohne Worte* which became for a time one of the most popular forms of short piano piece.

IX

ITALIAN OPERA

By WINTON DEAN

BETWEEN MOZART AND ROSSINI

AT the outbreak of the Revolution and for long afterwards Italian opera[1] was still an international commodity. Enormous numbers of works were produced, not only in Italy – where Naples, Venice, and Milan were the principal centres – and not only by Italians. The German cities (especially Vienna and Dresden), London, St Petersburg, and the Iberian peninsula saw the birth of countless Italian operas, many of them by visiting Italians, others by local composers who often transferred their activities to Italy. These included numerous Germans and Central Europeans, Martín y Soler and Portugal (Portogallo) from Iberia, and the occasional Pole or Russian. Between Mozart's death and the rise of Rossini none was an artist of the first rank, and few even aspired to the second. Many enjoyed wide success despite (or because of) the fact that they worked to a limited number of standard patterns.

Stylistically it was a period of suspended animation. While the foundations of the art were shifting in France, and later in Germany, Italian opera remained almost stationary. It was by tradition an entertainment industry geared to public taste, like Hollywood films and television in the twentieth century, not yet a vehicle for national aspiration. Its most gifted composer, Rossini, was the last man to disturb this equilibrium; at least until he left Italy for France he was a codifier, not an innovator. The position did not change until the late 1820s, when the Romantic spirit, which had entered the libretto some

[1] Conditions of performance and publication make Italian opera of this period much more difficult to assess with any approach to comprehensiveness than French or German opera. Any successful Italian opera was liable to appear in different cities, on stage and in print, with variants not always sanctioned or even composed by the ostensible author. Full scores were almost never published, vocal scores fitfully, inconsistently, and often in incomplete form. The painstaking research of Ludwig Schiedermair has made much of Mayr's work available. Philip Gossett has disentangled the complex early history of Rossini's operas. The other composers covered in this chapter, apart from Bellini, who wrote comparatively little, await detailed study.

time earlier, at last began to suffuse the music. Though Simon Mayr in particular was familiar with the works of the French Revolution school, as well as with Haydn and Mozart, he failed to match the passionate energy of Cherubini and Méhul even when his librettos were packed with extravagance and his ensembles and finales with violent action. This gulf between music and drama persisted in the serious operas of the next generation, including those of Rossini, and, though partly bridged by Bellini and Donizetti, did not finally disappear until Verdi's maturity. It is characteristic of Italian backwardness that Zingarelli should tell Spohr that if Mozart had studied for another ten years he could have written something memorable.

There was also a considerable stylistic overlap, of similar duration, between the three types of opera practised in Italy. The two traditional forms, *opera seria* and *opera buffa*, continued side by side while their musical language – not their conventions – became more and more assimilated. The third form, *opera semiseria*, which was to become important later, was not a true synthesis but a haphazard product of several strains, some of them literary and extra-musical. Rossini's shuttling of the same music between comic and serious works is notorious, but was by no means unique. Mayr did the same thing without scruple: the overture to *La rosa rossa e la rosa bianca* (1813) borrows from that of *Belle ciarle e fatti tristi* (1807), and both of Omphale's arias in *Ercole in Lidia* (1803) originated in *buffo* surroundings. In the absence of a composer of compelling genius there was nothing in the operatic climate to discourage this, and the tension between drama and music was so slack that the practice can seldom be deduced from the context alone.

Italian conservatism derived partly from the deep grooves worn by a successful tradition, partly from national character and partly from political circumstances. Where courts exercised strong control, for instance at Naples, opera after the Revolution was subjected to ever-tightening censorship, an incubus that continued to afflict the Papal dominions and the Austrian-occupied provinces of north Italy for much of the nineteenth century. A country divided into separate states whose allegiance was constantly changing offered meagre soil for new growth in an essentially social art. Unlike the French and Germans, the Italians were seldom tempted to theoretical or aesthetic experiment, and they had no strong tradition of classical spoken drama. Composers with more serious ambitions, like Cherubini and Spontini, migrated to Paris. The Gluckian reforms made little impact in Italy, though Luigi Serio's libretto for Cimarosa's *Oreste* (1783) endeavoured to reduce the recitative and integrate the chorus with the action throughout instead of confining it to finales. The greatest *opera seria* of the age, Mozart's *Idomeneo*,[1] was not produced in Italy until 1947, and his *opere buffe* – less successful even in Vienna than those of Cimarosa and Martín y Soler – were scarcely known outside a small circle before the Naples performances of 1812–15.

Of the Italian opera composers who practised between the Revolution and the rise of Rossini, Paisiello and Cimarosa were near the end of their active careers, though their successors imitated them as closely as they imitated themselves. The most prominent among the next generation, Simon Mayr (1763–1845) and Ferdinando Paer (1771–1839), both popular and prolific (between 1794 and 1824 Mayr produced more than sixty operas in all the current forms), are chiefly important as hyphens between the eighteenth century and the generation of Rossini, Donizetti, and Bellini. They initiated very little. Though their music has much in common, their careers were almost antithetical. Paer's took him from Parma to Venice in 1791, Vienna in 1798, Dresden in 1803, and Paris in 1807; he became an expatriate and wrote little for the stage in his later years. Mayr, a Bavarian by birth, went to Italy in 1787 to study with Bertoni, from whom he imbibed the tradition of Gluck, and apart from one opera for Vienna wrote exclusively for Italian theatres. He worked mainly at Venice (where he received encouragement from Piccinni) from 1790, and in 1802 settled permanently at Bergamo. He refused many foreign invitations, including one from Napoleon in 1806 to succeed Le Sueur as director of the Paris Opéra. A learned and cultivated musician, he revered Gluck, Mozart, and Haydn, on whom he wrote a monograph, and in 1809 conducted the first performance in Italy of *The Creation*. He was a more important influence on subsequent Italian opera than Paer, not least as a teacher (Donizetti was his most successful pupil); but though he was a respectable craftsman and introduced, rather tentatively, certain ideas from Austria and France that were to prove fertile in the long run, neither he nor Paer commanded the individuality to transcend conventions that had long outgrown their vitality or to leave more than a temporary mark on history.

OPERA BUFFA

Of the senior forms, *opera buffa* was the younger and more vigorous.[2] Many of its facets scarcely changed between Pergolesi's *La serva*

---

[1] Strictly it was a compound of *opera seria* and *tragédie-lyrique*, described in the first score as *dramma eroico*. Mozart called it a 'grosse Oper'.
[2] Its general characteristics are described in Vol. VII, pp. 47 ff.

padrona (1733) and Donizetti's *Don Pasquale* (1843), though later examples enjoyed the reversion of the wit and energy infused by Rossini. Giovanni Paisiello (1740–1816) reset the libretto of *La serva padrona* in 1781, adding little of his own except a hint, in Serpina's mock-pathetic minor-key aria in the second scene, of the plaintive sentiment that was the most personal feature of his style. Since *opera buffa* depended on intrigue rather than character, and still bore marks of its origins in the *commedia dell'arte* – in Naples characters often conversed in dialect or gibberish – the libretto carried as much weight as the music. The Italian genius for comic imbroglios and absurd situations threw up many gifted librettists (Goldoni, Da Ponte, and Bertati are only the best known) who were able to vary the basic situations and by some comparatively minor twist to keep them fresh. The same types – frustrated lover, scheming minx, heavy father, avaricious or amorous elder, rich fop, jabbering lawyer, decrepit aunt or governess, and the factotum who manipulates the plot, immortalized in the barber Figaro – recur again and again. (Carlo's part in Mayr's *Un vero originale* (1808) with its alternation between parlando passages, sudden fermatas, and changes of time has strong affinities with Rossini's *Barbiere*.) So do the situations. Multiple impersonations are frequent: the maid Ninetta in Cimarosa's *Chi dell'altrui si veste presto si spoglia* (1783), like Despina in *Così fan tutte*, indulges in a whole string of them, and in one scene she and Martuffo make mutual advances, each unaware that the other is an impostor. Lovers disguise themselves or their servants as philosophers, priests, doctors, lawyers, orientals, lunatics, or anything else, in order to outwit their elders. Sometimes they are secretly married, and occasionally – as in Mayr's *Amore non soffre opposizione* (1810) and Donizetti's *L'ajo nell'imbarazzo* (1824) – they have a child, legitimate or illegitimate, to explain away;[1] but the explanation is always successful in the end, after the household or village has been turned upside down in a series of frantic comings and goings whipped up into a fury of communal exasperation.

SATIRE IN *OPERA BUFFA*

There is little social satire of more than a superficial kind – Bertati's clever adaptation of a play by Colman and Garrick, *The Clandestine Marriage*, for Cimarosa's *Il matrimonio segreto* (1792) removed that

---

[1] This is also a feature of Francesco Puttini's libretto *La vera costanza*, set by Anfossi in 1776 and Haydn in 1779. The exploitation of the child as a pathetic element in the plot anticipates many operas of the post-Revolution period and may owe some of its popularity to Rousseau and his literary followers, though it occurs in Handel (*Rodrigo, Rodelinda*) and even earlier. We meet it again in Italian opera in Paer's *Camilla*, Rossini's *Zelmira*, Meyerbeer's *Margherita d'Anjou* and *Il crociato in Egitto*, and Bellini's *Bianca e Fernando, Il Pirata*, and *Norma*.

element altogether – but plenty of good-humoured fun at the expense of certain professions, especially lawyers and singers; it was too dangerous to place politicians or monarchs in compromising situations, as Verdi among others was to discover. The eccentricities, mannerisms, and vanities of those engaged in opera itself were a favourite target. Cimarosa in *L'Italiana in Londra* (1778) had indulged in elaborate parodies of *opera seria*, and in *Il maestro di cappella* treated the mishaps of a pompous composer-conductor with wit and humour. This gave opportunity for simple-minded jokes with voices imitating instruments, which were very popular and can still entertain an audience. They were not disdained by Haydn (*Orlando paladino*) and Mozart (*La finta giardiniera*), and were still going strong in Paer's *Le Maître de chapelle* (1821) and Donizetti's *Il fortunato inganno* (1823).

Mayr won most of his early successes with *farse* of this type in one or two acts, such as *Che originali* (1798) on an amusing libretto by Gaetano Rossi satirizing musical snobbery and the vogue for Metastasio and pasticcios, and *I virtuosi* (1801) which makes hilarious sport of backstage life in a Venice theatre. The principal targets here are the rivalry between the prima donna and the prima ballerina (who in the absence of a voice has an 'aria' with bassoon obbligato) for the favours of the public and the marquis who owns the theatre, the casual insertion of arias from other operas, and the absurd clothes and accoutrements: the *buffo* enters with a parrot in one hand, a cage containing a cat in the other, and a small dog on a lead. (He also has an aria that begins in G and ends in E minor after a middle section in E flat, a rare excursion into unorthodox tonal design.) There were numerous operas of this type, from Jommelli's *La critica* (1767) and Cimarosa's *L'impresario in angustie* (1786) to Donizetti's *Le convenienze ed inconvenienze teatrali* (1827); Mozart's *Der Schauspieldirektor* is a more refined example. One of the most popular was *Le cantatrici villane* (1799) by Valentino Fioravanti (1764–1837), the cast of which includes three village prima donnas, a male singer, and a composer-conductor. The music falls half way between Cimarosa and Rossini; like Mayr's *farse*, it uses the same language with rather less polish and balance. The *farsa*, *La prova d'una opera seria* (1805), by Francesco Gnecco (1769–1810) was revived repeatedly all over Europe for fifty years and became a favourite vehicle for Malibran.

MUSICAL STRUCTURE OF *BUFFA*

The musical design had become standardized well before 1790. Until the late 1770s most full-length *opere buffe* had three acts, but the third shrank to an appendix sometimes consisting (as in Haydn's *Il mondo della luna* and *La vera costanza* and a number of Cimarosa operas) of little more than a love duet and a perfunctory final ensemble, and it soon dropped off altogether. Act I was framed by an *introduzione* in which the plot was set moving, generally by secondary characters, and the now universal 'chain finale', essential for building up tension and supplying a selection of climaxes and anticlimaxes. Another such finale ended the second act, whether or not a third followed. The finales tended to increase in length, embracing movements of different type from accompanied recitative to love songs, and their popularity increased the number of ensembles in the opera. The castrato and the *travesti* hero were rejected as foreign to an idiom that depended on natural plots and earthy humour, and therefore required good singing actors able to declaim the words rapidly and clearly. (Mozart's *La finta giardiniera*, not composed for Italy, has a castrato as well as *buffo* parts.) Coloratura was reserved for parody, of which there was plenty. Paisiello in *Il mondo della luna* (1774), first produced as *Il credulo deluso*, an effective setting of Goldoni's libretto – theatrically superior to Haydn's if less distinguished – had made fairly extensive use of chorus and dancing, though these may have been introduced for the St Petersburg production of 1783. But the practice seems to have died out; later composers used the chorus sparingly. Mayr introduced a male group in *I finti rivali* (1802) and *Belle ciarle e fatti tristi* (1807), which has an entertaining episode for a body of lawyers singing through their noses, accompanied by two muted trumpets and strings alternating between *arco* and *pizzicato*. The Italian opera orchestra in the late eighteenth century was strongly weighted in favour of treble and bass against middle parts; that of the San Carlo Theatre, Naples, in 1780 contained 32 violins, four violas, three cellos, and five double basses.[1]

PAISIELLO AND CIMAROSA

Paisiello and Cimarosa each closed his *opera buffa* career in 1798, the former with *L'inganno felice*, the latter with *Il matrimonio per raggiro*, his last completed opera. (Paisiello went on to write one French grand opera, *Proserpine*, produced in Paris in 1803.) By that time the idiom was becoming threadbare, and their numerous followers could do little but repeat the same formulae directed to the same ends. The best operas of the period, such as Paisiello's *Il barbiere di Siviglia* (1782), which Rossini hesitated to challenge thirty years later, and Cimarosa's *Il matrimonio segreto* (1792), still retain a certain vitality, since a well-constructed libretto and a string of comic

[1] Michael F. Robinson, *Naples and Neapolitan Opera* (Oxford, 1972), p. 160.

situations can keep secondary music afloat – which was indeed the main purpose. Significantly, both were based on successful stage plays. Not that this was an infallible recipe. Salieri's *Falstaff* (1799) debases Shakespeare to the level of Viennese *Singspiel*: Mrs Ford, not her husband, visits Falstaff in disguise – as a German chambermaid, in which persona she converses with him in a mixture of Italian, German, and improper gesture. Salieri squandered his opportunities in a score with little sense of life or development.

It might be said (without implying a value-judgement) that Paisiello is closer to Mozart, Cimarosa to Rossini. A glance at Cimarosa's duet for two baritones in Act II of *Il matrimonio* ('Se fiate in corpo') at once reveals Rossini's debt, which he was happy to acknowledge: when asked to name his favourite among his own operas, he liked to reply '*Il matrimonio segreto*'. The technique of Paisiello and Cimarosa is neat, polished, light-fingered, but very limited in range, especially in harmonic vocabulary and the avoidance of the minor mode except as a temporary point of contrast (when it can be very effective if well timed, as in Carolina's solo leading to the quintet in Act II of *Il matrimonio segreto*). A favourite method of keeping the music on the boil was to give the principal melody to the orchestra, generally the strings, while the voices declaim against it and the wind add more or less standard punctuation. Cimarosa was a master of this device, which (like the cumulative crescendo) was used by almost everybody; it remained for Rossini to elevate it into a fine art by repeating the tunes in different keys and so timing the modulations that they advance the plot with a satisfying jerk. By comparison the transitions of his predecessors, though based on similar changes of rhythm and key, are more loosely geared to the action. The Act I finale of *Il matrimonio segreto*, which contains a powerful plunge from D to E flat and ends by recalling not only the initial tonic but the opening orchestral melody in altered form, is admirably constructed; but it leaves the dramatic situation exactly where it was before. Every idea is made to go a very long way; the music seldom penetrates below the surface, and never goes deep enough to touch the springs of passion. Cimarosa generally eschews any hint of strong emotion (Paolino's almost Mozartean aria with clarinet obbligato 'Pria che spunti' and Carolina's accompanied recitative on being ordered into a convent, 'Come tacerlo', both in Act II of *Il matrimonio segreto*, are rare exceptions); Paisiello more often strikes a vein of genuine poetry. There are examples in the garden scene (the supposed lunar landscape) in Act II of *Il mondo della luna* with its rustling strings and solo violin and clarinet, another garden scene from the second finale of *Gli astrologi immaginari,* and the Count's serenade with mandoline ('Saper bramate') in *Il barbiere di Siviglia,* which may have suggested Mozart's 'Voi che sapete'.

Opera buffa possessed one advantage in that it was relatively easy to carry on the plot in musical terms, sometimes for considerable stretches; but this was partly nullified by limited characterization. The persons are all types, dramatic and vocal, and generate a stock response. Moreover in ensembles and finales, however skilfully contrived (they often include much padding and repetition), they are apt to forfeit individuality by indiscriminate sharing of the same material. This helps to surmount such dramatic somersaults as Lord Robinson's transference of his affections from one sister to another in order to tidy up the plot of *Il matrimonio segreto.*

OPERA SERIA

The ossification of the joints revealed in *opera buffa* is even more conspicuous in *opera seria,* whose final phase, which persisted until the delayed flowering of Italian romantic opera around 1830, still clung to conventions a full century old. The castrato hero survived into the 1820s, when Meyerbeer wrote *Il crociato in Egitto* (1824) for Giovanni Battista Velluti, the last great operatic castrato, who sang the part in London the following year and did not die till 1861. (He made his début in 1800). Mayr, whose output included no fewer than 32 *opere serie,* wrote parts for Crescentini (*Saffo,* 1794), Marchesi (Ariodante in *Ginevra di Scozia,* 1801), and Velluti (*Raul di Crequi,* 1810), and called for two castratos in *Argene* (1802) and *Alonso e Cora* (1803). If none were available, the hero was sung by a woman soprano or mezzo *en travesti;* as in Handel's day, pitch rather than sex (or its absence) was the determining factor, and the tenor often sang the villain. (Mayr's late opera *Medea in Corinto* however, composed under French influence and produced at Naples in 1813, had two leading tenors, with Isabella Colbran as Medea.) Mayr wrote the chief male part in *Gli Sciti* (1800) for Angelica Catalani; the German heroes of *Adelasia ed Aleramo* (1806, set in the reign of the tenth-century emperor Otto II) and *I Cherusci* (1808, on the Arminio story) were sung by women, as were Achilles in *Il sacrifizio d'Ifigenia* (1811) – though this part was intended for a castrato – and King Alfred in *Alfredo il Grande* (1820). Romeo in the *Romeo and Juliet* operas of Nicola Zingarelli (1796), Nicola Vaccai (1825), and Bellini (1830) was more naturally the province of a woman mezzo; Guglielmi (1810) varied the pattern by making Romeo a tenor and Paris a soprano. Donizetti's *Zoraide di Granata* (1822) and Rossini's *Semiramide* (1824) had female heroes, and there are many *travesti* roles in later Donizetti operas, such as *Lucrezia Borgia* (1833), *Pia de'Tolomei* (1837), and *Maria di Rohan* (1843). Later they were reserved for pages and similar characters, as in *Les Huguenots* and *Un ballo in maschera*, though the heroic mezzo survives even in Wagner's *Rienzi* (1842), written partly under Italian influence.

SERIA LIBRETTOS

Many *opera seria* librettos continued to be based on Greek and Roman history and mythology and the Renaissance epics of Tasso and Ariosto. The French tragedies of Racine, Voltaire (*Sémiramis* was a particular favourite), Lemierre, and Marmontel became popular from the 1790s, followed a little later by English subjects, drawn not only from Shakespeare, Scott, and Byron (whom we encounter, variously transmuted, in Rossini, Donizetti, and Bellini) but from many lesser authors. Part of the success of Mayr's *La rosa rossa e la rosa bianca* (1813, on an early Felice Romani libretto) was attributed to its setting in the Wars of the Roses; the subject of Rossini's *Elisabetta, regina d'Inghilterra* (1815), which antedates Scott's *Kenilworth*, was probably suggested by the recent battle of Waterloo. More exotic settings were much in favour, with scenes laid in Scotland, Asia, and South and Central America; but this was reflected neither in the treatment of the characters nor in the colour of the music.

The eighteenth century offered two models for handling the libretto, the simplified pattern of Calzabigi and the intricate chessboard manoeuvres of Metastasio with their contrived happy end. A few librettists, such as Antonio Sografi in Cimarosa's *Gli Orazi ed i Curiazi* (1796) and Giovanni de Gamerra in Paer's *Achille* (1801), followed the first, which was to lead by way of *La Vestale* to *Norma*; but the second was much the more common until the 1820s. Metastasio's own librettos continued to be set well into the nineteenth century,[1] especially at Venice. Zingarelli's last opera (1811) was a version of Zeno's *Lucio Vero* under the title *Berenice, regina d'Armenia*. Mayr, who had set Metastasio's *Adriano in Siria* in 1798, closed his operatic career in 1824 with the same poet's *Demetrio*, scarcely altering the text apart from the addition of choruses. Although he obtained many librettos from French sources, original or adapted, and encouraged his collaborators to look in that direction, he thoroughly Italianized them. Tragedies by Voltaire (*Adelaide di Guesclino*, 1799; *Gli Sciti*, 1800), Lemierre (*Lanassa*, 1817, on the same subject as Spohr's

---

[1] The latest examples given in Alfred Loewenberg's *Annals of Opera* (Cambridge, 1943) are two works by Baltasar Saldoni, produced at Madrid in 1838 and 1840.

Jessonda), and Racine (*Fedra*, 1821) all emerged with soprano heroes and happy ends. Nothing could better illustrate the conservatism of Mayr and the Italian tradition in general than the treatment of librettos previously used in Paris. *Il sacrifizio d'Ifigenia* (1811) reworks that of Gluck's *Iphigénie en Tauride, Atar* (1814) that of Salieri's *Axur* (originally *Tarare*) with the *semiseria* elements suppressed; in both, earlier Metastasian traits are reinstated. *Alonso e Cora* (1803) is based on the text of Méhul's *Cora, Tamerlano* (1813) on that of Peter von Winter's *Tamerlan*; the former has both a rescue (cancelled by subsequent recapture) and a Metastasian clemency when the Inca decides to abolish the sacrifice of virgins to the sun-god. Mayr reset four *opéra-comique* subjects used by Cherubini (one of them twice), two by Gaveaux, one by Monsigny, and one by Dalayrac. Some of them are discussed below under *opera semiseria*, but several, stripped of their comedy and their revolutionary content, emerged as old-fashioned *opere serie*. The substitution of a soprano for a tenor hero in itself set the French spirit at a distance. The second setting of *Lodoiska* (1799; the first, of 1796, is lost), with a castrato hero, additional subplots and many changes of scene, belongs to a more antique world than the operas of Cherubini and Rodolphe Kreutzer.[1] *Raul di Crequi* (1810) transforms Dalayrac's simple rescue opera of 1789 into a web of Metastasian intrigue; its most prominent character does not appear in Dalayrac at all. *La rosa rossa e la rosa bianca* and *Medea in Corinto* have librettos by Felice Romani based respectively on plots used by Gaveaux (in 1809) and Cherubini (*Médée*). Romani, who gained much of his reputation from these two works and collaborated with Mayr in several others, was too good a dramatist to make Medea repent, but by adding a second pair of estranged lovers he reworked the text backwards towards Metastasio rather than forwards towards Bellini. The tragic dénouement was not unprecedented, as Cimarosa's *Gli Orazi ed i Curiazi* bears witness, but it was unpopular. Paisiello's *Elfrida* (Naples, 1792), like more than one of Rossini's operas, had to be sweetened with a happy end to satisfy the taste of other cities.

USE OF RESOURCES

The musical resources of *opera seria* were naturally more substantial than those of *opera buffa*. The orchestra was larger and more sumptuously deployed, especially by Mayr, who favoured marches and processional movements for instruments alone, though the military rhythms characteristic of all music of the Revolutionary and Napoleonic period are already prominent in Cimarosa's *Gli Orazi ed*

---

[1] Another *Lodoiska*, by Luigi Caruso, was produced at Rome in 1798.

i Curiazi. More extended opportunities were given to the chorus, not only in finales but in arias, ensembles, and separate movements, and here too the credit has been claimed for Mayr. He certainly used it with increasing freedom, at first male voices only (sometimes divided into two national groups, such as Poles and Tartars in *Lodoiska*), and from *I misteri Eleusini* (1802) mixed. But Paisiello, Cimarosa, and other Neapolitans had expanded the role of the chorus long before. Although Paisiello's quite extended treatment of chorus and accompanied recitative in *Fedra* (1788) suggests Gluck to a modern ear, the models are more likely to have been Traetta and Jommelli. In his late operas Cimarosa deployed the male chorus as an effective contrast of timbre with a soaring soprano soloist, sometimes as early as the *introduzione*.

The extreme virtuosity of the solo parts, especially the sopranos, who are regularly endowed with the most dazzling coloratura, is a feature of all *opere serie* of the period. The heroines of Cimarosa's *Oreste* (1783) and *L'Olimpiade* (1784), written for Marina Bertaldi, disport themselves like a piccolo up to G in alt, higher than Mozart's Queen of Night. Mayr liked to flatter his leading sopranos, for example Lodoiska and Cora, with all manner of athletic hurdles, including leaps of two octaves, as soon as they reach the stage. Tusnelda in *I Cherusci*, like Paer's Briseis in *Achille* and Marcellina in *Leonora*, goes rocketing up to D with no justification for the ascent except that, like Mount Everest, the notes are there. The castrato chief suitor in *Il ritorno di Ulisse* (1809) behaves in a similar manner. As with Cimarosa, there is sometimes an obbligato wind instrument in competition. The romantic weakness for lunacy in thirds with a flute can be traced back to Mayr; Donizetti may have remembered the soprano-flute imitations in the finale of the *opera semiseria Amor non ha ritegno* (1804).

The expansion of resources was not balanced by a corresponding increase in power and range of expression. Failure of the music to engage the drama on its own level was the besetting weakness of the whole period. Plots and characters designed to exhibit heroic virtues require dignity and a subtlety in the differentiation of emotions for which there was no place in *opera buffa*; a great figure has all the further to fall. The language of *opera buffa* had made inroads into every kind of music, including that composed for the church, and was not to be controlled except by a genius like Mozart. In one respect it was beneficial: the 'chain finale' modified the stiffness of the stereotyped *opera seria* concluding chorus, turning it into a concerted piece with action. Paisiello claimed this innovation for his *Pirro*

(1787). Otherwise the influence was disastrous: a note of flippant triviality, especially in quick movements, undermined any pretence of dignity in the more solemn scenes and left a vast gap between the aim and the achievement. Attempts to bridge the gap – and not every composer essayed it – led to the inflation of an idiom founded on farce into the insipid or the emptily pretentious just when the context demanded dramatic force and concentration.

PAISIELLO, CIMAROSA, AND OPERA SERIA

It was hardly to be expected that such masters of the soufflé as Paisiello and Cimarosa – though they turned out nearly as many serious as comic operas – should keep a straight face for long among the heroes of Greece and Rome. *Fedra* shows Paisiello wholly unfitted for tragedy. His harmonic vocabulary is too limited to express passion; if he has a good idea, he lets it slip through his fingers. Only Teseo's sombre prayer in Hades rises to the challenge of the text. Cimarosa's *Gli Orazi ed i Curiazi*, the most successful *opera seria* of its decade, has the advantage of Sografi's Calzabigian libretto, which does not dodge the issues. The plot, like that of Gluck's *Orfeo*, is simple in outline – too much so indeed, for it constantly presents the same situation: Orazia torn between love for her brother and her husband Curiazio (a soprano castrato), who must fight to the death for family honour. The story actually retraces its steps between the first two acts. The double tragedy in Act III, in which Marco Orazio after killing Curiazio loses patience with his sister's taunts and stabs her as well, finds Cimarosa at his best. The extended duet has more than his usual theatrical fire and a beautiful initial Andante mosso with long melodic lines over slow-moving harmony. While the language is basically that of *opera buffa* and Cimarosa still almost limits himself to major keys (and not many of them), there are faint romantic hints in Curiazio's short prayer before the oracle speaks in the second finale, in the free design of the previous movement, which contains a little tone-painting with solo clarinet and an imaginative C minor section, and in the tendency to dwell sentimentally on Orazia's predicament. The model here no doubt was Paisiello's *Nina*, a link with the *opera semiseria*. The second finale brings back some material heard earlier; the moral tone of the third, on the dangers of patriotic anger, has a clear contemporary reference.

FERDINANDO PAER

Paer, better known for his *semiseria* works, composed a number of

opere serie on classical subjects, including an *Idomeneo* (1794) and
Achille (1801). The latter, though uneven and untypical in that it was
written for Vienna and has no castrato or *travesti* roles, is one of the
more interesting works of its class. Gamerra, who had collaborated
with Metastasio and Mozart on *Lucio Silla*, presented the Homeric
story without subplots but included many changes of scene, seven in
Act II alone. The issue is love versus patriotism in the heart of
Achilles. The style reflects the cosmopolitan influences Paer had
encountered on his travels: Gluck in the accompanied recitatives and
many short action choruses and, more radically, Mozart. One
Mozartean duet (no. 20[1]) has an impressive modulating arioso, Adagio
non tanto over an ostinato, in which Briseis begs Agamemnon to
restore her to Achilles. But Paer conspicuously failed to grasp the
structural function of Mozart's ensembles and finales: one under-
developed idea is tacked on to another, especially in the finale of
Act II, where potentially fertile material goes to waste. The C minor
funeral march impressed Beethoven, as well it might:

Ex. 154

and there are other points of contact; the chorus in which the
priestesses urge the distressed Briseis to accept Agamemnon (no. 24)
combines charm with harmonic pungency (including semitone clashes)

[1] References are to the contemporary Simrock vocal score (Bonn, n.d.).

in a not dissimilar style. From time to time Paer rises to his theme, as in the unison chorus of Greeks abducting Briseis (no. 17), *sempre sotto voce*, ending in the tonic minor, and the multipartite duet with chorus (no. 26) for Achilles and Patroclus just before the latter's death. But Paer's dramatic sense is spasmodic and his melodic invention, though graceful, lacks profile and variety. *Buffo* mannerisms are still present; the quartet in the first finale makes good use of a running orchestral melody against independent voice parts. Both the opening and the close of the opera are unorthodox, though not particularly successful: the *introduzione* telescopes the functions of overture (four orchestral sections) and first chorus, as Gluck and Mozart had done; the finale, after quoting two themes from the *introduzione*, ends with 84 Allegro maestoso bars for orchestra alone, representing either a military parade or Achilles's fight with Hector.

SIMON MAYR

Mayr's serious operas employ a similar idiom, rather more purposefully in ensembles (especially in the later works). But he had little sense of character – he scarcely attempted to differentiate secondary persons – and his solo movements fall into a few restricted categories. The lively passages tend towards empty display, the slow towards a wan lyricism. Many of his scores, like others of the period – for example Zingarelli's *Giulietta e Romeo* (1796) and the *Romeo e Giulietta* (1810) of Pietro Carlo Guglielmi (1763–1817) – are sicklied o'er with prayers, often attractively scored (the harp was a favourite instrument in this context) but of distressing banality and even flippancy, like Penelope's address to Minerva in Act II of *Il ritorno di Ulisse*. Prayers were by now a regular feature of *opera seria*, whether as solos, duets, or choruses – Paer's *Achille* has examples of all three – and were often prominently placed at the beginning of acts or in finales. The famous examples in *Mosè* and *Nabucco* had many antecedents in Mayr and his contemporaries.

Mayr's operas are full of situations that seem ripe for romantic treatment, and sometimes received it in the work of his successors. In *Labino e Carlotta* (1799) the eloping lovers are held up by a broken bridge and the heroine saves the situation by snatching a pistol from the wicked Baron, an action parallelled of course in the Leonora operas; *Raul di Crequi* (1809) has an offstage chorus of sculptors working in a valley and praising their art while the disguised hero descends from a mountain; the hero of *I Cherusci* (1808) sings a cavatina with harp accompaniment outside a tower in which Tusnelda is imprisoned. There are big military spectacles, battles, storms, hunts, and nature pieces, sometimes several of these in combination. They clearly derive from the *opéra comique* of the Revolution; yet although Mayr makes liberal use of choral and orchestral forces, scarcely a hint of romanticism seeps into the music, and only a pale echo of Cherubinian energy. It is true that, although the armies of France overran Italy as well as Germany, French music was slow to make its mark, at any rate before the Naples productions of *Iphigénie en Aulide* and *La Vestale* in 1811–12.[1] But Mayr was a learned musician, whose library contained a number of French opera scores. Evidently his creative personality was not strong enough to digest or develop what he found; he merely reduced it to domesticity. There are hints of deeper commitment, for example the B flat minor march towards the end of Act II of *Telemacco* (1797), strikingly scored for wind, violas, and basses, and Carlo's big scene of remorse in Act II of *Adelaide di Guesclino* (1799) and the C minor chorus that follows. The chorus of hermits in *Ginevra di Scozia* (1801) and such violent finales as that of Act I of *Raul di Crequi* bring a whiff of the revolutionary spirit. So in a different way does the anticlerical propaganda in *Alonso e Cora* (1803), possibly an accidental survival from Méhul's libretto. But if Mayr borrowed a little from the French, he repaid them more liberally through Spontini, who learned much from his treatment of the orchestra and surely recalled in *La Vestale* the rather Glucklike funeral march when the heroine of *Alonso e Cora* is condemned to be buried alive.

A different debt is apparent in a group of middle-period operas – *I misteri Eleusini, Alonso e Cora, Zamori, I Cherusci* – which make a feature of solemn scenes of pagan religion in temples or hidden valleys, with a great deal of marching and ritual. The model is obviously *Die Zauberflöte*, which is often echoed in detail, and there is nearly always a sonorous bass High Priest; it is no surprise that the Chief Druid in *I Cherusci* is called Zarastro. Mayr's frequent storms, nearly always in D minor with chromatic scale figures and the full orchestra busily employed, have parallels in France, but the link is quite as strong with *Don Giovanni*. That opera left an obvious mark on Polinesso's music in *Ginevra di Scozia*, on much of *Adelasia ed Aleramo* (1806), on the raging heroine of *Medea in Corinto* (1813), and elsewhere. Mayr's serious operas leave the impression of a cenotaph waiting for an occupant; of an eclectic artist who never overthrew and seldom disturbed a convention, but left a building swept and garnished for his successors.

[1] Gluck's *Armide* and *Iphigénie en Tauride* were not performed in Italy until 1890 and 1922 respectively.

Medea in Corinto is probably his finest achievement, thanks to the grip that Medea's daemonic character exercised on his imagination. Her invocation in prison to the powers of hell, answered by a chorus of Furies, and the finale of Act II, while palpably indebted to Cherubini and *Don Giovanni* – the invocation is in D minor, the finale begins in C minor and ends the opera in D minor – develop genuine power and grandeur. Perhaps as a result of the recent Naples production of *La Vestale*, Mayr's contract specified that the opera should be composed 'in the French manner'. This and Cherubini's treatment of the same subject ensured that the latter's influence is stronger here than elsewhere. The Act I duet for Medea and Jason with its agitated accompaniment figures and the wedding chorus in the first finale seem to have been directly modelled on *Médée*. But it is only in the scenes for Medea herself that Mayr approaches the driving energy of his predecessor. Elsewhere, despite high technical finish, sensuous scoring (from solo woodwind to heavy brass) and in the ensembles a sense of harmonic movement undoubtedly derived from Mozart, he drops back into the superficial bustle of the *buffo* idiom, for example in the two vengeance duets for Medea and Egeo in Act II, where a serious situation is marred by inanely cheerful music. Too few of the ideas carry the weight placed upon them; the lyrical movements in particular incline to a self-indulgent blandness. The opera is historically important as one of Rossini's models for *Elisabetta*, produced in the same theatre less than two years later. Romani's superior dramaturgy enabled Mayr to increase the ratio of ensembles and abridge that of *secco* recitative; at the 1813 première he anticipated Rossini by dropping the latter altogether, but he reverted to it in revivals.

OPERA SEMISERIA

An intermediate type of opera combining features from *seria* and *buffa* was a logical development in an age when literary and political influences were impinging more and more on the theatre. The *opera semiseria*, first so-called about 1800, grew from a number of roots. Giovanni Battista Lorenzi in his preface to Cimarosa's *L'infedeltà fedele* (Naples, 1779) specifically claimed an intention to create something between the two older forms. About the same time Giovanni Bertati and Giovanni Battista Casti evolved the *dramma eroicomico*, sometimes, as in *Il rè Teodoro a Venezia* (Casti – Paisiello, 1784) combining the comic element with historical personages.[1] Other early and related examples were *Il cavaliere errante* (Bertati – Traetta,

[1] See Edward J. Dent, *The Rise of Romantic Opera* (Cambridge, 1976), pp. 35 ff.

1778), *Orlando Paladino* (Porta – Haydn, 1782), *La grotta di Trofonio* (Casti – Salieri, 1785), *Don Giovanni Tenorio* (Bertati – Gazzaniga, 1787, related to Mozart's opera, which itself almost qualifies as *semiseria*), *Axur* (Da Ponte – Salieri, 1788, an adaptation of Salieri's French *Tarare* of the previous year on a libretto by Beaumarchais), and several operas by Giuseppe Gazzaniga, Francesco Bianchi, and others in the 1790s. A little later came the *farsa sentimentale* and *melodramma sentimentale*, in which comedy bowed to bourgeois sentiment. Marcos Antonio Portugal's *La madre virtuosa* (Venice, 1798) is an early instance, and three of Mayr's operas based on *opéra comique* librettos bore this title.

The sentimental element can be traced as far back as Piccinni's *La buona figliuola* (Rome, 1760),[1] in which Goldoni blended traditional *buffo* comedy with a vein of sentiment drawn from his literary source, Richardson's *Pamela*. The catalyst however was *opéra comique*, first the pre-Revolution *comédie larmoyante*, linked with the writings of Rousseau and his followers and popularized by Grétry and (especially) Dalayrac, and later the *fait historique*, though its realism was considerably modified. The great majority of *semiseria* librettos for the next two generations were derived from French sources, plays, *opéras comiques*, *mélodrames*, and even ballet scenarios. The mingling of genres had at first only a mild effect on the music, but it led eventually, by way of such works as *La gazza ladra*, *Emilia di Liverpool*, *La sonnambula*, and *Linda di Chamounix* to the domestic drama of Verdi's *Stiffelio* and *La traviata*. The link with romantic opera becomes explicit in Donizetti's *Otto mesi in due ori* (*Gli esiliati in Siberia*) of 1827, which is specifically entitled *opera romantica*. From the start *opera semiseria* rejected castratos and classical heroes and heroines; it brought the serious characters down to the plebeian level of contemporary life, sometimes reducing comedy and intrigue to insignificance; but it carried neither the ideological drive of the French Revolution nor the German preoccupation with the supernatural.

One of the most successful and influential works of the age, originally given in one act with spoken dialogue (very rare in Italy, though sometimes used in Naples), later in two acts with recitative, was Paisiello's *Nina ossia la pazza per amore* (1789) with a libretto translated from Dalayrac's *opéra comique* of three years earlier. The

---

[1] See Vol. VII, pp. 49 ff.

very simple plot concerns a girl who goes out of her mind when her lover, rejected by her father, is reported killed in a duel, but re-enters it when he returns forgiven. This is the only event in the story. The opera begins after the dramatic climax (the rejection and departure of Lindoro) and plays continually on the same situation, from which librettist and composer extract the maximum of sentimental appeal, despatching the minor characters with the bare clichés of *opera buffa*. Paisiello's concentration of all his resources, melodic, harmonic, and orchestral, on a single target – slow drooping melodic lines, lachrymose lingering over Neapolitan sixth chords and mildly chromatic inner parts, plangent treatment of wind instruments, especially the flute but also bassoons and horns, local colour in the form of a shepherd's song evoking bagpipes and the open air (an idea taken straight from Dalayrac) – inaugurated a new operatic climate that was to have major consequences later. Nina's first utterance, a cavatina in free rondo form with an early modulation to the mediant minor and broken phrases at the end to indicate pathetic insanity

Ex. 155

(My love when he comes to see the unhappy girl)

and the G minor aria with female chorus 'Lontana da te', also in Act
I, in which she and her companions lament the loss of Lindoro and she
sinks into chromatic despair

Ex. 156

(Far from you, Lindoro my dear, Nina languishes for love.)

are fundamental sources for the style of Bellini.

PAER AND *SEMISERIA*

Paer devoted much of his career to *opera semiseria*. In *La virtù al
cimento* (1798), also known as *Griselda* and based on Boccaccio's tale,
the Marchese humiliates his low-born but faithful wife in order to
convince his proud sister that wealth is not everything, and further
torments her by pretending that their daughter is dead. *Camilla* (1799),
I fuorusciti in Firenze (1802), *Sargino* (1803), and *Leonora* (1804) all
derive from French rescue opera; *Camilla* and *Sargino* are based on
Dalayrac librettos, *Leonora* on the Bouilly text used by Gaveaux,
Beethoven, and Mayr. *Agnese di FitzHenry* (1809), from a novel by
Amelia Opie, is a development of the *Nina* idea: a mad father, who is
tended by two comic and ineffectual doctors, is cured by the music of
his daughter. *Camilla*, also set by Fioravanti, brings the child of a
broken marriage on the stage and gives him quite an important part;

the appeal is to our pity for the mother, imprisoned and condemned by her tyrannical husband. This makes room for two affecting prayers, one a duet with the boy. *Sargino*, a *dramma eroicomico* set in the reign of Philip Augustus of France and culminating in the Battle of Bouvines – which provides a spectacular Cherubinian finale (the opera's only piece in a minor key), during which a village is sacked and burned – has a rather silly plot about a timorous youth who is despised by his father because he has failed to achieve knighthood. The king however trusts the boy, who saves his life in the battle, thereby winning his spurs and the girl.

The serious element in the plots, which more and more outweighs the comic without transmuting the musical idiom, exposes the weakness in Paer's approach, in particular his inability to differentiate his characters. They all discourse in a facile sub-Mozartean idiom with little rhythmic or harmonic variety; the avoidance of the minor mode seems almost pathological. The melodies, like Mayr's and Winter's, are either mellifluously insipid or encrusted with parasitic coloratura, sometimes both. Griselda, for all her patience, is not averse to vocal leaps of a thirteenth. A modulation from E flat to C in the first finale of this opera appears to have been suggested by the Act II finale of *Figaro*, but the mild chromatic harmony, chiefly the product of appoggiaturas, always stops short of Mozartean bite. There is more vitality in episodes that to our ears prefigure Rossini, though they derive from Cimarosa: the simmering first finale of *Camilla*, the agitated male quartet in Act II with two characters on each side of a door (the timing of the early plunge from A to C sounds particularly Rossinian), and the spirited overture to *Sargino*. A few details show genuine imagination: a modulation in Loredano's Act I aria in *Camilla* (which has no counterpart in Dalayrac's opera),

Ex. 157

(Oh gods, what if she were to suffer because of my mistake! A thousand torments and pains)

the delightful canonic round for Adolfo and his parents, and the attractive main theme of the Act I love duet for Sargino and Soffia, which occurs only in the orchestra:

Ex. 158

moves through a series of expressive modulations (C – A minor – E flat), and could almost be by Bellini.

SEMISERIA OPERAS BY MAYR

Mayr adopted the *semiseria* type a little later, writing eight such works between 1801 and 1814. All have French literary connections. Two – *I due giornate* (1801, revived with much new music in 1807) and *Elisa* (1804) – cling to well-known librettos set by Cherubini, whose influence also appears in the music, as was tartly pointed out by the critic of the *Allgemeine musikalische Zeitung* after the 1816 revival of the former. This opera has an unusually high proportion of ensembles to solos, including four trios in Act I. Both works incorporate actual themes from Cherubini; Mayr had a faculty for carrying his imitations to the point of plagiarism, though his victim was more often Mozart. *I due giornate* is labelled *eroicomico*, *Elisa farsa sentimentale*, but there is no difference in style, and the comic element is very slight. It is more prominent in *Amor non ha ritegno* (1804), which has an amusing hunting scene by inversion, in which two comic lovers (attended by four horns, one pair on stage) are chased up trees by a wild boar. *La roccia di Frauenstein* (1805), with a libretto imitated from Paer's *I fiorusciti in Firenze* (1802), contains a typical hunt and storm, *Le due duchesse* (1814), on a French melodrama set in Saxon England during the reign of King Edgar, a wolf hunt. *L'amor filiale* (1811) goes right back to Monsigny's primitive rescue opera *Le Déserteur* with the scene transferred to Poland; in *Elena* (1814), as in the *Leonora* operas, the heroine is disguised as a man, and the action (near Arles) conforms to the Revolution terror type.

Le due duchesse is advanced in design, thanks to Romani's contraction of the *secco* recitative and complex lay-out of set numbers. The *introduzione* has eleven sections, including a French-style romanza for Loredano, Conte di Devonshire, accompanied by guitar and pizzicato strings. Some of the bigger pieces, such as Laura's Act I cavatina (in five sections) and the substantial duet for Malvina and Loredano in Act II – in the third (12/8) movement of which she begs her father not to betray her while the hunt is approaching in the distance – look forward in plan to the later Bellini and Donizetti. The

Act I finale contains a melody that strikingly anticipates the second subject of the *Euryanthe* overture, presumably by coincidence. Significantly, according to a report in the *Allgemeine musikalische Zeitung* for November 1814, Mayr was criticized for running movements together and combining opposed styles – which he did in more than one sense: Edgar's entrance aria begins as a siciliano and ends as a *Ländler*.

LÉONORE OPERAS BY MAYR AND PAER

Nothing could better illustrate the Italian debasement of the French Revolution style than the two works based on Bouilly's *Léonore*. Both omit the chorus of prisoners, and Mayr eliminates the political motive altogether.[1] In his libretto, which again transfers the action to Poland, Moroski (Pizarro) is less a blusterer than a cunning coward, a figure almost devoid of menace, and his motive is lust for Zeliska (Leonora); the avaricious Rocco becomes the bibulous Peters; Amorveno (Florestan) is rescued by the fortuitous arrival of his brother-in-law. Paer grossly expands Marcellina's role for a favourite singer with a high E flat. She is an outrageous flirt, and breaks into the dungeon scene (having stolen the key from Rocco) between Pizarro's exit and the reunion of the lovers, who have great difficulty in getting rid of her; Leonora is compelled to assure her of her love in a long duet in the presence of her husband. Mayr makes some attempt at continuity in the dungeon scene, which includes a 6/8 strophic romanza in French style and the minor mode for Zeliska, hoping that Amorveno may recognize her voice:

Ex. 159

U - na mo - glie sven - tu - ra - ta cui ra - pir lo spo - so a -

---

[1] For a full account of Mayr's opera (full score ed. Arrigo Gazzaniga, Bergamo, 1967) see Mosco Carner, 'Simone Mayr and his "L'amor coniugale"', *Music and Letters*, lii (1971), p. 239. On Paer's, see 'Paërs "Leonora" und Beethovens "Fidelio"', by Richard Engländer, *Neues Beethoven Jahrbuch*, Jg. iv, p. 118.

-ma - to   lo   ri - cer - ca in o - gni   la - to

(An unfortunate wife whose husband has been taken from her searches for him eveywhere)

But he muffs the trumpet signal and extends every movement to a length that becomes counterproductive. Both composers give each of the lovers an extended *scena* on an enormous scale (longer than Beethoven's), consisting of several linked movements with accompanied recitatives introduced by huge ritornellos. Their style is very similar: the ritornellos and recitatives expressive if sometimes bland, the later sections, especially the cabalettas, tailing off into Mozartean or Neapolitan formulae. That manner is not inapt for the minor characters, but most of the serious scenes fall below the implications of the text, a defect compounded in Mayr by palpable echoes of all four of Mozart's most popular operas. In Paer the influence comes almost exclusively from *Figaro*: Marcellina and Giacchino, especially in their duet, are pale reflections of Susanna and Figaro, just as the military episodes in his *Sargino* (1803) can scarcely escape from 'Non più andrai'. Paer's *Leonora* contains one fine stroke in the return of a Leonora motive, heard three times in the overture, when she gives Florestan a drink in the dungeon scene:

Ex. 160

There is even a momentary hint of Beethoven in the bleak octaves, answered by a warm phrase in the major,[1] during the C minor ritornello (38 slow bars) to Florestan's aria at the start of Act II. Moroski's outburst during Mayr's finale is one of many derivatives at this period from Cherubini's Dourlinski.

[1] Quoted in Engländer, op. cit., p. 129.

FORMS AND HARMONY

The serious scenes in the *Leonora* operas show the multipartite aria as Rossini was to take it up. In the 1790s (and earlier) most arias and duets in all types of opera, when they extended beyond a single movement – which could be in ternary or simple sonata form, the latter derived from the first part of the old *da capo* aria – adopted a rudimentary cavatina–cabaletta design without intervening recitative or dramatic development, the quick conclusion in a different metre. The strophic cabaletta came later. Orazia's E flat aria in Act II of *Gli Orazi ed i Curiazi* exceptionally has three sections, in the last of which she reacts to a changed situation. Paer's earlier works offered little advance, though he frequently added a *più allegro* coda in an effort to whip things up. The more ambitious expansion into four or five sections seems to have been largely due to Mayr, though he seldom achieved a cumulative tension. Usually one of the inner sections is a slow cantabile pitched a major or minor third away from the main key, which is restored in a cabaletta, but still in the major mode; an A flat cantabile in a C major aria was a favourite choice, as it was with Rossini. This tonal plan occurs again and again in set pieces, including finales, not so much to make a dramatic point as to give variety. Movements like the slow sextet with solo clarinet in the second finale of *Elena* are the ancestors of many cantabile ensembles at similar points in the operas of Rossini and still more of Bellini and Donizetti. Finales show little advance on the chain type, though their constituents are more varied. Mayr was seldom able to maintain a corresponding degree of tension in the music; Paer's ensembles and finales are often no more than a string of unstructured episodes that fidget from one tempo, key, or rhythm to another.

The switch of a third was much favoured for modulations within a movement, in serious and comic contexts, and in the wake of Mozart became a mannerism of the whole period. Cimarosa used it to good purpose in *Gli Orazi ed i Curiazi* and *Il matrimonio per raggiro* (in one duet as early as the third bar of the Allegro vivace), as did Paer in the hero's first aria in *Achille*. Mayr associated it with sudden changes of fortune (the capture of the fugitive lovers in Act II of *La roccia di Frauenstein*) and the thought of death (Penelope's lament in Act I of *Il ritorno di Ulisse*, the love duet in Act I of *Le due duchesse*, Bombarow's buffo aria in *L'amor filiale*, which modulates from C to E flat minor and later to E flat major in parody of the serious style). Paer in *Achille* marks the hero's resolution to return to the field and avenge Patroclus by a jump from B flat to C, and the quartet towards the end of the opera in which Achilles under the High Priest's threat of pestilence consents to restore Briseis to her father is so well articulated by harmonic means as to suggest contact with Beethoven. Mayr, as befitted a German, occasionally used fugal texture in finales (*Lodoiska, Belle ciarle e fatti tristi, Un vero originale*), but seems to have avoided the canonic round that became a common and often strikingly successful feature of the period. It is not clear who introduced this device into opera. There are two examples in Martín y Soler's *Una cosa rara* (1786) – one of them, a female trio, perhaps Mozart's model in *Così fan tutte* – and others before the turn of the century in the second finale of Paisiello's *Nina* and Act II of Paer's *Camilla*. These are both trios; Paer's is one of the finest movements in any of his operas.

As in France, the older dance forms like the minuet yielded to more plebeian types, of which the most popular was the polacca. If this was a French export, it spread very rapidly. Vocal movements in this catchy rhythm, not inspired by anything Polish in the text, became very common, especially in cabalettas. They appear in Winter's *I fratelli rivali* (1793), Paer's *L'intrigo amoroso* (1795), *Griselda*, and *Sargino*, and a whole range of Mayr's operas of all three types, from *Avviso ai maritati* (1798) to *Alfredo il Grande* (1820), where the soprano monarch releases one in the second finale. The waltz also made its operatic bow at this time. Mayr wrote vocal pieces in waltz or *Ländler* rhythm in *L'amor filiale*, the *introduzione* of *Elena*, and *Le due duchesse*, and there is a curious orchestral specimen in 3/8, marked *sgarbato* and deliberately crude, in Act I of Paer's *Camilla*. Another oddity is a minuet in common time during the male trio in Act II of *Sargino*.

MAYR'S TREATMENT OF THE ORCHESTRA

The one department in which important advances were made was the treatment of the orchestra. The credit for this belongs principally to Mayr, though Paer too showed enterprise, especially after he left Italy and had absorbed the lessons of Mozart. (Paer's treatment of the woodwind in *Leonora* is one of the most satisfying features of the opera.) Mayr's influence on the whole Italian school – Rossini, Mercadante, Pacini, Bellini, Donizetti, and the young Verdi – was far-reaching. Cimarosa wrote occasionally for mandoline (*La finta Parigina*, 1773), harp (*L'Armida immaginaria*, a comic opera, 1777) and trombones (*Chi dell'altrui si veste, presto si spoglia*, 1783; *Penelope*, 1794), but they were not part of his regular orchestra. Mayr carried much of Mozart's technique across the Alps, especially the rich concertato treatment of solo wind instruments, and something from the French: the triple division of the cellos in Méhul's manner[1] (*Ercole in Lidia, Amor non ha ritegno*), a theme and variations with solo violin, cello, and bassoon, as used by Gaveaux and Boieldieu, to accompany a scene change in *Di locanda in locanda* (1805), trumpet and horn signals in the rescue scenes of *Lodoiska, La roccia di Frauenstein*, and *I Cherusci*. Like several contemporaries (including Paer and Sebastiano Nasolini (1768–1816?)) but to an even greater degree, he wrote obbligato parts of the utmost elaboration for every instrument in the orchestra from the flute to the double bass, which accompanies an uncouth German lover in *Amor non ha ritegno*. A clarinet obbligato in *Il caretto del venditore d'aceto* (1800) recalls *La clemenza di Tito*. Mayr's first opera *Saffo* (1794) employs a cor anglais and two *cornettini* as well as the now not unusual quartet of horns. He was partial to the cor anglais, introducing a pair of them in at least seven operas between *Labino e Carlotta* (1799) and *Gli Americani* (1806), and obbligatos for a single instrument in several others. He used the harp freely, alone and as part of the orchestral texture, in solos (especially prayers), choruses, and sometimes in overtures. Seven of his lighter operas contain obbligatos for guitar; the earliest, for *chitarra francese* in *Che originali* (1798), may have been suggested by Mozart's treatment of the mandoline in *Don Giovanni*. The score of *Di locanda in locanda* calls for a piano.

Mayr often wrote for wind instruments without strings, in purely orchestral movements and in vocal pieces. Two horns by themselves are so used in *Che originali* and with growing frequency later. Part of an aria for the castrato hero of *Lodoiska* is supported by eleven wind instruments. The serious operas after 1800 are full of choruses and marches with wind accompaniment, supplemented on occasion by a sizeable battery of percussion; often they approach *come da lontano*, a favourite direction from *Ercole in Lidia* onwards. *Alonso e Cora*, set in Peru, has an exceptionally large wind band for the period in Italy: piccolo, two each of flutes, oboes, cors anglais, clarinets, bassoons, and trumpets, four horns, and 'contratuba', with percussion to match. *Zamori*, built on a similar scale, fields two stage bands, including a serpent. Such demonstrations were doubtless the models for Spontini's *Fernand Cortez* and the notorious *banda* of Mercadante and Verdi. Orchestral inflation increased with the passage of time: *Tamerlano* (1813) has a barbaric march in C sharp minor with fourteen wind instruments and full Turkish percussion, and a tuba part in the final

---

[1] In the overture to his *Ariodant*.

chorus. (Ludwig Schiedermair suggests[1] that this was the *tuba curva* of the French Revolution pageants and Méhul's *Joseph*, but there is no evidence that such an instrument crossed the French frontier.) *Medea in Corinto* of the same year has three trombones and a serpent.

Mixed chamber groups are a feature of Mayr's orchestration, again perhaps suggested by Mozart: two clarinets, two bassoons, two horns, two violins, and one cello to introduce a duet in *Lodoiska*, two violins and two oboes to suggest a nightingale in *Adelasia ed Aleramo*, two clarinets, two bassoons, three horns, and a solo double bass pizzicato for a Mozartean notturno in *Belle ciarle e fatti tristi*. A scene in *Alfredo il Grande* in which the hero, disguised as a bard, is accompanied by a solo group of violin, clarinet, cor anglais, horn, cello, and harp was hailed by contemporaries as a masterpiece. Donizetti inherited this technique, and Verdi was to employ it with rich effect from early in his career. Mayr often attempts orchestral tone-painting, from the pastoral in the garden scene of *I finti rivali* (with violin and four solo wind variously combined) to the barbaric (the Tartars in *Lodoiska*), and frequently in storms, which are associated with hunts, shipwrecks (*Telemacco* and the opening of *Il ritorno di Ulisse*), and a volcanic eruption and earthquake (*Alonso e Cora*). The boldness of the conception is seldom matched by the material; it was left to Mayr's successors to exploit the vein. His few supernatural scenes, like those of his Italian contemporaries and successors, never transcend the conventional treatment of oracles. Once or twice in his comedies a character masquerades as a ghost. When the heroines of *Amor ingegnoso* (1799) and *Amore non soffre opposizione* (1810) are thus disguised, Mayr writes in the *opera seria* manner, accompanying the voice in one instance with two horns and a bassoon, in the other with wind over a low cello tremolo. The intention was presumably parodistic, but the music could equally fit a serious context.

ROSSINI

Gioacchino Rossini (1792–1868) is in many respects a puzzling figure, by no means so simple as he appears at first glance. By far the most immediately successful opera composer not only of his own age but of any other, his active career lasted less than twenty years (1810–29); despite a few fiascos, most of them temporary like the notorious first night of *Il barbiere di Siviglia*, it brought him continuous public

---

[1] *Beiträge zur Geschichte der Oper um die Wende des 18. und 19. Jh.* (Leipzig, two vols., 1907 and 1910).

acclamation wherever his operas were played.[1] Nor did this fade during the 39 years that remained of his life, despite developments without precedent in the history of the form. While the twentieth century, until recently, remembered him as the author of one immortal comedy (not the most popular in his own day), his contemporaries ranked him among the greatest serious composers of the age.

Of his 34 Italian operas thirteen (five of them in one act) belong to the *buffa* type, three to the *semiseria*, eighteen to the *seria*. There was remarkably little overlap of time between the two main classes. Most of the comedies belong to the early peripatetic years in north Italy and Rome; Rossini virtually renounced the form with the production of *La Cenerentola* in January 1817 before his 25th birthday. In 1815 the impresario Domenico Barbaja engaged him as director of the two Naples theatres at a generous regular salary. Required to compose only one opera a year, he could devote more time and care to the work while continuing to accept outside engagements. Apart from a few comedies for which he may have been already contracted, he turned entirely to serious opera. Between mid-1817 and 1822 his more important operas were written for Naples, and all of them, like his last Italian opera *Semiramide* (Venice, 1823), belonged to the *seria* class.

It has been suggested that this change of direction was due to the influence of the great soprano Isabella Colbran, his prima donna in Naples, whom he married tardily in 1822, and that it represented a denial of his true gifts. It was more probably a deliberate choice. Rossini was not the man to abandon a profitable enterprise without a strong incentive; moreover he had already composed five serious operas, one of which, *Tancredi*, was an instant and lasting success. Posterity has accepted Beethoven's remark (to the composer in 1822) that Rossini was made for *opera buffa* and should stick to it; Beethoven in fact extended the dictum to cover all Italian composers. While Rossini's genius for *opera buffa* is incontestable, the revival in recent years of more than two dozen of his operas of all types – some of them in corrupt versions that can be justified neither by the defects of the originals nor by Rossini's own occasional misdeeds – has confirmed the evidence of the scores that the high rank once accorded to his serious works, though exaggerated, did not lack some foundation. It is possible with hindsight to see in him an artist born to rescue serious opera from the slough into which it had fallen and establish a style in

---

[1] Philip Gossett, *The Operas of Rossini: Problems of Textual Criticism in Nineteenth-Century Opera* (Diss. Princeton, 1970), lists the following numbers of printed librettos, each representing a different production, for some of Rossini's operas to the end of 1830 alone: *L'inganno felice* 26, *Tancredi* 41, *L'Italiana in Algeri* 44, *Il barbiere di Siviglia* 20, *Otello* 54, *La Cenerentola* 49, *La gazza ladra* 34, *Mosè in Egitto* (incl. the Paris revision) 42, *La donna del lago* 35, *Semiramide* 31.

which romantic content was balanced by classical form. He had a technical ability beyond Bellini, Donizetti, Meyerbeer or even Weber, and he began with greater natural advantages than Verdi. He also commanded the imaginative range, as some superb scenes in the Naples operas indicate. Yet having demonstrated that the task was within his range he left it incomplete, contenting himself with a single masterpiece written for a foreign capital.

The juxtaposition of exaggerated *buffo* mannerisms and hints of passionate, even tragic emotion worthy of middle-period Verdi, is a symptom, not the cause; the two styles were intertwined before Rossini began to compose. The transference of material from serious to comic operas and vice versa was not in itself a sin against the canons of art; nor was the re-use of old music, even when it remained unaltered, which was by no means always the case. Rossini generally confined himself to raiding scores that had been dismissed by the public;[1] this was the common practice of Bellini, Donizetti, and many others and not disdained by Weber or even Wagner. The score of *Il barbiere di Siviglia* (1816) contains at least ten self-borrowings, from three comic and three serious operas and three cantatas; but only the overture, from *Aureliano in Palmira* (1813) via *Elisabetta, regina d'Inghilterra* (1815)), and the storm, from *La pietrà del paragone* (1812), retain their identity. It was normal for composers to write new arias for singers at revivals, thereby producing several equally authentic versions of the same opera; this seldom involved alteration to the plot. Nor can Rossini's reversion to *secco* recitative after abandoning it in *Elisabetta* and *Otello*, or his willingness to sublet the composition of secondary arias even at the first performance of his works (to one Agolini in *La Cenerentola*, Michele Carafa in *Mosè in Egitto*, an unknown hand in *Adina*, Giovanni Pacini in *Matilde di Shabran*) be put down to anything worse than opportunism and haste. Much more open to censure is Rossini's failure to stand by his convictions in the matter of tragic ends. The most notorious example is the Rome revival of *Otello* in 1820, when he not only left the hero and Desdemona contentedly in each other's arms but cut the gondolier's offstage solo, threw in a duet from *Armida* and a finale from *Ricciardo e Zoraide*, and inverted the verbal sense of some of the recitatives.[2] This was not a unique instance. *Tancredi* as first composed had a feeble happy end; at Ferrara in March 1813, a month after the première, Rossini restored

---

[1] Not quite always: he borrowed from *Il barbiere* in *Cenerentola*, and from *Cenerentola* in *La gazza ladra*. Gossett, op. cit., has shown that the quotation from the famous 'La calunnia' crescendo from *Il barbiere* in Act III of *Otello*, which appears in the printed score, was at some time modified by Rossini in the autograph.

[2] This revival contained no new music, although Rossini was himself in charge: see Gossett, op. cit., pp. 316–21.

Voltaire's conclusion, in which Tancredi dies; but he hastily retreated when the public disliked it.[1] He gave *Maometto II* a happy end at Venice in 1823, signing off with the rondo-finale of *La donna del lago*.

Such evidence of a weak artistic conscience should perhaps be attributed not so much to the time-serving cynicism of which Rossini has been accused as to fear, a major defect in a creative artist. It seems likely that his early successes were too easily won, and that he was loth to cut himself off from the applause of the public when his subject demanded a leap into dangerous waters. He glimpsed the promised land, but a native insecurity that all his worldly success could not dispel prevented him taking the decisive step to occupy it. The artistic dilemma into which this led him – the instinctive knowledge that he ought to pull up his roots on the one hand and a fear of consequent failure on the other – is the most probable cause of his withdrawal from the theatre in 1829. He could still compose, and his style was capable of development, as the late works for private performance testify; but a refusal to face the hazard of public disapproval reduced his principal career to silence.

Rossini accepted only one libretto that had been used before (*L'italiana in Algeri*, set by Luigi Mosca in 1808), but he lacked literary taste and was a poor judge of a dramatic text. Here again early success may have been a disadvantage. The eighteen-year-old Rossini had enormous talent, and something more. His extraordinary facility and ebullience enabled him from the first to endow ill-constructed, chaotic, and uncouth librettos with a fund of intoxicating music. He must have thought that the public would swallow almost anything in the guise of an *opera buffa*. Nor was he far wrong. Not surprisingly it was the best libretto that inspired the most perfect of his comedies. *Il barbiere di Siviglia*, based on a literary classic, gave Rossini not only every chance to develop his comic genius, but a fool-proof framework in which to display it. In a sense it was a brilliant fluke. Had he insisted on a similar standard in his other librettos, he might have equalled or surpassed his acknowledged comic masterpiece.

LA GAZZA LADRA

It is surprising that Rossini did not grasp the opportunities presented by the *opera semiseria*, especially as in 1817, on turning away from *opera buffa*, he created in that form one of his most artistically successful and satisfying works. The libretto of *La gazza ladra*, based on a French *mélodrame*, springs from the domestic realism of the *opéra comique* of the Revolution, the tap-root of

[1] The Ferrara end, recently discovered by Gossett, was restored in the Rome production of 1977.

romantic opera. The heroine Ninetta is a servant girl condemned to death, at the instance of an official whose advances she has rejected, for thefts that prove to be the work of a magpie. (The bird has an acting, speaking, and singing part.) Ninetta's fate also involves her father Fernando, a fugitive from a capital charge (striking a superior officer), who gives himself up in the hope of saving her life. The swings of mood between comedy and near-tragedy allow Rossini to exploit both styles, and for the most part he keeps them admirably in focus with the development of the plot. The opening scenes are pure *buffo*, and so is the conclusion with its hint of a vaudeville. When the drama grows more serious, the music rises with it. The principal characters are all villagers, with whom Rossini clearly felt at home; they are among the most sharply drawn in any of his operas. Ninetta is a touching figure, as is her peasant-boy admirer Pippo, a coloratura mezzo; best of all is the Podestà, who begins with a *buffo* aria very like 'Largo al factotum' but soon emerges in the sinister role of a village Scarpia, a relative of Cherubini's Dourlinski and Beethoven's Pizarro. The Act I trio in which he tries to take advantage of Ninetta, the disguised Fernando rebukes him for abusing his official position, and Ninetta urges her father to escape before he gives himself away, is no mere comic imbroglio but a brilliant action-piece, with a vivid stroke of irony at the end as the magpie flies down unseen and steals a spoon. It begins with a round (a form Rossini generally reserved for serious contexts), exquisite in its part-writing, and reaches a taut climax in the cabaletta, the comic and serious elements in perfect equilibrium. The finale, couched in Rossini's now standard tonally balanced form, is still more impressive. The A flat ensemble after Ninetta's arrest, expressing the despair of all the characters except the jubilant Podestà, is remarkable for its beautiful melody, deeply serious tone, and unusually bold modulations (to G and E among other keys); here is the true spirit of Romantic opera. Act II preserves this level almost throughout the prison and trial scenes. The latter, beginning with a formidably scored C minor march, shows Rossini in full command of the sombre majesty of the law. The Adagio quartet of general horror is marred by fortissimo off-beat thumps, a *buffo* mannerism destined to mar countless serious operas, including Wagner's *Rienzi* (1842) and Meyerbeer's *Le Prophète* (1849), until at least the middle of the century; but the quintet after Fernando's surrender, aided by the combination of two ostinato figures heard separately earlier, has a tragic grandeur prophetic of the mature Verdi. Best of all is the C minor march and chorus, incorporating a short *preghiera* for Ninetta, as she is led to execution – which is cancelled at the last moment when the magpie's guilt is discovered. This whole movement, with its alternation of minor and major modes, sinister chromatic scales in the minor sections and mournful final diminuendo, has a sustained nobility more typical of Schubert or Beethoven than of Rossini's usual manner.

Rossini never followed up *La gazza ladra*, or apparently perceived that the *semiseria* form with its treatment of serious emotion in a vernacular context, and consequent demand for a mixed style that enlarged the comic manner without abandoning it, held the key not only to his personal dilemma but to the evolution of Romantic opera. His only other exercises in the form, the earlier *Torvaldo e Dorliska* (1815) and the later *Matilde di Shabran* (1821), based on well-known French librettos of the Revolution period, Cherubini's *Lodoiska* and Méhul's *Euphrosine*, are much less successful. Rossini lacked the sort of vision to perceive, by reason or instinct, the most promising way ahead for himself or the art he served.

ROSSINI'S EARLY *OPERE BUFFE*

He was able to develop his *buffo* style very early because none of its features was new. He merely systemized, invigorated, and perfected what was there already. Many details that strike us as Rossinian – melodies in the orchestra, often with staccato repeated notes, against non-committal voice parts, see Ex. 161(i), prancing marches with dotted and triplet rhythms (ii), sometimes reinforced by sforzandos on weak beats (iii), triplet cadence figures (iv) – were the common property of his predecessors in every type of opera.

Ex. 161

(i) PAER: *Camilla*
Allegro agitato

(ii) MAYR: *Medea in Corinto*
Allegro

(iii) PAER: *Achille*
Meno Allegro [after Presto]

(iv) PAER: *Camilla*

Some well-known Rossini melodies are almost borrowings; the main *allegro* theme of the overture to *L'Italiana in Algeri* echoes that in Paer's overture to *Sargino*:

Ex. 162

(i) PAER: *Sargino*

(ii) ROSSINI: *L'Italiana in Algeri*

The invention of the graded crescendo has been attributed to Luigi Mosca, Pietro Generali, and Mayr among others. Mayr used it in several of his early light overtures – *L'avaro* (1799), *I finti rivali, L'amor conjugale, Belle ciarle e fatti tristi* – and so did many others. Rossini simply improved it in energy, timing, and balance. It has been said that he exaggerated the farcical element in his comedies and dehumanized the characters, but this was universal in *opera buffa* outside Mozart and to some extent Paisiello. They were after stereotypes from the *commedia dell'arte*.

Rossini's first comedy *Il cambiale di matrimonio* (1810), composed at the age of eighteen, though it may suggest an immature wine opened too soon, has his personal bouquet. This is truer still of the first full-length piece *L'equivoco stravagante* (1811), in which he equals his senior contemporaries in technique and surpasses them in verve and often in invention. Both operas have amusing librettos; *Il cambiale* must be one of the earliest to make sport of a transatlantic millionaire, while *L'equivoco* (which lives up to its title) hinges on the tenor frightening off a pompous rival by pretending that the girl of their desire is a castrato in disguise – a joke then still topical. (For most of the eighteenth century the Pope required all female parts in Rome opera houses to be played by men.) The plot of *Il signor Bruschino* (1813), though scrappy, contains some entertaining scenes, notably a male trio in which the heavy *buffo* simultaneously complains about the weather and resists an attempt to father a supposititious son on him. However Rossini soon discovered that his muse could subsist quite well without reference to the libretto before him. *L'inganno felice* (1812) is an extraordinary rigmarole set among industrial iron mines; most of the characters belong to a ducal entourage, and all the motives and decisive actions lie ten years buried in the past. Rossini made no attempt to characterize the villain, but found room for (among other things) a beautiful trio with a strikingly Mozartean melody in the orchestra. *La pietrà del paragone* of the same year, like *Le Comte Ory* later, is a one-act piece with a tautological second act tacked on to fill the evening. It is full of jokes about poets and Turks; Rossini seems to have found Turks, whether genuine or simulated (they occur in *L'Italiana in Algeri, Il Turco in Italia* and *La gazzetta*), so hilarious that he drew the menacing central character of the *opera seria Maometto II* as a *buffo*. He was already skilful at controlling dramatic development by rhythmic and harmonic means. *L'inganno felice* has a tonally balanced *introduzione* and, like *La scala di seta* and Act I of *La pietrà del paragone*, a spirited and well-constructed finale. The influence of Mozart's *Figaro* is strong in this last opera, and the obbligatos for horn and clarinet (in the tenor aria 'Quell'alme pupille') have a beauty and shapeliness far surpassing Mayr.

ROSSINI'S *BUFFO* MASTERPIECES

With *L'Italiana in Algeri* early in 1813 Rossini's command of *opera buffa* was complete. Four of his last six works in this genre are among the liveliest ever written. (Of the other two, *La gazzetta* (1816), with a complex plot from Goldoni and an excess of recitative, never quite comes to the boil and borrows its best scene, the quintet in Act II, from *Il Turco in Italia*; *Adina* (1818), on a feeble version of the *Entführung* plot, was dashed off to a commission from Portugal – though not performed there till 1826 – and contains only three original numbers.) If Rossini's heroines show more sense than sensibility, the genre demanded nothing else. He does give Angiolina in *La Cenerentola* a touch of pathos in the sad little D minor 6/8 ditty that recurs with happy effect. But this is unusual; in his comedies Rossini uses the minor mode no more than Cimarosa. *La Cenerentola* has the weakest libretto of the four; it lacks genuine climaxes, and Angiolina's arrival at the ball is thrown away since no one recognizes her. The plot of *L'Italiana*, with an amorous Turkish potentate as the *buffo* butt, was a gift for Rossini's sense of fun; that of *Il Turco in Italia*, despite its title not a true companion piece, has an original twist – indeed a Pirandello-like ambiguity – in the appearance of a poet alongside his own characters, and others who turn up by chance, demand to be fitted in, and divert his plot beyond his control. This was the work of Felice Romani, the best librettist of the age. The first finale is a brilliant refinement of the old jokes about the mechanics of opera: the poet joins in a sextet to point out what a splendid finale it is, and Rossini more than justifies the claim.

Best of all is Cesare Sterbini's adaptation of Beaumarchais in *Il barbiere di Siviglia*, which sums up all that is most fruitful in the *commedia dell'arte* tradition. This, of course, lies behind the whole genre: Pantalone survives not only in Bartolo, but in Don Magnifico, the two Turkish autocrats, and later in Don Pasquale and even (much refined) in Falstaff. Figaro however is not simply Arlecchino; he has something of Rossini himself, manipulating all that happens on stage, as Prosdocimo tries to do with limited success in *Il Turco*, and laughing up his sleeve at his own antics as well as the other characters. It is this double focus, together with the admirable construction of the plot and its resource in the invention of comic incident, that elevates the work above its fellows. The characters lack Mozart's insight into the subtler complexities of human nature, but they are the ultimate crystallization of certain facets: Figaro's Protean resource in 'Largo al factotum' with its exceptional flexibility and variety of rhythm, the mettlesome flirt in Rosina's 'Una voce poco fà', Basilio's oily but menacing insinuations in 'La calunnia', the finicky wheedling Bartolo in 'A un dottor', the coarse but sharp wits of Berta in 'Il vecchietto'. Old devices too reach their peak: Almaviva's two disguises – especially the second, culminating in the brilliant quintet in which the false confronts the genuine priest while the lovers plan their escape and Figaro shaves the helplessly raging Bartolo – and the crescendo to end all crescendos in 'La calunnia', where it is not merely exciting but makes a dramatic point.

In this opera Rossini challenged one of the great successes of the day, Paisiello's 34-year-old setting of the same subject. His cautious approach is indicative of his temperament. He wrote a letter of apologetic explanation to Paisiello (and inserted a note to the same effect in the printed text), changed the title to *Almaviva o sia l'inutile precauzione* (the familiar title was first used at Bologna six months later, after Paisiello's death), and had a new libretto written, carefully choosing where to give battle to his predecessor and where to avoid it. Paisiello's libretto is closer to Beaumarchais; but much more of the action is left to the recitative, whereas Rossini gets it into the music, to the great advantage of his opera. He skipped some scenes that had been set incomparably by Paisiello, notably the trio for Bartolo and two servants, one sneezing, the other yawning, at the end of Act I. Elsewhere he set out to beat Paisiello on his own ground by taking his ideas and improving them, as in Basilio's slander aria and the quintet. He was so successful that all but the finest episodes in Paisiello's opera now sound like limp Rossini.

If *Il barbiere* enjoys an advantage over Rossini's other three comedies in the decisive cut of the arias, all four are outstanding in their ensembles, especially the first-act finales. (Two acts were now universal in *opera buffa*, and in most serious operas as well, though *Otello*, *Armida*, and *Mosè* have three.) This was the traditional point for concentrating the dramatic and musical climax, and no one executed it with greater skill than Rossini, who undoubtedly learned from Mozart's supreme mastery here. These finales are admirable in tonal architecture, in the balance between active and reflective sections, and above all in timing. Just when each situation has received its musical due, the energy is recharged by a new twist in the story, reflected in a change of key, rhythm, or orchestral resource (often all three at once), so that the listener is kept on tiptoe of expectation. The first finale of *Il barbiere* is the *locus classicus* in this respect, since music and drama play so consistently into each other's hands. The numerous other ensembles – quartets, quintets, and sextets

– though less complex in design are equally resourceful in bringing some dramatic imbroglio to the boil, especially the quintet in *Il barbiere*, the quintet with multiple disguises (two apparent Fiorellas and three Selims) in *Il Turco*, and the brilliant sextet of perplexity 'Quest'è un nodo' in *La Cenerentola*, each strategically placed in the Second Act to balance the finale of the First. The second finale is generally a simple rounding off of the plot, though that of *L'Italiana* extends the 'Pappataci' joke to its hilarious conclusion.

An unusual feature of these operas, which allowed Rossini to create a more interesting and varied texture, is the employment of low voices, especially for the heroines. Rossini showed a particular fondness for the coloratura contralto or mezzo-soprano, writing principal parts in *L'equivoco stravagante*, *La pietrà del paragone*, and *L'Italiana in Algeri* for Maria Marcolini (who also sang the hero in *Sigismondo*), in *L'inganno felice* and *La gazza ladra* (the boy Pippo) for Teresa Giorgi-Belloc, and in *Il barbiere* and *La Cenerentola* for Geltrude Righetti-Georgi – none of them sopranos. The leading male role in *La pietrà del paragone* and *L'Italiana* was a bass, Filippo Galli, who created all Rossini's Turks, including Maometto, and appeared in several of his other operas. The choice of vocal timbre colours all the scores, especially the ensembles; the quintets in *Il barbiere* and *La Cenerentola* employ three baritones or basses but no soprano, and much is lost if this balance is disturbed. In *La Cenerentola* the contrast between the mezzo heroine and the two soprano sisters is dramatically important.

ROSSINI'S *OPERE SERIE*

Rossini's task in *opera seria* was more difficult in view of the discrepancy between ends and means, between the congenial style he inherited and the heroic and tragic emotions generated by the plot. But if his success was fitful and the operas more deeply flawed than his comedies, they contain his boldest strokes of imagination and some of the finest operatic music of the period. The disappointing feature is not so much that cheerfulness keeps breaking in at unsuitable moments but that Rossini shrinks from consolidating his advances and facing their implications. Between his first important *opera seria*, *Tancredi* (1813), and his last, *Semiramide* ten years later, there is an enormous advance in technique but almost none in appreciation of how to approach a serious subject. The two have a surprising amount in common. Both librettos are based on Voltaire and follow the Metastasian rather than the Calzabigian line of development, with little individuality or emotional warmth in the characters. Both are stiffly formalized, and after rising to their peak in the first finale descend to the most perfunctory triviality in the second. Each exhibits the same awkward hiatus between music and drama as Paer's *Achille* and Mayr's serious operas, and in both Rossini writes for male chorus as if it were a military band. The hero of each was played by a woman contralto. Here Rossini was following current practice: *Aureliano in Palmira* had a castrato hero (Velluti), but in half his serious operas (including *Ciro in Babilonia, Sigismondo, Adelaide di Borgogna, Edoardo e Cristina, Bianca e Falliero,* and *Maometto*) he employed a woman, and several others (notably *Elisabetta* and *La donna del lago*) contain important *travesti* roles. Tenors are sometimes subsidiary (*Semiramide* and a few comedies such as *La pietrà del paragone*), but Rossini gave them more prominence in the Naples operas; there are two substantial tenor parts in *Mosè, La donna del lago* and *Zelmira*, and three in *Otello* and *Armida*.

Tancredi shows Rossini still in thrall to the eighteenth century. The stilted libretto is full of shop-worn devices like the intercepted letter and the champion fighting a duel in disguise for the girl he believes false, and Rossini's handling of them is weak. He makes no attempt to individualize the minor characters, and is scarcely more successful with the principals, who in his serious as in his comic operas are seldom more than types. The layout and language – prayers, laments, martial choruses, polacca rhythms, modulations by a third (often effective but overdone) – are largely taken over from Mayr, though Rossini infuses them with a stronger melodic impulse. Most of the arias are in simple cavatina or cantabile-cabaletta form, and the duets are equally conventional. The enormously long ritornellos to Tancredi's two cavatinas and Amenaide's Act II prison scene (the only piece in a minor key), though not obviously dramatic, have great beauty of line and detail. They may owe their inspiration to Mayr and Paer, but the exquisite scoring – especially for solo violin, woodwind, and horns – suggests Mozart and even (in Tancredi's first cavatina) Gluck's 'Che puro ciel'. The duet for Amenaide and Tancredi in Act I borrows an accompaniment figure from the *Zauberflöte* overture. Rossini's rhythmic vitality is much in evidence, but this is scarcely an advantage; it led him, as often later, to devalue the cabalettas with a great deal of *buffo* scampering, however serious the context.

While the opera as a whole is singularly shapeless, it contains one movement, the first finale, in which Rossini showed a mastery of dramatic architecture and established a model he was to follow, with occasional variations, for the rest of his career.[1] The principle is an

[1] See Philip Gossett's analysis, 'The "Candeur virginale" of *Tancredi*', *Musical Times*, cxii (1971), p. 326.

alternation of dynamic and static elements, the former of which (developing the action, usually flexible in design and tonality, and based on a generating motive in the orchestra) motivates the latter (in which the characters stand and deliver their reactions simultaneously in a closed form). In *Tancredi* the plan appears at its simplest: the first static section is a slow ensemble, the second a balancing cabaletta to discharge the accumulated tension. It is also particularly satisfying, since it not only reflects the dramatic situation (Amenaide, accused of treason, appeals in turn to the other characters, who reject her), but Rossini binds it together by using the same orchestral motive in both dynamic sections and then giving it to the voices in the cabaletta. Few of the innumerable vengeance cabalettas in Italian opera are so firmly motivated.

THE NAPLES OPERAS

The nine Naples operas show Rossini's serious style at its most polished, no doubt because the appointment allowed him more leisure. *Elisabetta* (1815) was the first in which he replaced *secco* recitative with string accompaniment and wrote out all the ornaments instead of leaving them to the singers[1] (hence a deceptive appearance of over-encrustation). In *Otello* next year he enriched the recitative with full orchestra, and in *Armida* (1817) incorporated the ballet as a constituent part of the score and enlarged the role of the chorus. This widening of scope is even more apparent in *Mosè in Egitto* (1818), which with the First Act of *La donna del lago* (1819) and much of *Maometto II* (1820) demonstrates that the more dignified manner of *Guillaume Tell* antedated Rossini's Paris period. If he did not employ it consistently, the fault lay partly in the librettos, or rather in his undiscriminating approach to them. He lacked the urge to transfigure a convention. Despite the high technical finish of *Elisabetta* (especially in orchestration) and the constant animation of its ideas, the plot is thin, its treatment perfunctory, and the characters are wanting in depth. Only occasionally, as in the gloomy chorus of Norfolk's followers lamenting his banishment (an antecedent of Verdi's Scottish exiles in *Macbeth*) and the first part of Leicester's prison scene, where flute and cor anglais solos colour his dreams, does humanity break through.

However we define Romanticism, its presence can scarcely be denied in Act III of *Otello*, Act I of *La donna del lago*, and certain scenes in *Mosè* and *Maometto*. The greater part of the libretto of *Otello* is a sad debasement of Shakespeare. Othello never leaves Venice and

---

[1] He later added ornaments and cadenzas to an aria by Giuseppe Nicolini inserted in *Tancredi*, probably for Pasta at the Bologna revival of 1829 (Gossett, Diss., pp. 234–5).

has no love scene with Desdemona, thereby undercutting the poignancy of the conclusion; Cassio does not appear; Roderigo and Desdemona's father Elmiro become the conventional rejected suitor and heavy father. Rossini reacts conventionally to these inhibiting factors; yet when he makes direct contact with Shakespeare he surpasses everything in his earlier work. In the last act, which follows the play closely, he abandoned set numbers and set the text to continuous music. The willow song,[1] interrupted by a sudden storm – most of Rossini's storms contribute something more than a diversion – and Desdemona's A flat prayer, its lingering woodwind cadences prophetic of the *Comte Ory* trio, are worthy of their context, and Rossini does not spoil their simplicity by overelaboration. (The willow song, like the earlier duet for Othello and Iago, left its mark on Verdi, who may have borrowed the idea of Desdemona's 'Ave Maria' from Rossini's prayer.) The most haunting moment in the opera, the introduction—just before the catastrophe—of a gondolier's voice in the distance singing the famous nostalgic verse of Dante 'Nessun maggior dolore che ricordarsi del tempo felice nella miseria',[2] while in keeping with Shakespeare's dramatic irony, was Rossini's own idea, against the wishes of his librettist, and is scarcely conceivable before the Romantic age.

The choice of a Shakespeare tragedy might be termed a gesture towards Romanticism. The treatment of Scott's poem in *La donna del lago* goes a little further. The nature-painting of the first scene, in which the strains of a hunting party greeting the dawn alternate with a barcarolle as the heroine makes her first entry rowing a boat across the lake, added a new flavour to Italian opera. The barcarolle, a popular novelty of the age, supplies the material of Elena's cavatina and her duet with Uberto (the disguised James V of Scotland) and recurs several times. The setting among the mountains, lakes, and forests of Scotland looks forward to *Guillaume Tell*, as do the gathering of the clans and the patriotic element in the plot, though these are much less boldly treated. The opera scarcely lives up to its opening, and goes badly to pieces in the Second Act. Nature also plays a role in *Mosè*, in the superb depiction of the sun's eclipse (the plague of darkness) and its effect on the superstitious Egyptians in the *introduzione*, and again in the raging seascape of the finale. When light is restored at Moses' bidding, Rossini, like Handel in *Samson* and

---

[1] See the long quotation in Handbook to *The History of Music in Sound*, viii (London, 1958), pp. 36–7.
[2] Ibid., p. 35.

Haydn in *The Creation* and with scarcely less effect, resorts to a symbolic blaze of C major, echoed in the closing bars of the opera when the C minor of the storm moves quietly to the tonic major.

It was no accident that the two operas Rossini chose to revise for Paris were *Mosè* and *Maometto II*. The plots of both are concerned with patriotism and a people or city at bay – Moses leading his people out of bondage in Egypt, the Venetians defending Negroponte against the besieging Turks. *Mosè* has the better libretto (*Maometto* is another cold collation from Voltaire full of Metastasian intrigue), and inspired in Rossini the strongest response in any of his Italian *opere serie*. In both operas the finest music occurs in the ensembles and the orchestra rather than in the solos or duets. Some of the latter are as regressive as the ensembles are advanced. The two basses in *Mosè*, Moses and Pharaoh, attain a powerful stature in the ensembles, where they represent their embattled peoples, but relapse into the language of Don Magnifico in the solos embodying their personal relationships. The arias of Pharaoh in Act I (substituted for a piece by Carafa sung at the first performance) and Moses in Act II (especially the cabaletta) are, like the Egyptian male chorus that follows the latter, quite unworthy of the opera's magnificent opening. Maometto's Act I aria with male chorus would be more appropriate to Mustafa in *L'Italiana*. The first and third finales of *Mosè* are perhaps the most imaginative movements in any of Rossini's Italian operas. In each of them Moses by raising his rod brings down the wrath of God on the Egyptians, and both conclude in a manner unorthodox for Rossini, the first in the tonic minor, the third with a movement for orchestra alone as the Red Sea swallows its victims. If the subtler aspects of human character were beyond Rossini's range, he could portray with absolute conviction an upheaval of nature at the furthest remove from *opera buffa*.

Rossini discarded formal overtures in his later Neapolitan works (a welcome move in view of the preposterous example with which he launched *Semiramide*), and *Maometto*, like *Mosè*, begins with an *introduzione* of exceptional power and grandeur. The chromatic progression in the orchestra conveying the idea of national crisis is all the more impressive for its contrast with Rossini's usual plain diatonic style. The Venetian leaders meet at night in their beleaguered city, uncertain whether to surrender or continue the struggle.

Ex. 163

They decide to resist, and the third section of the *introduzione* reflects the first, underpinned by the same ostinato figure, but at twice the speed and transformed from triple to quadruple march time. This idea may have been suggested by Spontini's *Fernand Cortez*, of which Rossini had conducted the first Italian performance earlier the same year. The whole episode launches the plot with a fine momentum, at the same time adumbrating the decisive part played by political and patriotic sentiment in Italian Romanticism.

Rossini also romanticized the prayer, especially in its choral form. The famous example in *Mosè*, added for the Naples revival of 1819 a year after the première, derives its emotional potency partly from the dramatic situation, partly from the emphatic sharpened-fourth appoggiatura of the melody and the radiant turn to the major as the soloists take over from the chorus in the last stanza. Both these operas are full of prayers, and of similarly accented appoggiaturas, for example the 2/4 Andante maestoso in G minor in the *introduzione* to *Maometto*, the duet for Elcia and Osiride ('Ah se puoi') in Act I of *Mosè*, and the chorus 'All' Etra al ciel' at the beginning of the first finale of the same opera. *Maometto* has two movements entitled Preghiera for the heroine Anna and female chorus, and a third, the A flat minor trio 'In questi estremi istante' in Act II (a round), that is clearly modelled on the *Mosè* prayer, though the singers are content to look forward to a heavenly meeting rather than request heaven's aid. All three are expressive movements in minor keys turning to the major. There is nothing sanctimonious about Rossini's prayers; he exploits not the stuffier associations of religion so often linked with squat rhythms and sugary harmony in French and German opera but his gift for long lyrical melodies and a distinct if oblique appeal to patriotism. His reputation as an unpolitical animal is not always supported by the music.

Maometto was not well received, and in his last Naples opera *Zelmira* (1822), based on another frigid French tragedy, Rossini beats a retreat. The movements are simple and conventional in plan (Polidoro's Act I cavatina is very short and lacks a cabaletta); despite another impressive first finale, balanced by a fine quintet towards the end of Act II, the style marks time. The flashy final 'rondo' for the heroine, which he had renounced in *Otello* and *Mosè* but retained in *Elisabetta, La donna del lago*, and *Maometto*, brings the opera to a tame conclusion. *Semiramide*, the most ambitious of his Italian operas, is even more of a regression. Rossini scarcely rises to the grand theme of matricide and incest; although he does not shirk the tragic end, he devalues it by crowning Arsace's perfunctory attempt at suicide with a brief chorus of vacuous cheerfulness hailing him as his mother's successor.[1] The libretto is defective in that the important character of Azema, loved by the three leading men, is confined to recitative (and not much of that); she is given a superfluous suitor in Idreno, who does not appear in Voltaire's play, simply to supply a tenor voice for the ensembles. The opera contains four big duets but no straightforward love music. This was never Rossini's strongest suit, and he was perhaps wise to avoid it; but the time spent on Idreno's two mediocre arias would have been better allotted to Azema.

The score leaves an impression of icy elaboration, its hieratic formalism undermined by the unevenness of the musical language. Much of the first finale – especially the impressive A flat minor ensemble at the appearance of Ninus's ghost and the even finer F minor Andante sostenuto that follows, on another ostinato – develops a power worthy of the mature Verdi; indeed the quintet 'Qual mesto gemito' surely lies behind the *Trovatore* 'Miserere', just as the *agitato* F minor section ('Deh! ti ferma') of Assur's Act II aria anticipates *Nabucco*. In view of most Italians' aversion to the supernatural (the fairy godmother in *La Cenerentola* becomes a benign Don Alfonso, a worldly figure from the age of rationalism, and the whole plot a satire on snobbery and avarice) it is surprising that Rossini makes so much of the ghost. The influence of *Don Giovanni* may be responsible; the

---

[1] Rossini became aware of the weakness: he first cut the last recitative to the point of unintelligibility, then rewrote it (for Paris in 1825) with a new final chorus expressing horror, the music of which however is lost (Gossett, Diss., pp. 496–9).

scene is decidedly more impressive than Verdi's dealings with Joan of
Arc's voices and the witches in *Macbeth*. But most of the best moments
in *Semiramide* occur in details and transitions. The agitated string
figures at the start of the duet for Arsace and Semiramide in Act II,
and still more the Andante maestoso when Arsace produces his dead
father's letter, suggest that Rossini's meeting with Beethoven in
Vienna the previous year had musical consequences:

But stylistic inconsistencies abound: chromatic passages proclaiming
Rossini the contemporary of Spohr (as co-heir of Mozart) sit oddly in
the trio 'Là dal Gange' early in Act I, the voice parts of which might
have been written for military band, and in the climactic Act II
chorus 'Un traditor', where Rossini uses the flippant main theme of
the overture's Allegro as an ostinato – and even repeats it when Assur
enters the tomb with murder in his heart. The beautiful canon quartet
in Act I, in which the heroine makes her initial entry as the second
voice, Arsace's first cavatina, and Semiramide's 'Bel raggio' are each
marred by fortissimo explosions off the beat. Almost all the solo and
duet cabalettas relapse into *buffo* language, rendered the more
incongruous by the extreme brilliance of the vocal writing. The
choruses in *banda* style, and the presence of a substantial *banda* on
stage, further distance the score from its solemn theme.

  Semiramide had an enormous influence on its successors, from
Meyerbeer's *Il crociato in Egitto*, which accentuated all its most blatant
features, to Donizetti and Verdi. But the rigidity of the procedures –
everything from tonal and structural design to rhythmic figuration
and the timing of modulations had become mechanical – marks a
decisive turning away from the dramatic and romantic potential of
Mosè. There was no future on these lines. The move to Paris seems
inevitable in retrospect if Rossini's career was not to come to a full
stop, and even that prolonged it for only a few years.

ROSSINI'S METHOD

  Rossini's contribution to operatic history lay not in the novelty of
his style but in its conservatism, though this judgement might have

astonished his contemporaries. He established a pattern for Italian romantic opera, necessary for its further development as well as his own convenience. His personal contributions – spontaneous exuberance, a rhythmic drive that propelled everything into a livelier orbit, and a melodic gift limited in range but long-spanned and skilfully articulated – supplied qualities conspicuously lacking in Mayr, Paer, and their contemporaries, but might have run to waste without strong formal controls. Rossini greatly admired Mayr, from whom he learned much, especially in the treatment of wind instruments. The obbligatos for cor anglais in *Il Signor Bruschino* and *Sigismondo* (transferred later to *Adina*), the use of two horns alone to accompany a solo voice in *La gazzetta*, and many other orchestral details have their prototypes in Mayr. But much was also due to his early study of Haydn and Mozart. Though not a learned composer, he had all his life an admiration amounting almost to reverence for German music. He conducted *The Seasons* at Bologna in 1810, and more than once echoed Haydn's music almost literally: for example 'In native worth' in Ninetta's *preghiera* 'Deh tu reggi' in the last scene of *La gazza ladra*, and the trio of the minuet of the 'Emperor' Quartet at the start of Desdemona's prayer in Act III of *Otello*. Later he extended his enthusiasm to Beethoven and Bach. His teacher Mattei nicknamed him *il Tedeschino*, and his Italian contemporaries often found his music oppressively Teutonic. Stendhal, who admired his work up to *Tancredi*, was distressed by what he considered increasing German influence and offered him back-handed applause for using the *buffo* idiom to revive the *opera seria*.

The need to galvanize the limp and amorphous structures of Mayr and Paer, which failed to reflect the climate of their librettos, presented a challenge not unlike that confronting Spohr and Weber. Their response led German opera into new channels; but Italy was neither ready nor suited for such a radical departure. Italian opera was still an art of the people requiring a high rate of production in a political climate discouraging experiment. To meet this demand Rossini evolved a system of minimizing the number of compositional decisions to be taken with each movement. (This is not to be equated with laziness: a lazy composer does not produce nearly forty operas in eighteen years.) Rossini's solution involved composition straight into full score (the two or three surviving sketches all concern the Paris operas); even the autographs contain remarkably few erasures and corrections. His systemization affected every part of the opera. The overtures show almost no variation in plan or mood. Having early settled on a satisfactory design – slow introduction, sonata form without development, crescendos to whip up excitement after the second subject and in the coda – he used it for comic and serious operas alike. The same overture could serve any opera, whatever its subject: that of *La gazzetta* was transferred to *La Cenerentola*, that of *La pietrà del paragone* to *Tancredi*, that of *Aureliano in Palmira* first to *Elisabetta* and then to *Il barbiere*. Much of the *Otello* overture had served for *Sigismondo*, and some of it before that for *Il Turco in Italia*.

Gossett[1] has analysed Rossini's method in the *introduzione* with the aid of an unfinished example left in skeleton form. It consists almost invariably of an orchestral introduction, a chorus in AA′ form, sometimes expanded to ABA′ if solos for minor characters are included, a slow movement involving a major character, and a cabaletta for the same character, combined with chorus or ensemble and restoring the original key. Arias and duets are equally stereotyped, though they grow more elaborate. Some early operas, like *Tancredi*, include single-section movements of primitive design. Later examples belong either to the slow-fast plan of the late eighteenth century, both movements in the tonic, or to a more extended design in three sections, of which the first is introductory and generally dynamic, the second slow and static, the third (motivated perhaps by the intervention of the chorus or another character) a cabaletta. Ensembles and finales use an extension of the same procedure. None of this was new. Rossini's only significant advance on Mayr,[2] whose forms are sometimes looser and more multipartite, lay in the greater firmness with which he handled the tension between music and drama and between the component musical sections.

In *opera seria*, as in *opera buffa*, the highest degree of organization is attained in the first finale, always the most carefully wrought part of the score, and usually the most successful in bringing music and drama into equilibrium. (The method has been described above in connection with *Tancredi*.) The Act I finale of *Maometto* follows exactly the same pattern, with a single orchestral theme propelling both dynamic sections. Some examples are more complex: the first finale of *Otello* has three dynamic-static alternations preceded by an introductory chorus. Constant features are the strophic cabaletta and the careful balance of tonality. (The last-act finale is always simpler, sometimes – in serious and comic opera – built round a brilliant show-piece for the prima donna known traditionally as a rondo, though it

---

[1] 'Gioacchino Rossini and the Conventions of Composition', *Acta Musicologica*, xlii (1970), p. 48.
[2] Mayr, though nearly 30 years older than Rossini, produced a dozen new operas after *Tancredi*. Some reciprocal influence is therefore possible.

has little in common with classical rondo form. This simplistic device, which survives in Bellini and Donizetti, occasionally serves the plot but is more often an appendage designed to gratify the singer.) The two-stanza cabaletta may not have been Rossini's invention, but he standardized it for movements of all kinds. The repeat, even when unvaried, is not a mere indulgence; it is needed for structural balance (as its omission in operas as late as *La traviata* often demonstrates). Like every other set piece it is rounded off with extra cadences and, especially in finales, extended by a coda containing a sudden internal modulation or harmonic switch, usually by a third and often back to the key of an earlier slow episode, as in the Act I finale of *La gazza ladra*, in order to increase tension and bring the movement to a satisfying climax. This was dictated as much by formal demands as by a call for applause, though of course it served that purpose as well.

The cabaletta in Rossini always restores the original tonic: at least one of the earlier static sections is slow – the characters holding a pose at some decisive moment in the drama – and, as in Mayr but with even greater uniformity, pitched in a key a major or minor third above or below the tonic, most frequently the flattened submediant. In tripartite arias and duets the key sequence C – A flat – C is as popular with Rossini as with Mayr; it occurs three times in *Maometto* and frequently elsewhere. The same third-relationships are found in all mature finales and larger ensembles (the early comedies are less regular), as the following basic plans indicate:

Barbiere I finale: C–E flat–C–A flat (slow round)–C.

Barbiere II quintet: E flat–G (Moderato)–B flat–E flat.

Gazetta I finale, *Cenerentola* I quintet, *Gazza ladra* I finale: C–E flat–A flat (slow)–C.

Otello I finale: C–F–B flat (slow round)–D–C–A flat (slow)–C.

Cenerentola I finale: D–G–C–E flat–G (slow)–B flat–D.

Cenerentola II sextet: E flat–B flat–G (slow)–E flat.

Zelmira II quintet: C–A flat (slow round)–E (Maestoso)–C.

Semiramide I finale: C–E flat (slow)–G (freely modulating)–A flat minor (slow)–F minor (slow)–C.

The *Semiramide* finale is exceptional in having two consecutive slow sections, and in using the minor mode for a principal movement; that is conditioned by the dramatic situation, the appearance of the ghost of Ninus.

Of the technical devices employed by Rossini within the body of a finale or any other substantial number, two are conspicuously successful, though he invented neither. One is the orchestral ostinato, a staple feature of dynamic sections and often carried though a succession of keys, which serves at once to hold the music together and tighten the drama. Though related to the ground bass and chaconne, it came through the *opera buffa*, where it gave sustenance to the texture while the voices indulged in rapid parlando. Rossini, though not the first to employ it in *opera seria*, refined and acclimatized it with complete success in serious contexts. The trial scene in *La gazza ladra* gains considerable lift from the creeping *sotto voce* bass figure that appears when Giannetto tells the judges there is a secret they do not know (just before Fernando's surrender) and returns both before and after the *andante* quintet 'Che abisso di pene!' The dynamic sections of the first finale of *Otello* are built on a whole series of ostinatos. The semiquaver figure that runs through the *introduzione* of *Mosè* (unusual in comprising a single ensemble in the same tempo) is worked with a Teutonic strength almost worthy of Bach, and recurs several times in the following recitative, to the great advantage of dramatic continuity. This technique never failed Rossini and retained its fertility in the operas of his successors.

His other successful device is the canonic round, which he employed – usually as a static element between two dynamic sections but sometimes to start a piece – with greater effect than any of his predecessors or contemporaries, the single examples in *Così fan tutte* and *Fidelio* excepted. These rounds are almost confined to slow tempos and serious contexts (though the first finale of *Il barbiere* contains a specimen, shortly preceded by a brief fast passage that feints in the same direction), and without exception of striking beauty. A large proportion of them (*Barbiere* I finale, *Maometto* II trio, *Mosè* II quartet, *Zelmira* II quintet, *Semiramide* I quartet) are in A flat. Elsewhere Rossini initiates the same procedure but does not pursue it. The very beautiful slow quintet in Act I of *Mosè* combines the method of a round with a sort of arch form, the same melody being presented successively in F, C, A minor, C, and F. All these movements are remarkable for the clarity, resource, and expressiveness of the part-writing. When the compass of the voices compels him to modify a melody (the *Mosè* quintet is for soprano, two tenors, and two basses), Rossini seldom fails to make capital by giving it some inventive new twist. He may have developed his gift for euphony from studying Mozart; indeed the *Mosè* quintet and the *preghiera* in F sharp minor for Anna and female chorus in Act I of *Maometto* exhibit an almost Mozartean harmonic warmth as well. Nor are such static movements dramatically null; like Beethoven in 'Mir ist so wunderbar' Rossini is able, if not to paint each character in every phrase, at least to prolong and intensify the suspense until it is time for the next move forward.

While Rossini's standardization of formal patterns, the respect in which the charge of sameness brought against his operas has most validity, was in the main a source of strength, like all conventions it became a millstone requiring a copious flow of genius to set it on the move. In association with the stereotypes of subject, situation, and sentiment imposed by the *opera seria* libretto it sometimes blocked his powers of expression. In duets and trios he tended, like his predecessors, to give the same music to characters expressing opposite sentiments, either to preserve an equal balance or to spare his invention. This is not universal even in the early comedies; in the male trio 'Pappataci che mai sento' in Act II of *L'Italiana in Algeri* each person sings different and appropriate music almost throughout. But it often mars the later operas. The duet at the start of Act II of *Mosè*, in which Pharaoh tries to force an unwelcome marriage on his son, suits neither the situation nor the emotions of the characters (the son's bitter grief, the father's hopes and puzzled insistence); their shared music evokes a mood of unseemly hilarity. The same applies to the cabalettas of the Act II duets for Anna and Maometto and for Semiramide and Arsace. Even in arias and choruses Rossini can write music utterly unsuited to the situation. The text of the chorus 'Regna il terror nella città', in Act II of *Tancredi* suggests a reign of terror; the music would do nicely for a bridesmaids' procession. The *maestoso cantabile* of Maometto's Act II aria, in which he threatens to wash away the shame of defeat in Venetian blood, is as floridly genial as the summons to battle in the cabaletta is chirpy.

The serious cabaletta, apart from sometimes defeating the ingenuity of librettists, found Rossini's resources insufficient. The results are less damaging in finales, where the characters have generally worked themselves into a lather of excitement and confusion, than in arias and duets expressing heroic determination in essentially frivolous music. Neither Rossini nor Bellini found a key to this problem, which notoriously troubled Verdi until he swept away the cabaletta altogether. Only Donizetti in his later tragic operas, with his evolution of a slow lyrical cabaletta, often charged with dramatic irony, produced a satisfactory answer, confined, however, to a limited range of situations. In all Italian opera of this period the conventions of the libretto were liable to cramp the development of the plot, a situation made more acute by the influx of literary Romanticism. Rossini was not the man to bend conventions or badger librettists in Verdi's manner; nor was he concerned with the psychological exploration of character. He preferred to treat the situations presented to him without investigating new possibilities.

Nevertheless, having codified the formulae of *opera seria* by the time of *Elisabetta*, he occasionally allowed himself to relax them in response to special circumstances. As we have seen, in Act III of *Otello*, the first scene of *La donna del lago*, and the first and last of *Mosè*, he was able to retain his points of reference while slightly modifying them to admit a wider range of expression. From early days he commanded a strong sense of the individual *coup de théâtre*. His interior modulations, though often taking the same steps as Mayr and even Cimarosa, are far more decisively timed: the stroke, when it comes, hits the nail on the head and drives it home. But his conception of musical drama on the larger scale was bounded by tradition. He was not prepared to break his own mould. The furthest he went in that direction was in *Mosè*; when the intermediate genre of *opera semiseria* offered him a promising line of advance in *La gazza ladra* he either shrank from it or, more probably, failed to notice it.

MEYERBEER'S ITALIAN OPERAS

By 1820 Rossini had riveted his mannerisms on the flaccid body of Italian opera. It was the *buffo* element, the pounding rhythms and rocketing cabalettas, that dominated his contemporaries, even in *opera seria*, to the exclusion of almost everything else in the early works of Mercadante, Donizetti, and Pacini. His most committed and for a time one of his most successful followers was Meyerbeer, who spent the years 1815–25 largely in Italy, fell at once under the spell of *Tancredi*, and produced six Italian operas, the first of them, *Romilda e Costanza*, in 1817. They are important for the development of his style, if not for the history of Italian opera. Meyerbeer anticipated Puccini's knack of exploiting all the newest devices (including religion as a theatrical prop) without letting go of the old, and also his tendency to aim too low; the opportunism that was to mark his career in French grand opera was already conspicuous in Italy. His choice of librettos was eclectic. *Semiramide riconosciuta* (1819) is a setting of Metastasio. *Margherita d'Anjou* (1820), an aberrant specimen of the *semiseria* class with historical characters jostling buffoons, has a libretto by Romani – who was also responsible for *L'esule di Granata* two years later – based on a French *mélodrame* by Pixérécourt. *Il Crociato in Egitto* (1824), the last and most successful of the group, whose Paris production was the turning-point in Meyerbeer's career, is an extraordinary compound of the old *opera seria* with every Romantic effect except the supernatural.

These librettos read like Scribe *avant la lettre*. The action of

Margherita takes place near Hexham during the Wars of the Roses, and is full of battles, disguises, conspiracies, and tergiversations of every kind, with a most unconvincing happy end.[1] It contains a duet for the Grand Seneschal of Normandy and his disguised wife, whom he fails to recognize and enlists as his page (later requiring her to carry his vows of love to her rival the Queen), and a trio for Richard Duke of Gloucester, an English outlaw (Norcester by name) disguised as a Scottish chieftain, and a cowardly Gascon surgeon – all basses, the last a *buffo*. Norcester has already saved the plot from reaching a premature end in the finale of Act II by quixotically joining the beaten side when his own has conquered and avenged his wrongs. *Crociato* anticipates *Les Huguenots* and *Le Prophète* in its religious warfare, here between Saracens and Crusaders. The behaviour of the hero (a castrato part written for Velluti) and the villain is equally inconsequent, and that of the former contemptible; there are two long-suffering heroines of different races, both of whom he has wronged, and (as in *Margherita*) a mute child, his illegitimate son by a Saracen princess, who is tossed hither and thither by marital and dynastic disputes. Meyerbeer's cynical attitude to consistency of characterization was not a novelty in his French operas.

His music is a jumble of styles, Italian, French, and German. Even the national influences do not belong to the same period: archaic Mozartean formulae jostle harmonic *frissons* derived from *Der Freischütz*, expecially in *Crociato*. Each act of *Margherita* begins, not with an Italian-style *introduzione* but with a 'character' chorus: French soldiers drinking, wenching, and playing cards in Act I, English soldiers denouncing the French in Act II, villagers hailing the sunrise in Act III. The grandiose paraphernalia of *Crociato*, with two stage bands, Egyptian and Christian, to bolster a big double chorus in the first finale (which culminates in a declaration of war), reflect Spontini by way of *Semiramide* and anticipate Meyerbeer's French operas. The prayers and hymns are much closer to the windy rhetoric of *Le Prophète* than to the straightforward lyricism of *Mosè*, if only because Meyerbeer was not an Italian. The main theme of the quartet in the first finale of *Margherita*, which concludes with a cabaletta in block harmony as the Queen makes all swear to die for their country, speaks for itself; it is a borrowing from the first finale of *Emma di Resburgo*.

[1] There are several versions of the opera, as of so many others at this period, all produced within a few years; the published scores are not dated. The one described here appears to be a Paris arrangement made in 1826, expanded from two to three acts with extra music borrowed from *Emma di Resburgo*. Romani should not be held responsible for every extravagance, though the essentials of the plot and the characters remain; the music all dates from Meyerbeer's Italian years.

Ex. 165

(The lovely hope of joy, of peace. Brief flash that appears and vanishes.)

Rossini is however the dominant influence, with every detail exaggerated out of proportion: for example the heavy accentuation of the third quaver of each beat in the 12/8 chorus of Egyptian priests and Christian knights in Act I of *Crociato* and, a little earlier, the extravagant entrance aria of the Crusader leader Adriano di Monfort, a freak tenor with a compass of nearly three octaves, whose coda explodes in a noisy antiphony between pit orchestra and stage band. The coloratura is applied rather than organic. Like Le Sueur, and for the same reason – an urge to express more than he really feels – Meyerbeer lards the voice parts, including the choruses, with hortatory instructions. *Crociato* is full of such markings as *molto vibrato, vibratissimo, soffocato, con trasportita di disperazione, con voce cupa, con amara ironia*, and so on. Meyerbeer retains the third-relationships and some of the structural features of Rossini's ensembles – the second finale of *Margherita* has an *andante sostenuto* quintet in A flat, the first of *Crociato* a canonic round in the same key – but not the tonal balance. He does however make a genuine attempt at cumulative tension by running movements together at any point during the course of an act, and endeavours to get as much action as possible into the set numbers. This is a feature of *Margherita*, and may owe something to Romani.

Meyerbeer's most positive contribution is a power of evoking atmosphere, especially in scenes of darkness, mystery, or horror, that goes beyond Rossini and reflects his German origin and perhaps contact with Weber. The opening 'Pantomima ed introduzione' of *Crociato*, in which Christian prisoners, set to work on fortifications, are maltreated by their Egyptian guards and sing a chorus of yearning (*con impeto doloroso*) for their lost families and country, is an original and unmistakably romantic conception, though more striking for its dramatic and harmonic than its melodic ideas. The prison scene in Act II, especially Adriano's scena with its long brooding introduction and the Hymn of Death for four-part male chorus, approaches the world of early Verdi, as does much of the preceding quintet. The phrases are longer than usual, the harmony with its unprepared alien chords bolder than Rossini's; the orchestration of the whole opera, with a rich tapestry of solo instruments and prominent dark colours, already shows Meyerbeer's personal stamp. The nocturnal trio for three frightened and bewildered people in Act II of *Margherita* and the early part of the connected finale, where the voices of Norcester's soldiers, searching for the Queen, answer one another in the darkness over a creeping ostinato, combine a vivid sense of atmosphere with unusual lightness of touch. Meyerbeer was helped here by the presence of a comic character, as he was again in the Act III trio for three basses, a clever action piece that exploits the link between comedy and political intrigue, like the male-voice trio 'Sous votre bannière' in Act III of *Le Prophète*. (The conspiracies of Verdi and his contemporaries are essentially *buffo* ensembles writ large.) But Meyerbeer employs the same manner, grossly inflated, when he deals with serious episodes such as the chorus of Egyptian conspirators (no. 13) and the double chorus of Emirs and knights (no. 17) in Act III of *Crociato*. In the former he destroys the effect of a splendid modulation, followed by a gradual and well-contrived return, by dropping into a jaunty tune prophetic of Sullivan's policemen. This is symptomatic of his whole style, not only in Italy: if flashes of inspiration sometimes redeem a dull idea, they are often expunged by lapses into shameless banality.

DONIZETTI AND MERCADANTE

The early comedies of Gaetano Donizetti (1797–1848) (he seldom essayed *opera seria* before 1829) add nothing to Rossini's resources. They possess humour, high spirits, neatness of touch, and a melodic gift that, while fresh and fluent, wants the undercurrent of pathetic sentiment in the later *L'elisir d'amore* and *Don Pasquale*. *Il borgomastro di Saardam* (1827, on the same story as Lortzing's *Zar und Zimmermann*) has not a single movement in a minor key. The single mild deviation from tonal orthodoxy is the placing of the two central movements of the first finale in G and A flat (the tonic is C). *Le convenienze ed inconvenienze teatrali* (1827, expanded 1831) burlesques the offstage antics of opera singers and their relatives. The central role is the *seconda donna*'s mother, a baritone part sung in falsetto; her father too takes a hand, boasting of their daughter's chromatic scales while still in her mother's womb. Donizetti, who wrote his own entertaining libretto, made no bones about quoting and parodying Rossini with a take-off of Desdemona's willow song. The *opera semiseria Emilia di Liverpool* (1824, rewritten 1828[1]) has a quaint interest for British ears in its setting,[2] an Alpine landscape (with a hermitage and a Gothic temple) inhabited by wild mountaineers and afflicted with a barbarous climate. It begins with a road accident in a thunderstorm and features an unscrupulous seducer called Colonel Tompson. The later Donizetti is faintly foreshadowed in the major-minor switches of the duet for Emilia and Claudio in Act II.

Saverio Mercadante (1795–1870), whose later years, like Donizetti's, were devoted to serious opera, made his reputation with an *opera buffa, Elisa e Claudio* (1821), that apes Rossini's manner with no little spirit. It contains an A flat round in the Act I trio (in 9/8 time, commoner in Meyerbeer and Bellini than in Rossini himself), a first finale very much after *La Cenerentola*, and a slow florid ensemble in the Act III quintet very close to his mentor's voice except for an unexpected suggestion of a Germanic part-song:

---

[1] Its history is disentangled by Jeremy Commons, 'Emilia di Liverpool', *Music and Letters*, xl (1959), p. 207.

[2] It is not the oddest of Donizetti's dealings with a British subject: the early *opera seria Alfredo il Grande* (1823) has a Danish general called Atkins, and Alfred and his queen are required to make an important entry on all fours.

Ex. 166

(From the flash of that brow, from the sound of that voice, there's no hope of escape, of pardon/His every look is a flash and his voice a sound from which there's no escape or pardon)

This and a weakness for the 'German' augmented sixth were prophetic. In his middle-period operas, notably *Il Giuramento* (1837), Mercadante was to claim – not wholly without justification – the outlawry of trivial cabalettas, crescendos, repetitions, long solos in concerted numbers, and brassy scoring, and concentration on dramatic conciseness by harmonic means. But he fell more and more under the influence of French grand opera, especially Meyerbeer, and his later operas, such as *Gli Orazi ed i Curiazi* (1846), slide back into everything he had renounced – sectional design, conventional cabalettas, weak characterization, heavy scoring, and much pounding rhetoric. His lyrical impulse, never strong, sank into harmonic vacillation and a turgid striving after effect.

BELLINI

The one composer to introduce something new before 1830 was Vincenzo Bellini (1801–35). He is commonly regarded as the first Italian romantic, and there is some truth in this. His romanticism was not political. Although the Druid choruses in *Norma* excited nationalist enthusiasm, there is no evidence that Bellini intended to identify Roman with Austrian oppression, nor does their music strike a deeper note than the rest of the score, as Rossini's patriotic scenes in *Mosè, Maometto*, and *Guillaume Tell* emphatically do. The abandonment of the half-composed opera on Hugo's *Hernani* in 1830 suggests a cautious approach. The vital element in Bellini sprang from a single source, the languid melancholy of his slow melodies; he was not ahead of his time in harmony, orchestration, construction, or choice of subject. His career illustrates the importance of melody as an operatic driving force and its insufficiency when unsupported by other qualities. The full fruits were to be gathered by Donizetti and especially Verdi, who developed a specifically Italian romanticism distinct from, and later than, their contemporaries in France and Germany.

Bellini's lyric gift grew from eighteenth-century roots. Like Mercadante, who developed in a very different direction, he was a pupil of Zingarelli at Naples, a city once in the vanguard of Italian opera but now a backwater. Zingarelli, nearly half a century older than Bellini (he was born in 1752), had composed the last of his many operas in 1811. His style, like Paisiello's, derived from Pergolesi and the *comédie larmoyante* of pre-Revolution France, not least in his very popular *Giulietta e Romeo* (1796). Bellini, inheriting this conservative and indeed obsolete tradition, found a particular affinity with Paisiello, whose operas contain many episodes – for example the pathetic utterances of Rosina in *Il barbiere di Siviglia* and the garden scene in *Gli astrologi immaginari* – prophetic of his successor. The closest link is with *Nina pazza per amore*, which served Bellini as a model not only in his first opera but, more significantly, in his last.

Adelson e Salvini (1825), performed by Bellini's fellow students with spoken dialogue (like the original *Nina*), is an *opera semiseria* of the same inconsequent type as *Emilia di Liverpool*, which Bellini had almost certainly heard in its first version the year before. The characters include a sympathetic Irish peer (the scene is laid in Ireland), a visiting Italian painter, his *buffo* Neapolitan servant, and a rascally colonel who tries to abduct the heroine and ends by receiving a shot in the neck. The libretto had been set previously by Fioravanti; Bellini changed the opening to bring it closer to *Nina*, with the lovelorn heroine's first entry preceded and prepared by cavatinas for two basses, one serious and one comic. While the music[1] is technically

---

[1] The published vocal score (Milan, 1836?) gives a revised version, in two acts with recitatives, dating from a year or two later, but the incomplete autograph of the three-act original survives: see Francesco Pastura, *Bellini secondo la storia* (Parma, 1959), pp. 77–80. The opera was never professionally performed.

primitive, with little feeling for character or design (the arias are all single-movement cavatinas), and saturated with unassimilated Rossini mannerisms, the Paisiello element stands out sharply from the rest. It appears in patches of mild chromatic harmony, in the cavatina of the Act II duet 'Torna, O caro' for Adelson and Salvini, in Salvini's 'Ecco, signor, la sposa' in the second finale (added in the second version and used later in *La Straniera*), and most strikingly in Nelly's F minor romanza 'Dopo l'oscuro nembo' in Act I. The limpid melody with arpeggio accompaniment, orchestral echoes, and final turn to the major is the clearest anticipation in the opera of Bellini's later style (he was to re-use it in *I Capuleti e i Montecchi*); it is also directly modelled on Nina's 'Lontana da te':

Ex. 167

Andante flebile

Do - po l'os-cu - ro   nem - bo   il ciel___ spe - rai___ se -
- re - - no   e al mio   te - so - ro   in

(After the dark cloud I hoped the sky would clear for me to enjoy in peace the treasure in my heart)

The wide split between what may be called the masculine and feminine aspects of Bellini's temperament – represented by Rossini's driving energy, with which every composer had to come to terms, and Paisiello's sentimental lyricism – is no cause for surprise in a first opera. That he never achieved a satisfactory balance between them was not due merely to his early death. He was a cautious developer and a man divided against himself, in his music and his personality. Encouraged from the first by his family and his teachers, he had an exceptionally easy passage with the public. His early operas were warmly acclaimed; his only failures were *Zaira* (1829) and – temporarily – *Beatrice di Tenda* (1833), by which time his fame was assured. Yet he suffered from an inner insecurity that made him bitterly jealous of all possible rivals, especially Donizetti, and even at the end of his life he remained almost morbidly dependent on Rossini's approval.[1] His last two operas do suggest that he was slowly advancing into new territory and eliminating weaknesses; but they reveal basic limitations from which Donizetti, who had by then forged ahead, was largely free.

[1] See his letters of 3 March and 1 April 1835 in Luisa Cambi, *Vincenzo Bellini Epistolario* (Verona, 1943), pp. 531–2 and 536 ff.

BELLINI'S LIBRETTOS

The most obvious was his restricted attitude to opera as a dramatic entity. When after *Beatrice di Tenda* a quarrel with Romani deprived him of the services of his regular librettist, he was forced to work with an inexperienced amateur, Count Pepoli, and to explain just what he wanted. His letters about *I Puritani* (1835) show him more concerned with the part than the whole. It was not the conflict between the characters or the coherence and credibility of the plot that interested him, but the provision of opportunities to assault the tear ducts of the audience. This emerges clearly from the letter to his uncle[1] explaining why he was so attracted by the subject, a French play recently produced in Paris. Bellini expressed boundless delight[2] with the incredible scene in Act I of the opera where Elvira learns, at the very last moment and not even from her father, that she is to marry Arturo (whom she loves) instead of Riccardo (to whom she is betrothed). Bellini transformed the play's spiritless heroine into an emotional ninny whose wits desert her when she sees Arturo escorting a veiled woman out of the camp, and return when the woman is identified as the widow of Charles I. This was a conscious reversion to Paisiello's Nina, as several mentions in Bellini's letters indicate; he told Florimo that the part of Elvira would suit Malibran 'because it is of a genre like *Nina pazza* and has harrowing situations (*situazioni laceranti*)'.[3]

The result of this preoccupation with harrowing situations was to place a heavy emotional burden on the heroine. Bellini's operas all revolve round the sopranos (so do many of Donizetti's, perhaps a legacy from Bellini); their sufferings motivate the drama. Imogene in *Il Pirata* and Elvira go mad; Alaide becomes delirious in the first finale of *La Straniera* when Arturo wounds her brother and throws him in a lake; Amina compromises herself by sleep-walking (the *semiseria* equivalent of a mad scene, and so treated); Giulietta cannot make up her mind to elope with Romeo and takes refuge in a drug. (In Romani's original libretto for Vaccai the potion is her own idea, not Lorenzo's, and she is a more positive and consistent character; this and other changes were almost certainly made at Bellini's instance.) This tends to pull the other characters out of focus. The Bellini tenor is passionate, even hysterical, and scarcely able to control his emotions; Salvini in his first opera tries to commit suicide out of hopeless love as soon as he reaches the stage. The violence of each

---

[1] Pastura, op. cit., pp. 412–13.

[2] In a letter to Pepoli, Cambi, op. cit., p. 402.

[3] Ibid., p. 455. See also Pierluigi Petrobelli, 'Bellini e Paisiello. Altri documenti sulla nascita dei *Puritani*', in *Melodramma Italiano dell'Ottocento, Studi e ricerche per Massimo Mila* (Turin, 1977), p. 351.

tenor's behaviour seems a compensation for some inner fear, a reflection perhaps of that of his creator. The most balanced of Bellini's heroes is Romeo, composed for a mezzo-soprano. The baritone is either benevolent and more or less detached or torn by jealous fury (as in the first three operas and *Beatrice di Tenda*); Bellini declared emphatically that 'a baritone cannot play a lover'.[1] A secondary feature, which Bellini shares with Puccini, is a fondness for introducing his sopranos as offstage voices, as Cherubini had done in *Lodoiska*. Alaide's cavatina in the distance adds to the romantic mystery of her identity. Agnese, the *seconda donna* of *Beatrice di Tenda*, sings a long cavatina before she appears. Elvira in all three acts of *I Puritani* (though not at her first entry) anticipates an important melody in the wings.

Bellini's long collaboration with Romani, in six consecutive operas as well as the 1828 revision of *Bianca e Fernando*,[2] is justly famous; he described Romani as a necessity. Its importance lies not so much in the latter's undoubted skill with words as in his ability to keep Bellini on a steady dramatic course. Pepoli's failure here handicapped *I Puritani* from the start. Romani was surely in great part responsible for Bellini's greatest and least typical heroine, Norma, whose stature derives from a balance, as much classical as romantic, between passionate emotion, strength of character, and an inflexible sense of duty. She is a more heroic figure than in Soumet's play, where she implores Pollio to take her to Rome, even as his slave; in the last act, not used in the opera, she goes mad and throws herself and her children over a precipice. It is hard to imagine Bellini abandoning these features without Romani's prompting. Romani was not a faultless librettist: three of his collaborations with Bellini – *Il Pirata, La Straniera*, and *Beatrice di Tenda* – have complex plots in which so many important events have occurred before the rise of the curtain that the action is sometimes obscure and sometimes improbably melodramatic. A fourth, *I Capuleti*, was a hasty refashioning of an earlier piece, not for the better. It is no accident that the two simplest librettos, *La Sonnambula* and *Norma*, inspired Bellini's two most satisfying operas.

BELLINI'S MELODY

That Bellini did not depend for inspiration on Romani's words, or

[1] In a letter to Florimo (24 September 1828), who had suggested giving the part of Arturo in *La Straniera* to the baritone Tamburini (Cambi, p. 159).
[2] First produced in 1826 as *Bianca e Gernando*, to avoid the taboo of using the name of the heir to the throne of Naples in the theatre.

anyone else's, is clear from his method of composition. His first biographer's emphasis on a demonstrably spurious letter to Agostino Gallo, in which Bellini is supposed to have said that he put himself into the mind of each character, shut himself in his room, and declaimed the words 'with all the heat of passion' until the music came, has propagated a totally false picture. Bellini's melodies were seldom dependent on words; he jotted them down for future use as they occurred to him,[1] and often required Romani to supply words for music already written. This was obviously necessary in adaptations such as the revised *Bianca e Fernando* and *I Capuleti*[2] (which uses many themes from *Zaira*, not always in parallel contexts), but it occurred on other occasions. Romani himself complained of it in connection with *Beatrice di Tenda*. Bellini began the composition of *La Straniera* without the text, to save time while Romani was ill. The probable truth is, as Charlotte Greenspan has suggested, that 'Bellini's great melodic gift is due not so much to sensitivity to the text as to its unfettered freedom, somewhat in disregard of the text'.[3]

Bellini's career can be seen as a gradual attempt to expand the lyrical element, first evident in simple melodies like Ex. 167, towards a permeation of the whole score, recitative on the one hand, ensemble and the longer scenic complex on the other. It was a matter of discovering, or knowing by instinct, where his strength lay and building on it. He may never have understood the structural principles underlying Rossini's work, though he began by imitating them. The standard multipartite aria forms, which he first adopted in his second opera *Bianca e Fernando*, and as late as *I Capuleti* the ensembles and finales regain their original tonic. Bellini's feeling for overall tonal balance was at first so weak that long stretches of *Bianca e Fernando* threaten to settle in B flat with occasional excursions to F. The first finale of this opera contains an attempt at a round (predictably in A flat in a C major context), and there is another in the second finale of the revised *Adelson e Salvini*, but neither carries much conviction. A better example in *Zaira* reappeared in *Beatrice di Tenda*. There is little tension in these early finales, which like the other movements find issue in fidgety cabalettas so lacking in rhythmic and harmonic tension that they often sound like slow pieces played too fast. Hence the sluggish pace characteristic of Bellini's operas.

He never overcame this inability to write lively tunes possessing

[1] Pastura (op. cit., pp. 588–95) discusses two groups, one dating from the last months of Bellini's life after the production of *I Puritani*; see the page reproduced opposite his p. 400.

[2] All Bellini's later operas contain self-borrowings, including three from the abandoned *Ernani* in *Norma*.

[3] *The Operas of Vincenzo Bellini* (Diss., Berkeley, 1974), p. 121.

both character and animation. Unlike many of Donizetti's in his later operas, Bellini's cabalettas are nearly always a sad falling off after the cantabile; it is difficult to think of more than two – 'Se ogni speme' in the first finale of *I Capuleti* (originally for *Zaira*) and 'Il mondo che imploro' in the Act I duet for Beatrice and Filippo in *Beatrice di Tenda* – that decisively raise the dramatic temperature. The overtures seldom display anything beyond a limp agitation. Most of the choruses in the early operas are similarly afflicted. Bellini gave the chorus an enlarged dramatic role in *Il Pirata* and *La Straniera*, where it sometimes initiates action, but the music, like that of the *banda* marches, is often trivial. The storm and shipwreck in the first scene of *Il Pirata* is a partial exception; the rare slow choruses, such as the barcarolle that begins *La Straniera*, are naturally written *con amore*. Not till the Druid outbursts in Act II of *Norma* did Bellini write a chorus of genuine power.

In *Bianca e Fernando* he found an unsuitable subject, a rescue opera of French cut (though in fact based on a recent Neapolitan play) with no straight love interest. The hero and heroine are widowed sister and exiled brother oppressed by a malevolent baritone usurper who has imprisoned their old father Carlo (bass). The two most characteristic movements, the *andante flebile Romanza a due voci* (both sopranos) 'Sorgi, O padre' and Carlo's striking F minor cavatina, almost Verdian in atmosphere, are both concerned with the imprisoned father. Romani in his revision brought on Bianca's little son as a pawn, a favourite romantic device he was to repeat in *Il Pirata* and *Norma*. But Bellini's music, with its repetitions, Rossini echoes, and excessive reliance on certain mannerisms (interminable dominant pedals and hammering at the chord on the flattened seventh to work up climaxes) shows no great advance.

IL PIRATA

Il Pirata (1827), though almost as uneven in style, is a historical landmark. It was Bellini's first full collaboration with Romani, his first opera with a tragic end, and his first international success. Imogene is his earliest convincing heroine, and it was her music that haunted contemporaries. The plot, from a Maturin tragedy of 1816 by way of a French play, revolves round that typical hero of literary romanticism, the farouche Byronic outlaw. Romani softened and sentimentalized him; Bellini, temperamentally unfitted to express the daemonic, could only make him brutal and unsympathetic. But Imogene, who once loved the pirate Gualtiero and later married his successful rival, fired the composer's imagination. Her two big arias

PLATE III. ITALIAN OPERA

Two of Alessandro Sanquirico's stage-designs for the first performances of (above) Rossini's *La gazza ladra* (31 May 1817), (below) Bellini's *Il pirata* (27 October 1827), at the Teatro alla Scala, Milan.

show the Bellinian cantilena for the first time at full span. The slow sections of the second (before a much weaker cabaletta ends the opera), a long F minor *parlando* introduced by cor anglais and harp and an F major *andante sostenuto* with flute, left echoes far and wide, the former for example in Donizetti's 'Una furtiva lagrima', the latter in Lucia's mad scene, a similar situation, as well as in 'Casta diva'; the whole episode lies behind Anna Bolena's sufferings in prison and Lady Macbeth's sleepwalking. Bellini's obbligato technique is still that of Mayr and Rossini in *Tancredi*, softened by the languorous melancholy of the tunes themselves. He was to continue it in the exquisite obbligatos for horn, cello, and clarinet in *I Capuleti* before dropping it in favour of a more symphonic treatment of the wind instruments, especially in *I Puritani*, where he could write for a first-rate Paris orchestra. Elsewhere in *Il Pirata*, amid a mass of formulae, Bellini's personal voice is heard in occasional details, again generally in connection with Imogene: the *maestoso* introduction to her first recitative, the little A flat arioso just before her duet with Gualtiero, and the expressive modulations in her Act II duet with Ernesto when she admits her love for Gualtiero.

LA STRANIERA

Despite the example of Rossini, Bellini had not yet adapted the long melody to ensembles. The quintet before the first finale is weakened by short phrases and the want of just such a clinching tune, and so is the quartet in Act II of *La Straniera* (1829) (based on an early 'Tantum ergo'). Nevertheless the latter opera shows a notable advance in its ensembles, especially the love duet and the two trios, all in Act I. Bellini begins to work action and the development of character into lyric movements. The *allegro moderato* cabaletta of the duet, a moment of tender farewell, and the last section of Valdeburgo's Act II aria hint at the expressiveness of Donizetti's better cabalettas, though Bellini scarcely followed this up. The second trio (terzettino), in which Arturo overhears the meeting of brother and sister and mistakes them for lovers, is a remarkable piece; Bellini depicts the friction and cross-purposes of the situation by means of a half-sinister Rossinian ostinato, Alaide's lyrical but unsymmetrical phrases (of seven and five bars), and an abrupt leap from the tonic E flat to E major at Arturo's outburst of jealousy. The piece ends in Arturo's key; the opera's other ensembles are tonally balanced. Bellini had used the semitone shift in plunging from the chord of B flat into B major during Imogene's Act I cavatina. Though not unprecedented (it occurs in Spontini and for comic effect in Cimarosa and Mayr), it is not characteristic of Rossini, but was to become a favourite pattern for a strong dramatic gesture throughout Italian romantic opera. A less distinguished anticipation is the bridal chorus in the last scene, which strikingly resembles that in Verdi's *Attila*. *La Straniera* creates an aura of romantic mystery by presenting the unnamed and veiled heroine as a figure of doom who destroys the happiness of the other characters and drives Arturo to suicide. For much of the opera the leading figures are unaware of each other's identity, as is the audience; only in the last scene do we learn that the stranger of the title, who so rouses the suspicions of the chorus, is the Queen of France, separated from her husband by Papal decree. The background of lake, forest, and storm is paralleled in Rossini's *Guillaume Tell* of the same year and his earlier *La donna del lago*. Bellini took a hint from the latter opera, which he knew well, by introducing his heroine in a boat and characterizing her with an *andante* barcarolle, first sung offstage. Bellini's melody is more fluid and open-ended, and to that extent more romantic.

I CAPULETI E I MONTECCHI

La Straniera was an even greater success than *Il Pirata*, and it is significant that the Milan press congratulated Bellini on restoring the pre-Rossini style of the eighteenth century, thereby pinpointing an important truth. Much the same could be said of *I Capuleti* (1830), two of whose strongest features are regressive. In wealth of slow melodies it surpasses all his other operas, perhaps because he could utilize a store salvaged from *Zaira*, his failure of the previous year. A study of the re-used material[1] tells us much about the evolution of the mature Bellini melody with its long line alternately drooping and recovering, swaying rhythms, expressive decoration, artfully delayed climax, and such personal mannerisms as the falling triplet on the second or fourth beat and the high note on a weak beat towards the end of a phrase. Bellini was evidently concerned to increase suppleness of rhythm in melismas, extend the vocal compass at moments of particular expression, and avoid exact repetitions so that the principal phrases gain in intensity at each return. This is not the work of a man declaiming a text or surrendering to passion, but of a conscientious craftsman polishing a gem. For Giulietta's Act II cavatina 'Ah non posso partire' the *Capuleti* autograph supplies an intermediate stage that throws further light on the process:

[1] Greenspan, pp. 144 ff.; Pastura, pp. 196 ff.

Ex. 168

del mi o se-pol - cro in sen, ah pa-dre mio— per - do - na un cor che —

mi - o se-pol-cro in mi - o per

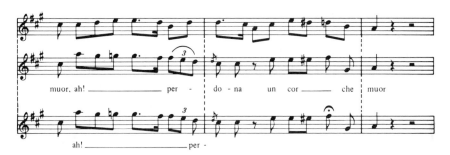

muor, ah! _____ per - do - na un cor _____ che muor

ah! _____ per -

A second conservative feature is the mezzo-soprano Romeo. But Bellini was not blindly following convention or the example of Zingarelli and Vaccai, or acceding to the demands of a great singer (Giuditta Grisi). He made this the corner-stone of the opera both musically and dramatically (as Wagner was quick to notice), by contrasting Romeo's mezzo tessitura with the male chorus of embattled Capulets in the first scene and with his tenor rival Tebaldo in Act II, and most of all in the first finale, where the voices of the lovers singing their bounding triplet melody in unison against the muttered *sotto voce* of the all-male chorus become a symbol of innocence in a hostile world. This was the most literal of the borrowings from *Zaira*, extending to words as well as music, but the substitution of unison for octaves was new – and a stroke of genius. Bellini's object, like Handel's in many of his heroic roles, was to emphasize Romeo's youth. He was so pleased with the result that he planned his next opera, the abortive *Ernani*, with a mezzo-soprano hero.

In another respect *I Capuleti* marks an important advance. Hitherto Bellini had ended all his operas except *Adelson e Salvini* with an extended rondo-finale for soprano culminating in a showy cabaletta,[1] and he was to return to the gambit with deplorable results in *Beatrice*

---

[1] There are signs that *Il Pirata* was designed to end with Gualtiero's surrender and suicide; but Imogene's mad scene was placed after instead of before it, perhaps at the instance of the prima donna, Henriette Méric-Lalande.

di Tenda and the Malibran version of *I Puritani*, and more justifiably in *La Sonnambula*. Only in *La Straniera*, where Alaide's aria is punctuated by the offstage wedding music (as in Act II of Cherubini's *Médée*) and Arturo kills himself between the stanzas of her cabaletta, had some tension been preserved. In the final scene of *I Capuleti* Bellini dispenses not only with a cabaletta but with a set duet of any kind. Romeo's lament, a mixture of recitative and arioso with occasional snatches of distant male chorus, eschews regular periods and coloratura; when Giulietta awakes the lovers exchange a few broken phrases; Romeo dies in the middle of pronouncing her name, an idea borrowed from Vaccai; and the curtain falls immediately on Capulet's discovery of the bodies and his own guilt. The music expresses the drama with a directness worthy of Verdi and the later Donizetti. This restraint was too much for contemporary singers. As early as 1832 Malibran substituted Nicola Vaccai's penultimate scene for Bellini's finale, and the opera was often performed in this bastard version,[1] which gives Romeo more opportunity for display and Giulietta a valedictory top C. Vaccai's opera (1825), springing from the same tradition as Bellini's – he was a pupil of Paisiello at Naples – deploys a similar though less personal vein of elegiac sentiment and even flimsier cabalettas.

LA SONNAMBULA AND NORMA

Bellini came closest to establishing a satisfactory balance in *La Sonnambula* and *Norma*, both produced in 1831. They belong to different genres (Romani called the former *melodramma*, the latter *tragedia lirica*), and may be said to represent the French forms of *opéra comique* and grand opera as transmuted through an Italian imagination. *La Sonnambula*, based on a Scribe ballet set by Hérold, is Bellini's only *opera semiseria* apart from *Adelson e Salvini*. It typifies the form in its contemporary domestic setting (a Swiss village), proletarian characters (no one of higher rank than the lord of the manor), and sentimental treatment of a situation that in other circumstances might have issued in tragedy. There is no *buffo* part, the comedy being to some extent taken over by the chorus, who converse on a level with the principals, but in the main softened into cosy sentiment. The plot depends on misunderstanding rather than conflict, which allows Bellini to treat Amina's two sleep-walking excursions as embryo mad scenes, with the usual pathetic thematic reminiscences but no graver implications. 'Ah! non credea', which would be scarcely tolerable in

---

[1] The Ricordi vocal scores still include Vaccai's scene in an appendix as an alternative generally substituted for Bellini's.

a tragic context, is perfectly apt here. A mild romanticism infects the harmony in the oblique approach to this aria and to Teresa's Act I solo about the ghost and the following chorus. The drama suited Bellini in much the same way as *La gazza ladra*, a story of very similar cut, suited Rossini. Moreover the residual Rossini element in Bellini's music coheres with the gentle 6/8 and 12/8 Neapolitan rhythms more happily than in an *opera seria*.

Like the sleep-walker, the priestess who betrays her vows was a popular theme in the romantic theatre, from Spontini to Mercadante (1840) and Bizet. Pacini, who tackled subjects classical, medieval, and oriental and wrote an opera on Mérimée's *Colomba*, approached Bellinian territory with *La sacerdotessa d'Irminsul* (Trieste, 1817). *Norma* is almost classical in its simplicity and freedom from dramatic extravagance, and by no means advanced for its date. 'Casta diva', perhaps the supreme example of the romantic *preghiera* for solo voice, has a statuesque quality redolent of Gluck, in temper if not in style. The slow pace of the opera, due partly to concentration on only three characters (the confidantes are restricted to recitative, and even Adalgisa is left out of the finale), reflects both the strength and weakness of the composer and imposes a heavy burden on the singers. Norma herself is a noble creation, happily contrasted with the younger and more pliant Adalgisa, who is beautifully drawn at her first entry and in both her duets with Norma, especially the second; Pollione emerges as a shallow hedonist whom we can scarcely imagine fighting a battle or governing Gaul. There is a new power in the ceremonial scenes, notably the sombre opening march of the Druids and the whole Act II finale, whose sacrificial dignity prefigures the end of *Aida*. Prophetic too is the atmospheric prelude to Act II and the arioso in which Norma contemplates the murder of her sleeping children; Verdi was to strike a similar mood in Act II of *Simon Boccanegra* when the Doge drinks the poisoned water. Bellini cannot sustain it; Oroveso's 'Ah! del Tebro' singularly belies its marking *con ferocia*. But he is more successful in combining lyricism with dramatic thrust, for example in the duet 'In mia mano', whose first (F major) section, while giving full value to the conflict between Norma and Pollione, is a beautifully proportioned paragraph, beginning ominously on Norma's low C and rising nearly two octaves to the climax. The deceptively simple arpeggio accompaniment makes a positive contribution by focussing attention on the voices. Until the cabaletta this is a new type of duet, with one voice confined to short breathless interjections and no shared material. The autograph of *Norma* shows Bellini taking considerable trouble, with many changes of mind, over the pacing of the recitative and over the orchestration: in several pieces, including 'Casta diva' and the start of the Act I duet 'Sola furtiva al tempio', the spare accompaniment was the outcome of steady paring down of a much ampler original.[1]

MUTUAL INFLUENCE OF BELLINI AND DONIZETTI

By this time an important new voice had been heard in Italian opera. Donizetti's *Anna Bolena* had its first performance in Milan in December 1830, less than a week before Bellini began to compose *La Sonnambula* in the same city, for the same theatre, and with the same librettist. While Donizetti's mature work lies beyond the scope of this volume, something must be said on the difficult question of mutual influence. There was a strong rivalry between the two composers, generous on Donizetti's side, mean and envious on Bellini's, and the public encouraged it. It seems likely that Bellini's lyrical cantilena in *Il Pirata* and *La Straniera* played a decisive part in weaning Donizetti from the constricting influence of Rossini, and in turning his attention towards *opera seria*, in which he had previously shown scant interest. After 1828 he concentrated on little else; the comparative familiarity of his only three full-length comedies of this period has concealed the fact that it saw the birth of no fewer than 29 serious operas. They represent by far his most impressive achievement. His mature melodic style, more varied and energetic than Bellini's and quite as distinctive (the prayer 'Divo spirto' in Act II of *Pia de'Tolomei* and Queen Elizabeth's slow cabaletta 'Quel sangue versato' at the end of *Roberto Devereux* are among the finest and longest melodies of the age), seems to be the product of a fusion between Bellinian cantilena, less encrusted with decoration and more often built from the varied repetition of short rhythmic units, and the lilting Neapolitan popular song with its ambiguous attitude to the major and minor modes. It can be clearly detected in *Il paria* (1829), a tragedy dealing with the Indian caste system. Donizetti's next opera of the same year, *Elisabetta al castello di Kenilworth*, based remotely on Scott with some hints from Scribe's libretto for Auber's *Leicester*, veers back towards Rossini, as was only too likely with this subject. Donizetti's Queen is very like Rossini's, changing abruptly from termagant into angel of mercy to ensure a happy end; the music reflects *La Cenerentola* as well as *Elisabetta*. There are a few traces of Bellini. Most of the best music is concerned with the wronged Amelia (Amy Robsart), who is close kin to Imogene. Her melancholy Act III cavatina, the finest piece in the

---

[1] Greenspan, pp. 239 ff., Pastura, pp. 559 ff.

score, with obbligato for glass harmonica and harp prophetic of *Lucia di Lammermoor*, and the beautiful cor anglais obbligato of the Queen's last cavatina owe a debt to *Il Pirata*; whereas the Act II garden scene for Amelia and the Queen, especially the arioso at the start, looks forward to the more famous confrontation in *Maria Stuarda*.

DONIZETTI'S *ANNA BOLENA*

The advance in *Anna Bolena*, less than eighteen months later, is startling. While the pathos of the last scene no doubt owes something to Bellini, and specifically to the close of *I Capuleti*, in several important respects Donizetti carried the *opera seria* beyond anything that Bellini had achieved or would achieve, and brought it close to middle-period Verdi. Despite the survival of some Rossinian dross, the pervasive atmosphere of suspicion haunting Henry VIII's court, the astringent menace of the monarch himself, who has no aria but exercises a numbing grip on everyone else through the ensembles, the sombre orchestration, and the psychological range of the characterization added a new dimension to Italian opera. The quintet in the second scene, in which Anna, though warned by her brother, reveals her love for Percy while the King sets Hervey to spy on them, unites dramatic momentum, personal tension, and a melody of noble span with a potency new in Italian opera. Donizetti's gift for dramatic irony, which he shares with Verdi rather than Bellini and was to develop extensively later, is conspicuous here for the first time. There is a striking instance in the last scene when the offstage march for the King's marriage with Jane Seymour, a trivial tune in itself and appropriately so, crashes in on the condemned Queen's exquisite arioso 'Cielo a' miei lunghi spasimi' (based on the melody of 'Home, sweet home', an inspired touch whether or not Donizetti knew its true origin) and turns her mind back from the borders of insanity to denounce her supplanter. The whole finale, between the sad F minor chorus of Anna's ladies-in-waiting (with its melting cadence in the major) and her final cabaletta, is built up from a mosaic of recitative, orchestral fragments, and ariosos, mostly very short but extraordinarily eloquent of the passing moods of the characters, who include Hervey, Rochfort, Percy, Smeton, and the female chorus as well as Anna. It holds together firmly as a dramatic unity, based on a kind of progressive tonality that moves from F minor to D major, shifting its tonal centre with each development of the action. The technique was perhaps suggested by the last scene of *I Capuleti*, but evolves on a much broader scale. Donizetti introduces pregnant ariosos, vocal and instrumental, elsewhere in the opera, for example before the duet for

Anna and Percy in Act I, as he had already done in *Il paria*. They often
concentrate a world of feeling in a very few bars, as in the haunting
string phrase before Anna's first words in the Act II finale (Ex. 169i),
the fragment in which Percy in Act I proclaims his devotion to the
Anna he has lost (ii), and the flute melody introducing Anna's
confused recollections of the past (iii) in Act II. The last two reappear
almost literally, not in Donizetti's opera but in *Rigoletto* and *Macbeth*,
in the same keys and identical dramatic situations.[1]

Ex. 169

---

[1] On Donizetti's later works see Vol. IX.

(No, no, no, for me you are Anna, only Anna)

BELLINI'S LAST OPERAS

Bellini had used arioso to a limited degree as early as *Bianca e Fernando*, but never in such concentrated form. The blurring of the fixed line between recitative and set number and the freer use of the chorus characteristic of *La Sonnambula* and *Norma* may be independent of Donizetti; they are prefigured in *La Straniera*. Whereas most movements in *Anna Bolena*, with the important exception of the finale, are tonally balanced, Bellini abandoned this practice in *Norma*[1] and seldom adopted it later. His last two operas are by common consent less satisfactory than their two predecessors, but their obvious imperfections have obscured their virtues, in particular the growing flexibility of form and greater enterprise in harmony and scoring. It is possible that the impact of *Anna Bolena* unsettled his precarious balance. Certainly its shadow lies heavy on *Beatrice di Tenda* (1833). Bellini was aware of the dangerous similarity of the librettos, both by Romani: the baritone tyrant rejecting his wife for a younger rival, who (like Eboli) repents too late for the suffering she has caused, the arrest of the heroine in an apparently compromising situation in the first finale, her rigged trial, condemnation, and execution together with the tenor who loves her, the grim atmosphere of Renaissance cruelty and suspicion. Bellini had the weaker libretto in that Beatrice, one of opera's rare middle-aged heroines, is wholly innocent and undisturbed by inner conflict, whereas Anna has loved Percy in the past (and has a second admirer in Smeton, whose actions are enough to rouse suspicion). In view of this, Filippo's brutality is too unredeemed (he has a single brief moment of humanity when he remembers that he owes his power to Beatrice and hesitates before signing the death sentence), Beatrice's and Orombello's sufferings too unmerited, and Agnese's repentance perhaps too tardy for genuine tragedy. Moreover there is no reciprocated emotional relationship in

[1] The cantabile of 'Casta diva', though published in F major, was composed in G. Tonally balanced movements are the exception in later Donizetti and Verdi.

the opera: Beatrice loves Filippo, who loves Agnese, who loves Orombello, who loves Beatrice, and all are doomed to frustration. This was perhaps a subject for Verdi rather than Bellini.

It seems likely that Bellini was deliberately challenging *Anna Bolena*, for the musical parallels are equally striking: the similar handling of a romanza for the mezzo-soprano with harp accompaniment in the Act I *introduzione*, the tendency (untypical of Bellini) for the melodies to be built from repetitions of a single unit, the introduction of arioso fragments like the exquisite four-bar *andante* for strings in the recitative before the Agnese-Orombello duet, the darker scoring, the vivid male chorus with its bustling orchestral obbligato before the first finale, and the greater energy of the ensembles, especially the Act I duets for Agnese and Orombello and Beatrice and Filippo (with its stirring cabaletta) and the magnificent quintet in the trial scene, which has much in common with the *Anna Bolena* quintet and far surpasses that in *La Straniera*. By the same token this is the most Verdian of Bellini's operas. Although both finales collapse at the end, the second into an inept and trivial cabaletta for Beatrice (borrowed from *Bianca e Fernando*), each has its centre-piece in a beautiful cantabile. The E flat *largo* for quintet and chorus in Act I, like the *andante* sostenuto in the same key at the corresponding point in *La Sonnambula*, looks forward to the first finale in *Macbeth*, whose grandiose theme ('L'ira tua formidabile') it faintly foreshadows; likewise the harp-accompanied trio 'Angiol di pace', an A flat round adapted from *Zaira*, begun by Orombello from his offstage cell, evokes memories of Manrico in his tower.

I Puritani (1835),[1] despite its creaking libretto, is structurally the most interesting of Bellini's operas. Arias in set form are heavily outnumbered by duets and ensembles. The beautifully prepared first entry of the tenor, with its romantic horns, leads not to an aria but to a quartet – and 'A te, O cara' is surely an ancestor of the quartet in *Rigoletto*. All Elvira's solos are combined with one, two, or three other voices. By contrast the duet for two baritone Roundhead colonels (one retired) that ends Act II seems old-fashioned, especially as they begin by singing opposed sentiments to the same music. Yet the cabaletta ('Suoni la tromba') represents an enduring strain in Italian opera that reappears in *Ernani* and even the march in *Aida*. The blatant trumpet obbligato is not typical of the scoring of *I Puritani*, which has greater

---

[1] The original title *I Puritani di Scozia* was a product of the literary cult of Scott. While the source play, *Têtes Rondes et Cavaliers*, bears very faint traces of *Old Mortality*, these were entirely eliminated in the libretto; but the earlier appearance of a translation of the novel as *Les Puritains d'Écosse* was enough to drag across the border a story that takes place in Plymouth.

variety and a warmer blend than in earlier operas, especially in the treatment of woodwind and horns. The flexibility of the ensembles shows Bellini beginning to think in longer periods and anxious to incorporate more action instead of leaving it to the recitative, of which there is comparatively little. The duet during the first finale in which Arturo plans the escape of the disguised Enrichetta (widow of Charles I), with the voices conversing *parlando* over a symphonic accompaniment, develops a high degree of suspense, sustained when the couple are intercepted and challenged by Riccardo. The first half of Act III is exceptionally fluid in design. After a storm prelude Elvira begins a romanza offstage, answered a tone higher by Arturo, who is on the run. Interrupted while he hides from the searching Roundhead patrols, he resumes the romanza, which never reverts to its original key or to Elvira, but leads by way of reminiscences of Act I as Elvira's sanity returns to a duet in which Arturo has to explain Enrichetta's identity. However dramatically absurd, the scene is musically convincing, at any rate until the cabaletta of the duet. The working of ostinato figures when the soldiers search for Arturo on two occasions in Act III, in the D flat *largo maestoso* of the finale, and in the Act II chorus 'Quaggiù nel mal', shows an increased certainty of control, supported as it is by greater freedom of modulation. So does the handling of reminiscence motive. Bellini had used it in *Norma*, rather stiffly with the march in Act I, effectively at the recall of the theme associated with Norma's children in the second finale. In *I Puritani* he carried it further, bringing back earlier material, always in the orchestra, for dramatic and structural purposes in all three acts.

X

GERMAN OPERA

By WINTON DEAN

FOREIGN INFLUENCES

AT Mozart's death the status of German opera – opera in the German language – was very different from that of French or Italian. In those countries opera had been a flourishing concern for generations and had developed a sturdy root system. Since the demise of the Hamburg Opera in 1738 serious German opera, except in a fragmentary and discontinuous form, had scarcely existed. One determining factor was the absence of political unity; the country was divided into innumerable states, great and small, of which the most important were Austria, Prussia, Bavaria, and Saxony. The opera houses were controlled by the courts (as they were in Italy and almost everywhere else in the eighteenth century), and were to remain so for another two generations. The ruling princes, in so far as they encouraged opera at all – and this was largely for reasons of prestige – preferred foreign imports, sometimes French but generally Italian. Berlin (until 1806), Munich (until 1826), and Dresden (until 1832) maintained permanent Italian companies; Vienna had a regular annual season of Italian opera subsidized by the state. Even the theatres giving performances in German – there were 24 of them in 1804 – relied for the greater part of their repertory on French *opéra comique* and Italian *opera buffa* in translation.[1] After 1815 Vienna, the Habsburg capital, fell more than ever under Italian influence and, thanks to the Neapolitan impresario Barbaja and the infectious music of Rossini, became for a time almost an Italian satellite. As had happened before, Italy recovered on the artistic front much of the power and prestige she had lost on the political.

Although the origins of the German Romantic movement lay well

[1] Siegfried Goslich in his exhaustive study *Beiträge zur Geschichte der deutschen romantischen Oper* (Leipzig, 1937, pp. 38–40) gives statistics showing that this was still true for the period 1820–50, and emphasizes that German operas before *Lohengrin*, with a few notable exceptions, enjoyed only restricted local runs. Goslich's book was later revised and expanded as *Die deutsche romantische Oper* (Tutzing, 1975).

back in the eighteenth century, it was slow to make productive contact with music. It was natural that its driving force should be primarily literary, philosophical, and political, but fortuitous and unlucky that its leaders, with rare exceptions, showed little feeling for the other arts – much less than their contemporaries in France. Goethe wrote *Singspiel* librettos, but was singularly ham-handed in his contacts with musicians; turning his back on Beethoven, Schubert, and Weber, he rested his faith in the academic conservative Zelter who was hostile to opera. This block between music and letters was to be a chronic hindrance to the development of German Romantic opera. As the early history of the form in Italy and France – and in other countries later – sufficiently demonstrates, the establishment of an operatic tradition is not a simple affair. Opera is a composite art; its constituent parts jostle and struggle for supremacy before they can achieve even a precarious balance. If the history of German opera at this period is one of confusion, false starts and blind alleys, the whole blame cannot be laid at the door of composers.

They were confronted at the outset with a divorce from their native tongue. Gluck, an Austrian citizen, wrote operas in French and Italian for Vienna but never set a word of German for the theatre. Much the same had been true of Handel and Hasse. German composers went regularly to study in Italy, and were still doing so in the time of Meyerbeer and Nicolai. The Bavarian Mayr became so italianized that he settled permanently in Bergamo. Most German composers with operatic ambitions wrote chiefly in Italian, because it offered more openings, and some also in French. This cosmopolitanism was typical of the age; Winter, Reichardt, and Meyerbeer among Germans, Cherubini, Spontini, Paer, Paisiello, and Salieri among Italians set librettos in all three languages. Gyrowetz, a Czech, was Court Kapellmeister at Vienna from 1804 to 1831 but continued to set Italian as well as German texts. Mozart's career is less remarkable for his many Italian operas than for its inclusion of two major works in German.

When a composer did attempt a serious German opera, he was faced with a struggle on two fronts: outwardly against the powerful and jealous Italians (as Mozart found in Vienna and Weber in Dresden), internally with a medium that offered few holds to grip and fewer examples to follow. No German poet had studied the libretto in depth, or seen any necessity to do so, with the result that every composer ran into the same difficulties of incompetence and irrelevance, until Wagner solved the problem for himself by writing his own texts. Nor were suitable musical forms easily available. The

German *Romanze* and *Lied* – and still more the *Volkslied*, which was
generally not a folk-song but a popular song, a simple ditty intended
for domestic or convivial use, or as incidental music in a play –
possessed nothing like the scope for development of the Italian aria or
its French equivalent. While Italian vocal writing was primarily
melodic, and French declamatory, that of the Germans tended to be
instrumental. Having no tradition of recitative on the one hand or
coloratura display on the other, but a growing experience of the
symphony and concerto, they were apt, when endeavouring to enlarge
their solo forms,[1] to treat the voice as if it were a clarinet or bassoon.
Mozart's thorough training in the Italian style had saved him from
this danger, but Weber with his innate and increasing hostility to
Italian opera never overcame it. Winter's opera airs regularly combine
simple *Lied* melodies with outbursts of frantic coloratura unsuited
both to the voice and to the context.

Mozart's two *Singspiele* could not provide an adequate model to
men of lesser powers, since they were themselves, in words and music,
eclectic *mélanges* of bewilderingly wide provenance, from low farce to
high-flown *opera seria*, held together only by the genius of their creator.
Various attempts were made to discover a suitable root-stock in
French and Italian tradition, some of it long outmoded. Even after the
fall of Napoleon German composers were still struggling with librettos
based on Metastasio: Johann Nepomuk von Poissl (1783–1865) in *Der
Wettkampf zu Olympia* (1815) and *Nittetis* (1817), Ignaz Franz Mosel
(1772–1844) in *Cyrus und Astyages* (1818). Poissl also tried Racine in
Athalia (1814), an opera that Weber produced at Prague two years
later and on which he gave the composer extensive advice. This was
a case of the blind leading the blind. Weber, though brought up in the
theatre and capable of achieving individual *coups de théâtre* of
stunning effectiveness, made repeated miscalculations in attempting
to impose an over-all design. Beethoven struggled for years with a
single opera without reaching a satisfactory solution. Schubert,
endowed with a love of the theatre but little understanding of its
artistic requirements, was further handicapped by inability to get his
operas produced at all. German operas before Wagner, whether in
Singspiel or through-composed form, are almost invariably looser in
construction than their French and Italian contemporaries and less
adept at integrating music and drama. The endeavour to supply their
deficiency was a major factor in their growing pre-occupation with the

---

[1] The various types of vocal solo, native, borrowed, and mixed, in German Romantic opera are
comprehensively analysed by Goslich, op. cit.

reminiscence motive,[1] an idea borrowed from the French. But it was a long time before any German composer (Mozart always excepted) achieved that quality of theatrical movement in the set numbers reached again and again by a comparatively minor figure like Dalayrac. Eventually the catalyst was found in the French *opéra comique* of the Revolution; but the seed could not thrive in German soil until native composers supplied a powerful fertilizer derived from their gift for the symbolic and the supernatural, and until they solved the problem of through-composition. The early history of German Romantic opera is largely concerned with these two important developments.

THE LATER VIENNESE *SINGSPIEL*

The nearest approach to a German operatic tradition in 1790 was the Viennese *Singspiel*, which was almost as much a literary as a musical form, corresponding to the French pre-Revolution *opéra comique* and the Italian *opera buffa*, from both of which it borrowed extensively. But it lacked the sophistication of the former and the consistency of the latter with its linking *secco* recitative. Its two principal types more or less reflected the practice of the court and the suburban theatres. One of the former, the Burgtheater, had been the scene of a worthy attempt to establish a National *Singspiel*, patronized by the Emperor Joseph II, between 1778 and 1787; but after producing one work of genius in Mozart's *Entführung* it petered out and fell back on translations. Italian opera remained dominant there and in the other court theatre, the Kärntnertor, which between them saw the production of popular works by Salieri, Paisiello, Martín y Soler, and Paer (and also Storace's two Italian operas). There were a few German successes, notably Johann Schenk's *Der Dorfbarbier* (1796) at the Burgtheater and Dittersdorf's *Doktor und Apotheker* (1786),[2] Winter's *Das unterbrochene Opferfest* (1796), and Süssmayr's *Soliman der Zweite* (1799) at the Kärntnertor. The suburban theatres, Marinelli's in the Leopoldstadt (opened in 1781) and Schikaneder's Theater auf der Wieden (opened 1787, replaced in 1801 by a new building, Theater an der Wien) catered for a lower taste. Their rivalry, while as strenuous as that of the *opéra comique* theatres in Paris, operated on a less idealistic level; the more basic competition was between the German and Italian languages. The works produced at the Leopoldstadt, which from 1786 was directed by Wenzel Müller, a pupil of Dittersdorf, have

---

[1] See Karl Wörner, 'Beiträge zur Geschichte des Leitmotivs in der Oper', *Zeitschrift für Musikwissenschaft*, xiv (1931–2), p. 151.

[2] See Vol. VII, pp. 95–6.

with reason seldom troubled historians; the most successful were those of Müller himself and such similar pieces as Dittersdorf's *Hieronimus Knicker* (1789) and the immensely popular *Das Donauweibchen* (1798) of Ferdinand Kauer (1751–1831). Schikaneder's theatre had a chequered but more honourable career. Its production of the first two masterpieces of German opera, *Die Zauberflöte* (1791) and *Fidelio* (1805), would alone distinguish it; but it saw the birth of a number of secondary works by Paul Wranitzky (*Oberon*, 1789), Karl Ditters von Dittersdorf, Franz Süssmayr, Franz Hoffmeister, Joseph Weigl, Peter von Winter, and Georg ('Abt') Vogler (*Samori*, 1804).

One type of *Singspiel*, represented by *Doktor und Apotheker* and *Der Dorfbarbier*, was a domestic operetta much influenced, in words and music, by *opera buffa*. We meet all the stock characters and situations – heavy father, drunken soldier, bogus notary, amorous dotard; an elopement or some other escapade of the young lovers is first frustrated and then crowned with a satisfactory reconciliation, the comic bass being tricked or laughed into abandoning his opposition. There is no social satire. The plots can be entertaining on a crude level: Schenk's barber-surgeon has a sovereign remedy – ham, 'indispensable for tailors, harmless for smiths' – which undoes him in the end. The subplots introduce superfluous characters, some of whom sing very little if at all; they were presumably played by actors with untrained voices. The music is tuneful, high-spirited, formally elementary and, when not predictable, often clumsy in execution. The ensembles, especially in *Doktor und Apotheker*, are livelier than the solos, most of which imitate the Italian AB design, the second section in a different time and mood, without establishing a balance between the components. The harmony is very limited; the rhythms incline to an amiable 6/8 or a skittish 2/4. *Der Dorfbarbier* has an early German example of the vocal polonaise[1] and a simple *Lied* with five identical stanzas (sung by the barber's apprentice, a paler Papageno) – both forms that survived into Romantic opera. The entire style is rendered insipid to modern ears by Mozart's transfiguration of it. His contemporaries, without his sense of design or timing, not to mention his powers of invention, characterization and scoring, merely deposit their numbers at intervals in the dialogue.

SPECTACLE AND FANTASY IN *SINGSPIEL*

This is also typical of the second type of *Singspiel*, in which Hanswurst buffoonery and copious dialogue are combined with

[1] Schenk was anticipated by J. G. Naumann, but in an Italian opera, *La dama soldato* (Dresden, 1791).

elaborate stage spectacle and a strong element of the fantastic and magical – another contributory stream to Romantic opera. There was less consistency here and much more eclecticism. The type is familiar from *Die Zauberflöte*; the failure of other composers to approach its integrity can cause no surprise. Most of them scarcely made the attempt. Schikaneder was not alone in devising this type of entertainment, though he provided many examples in association with Weigl, Winter, F. A. Hoffmeister, and Süssmayr as well as Mozart: Wenzel Müller (1767–1835) at the Leopoldstadt turned them out in dozens over a long period. Many bear such subtitles as *heroisch-komisches Singspiel* or *romantisches komisches Volksmärchen mit Gesang*, which indicate the subordinate status of the music.

One of the curiosities of opera at this period is the popularity of Shakespeare's *Tempest* as a source: the years 1798–9 saw the production of eight operas based on it, seven in Germany and one in Italy. It is easy to see why the plot's double intrigue of courtly conspiracy and low comedy, crossed with the spectacular elements of storm, shipwreck, and supernatural manifestations and the allegory of good and evil, appealed to the German temperament, especially after the success of *Die Zauberflöte*. There is an obvious correspondence between Prospero, Miranda, Ferdinand, and Caliban on the one hand and Sarastro, Pamina, Tamino, and Monostatos on the other, and no great ingenuity is needed to work Ariel into the posture of the three genii and Trinculo or Stephano into that of Papageno; Shakespeare even has a Queen of Night in the wings in the person of Sycorax, as more than one German composer discovered. Müller's version (*Der Sturm, heroisch-komische Oper nach Shakespeare*, 1798) makes less of the allegory than those of his northern compatriots mentioned below; indeed it suggests the English pantomime in its mixture of buffooneries, sensational transformation scenes (several in each finale, with a whole string of tempests), and more of less extraneous music. Shakespeare's comic roles are expanded and increased in number: Stephano has a sister, Rosine, who employs wrestling technique to defeat the Polyphemus-like advances of Caliban and eventually joins with Trinculo in establishing a *Narrenfabrik* to keep the court supplied with jesters. Bianka (Miranda), promised a young man by her father, makes uninhibited advances first to Trinculo, then to Rosine, and finally to an embarrassed Ferdinand. Ariel teases the conspiring comics by conjuring up three seductive females, who disconcertingly turn into three bears; Bruno (Prospero) presently buries the malefactors up to their necks. Another suggestive incident is his presentation of a magic horn, not to Ferdinand but to Ariel.

Although Müller occasionally wrote quite substantial finales,[1] most of the music offered little but sentimental songs in the popular Viennese style, in which echoes (and borrowings) from Mozart and *opera buffa* were frequent. Some use was made of *mélodrame*; Benda's works in this form were very popular in Vienna. It is not surprising that Beethoven, a one-time pupil of Schenk, found little in the Viennese operas of the 1790s except themes for variations, which alone have preserved many of their names.

PETER VON WINTER

A more ambitious but scarcely more homogeneous method was adopted by Peter von Winter, a pupil of Vogler and a servant of the Bavarian court, whose long career embraced German, French, and Italian operas (some written for the London Haymarket) and included settings of Metastasio (*Catone in Utica*, 1791) at one end and Romani (*Maometto II*, 1817) at the other. His most popular work, *Das unterbrochene Opferfest*, the most successful German opera in the thirty years between *Die Zauberflöte* and *Der Freischütz*, belongs to a strange mixed convention combining elements from *Singspiel* with the old (pre-Gluck) *opera seria* and a dénouement influenced by French rescue opera: Murney, an Englishman about to be sacrificed to the Sun-God, is released by the son of the Inca whose life he has saved. The comic scenes were cut in later revivals with the emphatic approval of Weber. Like Winter's subsequent success *Marie von Montalban* (Munich, 1800), which is entirely serious, it has a stiff Metastasian plot set in an exotic climate (Peru in the one case, India in the other) without the remotest trace of exoticism in the music. Both stories are full of menaces, battles, and violence, but the central situation remains static: the threat of execution hangs over the hero or heroine until it is dissipated by an unconvincing happy end. The finale of *Marie von Montalban*, some of whose characters we meet again in Spohr's *Jessonda*, is absurdly perfunctory. The tangled amorous motives receive much more attention than the political; there is no trace of the idealism of the French.

The music is overwhelmingly influenced by Mozart's comedies, and even contains echoes of his instrumental works; it shows little sign of Gluck or *Idomeneo*, which would have been more suitable models. Winter commanded a feeling for the stage and for felicitous modulation, including a fondness for contrasting keys a third apart;

[1] For example in *Die Schwestern von Prag* (1794) and *Die unruhige Nachbarschaft* (1803). See Peter Branscombe, 'Music in the Viennese Popular Theatre', *Proceedings of the Royal Musical Association*, xcviii (1970/71), p. 111.

this anticipates a favourite gambit of Romantic opera but was probably derived from Mozart. He is weak in characterization and structural design; the numerous ensembles and long finales are poorly articulated despite the occasional recall of their opening themes at a later stage. His happier ideas, such as the effective ostinato in the second finale of *Opferfest* and the use of the same material in differently paced sections of Enrichetta's aria (no. 20) in the Italian opera *I fratelli rivali* (1793), are apt to draw attention to the flaccid level of the rest. A more striking feature, again clearly derived from *Die Zauberflöte*, is the attempt to impose a tonal unity on a whole opera: *Opferfest, Das Labyrinth* (1798) and *Marie von Montalban* all revolve round the keys of C major and minor, and E flat major.

Winter's arias suffer from short-winded melodies, usually square in ·rhythm, and stunted development, incongruously yoked with coloratura of the most formidable difficulty. His sopranos are embryo Queens of Night with a tendency to fire rockets into the stratosphere on the slightest provocation. Elvira's aria in Act I of *Opferfest* (no. 11) decorates the second syllable of the word 'verzehren' for 15 bars of quavers and semiquavers in common time, several times hitting the E above the treble stave, and in the second finale Myrha delivers the following in a quartet against detached crotchet chords from three other sopranos:

Ex. 170

(He is dying, already the flames are crackling wildly, I must see him again)

Enrichetta, the mezzo-soprano heroine of *I fratelli rivali*, seems to have been conceived in terms of the clarinet:

Ex. 171

(There is nothing sweeter, clearer, than peace of the soul, of the heart, nothing more beautiful or more treasured when it is united with tender love.)

Bass voices are treated similarly; the compass (C♯–e′), agility and huge vocal leaps demanded of the Priest of Brahma in no. 22 of *Marie von Montalban* might be assumed to presuppose a liaison between Sarastro and the Queen of Night. In this opera the chief male voices are all low; there are three basses or baritones and only a minor tenor. Winter's inability to develop his ideas beyond a short span is underlined by an almost Wagnerian propensity for common time (except in a few slow pieces and the comic scenes of *Opferfest*, where a 2/4 or 6/8 signature is a sign that a servant is about to give tongue) and a sparse use of counterpoint. His rare chromaticism, also stemming from Mozart, adds a certain savour, as in the trio for three basses (no. 15) in *Opferfest* and the A flat *adagio* for two sisters welcoming death (characteristically following C major) in the second finale of *Montalban*. This act contains a powerful D minor quartet very redolent of *Don Giovanni*,[1] beginning on a diminished seventh.

Winter's most interesting opera – though it was a failure in its day and provokes such odious comparisons that it could not be revived except as a curiosity – is his sequel to *Die Zauberflöte*, *Das Labyrinth*. This was commissioned by Schikaneder, who virtually duplicated his earlier part, giving even greater prominence to his own role: Papageno appears not only with his wife, but with his old parents and a whole chorus of brothers and sisters all rejoicing in the same name. Tamino

---

[1] There are several other contemporary echoes of *Don Giovanni's* characteristic D minor mood, for example in the overture to Müller's *Die Teufelsmühle am Wienerberg* (1799).

and Pamina are just married, but the Queen of Night and her minions, including Monostatos, hatch a plot to kidnap Pamina and marry her to a suitor of their choice. Winter as well as Schikaneder set out to mimic the earlier opera both in general plan and in individual scenes. He borrowed two of Mozart's themes, the triple chord (slightly varied) and Papageno's upward scale figure, which appears constantly, sometimes with echoes. All the characters operate in Mozart's keys and with similar accompaniment figures and other accessories (for example Monostatos's repeated notes); flute and glockenspiel are prominent (Papageno makes the three ladies dance to the latter); there are solemn temple scenes, Sarastro puts the lovers through tests in the labyrinth and sings two sonorous E major *larghettos*, the Queen of Night delivers fiery coloratura in C minor and D minor, and so on. Winter, who was notoriously hostile to Mozart (the sentiment was mutual), made an obvious attempt to beat him at his own game. Needless to say, he did not succeed; but the challenge raised him above his normal level in invention, imagination, and sometimes in construction. The music has greater continuity, rhythmic vitality, and harmonic spice: the occasional romantic appoggiaturas sound almost bold for their period. The two enormous finales, though they do not approach the models, are not spineless and contain episodes that are impressive in their own right: in Act I the E flat *grave* when the Queen of Night and four Moors lie in wait for Pamina and Tamino's flute is heard inside the labyrinth (Ex. 172) and the sudden pianissimo coda after Pamina's abduction at the very end (Ex. 173); in Act II the C minor *maestoso* as two male choruses prepare to fight while Pamina's soprano soars high above.

Ex. 172

(Already they are wandering in the dark labyrinth)

Ex. 173

(Woe to us! Pamina has gone!)

Winter has nothing of Mozart's sublime wisdom or his spiritual unity;
otherwise one is most conscious of his inferiority in the Papageno
music, where the manner is very close to Mozart's but a deceptively
narrow chasm separates triviality from genius.

INFLUENCE FROM FRANCE

If one element in Winter's style came from Mozart, its other source was the insipid feminine strain in the Italian operas of Paer and Zingarelli. The combination held no future for German opera. But a new force appeared at the turn of the century when the major works of the French Revolution school reached Vienna and made all the greater impact because they were filling an artistic vacuum. A few of Dalayrac's early operas and Méhul's *Euphrosine* had been given up to 1795, but were little noticed. In 1800 Süssmayr based his *Gulnare* on Dalayrac's libretto of two years earlier. The decisive moment came in 1802 with the arrival in quick succession of four important operas by Cherubini, all in German translation: *Lodoïska* in March, *Les Deux Journées* in August (at two different theatres on successive nights), *Médée* in November, and *Élisa* in December. *L'Hotellerie portugaise* followed in 1803, together with Le Sueur's *La Caverne* (also at two theatres) and no fewer than five operas by Méhul, including *Héléna*, which had its Paris première only five months earlier. 1804 brought a veritable spate of French operas, among them *Ariodant* and works by Dalayrac, Della Maria, Devienne, Berton, Boieldieu, and Isouard. The stage was set for *Fidelio*.

OPERA IN NORTH GERMANY

In north and central Germany sporadic attempts by Schweitzer, Holzbauer, Benda, and others to establish vernacular opera, serious and comic, had come to nothing[1] for the reasons outlined at the beginning of this chapter. The Gotha poet, Friedrich Wilhelm Gotter, who had collaborated with Schweitzer and Benda, was no more successful with Johann Friedrich Reichardt (1752–1814), Kapellmeister in Berlin from 1776 to 1794 and active as reformer, impresario, and critic. Reichardt, who travelled extensively in his youth, visiting Paris and London in the 1780s, was a man of more enterprise than creative talent. In his early *mélodrame Ino* (1779), modelled on Benda, he experimented with reminiscence themes – the *mélodrame* form would seem a natural seed-bed for such a device – and he introduced three stage bands in addition to the pit orchestra in the Italian opera *Brenno* (1789). The first consists of woodwind (including basset-horns, double bassoon, and serpent), the second of 'Turkish music', the third of four trumpets and drums; they play separately and then together. In 1798 Reichardt was one of four composers to set *Die Geisterinsel*, a libretto based on Shakespeare's *Tempest* by Gotter and F. H. von Einsiedel. The libretto is of some historical interest: Goethe called it a masterpiece, and its authors considered many possible composers,

[1] See Vol. VII, pp. 65–89.

including Haydn, Grétry, Dittersdorf, Wranitzky, and Friedrich Himmel: in 1791 they offered it to Mozart, who is said to have accepted it shortly before his death. The plot emerges as a struggle between black and white magic, represented by Sycorax who rules by night and Prospero who rules by day. Sycorax and Maja, a deceased good spirit who is restored to life by Ariel, are played by dancers. Prospero ensures that Ferdinand and Miranda do not fall asleep, and so into the enemy's power, by keeping them up all night counting corals – an episode used later by Weber in *Rübezahl* and Spohr in *Der Berggeist*. There is a great deal of spectacle, including a volcanic eruption staged by Prospero. The low buffoonery of the Caliban scenes is set off by much sententious moralizing after Sarastro's manner from Prospero, and still more from Ariel, who offers worldly advice seasoned with oracular pronouncements about the realm of shadows resting under a sevenfold seal. The opera ends with Caliban, after a formidable curse, diving into the sea to join his mother, and the entire company singing a hymn in praise of the fatherland.

Here are to be found almost all the literary ingredients of German Romanticism as exploited by the generation of E. T. A. Hoffmann, Spohr, and Weber. Reichardt was not equal to the challenge. His score, overwhelmingly influenced by Mozart (*Don Giovanni* in the overture and storm music, *Die Zauberflöte* in the magic scenes), resembles Winter in its short-winded melody, limited rhythmic and harmonic vocabulary, and inappropriately showy coloratura. Caliban's compass extends from the E below the bass stave to top G. With this goes a propensity for demure little *Volkslied* tunes that suggest a parody of an amateur German choral society. There is some attempt at characterization, with the aid of varied scoring, and Caliban takes off the latest fashion for a vocal polonaise; but the ensembles and finales are structurally helpless. The most interesting feature is the overture, based on four themes from Act I, into which it runs without a break. This is undoubtedly due to French influence; Reichardt, an admirer of the Revolution, had revisited Paris in 1794. The setting of the same libretto by Johann Zumsteeg (1760–1802), produced at Stuttgart four months after Reichardt's,[1] though weakly characterized – Ariel, Prospero, and Caliban are musically indistinguishable – is much more accomplished; melody, harmony, and rhythm move with a sense of purpose, the ensembles are soundly constructed, and the German choral society is set at a distance. The style, though somewhat anonymous, suggests early Beethoven as much as Mozart.

---

[1] The other two settings, by Friedrich Fleischmann and Friedrich Haack, were not published.

Reichardt and Zumsteeg were to leave their principal mark on the *Lied* and ballad, but the former was an assiduous opera composer who drew on a wide variety of literary sources, including Ariosto and Schiller as well as Shakespeare. He set Metastasio and others in Italian, three *Singspiel* texts by Goethe, and three French librettos, one of which (*Tamerlan*) was used later by Winter. After returning to Berlin at the end of the century he devised, in *Lieb' und Treue* (1800), a new form known as *Liederspiel*, a primitive ballad opera or vaudeville with few pretentions to artistic stature. Its most popular example was *Fanchon das Leiermädchen* (1804) by Friedrich Himmel (1765–1814), Reichardt's successor at the Berlin Court, who had begun his career with several Italian operas. The *Liederspiel* reached its peak of accomplishment in the young Mendelssohn's *Heimkehr aus der Fremde* (known in England as *Son and Stranger*), written for private performance in 1829 and not given in public until 1851. The deft music owes much to Weber; the plot contains curious anticipations of Beckmesser.

Cherubini's most important operas reached Berlin even before Vienna (*Lodoiska* as early as 1797), thanks to the enterprise of the conductor Bernhard Anselm Weber (1764–1821). An enthusiastic supporter of German musicians and one of Meyerbeer's early teachers, Weber had already introduced many works of Gluck and Mozart, but although he sometimes supplemented operas by Dalayrac, Gaveaux, and others he failed as a stage composer in his own right, and no one else was competent to seize the opportunity. Berlin had to wait until 1816 for its first important German opera, the *Undine* of E. T. A. Hoffmann (1776–1822); even after that and *Der Freischütz* it was for many years subject to the foreign domination of Spontini.

FIDELIO

Beethoven's single opera, quite apart from its artistic merits, is a historical landmark because, by assimilating the French Revolution style, it gave German theatre music a robustness, musical, dramatic and philosophical, of which it was badly in need. Owing to the failure of the first two versions and adverse external circumstances – the French army had just occupied Vienna – this was not at once appreciated. *Fidelio* stands in splendid isolation as the one German opera composed between Mozart's death and 1816 to retain a spark of vitality, apart from the early attempts of Weber. Beethoven, though strongly attracted to the theatre, was repelled by the triviality of contemporary German librettos and the scrappiness of the music; to his ethical cast of mind Mozart's subjects, apart from *Idomeneo* and parts of *Die Zauberflöte*, were antipathetic, lacking in dignity and morally degenerate. He needed a theme to reflect his ideals for humanity, and a style to do justice to them. He found both in Cherubini, whom he considered the greatest composer of the age, and not only in opera. He likewise gave high rank to Méhul and later to Spontini, and declared in 1823 that the best librettos he knew were those of *Les Deux Journées* and *La Vestale*.

Fidelio in all three versions, especially that of 1805, belongs in form and spirit to the French Revolution school, of which it is the true climax. This is not merely because its libretto is French in origin; so is its whole ambience and almost every technical device it employs. The background of dramatic realism, on which is superimposed a heroic story involving a conflict between black menace and almost superhuman endeavour, set in a confined space (often in darkness) and resolved in the nick of time not primarily by a *deus ex machina* but by an act of supreme courage, is that of *Lodoiska* and many other rescue operas. The slow approach to the serious business of the plot by way of a series of genre scenes is as typical as the powerful overtures of the first two versions (at once symphonic and programmatic) encapsulating the kernel of the action, the graded use of spoken dialogue merging at moments of crisis into *mélodrame* and recitative, the fundamentally serious approach to the lighter scenes, and the massive ensembles combining rhythmic energy, slow-moving harmony, and trenchant modulations. Even the most Beethovenian factor of all, the generic treatment of the characters as personifications of love, hope, faithfulness, and villainy, is modelled on the Cherubini of *Les Deux Journées*.

The history of the opera is complex. Early in 1803 Beethoven began to set a libretto by Schikaneder, *Vestas Feuer*, for which he was offered very favourable terms. He may have been attracted by the idea of working with Mozart's collaborator in *Die Zauberflöte*; but only inexperience and the absence of suitable Viennese models can account for his acceptance of this frigid story of conspiracy in ancient Rome. It was perhaps at this time that he copied for study substantial sections of a French *tragédie-lyrique*, Salieri's *Les Danaides*. He set the greater part of Schikaneder's first scene, including a trio of reconciliation whose music was later adapted for the duet 'O namenlose Freude' in *Fidelio*. The most interesting point about *Vestas Feuer* is that it was planned not as a *Singspiel* but as a through-composed grand opera with the numbers linked by arioso. An unexpected and perhaps unfortunate result of the discovery of Cherubini was the deflection of Beethoven and many other Germans back to *Singspiel*. By January

1804, disillusioned with *Vestas Feuer*, he had found Bouilly's libretto of *Léonore*[1] and given it to Joseph Sonnleithner to arrange. In an interesting letter to Rochlitz (4 January) he remarked that Schikaneder's empire had been 'entirely eclipsed by the light of the brilliant and attractive French operas', and he refused the first act of a libretto by Rochlitz because it was based on magic (he reacted similarly in 1808 when Matthäus von Collin submitted a libretto on the Alcina story, subsequently set by Reichardt). Nothing could illustrate more clearly Beethoven's affinities with the French and his aversion from both the past and the future diet of German opera.

It is easy to understand the appeal *Léonore* made to him. Here was a credible story of daily life (some of Bouilly's characters talk in dialect), wholly free from the stagey conventions of Italian *opera seria* and German comedy. Moreover it had a strong ethical content, and contained an attractive presentation of what Beethoven had been unable to find in person: an ideal heroic woman. Sonnleithner's libretto is much closer to Bouilly than those set by Paer and Mayr, or than the two later versions of *Fidelio*; it is virtually a translation, with inserted movements to increase the opportunities for musical expression. In Pierre Gaveaux's opera, almost a play with songs, Pizare does not sing at all, and the decisive trumpet-call occurs during spoken dialogue. Sonnleithner gave Pizarro two arias and an important part in several ensembles; he was responsible for both quartets, two trios in Act I, and the duet in which Pizarro and Rocco plan the murder. His set pieces are well-contrived, but he made the grave mistake of expanding the earlier, domestic, and less dramatically crucial part of the story and dividing Bouilly's first act into two, making three in all. Apart from enlarging Marzelline's part out of all proportion, this postponed Pizarro's first appearance till Act II and Florestan's till Act III. Sonnleithner's final act is an improvement on Bouilly; but the main action does not begin till far too late.

Beethoven, inexperienced in the theatre, accentuated the disproportion. His music with its expressive forms and regular periods seems geared to abstract design rather than dramatic pace, and as a result sounds diffuse. It is more Cherubinian in plan and more Mozartean in idiom than his 1814 score, expecially in the first two acts, but wholly lacks that dramatic ruthlessness that impelled Mozart to cut some of his finest music from Act III of *Idomeneo*. All the movements except the march are longer than in 1814 (some of them a great deal longer), and three subsequently disappeared: a trio in which Marzelline and

---

[1] See above, p. 32.

Rocco dash Jaquino's hopes of marriage, a duet (straight from Bouilly) in which Marzelline looks forward to marriage with 'Fidelio' while the latter dissembles, and an air for Pizarro with male chorus at the end of Act II. The first two are dramatically otiose; the third has the weakest music in the score. Act III on the other hand is at several points more striking than the corresponding Act II of 1814. Florestan's air ends, not with his radiant F major vision of Leonore but with an agitated F minor *andante* expressing a stoical defiance of destiny that enlarges our view of the character. At the end of the quartet Rocco snatches the pistol from Leonore, who falls senseless. Instead of the tame 1814 dialogue (generally cut) there is a long recitative of superb quality in which the shackled Florestan, fearing that she may be no sooner regained than lost, tries to reach her, she gradually recovers, and they fall into each other's arms. Based on a beautiful oboe melody, this has a quality of overwhelming suspense paralleled only by the passage introducing the finale of the Fifth Symphony. It leads into the duet 'O namenlose Freude', which is launched with tremendous impact, reinforced by the fact that both voices enter together and the melody is carried up to the top B (though the words are a much more awkward fit than in *Vestas Feuer*).

Ex. 174

(i) Vestas Feuer

Moreover Leonore and Florestan, though re-united, have no reason to consider themselves safe. They have lost their only weapon, and naturally take the offstage cries of vengeance (another detail lifted from Bouilly) as directed against themselves. The drama, instead of subsiding, is thus extended into the finale, in which the tumultuous crowd, followed by Don Fernando, burst into the prison as if into the Bastille (there is no change of scene). The A major episode, which in 1814 occurs in broad daylight after all is solved, represents the lovers' instant response to their rescue. While the finale was later shortened and musically strengthened, it lost its dramatic tension. The slightly modified quotation from Schiller's 'Ode to Joy', which so strikingly links Beethoven's two most heartfelt statements of faith, is already present in 1805, though it was reinforced in 1814 by Don Fernando's lines beginning 'Es sucht der Bruder seine Brüder'. Present too is the remarkable self-borrowing from the 1790 *Cantata on the death of the Emperor Joseph II*, perhaps also suggested by the original words ('Da stiegen die Menschen an's Licht'): this F major *andante assai*, progressivly reduced in length, occurs in all three versions of the opera.

The first *Fidelio*, produced on 20 November 1805, had three performances. Beethoven wished to keep the title *Leonore*, and used it for the 1806 libretto and the incomplete vocal score of 1810; but the management insisted on a change because Paer (who had links with the theatre) had pre-empted it for his setting, produced at Dresden on 3 October 1804.[1] Beethoven's second version, given twice only on 29 March and 10 April 1806 and still unpublished in full, was in the main a hasty attempt to remedy the weaknesses of the first. His friend Stephan von Breuning overhauled the libretto, compressing the first two acts into one and altering the order of movements. Only Rocco's air and the Act II *Melodram* were omitted, but many movements, including both finales, were drastically shortened. All three trios and Florestan's scena, which lost the ritornello of its *adagio*, suffered clumsy mutilation. Breuning, though he failed to get rid of the main defect, Marzelline's undue prominence, introduced a number of improvements commonly attributed to Treitschke in 1814.[2] Pizarro posts the trumpeter after his aria, not before; Leonore, not Marzelline, releases the prisoners. Beethoven made some interesting changes in the orchestration, adding the double bassoon to the grave-digging duet and removing the trombones from Pizarro's 'Ha! Welch ein Augenblick!', and quickened many of the tempo indications. He eased the extravagant difficulties in Leonore's aria and 'O namenlose Freude'; his vocal writing is nowhere more brutal than in the 1805 *Fidelio*. The strengthened coda of 'O namenlose Freude' dates from 1806, as does Leonore's part in the final ensemble, where she had previously been silent; but the most important addition was the new overture, Leonore, no. 3, which replaced no. 2. Recent study of the sketches suggests that no. 1 was composed about 1806–7, not (as Schindler said) before the 1805 production.

A third librettist, Treitschke, was employed in 1814. His changes in Act I were all for the better: he reduced Marzelline to scale, removing the superfluous duet and trio, and tightened up the first finale, working in more action and substituting the second prisoners' chorus for Pizarro's second aria. Beethoven reversed the order of the first two movements, so that the A major duet began the opera instead of Marzelline's C minor-major aria. This, in conjunction with the new E

[1] See above, pp. 398.9.
[2] For a full account of the different versions, see Winton Dean, 'Beethoven and Opera' in *The Beethoven Companion*, ed. Denis Arnold and Nigel Fortune (London, 1971).

major overture (designed perhaps to pick out the key of Leonore's great aria), altered the tonal plan of the opera, which had previously been strongly orientated towards C major and minor. Leonore's aria was introduced by the new recitative 'Abscheulicher!', based on the corresponding words in Paer's setting, which had its first Vienna performance (attended by Beethoven[1]) in February 1809. Treitschke's changes in Act II, by sentimentalizing Rocco, virtually terminating the drama with the quartet, and substituting the flattest dialogue[2] for the recitative before 'O namenlose Freude', radically transformed the dénouement. The duet is the one movement unmistakably weakened. The change of scene for the finale, which now includes a political pronouncement from Don Fernando, is saved from anticlimax only by the nobility of Beethoven's hymn to freedom.

This was a deliberate change of emphasis. In the 1805 score, as in Bouilly, the fate of Leonore and Florestan is all-important; the other prisoners are no more than a background, and the moral is allowed to emerge by inference. In 1814 Beethoven rams it home by increasing the prominence of the prisoners and presenting them as symbols of suffering mankind. The finale, with its general amnesty, becomes a cross between the day of judgement and a sermon on the brotherhood of man. This springs less convincingly from the plot, since there is no reason to suppose that all the prisoners are victims of political oppression. The newly emphasized symbolism (light to darkness in Act I, darkness to light in Act II) underlines the parallels with the Ninth Symphony and the message of the Revolution, but drains Leonore and Florestan of individual personality. The 1814 *Fidelio* is a different sort of opera.

The musical changes reflect an enormous advance in Beethoven's style, most conspicuously in the urge to break down symmetrical phrase-lengths and blur transitions. The symphonic development of the duet in which Pizarro and Rocco plan the murder, if it looks back to Act II of *Médée* on the one hand, prefigures the evolutionary method of Wagner on the other. All the numbers Beethoven retained were altered, chiefly in detail by the removal of idle bars and ornamental passages; the cumulative effect is considerable. While generally shortening the music, Beethoven repaired the 1806 mutilations in the early part of Florestan's aria and two of the trios (the third disappeared) without reverting to the leisurely procedures of 1805. The further simplification of the voice part of Leonore's aria was due

[1] There is no evidence that he was aware of Mayr's setting, *L'amor conjugale* (see p. 398.9), produced at Padua in July 1805.
[2] Beethoven considered writing a new recitative at this point.

to the insistence of the singer, Anna Milder, but Beethoven gave the piece a terser, more concentrated form. An outstanding addition was the second prisoners' chorus, 'Leb' wohl, du warmes Sonnenlicht'; the first finale, though shorter than either of the earlier versions, sounds much more massive and spacious. Leonore's aria was first heard at the seventh performance (18 July 1814), when Beethoven also restored Rocco's aria; an earlier 'Abscheulicher!' without the 'komm, Hoffnung' section, sung at the first six performances, has disappeared.

Behind all three versions the example of the French school is manifest. The basic ideas of several pieces, including the arias of Marzelline and Rocco, the accompaniment of the grave-digging duet, and the introduction to the first prisoners' chorus, were clearly suggested by Gaveaux's *Léonore*, though Beethoven far transcended the model. Both the conception and the execution of the trumpet-call in the quartet and the two overtures of 1805 and 1806 derive from Méhul's *Héléna* (on another Bouilly libretto), in which the arrival of 'Le Gouverneur' in the first finale is announced by backstage trumpets in a foreign key; the repetition of the fanfare, the slow-moving harmony with pedal and string ostinato, and the anticipation of the whole process in the overture all occur in Méhul.[1] The influence of Cherubini is more far-reaching. Apart from the obvious modelling of Pizarro on Dourlinski in *Lodoïska* (see p. 40), it would scarcely be too much to say that Beethoven's entire instrumental style, in the symphonies and overtures as well as in *Fidelio*, is a transfiguration of Cherubini's, with its balance of structural masses, its combination of a rhetorical melodic thrust with seething orchestral textures, its sharply contrasted dynamics, and intense rhythmic energy.[2] The Mozartean element in *Fidelio* derives chiefly from *Die Zauberflöte*. Something of its Masonic idealism – which may reflect Mozart's response to the underlying spirit of the Revolution – appears in the Sarastro-like pronouncements of Don Fernando and in the treatment of Leonore and Florestan, whom Dent likened to Pamina and Tamino grown up and brought down to earth.[3] There is also a palpable echo of *Idomeneo* in the *allegro con brio* melody ('Ich folg' dem innern Triebe') of Leonora's aria, whose rhythmic and melodic outline recalls Electra's first aria and several other movements in Mozart's opera.

---

[1] Similar trumpet-calls, on or behind the stage, are found in earlier French operas, for example in the first-act finales of Cherubini's *Lodoiska* and Dalayrac's *Léhéman* (1801).
[2] The orthodox view, stated by Goslich among others, that Beethoven's symphonies supplied material to Romantic opera is almost an inversion of the truth; as Dent argued in *The Rise of Romantic Opera* (Cambridge, 1976), p. 185, the symphonic style of Beethoven and all the German Romantics is basically operatic in origin.
[3] *Mozart's Operas* (London, 2nd edition 1947), pp. 258–9.

We know that Electra's aria made a profound impression on Beethoven in Bonn.[1]

While the Mozartean strain supplied the lyrical deficiencies of the French style, what Beethoven created in *Fidelio* was very much his own. Only a consummate artist endowed with dramatic genius could have conceived the two quartets, especially the canonic 'Mir ist so wunderbar', in which Beethoven's concentration on Leonore's rapture draws the other characters into her orbit, although their feelings at this point bear no comparison with the depth of hers. Yet having forged a style for heroic German opera, he never used it again. Among the many further projects he considered, the most interesting is Grillparzer's *Melusine* (1823), a subject very similar to Hoffmann's *Undine* and a favourite of the German Romantics. Beethoven had long discussions with the poet, who suggested the use of 'a recurrent and easily grasped melody' to be heard first in the overture and thenceforward 'to mark every appearance of Melusine or of her influence in the action'. Beethoven's failure to compose another opera was not primarily due to the inadequacy of the subjects proposed. The attraction of *Fidelio* lay partly in the idealism of the theme – it is significant that the more he revised it, the more he emphasized the spirit of 1789 – and partly in the search for the ideal woman. Yet having found her he proceeded to depersonalize her by placing her on a pedestal. In the last resort humanity in the mass was more important to him than any individual. This is not the mentality of the natural opera composer.

WEIGL'S *SCHWEIZERFAMILIE*

Although the popularity of French operas in Vienna led to an invitation to Cherubini to compose one in German – this was *Faniska*, on a Polish subject very like that of *Lodoiska*, given on 25 February 1806 between the first two productions of *Fidelio* – Beethoven's opera was for long the only artistic fruit of any consequence in Germany. Joseph Weigl, a godson of Haydn and a typical easy-going Viennese in art and manners, who was attached to the court theatre from 1792 to 1823, continued to turn out a long series of popular *Singspiele* dependent on light, graceful melody, lilting rhythms (with a preponderance of 2/4 and 6/8), sedate tempos (a great deal of *andantino* and *moderato*), simple harmony resting on pedals and well-worn accompaniment figures (though with occasional deft modulations), and a notable absence of counterpoint or formal development. The

[1] The witness is Antonín Reicha: see Adrienne Simpson, 'Beethoven through Czech Eyes', in *Musical Times*, cxi (1970), p. 1204.

very successful *Die Schweizerfamilie* (1809), which was played all over Europe, made a gesture towards local colour, incorporating a Swiss folk-song and yodelling, but was essentially a bourgeois entertainment with a debt to Papageno and more than a touch of sentimentality. This was the *Biedermeier* style against which Weber and Schubert grew up, and there are anticipations of both in *Die Schweizerfamilie*: of the A major duet for Agathe and Ännchen in *Der Freischütz* in the duet no. 6 (same key, time, mood, and principal modulation to C major) and Weber's hunting chorus in no. 15; of the *Rosamunde Romanze* in Jacob's *Lied* (no. 11) and Schubert's harmonic idiom in general in the duet no. 13.

THE ROMANTIC FLAME

The year 1816 was crucial to German Romantic opera. Within a month it witnessed the first productions of Hoffmann's *Undine* in Berlin (3 August) and Spohr's *Faust* under Weber in Prague (1 September), though each had been composed some three years earlier. The subjects are significant: the union of a mortal with a fairy (who cannot otherwise acquire a soul), so that both are trapped in the limbo between two worlds; and the man who mortgages his future in either world in order to regain or prolong the joys of his youth. Both recur again and again, with slight variants, in German opera of the Romantic generation (and of course elsewhere): the former in the many *Undine* and *Melusine* librettos, in Lindpaintner's *Der Bergkönig* and Spohr's *Der Berggeist* (both early 1825), in Marschner's *Hans Heiling* (1833) and Wagner's *Der fliegende Holländer* (1843); the latter not only in settings of the Faust story but in *Der Freischütz* (1821), the *Vampyr* operas of Marschner and Lindpaintner (both 1828), and on a debased level in Meyerbeer's *Robert le Diable* (1831). The two subjects have much in common, in particular the mingling of the natural and the supernatural and the idea of redemption, which was to form a central strain in Wagner's work as late as *Parsifal*. The fascination of this psychological nexus is underlined by the repeated recourse of every prominent composer to the same themes; apart from the operas that reached the stage, Spohr began an opera on the *Freischütz* story and Weber had a libretto prepared on that of Tannhäuser. Lortzing wrote a *Hans Sachs* (1840) as well as an *Undine* (1845). (Though chiefly remembered as the author of light *Singspiele*, Lortzing, who wrote his own librettos, was a not unimportant link between Hoffmann and Wagner.)

The ideas themselves were not new; they are found in a number of earlier librettos, such as the *Doktor Faust* (1797) of Ignaz Walter

(1759–1822) and Kauer's *Das Donauweibchen* (on the Undine story) in 1798; Wranitzky's *Oberon* dates from 1789. But it took some time for them to penetrate the music, and when they did they produced confusion. German literary Romanticism, in the works of Wieland, Goethe, Schiller, Tieck, and the Schlegels, was at least a generation ahead. The decisive factor in opera was not the discovery of nature or the supernatural as material for art but the perception of the symbolic relationship between those elements and the hidden forces of human personality, the subconscious urges, fears, and aspirations that underlay – and undermined – the supposedly rational man of the Enlightenment. This central strain of Romanticism led not only to Wagner but to Freud, and was to provide copious material for the modern science of psychology. Significantly it was a writer of fiction, Hoffmann, who established the link with opera, an art-form perfectly suited to explore the recesses of the subconscious mind, since its use of a double means of expression – words and notes, dramatic action and musical development – enabled it not only to say two or more things at once but to draw on music's hitherto scarcely exploited power to evoke memories and verbal concepts and to suggest what is not explicitly stated. When words failed, the orchestra could take over.

The suddenness of the Romantic transformation is remarkable. In the early years of the century genius in all the arts, especially music and poetry, tended to burn itself out quickly, followed either by early death or by decline into mediocrity or a sour and superannuated old age. One thinks of Schubert, Weber, Mendelssohn, Chopin, and Schumann, and of Keats, Shelley, and Byron on the one hand; of Coleridge, Wordsworth, Cherubini, Spontini, and Marschner on the other. Spohr is an interesting case on a lower level; though he had a good conceit of himself from the first, the priggish moralizing tone so prominent in his autobiography increased as his creative powers waned. This decline is not characteristic of the generations of Byrd and Monteverdi, of Bach, Handel, Scarlatti, and Rameau, of Gluck and Haydn, or of Wagner and Verdi; indeed it is difficult to think of a historical parallel. Romantic music is young man's music, and the same is true of much Romantic poetry. It is as if the creative gift could not survive the convulsive birth of a movement more radically new than anything since the spiritual and artistic disturbances of the sixteenth century. One odd result of the speed with which events moved was an overlapping and apparent foreshortening of the generations. Salieri and Winter died within a year or two of Weber, Beethoven and Schubert; Gossec, Cherubini, and Mayr outlived all

three; Spontini outlived Mendelssohn, Chopin, Bellini, and Donizetti
as well.

Other distinguishing features of Romantic art are a love of
grotesquerie and exaggeration, in incident and emotion, and an urge
towards comprehensiveness. The former led to a subjective approach
and a loss of detachment, the dramatist or composer tending to
identify himself with one or more of his characters. The blending of
genres, typical of the whole period and apparent in French *opéra
comique* and Italian *opera semiseria*, was carried to extremes by the
Germans. They became preoccupied not only with the natural and
supernatural worlds, the pull between the life of reason (symbolized
by light) and the mysterious operations of instinct and half-compre-
hended impulses (symbolized by darkness and mythical figures of
menace and evil); they combined legend with history, the epic with
the contemporary, tragedy with humour and fantasy, the aristocratic
with the vernacular. This led them in many contradictory directions.
One manifestation was nationalism, which in Germany (and later in
Bohemia, Russia, and other countries) sprang from a mixture of
political fervour, local history or legend, and the peasant earthiness of
traditional songs and dances. Another was parody, the juxtaposition
of straight sentiment and its distortion, whether as a dramatic feature
introduced by another character (Mephistopheles mocking Faust) or
at the whim of the composer; Lindpaintner's *Der Vampyr* has two
consecutive cavatinas, and Schubert's *Die Verschworenen* two consecutive ariettas, of which the second parodies the first. But the most
immediate consequence was incoherence on many levels, symbolic,
dramatic, musical, and structural. The world of German Romantic
opera seems peopled largely by knights, huntsmen, bridesmaids,
hermits, goblins, and spectres behaving in a singularly inconsequent
manner at variance not only with common sense but with their own
supposed natures.

NEW TYPES OF LIBRETTO

Romantic composers were haunted by the shimmering mirage of an
ideal fusion of the arts. Most of them dabbled in more than one, and
many were active in politics and social agitation. Not only Hoffmann,
but Weber, Schumann, Wagner, Berlioz, and Liszt were copious
writers and influential critics. This did not qualify them as librettists
or even as judges of a libretto; only Wagner, and Berlioz in a single
masterpiece, were to solve that knotty problem by taking it into their
own hands. Here the divorce between music and letters was disastrous,
partly because the leading German poets were more than usually

unmusical, partly because the new type of opera demanded a totally different approach from that of the traditional librettist. The composers were aware that something had to be done. Weber (12 March 1813), Marschner (early 1820), and Spohr (16 July 1823) all made public appeals for decent German librettos – and the Leipzig *Allgemeine musikalische Zeitung* lent its support to the search – yet all three jeopardized their chances by accepting poor texts because they did not know how to identify or construct a good one. Spohr wrote vaguely that a satisfactory libretto should offer sturdy humour or devilry (*Teufelsspuk*) or beautiful sets and costumes, and he wanted it to appeal to the educated and uneducated alike. His ideas were more progressive than those of his contemporaries; he came to advocate through-composed opera and the abandonment of verse; but no one grasped the full implications with regard to form, metre, or language. Most German Romantic librettos are deplorably bad in all three respects. The authors, many of them amateur writers with little idea of dramatic or musical requirements, were drawn to ballad metres, quatrains with alternate lines of eight and seven syllables. This not only blurred the distinction between the requirements of recitative and aria or ensemble – words that must be sung rapidly and clearly to convey essential information, and words suited to lyrical expansion; it tended to clamp the set pieces in square melodic periods of four or eight bars. The consequences appear at their most extreme in the operas of Schubert; the slowness with which Wagner rid himself of this rhythmic incubus doubtless relates to the age's fondness for the ballad.

Romantic librettists – and some composers – began to take themselves with a deadly seriousness that provided ample opportunities for bathos, especially in their dealings with the supernatural. Nor were they nice about literary sources, drawing indiscriminately on the vogue for medieval legends and romances, Gothic horror stories, the plays of Shakespeare, Calderón, and Gozzi, Scott's novels (very popular because of their aura of chivalry), and the *mélodrames* of Pixérécourt and his school, and reducing all to a common denominator. In the most solemn context the ludicrous was seldom far to seek. Josef Kupelwieser in *Fierrabras*, a grandiose Romantic libretto set at Charlemagne's court, saddled Schubert with two mortal enemies called Roland and Boland, which instantly evoke the aroma of Burnand's Cox and Box or Gogol's Bobchinsky and Dobchinsky. A very successful opera, Franz Gläser's *Des Adlers Horst* (Berlin, 1832), has a libretto (written in the first place for Meyerbeer) by a respectable dramatist, Karl von Holtei, based on a story by Schopenhauer's mother, which would be inconceivable at any other period. The central characters are an estranged husband and wife whose baby is seized by an eagle and carried off to its eyrie. Each climbs a steep mountain with a chasm in between, against a background of drinking choruses, rustic dances, and convivial scenes for farm labourers, and they are finally reconciled, and the baby recovered, when a tree struck by lightning forms a bridge across the chasm.

HOFFMANN'S *UNDINE*

'In romantic art', according to Jules Combarieu, 'the imagination gives a lively colour to the language, and the thought has such lyrical intensity that it freely determines the form'.[1] Ideally this may be true, but the thought needs to be clearly conceived and firmly directed; free-ranging imagination is not enough. The difficulty with opera was that a vessel capable of holding the heady new liquor could scarcely be invented in a vacuum before the brew had been tested. The Romantic libretto was no field for theatrical amateurs; hence Wagner's assumption of his double role. Hoffmann's *Undine* has an importance out of proportion to its merits because he took the plunge; if he failed as musician and dramatist, his efforts so excited his successors, Weber in particular, that they were impelled to follow his initiative. A lawyer by profession, and deservedly remembered as a writer of fantastic tales, he had from 1808 acted as musical director of theatres at Bamberg and elsewhere and composed his first opera, on a libretto of his own, as early as 1799. In *Undine* he found a subject that suited his peculiar gifts and a libretto (adapted by La Motte Fouqué from his own story) of stauncher quality than many at this period. Hoffmann held that the perfect opera should embrace the comic and the tragic, the realistic and the fantastic, and his attempt to put this into practice was nothing if not ambitious. The plot presents a series of antitheses, between the human and the spectral, between courtiers and humble fisherfolk (the latter much the more convincingly drawn), between Christianity in the person of the pastor Heilmann – an antecedent of the Hermit in *Der Freischütz* – and superstition. All are viewed on the level, but with a certain ambivalence (and scarcely veiled social satire), against a background of raging natural forces; Hoffmann tried to express all this – and more – in the music. If the mixture of the supernatural and the homely (as when Undine and her foster-mother, after the storm in Act I, settle the parson by the fire with a drink) suggests the world of *Der Freischütz*, the symbolic content looks forward to *Tannhäuser* and beyond. The finale, with Huldbrand's

[1] *Histoire de la musique.*

death on Undine's kiss, broaches the idea of redemption through love, and the word 'Liebestod' occurs in the text.

Hoffmann's chief models were Mozart and Cherubini. He was a passionate admirer of *Don Giovanni*, on which he wrote a celebrated story in the same year as *Undine*. He called it 'the opera of all operas', and Mozart 'the inimitable creator of romantic opera'. The character of Don Giovanni, the superman doomed to bring destruction on others and on himself, fascinated Hoffmann as it fascinated so many of his generation. He became the typical Romantic hero, related to Milton's Satan, to Byron in his private and his literary persona, and to Faust, who has been called the Don Giovanni of the north. Hoffmann's Huldbrand is inevitably a baritone. The other important male role, the grim water-spirit Kühleborn, is a bass of phenomenal depth and compass; there is no tenor part of consequence. This distribution of voices was to become characteristic of many Romantic operas, including some of Donizetti's and Verdi's. Mozart's musical influence is apparent in the storm music and elsewhere, but Hoffmann's indebtedness to the French is even greater. The extensive use of *mélodrame* with speech and recitative, the attempt to build up substantial blocks of through-composed music (sometimes embracing a scene-change), and many stylistic mannerisms came from Cherubini. Méhul suggested the ending of musical numbers on interrogatory and imperfect cadences and the treatment of recurring motives, though Hoffmann widened their scope by attaching them chiefly to supernatural elements. The anticipation of later music in the overture and act introductions owes as much to France as to Mozart.

But Hoffmann's dramatic reach exceeded his musical grasp. He lacked the technique to reconcile the Mozartean and Cherubinian strains, or to raise the execution to the level of the conception. The fragmentation of forms, though prophetic (especially of Marschner), does not yield a coherent arioso. The melodic idiom is short-spanned and in lyrical passages falls back on the *Volkslied* type of ballad, adorned with occasional Italian clichés. The harmony is over-dependent on a few chords and progressions such as the diminished seventh and 'German' augmented sixth. There is little counterpoint; the accompaniment figures, formulae derived from Cherubini, produce an effect of fidgety agitation that grows monotonous. The music seldom flows or soars; the restless shifts in tempo, dynamics, and tonality, though clearly inspired by the text, are so architecturally uncontrolled that they allow no time for establishing contrasts of mood. The most successful features are Hoffmann's evocation of the forces of nature – not only the waters and forests themselves but their impact on the characters – and of the supernatural, especially in the person of Kühleborn. His Act II aria 'Ihr Freund' aus See'n und Quellen', while indebted to Cherubini's Dourlinski (and so related to Pizarro), has a strength and spaciousness beyond most of the score, and the characterization by means of low tessitura, huge vocal leaps, and menacing figures in the bass is impressive.

Ex. 175

(Friends from lakes and springs, brother beings)

The second finale, in which Undine, cursed as a witch by her mortal husband Huldbrand, returns to her watery element as a storm rises, has a power of atmospheric suggestion not lost on Weber and Wagner. In Italian and French opera (apart from Le Sueur) the supernatural, generally in the form of oracles, was conventionally depicted by solemn trombone chords as late as Mercadante and Verdi; the *frisson* associated with Samiel, Hans Heiling, and the various vampires and other diabolic shapes entered opera with *Undine*. Some of the *mélodrames*, notably that following the Act III terzetto when the thoughts of Huldbrand, torn between his mortal and his fairy love, revert to Undine as the orchestra quotes the music to which she disappeared, are prophetic of Marschner. The orchestra begins to represent the forces of nature and super-nature against which man has to struggle to preserve his balance, one of its roles in *Der fliegende Holländer*. It is easy to see why Weber in an article of 1817, while criticizing its faults, called *Undine* 'one of the most gifted works we have been given in recent times'. If Hoffmann could not bring the two worlds into focus, he was the first to make the attempt and to demonstrate an untapped reservoir of new life for the musical drama.

SPOHR'S WEAKNESSES

Although Weber, before he knew *Undine*, proclaimed in 1816 that the dark romantic spirit world of Spohr's *Faust* had done precisely that, Spohr's approach was more timid. Like Hoffmann, he was influenced by Cherubini and Mozart, but with different results. According to his autobiography Spohr (1784–1859) became familiar with French opera while playing in the Brunswick orchestra in 1799.[1] He then fell under the spell of Mozart, who 'became for my whole lifetime my ideal and model'. He confessed that his early operas *Alruna* (1808, not performed) and *Der Zweikampf mit der Geliebten* (Hamburg, 1811) were full of Mozartean reminiscences, but considered that he had outgrown them by the time of *Faust* (1816). Here he deceived himself. The most conspicuous features of Spohr's style are its failure to develop – if anything, it retrogressed – and its excessive dependence on a mannered chromaticism regardless of context. The daemonic element in *Don Giovanni* touched him only superficially, though that opera was doubtless responsible for his casting Faust as a baritone and stressing his sexual appetite; the link between the two characters so typical of the German artistic response seems to have begun with Spohr. But he was seduced by the quicksilver chromaticism of the later Mozart, especially in inner parts and quick tempos. Spohr adopted it, slowed it up, and lingered over it so lovingly that he often brought all momentum to a standstill. The devitalized impression conveyed by so much of his music is due to the absence of any corresponding strength in melody and rhythm.

His melodic ideas are almost uniformly short-winded and often insipid; at their best they suggest the milder felicities of Weber or Mendelssohn. His rhythmic limitations are even more conspicuous. Distinctive melodies and irregular phrase-lengths are rare in his operas, cross-rhythms and misplaced accents rarer still, with the result

[1] *Selbstbiographie* (Kassel, 1860), i, p. 12.

that long stretches consist of an enervated line sinking into a morass of stagnant harmony. The ambling complacency in compound metres (or triple and common time with triplets), whether combined with succulent harmony or jerked into spasmodic activity by an *allegro agitato* tempo mark, which wrapped itself like a convolvulus round the later Mendelssohn, is a direct legacy of Spohr. In this respect, and in a certain intellectual flabbiness, Spohr was a disastrous influence not only on Mendelssohn but on the church music of Victorian England, which converted the organ voluntary in the wedding scene of *Faust* into an Anglican hymn.

Although he adopted a number of Romantic practices, including the baritone hero (in *Jessonda* and *Der Berggeist* as well as *Faust*) and the reminiscence theme, Spohr was not at heart a Romantic but a reactionary chained to a single aspect of one great predecessor. He shrank from the counterpoise offered by the virility of Cherubini and Beethoven. He thought Cherubini would have been a far better composer if he had written for the Germans instead of the French. He could stomach Beethoven only as far as the end of the first period, considered his late works (twenty years after his death) 'eccentric, unconnected and incomprehensible', and criticized the Ninth Symphony as 'wanting in aesthetic feeling and a sense of the beautiful'. He despised Weber as an amateur and was baffled by the success of *Der Freischütz*, but (with some reservations) admired Wagner's early operas and personally introduced *Der fliegende Holländer* and *Tannhäuser* at Kassel, where he served as Kapellmeister from 1822 until his death in 1859; he would have added *Lohengrin* if the Elector had allowed it.

Spohr's fatal weakness as an opera composer was his limited gift for the theatre, and especially for the theatre he chiefly attempted, the half-light between peasant humanity and the supernatural. He commanded neither pole. His characters, compared with those of Weber, and even Marschner, are cardboard cut-outs, lacking depth, fire, and intellectual commitment; in this they reflect perhaps the personality of their creator. His sense of dramatic timing was poor; it is typical that he criticized Rossini for insipidity and the failure to balance music and drama – his own faults, from which Rossini was conspicuously free – and that he thought Rossini should have devoted more study to Mozart. Spohr had little or no feeling for the open air. He shrank from the darker aspects of human psychology that could alone give conviction to his subjects, and consequently failed to bring out their symbolic content.

SPOHR'S HISTORICAL IMPORTANCE

Nevertheless Spohr is of major importance in the history of German opera, an importance that derives paradoxically from his limitations. His dependence on harmony as almost his sole expressive resource, accentuated by a growing tendency to abjure counterpoint in opera, brought him to a dead end. Craving variety, he sought it in ever more frequent modulation – especially enharmonic modulation – in prolonged suspensions, yearning upward-resolving appoggiaturas, chromatic inner parts often moving in thirds or contrary motion, and a susceptibility to the diminished seventh in every imaginable context. He used this chord not primarily (as the French Revolution composers did) to make a dramatic point, but self-indulgently for its own sake. The effect is peculiarly enervating in major keys. Spohr's harmonic excursions soon degenerated into cliché; but they left a deposit in the minds of his successors. A number of them anticipated procedures characteristic of Wagner, for example the progression that introduces the 9/8 *andante* in Act II, scene 1, of *Der Berggeist*.

Ex. 176

Spohr's fondness for richly harmonized chromatic scale passages left its mark on Lindpaintner (Isolde's swoon in his *Vampyr* of 1828) and the 'magic sleep' motive in *Die Walküre*. Here no doubt lies the explanation of this arch-conservative's unexpected warmth towards Wagner.

Equally significant, and equally inspired by the imbalance of his technique, are the advances he made towards a continuous musical texture and the development of the reminiscence theme. *Jessonda*

(1823) and *Der Berggeist* (1825) are, with Weber's *Euryanthe* (1823),
the earliest through-composed German operas of any consequence,
and the libretto of *Der Berggeist* was at Spohr's request written in
prose. Act III of *Jessonda* flows on continuously with no full closes
between numbers. The arioso 'Was für ein Fest seh' ich bereitet!', in
which Tristan sees a vision of Jessonda being burned alive, with its
many changes of tempo and its symphonic development of a phrase
in the bass, owes something to Cherubini and Spontini; but it is closer
to Marschner and early Wagner. In *Der Berggeist* the recitative is
penetrated by patches of orchestral elaboration in which earlier
motives recur, though there is little sense of symphonic direction and
sometimes the result is a chromatic morass, as in the finale of Act III
or this complete arioso from Scene 4 of the same act, which illustrates
the extent to which melody and rhythm are subordinated to harmony:

Ex. 177

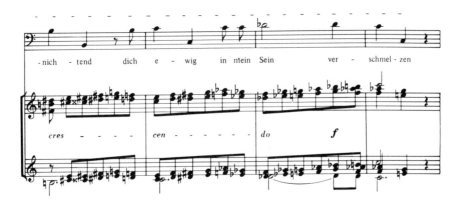

(Know then: Directly the flame has permeated my whole being it will take hold of thee and, painfully destroying thy earthly body, melt it away for ever in my essence.)

Reminiscence motives are used in all Spohr's operas, especially the two last named, sometimes with a certain aptness. But he does not consolidate his gains – less so indeed than Méhul or Weber – partly through uncertain placing in relation to the drama and partly because many of the motives lack flavour. One of the most prominent in *Der Berggeist* is a chromatic scale, a device common among the French and one to which Spohr is so prone in any circumstances that we are often left in doubt whether or not a specific reference is intended. Spohr's mastery of fluent orchestration on the other hand, derived from his long experience as a violinist, put a well-oiled tool in the hands of his successors.

SPOHR'S *FAUST*

Only the *Zeitgeist* and Spohr's lack of self-criticism can account for his choice of the supernatural, a realm he was unfitted to penetrate, for three of his principal operas. *Faust* was originally a two-act *Singspiel*; Spohr added some new music in 1818 and full recitatives, with a division into three acts, for Covent Garden in 1852. The libretto, not based on Goethe, is highly melodramatic. Faust is a typical Romantic hero in whom lofty ideals for humanity alternate with bouts of frantic sensuality; but Spohr, while retaining the tragic end, possessed neither the imagination nor the intellectual grip to bring him to life. He merely paints Faust's moods, with a predictable emphasis on the lures of the flesh, conveying very little of his idealism and nothing at all of the hubristic side. (Faust has made his bargain before the opera begins.) Mephistopheles, though his air in Act II, 'Stille noch dies Wuthverlangen', is one of the stronger pieces, is sinister in a wholly mundane way. The overture is unorthodox in form and tonality. According to Spohr's own detailed programme it represents the conflicting forces in Faust's character, sensual debauchery in the *allegro vivace*, a gradual burgeoning of good intentions and renunciation in the fugal *largo grave*; but the music has so little profile that the application could as easily be reversed. The witches' unison chorus at the begining of Act II would serve equally for shepherdesses or mermaids. The idiom of *Faust* is sometimes close to Weber, for example in the instrumental melodies that permeate the second finale, and the extended sectional design of Kunigunde's scena and aria 'Die stille Nacht entweicht', Hugo's scena and aria 'Beflügle den Lauf', and Faust's 'Wie ist mir! Welch ein Zwist' unquestionably influenced him. Weber's later heroes and heroines all have multipartite arias of just this type.

JESSONDA

Zemire und Azor (Frankfurt, 1819) uses an adaptation of Grétry's libretto; the overture includes a storm in the French style. Spohr's treatment of the fairy story suggests not so much the wonder and delicacy of similar episodes in Weber and Mendelssohn as the cushioned domesticity of a suburban lounge. Spohr admitted the influence of *Tancredi*, which appears perhaps in the canonic Act I trio, but like the whole plot this is grossly sentimentalized. The same weakness is more damaging in the two through-composed operas because they attempt more ambitious themes. That of *Jessonda* (to which Winter's *Maria von Montalban* is the dramatic sequel; its libretto is quoted in Spohr's) concerns the Indian custom of suttee, the ritual suicide of a widow on her husband's death. Spohr, as one might expect, removes the political and revolutionary content of the source (a play by Antoine Lemierre) and emasculates the character: Jessonda, though a widow, is also a virgin, and her compatriots behave with such nonchalance that she is rescued from the pyre by a former Portuguese admirer. The confrontation of Brahmins and Portuguese Christians cries out for local colour or at least differentiation in style, but receives none. The introduction of the overture represents the two parties, the Portuguese in polonaise rhythm; this however permeates the whole score, including the Indian scenes, and in Jessonda's Act III aria, 'Mit muthigen Verlangen', is incongrously yoked with a fulsome prayer (*larghetto* 9/8). The influence of French rationalism appears in the treatment of religion as a mere device, as in Scribe's librettos, and there are links with all three of Spontini's principal operas. The librettist took the name of Jessonda's sister Amazili from *Fernand*

Cortez, confusing the West and East Indies. The languor of Spohr's harmony with its prolonged suspensions and appoggiaturas (the hero's name, Tristan, has a prophetic aptness) reaches its apogee in this opera. It is not confined to the erotic, nostalgic, or oriental but crops up everywhere, even in the chorus of Portuguese warriors that begins Act II and the vengeance trio in Act III; the ferocious finales reveal Spohr as a sheep in wolf's clothing. Nevertheless, despite resemblances to the most supine movements of *Elijah* in the Brahmin choruses and the use of an ambling 6/8 rhythm derived from *opera buffa* for the bayaderes' dance round the bier at the beginning of Act I, *Jessonda* is the best of Spohr's operas. The dissolution of forms begun by the *tragédie lyrique* of Gluck's successors in Paris and extended by Spontini, though delayed in Germany by a combination of the *Singspiel* tradition with that of the French Revolution *opéra comique*, is at last gathering way. In several movements Spohr employs the juxtaposition of remote or unrelated keys to good structural purpose, again perhaps learning from Spontini: E minor, G minor, and A flat major in Jessonda's first recitative and aria, B minor, C major, and A flat major in the first finale, A flat and B major in the duet for Amazili and Nadori ('Schönes Mädchen'). Here the B major section looks startling on paper, since the orchestral parts are written in that key without signature and the vocal in C flat with a signature of four flats.

DER BERGGEIST

Der Berggeist, on the Rübezahl legend, reveals even more than *Faust* Spohr's inability to differentiate in musico-dramatic terms between the human and supernatural worlds or between good and evil. The opera begins with earth-spirits mining ore, as in *Hans Heiling* and *Das Rheingold*. Their ruler, learning of the delights of earthly love, decides (like Hans Heiling) to sample it, abducts Alma just before her wedding to Oskar, and conveys her into the bowels of a mountain. From this point Spohr topples first into the sentimental and then into the ridiculous, by evading the psychological problems and treating the story in a style of bourgeois realism that sets the potential symbolism at nought. On one side a simpering virtue gets its way by deceit and broken promises, on the other supernatural powers are so ineptly handled that they carry neither menace nor conviction. The demon hero, instead of taking the obvious step, allows himself to be tricked into counting flowers while his victim escapes, whereupon with an abrupt gesture he decides that human love is no occupation for a pure spirit. While outwardly the music stretches the free structures and fluid tonality of *Jessonda* to the extent of sometimes dispensing with fixed key signatures, its content suggests nothing more outlandish than a cosy *Gemütlichkeit*. Spohr's goblins are innocent of the daemonic menace of Samiel, Ruthven, and Heiling, and still more of Mime and Alberich, all of whom sprang from the same tradition and benefited from Spohr's procedures. They do enjoy attractive music, for example the dances in the second finale, but it is unpretentious stuff more suited to a village hop.

WEBER'S HISTORIC ROLE

In strong contrast with Spohr, Weber's life-work is a paradigm of German Romantic opera in its glories, its hesitations, and the obstacles with which it was confronted. His peripatetic life and his upbringing – no composer, not even Wagner, had a wider early experience of conditions inside the theatre – allowed him to hear innumerable operas of every current type and to take an active part in their performance. Apart from residence in many towns and employment at several Courts, he exercised artistic control over three opera houses, at Breslau (1804–6 – he was appointed at the age of seventeen), Prague (1813–16), and Dresden (1816–26). His views on opera were in many respects enlightened and in advance of his time. An articulate writer, he introduced the operas he conducted in the local press and paid close attention not only to the musical execution but to every detail of the staging and scenic representation, with special reference to ensemble work and lighting. He had outstanding creative gifts, and he was an industrious worker. Yet although he established the foundations on which Wagner and the whole German Romantic theatre were to build, his achievement seems in retrospect spasmodic and disjointed. All three of his mature operas have major flaws, and the two in which his genius burns brightest present such formidable practical problems that they are heard in the theatre far less frequently than their musical merit warrants.

There were personal, technical, and social reasons for this. Weber's musical education, largely under his father (a more mercurial but equally exacting counterpart of Leopold Mozart), was fitful and unsystematic. He studied under Vogler at Vienna in 1803–4 (when he arranged the vocal score of his master's opera *Samori*) and again, with Meyerbeer as a fellow-pupil, at Darmstadt in 1810; but it is not clear what he learned from that eccentric figure. He never quite overcame a certain amateurishness of technique, and never mastered the peculiarities and limitations of the human voice. His ingrained hostility to Italian music – though in his later years he enjoyed the operas of Cimarosa and Rossini and conducted the latter's *La donna del lago* at Dresden – was in part a response to what he saw as a serious threat to German opera; but it unbalanced his resources for creating a solid alternative. He had to fight against strong Italian opposition, especially from Francesco Morlacchi and his company at Dresden, and to win over a public divided in its allegiance. Moreover he was not the soul of tact.

Of his German predecessors only Mozart (his cousin by marriage) could be of much service; but he lacked Mozart's all-round genius and his innate sense of form, not least theatrical form. His reverence for Mozart caused him to quarrel with the influential Berlin conductor Anselm Weber but failed to endear him to Spohr, whom he found rough and arrogant in manners. Like Mozart – but unlike Spohr – he disliked Winter, described by Weber's son and biographer as mean-minded, envious, and crotchety. Like most German composers of his day he was treated with lordly disdain by Goethe and received little help from men of letters. Even after the sensational success of *Der Freischütz* at Berlin in 1821, when Weber became a national hero, especially to those who resented Spontini's power at court, his opera met strong criticism from his countrymen. Zelter, writing to Goethe, called it 'a nothing of colossal size', Tieck 'the most unmusical row that ever roared upon a stage'. Spohr could attribute its success only to Weber's gift for writing down to the masses, and Hoffmann damned it with faint praise, ridiculing the supernatural effects as childish and accusing Weber of plagiarism from Spontini of all composers.[1] With Beethoven on the other hand, Weber was on cordial terms, and (again unlike Spohr) he admired his mature music, calling *Fidelio* 'one of the greatest operas ever created by mortal mind'. His reputed hostility to Beethoven's symphonies seems to have been a legend manufactured by Schindler.[2]

WEBER'S EARLY OPERAS

Repelled by the Italians and finding little sustenance in the Germans, Weber turned like Beethoven to the French. As we have seen, the most important operas of the French school – apart from Gluck and Spontini, whose bent towards heroic classicism was out of tune with Weber's temperament – were *opéras comiques* with spoken dialogue. They were excellent models in style and technique, but offered insufficient help towards the realization of the comprehensive new ideals of the German Romantics. Weber recognized the gap, at

[1] Hoffmann's authorship of this anonymous attack has been questioned by Wolfgang Kron, *Die angeblichen Freischütz-Kritiken E. T. A. Hoffmanns* (Munich, 1957).
[2] See John Warrack, *Carl Maria von Weber* (London, 1968), pp. 93–4.

least intermittently, but was unable to fill it. Gifted with a sure eye for
what was immediately effective, and intoxicated by his ability to enter
into picturesque backgrounds and superheated states of mind, he
could not stand back and view his creations as a whole. The weakness
is at once apparent in his choice of librettos and his inability to correct
or control the vagaries of his collaborators. Only one of his stage
works, the little *Singspiel Abu Hassan* (1811), achieves a satisfactory
balance of music and drama, and that on an unambitious level of light
comedy.

Two of Weber's early operas, *Das stumme Waldmädchen* (1800) and
Rübezahl (1804–5) survive only in fragments, though he treated the
subject of *Waldmädchen* again in *Silvana* (1810).[1] The latter was
probably never finished, and is chiefly interesting for its choice of
subject, but we do not know how Weber treated it. The dominant
influences here, and in *Peter Schmoll und seine Nachbarn* (1803), are
Mozart and the Viennese *Singspiel* of Dittersdorf and Schenk. The
ungainly coloratura of Mathilde's aria in *Das Waldmädchen* and
Mechtilde's 'Weh mir, es ist geschehn' in the first version of *Silvana* is
very close to Winter; like him Weber was susceptible to the *Volkslied*
element in *Die Zauberflöte*, and no more successful in reconciling the
strains. The characters of Hans Bast in *Peter Schmoll* and Krips in
Silvana derive straight from Papageno. Modulations between keys a
third apart also belong to this tradition, but that from D to E flat on
the word 'Todt' in the middle of Mathilde's aria is striking for its date.

Peter Schmoll is a remarkable achievement for a boy of sixteen. The
libretto, inconsequent and clumsily handled (the dialogue is lost), is
one of the earliest in Germany on a contemporary political subject,
the fate of refugees from the French Revolution. Its sententious moral
tone derives from the school of Rousseau, and the treatment is
sentimental, not realistic. Although Weber could have encountered
some of Dalayrac's operas at Munich in the winter of 1798–9, there is
little sign of French influence in the music (except perhaps in the use
of five themes from the opera in the overture) and still less of Italian.
Die Zauberflöte haunts the score; Hans Bast even has a duet, 'Der edle
schöne junge Mann', with the serious heroine. The carefully planned
tonal layout – the overture, introduction to Act I, both finales, and the
principal love scene are all in E flat – no doubt derives from the same
source. The orchestration however is original, not merely in its revival

[1] *Das stumme Waldmädchen* is ed., with *Peter Schmoll*, by Alfred Lorenz, *C. M. von Weber: Musikalische Werke. Erste kritische Gesamtausgabe*, i (Augsburg, 1926), *Rübezahl* and *Silvana*, ibid., ii, ed. Willibald Koehler (Augsburg, 1928).

of obsolete instruments (two *flauti dolci* and two basset-horns with bassoon and strings in the Act II trio 'Empfanget hier', which also attempts a canonic round in the manner of *Così fan tutte*) but in its almost Berliozian blend of colours and its free use of solo wind instruments in dialogue, a trait that persisted in Weber's mature style. Minette's *Romanze* 'Im Rheinland eine Dirne war', later adapted for Fatime's 'Wird Philomele trauern' in *Abu Hassan*, employs solo flute, horns, bassoons, and divided violas without violins; the dark colour, prophetic of the solo viola with Ännchen's soubrette voice in *Der Freischütz*, is nicely set off by flute solos, including four bars for the instrument by itself at the very end. The D minor bass aria 'Wie der bange Pilger zittert', scored for two piccolos, two horns, two trombones, and strings, the only piece in a minor key, takes the hint of a storm simile to reflect *Don Giovanni*; hence the trombones, which occur nowhere else in the opera. The appearance of two piccolos in several movements is noteworthy, though they have not yet acquired the sinister associations of Caspar. The bassoon is much more prominent than the clarinet, which plays in only four of the twenty numbers.

It seems unlikely that the theatres Weber had hitherto frequented possessed more than a meagre orchestra, or that he knew anything yet of Vogler, who was given to orchestral experiments. If so, Weber's sensitivity to instrumental timbre was born in him. There is little feeling for continuity or characterization, harmony and part-writing are sometimes gauche, and most of the tunes are of simple *Volkslied* type; but the hero Carl's impassioned recitative and aria, 'O Hoffnung, gütigste der Feen', the most individual piece in the opera, looks forward to the later Romantic scenas, both in its tripartite form and in the appearance of the second subject of the overture on a climax, as in *Silvana* (Rudolph's aria in Act I) and *Euryanthe*. Another characteristic feature is the disposition of quick melodies with two quavers to each syllable; and the *largo* for wind alone before the recapitulation of the overture even hints at the *Euryanthe* ghosts:

Ex. 178

SILVANA

French influence is more marked in the next two operas, *Silvana* (1810, partly a reworking of *Das Waldmädchen*) and *Abu Hassan* (1811). *Silvana* was described in the autograph as *heroisch* and in early productions as *romantisch* and *heroisch-komisch*. This confused terminology, already encountered in the Viennese *Singspiel*, accurately reflects the style, which is a hotchpotch of all the elements later incorporated into Romantic opera with the single exception of the supernatural. The libretto combines the trappings of literary Romanticism – medieval chivalry, a tournament won by an unknown knight, the long-lost daughter recognized by a mole on her arm, the mysterious forest, a nocturnal thunderstorm – with relics of the *Singspiel*, notably the comic squire Krips, who seems ill at ease in these surroundings. In the music Weber alternates between *Volkslied* and *Kunstlied*, between superficial dance tunes (often in polonaise rhythm) and extended structures such as the second finale (much improved in the Dresden revision of 1817), which with its pageantry – including stage trumpets – stronger grasp of large-scale design, and well-managed climax shows acquaintance with Cherubini. The woodland scenes of Act I owe something to Méhul, but there are already signs of the mellow tone-painting of *Der Freischütz*, especially in the *adagio* opening bars. Weber had digested some of the lessons of *opéra comique*, including the importance of expressing action through music, though the attempt to achieve this sometimes defeated his sense of form, as in the Act III trio 'Nieder mit ihr!'. The most unusual feature of the plot (a Romantic conception in itself), the dumb heroine – dumb of intent; she speaks in the final dialogue – inspired some of the finest music, less in the dance sequences than in the scenes with Rudolph. Here her thoughts and emotions are represented by solo instruments, notably a cello against muted violins in her scena with Rudolph, 'Willst du nicht diesen Aufenthalt'. This 'duet' and the later dance scene in Act II, in which neither party sings, are wholly individual conceptions, even if indebted to earlier experiments with *mélodrame*. The introduction to Act I, which begins with a hunt (four horns echoing each other on stage) and continues with Silvana's first timid entry, is also characteristic, though Silvana's polonaise led by solo oboe suggests the ballroom rather than the bush.

While the score is very uneven, its best pages have an open-air quality, a freedom from stuffiness, and an epigrammatic wit rare in German Romantic opera and unknown to Hoffmann, Spohr, and Marschner, but common in the lighter *opéras comiques* of Boieldieu and Isouard.[1] It appears most happily in codas, where the music either takes an unexpected turn or rounds things off with a deft reference to earlier material. Examples are the *ppp* end of the first finale (answering the opening of the Act) and the closing bars of the garden quartet (see Ex. 179), Krips's 'Tempo d'un tedesco' song 'Sah sonst ich ein Mädchen', and the storm chorus in Act III. There are significant anticipations of *Euryanthe*, the nearest in subject of the later operas, in the passionate music of Adelhart (a forerunner of Lysiart and the most convincing character), and in the 1812 Berlin revision of Mechtilde's scena 'Er geht! Er hört mich nicht!', especially the main theme of the *allegro*:

Ex. 179

ABU HASSAN

Abu Hassan is much less ambitious, and partly for that reason more successful. The specifically Romantic qualities are in abeyance. Weber's models are Dalayrac and the Mozart of *Die Entführung*. The former's graceful melodic style, for example in Ex. 180 from Act I of his *Léon* (1798), is very close to that of *Abu Hassan*.

Ex. 180

Mozart's opera lies behind several movements, notably the trio 'Ängstlich klopft es mir', which has the same youthful ebullience. Weber almost rivals his predecessor in delicacy and economy, though

---

[1] They have many points of contact with Weber, for example in Mme de Melval's offstage *romance* with harp in Act II of Boieldieu's *Les Voitures versées* (1808) and the duet for Édile and Robert, very suggestive of Ännchen, in Act I of Isouard's *Joconde* (1814).

without the undercurrents of pathos and potential tragedy. What he wrote of *Die Entführung* in an article of June 1818 – that Mozart's artistic experience was now complete, and only his experience of the world was to increase later – could almost be applied to his own opera. The plot and characters are purely comic; the music exhibits a nice vein of tender sentiment, but attempts nothing beyond its reach. The scoring has little of the exotic, apart from conventional Turkish effects and the two guitars in Abu Hassan's aria 'Was nun zu machen'. But the whole work is happily integrated, and the humour, unlike that of Bast and Krips, is intrinsic rather than applied. Weber also shows a nice gift for parody, momentarily in the opening duet and more substantially in Fatime's mock lament, 'Hier liegt, welch martervolles Loos' (added for Dresden in 1823), which pokes delicious fun at the exaggerations of Romantic opera while it was still young.

WEBER'S REPERTORY AS OPERA CONDUCTOR

Ten years, more than half of Weber's mature creative life, separate *Abu Hassan* from *Der Freischütz* (1821). They were not years of idleness: apart from concert and domestic works, he was busy forwarding the cause of opera in the theatre and with the pen, Most of his critical articles date from the years 1810–12 and 1815–20. He also worked on a semi-autobiographical novel, *Tonkünstlers Leben*, begun in 1809 and never finished, which echoes the manner of Hoffmann's fantastic tales. Yet there must have been inner reasons for the block in his operatic career. He did consider a number of subjects, including *Tannhäuser* with Brentano in 1814, but even after settling on *Der Freischütz* in 1817 he postponed serious work on the music for another three years. The explanation probably lies in the absence of suitable models and the need to discover and then to embody some fixative for the disparate elements that had jostled one another in *Silvana*.

A study of his repertory throws light on the way his mind was moving. At Breslau he had produced mostly Italian operas, including three by Mozart, and German *Singspiele*. Ten of the first eleven works he conducted at Prague were French, all of them very recent; only *Les Deux Journées* was more than seven years old. Although they included *Fernand Cortez*, with which he opened, and *La Vestale*, the vast majority – then and later – were *opéras comiques*. Weber's French repertory at Prague comprised five works by Isouard, three by Méhul and Boieldieu, two by Cherubini, Spontini, Grétry, and Dalayrac, one by Catel, Berton, Gaveaux, and Salieri. The lighter pieces of Dalayrac, Isouard, and Boieldieu, and Catel's *Les Aubergistes de qualité* (1812), were immensely popular all over Germany, and several of them appeared within a year or two in as many as five different versions. Weber's Italian repertory, apart from Mozart, consisted only of three operas by Paer and one by Fioravanti. As a committed supporter of German products he put on as many as he could find, but nearly all were trivial *Singspiele* in which the public took no interest. The only exceptions, apart from Spohr's *Faust*, were *Fidelio* in 1814 and Meyerbeer's early *Alimelek* (*Wirth und Gast*) in 1815. At Dresden Weber added Mozart's two German *Singspiele, Jessonda,* and Marschner's *Heinrich IV und Aubigné,* as well as *Lodoïska, Olimpie,* and (with little enthusiasm) two of Meyerbeer's Italian operas.

MEYERBEER'S FIRST OPERAS

Meyerbeer had begun from a position very close to Weber. His first opera, *Jephtas Gelübde* (1812), understandably mixed in style, shows the influence of Cherubini and Spontini and in its orchestral experiments (including a canon for double bass and bassoon while Jephtha broods over his predicament) that of Vogler. It employs a large orchestra, heavy in brass, and choral masses after Spontini's manner. The overture and prelude to Act III are based on motives used later in the action, which they handle with some enterprise. This motival development was extended in *Alimelek* (1813), but some of the orchestral effects singled out by Edgar Istel,[1] such as solo viola and three cellos at the start of Act II, were borrowed from the French. Weber detected divided aims in *Jephtas Gelübde* between the harmonic complexity of the ensembles, which he attributed to inner conviction, and an urge to humour the singers with brilliant coloratura in the solos. When Meyerbeer went to Italy and succumbed to the domination of Rossini, Weber scorned him as a traitor to the cause, contrasting his Italian operas unfavourably with *Alimelek*.

WEBER'S CRITICISM AND EXPERIMENTS

Weber's critical articles reveal an intimate knowledge of the French school, especially Cherubini and Méhul. He regarded *Les Deux Journées* and *Lodoïska* as classic masterpieces, emphasizing the gripping dramatic truth of the former and the gigantic stature and all-embracing technique of the latter, which 'belongs to the dominating trend of our time – the romantic'. Defending Cherubini against the charge of melodic weakness, he considered all means subordinate to the total effect, so that the melody lay not in the vocal line but in the fabric as a whole – a pointer towards Wagner. He laid repeated stress

[1] 'Meyerbeer's Way to Mastership', *Musical Quarterly.* xii (1926), p. 72.

on dramatic truth, which he discovered in lesser French operas such as Dalayrac's *Léhéman* (1801; produced at Munich in 1811 and 1819 under the title *Macdonald*), where the overture takes the listener right into the action, and the music, combining popular and classical elements, always propels the plot forward. This was a perceptive judgement. Weber was also attracted by the humanist ideals of the French librettos. He welcomed romanticism in Grétry, wit and intelligence in Boieldieu, grandeur in Catel's *Sémiramis*, and a many-sided genius in Méhul, seven of whose operas he named in a Dresden article on *Joseph* in January 1817. All this he was to turn to fruitful account.

About the time of *Der Freischütz*, under the influence of Tieck, Weber was much preoccupied with Spanish subjects. Besides the oriental *Alcindor* (with Kind, 1819) he considered or planned operas on Pizarro, Don John of Austria, Columbus, and the Cid, composed the incidental music to Pius Alexander Wolff's *Preciosa* (1820), and sketched *Die drei Pintos* (1820–1, completed later by Mahler, who was unable to match Weber's style). Both these works make good use of local colour (Spanish melodies and gypsy rhythms in *Preciosa*). Although Weber called *Preciosa* 'more than half an opera', it has only one singing character apart from the chorus; its principal interest lies in the *mélodrames*, which led Weber not only to thematic reminiscence but to a primitive form of *Sprechgesang*, and in the brilliant orchestration, with a battery of four horns on stage answering another in the pit. There is a hint of Rossini in 'Es blinken so lustig die Sterne' in Act IV, a chorus with a continuous melody running in the orchestra.

DER FREISCHÜTZ

If Weber's introduction of local colour represented one aspect of his search for a distinctive Romantic opera, the catalyst that precipitated it in *Der Freischütz* was his realization of the supernatural, not as an excuse for decoration and spectacle but as a live force, potent, sinister, mysterious, the shadow behind the reality. Some of the French Revolution composers, notably Méhul, had been unconscious or potential Romantics, interested in nature as a force governing human actions and in remote or medieval backgrounds, but expressing the darker emotions only in human terms. Weber's achievement was to make the supernatural theatrically credible and symbolically signifi-cant. *Undine* and *Faust*, by pointing the way, released him from his temporary silence. Like Hoffmann and Spohr he found his starting-point in German legend, reaching back to the Middle Ages and bringing with it the immemorial confrontation of good and evil, holy church and heathen superstition. The characters of *Der Freischütz* are all villagers; the audience could identify with them and still more with the chorus, a character in its own right employing the *Volkslied* idiom. The opera makes sense only if Caspar's subjection to Samiel (with its obvious Faustian connections) and his bargain with Max are treated with absolute seriousness. The symbolism is not philosophical as in *Die Zauberflöte* but psychological in a more modern sense: for the first time in opera suppressed and half-understood aspirations are given musical utterance on a level with acknowledged emotional and intellectual content. This great Romantic discovery provided the infrastructure of all Wagner's major works from *Der fliegende Holländer* to *Parsifal*.

The central theme of *Der Freischütz* is not love, jealousy, and ambition but the struggle between good and evil, a struggle of which the characters are only half aware. Powerful personalities abounded in the operas of Handel, Cherubini, and others. Mozart had explored almost every intricacy of character on the human level, and in *Don Giovanni* hinted at something beyond – hence its fascination for Hoffmann. Weber, like many men of his age, including the poet Wordsworth and the philosopher Schelling, identified natural phenomena with human moods and emotions (he was regularly moved to compose by scenery and travel); the next step was to take in supernature as well, and to express atmosphere and perspective, whether of time, place, or idea, in moral terms. The obverse of his achievement was a tendency to distance and depreciate the characters, especially the agents for good, who in all Weber's operas (and some of Wagner's) appear intellectually and emotionally flabby by contrast with the evil or the doomed. Adelhart in *Silvana*, Caspar in *Der Freischütz*, Eglantine and Lysiart in *Euryanthe* are far more powerfully drawn, as individuals and therefore as symbols, than their virtuous counterparts. It is no accident that the three men, like Beethoven's Pizarro, are related to the villains of French Revolution opera, especially Cherubini's Dourlinski and Méhul's Othon. Weber can establish elementary contrasts on a more human level, for example between Agathe and Ännchen, Huon of Bordeaux and his squire Sherasmin, or Reiza and Fatima; but he is no master of characterization in the Mozartean sense. In the last resort it is the background of his operas, rather than the individual actors, that haunts the memory.

This is reflected in the weight placed on the overtures, which, though based on French models, far surpass them in concentration and quality of invention and, like Beethoven's *Leonore* nos. 2 and 3, emerge as symphonic compositions able to stand unsupported. The *Freischütz* overture establishes at the outset – and in a coherent and satisfying form – not only the principal motives of the characters but their environment, physical in the forest music of the introduction with its evocative horns, spiritual in Samiel's diminished seventh. It was a considerable feat of imagination and economy to take this much-used chord and invest it, largely by means of orchestral colour and spacing, with such potency that we recognize it throughout the opera as a symbol of evil. The Wolf's Glen scene, for all its pantomime trappings, can still grip an audience because it is much more than an attempt to send shivers down the spine: it enshrines the central conflict of the opera. Weber in Act I has established the sinister power of Caspar and the weakness in Max on which he feeds; the C minor middle section of 'Durch die Wälder' shows the poison beginning to work. The means by which Weber builds up his great central scene all derive from *opéra comique*: the extended use of *mélodrame*, alternations of sung and spoken word, ostinato figures, reminiscences of earlier music (Caspar's drinking song), and the omnipresent diminished seventh, whose notes outline the successive tonal centres. But their strength is redoubled because they represent, besides the Glen itself, the guilt and anguish in Max's mind. The opera's weaknesses derive from the libretto, which Weber was insufficiently critical or too preoccupied to modify: the sprawling verbosity of the dialogue, the gratuitous appeal to sentimentality in the reference to Max's mother (not previously mentioned) and the feeble dénouement with its ludicrous dependence on a feat of marksmanship straining ballistic credibility. Even before the hermit turns up as a comfortable *deus ex machina*, Act III has tailed off into a mixture of sentimentality and irrelevance. Ännchen's aria about her aunt's dream, 'Einst träumte meiner sel'gen Base', added to please the singer, is a clever parody (diminished seventh and all), but fits the context far less well than the not dissimilar addition to *Abu Hassan*.

EURYANTHE

Euryanthe (1823) illustrates Romanticism's striving towards union of the arts. This too Weber had singled out in his analysis of *Undine*, and he had advocated it earlier in *Tonkünstlers Leben*: German opera must be an organic form in which all elements combine to create a new whole. In a letter to the Musical Academy of Breslau (20 December 1824) Weber declared that *Euryanthe* required a full union of the sister arts to make its proper impact. It is one of the ironies of operatic history that while this was a regular theme of his writings, a

PLATE IV. THE WOLF'S GLEN SCENE IN *ROBIN DES BOIS*
Castil-Blaze's adaptation of *Der Freischütz* was produced at the Odéon, Paris, on 7 December 1824.

fatal blind spot prevented him from achieving it, and nowhere more disastrously than in his most ambitious essay. Librettist, subject, and treatment were his own choice; the much maligned Helmine von Chezy has received a dusty deal. Weber began by giving her good advice: to use the libretto of *La Vestale* as model and to give him strange metres and distorted rhythms. But he then made a fatal mistake by insisting on the inclusion of the ghosts, thereby obscuring the plot and undermining the characterization, especially of his spotless heroine. A man of his theatrical experience should have seen that her failure to tell the truth when unjustly accused in Act II, and the importance allotted to a *serpens ex machina* in the first scene of Act III, were major defects in a design dependent on the clash of human temperaments. Weber left himself with a plot in which two of the characters are dead and a seminal dramatic action is over before the opera begins, and the survivors belie their own natures to prevent it ending too soon. Much of this could easily have been remedied. When Tieck advised Weber to restore the more realistic treatment of the story used by Shakespeare in *Cymbeline*, he made failure inevitable by a flat refusal.

Weber was not devoid of self-criticism. When the critic Friedrich von Drieberg pronounced a severe judgement on *Silvana*, he re-wrote two of the principal arias, and after the successful Berlin performance of 10 July 1812 noted in his diary: 'In my melodic shapes the suspensions are too frequent and too prominent, and in future I must try for more variety of tempo and rhythm.' Yet he lacked the synoptic vision of the true dramatist. And we may suspect that another factor was at work. The story of *Euryanthe*, involving envy, jealousy, and malice against a background of knightly chivalry, links *Ariodant* with *Lohengrin*; the resemblances between Ortrud and Telramund on the one hand and Eglantine and Lysiart on the other have often been pointed out, and can hardly be fortuitous; but there is no reason why ghosts should come into it at all. It would seem that Weber, having tapped a new vein in the supernatural scenes of *Der Freischütz*, could not bring himself to relinquish it. The intoxicating discovery that he could make such things convincing by the sheer force of musical imagination overthrew his judgement. His desperate attempt to obtain the best of both worlds by suggesting a *tableau vivant* during the overture,[1] to show Euryanthe kneeling at Emma's tomb while her restless ghost hovers above, was bound to fail because the whole episode is extraneous. This does not justify modern attempts to rewrite

---

[1] Weber probably got this idea from *opéra comique*, e.g. Kreutzer's *Lodoïska* and Grétry's *Le Magnifique*.

the opera. The musical plan, dependent on reminiscence motives and the alternation of sunny and stormy pieces – Adolar's confidence in Act I before the start of the intrigue, the love scene in Act II before Lysiart's denunciation, the May song, hunting chorus, and wedding march in Act III between Euryanthe's abandonment and the murderous dénouement – is precisely calculated and impossible to fault. To disturb this by cutting and rehashing is to destroy the opera's strength without remedying its weakness.

Euryanthe is by far the most advanced of Weber's operas, and the most influential; it left a deep mark on Marschner, Wagner (*Tannhäuser* and *Lohengrin*), Schumann (*Genoveva*), and Smetana (*Dalibor*), and at its best surpasses them all. Tovey called it 'both a more mature work of art and a more advanced development of Wagnerian music-drama than *Lohengrin*,[1] a judgement that can be sustained if the music is considered alone. The greatness of *Euryanthe* lies not in the arias and ensembles but in the extraordinary force and emotional intensity of the dramatic monologues and duologues, where Weber evolved an art of passionate expression foreshadowed in Méhul but handled with much greater freedom and certainty. His technique rests on through-composed form, the extensive use of reminiscence themes for structural and psychological purposes in a manner anticipating Wagner's *Leitmotiv*,[2] and the very bold treatment of tonality, which in certain scenes (notably the opening of Act III) foreshadowed its progressive dissolution under Wagner and indeed made that inevitable in the long run. The relaxation of set numbers owes something to Spohr and the simpler overlappings of Spontini; but Weber took it further, developing in key passages a flexible seamless texture in which recitative merges into arioso, monologue, or duet, so that the scene (in the modern sense of the term) becomes the unit. The most notable examples are the second scene of Act I, where Eglantine worms her secret out of Euryanthe, and the first of Act III, where Adolar abandons in the desolation of the forest the wife he intended to kill. *Euryanthe* and *Jessonda* were not the first German operas to eliminate spoken dialogue; it was no doubt the earlier ventures of Mosel and Poissl[3] in that direction that won Weber's approval for those long-forgotten composers, whose work was doomed by creative impotence.

The principal recurring themes, like Wagner's in the *Ring*, are

---

[1] *Essays in Musical Analysis*, iv (London, 1936), p. 54.
[2] F. W. Jähns, in his thematic catalogue of Weber's works (Berlin, 1871), actually used the term *Leitmotiv* – 'Er [Weber] *zuerst* planvoll angewendete *Leitmotive* einfürht' (p. 2) – earlier than Wagner or his disciples. On p. 366 he enumerates the *Leitmotive* in *Euryanthe*.
[3] See p. 454, above.

primarily rhythmic and harmonic, and therefore lend themselves to metamorphosis. The slithering wheedling motive of Eglantine heard first before her 'So einsam bangend find' ich dich?' on strings *pianissimo lusingando dolcissimo* in association with diminished seventh harmony, paints the false friend to the life.

Ex. 181

It is naturally prominent when Eglantine tries to discover Euryanthe's secret and, combined with a new cello melody, in her scena, 'Bethörte!', torn between hatred of Euryanthe and love for Adolar. Weber uses it later to suggest Eglantine's malign influence in her absence: when Lysiart, as a result of her treachery, denounces the innocent Euryanthe in the finale of Act II and at 'Eglantinens flehend Kosen' when Euryanthe at last tells the King the truth. The motive associated with the dead Emma and her ring, first heard in the middle of the overture and in its veil of chromatic mystery immensely potent in its own right, looks as far forward as *Die Walküre* when Euryanthe tells her secret to Eglantine in Act I:

Ex. 182

weint um mich! nicht eh' kann Ruh' mir wer-den, bis dies-en Ring, aus dem ich Tod ge-trun-ken, der

Un-schuld Thrä-ne netzt im höch-sten Leid, und Treu' dem Mör - der Ret-tung beut für Mord!

(Parted from Udo, I wander through the nights! O weep for me! I'll never rest until this ring from which I've drunk death is wetted in deepest sorrow with innocent tears, and murder is requited by loyalty to the murderer!)

At the end of the opera its single appearance in a major key, as the unquiet spirits are laid to rest, is marvellously apt. Lysiart is characterized by leaping dotted figures associated with jealousy, hatred, and revenge. If Euryanthe's purity wears a more conventional dress, the music associated with her abandonment in Act III is harmonically the boldest in the opera. The introduction's bleak horn solo is much closer to Wagner than to the hunting associations of *Der Freischütz*, or indeed of the *Euryanthe* huntsmen later in the Act. Like Lord Berkley in *Der Vampyr* and Mark in *Tristan*, the King hunts by night; the quarry is not specified.

OBERON

Oberon (1826) suffers from another notoriously recalcitrant libretto; but Weber was fully aware of the central flaw, the fact that so much of the action and characterization is confined to spoken dialogue and cannot be expressed in the music. He protested in letters to James Robinson Planché, his English librettist, but had no chance of prevailing against the fatal divorce that had bedevilled English theatre music from the days of Purcell and persisted in ballad opera. English audiences preferred the spectacular frivolity of pantomime to an art-form that made sense. Weber did not mean to leave *Oberon* as we have it; death intercepted his plan to rewrite the score with recitatives for the German theatre. While the libretto inhibited the symphonic development of *Euryanthe*, it appealed to another side of his genius by throwing the emphasis on nature-painting, genre pieces, and the fairy world, an aspect of the supernatural he had not yet tackled. By the same token it evoked his gift for the delicately poetic and the epigrammatic, which had emerged in *Abu Hassan* and parts of *Silvana* but (except in the delicious May song) found no place in *Euryanthe*. It is not surprising that on his way through Paris to London early in 1826 he was so captivated by *La Dame blanche* that he urged Marschner to produce it in Dresden. Mendelssohn's *Midsummer Night's Dream* music is full of *Oberon* echoes, for example of the fluttering staccato figures on flutes and clarinets in the first chorus and the introduction of the overture; it has often been pointed out that Mendelssohn's overture, composed in the same year as *Oberon*, actually quotes the mermaid's song, and in the same key.

Oberon presented Weber with three worlds, the magic, the chivalrous, and the oriental. He had conquered them individually before; he now evoked and distinguished them with absolute certainty in the same work, chiefly by means of orchestral colour and harmony. The musical numbers are mostly short, but they are wrought with an exquisite blend of richness and economy. The overture uses material from seven different movements. The three-note opening motive of Oberon's horn-call could scarcely be simpler (it was evolved perhaps from the main principle of two oriental melodies used in the first and third finales); yet while giving birth to many episodes in the opera and acting as a unifying factor, like Samiel's diminished seventh it is always instantly recognizable. This power of pregnant utterance distinguishes the first few notes of all three mature overtures; the bare string octaves in *Der Freischütz* and the dotted rhythm and leaping triplet arpeggios in *Euryanthe* likewise set the scene with a single gesture.

WEBER, WAGNER, AND HOFFMANN

There was a lesson here for Wagner, who learned almost as much from the deceptively simple English pantomime as from its *grosse romantische* predecessor. We can sense his presence in the wings in Oberon's aria, 'Fatal vow!', where the voice is mainly declamatory while the orchestra, with its distinctive motives thrusting upwards in the bass, has the most important material and carries the argument; in the tremendous Act II storm, indebted to Hoffmann's *Undine* but much nearer *Der fliegende Holländer*; in 'Ocean, thou mighty monster', which anticipates not only the 'sword' motive in the *Ring* but, when the sun breaks through on arpeggios of the tonic major chord, Brünnhilde's awakening in *Siegfried*, and perhaps the Valkyrie's war-cry in Reiza's repeated cries of 'Huon!'; in the Act III seduction scene with its hint of the *Parsifal* flower maidens; and in the sheer sound and texture of the orchestral writing in the serious scenes. The idea of redemption through love is also present in the plot. Nor had Weber exhausted his debt to *Undine*, underlined by the marine episodes and more explicit in the chorus of spirits before dawn in Act II. The linking of music with action and dialogue, notably in the vision of Reiza with guitar accompaniment, 'O, why art thou sleeping?', and the magic transformation to Baghdad in the following ensemble, is a refinement of the same source, though Weber's control is firmer and his invention infinitely superior. The song of the mermaids with its haunting solo horn (derived like so much else from the first bar of the overture) is perhaps the purest evocation in music of the Romantic spirit in its untroubled youth. The finest parts of the score are associated with the orchestra rather than the voice, for which Weber now writes inconsistently as well as unidiomatically. It is notorious that Reiza requires two different voices, those of an Agathe and a Brünnhilde; her part in the first finale must be one of the most unvocal ever penned by an experienced opera composer. Huon's tessitura too has a high potential for the slaughter of tenors. Weber's most unusual vocal idea was never carried out: like Britten later, he planned to cast Oberon for a mezzo-soprano.

WEBER'S TREATMENT OF TONALITY AND ORCHESTRA

Weber's ultimate failure on the dramaturgical level is the more disconcerting in view of his subtle and systematic treatment, in the mature operas, of the musical design as exemplified in orchestration and tonality. He himself explained his choice of horn colour for the forest and hunting scenes in *Der Freischütz*, and the lower register of strings and clarinet, deep tremolandos, and off-beat pizzicato basses, reinforced on occasion by heavy brass and drums, for the powers of evil. The wicked glitter of the piccolos in Caspar's 'Hier im ird'schen Jammerthal' makes a telling contrast. The progress from light to darkness and back is reflected in the alternation of C major and C minor. A more complex pattern governs *Euryanthe*: E flat major, trumpets, and a basic squareness of rhythm with heavy tonic and dominant accents for the outer aspects of chivalry, diatonic lyricism with many string and woodwind solos for Adolar and Euryanthe in their happier moods (especially Adolar's 'Wehen mir Lüfte Ruh'?' and Euryanthe's 'Glöcklein im Thale'), sharp keys, such as the B major of the climactic Act II duet, a violently contorted chromaticism, restless string figures and heavy brass for Eglantine and Lysiart, and by extension for Euryanthe when she is caught in their toils in Act III. The lighter psychological climate of *Oberon* demanded less concentration, but the tonal plan, based on D major, with excursions to E flat for two big 'chivalrous' arias, is entirely appropriate, and the three levels – the gossamer texture of the fairy scenes, the sinister trampling of the orientals, and the gallant fanfares of Huon and Charlemagne's court – are precisely differentiated (and sometimes combined) in terms of sound.

The orchestration is one of the glories of these operas. While Weber made full use of French experience, the idiomatic feeling for the colour – one might almost say the personality – of each instrument, especially the woodwind, was his own. Perhaps as the result of his friendship from 1811 with Heinrich Bärmann, he signally enriched the repertory of the clarinet, whose solos before the second subject of the *Freischütz* overture and before the main theme of 'Durch die Wälder' seem to distil the essence of Romanticism. The bassoon (in Euryanthe's chromatic Act III cavatina, 'Hier dicht am Quell') and the cello (in Agathe's 'Und ob die Wolke') are almost as sensitively endowed, and there are many trouvailles in fuller passages, such as the layout of the accompaniment of 'Leise, leise' for violas and muted violins in four parts and the remarkable scoring of the ghost music in *Euryanthe* for violas and eight muted solo violins.

Except in *Euryanthe*, where the unbridled passions of the characters led Weber to explore abstruse areas of experience, his harmonic style is more remarkable for imaginative judgement than for novelty. Like many contemporaries he employed great freedom of modulation, but he surpassed all except Beethoven in the exactitude of his timing. The now familiar shifts of a third are invested with maximum value in 'Leise, leise', 'Und ob die Wolke', and the hermit's entry in *Der Freischütz*. There is theatrical mastery in the magical change from the chord of G major to F sharp major when Agathe opens her balcony door to let in the moonlight, in the plunge from C to D flat as Lysiart stakes his claim against Euryanthe in the second finale, and in the modulation from F to D via F minor and D flat when in Act I Oberon transfers the scene from France to the banks of the Tigris. Not all Weber's modulations represent theatrical gestures. The breath-taking sideslip from E major to C major and back in the coda of the Mermaid's song is worthy of Schubert in its hint of inspired improvisation. Spontaneous lyricism is the most memorable feature of Weber's melodies (especially their initial phrases), which have a freshness and a youthful impulsiveness that belong to the brave new world of German Romanticism and generally evaded the coarser-grained Marschner and the more sophisticated Wagner. The second subjects of the overtures are sung by hero or heroine at a decisive point in the action, but they were surely conceived in terms of the orchestra, and sometimes of a particular instrument. Weber's tendency to embroider his voice parts with quaver or semiquaver figuration in quick tempos suggests the woodwind, his liberality with scale and arpeggio figures the keyboard. The melodic turn followed by an upward leap in the second subject of the *Freischütz* overture was to haunt Wagner as late as *Parsifal*. If it seems paradoxical to derive so much of an opera-composer's inspiration from the orchestra rather than the voice, this is perhaps a national characteristic, from which only those like Handel and Mozart who received much of their training and early experience in Italy are wholly exempt.

HEINRICH MARSCHNER

After Weber's death German Romantic opera flew rapidly to extremes. Marschner and Lindpaintner became intoxicated by the licence to horrify, without commanding Weber's invention or musical control. Wagner's first three operas swung violently between the styles of Weber, Marschner, Meyerbeer, Auber, Halévy, and Bellini before he settled on a steady personal course. Marschner, an important link between him and Weber, achieved rapid fame with two dramas on supernatural themes, *Der Vampyr* (1828) and *Hans Heiling* (1833); his third major opera, *Der Templer und die Jüdin* (1829), was popular for a time, but later works – one of them, *Kaiser Adolph von Nassau* (1845), brought out by Wagner at Dresden – showed a steep decline. In *Das Schloss am Ätna* (1836) he tried to repeat the formula of *Der Vampyr* and *Hans Heiling* in a Sicilian context, but merely diluted a Teutonic conception with Italianisms.

Marschner had worked with Weber at Dresden in 1823–6, and his imagination (like Lindpaintner's) was haunted by the dramatic and musical climate of *Der Freischütz* and *Euryanthe*. He had a gift for the macabre, which (unlike Weber) he was tempted to overplay, going all out for the *frisson* with insufficient regard for character or context. Hence, except to a limited degree in *Hans Heiling*, he jumped the symbolic element and lost a potential source of strength. This is most evident in *Der Vampyr*, which attracted attention by its scandalous and repulsive subject, a mixture of diabolism and sexual pathology based on a story attributed to Byron but in fact by his secretary John William Polidori. The central character, Ruthven (a Scottish earl), is a psychopath who murders and drinks the blood of his virgin-victims, apparently during intercourse. These exploits are a condition of his pact with the devil, but we are not shown how he came to such a desperate pass; the authors (the librettist was Marschner's brother-in-law Wilhelm August Wohlbrück) treat his performances with relish, wasting little time or sympathy on the victims or their bereaved relatives. The religious element that saves Malwina, the heroine and potential third victim, is handled rather superficially, as in *Robert le Diable* (which owes something to *Der Vampyr*) and indeed in *Der Freischütz*. The fascinated authors – like those of Lindpaintner's contemporary opera on the same story, produced six months after Marschner's – saw Ruthven as a linear descendant of Don Giovanni, with whom he shares not only his diabolism but several musical traits, including the baritone voice (which takes the leading part in all three of Marschner's principal operas) and the prevailing D minor tonality, culminating in a storm as the earth opens and swallows him up.

The hero of *Hans Heiling* (the libretto was intended for Mendelssohn) is a kind of inverted Faust. The offspring of the Queen of the Earth Spirits and a mortal father, he falls in love with a peasant girl (it is not clear how they met) and travels up from the underworld to marry her. His sombre manner, inability to enjoy the pleasures of rural life, and pathological jealousy of Anna's peasant admirer Konrad terrify the girl, despite the rich jewellery he bestows on her, and drive her into Konrad's arms, whereupon Heiling abandons human love and returns chastened to the underworld. Comparisons with Spohr's *Berggeist* are interesting. Ruthven, like Don Giovanni, at least has the courage of his convictions (if they can be so termed) and commits two murderous rapes in the course of the opera, whereas Spohr's Mountain Spirit, endowed with true supernatural powers, merely dithers. Heiling achieves little, beyond wounding Konrad in a bungled attempt at murder, but he is never contemptible. The libretto fails to define the powers of the earth spirits – in begging Anna to restore Heiling they behave like spoiled mortals – but Marschner makes Heiling's divided nature, his love for Anna, and his inner torment dramatically convincing. Heiling also possesses some symbolic significance as the Romantic outsider, longing to share ordinary human joys but inhibited by his split personality.

In both operas Marschner, following *Der Freischütz*, contrasts the supernatural world with that of the peasantry; drinking songs, ballads, and other strophic convivialities jostle the freer forms developed by

Weber and Spohr. *Der Vampyr* adds the gentry in the persons of Sir Humphrey Davenant and his daughter Malwina (Ruthven draws his victims from all ranks of society). *Der Templer und die Jüdin*, based on Scott's *Ivanhoe*, omits the supernatural but exhibits every other ingredient of Romantic opera: big crowd scenes, frequent battles, the paraphernalia of chivalry, a witchcraft trial, the comic Friar Tuck, even a village idiot. The librettist (Wohlbrück again) tried to work in so many strains from the novel that the plot is overcrowded with incident and few of the characters have room to develop. But it is clear that Marschner needed the spur of the grotesque and daemonic. He could draw peasants, perhaps because he was himself a peasant at heart, but was not at home with chivalry or court life. This is the weakest of the three operas, in style and characterization. The recurring motives have less distinction than those of *Der Vampyr* and *Hans Heiling*; that of the Norman soldiers is deplorable. Ivanhoe greets his sovereign in Act II with a fashionable polonaise, 'Es ist dem König Ehr' und Ruhm'. Religion is again treated as a mere device, and there is a great deal of it; Rebecca's part is a long succession of prayers. The characters with one notable exception remain flat. King Richard is a shadow, Ivanhoe and Rowena (who have no music together) not much more. Friar Tuck's strophic songs are within Marschner's compass, but they consort awkwardly with the extended arias and duets and the massive finales. The single impressive character is the baritone Bois-Guilbert, another doomed hero-villain in the Don Giovanni tradition: having stabbed the woman he loved and her bridegroom and taken the Templar's vow in repentance, he lives without hope of happiness unless he can obtain it from Rebecca. His big scena of self-torment, 'Mich zu verschmähen!', owes something to Spohr but develops considerably greater energy and brings him momentarily into touch with Lysiart and Telramund; Wagner described this scene as 'a creation of the greatest originality of feeling'. Its final *allegro brillante* echoes Weber's mermaids (with more panache but less poetry) in twice plunging from E to C major and back, a modulation that recurs at the same pitch towards the end of the finale of Act III and again in the coda of Hans Heiling's first aria, 'An jenem Tag'.

Marschner's strength lay in his gift for the theatre: *Der Vampyr*, for all its gaucheries of plot, comes off remarkably well even today. His sense of timing, though less subtle than Weber's, was much stronger than Spohr's, and his ensembles and finales, especially in *Der Vampyr* and *Hans Heiling*, can generate and maintain considerable tension. The two trios in *Der Vampyr*, 'Wie? Mein Vater!' in Act I and 'Ihr

wollt mich nur beschämen' in Act II, depict the individual characters
and their conflict with a fire surpassing that of the solo music. The
apparently irrelevant scene in Act II, in which four yokels with the
Shakespearian names of Gadshill, Richard Scrop (*sic*), Green, and
Toms Blunt drink themselves into a stupor and are hauled over the
coals by Blunt's indignant wife, gives rise to a brilliant *coup de théâtre*.
It follows Ruthven's wooing of the peasant bride Emmy, and is
terminated abruptly by shots as her bridegroom, finding her ravished
body, fires at the escaping murderer; the chill realization of what has
been going on offstage is immensely effective. *Hans Heiling* has several
moments of strong drama, especially in Act II, and some that are
contrived by the skilful handling of reminiscence motive: for example
the recall of Heiling's passionate love song, 'An jenem Tag', when he
asks Anna why she has betrayed his love, and of his promise (in the
Prologue) to return to the underworld when his garland is withered
and his heart broken, both in the finale of Act III.

Marschner's range is more limited than Weber's. He lacks the
lightness of touch – he deals in goblins and demons, never the fairies
of *Oberon* – and the power of epigram. His peasants are more boorish,
though not without rough humour; his nature pieces evoke the
nocturnal and sinister more memorably than the fresh air of the open
countryside. His orchestration, if coarser, has undeniable power,
again chiefly in sombre contexts. The growling of the double bassoon
in the second *Vampyr* seduction duet, 'Leise dort zur fernen Laube',
may have been suggested by the grave-digging episode in *Fidelio*, but
like the shuddering double basses and eerie high woodwind when
Ruthven is at his exercise it hits the mark. One of Marschner's most
successful gambits is his use of *mélodrame* in scenes of darkness,
terror, and extreme emotion, for example twice in Act I of *Der
Vampyr*. A vigorous ensemble and chorus during which Ianthe, the
vampire's first victim, is found dead in a cave, ends with a pianissimo
mélodrame as the wounded Ruthven fears he may die before a shaft of
moonlight can revive him. (The sudden change of mood and texture
at the very end recalls Méhul.) And then when Aubry carries Ruthven
to safety and flees in horror, he does not utter a word, Ruthven only a
sentence or two. Marschner's finest achievement in this line is in Act
II of *Hans Heiling*, a mixture of *mélodrame*, song, and tone poem.
Gertrude waits by lamplight for her daughter Anna's return through
the wood as the wind begins to howl. Fearing Anna has lost her way,
she begins to spin, humming to herself, singing snatches of gloomy
Volkslied, 'Des Nachts wohl auf der Haide', and breaking off at
intervals to comment on the rising storm. This is the most original

piece in the opera, its suspense heightened by the dark scoring for divided and muted lower strings, low woodwind and horns, and a wind machine.

Reminiscence motives are used freely and with considerable impact, but seldom symphonically, and the themes themselves have less pith and flexibility than Weber's. *Der Vampyr* contains at least eleven, of which four appear in Ruthven's D minor aria, 'Ha! Welche Lust!', and seven in the first finale. The two seduction duets, 'Theurer Eltern einz'ge Freude' and 'Leise dort', are quite different in mood, as befits the social status of the girls, but both are penetrated by Ruthven's characteristic triplet rhythms, often against a basic duple metre. There are occasional rhythmic subtleties, for example in Emmy's *Lied*, 'Dort an jenem Felsenhang', where a not quite regular alternation of 3/4 and 2/4 bars hints at quintuple time without establishing it. Marschner sought to unify his operas by tonality: D minor dominates *Der Vampyr*, E major (the equivalent of Weber's chivalrous E flat in *Euryanthe*) *Der Templer und die Jüdin*, C sharp minor the Second Act of *Hans Heiling*. He shared Spohr's fondness for enharmonic modulations and contrasts between adjacent keys, for example E flat and E, and E flat and D, in the trio, 'Wie? Mein Vater!', in *Der Vampyr*.

He essayed a few experiments in design. The Prologue to *Hans Heiling*, which shows the hero's departure from the underworld and by an original stroke precedes the overture, is an extensive through-composed scene, with many changes of key and tempo, which establishes the conflict in Heiling's mind and the prevailing climate of the drama. The overture itself has a programmatic function: it represents Heiling's ascent to middle earth, and as the curtain rises the voices of the underworld die away backstage. Not infrequently Marschner links movements together without benefit of cadence, and he breaks up strict forms into free arioso monologues; weakness of melodic invention may have impelled him, like Spohr, in this direction, though of course he had the examples of *Euryanthe*, *Jessonda*, and *Der Berggeist* before him. A striking instance is the *Grosse Scene*, 'Wohl, du zwingst mich zum Verbrechen', in which Ruthven reduces Aubry to despair by warning him that if he breaks his oath he too will become a vampire. The voice parts are declamatory; the music is propelled by the orchestra, which goes its own way, based on tremolando, diminished sevenths, harsh suspensions, restless modulations, and brief snatches of lyricism. The intention is perhaps more impressive than the achievement, but there is no doubting the urgent dramatic impulse. In view of this it is surprising that Marschner did not take the plunge and adopt the through-composed form his methods and initiative would seem to demand. In all three operas the resort to dialogue aborts progress, and in *Der Vampyr* it produces a major flaw: Aubry's oath not to expose Ruthven, on which the whole action depends, occurs in dialogue and consequently carries no musical force (though it is endowed with a motive later). Marschner may have wished to maintain contact with peasant life, regarding through-composition as a mark of grand opera; or he may have been restrained by Cherubini's example. Certainly Cherubini was a persistent influence. The first finale of *Der Templer und die Jüdin*, with its stage fighting and the collapse of a tower in flames, looks back to *Lodoïska*; all three finales of *Hans Heiling*, especially the first (Heiling's jealous fury against the waltz rhythm of the stage band) and second (the conflict between Heiling and Konrad over a symphonically worked scale-figure in the bass) are indebted to *Médée*. It is difficult to resist the conclusion that Marschner lacked the intellectual fibre to see his course clearly and follow it without deviation.

MARSCHNER'S MUSICAL LIMITATIONS

Nor was his musical endowment strong enough to carry him to the conquest of new territory. He remained half-shackled to Weber and Spohr, and never managed to transcend their influence or unify his style. His lyrical movements, especially the solos and duets of his lovers, again and again sound like pale echoes of Weber's, and they are built on similar lines. The peasant scenes owe an equally obvious debt to *Der Freischütz* and the May song in *Euryanthe*. *Hans Heiling* even has in Act III a bridesmaids' chorus – as does Lindpaintner's *Vampyr*, where it is distorted later as in Marschner – enlivened by polonaise rhythm. The overture to *Der Vampyr* is modelled almost slavishly on that of *Euryanthe*, with a very similar second subject (used later in the duet for Aubry and Malwina, 'Halt ein! Ich kann es nicht ertragen'), a fugato development, and the same inflation and acceleration of the second subject in the coda. The opening scene of the opera is diluted Wolf's Glen, with flaring will-o'-the-wisps, horrific nocturnal apparitions, eldritch woodwind squeals, raucous diminished sevenths, and an intermittently darkened moon. (The second finale of Lindpaintner's *Der Vampyr* is based on the same model.) The high-flown chivalry of *Der Templer und die Jüdin* is that of *Euryanthe* grown stale and transposed up a semitone. The direction *allegro agitato* is almost as common as in Spohr and Mendelssohn, though (thanks to greater rhythmic urgency) less frequently sapped by chromatic harmony. In *Der Templer und die Jüdin* Marschner employed Spohr's chromatic mannerisms in straight scenes (the 9/8 passage in the second finale when Rebecca unveils at her trial) and also for parody (Friar Tuck's 'Ora pro nobis' in the drinking song). There are borrowings from further afield: Konrad's 12/8 'Gönne mir ein Wort der Liebe' with obbligato horn in the second finale of *Hans Heiling* almost reproduces the melody of Schubert's 'Ungeduld', and the comic quintet in Act II of *Der Vampyr* suddenly plunges from the most Teutonic of drinking-songs into the world of Rossini, with a jocular theme in rapid repeated notes running through the orchestra. *Hans Heiling* is the most consistent in style of the three operas, but in the last resort its not inconsiderable merits are undermined by lack of individual contour in the melodic lines.

MARSCHNER'S INFLUENCE ON WAGNER

If Marschner never digested the music of his predecessors, he sometimes anticipated that of his successors. The parallels with Schumann and Mendelssohn may derive from common influences, but those with Wagner are in a different category. That supreme snapper-up of unconsidered trifles, who in 1833 composed an extensive new *allegro* for Aubry's 'Wie ein schöner Frühlingsmorgen' in *Der Vampyr*, found plenty to devour in Marschner. The strophic *Romanze* with choral refrain in which Emmy tells the story of the Vampire, 'Sieh, Mutter, dort den bleichen Mann', an atmospheric piece all the more potent for its restrained scoring, was one of the models for Senta's ballad, in the words ('der bleiche Mann') as well as the music. The already-mentioned *Grosse Scene* in Act II comes close to the rhetorical declamation of *Tannhäuser*. The resemblances are still closer in *Hans Heiling*, whose theme, the half-spectral hero's anguished renunciation of earthly love, is central to *Der fliegende Holländer*. The Prologue with its free design and its Nibelung-like earth spirits toiling away in the dark, the overture depicting Heiling's journey, and his impressive *mélodrame* and scena of disillusionment and despair at the start of Act III, whose initial horn motive (i), which also begins the overture, provides a symphonic underpinning of the texture when the earth spirits rise up (ii) and when Heiling cries 'Sprecht Ihr eurem König Hohn?' (iii), are all distinctly Wagnerian:

Ex. 183

So, more specifically, is the aria of the Queen of the earth spirits, which prefigures Brünnhilde's 'death announcement' in *Die Walküre* in the notes, atmosphere, and accompaniment for low trombones:

Ex. 184

(Else thou art forfeited to the vengeful fury [of the mighty spirits])

Of course Marschner is not equal to the implications, structural or symbolic; the status and powers of his earth spirits are ill-defined, and his hero lacks the concentrated projection of the Dutchman. But without Marschner Wagner would not have been the same composer.

SCHUBERT AS OPERA COMPOSER

Neither influence nor historical importance can be claimed for Schubert's operas, of which only the one-act *Die Zwillingsbrüder* and the melodrama *Die Zauberharfe* were produced during his life (both in 1820), and none was published till long after his death. Yet Schubert's status as a great composer, his manifest love for the theatre, and the profusion of fine music to be found in his operas demand their examination. Of the seventeen projects on which he embarked, seven were never finished and one survives incomplete. Four of the remainder are light pieces in a single act, but three – *Des Teufels Lustschloss* (1813–14), *Alfonso und Estrella* (1821–2) and *Fierrabras* (1823) – are among the most ambitious of Romantic operas. As works of art they are total failures. Like Haydn, but to an even greater degree, Schubert had no innate gift for the theatre. He was either unaware of this or thought it of no importance, for he never attempted to gain practical experience; and he compounded the deficiency by accepting librettos from personal friends with even less flair for drama or literature. His one setting of a major poet, Goethe's *Claudine von Villa Bella* (1815), was subsequently mutilated by a housemaid in search of tinder. The librettos were a major handicap, but not the only one. Almost all are vitiated by monotonous ballad metres, insipid verses, and a crass inability to create character or a coherently motivated plot. Those of *Alfonso und Estrella* and *Fierrabras*, the two big operas of Schubert's maturity, were deliberately planned to exploit his gifts as a composer of concert songs and choruses, the worst possible model for a drama. Inevitably they led him to luxuriate in lyrical sentiment, whether or not it was appropriate to the context, and to write accompaniments of a type suited to the drawing-room, with otiose orchestral interludes between lines and at the end of stanzas or sections. Partly because he eschewed recitative, the time-honoured and indispensable method of despatching stage business between movements requiring lyrical or dramatic expansion, he was unable to vary the dramatic pace or adjust the music to the demands of the action. This is reflected in his modulations; often thrilling in themselves, they are geared not to structural changes or stage incidents or points of character, but to an abstract musical design or a passing verbal image. Hence the drama moves by fits and starts, and for long stretches hardly at all. In the theatre this is a recipe for tedium.

One of Schubert's most disconcerting habits is to waste time over side-issues. It scarcely matters that he dragged into the Second Act of *Die Freunde von Salamanca* (1815), an intricate love story, a duet for two guerrillas enlarging on the joys of their profession. But every act of *Alfonso und Estrella* and *Fierrabras* begins with an episode that would be better out of the way or severely pruned. Act I of the former starts with an enormously long and slack greeting to the sun from the exiled monarch Troila, Act II with the same character, at his son's request, singing a pointless narrative aria about a cloud-maiden (one section ended up, with similar words, in the *Winterreise* song 'Täuschung'), Act III with a stormy battle scene which is at once duplicated in a description by a group of terrified women. *Fierrabras* offers in Act I a spinning scene for the heroine Emma and chorus, in Act II a *Lied* for Eginhard, Roland, and the Frankish knights saluting the fatherland (they are on a military expedition in no-man's-land, but Eginhard carries a harp, and the knights retire at the end, leaving him to be captured), in Act III another extraneous scene for Emma and female chorus. It comes as no surprise that when left alone in prison the knights divert themselves with an unaccompanied partsong. No opera, especially one with a complex plot, can afford to mark time with such regularity at the beginning of each act.

STYLISTIC INFLUENCES ON SCHUBERT

In matters of style Schubert was a veritable magpie, borrowing from all quarters. Whereas he was able to digest the influences in his finest instrumental works, they obtrude in the operas owing to the lack of formal discipline. The most persistent were Mozart, Gluck, and the French school – Cherubini, Catel, and Spontini in the grander works, Dalayrac, Boieldieu, and sometimes Méhul in the lighter *Singspiele*, which also reflect the Mozart of *Figaro* and the popular idiom of Weigl. The freedom of modulation in the overture to Méhul's *Le Trésor supposé* and the melodic and harmonic savour of Zulmé's romance in Act II of Dalayrac's *Gulistan* are very close to Schubert; both operas were popular in Vienna. The Gluck influence, strengthened by Schubert's admiration for *Iphigénie en Tauride* and perhaps by his early studies with Salieri, is obvious in *Des Teufels Lustschloss* and the fragmentary *Adrast* (1819); it mingles with that of *Die Zauberflöte* in the noble *Trauermusik* that is a feature of both operas (nos. 10 and 16 in the former, the funeral march, no. 4, in the latter) and recurs in Act III of *Fierrabras* ('Der Rache Opfer fallen'). These pieces, sometimes combined with *mélodrame*, are all in minor keys and scored chiefly or entirely for wind instruments;[1] the large stage band in *Fierrabras*, including trombones, may have been suggested by Spontini. *Adrast* contains some of Schubert's most impressive theatre music, chiefly sombre or pastoral in mood (sometimes both at once) and very like the song settings of the same poet, Johann Mayrhofer; Schubert's genius was more at home with classical tragedy than with the pomp of chivalry. The approaching trumpet signals of *Fidelio* left their mark on several scenes of *Fierrabras*, especially the second finale, where the last of them is followed by the same modulation as in Beethoven. In the ensemble 'Sie haben das Rufen vernommen' in Act III of *Alfonso und Estrella* Schubert makes similar play with horn calls, a common feature in French Revolution operas. The canonic round, of which there are several instances – the trio 'Ich lach', ich wein'' in *Des Teufels Lustschloss*, the quartet 'Freund, eilet euch zu retten' in *Der vierjährige Posten* (1815), where it is dramatically apt and beautifully wrought with overlapping entries, the Act I finale of *Alfonso und Estrella* – came from Italy,[2] though it is most familiar today in *Così fan tutte* and *Fidelio*. There are strong traces of Rossini in the later operas, *Die Verschworenen* (1823), *Alfonso und Estrella* ('Versammelt euch, Brüder', a chorus and ensemble in Act I, where a bouncy tune in sharply accented rhythm with triplets runs in the orchestra against the voices), and *Fierrabras* (the quintet 'Verderben denn und Fluch'). The male-voice partsongs, sometimes introduced in the most inappropriate places, recall Weber, but may have a common origin in the patriotic choral societies that sprang up all over Germany during the Napoleonic Wars.

MUSICAL CHARACTERISTICS

A glance at the three big operas shows that, except in quality of musical invention, Schubert scarcely developed at all. *Fierrabras* is as disproportionately mis-shapen and as dramatically preposterous as *Des Teufels Lustschloss*, the first opera he completed. Both use Cherubini's compound resources of spoken dialogue, *mélodrame*, recitative, formal aria, and ensemble, but never with an effect equal to that of the second finale of *Médée*. In *mélodrame* Schubert sometimes achieves conspicuous success, as in Florinda's running commentary on the battle at the end of Act II of *Fierrabras*, where a surprisingly concise finale ends in E flat minor. His most extensive use of the form in *Die Zauberharfe* is marred by weaknesses of timing and the

[1] There is a good deal of this kind of scoring in *Die Zauberharfe*, where Schubert places a wind band under the stage, and the incidental music to the lost play *Rosamunde* (1823).
[2] See p. 401.

inappropriate length of the movements, not to mention the exagger-
atedly romantic plot about an heiress on a hunting-party lost in a
magic forest. All three operas are immensely long and (like *Die
Zauberharfe*) make practical demands only realizable on Wagnerian
terms, including large casts (not all of whom sing), elaborate spectacle,
and numerous changes of scene in each act. The scoring is
correspondingly massive, especially in the use of wind instruments;
when he treats them with restraint or as soloists, Schubert often
produces exquisite results, but he is as likely to drown the voices by
keeping the whole orchestra at full blast for pages on end. He gives
greater prominence to trombones than any earlier composer outside
France (another possible legacy from Spontini), both to reinforce the
tutti and as a group to add an extra strand of colour; like some French
composers he often strengthens the bass line with the bass trombone
without its fellows. *Adrast* has four trombones; but the orchestra in
this opera, though massive, is handled more sensitively than elsewhere,
with emphasis on the dark colours of divided violas and cellos.

Kotzebue's libretto for *Des Teufels Lustschloss*, an eccentric
specimen of the Gothic-Romantic type, has points in common with
Lodoïska and several of Dalayrac's operas, notably *Léon*. It is called
eine natürliche Zauberoper, which means that the magic episodes that
dominate the first two acts and much of the third turn out to be faked.
The hero Oswald is subjected to every imaginable Gothic horror and
temptation, including a giant hand, an iron cage, armed statues that
come to life and fight, a mock-execution, a flood, and the seductions
of an Amazon and a bevy of flower maidens playing Turkish
instruments. We discover in the event that these have all been devised
to test Oswald's constancy by the heroine Luitgarde's uncle, with the
aid of his estate staff and machinery brought from Italy; the Amazon
is his gardener's daughter. This pretence devalues the rescue scene
during a thunderstorm in the middle of Act III (as lurid as that in
Lodoïska), in the course of which Oswald knocks down several men in
armour, throws the executioner and his chopper over a cliff, and saves
the fainting Luitgarde from the flood. It might work as parody or as
symbolism in the manner of *Die Zauberflöte*; but Schubert's music is
innocent of either. He takes everything with absolute seriousness, at
no time distinguishing between genuine and simulated emotion. The
Amazon is presented as a woman scorned; she and Luitgarde both
sing in the style of the Queen of Night; and there is little distinction
between the music of Oswald and his bibulous servant. The finest
thing in the opera is the overture, which runs on into the first ensemble.

Alfonso und Estrella is Schubert's only through-composed opera;

but although he several times dispenses with cadences between set pieces (a process slightly extended in *Fierrabras*), he scarcely advances beyond Spontini in this respect. Franz von Schober's jumbled libretto makes its bow to Metastasian *opera seria*, French rescue opera, Rousseau, and German Romanticism (forests, chivalry, a gold chain as talisman). As with *Fierrabras* and several other Schubert operas, the scene is set in Spain, but there is no attempt at local colour. The predominance of low male voices (a rightful king in exile, a usurper, and a vile but ineffective seducer) over the single tenor reflects the practice of the period, without any of its fashionable diabolism, which was scarcely compatible with Schubert's *Biedermeier* temperament. Although the action moves between a happy valley and the usurper's court, and several scenes are set in the open air, the climate is that of the drawing-room. The music flows smoothly along with all the leisure in the world, throwing off wonderful ideas but putting them to no dramatic purpose. That of the villains, with the exception of the defeated usurper's G minor aria, 'Wo find' ich nur den Ort' in Act III, is as amiable as the rest, and it comes as no surprise when the restored monarch bestows a chivalrous forgiveness on everyone. The scale is indicated by the presence of no fewer than thirteen duets, the longest love scene before *Tristan* (a string of two arias and three duets in Act II) and, immediately after it, perhaps the longest conspiracy as well. Apart from the numerous double choruses, many of them square military pieces for male voices, almost every movement is an extension of *Lied* or aria form.

FIERRABRAS

Fierrabras is a *heroisch-romantische Oper* with the same chivalrous background as *Euryanthe*, which Schubert condemned as formless. His own opera has a libretto (by his friend Leopold Kupelwieser) beside which that of *Euryanthe* is a model of sweet reason. The action takes place in Spain during the struggle between Charlemagne and the Moors, and concerns the adventures of two pairs of lovers on opposite sides. Charlemagne always acts before he thinks; Fierrabras, son of his Moorish enemy, displays a quixotic nobility that is singularly ill-rewarded; he and Emma, Charlemagne's daughter, vanish for the whole of Act II. Eginhard, whose behaviour is that of a coward and a cad, wins the girl, and Fierrabras has to be content with a fruitless conversion to Christianity. There are many other characters, all of cardboard, an exceptional number of coincidences, and a long series of battles, sorties, sieges, and abortive executions. The Calderón play on which the story is based treats it ironically (as it might seem to demand); the opera refuses this approach and omits the magic element – the exact opposite of Weber's procedure with *Euryanthe* in the same year.

Schubert offers no differentation in the music of Franks and Moors. While the last two acts in particular contain much empty note-spinning, and the whole opera is full of enormous ensembles in which the characters join without expressing any individuality, there are scenes in Act I where Schubert does develop tension and conflict, chiefly in *mélodrames* and arioso passages. One is the *mélodrame* at the end of the A major ensemble 'Der Landestöchter fromme Pflichten' in Act I, when Fierrabras recognizes Emma as the girl he fell in love with at Rome four years earlier. The long first finale, in which Eginhard, after serenading Emma, is admitted to her room but allowed to escape with the connivance of Fierrabras, who is himself suspected and arrested by Charlemagne, is musically and dramatically the finest piece of sustained writing in Schubert's operas. The Act III quartet 'Bald, bald', which begins as a duet, continues as a trio, and jumps from D minor to B flat minor at the appearance of Eginhard, does help to advance the action, but is weakened by the incredibility of the characters. A feature of some interest is Schubert's use of a personal theme (Ex. 185) for Fierrabras. It appears during ensembles, generally in recitative or arioso, and is handled with a certain flexibility. Introduced by the bassoons when Charlemagne first sees Fierrabras as a prisoner (i), it recurs in modified form when some other character refers to him or merely thinks of him (ii and iii), and finally becomes part of the march for the entry of the Moors with him as a prisoner in Act II (iv). Schubert does not fully exploit its rhythmic or harmonic potential, and he abandons it altogether half way through the opera. He seems to have been feeling his way by instinct rather than following a settled plan.

Ex. 185

SCHUBERT'S *SINGSPIELE*

The most viable of Schubert's operas are the modest one-act *Singspiele*, especially *Der vierjährige Posten*, which has an amusing dramatic idea, and *Die Verschworenen*, based on a mild variant of Aristophanes's *Lysistrata*. There is little tension or characterization, but in such unpretentious contexts Schubert's effervescent lyricism, like a stream of *Schöne Müllerin* songs, his attractive woodwind writing, and general high spirits can give much pleasure. The two-act *Die Freunde von Salamanca*, looser in plan, has many Mozartean echoes, including an initial trio of male voices hatching a sexual intrigue in the manner of *Così fan tutte*, and a tendency to spin out the chromaticism in the direction presently abused by Spohr.

Ex. 186

All the operas are rich in melody, strokes of harmonic imagination, and passages of deft economic writing for the voices, the more striking for the comparative absence of counterpoint in the orchestra. If a fraction of the craftsmanship Schubert bestowed on musical detail had been devoted to bringing the drama into focus, his immense expenditure of effort would not have issued in such a mouse-like achievement.

XI

OPERA
IN OTHER COUNTRIES

By GERALD ABRAHAM

THE German-speaking lands were not alone in attempts to free themselves from the domination of Italian and French opera, but no others had composers comparable with Spohr, Weber, and Marschner. As in Germany and Austria, vernacular opera usually took the form of *Singspiel*; composers were apparently nervous of setting prosaic dialogue as recitative. And, as in Germany, patriotic and romantic subjects became particularly popular after the close of the Napoleonic War. In several cases the composers were not even natives; the pioneers of Danish *syngespil*, Friedrich Weyse (1774–1842) with his *Sovedrikken* (1809), *Faruk* (1811), and other works, and Friedrich Kuhlau (1786–1832) with *Elverhøj* (1828), were respectively North German and Hanoverian by birth; one of the leading composers of Polish opera, Jósef Elsner (1769–1854), came of Silesian stock, and the first outstanding composer of Russian opera after Fomin,[1] was Catterino Cavos (1775–1840), a Venetian. In England Henry Bishop (1786–1855), after composing two three-act operas, *The Circassian Bride* (1809) and *The Maniac, or The Swiss Banditti* (1810), declined into a compiler of pasticci and shocking English derangements of foreign masterpieces (including *Don Giovanni*, *Figaro*, *Il barbiere di Siviglia*, and *Der Freischütz*). His own *Clari, or The Maid of Milan* (1823) is remembered only because he introduced in it his song 'Home, sweet home', treating it as a reminiscence theme.

POLISH OPERA

The last opera produced in the independent Kingdom of Poland was *Krakowiacy i Gorale* (Cracovians and Mountaineers) (1794) by the Czech-born Jan Stefani (1746 or 1748–1829), It contained music more genuinely Polish than any earlier opera, for Stefani modelled a number of his melodies fairly closely on actual folk-tunes[2] and adopted not

---

[1] See Vol. VII, pp. 278–81.
[2] See Jan Prosnak, *Kultura muzyczna Warsawy XVIII wieku* (Cracow, 1955), pp. 140–2.

only mazurka, polonaise, and krakowiak rhythms but the occasional sharpened fourth of the scale characteristic of Polish melody. Even the plot has one striking feature: the decisive 'god' appears not *ex machina* but with a machine, an electrical one, with the help of which he routs the marauding mountaineers. The immense popularity of the work at the time was also partly due to its being 'the opera of the Kościuszko rising' which broke out a month after the first performance. The libretto of *Krakowiacy i Gorale* was the work of Wojciech Bogusławski (1757–1829), librettist, playwright, theatre director, actor, and bass singer, who has been called not unjustly 'the father of the Polish theatre'. And it was Bogusławski, then director at Lwow, who provided the theatre conductor Elsner with the libretto of his first notable opera *Amazonki czyli Herminia* (The Amazons, or Herminia) (1797). Two years later the pair were appointed to the National Theatre at Warsaw and in 1810 Bogusławski recruited a second conductor, Karol Kurpiński (1785–1857), who soon scored an operatic success with *Lucypera* (Lucifer's Palace) (1811). Elsner and Kurpiński were the mainstays of Polish opera throughout this period.

ELSNER'S OPERAS

Elsner had a penchant for libretti translated from the French and he also slipped easily into Italian idioms; Irena's Act II aria[1] in *Amazonki* is typical:

Ex. 187

---

[1] Complete in full score in Alina Nowak-Romanowicz, *Józef Elsner* (Cracow, 1957), supplementary volume of musical examples, pp. 14–21.

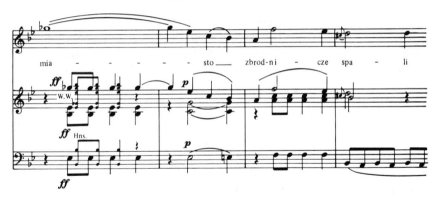

mia - - - - sto___ zbrod-ni - cze spa - li

(Let that wicked city be burned by its fiercest foes)

But there is a genuine national vein in his two best operas, the two-act
Leszek Bialy czyli Czarowicna z Lysej Góry (Leszek the White, or The
Witch from the Bare Mountain) (1809) and *Król Łokietek czyli
Wiśliczanki* (King Dwarf, or The Girls of the Vistula) (1818), also in
two acts, both on libretti by Ludwik Dmuszewski. The polonaise
which provides the main section of the overture to *Leszek*[1] is a good
example:

Ex. 188

(Oboe, doubled 8ve lower by solo cello; acc. by W.W. and pizzicato Str.)

A slow polonaise-like opening to the *Król Łokietek* overture[2] suggests
Poland under the Bohemian yoke from which it was freed by
Władysław I, nicknamed 'King Dwarf' from his stature. But the king
himself has only one song; the rest of his part is solely recitative.
Much of the score consists of krakowiaks and mazurkas, one of which
– sung by two of the 'girls of the Vistula' – became a quasi-folk-song
with different words, and Paganini composed variations on it in 1829.
Łokietek is also notable for a dream episode in which one of the
characters sees a series of tableaux from Polish history which Elsner
accompanied with music partly from his own earlier works, partly
borrowed, but all strongly evocative to a patriotic audience.

[1] Ed. Grzegorz Fitelberg (Cracow, 1950).
[2] Complete full score in Nowak-Romanowicz, pp. 38–55.

KURPIŃSKI

Like Elsner, Kurpiński was attracted by librettos translated from the French though he usually provided them with Polish music; one of the earliest, the one-act *Marcinowa w seraju* (Marcinowa in the Seraglio) (1812), has an overture in sonata form[1] 'sur le thème de Mazurek' which is treated fugally in the development section. But his most popular opera, *Zabobon czyli Krakowiacy i Górale albo Nowe Krakowiaki* (Superstition, or Cracovians and Mountaineers, or The New Cracovians) (1816), is an entirely new setting of a complete reworking of Bogusławski's libretto of 1794 with the same characters. But Kurpiński was a better musician than Stefani, as he shows by his version of the student Bardos's song:

Ex. 189 (i)

(Cruel world, perverse world, everything goes wrong)

(ii)

(When you look at the world, what is revealed for me there?)

Its lack of national flavour was perhaps deliberate; Bardos, unlike all the other characters, is not a peasant.

In the three-act *Jadwiga, królowa polska* (Jadwiga, Queen of Poland) (1814),[2] like Elsner in *Król Łokietek*, he turned to a patriotic Polish monarch of the fourteenth century. (Under severe pressure from her subjects, the young Jadwiga renounced the Austrian prince to whom she was betrothed, and whom she deeply loved, to marry the Lithuanian Prince Władysław Jagiello.) Here national colouring is minimal owing to the predominance of princely characters, two of whom are not even Poles, but when the Polish people make themselves heard, as in the final chorus of Act I, the music is appropriately Polish.

---

[1] Complete full score in Tadeusz Strumiłło, *Źródła i początki romantyzmu w muzyce polskiej* (Cracow, 1956), supplementary volume of musical examples, pp. 30–70.
[2] Full score ed. Nowak-Romanowicz, *Opery polskie*, v (Cracow, 1980).

And the text is said to be very sensitively treated, as in Jadwiga's first recitative,[1] while her aria following the recitative, if not strikingly original, shows Kurpiński's mastery of the type of Italian melody which still lingered on almost everywhere in Europe:

Ex. 190

(A beloved mother's words remain sacred in my heart)

[1] According to Zdzisław Jachimecki, *Muzyka polska w rozwoju historycznym*, i.2 (Cracow, 1951), p. 165.

The most successful of Kurpiński's other operas was *Zamek na Czorstynie czyli Bojomir i Wanda* (The Castle of Czorstyn, or Bojomir and Wanda) (1819).[1] This is the most 'romantic' in subject of all his operas: heroine imprisoned in haunted castle by cruel father and out of her mind, rescued by lover returning from the Turkish wars. (The year is 1683.) But both Wanda and Bojomir are musically rather colourless, whereas the peasant Nikita, who guides Bojomir but warns him of the terrors of the castle, is characterized by folk-idioms.

RUSSIAN OPERA

Besides Fomin's *Amerikantsy*,[2] produced at last in 1800 though composed twelve years earlier, a Spaniards-and-Indians opera which thus anticipated Spontini's *Fernand Cortez*, the Russian stage during the first decade of the century saw a number of native works in not very successful rivalry with Boieldieu, who dominated the St Petersburg scene until his expulsion in 1812. Among these were a so-called trilogy by the amateur Aleksey Nikolaevich Titov (1769–1827): *Yam* (The Post-boys' Village) (1805), *Posidelki* (Evening Meeting in the Village) (1808), and *Devichnik* (Wedding Eve Party in the Bride's House) (1809).[3] As the titles – which must be defined rather than translated – indicate, these are little more than scenes from peasant life and Titov was not a very skilful composer, but his unpretentious little works enjoyed considerable popularity for a time. Particularly interesting is a mostly unison female chorus in *Devichnik*:

Ex. 191

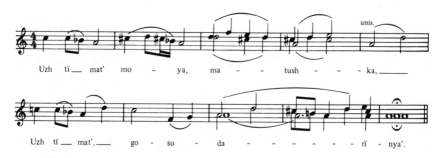

Uzh tï — mat' mo - ya, ma - - tush - - ka, —

Uzh tï — mat', — go - su - da - - - - - rï - nya'.

(Ah, mother, little mother, mistress!)

[1] Full score ed. Anna Papierzowa and Włodzimierz Poźniak, *Opery polskie*, i (Cracow, 1968).
[2] See Vol. VII, p. 280.
[3] Excerpts in S. L. Ginzburg, *Istoriya russkoy muzïki v notnïkh obraztsakh*, ii (Moscow-Leningrad, 1949), pp. 85–102.

with a note in the score: 'Wedding song. This chorus of girls is without orchestra. It begins behind the scenes quietly, but as they appear on the stage it is sung loudly and in such a way that when they cross the stage and recede behind the scenes it becomes weaker and finally dies away altogether'. It is clear that Titov was trying to reproduce, or perhaps had actually noted down, folk-polyphony.[1]

Influence from German *Singspiel* was rare but there was one outstanding exception, Kauer's *Donauweibchen*.[2] In Vienna this had been so successful that librettist and composer produced a sequel almost immediately and a third part was concocted three years later by another librettist and composer. A Russian version of the original *Donauweibchen*, as *Rusalka*, appeared in 1803 with Kauer's music and additional numbers by Stepan Ivanovich Davïdov (1777–1825), and the second part, as *Dneprovskaya rusalka*, in which the Venetian, Catterino Cavos (1775–1840) also collaborated, in 1804. Finally in 1805 and 1824 Davïdov alone was responsible for the third and fourth parts: *Lesta, dneprovskaya rusalka* (Lesta, the nymph of the Dneper).[3] The libretti of the first three parts were provided by N. S. Krasnopolsky, that of the fourth by A. A. Shakhovsky. In Davïdov's hands the original *Singspiel* became more and more a pre-romantic opera. He was not only a more gifted composer than Kauer technically; he gave the young hero, Prince Vidostan, romantic warmth, and Lesta – who bewilders him as in turn an ugly old woman, a charming young peasant girl, a gypsy singer – touching humanity. One example will suffice to show how Davïdov transfigured the pantomime trivialities of his librettist. In one comic scene of Act III a Negro boy was supposed to pop out of a basket of apples and play a trumpet; by substituting a horn for the trumpet, Davïdov translated this into an idyllic interlude:

Ex. 192

---

[1] Cf. Vol. VII, p. 280.
[2] See chap. X, p. 456.
[3] Excerpts in Ginzburg, op. cit., pp. 119–63.

Davïdov's instrumental ideas are often charming; in the very first scene the invisible Lesta is suggested by a dialogue of flute and glass harmonica; Vidostan's big aria in Act II is anticipated by solos for cor anglais and then cello.

CATTERINO CAVOS

Having contributed to the second part of *Dneprovskaya rusalka*,[1] Cavos embarked on works of his own in the same genre of semi-comic *féerie*: *Knyaz-nevidimka* (The invisible prince) (1805) and *Ilya-bogatïr* (Ilya the hero) with a libretto by the fabulist I. A. Krïlov (1806); another very successful work was the 'opera-vaudeville' *Kozak-stikhotvorets* (The Cossack poet) (1812).[2] Cosmopolitan though much of his music was, Cavos assiduously strove, not without success, to imitate Russian – particularly Ukrainian – folk-idioms and by the time he came to write the work on which his fame principally rests, *Ivan Susanin* (1815), he had really absorbed them. The subject of *Susanin* is the same as that of Glinka's *Life for the Tsar*, the first performance of which he was to conduct twenty years later; it is a 'rescue opera' in the French tradition, with spoken dialogue, and differs from Glinka in that it ends happily with Susanin saved from the Poles in the nick of time. The national note is sounded at once in the opening chorus of peasants, 'Do not blow the yellow leaves from the forest oaks, O storm-winds':[3]

[1] Two excerpts in M.S. Pekelis, *Istoriya russkoy muzïki*, i (Moscow-Leningrad, 1940), p. 298. One, Lesta's song in Act II, is based on Ukrainian folk material; the other, from her duet with the buffoon, might well be a French *romance*.
[2] Excerpts from all three in Ginzburg, op. cit., pp. 168–91.
[3] Complete in ibid., p. 194.

Ex. 193

And it is heard again and again, e.g. in the First Act trio when
Susanin's son-in-law, Matvey, sings:

Ex. 194

(Let the wicked dread and mourn for ever; the good man must rejoice.)

Susanin himself repeats the same words to a broader modification of
the melody in the finale of Act I when he is about to be led off by the
Poles, and again in his couplets at the end of the opera. Cavos makes
no attempt to characterize the Poles musically as Glinka was to do;
the only quasi-polonaise in the score is sung by Matvey with chorus in

the second number of the First Act; it has already been heard in the overture where it is marked 'Tempo di minuetto'. Surprisingly, even the Russian flavour seems to have evaporated from Cavos's later works, such as *Zhar-ptitsa* (The Fire-bird) (1823).[1]

VERSTOVSKY

The next considerable composer of Russian opera was Aleksey Nikolaevich Verstovsky (1799–1862). Unlike Fomin and Davïdov and Cavos, he was a dilettante – but a very talented one. His earliest stage-works were vaudevilles produced in St Petersburg during 1817–22, one of which *Karantin* (Quarantine) (1820)[2] was for a long time immensely popular. In 1823 he was sent to Moscow as administrator of the Imperial Theatres there; his first Moscow 'opera-vaudeville', *Kto brat, kto sestra, ili Obman za obmanom (Brother or sister? or Cheat for cheat)*[3] was produced in 1824. But Verstovsky became more ambitious and in 1828 his romantic opera, *Pan Twardowski* (the legendary 'Polish Faust')[4] appeared on the Moscow stage. (All the operas previously mentioned in this chapter were originally given in St Petersburg.) Like *Susanin* it derives from Cherubini and Méhul, and also to some extent from *Der Freischütz*, with spoken dialogue. Verstovsky was technically weak; it is said that he entrusted the orchestration to the Moscow theatre conductor who, if not the composer himself, had the idea of opening the overture to *Twardowski* with a quartet for solo cellos a year before *Guillaume Tell*. The actual musical invention is very uneven; Twardowski's First Act aria begins with powerful declamation admirably conveying the character's evil which is not sustained in the cabaletta. Even the first aria of the young hero, Krasitsky, never surpasses its opening phrase, the prototype of sentimental-romantic Russian melodies for another fifty years:

---

[1] One aria, ibid., p. 205. The *romance* from the ballet *Raoul de Créqui* (1819), ibid., p. 204, is wrongly attributed to Cavos; the entire ballet was composed by his pupils.
[2] Excerpts in Ginzburg, *Istoriya*, iii (Moscow-Leningrad, 1952), pp. 9–13.
[3] Excerpt, idem, p. 14.
[4] Excerpts, idem, pp. 39–64.

Ex. 195

(O days of happy pleasures, of my heedless youth)

Verstovsky went on to compose *Vadim* (1832) and *Askoldova mogila* (Askold's Grave) (1835) but these belong to the period of Glinka and 'exportable' Russian opera and must be considered in that context.[1]

---

[1] See Vol. IX.

XII

SOLO SONG

(a) Germany and Italy

By LESLIE ORREY

POETIC SOURCES

THE development of song in Germany during the period 1790–1830 and its culmination in the work of Franz Schubert was bound up with an interplay of literary, musical, technological, and social forces that from about 1770 seemed more pronounced in the German-speaking lands than in other countries of Western Europe. The raw material, in the shape of lyric poetry amenable to musical treatment, was there in abundance. Schubert set the words of over seventy poets, with Goethe numerically at their head.[1] The forty or so writers drawn upon by Schubert's senior, Carl Maria von Weber, overlap Schubert's choice hardly at all, and the vast extent of the material is further illustrated by the fact that Beethoven, working in the same city as Schubert, could draw many of his texts from yet a third circle of writers. The poems appeared in numerous collections, often with rather fanciful titles such as Reissig's *Blümchen der Einsamkeit*; and also in a variety of *Musenalmanache*,[2] *Taschenbücher*, and other periodicals such as the magazine, *Selam*, edited in Vienna by Castelli.

These publications and periodicals were a consequence of the rapid growth of a new middle class whose patronage of the arts was more and more replacing that of the nobility of the previous century.[3] Their musical needs were catered for by an ever-lengthening list of publishers in many of the chief cities.[4] The same activity is to be noted in the

[1] About three thousand settings are listed by Willi Schuh in the Artemis-Verlag edition of Goethe's collected works, ii (Zürich, 1953). A large proportion of these settings are from this period.

[2] For a discussion and history of the best-known of these, see H. Grantzow, 'Geschichte des Göttingen und des Vossischen Musenalmanach', in *Berliner Beiträge zur germanischen und romanischen Philologie*, xxxv (Berlin, 1909). Others such as those of Vienna, Salzburg, and that of Schiller, have not been so carefully studied.

[3] See Leo Balet, *Die Verbürgerlichung der deutschen Kunst, Literatur und Musik im 18 Jahrhundert* (Strasbourg, 1936).

[4] Among the more important were: the Leipzig firm of Breitkopf & Härtel, founded by Bernard and Christoph Breitkopf in 1719, musically influential from about 1750; the Bonn firm of Simrock, founded 1790; Schott of Mainz, founded 1773, and Artaria, who opened the first music printing press in Vienna in 1776.

British Isles, with firms too numerous to mention.[1] By contrast Italy, which had been a pioneer of music printing in the sixteenth century, and where the trade had flourished, notably in Venice and Bologna, during the next two hundred years, was comparatively inactive until the house of Ricordi began to dominate the scene in the middle years of the nineteenth century. A quantity of domestic Italian vocal music was, in fact, published in London.

INFLUENCE OF THE PIANO

On the purely musical side we must note first of all the consolidation, by the Viennese composers, of a self-sufficient instrumental style. This was an important prerequisite for the full flowering of Schubertian song, as was recognized for example by Walter Vetter who wrote: 'Beethoven did more for the furtherance of Schubert's *Lieder* through his instrumental music than all the *Lied* composers of the eighteenth century put together'[2] – though this rather overstates the case. This development coincided with the emergence of the pianoforte as the principal keyboard instrument, which already in the 1770s, in the sonatas of Haydn and Mozart and in the latter's concertos, had become stamped with its own distinctive style. Its versatility and greater range of dynamics gave it a pull over the harpsichord; its reluctance to blend with strings invited soloistic treatment[3] and encouraged the virtuoso approach. Its ability to suggest a wide variety of orchestral effects, another aspect of its superiority to the harpsichord, undoubtedly influenced the new fashion for piano transcriptions of operas. These scores, by Sterkel, Neefe (who made a pianoforte score of Salieri's *Axur*), and others, became progressively more numerous from about the mid-1780s. In 1785, for example, Simrock of Bonn was advertising for sale piano reductions of Schubaur's *Dorfdeputierten* and Mozart's *Entführung aus dem Serail*.[4] Such scores, which replaced the older type where the accompaniment was simply given as a figured bass, helped to draw the attention of composers, performers and public to the expressive and illustrative potentialities of the new instrument in accompanying the voice.

With all these developments the stage was set for the transformation

[1] See Charles Humphries and William C. Smith, *Music Publishing in the British Isles* (London, 1954; second edition, Oxford, 1970).
[2] *Schubert* (Potsdam, 1934), p. 132.
[3] We find confirmation of this in the virtual disappearance, during this period, of the 'sonata for clavier with violin or flute accompaniment' in favour of the 'sonata for pianoforte'.
[4] See Ludwig Schiedermair, *Der junge Beethoven* (Leipzig, 1925) p. 70.

of German song from the simple, artless *Volkslied* into a more complex art form.

THE NORTH GERMAN COMPOSERS

In their songs the North German composers such as J. A. P. Schulz (Schultz) and Johann Friedrich Reichardt[1] seem deliberately to have curbed their purely musical invention. Schulz for example in his *Six diverses pièces pour le pianoforte*[2] shows a command of keyboard style at least as developed as that of C. P. E. Bach; while St. Phar's aria 'Si jamais du sein des montagnes' in his opera *Aline, Reine de Golconde* (1787), with its vocal compass of a thirteenth, its extended melismata, and its range of harmony, is quite comparable in technique to the more Italianate *Singspiele* of Hiller or Neefe. But there is no trace of such sophisticated composition in his sets of *Lieder im Volkston*, written in accordance with the theories of song composition associated with Voss and Goethe, and which he certainly subscribed to.[3] By the 1790s however, some other composers of the North German School were beginning to see the possibilities of the pianoforte accompaniment. 'Das Clavier' by Johann Gottlieb Naumann (1741–1801), in his *Sammlung von deutschen, französischen und italiänischen Lieder beym Clavier zu singen* (Leipzig, 1799), though elementary in harmony, shows an attractive interplay between voice and piano, with at least the beginnings of a feeling for piano style:

Ex. 196

[1] See Vol. VII, pp. 350–2.
[2] Berlin, 1776; modern edition, Mainz, 1934.
[3] See the preface to the 1785 reprint of his *Lieder im Volkston* quoted in Vol. VII, p. 351, also *Briefwechsel zwischen Johann Abraham Peter Schulz und Johann Heinrich Voss* (Kassel, 1960). See also *Briefwechsel zwischen Goethe und Zelter* (Berlin, 1833–4; selection in English translation by Arthur Duke Coleridge, London, 1887); and Goethe's remarks on 'Erlkönig', below, p. 562.

Kla - gen   Mein treu - es Sai - ten-spiel.___   Nun

kömmt   nach trü - ben ___ Ta - gen,   Die   Nacht, ___ der Sor - gen

Ziel!   Ge - horcht   mir   sanf - te

fp

Sai - ten,   Und   helft   mein Leid ___ be -

- strei - ten,   Doch nein, _____ lasst mir _____ mein Leid, __   und __

mei - - - ne Zärt- lich - keit.

(two more stanzas follow)

(Thou echo of my lament, my faithful music. Now after dreary days comes night, the time of cares. Listen to me, gentle strings and help to bear my sorrow. But no, leave me my sorrow and my tenderness.)

REICHARDT

The most commanding figure of the North German School was Johann Friedrich Reichardt (1752–1814), a widely travelled, well educated man whose activities embraced criticism, journalism and writing on aesthetics as well as composition.[1] Of his more than seven hundred songs[2] the first appeared in the Göttingen *Musenalmanach*, but his most important song publications were the four volumes of *Goethes Lieder, Oden, Balladen und Romanzen mit Musik* (Leipzig, 1809–11) and the two volumes of *Schillers lyrische Gedichte* (Leipzig, 1810) – volumes certainly known to Schubert. These 57 Schiller songs range from tiny miniatures eight bars long ('An die Frühling', 'Punschlied') to lengthy operatic scenas or cantatas ('Aeneas zu Dido', 'Monolog der Thekla'). As might be expected from their date, they are songs with true accompaniments, embodying idiomatic piano writing which is usually independent of the vocal line but not always of poetic

---

[1] See Walter Salmen, *Johann Friedrich Reichardt* (Zürich, 1963). On Reichardt's earlier songs, see Vol. VII, pp. 350–1.
[2] Selection ed. Salmen, *Das Erbe deutscher Musik*, lviii–lix.

significance. Some of the songs, however, show a harmonic technique used with thought and consistency. 'Des Mädchens Klage', for instance, a strophic song with an arpeggiated accompaniment, contains a Neapolitan sixth, an augmented sixth, and a grinding minor ninth, all springing directly from the sense of the words. It is quite romantic in conception; the detailed dynamic markings in the second half are especially noteworthy:

Ex. 197

seuf - zet hin - aus in die fin - stre Nacht, das

Au - ge von Wei - nen ge - trü - bet.

(The oak-wood roars, the clouds pass, the young girl sits on the grassy brink; the waves break loudly and she sighs out into the gloomy night, her eyes dull with weeping.)

The following, from 'Hektors Abschied' – a wandering unison passage illustrating the words 'Wenn der finstre Orkus dich verschlingt!' – glances backward to 'The people that walked in darkness' from *Messiah* and forward to similar passages in Schubert, Schumann, and Brahms:

Ex. 198

Wenn der fin - stre Or - kus dich ver-schlingt! Wenn der fin - stre Or - kus

dich ————————— ver - schlingt

(When dark Orkus swallows thee!)

Another interesting song is 'Amalia' (set also by Schubert, D. 195). Its wide vocal compass (an octave and a sixth), and its agility are closely related to the poetic content. The upsurging opening phrase derives directly from 'Schön wie Engel voll Walhallas Wonne', and the sudden side-slip from E major into F major at 'Himmlisch mild sein Blick' parallels the poetry-inspired modulations of Beethoven and Schubert:

Ex. 199

Schön ___ wie En - gel voll ___ Wal - hal - las _____ Won - ne, Schön vor

al - len Jüng - ling - en ___ war er, Himm-lisch mild sein Blick wie ___

Mai — en - son - ne, Rück - ge - strahlt ___ vom blau - en Spie - gel - meer,

Er ___ ist hin ver - ge - bens, ach ver - ge - bens stöh - net

Ihm der ban - ge ___ Seuf - zer nach! Er ist hin und al - le Lust ___ des

Le - bens wim - mert hin __ in __ ein __ ver - lor - nes Ach!

(He was beautiful as an angel filled with heavenly joy, more beautiful than any youth, his gaze heavenly mild like the May sun, radiant from the blue mirror of the sea. In vain he is gone, ah vain to sigh anxiously after him. He is gone, and all joy of life sobs away in a lost sigh!)

It is in the bigger songs and the ballads that Reichardt's weaknesses are most apparent. His 'Monolog der Johanna' (Schiller) is a bulky composition, thirteen pages of oblong folio; like Zumsteeg's ballads (see below) it is indebted to the operatic scena. The first section, ten pages long, is mainly recitative; the accompaniment is obviously orchestrally inspired, with crisp, rhythmic interjections between the recitative fragments, and with occasional passages that threaten to blossom into expressive arioso but never quite do so. The culminating aria, *larghetto*, in 3/8 time, is a poor little affair, in stiff, four-bar phrases. Its one point of interest is that, strophic in form, it employs the same technique of variation in the piano part that so appealed to Beethoven.[1] The ballads, for example 'Ritter Toggenburg' or 'Der Graf von Habsburg', are even duller, the rhythm congealing into the plodding ♩ ♫ that threatens every setter of German narrative verse.

ZUMSTEEG

The composer whose name is most associated with the development of the ballad is Johann Rudolf Zumsteeg (1760–1802).[2] His main work in this field began in 1791 with the composition of Bürger's 'Des Pfarrers Tochter von Taubenheim'. The pattern had in fact been established a few years earlier by the through-composed setting of Bürger's 'Lenore' by Johann André (1741–99).[3] The ballad was sharply differentiated from the simpler *Lied* not only by its length – André's and Zumsteeg's settings of 'Lenore' run to about 950 bars – but by the sectionalized treatment and the pictorialism of the piano's contributions. Such fragmentary treatment calls for a high degree of musical organization, which Zumsteeg did not possess. The parts, interesting in themselves, never coalesce into a whole. It must be confessed also that his melodies are often stiff and formal, or flat and insipid. By contrast, some of his simpler songs such as the *Zwölf Lieder mit Klavierbegleitung* (1797) are unpretentious and attractive.

[1] See below, p. 554.
[2] See Ludwig Landshoff, *Johann Rudolf Zumsteeg, ein Beitrag zur Geschichte des Liedes und der Ballade* (Berlin, 1902); Franz Szymichowski, *Zumsteeg als Komponist von Balladen und Monodien* (Frankfurt, 1932). See also K. E. Schneider, *Das musikalische Lied in geschichtlicher Entwicklung* (Leipzig, 1863–5) p. 330, for a discussion of the evolution of the ballad. *Das Erbe deutscher Musik*, xlv, contains settings of ballads by Bürger, Zumsteeg, André, and others.
[3] Of the two versions reprinted in *Das Erbe deutscher Musik* the second shows a much freer, more advanced, orchestrally inspired accompaniment.

SONG IN AUSTRIA

The development of the *Lied* in Austria from the first showed differences compared with that in North Germany.[1] To begin with, the lack of a vigorous literary tradition must be noted; Austria contributed little of note to the body of German poetry before Franz Grillparzer (1791–1872) and Viennese verse was hardly drawn on at all before Beethoven and Schubert. Then it has been observed above that the development of the *Lied* from about 1790 was essentially linked with the consolidation of an instrumental style closely associated with Vienna. Thirdly, this development was in the hands of composers whose training and upbringing was Italian rather than German. The young Schubert, for example, singing in the Viennese Hofkapelle from the age of about eleven, must have been influenced more than we can tell by the predominantly Italian repertory sung there under Salieri. When Beethoven arrived in Vienna in 1792 he turned to Salieri for instruction in the current Italian style, and in writing *ariette* to Italian words he followed a well established precedent set by such composers as Adalbert Gyrowetz (1763–1850), Leopold Kozeluch (1747–1818), Johann Franz Sterkel (1750–1817), and Vincenzo Righini (1756–1812).

The number of pre-Schubert song composers in or associated with Vienna, Bohemia, and South Germany is considerable. Some of the more important, apart from Beethoven and those just mentioned, are: Emanuel Alois Förster (1748–1823), Peter von Winter (1755–1825), Friedrich Franz Hurka (1762–1805), Anton Eberl (1765–1807), Friedrich Heinrich Himmel (1765–1814), and Nikolaus von Krufft (1779–1818).[2] The songs are mainly 1790 or later, by which time certain significant patterns can be seen. They are usually laid out on three staves, and the piano part has become idiomatic, with figured, on-running accompaniments which, if not attempting any elaborate word-painting, are often more than just a neutral support and frequently reflect the moods of the poems. Composers in fact are no longer writing *Melodien*, whether *beym Clavier zu singen* or not, but are conceiving their songs as a unified interplay between voice and piano, if not indeed seeing their compositions from a predominantly instrumental standpoint. The piano has the last word; though preludes

[1] See also Vol. VII, pp. 352 ff.

[2] A number of others are discussed in 'Die Wiener Liedmusik von 1778 bis 1789', by Irene Pollak-Schlaffenberg, and 'Das Wiener Lied von 1789–1815' by Editha Alberti-Radanowicz, *Studien zur Musikwissenschaft*, v (1918) and x (1923). Songs by Anton Teyber (1754–1822), Eberl, Emilian Gottfried von Jaquin (1767–92), Moriz von Dietrichstein (1775–1864), Johann Fuss (1777–1819), Sigmund Neukomm (1778–1858), Krufft, and Conradin Kreutzer (1780–1849) are reprinted in *Denkmäler der Tonkunst in Österreich*, lxxix.

or introductions[1] are still infrequent, a song that lacks a postlude has become a rarity.

The *Zwölf neue Lieder*, Op. 13, by E. A. Förster, published by Artaria in about 1791, may be cited as typical. They are all strophic, the number of stanzas varying between two and six. The poems, light, of a pastoral or anacreontic type, have a certain elegance. Many, for example 'Der Arzt und Phyllis', still employ the old-fashioned two-stave layout, and are close in type to the North German song, though they are rounded off with postludes. On the other hand the first song, 'Chloe an Thyrsis', is nearer to the operatic aria, with a long introduction and with much repetition of words – a practice frowned upon by the North German school.[2] Another interesting song is 'An den Traumgott', with a patterned, on-running accompaniment in persistent semiquaver triplets. It is quite possible that these songs were known to Beethoven, who was acquainted with Förster and indeed had composition lessons from him (*c.* 1794).

The various collections by composers such as Gyrowetz and Leopold Kozeluch show similar characteristics. Kozeluch, a Czech, who worked in Prague and later in Vienna, was sufficiently esteemed for Thomson of Edinburgh to engage him to make arrangements of Scottish songs.[3] His published songs include a set of twelve *Ariette* to Italian words, issued by J. Bland of London, *c.* 1790. Gyrowetz, another Czech, travelled extensively, visiting Italy, France, and England; he was in London during Haydn's first visit, in 1792. He published about sixty songs between 1793 and 1815. His six Italian *Ariette* (published by Artaria in 1793) are all short songs, with idiomatic piano accompaniments, fully worked out.

STERKEL AND RIGHINI

Among the more than one hundred and twenty songs of Sterkel (1750–1817) several reveal a vein of poetry that lifts them above the general level. The early 'Am Fenster bei Mondenschein' (published *c.* 1788), though modest in scale and unpretentious in technique, breathes a gentle, nocturnal atmosphere:

---

[1] An introductory passage ending with a full close is called here a 'prelude'; one that ends expectantly, leading directly to the entry of the voice, an 'introduction'. See especially the discussion of Schubert's songs below.

[2] See for example Voss's letter to Schulz, in which he criticizes Neefe's setting of his own 'Selmas Lied' on the grounds that the repetition of the last line in each stanza was *nicht Natur, sondern Komponistenbequemlichkeit* (not nature, but composer's convenience); see *Briefwechsel*, op. cit., letter 5.

[3] See Cecil Hopkinson and C. B. Oldman, *Thomson's Collections of National Songs* (Transactions of the Edinburgh Bibliographical Society, 1940).

Ex. 200

Nacht und Still ist um mich her, Kaum ein Lüft-chen regt sich

mehr, Nur der lie - be Mond be - scheint Noch so treu - lich sei - nen

Freund. Tau - send Thrä - nen sind ver - siegt, Tau - send Sor - gen ein - ge -

- wiegt, Und so man - chen Lei - den - den Zeigt ein Traum E - li - si -

(Night and stillness are around me, scarcely a breath of air stirs, only the dear moon still shines so faithfully on his friend. A thousand tears are dried, a thousand cares are rocked to sleep, and an Elysian dream appears to many a sufferer.)

while in other songs we can detect distinct anticipations of Schubert, as for example in this non-related postlude from his setting of Kosegarten's 'O Blümchen, eurer jedes ruft', in his 1805 collection:

Ex. 201

(A little flower from a loved hand.)

Beethoven may well have come across some of Sterkel's songs during his Bonn period, for the latter's *Zwölf neue Lieder* were being advertised for sale in Bonn in 1787.[1] Whether or not this is so

[1] See Ludwig Schiedermair, op. cit., p. 70.

Beethoven certainly knew some of the works of the Italian Righini (1756–1812), who, born in Bologna (where he studied with Padre Martini) spent most of his life in Austria and Germany. He visited Bonn in 1788. Some of his songs were performed in the Elector's Palace there,[1] and one of them proved sufficiently attractive for Beethoven to write a series of brilliant variations on it. This was 'Venni Amore', the last of a set of twelve Italian *ariette*. These are all strophic songs,[2] with fully worked out accompaniments and often supplied with introductions rather than preludes, and postludes. Two of these songs, as well as several others by Righini and some by Sterkel, are important for their clues to the performance of strophic songs; the voice part is varied in each stanza and in 'Venni Amore nel tuo Regno' the variations reflect to some extent the differing sentiments in each stanza. The following illustration comes from an interesting song by Sterkel, 'Wiederseh'n', from his 1805 set. It is subtitled 'Rondeau', and is in five sections, ABABA. The third time the A section appears it is varied:

Ex. 202

[1] Schiedermair, p. 87.
[2] Published by Böhme of Hamburg; also Longman and Broderip (London, 1791).

(See-you-again – word of consolation and life, invented by love, balm to the wounds of parting, light by the grave [in hope of] resurrection.)

Singers, of course, were well versed in this kind of extemporization, and the instruction books such as those by J. A. Hiller and Peter Winter devote much of their space to this still essential side of the singer's art and Michael Vogl (1768-1840), who added such embellishments to Schubert's songs, would have been brought up in this tradition.

ITALIAN SONGS AND DUETS

The continued popularity of Italian songs and duets, whether described as 'ariette' or 'canzonette', is attested by the quantity of them in the catalogues of Breitkopf & Härtel, Simrock, and other publishers. Many were printed in London, mainly by Italian or Italianate composers such as Giuseppe Aprile (1732–1813), Bonifazio Asioli (1769–1832), Antonio Benelli (1771–1830), Francesco Bianchi (*c.* 1752–1810), Tommaso Giordani (*c.* 1730–1806), Vicente Martini y Soler (1754–1806), Simon Mayr (1763–1845), Giovanni Paisiello (1740–1816), Stephen Storace (1762–96), and others. Dating from 1790 or so, they tend to have fully worked out accompaniments, though these are not as a rule attributable to the poetic content except in the most general way. They do, however, often show the distinctive postlude, which may or may not be related thematically to the vocal portions. A prelude, related or non-related, or an introduction, is somewhat rarer. The set of twenty-four duets by Paisiello, *La Libertà*

e Palinodia, words by Metastasio, published in London in 1794, is for
that date exceptional in that it employs the by then old-fashioned
thorough-bass technique; the highly-wrought first set of *Original
Canzonettas* by Haydn, published in the same year[1] – issued with both
English and Italian words – offer an illuminating contrast. In all these
songs the voice is the dominant partner; the pianist's role is little more
than that of a humble accompanist, as we can see in Mayr's delightful
'La farfaletta', from his 12 *Venetian Ballads* (Lewis Lavenu, London,
1797):

Ex. 203

(The butterfly that flutters gaily through the grass, stripping now this plant now that according to its whims and then flying away.)

The high-water mark in Italian song during this period is reached in the handful of compositions by Vincenzo Bellini (1801–35).[1] It would be wrong to think of these simply as chips from his operatic workshop, though one or two are operatic scenas in all but name. 'Torna, vezzosa Fillide', for example is an extended cavatina and cabaletta. Nor are they the casual offspring of idle moments; they have been worked over with the utmost care and affection. 'Il fervido desiderio', for example, is a miniature, thirty-one bars long, in which voice and accompaniment are welded into a unity equalled by, say, Beethoven's 'Wonne der Wehmut', but not surpassed by it. 'Vaga luna, che inargenti' is a simpler scheme, a strophic song, a melody

[1] Fifteen are published in *Composizioni da camera* (Milan, 1935; reprinted 1966).

sustained over an undulating accompaniment; but the melody is of quite exceptional beauty and serenity. (The poem is addressed to the moon, whose beams bathe the landscape in a flood of silvery light and inspire the elements to speak the language of love). These and others only slightly less striking such as 'Dolente immagine di Fille mia', 'Malinconia', 'Ninfa gentile', 'Almen se non poss'io' and even the early 'Farfalletta, aspetta aspetta', attributed to him at the age of twelve, give Bellini an assured place beside the German song-writers.

BEETHOVEN

A new chapter in the history of song was opened with the advent of Ludwig van Beethoven (1770–1827).[1] As a boy in Bonn his musical experiences had been extremely varied, ranging from Italian opera of various kinds, through German *Singspiel* to French *opéra comique*.[2] By the age of eleven he had come under the beneficent influence of Neefe, who had contributed *Melodien* to the Göttingen *Almanach* and had had several collections of songs published.[3] Whether or not Neefe drew Beethoven's attention to the poets of the Göttingen *Almanach*,[4] some of his early songs were settings of these North German writers: for example 'Mollys Abschied' (Bürger), 'Lied' (Lessing, 1793 or earlier), 'Marmotte' (Goethe, 1793 or earlier), or 'Das Blümchen wunderhold' (Bürger, 1793 or earlier). They show similarities to songs by Schulz and Zelter as well as to those by Neefe himself. They are strophic (about thirty of Beethoven's songs are in this form), with a piano part that duplicates the vocal line and shows little development beyond a simple 'patterned' accompaniment with little specific connection with the sense of the words. The songs without exception are provided with instrumental postludes, and a very early song, 'An einen Säugling' (1784), an eight-bar prelude and a five-bar postlude which also serves as interludes between the four stanzas.

These songs are largely syllabic; or, if not strictly so, they employ the paired semiquavers sanctioned by the North German school, as for example in Lessing's 'Lied'.[5] The *Vier Arietten und ein Duett. Op.*

[1] On his songs consult: Hans Boettcher, *Beethoven als Liederkomponist* (Augsburg, 1928), and Henri de Curzon, *Les Lieder et airs détachés de Beethoven* (Paris, 1905). See also Leslie Orrey, chap. 11 on 'The Songs', *The Beethoven Companion* (London, 1971).

[2] For details see Schiedermair, op. cit., Adolf Sandberger, *Ausgewählte Aufsätze zur Musikgeschichte* (Munich, 1924); Boettcher, op. cit., p. 161 ff for parallels between opera and Beethoven's songs.

[3] See Vol. VII, pp. 349–50.

[4] It certainly circulated in Bonn (see Grantzow, op. cit.). See also Boettcher, op. cit. p. 39, for sources in the Göttingen and other almanachs.

[5] Examples are not lacking in Beethoven's later work. The same technique is exploited in the 'Freude trinken alle Wesen' variation in the Ninth Symphony.

82, are in every way wider in range. Their indebtedness to Italian opera is obvious – there is a clear reminiscence of 'Dove sono' from *Figaro* at bars 20-21 of no. 2, 'T'intendo . . .' – but the outstanding feature of these five songs is the pianistic nature of the keyboard writing. They exploit the piano's dynamics, its range and idiosyncrasies to a greater extent than any previous song accompaniment had done. The range is particularly surprising; no. 1, 'Dimi ben mio', extends over five octaves, from A to a$'''$, while the final duet, 'O di, l'aura', goes a whole tone higher to top B. Whether these songs were written in 1790[1] – that is, before the move to Vienna and the contact with Salieri (1792), but after the first visit to Vienna (1787) and the meeting with Mozart – or a little later, they date from the period when he was in his first triumphant flush as a piano virtuoso. These songs incorporate something of this brilliant style, which is equally in evidence in the piano sonatas and chamber music.

Beethoven's first large-scale song, 'Adelaide', Op. 46, shows a clear advance in the deployment of both pianistic and vocal resource. It is an aria of the cavatina-cabaletta type; the wide-arching vocal phrase of the opening Larghetto and the richness of the treatment suggest a deeper emotional involvement than had previously been made manifest. In some earlier songs Beethoven had been quick to seize any opportunities for word painting; here the musical realization of such phrases as 'Abendlüftchen im zarten Laube flüstern' ('Evening breezes whisper through the leaves') or 'Nachtigallen flöten' ('Nightingales warble') is accomplished with ease and grace, and without disrupting the over-all musical design in the piecemeal fashion of Zumsteeg. The kinship with instrumental forms is very apparent; the Adagio of the Piano Sonata, Op. 2, no. 1, written at about the same time (*c.* 1795), with its upward soaring leap of a major sixth from the dominant to the upper mediant and its subsequent sinking by step back to the tonic, is very similar in feeling to the song's opening phrase. The main theme of the cabaletta, too, has 'sonata material' stamped all over it, and indeed in this Allegro molto Beethoven, in his preoccupation with the instrumental side, seems to have lost contact with Matthisson's poetry.

Two other big songs dating from this period are the concert aria with orchestra, 'Ah! perfido!', written or at any rate first performed in 1796 (in Prague, by Josefa Duschek), and a setting of some words by Bürger, 'Seufzer eines Ungeliebten'. 'Ah! Perfido!', written at the same time as the First Symphony was being sketched, was almost his first important handling of the orchestra, and 'Seufzer eines Ungelieb-

---

[1] The date suggested in Kinsky-Halm, *Das Werk Beethovens. Thematisch-bibliographisches Verzeichnis* (Munich, 1955); they were first published in 1811.

ten' may possibly have been intended for orchestral treatment; the piano part reads very like a transcription of an orchestral score. The two are so similar in mood and technique that 'Seufzer eines Ungeliebten' may have been a preparatory study for 'Ah! Perfido!'

Beethoven's song output included only a few large-scale songs. Besides the three just mentioned the only other important ones are 'Lied aus der Ferne' (Reissig, 1809), a big ternary-form song of 146 bars, the piano writing harking back to his earlier style – florid, external, reminding one of the mood of the two early piano concertos; and the second 'An die Hoffnung' (Tiedge, 1815), which is also a fairly extended ternary-form song, with the second A section here repeating not only the music but the words. The device that seemed increasingly to appeal to him in constructing larger units was variation. Examples of this have been noted in Righini and Sterkel; but whereas they had varied the vocal line Beethoven applied the process to the piano part, leaving the vocal line unadorned. It is a method almost exclusively his own; Schubert for example hardly ever uses it. It first appears in 'Busslied', the last of the six Gellert songs of Op. 48 (1803). These strophic songs have a bare, chordal texture, suggestive of the hymn, utterly unlike any songs he had previously written and, indeed, not paralleled in any of his subsequent ones. Only the last song, 'Busslied', moves away from this simple scheme. It is in two sections: the first, in A minor, Poco adagio; the second, in A major, Allegro ma non troppo, three stanzas to identical vocal music, with an ornate, flowing piano part which is derived only very loosely from the words.

Other songs that make impressive use of this technique are the beautiful 'Sehnsucht' (Reissig, c. 1815), the late 'Abendlied' (Göble, 1820) and the six songs of *An die ferne Geliebte*, Op. 98 (Jeitteles, 1816). This, almost his last venture in song writing, is often considered the summit of his achievement in the *Lied*, though at least one isolated song, his 1810 setting of Goethe's 'Wonne der Wehmut', is superior in its perfect matching of poetic content with voice and accompaniment. *An die ferne Geliebte* was published (by S. A. Steiner of Vienna) as 'Ein Liederkreis' though Beethoven's manuscript simply calls it 'An die entfernte Geliebte; 6 Lieder von A. Jeitteles in Musik gesetzt von L. v. Beethoven'.

SONG-CYCLES

Its claim to be the first 'song-cycle', though often made, cannot be substantiated. The three Mozart songs, K. 472, 473, and 474, composed on the same day in May, 1785, to attractive but frivolous words by Christian Felix Weisse, are organized in a coherent key scheme and exhibit some motivic connexions that can hardly have been entirely fortuitous. Nor are Beethoven's own Italian ariettas, Op. 82, without some links of sentiment and style. If these show the song-cycle in its embryonic stage, it is already fully formed in Friedrich Himmel's *Die Blumen und der Schmetterling* (Berlin, c. 1805). The words are by Karl Müchler, whose name appears with some frequency in the songs of the time. There are ten songs. The first is entitled 'Zueignung an Deutschlands Töchter'; then follow seven 'flower' songs – 'Das Schneeglöckchen', 'Das Veilchen', 'Die Myrthe', 'Die Narzisse', 'Das Vergissmeinnicht', 'Die Palme' and 'Die Rose'. The ninth song, entitled 'Wechselgesang der Blumen', recapitulates portions of the various songs in their appropriate keys, with little modulatory links for piano between them, much as Beethoven does between his songs in Op. 98. The cycle is rounded off by no. 10, 'Der Schmetterling'. Though a little faded it has charm and is skilfully put together. Other sets by Himmel that suggest something of the cyclic principle are 6 *Romanzen aus Florian* (1805), *Gesänge aus Tiedges Urania* (1810?),[1] and – very significantly when we think of Schubert's *Die schöne Müllerin* – *Alexis und Ida*, 'ein Schäferroman in 46 Liedern von Tiedge' (1810?). This moves too slowly and covers too narrow a range to be acceptable as a whole today, but it contains one gem, 'Die Sendung' ('An Alexis send ich dich') which any composer would be proud to acknowledge and which inspired Schumann to compose a little canon on it for piano. Beethoven met Himmel in Berlin in 1796, but how much of his music was known to him is hard to say.[2]

NATIONAL SONG AND FOLK-SONG

The beginnings of eighteenth-century interest in 'popular' music and dance in the British Isles have already been traced.[3] This received an immense impetus through the enterprise of the Edinburgh publisher George Thomson (1757–1851), who in the last decade of the eighteenth century and the early years of the nineteenth enlisted the aid of such composers as Pleyel, Haydn, and Beethoven for his arrangements of national airs. These appeared in vast quantities; Haydn alone set about 250, Beethoven's contribution was about 150.[4] The success of

---

[1] *Urania über Gott, Unsterblichkeit und Freiheit*, a 'lyrisch-didaktisches Gedicht', first published in 1801, was the source of the two Beethoven 'An die Hoffnung' songs.

[2] Schubert certainly heard some Himmel songs; see O. E. Deutsch, *Schubert: a Documentary Biography* (London, 1946), p. 630. Further to Beethoven's Op. 98, see Joseph Kerman, *An die ferne Geliebte* in *Beethoven Studies* (New York and London, 1973), p. 123.

[3] See Vol. VII, p. 340.

[4] See Cecil Hopkinson and C. B. Oldman, op. cit. Beethoven's arrangements are published in the *Gesamtausgabe*, Series 24.

Thomson's volumes, in which Robert Burns had had a large part in providing the words, encouraged the Dublin publishers James and William Power to undertake a similar venture. The literary side was entrusted to Thomas Moore, and the collections of *Irish Melodies* published at various times between 1807 and 1834 attained enormous popularity. Their vogue was not confined to the British Isles but spread to France and Germany. The musical side was at first entrusted to Sir John Stevenson, but for the later volumes Sir Henry Bishop took over. The airs were taken from Edward Bunting's two volumes, *A General Collection of Ancient Irish Melodies* (London, 1796 and 1809).

In Germany, the *Volkslied* movement, which had really begun in the 1770s with Herder's *Volkslieder* (1778), entered a new phase with the publication, in 1805, of the first volume of the great collection by Ludwig Achim von Arnim and Clemens Brentano, *Des Knaben Wunderhorn*. (Two further volumes appeared in 1808.) Another contributing factor was the upsurge of patriotism released after Napoleon's retreat from Moscow by the ensuing War of Liberation (1813–15). A third ingredient, not entirely unconnected with the other two, was the nostalgic romanticism of the time – a harking back to a mythical Golden Age in Germany's past, in the Middle Ages.

WEBER

All three elements are strongly in evidence in Carl Maria von Weber (1787–1826). Weber wrote about seventy songs; the first extant one dates from 1802, the last from 1822.[1] As with Beethoven, they form only a minor part of his output, but they are important in his own development as a composer and in the history of song generally. He was a singer, trained under Johann Wallishauser (better known under the Italianized form of his name, Valesi) and used to sing his songs to his own accompaniment on guitar or piano; three sets (Op. 15, Op. 25, and the *Tre Canzonette* of Op. 29) were given specific guitar accompaniments. And since he was a pianist the instrumental side of his songs gets as much attention as we find in Beethoven.

On the whole the songs with the most elaborate textures are early ones. A setting of Matthisson's 'Ich denke dein' (written in 1806, thus antedating both Beethoven's and Schubert's settings of the same poem) is through-composed, and written in a decorated style similar to Haydn's canzonets. The accompaniment is illustrative: simple

[1] The most comprehensive survey of his songs is Max Degen, *Die Lieder von C. M. von Weber* (Basle, 1923). See also André Coeuroy, *Weber* (Paris, 1925) and John Warrack, *Carl Maria von Weber* (London, 1968). The numbering of the songs is from the thematic catalogue compiled by F. W. Jähns, *Carl Maria von Weber in seinen Werken* (Berlin, 1871).

chords for the first stanza, arpeggios for the second (suggested by the words 'im Dämmerschein der Abendhelle am Schattenquelle' – 'in the soft shades of evening's twilight glow'), and more agitated for the third stanza ('Ich denke dein mit süsser Pein, mit bangem Sehnen und heissen Thränen!' – 'I think of thee with sweetest pain, with anxious longing and scalding tears'). The song is rounded off in the fourth stanza by a return to the opening simplicity. Some of the early songs also display a considerable range of modulation and chromatic harmony. One of these is 'Süsse Ahnung dehnt den Busen' (J. 71, written in 1809). The poem, by Georg Reinbeck, is on a theme often treated by greater writers – broken-down and ivyclad walls evoking nostalgic dreams of departed glory: its full title is 'Romanze der Laura aus Reinbecks *Giovanni*. In den Ruinen eines alten Bergschlosses gesungen'. Written in rondo form, it exploits the 'pathetic' chromatic harmony of the augmented sixth, landing on E major, the dominant of the main key. There is a move to the tonic minor and a sudden plunge from the *chord* of E major to the *key* of C major, and using such expressive melodic dissonances as the following:

Ex. 204

füllt   den   Blick   mit Thrä - nen   mir

(My gaze fills with tears.)

Another song, 'Was zieht zu deinem Zauberkreise' (Op. 15, no. 4, 1809), not only exhibits this 'classic' augmented sixth/dominant progression, but is notable for a sudden, dramatic modulation in the middle, when at the words 'Mein Herz fängt stärker an zu schlagen' – 'my heart begins to beat more fiercely' – the music plunges from B major to G major, the progression of keys a third apart that was to become so noticeable in Schubert, but which Beethoven was already using. (Of course, neither Beethoven nor Weber was a pioneer in the use of such progressions and modulations, as a glance at Mozart's deceptively simple-looking 'Das Veilchen' will show.) A parallel modulation, from D major to B major, is also found in 'Abschied vom Leben' (Op. 41, no. 2) at the words 'Viel goldner Bilder sah ich um mich schweben' (A myriad golden visions swirled around me). This is one of the *Leyer und Schwerdt* poems by the young Karl Theodor Körner, killed at the age of twenty-three at the Battle of Leipzig in 1813; the popular, patriotic appeal of these settings did much to spread Weber's reputation throughout Germany. Unlike Beethoven's patriotic songs they are far from being simple strophic settings. The first song, 'Gebet während der Schlacht' is particularly noteworthy. Weber in a letter to his friend Hinrich Lichtenstein asks that the piano accompaniment should not be looked upon as descriptive of a battlefield; what he tried to express, he says, was the swelling feeling of the agitated soul praying to heaven during the battle. It is difficult, however, not to see in this brilliant piano writing at least a suggestion of the rumble and roar of cannon. Into the last of the Körner songs, 'Bei der Musik des Prinzen Louis Ferdinand von Preussen' Weber wove a number of quotations from Louis Ferdinand's F minor Piano Quartet (see p. 307).

Six songs composed in Berlin during a little more than a week in the late autumn of 1816, 'Die gefangenen Sänger' and 'Die freien Sänger', and the set of four *Temperamente beim Verluste der Geliebten* – are delightful character-pieces, and a simpler style becomes apparent after his move to Dresden; the two sets Op. 54 and Op. 65, written between 1817 and 1819, are in fact specifically entitled *Volkslieder*. They are settings of poems taken from collections such as *Des Knaben Wunderhorn* and Büsching and von der Hagen's *Deutsche Volkslieder*. Whether or not it is true, as André Coeuroy has suggested,[1] that Weber's interest in folk-song had first been aroused by his teacher, Abt Vogler, the preference for strophic song and folk-song was certainly intensified by his contacts with the literary circle revolving round Friedrich Kind, the librettist of *Der Freischütz*, at Dresden. But this was no longer the unaffected utterance of Voss or Schulz, where the vocal line was all.

The simple style is continued in Op. 80, written between 1819 and 1821, five out of six of which are strophic. So too is one of Weber's last songs, 'Das Licht im Tale' (1822, J. 286) – a ballad, harking back to Kirnberger rather than looking forward to Loewe. Several songs show the influence of the folkdance. Instances are 'Bettlerlied', Op. 25, no. 4 (1812) and 'Reigen', Op. 30, no. 5 (1813) – an energetic peasant dance with bagpipe suggestions in the piano accompaniment. In 'Mein Schatzerl ist hübsch', Op. 64, no. 1 (1818) the typical, lumpish dance of the mountain peasantry is lightened by a touch of yodel. Another yodelling song is 'Schwäbisches Tanzlied' (J. 135, 1812).[2]

Nevertheless, strophic, folk-song simplicity did not entirely dominate this Dresden period, and one of the most sophisticated of all Weber's songs dates from 1819. This is 'Das Mädchen an das erste

[1] Op. cit., p. 108.
[2] For a Schubert yodelling song, with yodel transformed into the highest art, see 'Der Hirt auf dem Felsen', D. 965.

LEYER und SCHWERDT

und

THEODOR KÖRNER

in Musik gesetzt und mit Begleitung des Pianoforte von Carl Maria von Weber.

Theodor Körners Monument.

HEFT III

Ihro königl. Hoheit der Prinzessin Louise von Preußen Fürstin Radzivil unterthänigst zugeeignet vom Verleger.

Eigenthum des Verlegers.

Berlin bei A. M. Schlesinger.

150.

Op. 43.

Pr. 1 rthlr. 8 g.

PLATE V. TITLE-PAGE OF WEBER'S *LEYER UND SCHWERDT* SONGS, HEFT 3 (1816)

The words are by Theodor Körner, whose poem is entitled 'Bei der Musik des Prinzen Louis Ferdinand von Preussen'; Weber's setting is based largely on themes from the Prince's F minor Piano Quartet and other compositions. The vignette shows the Körner monument at Wöbbelin.

Schneeglöckchen,' Op. 71, no. 3. The poem, by Gerstenbergk, is of the
slightly sentimental, delicate 'flower song' type that Schubert
sometimes set; the maiden compares the snowdrop yearning for the
blue sky, frozen almost before blooming, with her own lonely state,
and in the last lines of the second and final stanza invites the snowdrop
to go with her to her grave. The modulatory range is wide – G minor,
G major, E minor, D major, G minor (end of first stanza) – a sudden
move to E flat major, then back to G minor via an augmented sixth on
E flat (V^7 in A flat). But this is exceptional, and the remaining songs
of Op. 71 – some of them dating from much earlier – are on the whole
musically unadventurous.

SCHUBERT'S BACKGROUND AND EARLY SONGS

Like Weber, Schubert had training as a singer. He was accepted in
the Imperial Court Chapel in 1808, and remained there until his voice
broke. At the same time he became a pupil of the Imperial Seminary,
the Stadtkonvikt, where he remained until 1813. Most biographers
stress the importance of the music he experienced at the Stadtkonvikt,
where he played in the orchestra and got to know symphonies and
overtures by Haydn, Mozart, and Beethoven; but the Catholic church
music he sang under the Italian Salieri must have been equally
important in these early, formative years.

His friends at the Stadtkonvikt included musicians such as Josef
von Spaun, Anton Holzapfel, Anton Hauer, and Johann Hellmesberger; the actor and playwright Johann Nestroy; and others such as
Josef Kenner, Johann Senn and Albert Stadler, who were later to
furnish poems for him to set. After leaving the Konvikt he was drawn
into a remarkably wide cross-section of the literary, musical, and
artistic life of Vienna – the dramatists Eduard von Bauernfeld, Franz
Grillparzer; the artists Leopold Kupelwieser, William August Rieder,
Moritz von Schwind, and Ludwig Mohn; the composer and conductor
Franz Lachner and the singer Michael Vogl. Those with even closer
personal ties with Schubert included the already mentioned Spaun,
Anselm Hüttenbrenner, Johann Mayrhofer, and Franz von Schober.
The list could be enormously extended. It is interesting that there is
very little overlap with Beethoven's circle. There was no aristocratic
patronage – no Lobkowitz, Lichnowsky, or Archduke Rudolf; instead,
we find encouragement coming almost exclusively from the best of
Vienna's intellectual middle class such as Franz von Bruchmann and
Franz von Hartmann.

There was, with Schubert, no question of the simple *Lied* as Goethe,
Schulz, and Zelter had understood it, at least at first. His earliest

extant song, 'Hagars Klage' (Schücking, D.5,[1] 1811), owes nothing to the Berlin School, nothing to his Viennese predecessors, everything to Zumsteeg, whose setting of the same poem had been published in 1797.[2] His first genuine *Lied*, Rochlitz's 'Klaglied' (D.23, 1812), is already a unity, the vocal portions framed within a 2-bar introduction and a 4-bar postlude; and already the piano at the words 'In dem Säuseln der Lüfte, in dem Murmeln des Bachs' ('in the sigh of the winds, the murmur of the brook'), becomes pictorial, in a manner alien to the mere unobtrusive keyboard support of the earlier style. It is true that among the many strophic songs of 1815–18 some display a Schulz-like simplicity; 'Heidenröslein' (D.257, 1815) for example opens in a style not dissimilar to Reichardt's setting.[3] But on the whole Schubert, singer though he was, took the modern view that by the fusion of word and tone a new art structure was being created – with word, be it said, as the inferior partner. This is not at all to imply that he was insensitive or indifferent to the poetry he set.[4]

1814 was a crucial year for the young Schubert. He was no longer a schoolboy; he enjoyed his first public performance, the Mass in F (D.105), which he himself directed; and he fell in love, with the rather plain girl with the enchanting soprano voice who sang the solos in his Mass. This affair of the heart could hardly fail to have its bearing on his song production. The quickening pulse of adolescence was already reflected in the choice of poems – Matthisson's 'Adelaide' (D.95, 1814), for instance, or his 'Andenken' (D.99, 1814).[5]

SCHUBERT AND GOETHE

The same year brought the first Goethe song, 'Gretchen am Spinnrade' (D.118, 1814).[6] This, his first imperishable masterpiece, was the prototype of the aspect of Schubert's song technique that springs to the popular mind – a vocal line, strictly ordered rhythmically yet sufficiently varied, and melodically supple enough to reflect the prosody, with a patterned, on-running piano part that at one and the same time gives support to the voice, makes manifest the harmonic

---

[1] D. numbers refer to Deutsch, *Schubert: Thematic Catalogue*.
[2] Reprinted in *Franz Schuberts Werke. Kritisch durchgesehene Gesamtausgabe*, Series XX, iii, supplement, p. 1.
[3] Reprinted in *Das Erbe deutscher Musik*, lviii.
[4] For a full discussion, see Thrasybulos G. Georgiades, *Schubert: Musik und Lyrik* (Göttingen, 1967).
[5] Set by both Zumsteeg and Beethoven. For a discussion of the three settings, see Georgiades, op. cit., pp. 41–5.
[6] Composed on 19 October, three days after Therese Grob had sung in his Mass. For a facsimile of the fair copy, made for Goethe, see *Franz Schuberts fünf erste Lieder*, ed. Deutsch (Vienna, 1922).

structure, provides graphic illustration of the poem (in this case depicting the whirl of the spinning-wheel), and paints in the psychological or emotional background. The taste for Goethe once found, other settings quickly followed. Their merits were recognized at once by Schubert's circle and in 1816 Spaun, who all his life worked unremittingly for Schubert, sent a batch of Schubert's settings of Goethe's poems to the great man.[1] This was done with the best intentions, Spaun not realizing the unbridgeable gap between Goethe's *Lied* aesthetic and the newer, instrumental-pictorial approach. The sixteen songs included 'Erlkönig' (D.328, 1815) – itself sufficient to make Goethe's hair stand on end. Goethe's attitude to the performance of his songs is well known, and documented.[2] The 'Erlkönig' ballad had been included in his *Singspiel Die Fischerin* (1782), and he gives some exceedingly interesting directions as to its performance:

> Unter hohen Erlen am Flusse stehen zerstreute Fischerhütten. Es ist Nacht und Stille. An einem kleinen Feuer sind Töpfe gesetzt, Netze und Fischergeräthe rings umher aufgestellt. Dortchen (beschäftigt) singt: 'Wer reitet so spät'. Wir sehen, die Fischerin singt bei der Arbeit, halb mechanisch, das ihr längst vertraute Lied etwa wie Gretchen sich den 'König vom Thule' vorsummt.[3]

> (Under lofty alder trees are fishers' huts by the side of the stream. It is night, all is quiet. Some pots can be seen on the fire, nets and fishing gear are strewn around. Dortchen, busy with her work, sings 'Who rides so late'. We note, the fishergirl is singing as she works, half mechanically, her long familiar song much as Gretchen hums to herself 'The King of Thule'.)

Bearing this in mind, and recollecting the care with which Goethe drilled his singers into letting a single melody be varied to accommodate the diverse needs of different stanzas, one can understand the repugnance he must have felt for this, to him, over-dramatized effusion.[4]

---

[1] The accompanying letter is reproduced in Deutsch, *Documentary Biography*, p. 56.

[2] See *inter alia* Hermann Abert, *Goethe und die Musik* (Stuttgart, 1922) and Frederick Sternfeld, *Goethe and Music* (New York, 1954).

[3] Quoted in Max Friedlaender, *Das deutsche Lied im 18. Jahrhundert* (Stuttgart, 1924), who prints the version by Conradin Schroeter sung at the 1782 performance.

[4] Note the stage direction, 'under lofty *alder* trees' (Erlen). There is no such word in German as 'Erl'; the German for elf, goblin, is *Elfe*. When Herder translated the Danish poem telling of the fairy princess who lures King Oluf to his death (set by Loewe, see below) he translated the Danish 'elle' not by *Elfe* (goblin), but coined a new German word, *Erl*. J. Rissé, *Franz Schubert und seine Lieder* (Hanover, 1872–3) points out that the alder tree played a great part in the times of our pagan ancestors: it was 'das Sinnbild des Verderblichen, des Todes'. Goethe's *Erlköng*, then, is not 'King of the Elves', nor is it, as the French have it, 'Roi des Aulnes' or 'King of the Alders', but a conflation of the two, the malignant elf spirit combined with the menacing symbol of the alder tree.

As a ballad setting 'Erlkönig' was never surpassed, though 'Die junge Nonne' (D.828, 1825) approaches it, and stands high among the great, but not supreme, masterpieces. Schubert's interest in the ballad form and his profound but misguided admiration for Zumsteeg's confused and piecemeal constructions led him down a number of blind alleys. There are cumbersome settings of ballads by Schiller ('Der Taucher,' D.77 and D.111, 1814, 'Die Bürgschaft,' D.246, 1815) and settings of Ossian or his imitators which are even more unmanageable ('Der Tod Oscar's', D.375, 1816; 'Loda's Gespenst', D.150, 1815–16; 'Minona', D.152, 1815). The 1816 setting of Schiller's 'Ritter Toggenburg' (D.397) shows Schubert so convinced that Zumsteeg has something to teach him that he has gone to the length of modelling the whole of his setting on the earlier composer's work. Cadences, modulations, piano interludes occur in the same places; and he even, like Zumsteeg, finally abandons the through-composed treatment and finishes strophically.[1]

All told there are about two dozen of these lengthy rhapsodies, each amounting in bulk to a fair-sized[2] sonata movement. Though mainly early works, they include Schober's 'Viola' (D.786, 1823) which, though diffuse in the Zumsteeg manner, does at least have one section which recurs, giving a vestige of musical coherence, and two remarkable works from the last years of his life, 'Auf dem Strom' (Rellstab, D.943, 1828),[3] and his last considerable work, 'Der Hirt auf dem Felsen' (Müller and Chezy, D.965).

SMALLER SONGS

Unquestionably Schubert's real contribution to song literature lies, not in these Herculean efforts, but in the smaller songs, whether strophic or through-composed. The years 1815, 1816, and 1817 account for about half his total output. Many of these are slight, though there are few that lack some distinctive touch; many, such as Schober's 'An die Musik' (D.547, 1817) or his best Schiller setting, 'Gruppe aus dem Tartarus' (D.583, 1817) display his song technique to perfection. The Goethe settings of this period, all on a high level, include the *Volkslied* 'Heidenröslein' (D.257, 1815), 'Meeres Stille' (D.216, 1815) and 'Ganymed' (D.544, 1817), besides the already mentioned 'Gretchen am Spinnrade' and 'Erlkönig'. Some of the best of the forty-seven

---

[1] Zumsteeg's version is printed in the *Gesamtausgabe*, series XX, iii, supplement, p. 11.

[2] Or even larger: 'Adelwold und Emma' (Bertrand, D. 211, 1815) runs to a daunting twenty-six pages in the *Gesamtausgabe*.

[3] This was written for and performed at Schubert's only public concert of his works, on 26 March 1828.

Mayrhofer songs such as 'Memnon' (D.541, 1817) and 'Lied eines Schiffers an die Dioskuren' (D.360, 1816) came in these very fruitful years. Song production slackened off somewhat during the next year or two, but 1819 gave us the magnificent 'Prometheus' of Goethe (D.674). 1821 was a crisis year, with fewer important compositions, of all kinds, than any other; but it did include the companion piece to 'Prometheus', 'Grenzen der Menschheit' (D.716).

SCHUBERT: THE LAST PHASE

The songs of his last phase include the two Wilhelm Müller cycles, *Die schöne Müllerin* (D.795, 1823) and *Winterreise*[1] (D.911, 1827), and the remarkable Rückert, Platen, and Heine songs. These last, particularly 'Der Atlas', 'Die Stadt', and 'Der Doppelgänger' (D.957, in the set known as *Schwanengesang*), stand at the very pinnacle of Schubert's song production, and show him on the verge of new and unimaginable developments when death overtook him. In 'Die Stadt' for instance the shimmering arpeggios suggest both the mist enshrouding the city and the fitful breeze just ruffling the surface of the water; the diminished seventh never *re*solves, but simply *dis*solves. Of the four Rückert songs of 1823 'Du bist die Ruh' (D.776) and 'Lachen und Weinen' (D.777) are justly admired and much sung, but the sensitive and highly evocative 'Dass sie hier gewesen' (D.775) is even more remarkable and prophetic.

The twenty poems of *Die Schöne Müllerin* had their origin in a tiny five-act play with songs performed by Müller's family and his immediate circle.[2] They were published, with a prologue, an epilogue, and three poems not set by Schubert, in *Gedichte aus den hinterlassenen Papieren eines reisenden Waldhornisten* (Dessau, 1821). The songs were issued, in 1824, in five books, which correspond to the five acts of Müller's play. The twenty-four poems of *Winterreise* were first published in 1824, in the second volume of the *Gedichte aus der hinterlassenen Papieren.*, but the first twelve had been previously published in 1823, in the almanach *Urania*, in a slightly different order from the final version. This was Schubert's source for the first

---

[1] On *Die schöne Müllerin* see Hermann Kretzschmar, 'Franz Schuberts Müllerlieder', *Gesammelte Aufsätze*, i (Leipzig, 1910); Thomas Archer, 'The formal construction of *Die schöne Müllerin*', (*Musical Quarterly*, xx (1934), p. 401); F. W. Damian, *Franz Schuberts Liederkreis, Die schöne Müllerin* (Leipzig, 1928); Max Friedlaender, *Die Entstehung der Müllerlieder* (Leipzig, 1892); H. M. Schletterer, *Die schöne Müllerin* (Leipzig, 1878); Thrasybulos Georgiades, *Schubert: Musik und Lyrik* (Göttingen, 1967). The literature on *Winterreise* is not so extensive, but see Georgiades, op. cit.; Erwin Schaeffer, *Schubert's Winterreise* (on the autograph) *Musical Quarterly*, xxiv (1938), p. 39. Arnold Feil considers both cycles in *Franz Schubert: Die schöne Müllerin – Winterreise* (Stuttgart, 1975).

[2] See *Franz Schuberts Werke*, Series XX, i, supplement, and Friedlaender op. cit.

twelve.[1] The two cycles invite comparison – the first springlike, full of hope, the second wintry and despairing. The confident, buoyant phrases of the first cycle, with melodies swinging upwards in leaps of a sixth, yield in the second cycle to drooping patterns. The music is now subdued, the tempo restrained; there is a uniform gait in either the vocal line, plodding along in notes of equal value ('Gute Nacht', 'Die Krähe', 'Der Leiermann') or in the accompaniment ('Erstarrung', 'Wasserflut', 'Einsamkeit'). The bass line, usually in Schubert so lively, shows a tendency to immobilize itself into pedal points ('Gute Nacht', 'Rast', 'Einsamkeit') until in 'Der Leiermann' it freezes up altogether.

SCHUBERT'S STYLE

Schubert's songs provide ample material for the study of his musical style;[2] the following observations can be no more than a pointer to such a study.

The problems of abstract musical design are less tyrannical in vocal music than in instrumental music; words, even when they do not impose their own form, can supply the necessary continuity. But this is permissive, not obligatory; and in even the simplest poetic scheme of stanzas with identical rhythms the composer is at liberty to reject the strophic solution. The inherent superiority of the non-strophic form was assumed as axiomatic by some later composers, for example Wolf, but never by Schubert, who to the end of his life cultivated the strophic form side by side with the non-strophic, as such songs as 'Fischerweise' (Schlechta, D.881, 1826), 'An Sylvia' (D.891, 1826) and Scott's 'Ave Maria' (D.839, 1825) illustrate. Sometimes as in Rochlitz's 'Alinde' (D.904, 1827) the poetic structure demands it. More often it is something in the mood of the poem, less easily definable – a simplicity or freshness that calls for a like directness in the music. Poems with a pastoral flavour or a light narrative touch, nature poems, the easy, elegant verse of the Anacreontic poets or the later imitators, poems with a religious sentiment (for example Silbert's 'Himmelsfunken', D.651, 1819) – for all these types the strophic was the appropriate, and sometimes the only appropriate, treatment.

The table overleaf[3] shows the distribution of strophic and non strophic songs throughout Schubert's working life. The figures exclude unfinished songs and those to Italian texts.

[1] See Erwin Schaeffer, op. cit.

[2] Moritz Bauer's *Die Lieder Franz Schuberts* (Leipzig, 1915) was left incomplete, with one volume only published. The centenary in 1928 produced two notable books, Paul Mies, *Schubert, der Meister des Liedes* (Berlin, 1928) and Richard Capell, *Schubert's Songs* (London, 1928). Edith Schnapper, *Die Gesänge des jungen Schuberts* (Bern, 1937) is a valuable study of a limited field.

[3] Chronology based on the list in Maurice Brown's *Schubert: A critical biography* (London, 1958).

		Strophic	Non-strophic
1811		0	4
1812		1	2
1813		0	7
1814		8	16
1815	Jan. to Mar.	7	9
	Apr. to Jun.	19	12
	Jul. to Sep.	52	14
	Oct. to Dec.	18	10
1816	Jan. to Mar.	21	4
	Apr. to Jun.	19	9
	Jul. to Sep.	19	10
	Oct. to Dec.	10	7
1817	Jan. to Mar.	9	19
	Apr. to Jun.	10	9
	Jul. to Dec.	3	8
1818		5	6
1819		8	16
1820		4	9
1821		1	10
1822		2	20
1823		10	27
1824		1	4
1825		7	19
1826		10	13
1827		5	35
1828		3	15

The table naturally also shows the distribution of song composition generally. The large number of strophic songs in the summer of 1815 is noteworthy; the high number of non-strophic in 1827 is explained by the fact that twenty-three of the twenty-four songs of *Winterreise* are of this class, though they are in the main very short poems.

The strophic songs include only those that are strophic with no variation; the non-strophic list contains the true through-composed songs, those based on some clear musical structure such as ternary or rondo form, and those that, though basically strophic, show some significant variation from the pure form. These variations are fascinating in their diversity. Leitner's poem 'Die Sterne', for example, has four 4-line stanzas, with all the lines end-stopped; Schubert's treatment of each stanza is identical except for the third line which is varied each time (D.939, 1828). Another late song, 'Der liebliche Stern' (Schulze, D.861, 1825) shows the strophic form almost completely transformed into the through-composed.

The relationship between introduction or prelude, interlude, and postlude can be subtle. Only a few such as 'Meeres Stille' lack entirely prelude and postlude; a somewhat larger number have preludes but no postludes, though some of these have a coda. Songs with a postlude but no prelude form a much more numerous class, about 80. Most of these are comparatively early works, left unpublished at Schubert's death. It is likely that if he had seen these through the press he would have added preludes to many of them, as in fact he did to several.[1] A large class – upwards of 100 – have preludes and postludes identical, or nearly so. These are usually middle or late songs, and this rather formal framing of the vocal portion between two statements of piano material is much more noticeable after about 1818. Indeed, the presence of such identical preludes and postludes, whether related (i.e., with material common to the vocal portion) or non-related, is almost a guarantee of a late date. We can thus feel fairly sure that the prelude and postlude to 'Des Mädchens Klage' (Schiller, D.191), originally written in 1815, were added by Schubert when he prepared the song for publication in 1826. The form can be seen, typically, in the Müller songs, where no fewer than nineteen out of a total of forty-four are of this kind.

This device is not peculiar to Schubert, but can be found in the songs of Beethoven, Weber, and others. But some procedures one might have thought common among song writers seem to be Schubert's own. A number of his songs show a right-hand part in chords, repeated or arpeggiated, while the left hand is mainly occupied with a bass of considerable melodic development, often alive with rhythmic interest. 'An Sylvia', 'Erlkönig', 'Des Mädchens Klage', 'An die Musik', 'Der Einsame', 'Auf der Bruck, 'Fischerweise' and many others show this in a greater or lesser degree. It also invades longer songs, for instance 'Viola'. This is an obvious enough device, one, it might be thought, that would be common to many composers; in fact it is personal to Schubert. Beethoven for example never uses it. In 'Sehnsucht' I and II there are repeated chords over a single-line bass, but this left-hand part never becomes more than a bass; it is not imbued with the life and character of Schubert's basses in similar situations. It forms no part of Mozart's technique, though there is a suggestion of it in 'Als Luise' (K.520); nor does it belong to Schumann. Liszt has a fondness for expressive, melodic fragments in the tenor or baritone register, but they never combine a good bass line with crisp motivization, as Schubert's do. This is Schubert's unique and individual contribution to song writing.

[1] About a quarter of his songs were published during his lifetime (see Deutsch, *Documentary Biography*, p. 938). Nearly all the songs composed from 1821 on, and indeed a considerable proportion of other works, were thus published.

Other points concern the cadence. The ending of 'An die Musik' with its two dropping sixths can be paralleled frequently, in Schubert himself, Mozart, and many other composers, though there is no example in Beethoven's songs – unless one argues that bars 44–5 of the second 'An die Hoffnung' show an ornamental version of it. Here Schubert is working with common property. He also uses quite frequently another decoration of the 6/4 – 5/3 cadence – a little curl, tonic, mediant, supertonic, tonic, often in the rhythm ♫♫| ♩ or ♩ ♫| ♩. It occurs perhaps thirty or forty times; 'Heidenröslein' offers a familiar and typical illustration. This seems characteristic; but it is not confined to Schubert. A few examples can be found in Beethoven, rather more in Mozart; it is very frequent in Sterkel, Righini, and others. But another version of this 'curl' *not* at a final cadence seems peculiar to Schubert. This is a decoration, usually on the dominant, sometimes at the beginning of a phrase sometimes at the end, and often in the selfsame rhythm or a variation of it ♪ ♫ ♩. It can be seen typically in 'Der Wanderer' (Schmidt, D.493, 1816) bar 23. When it is in the minor, as here, it frequently involves a cross-relation clash. It appears in about forty songs including 'Morgengruss' and 'Des Müllers Blumen' from *Die schöne Müllerin*, 'Am Meer' (D.957, 1828) and 'Der Doppelgänger' (both in *Schwanengesang*), 'Schäfers Klagelied' (Goethe, D.121, 1814), 'An die Freunde' (Mayrhofer, D.654, 1819) 'Wandrers Nachtlied' (Goethe, D.224, 1815) – to name a few drawn from all periods. In most instances the songs are solemn in intent and slow of gait; they can be atmospheric, eerie, or sinister ('Colma's Klage', Ossian, D.217, 1815; 'Der Doppelgänger'), but sometimes, as in 'Das Heimweh' (Pyrker, D.851, 1825) or 'Grenzen der Menschheit', are more concerned with nobility of thought, with striving or aspiration. Its use, in short, is never perfunctory or purely ornamental; it is as significant and fundamental as the turn used so strikingly by Schumann in some of his songs.

Schubert's harmony and texture are classical in their clarity; his music is, so to speak, always in focus. His free treatment of tonality, his chromaticism, his range of modulation, were in line with the most up to date practice of his time, if not somewhat ahead of it. As an example of his originality in matters of modulation one might cite the two Platen songs, 'Die Liebe hat gelogen' and 'Du liebst mich nicht' (D.751 and 756, 1822); while the extraordinary opening of 'Dass sie hier gewesen' looks forward to Wolf's handling of discord in 'Herr, was trägt der Boden hier' in his *Spanisches Liederbuch*.

One harmonic trait is sufficiently characteristic of Schubert's style to warrant some slight discussion – the major-minor false relation.

The juxtaposition of the two modes was not new, but it seemed to have a special attraction for Schubert, who took a peculiar delight in thrusting the two modes into close and even violent proximity. It is not so much a question of a whole section in a changed mode, as when a portion of a through-composed song or the last stanza of a strophic one becomes transposed from tonic minor to major, but rather the alternation of the two as in 'Atys' (Mayrhofer, D.585, 1817) or 'Schwanengesang' (Senn, D.744, 1822). It was a habit that became more prevalent as he grew older. It appears in nine of the *Schöne Müllerin* cycle, sometimes in quite striking form as in 'Die böse Farbe', in both prelude and postlude. The contradiction comes not infrequently right at the end of a song, as in 'Drang in die Ferne' (Leitner, D.770, 1823), where an emphatic move to the tonic major in the last few lines of the voice part is repudiated by a postlude in the tonic major, or in 'Die Rose' (Friedrich von Schlegel, D.745, 1822), where the reverse occurs. 'Ihr Bild' (D.957) and 'Muth' (D.911) are other examples of the move to the major being over-ruled by the piano postlude. One of the oddest endings is that to 'Der Pilgrim' (Schiller, D.794, 1823); the whole of the last section (beginning at *sehr langsam*) oscillates between major and minor, a final *tierce de Picardie* in the vocal line being answered by two *sforzando* minor chords. A similar indecision is voiced in the postlude to 'Pause' (D.795). But it is perhaps in 'Geheimes' (Goethe, D.719, 1821) that this major-minor alternation is found at its most effective and delightful, the blending of the two contradictory modes symbolizing, maybe, the pleasurable conflicts in the lovers' hearts.

LOEWE AND THE BALLAD

The rather obvious theatricality and superficial effectiveness of Zumsteeg were carried over into the ballads of Schubert's coeval Carl Loewe (1796–1869), a versatile musician – pianist, organist, conductor, singer, and composer. On the whole the most striking and original of his songs are the early ones. His Op. 1 contained two masterpieces, 'Edward' and 'Erlkönig', written in 1818 while he was still a student at the University of Halle. The first of these, a tragic, gloomy, dramatic song, is as much a landmark in his career as 'Gretchen am Spinnrade' in Schubert's. The freely handled piano part ranges widely over the whole keyboard, and in the last frenzied climax as Edward curses his mother the chords are spread over almost five octaves. 'Erlkönig' has, inevitably, been compared and contrasted with Schubert's, also Op. 1, and in the same key, G minor.[1] Loewe's is the more illustrative, the

[1] See Albert B. Bach, *The Art Ballad. Loewe and Schubert* (Edinburgh and London, 1890).

more nearly faithful to the externals of the narrative. Thus while Schubert's agitated octave triplets suggest terror at the very outset, Loewe's more tranquil opening merely sketches in the initial scene, the leaves rustling in the night breeze. The galloping rhythm so prominent in the latter part of the song makes its first appearance only *after* the child has heard the first seductive whisperings of the elf-king; it is as if the father began to realize the urgent need for haste and spurred on his horse at that point. And whereas Schubert's 'Mein Vater, mein Vater' is a cry of terror, *forte*, Loewe's child, sick and feverish, can only whimper.

Loewe's best songs are those which call for little psychological insight, but which offer the excitement of straightforward narrative and pictorialism. Such a one is 'Herr Oluf', Op. 2, no. 2 (1820?). The text, a translation by Herder from Danish, is interesting in that we meet the 'elf-king's daughter' dancing King Oluf to his death. The impatience of the horseman is well portrayed, and is clearly differentiated thematically from the fairy dance. The *dénouement* (the bare statement 'da lag Herr Oluf und war todt', followed by a single *fortissimo* chord) is both simple and effective. Another early ballad, 'Die drei Lieder' (Uhland), Op. 3 (1825), is fine and imaginative. King Sifrid calls for the one among his harpers who can sing the finest song. A youth steps forward, harp in hand, sword at his side:

Three songs I know. The first you have forgotten – how you treacherously slew my brother. The second came to me one dark and stormy night, how that we must fight to the death. And now the third, of which I shall never tire, how King Sifrid lies in his own red blood.

Loewe sticks close to the Zumsteeg pattern; he draws freely on the operatic conventions of the time, and the piano part is busy with *tremolandi*, rushing scale-passages and flashing arpeggios.

Loewe also wrote a large number of smaller songs, often grouped in cycles. They include settings of the nine poems of Chamisso's *Frauenliebe und-leben*, Op. 60 (1836, thus ante-dating Schumann's settings) and all twenty-four of Theremin's *Hebräische Gesänge* after Byron. As with the ballads, the earlier songs are the more attractive. Songs such as 'An die Natur', 'Das Blumenopfer', and 'Sehnsucht', from his *Jugendlieder*[1] charm by reason of their piquant melodies and well-written, pianistic accompaniments. But Loewe never developed in later years, and seemed quite unaware of the harmonic advances of Schumann, Chopin, Liszt, and Wagner. The very late 'Archibald Douglas', Op. 128 (1857), can still make its effect, given a rich voice

[1] Vol. 1 of the *Gesamtausgabe*, ed. Max Runze (Leipzig, 1904).

and a commanding presence; but the musical material out of which it is built is almost totally undistinguished, with commonplace pianistic texture and insipid, complacent melodic style.

(b) The Slav Lands

By GERALD ABRAHAM

BOHEMIA

The Czech, Moravian, and Slovak composers internationally famous during the eighteenth century wrote primarily for instruments. If they composed songs, they set German or Italian texts; only Kozeluch and Gyrowetz composed a few trifles with Czech words. Czech was a lower-class language and its poets were humble village schoolmasters and cantors. Indeed the overpowering cultural influence of Austria persisted into the second half of the nineteenth century, long after the literary revival. The real pioneer of Czech song was a pupil of Kozeluch, Jakub Jan Ryba (1765–1815), a cantor's son, who published *Zwölf böhmische Lieder in Musik gesetzt von Franz* (sic) *Ryba* (Prague, 1800), a second collection of *Neue böhmische Lieder* (Prague, 1808), and the earliest Czech through-composed ballad, modelled on Zumsteeg, a setting of Vojtěch Nejedlý's 'Lenka' (also 1808). It is characteristic of the milieu that settings of Czech words were published in the chief Czech city under German titles and the composer given a false German forename. Ryba's melodies are naïve and short-breathed, as in 'Spokojený sedlák' (The contented peasant)[1] from his first set:

Ex. 205

S mo - cí Bo - ží, v po - li zbo - ží po - čí - na mi zrát,

(With God's help crops are beginning to ripen.)

[1] Complete in Jaroslav Pohanka, *Dějiny české hudby v příkladech* (Prague, 1958), no. 155.

and the pianist's right hand doubles the voice; yet one can detect a slight Czech flavour. The *Czeské Písně v hudbu uvedené* (Czech songs set to music) (Vienna, 1812) of Jan Emanuel Doležálek (1780–1858) pupil of Albrechtsberger and friend of Beethoven, are less ingenuous though he also tends to preserve voice and right-hand doubling:[1]

Ex. 206

(O how sweet is life now, with love and pleasure – and Pinka likes me.)

He set Goethe in the original – *6 Lieder von Schiller und Goethe* published by Diabelli in Vienna – and in translation. (His song 'Toužení' (Longing) published in the journal *Dobroslav* in 1820, is a Czech version of 'Die Nähe des Geliebten'.)

The songs of Václav Tomášek (1774–1850) are much more numerous and more accomplished. From 1800 onward he composed a great many *Lieder*, among them Bürger's 'Lenore' (1805), seven sets of Goethe songs, and four Schiller sets. But in 1813, 'for fear of quite forgetting my native tongue', he published in Prague *Šestero písní v hudbu uvedených* (A half-dozen songs set to music), Op. 48, and two more *Šestera* followed, Opp. 50 and 71. 'Měj se dobře', the second song of Op. 71 (1823),[2] is a good example of his work. The poem, like nearly all his Czech song-texts, is by his friend Václav Hanka. And in the same year he published another set of six songs, *Starožitné písně z Královédvorského rukopisu* (Ancient songs from the Králové Dvůr manuscript), also by Hanka,[3] which show more originality, e.g. Op. 82, no. 5, 'Žežhulice' (The Cuckoo):

---

[1] Complete in ibid., no. 160.
[2] Complete in ibid., no. 158.
[3] Hanka claimed to have discovered a collection of ancient Czech poems in 1817; their authenticity was at first generally accepted, then long disputed, but only finally demolished by Tomáš Masaryk.

Ex. 207

(In the broad fields stands an oak, in the oak a cuckoo; it cuckoos and laments that
it is not always spring.)

POLAND

Despite their political disasters, the Poles did not – like the Czechs – suffer degradation of their language. Vernacular opera during the last two decades of the eighteenth century, something impossible in Bohemia, naturally gave birth to solo song; opera-songs were extracted with piano accompaniments and sometimes new words. French songs were popular and provided with Polish words as well as offering models; intense patriotic feeling in the 1790s suggested vocal mazurkas and polonaises.[1] But the first significant Polish songs with piano appeared in a short-lived periodical publication, *Wybór pięknych dzieł muzycznych i pieśni polskich* (Selection of fine musical works and Polish songs). The first year's issue (1803) contained ten songs, of which eight were by the opera composer Elsner;[2] the second year (1805) brought thirteen more songs by Elsner. His place in the history of Polish song is roughly equivalent to Tomášek's in Bohemia and, as it happens, both thought it necessary to defend the suitability of the Slav languages for musical treatment, Tomášek in a preface to his first *Šestero*, Elsner five years later in a treatise on 'the metrical and rhythmical treatment of the Polish language, with special reference to Polish verse from the point of view of music' (1818). Three of Elsner's songs in the *Wybór* are styled *duma*, a term coined by the poet Julian Niemcewicz to denote a type of elegiac song, e.g. 'Duma Luidgardy'.[3] (Luidgarda was a medieval princess strangled on her husband's orders and she tells the east wind to let her dear ones know of her suffering):

Ex. 208

[1] See the examples in Jan Prosnak, *Kultura muzyczna Warszawy w XVIII wieku* (Cracow, 1955), pp. 240 ff. Prosnak also gives Polish adaptations of the Marseillaise and 'Ça ira'.
[2] See p. 524.
[3] Complete in Alina Nowak-Romanowicz, *Józef Elsner* (Cracow, 1957), supplementary volume, p. 5.

Another Niemcewicz setting in the *Wybór* is the vocal polonaise
'Życzenia w samotności' (Longing in solitude),[1] but more typical of
Elsner's sung polonaises is 'Muza wiejska' (The rustic muse),[2] one of
a set of six songs published in 1818:

Ex. 209

(I was born in a quiet village; shepherdesses reared me and, knowing no cares, I ran
about the fields.)

[1] In Jerzy Gabryś and Janina Cybulska, *Z dziejów polskiej pieśni solowej* (Cracow, 1960), p. 152.
[2] Nowak Romanowicz, p. 142.

Niemcewicz's publication of his *Špiewy historyczne* (Warsaw, 1816), a collection of thirty-three ballads – but including a few *dumy* written in his youth – glorifying the heroes of Polish history and legend, gave a powerful new impulse to song composition. Elsner had begun to collaborate with the poet and actually set the 'Duma o Stefanie Potockim' but then withdrew and it was left for composers of a younger generation to draw inspiration from the *Historical Songs*: Franz (Franciszek) Lessel (*c.* 1780–1838), Karol Kurpiński (1785–1857), and Maria Szymanowska (1789–1831). Lessel had spent some time in Vienna as a disciple, if not pupil, of Haydn and was technically much better equipped than Elsner and his predecessors. Among the best of his simpler songs are 'Stefan Batory' and 'Zawisza Czarny' ('Black' Zawisza, killed by the Turks in 1420), in the latter of which something of the spirit of the polonaise is embodied in 4/4 time. Harmonically more subtle are 'Jan Tarnowski: Płacz starego Rycerza na jego pogrzebie' (The old knight's lament at Jan Tarnowski's burial) and 'Pogrzeb księcia Józefa Poniatowskiego' (The funeral of Prince Józef Poniatowski), the epilogue to Niemcewicz's collection. The beginning of 'Jan Tarnowski' exemplifies Lessel's chromaticism:

Ex. 210

zo - sta - wi - ły?

(Why are the fates so pitiless to me?)

Kurpiński, mainly an opera composer, had already collaborated with Niemcewicz in his *Jadwiga* (see p. 526) and he set six of the *Historical Songs*. He lacked Lessel's keyboard sense and a song like 'Michał Korybut', depending entirely on its fine swinging melody, would be equally effective in the theatre. On the other hand, another lament for Poniatowski, 'Duma włościan Jabłonny o panu' (*Duma* of the farmers of Jablonna for their master) – the words are by Dionizy Minasowicz, translator of Goethe and Schiller – might just as well be a piano piece, a slow mazurka, for the voice doubles the piano throughout.

Maria Szymanowska, a pianist of European reputation, set three of Niemcewicz's *Historical Songs*, 'Jadwiga, królowa polska' (Jadwiga, Queen of Poland), 'Jan Albrycht', and 'Duma o Michale Glińskim'. Here the dramatic, quasi-orchestral writing is more surprising; the 'Duma o Glińskim' begins with dramatic tremolos and the voice part is no less operatic; the sad song about Queen Jadwiga, who gave up her lover and 'turned her eyes and heart to the Poles' ends with a triumphant polonaise-like flourish for the piano which suggests a tutti at the end of an aria. But for Szymanowska it was the narrative, the ballad element, that mattered supremely and it was a true ballad, Mickiewicz's 'Switezianka' (The nymph of Lake Switeź), that pointed a way forward for herself – for instance to the Mickiewicz 'Alpuhara' – and for a greater Polish musician. Her setting was published in Moscow in 1828 and its narrative tone:

Ex. 211

(Who is that fine young lad? And who the girl by his side?)

was to be caught not in songs but in Chopin's *ballades* for piano solo
which, he told Schumann were 'durch einige Gedichte von Mickiewicz
angeregt'. The earliest of Chopin's songs, 'Dzie lubi' (Where she likes)
and 'Życzenie' (The wish), came the year after 'Switezianka', and
'Życzenie' remains the only really well-known of his songs. He never
became a great song-writer but remained a faithful follower in the
tradition of Polish solo song, with a leaning to the vocal mazurka, and
– like Szymanowska – he rejected stylish keyboard writing in his
accompaniments.

RUSSIA

Accompanied solo song in Russia at first consisted mostly of folk-
song arrangements or adaptations rather than original compositions,
though as early as the 1750s Grigory Nikolaevich Teplov (1711–79)
published a collection of seventeen songs entitled *Mezhdu delom
bezdel'e ili Sobranie pesen s prilozhennïmi tonami na tri golosa* (Mid
work, idleness, or A Collection of songs with the addition of music in
three parts.)[1] They are extremely jejune; Teplov gives no indication of
the way the three parts are to be performed but the highest is obviously
to be sung, the lowest to be played; but he had the sense to set seven
poems by Sumarokov, the least frigid Russian poet of the time and he
sometimes manages to give his music a faintly Russian flavour.
   During the last quarter of the century there were more and more

---

[1] There were very small later editions in 1795 and 1776, and individual songs were reprinted
throughout the century; complete reprint in Tamara Livanova, *Russkaya muzïkal'naya kultura
XVIII veka*, i (Leningrad and Moscow, 1952), pp. 189–245.

publications of so-called 'Russian songs', which might be genuine
folk-songs, urban or peasant, imitations of them in the operas of
Catherine II's reign, or even Western compositions with Russian
words. Collections of them were published: the four parts (1776, 1778,
1779, and 1795) of Vasily Trutovsky's *Sobranie russkikh prostïkh pesen
s notami* (Collection of Russian simple songs with music) and the
famous collection by the Czech Ivan Prach (Johann Pratsch or Prač)
(1790; second edition 1806) which was the first to introduce the word
narodny (folk or popular) in the title.[1] Trutovsky supplied only simple
basses for his first three sets but in emulation with Prach, who gave
genuine piano accompaniments, he did the same in his fourth set. Not
quite all the songs in these collections are genuinely 'folk'; no. 42 in
Prach has words by Sumarokov.

During the 1790s the quantity of music published at St. Petersburg
increased enormously. Solo song naturally figured prominently in the
output, both 'Russian songs' and *romances* in the French style often
with texts by Jean-Pierre Claris de Florian. Some of the composers
were amateurs and preferred to remain anonymous, as did Fyodor
Mikhaylovich Dubyansky (1760–96), a Petersburg banker. One of his
six 'Russian songs', 'Stonet sizïy golubochek' (The grey dove moans
day and night):[2]

Ex. 212

became for a time as popular as a folk-song. Dubyansky's contemporary Józef Kozłowski (1757–1831), a completely Russified Pole,
described himself in at least one of his dedications as 'J. Koslovsky,
amateur' but he was a professional musician. He contributed to a
Sobranie nailuchshikh rossiyskikh pesen (Collection of the best Russian

[1] Modern editions of Trutovsky (Moscow, 1953) and Prach (Moscow, 1955), both ed. with
introductions by V.M. Belyaev.
[2] In S.L. Ginzburg, *Istoriya russkoy muzïki v notnïkh obraztsakh*, i (Moscow, second edition
1968), p. 423, with two other songs by Dubyansky.

songs) published at St. Petersburg in 1781, followed the vogue for French *romances* in *Six romances de Florian avec l'accompagnement de fortep. Op. 11* in the 1790s, and seems to have been equally happy in setting Russian, Polish, French, and Italian texts. 'Prezhestokaya sud'bina' (Most cruel fate), which appeared in the publisher Gerstenberg's *Karmannaya knizhka dlya lyubiteley muzïki na 1796 god* (Pocket booklet for lovers of music, for 1796),[1] gives an idea of his expressive power, conventional though the idiom is:

Ex. 213

Pre - zhe - sto - ka - ya   sud' - bi - na   raz - lu - cha - et mne s to - boy;___ Ya tvo-

- ya,   moy svet,   ne bu — du,   akh! i tï   ne bu — desh moy!___

(Most cruel fate severs me from thee; I shall not be thine, my darling, and thou wilt not be mine!)

Of the same generation as Dubyansky and Kozłowski were Shaposhnikov (dates and other names unknown) a pupil of Sarti, whose 'Potoplenie' (Drowning)[2] is a setting of Derzhavin's elegy on Dubyansky, the blind composer Aleksey Dmitrievich Zhilin (*c.* 1767–*c.* 1848),[3] and Daniil Nikitich Kashin (1769–1841), another pupil of Sarti and a serf until 1809.[4]

The next generation – headed by Aleksandr Aleksandrovich Alyabiev (1787–1851) and the gifted dilettanti Nikolay Alekseevich Titov (1800–75), his brother Mikhail Alekseevich (1804–53), and cousin Nikolay Sergeevich (1798–1843) – were fortunate in having better poets to collaborate with: Zhukovsky, pioneer of the Russian narrative ballad and superb translator of English and German poems, the young Pushkin, Delvig. But at first poets and musicians were ill matched. N. A. Titov began by setting French texts and modelling his

---

[1] In Ginzburg, with three other songs by Kozłowski, both op. cit., pp. 434 ff, and ii (Moscow and Leningrad, 1949), pp. 9 ff.
[2] In Ginzburg, ii, p. 337, with one of Shaposhnikov's four 'Anacreontic songs', 'The drunk and sober philosophers'.
[3] 'Malyutka' a setting of a translation of Népomucène Lemercier's 'Un jeune enfant, un casque en main', and another of Zhilin's *romances* in ibid., pp. 330 ff.
[4] A *romance* and six folk-song arrangements, ibid., pp. 218 ff.

songs on Boieldieu, and turned for his earliest Russian songs in the early 1820s to his friend M. A. Ofrosimov, while his cousin Nikolay Sergeevich set Pushkin's 'Talisman'[1] to a banal tune and a piano accompaniment of unsurpassable dullness. The partnership with Ofrosimov did, however, give Nikolay Alekseevich two of the most popular *romances* of the day, 'Yedinennaya sosna' (The lonely pine) and 'Kovarnïy drug' (Insidious friend).[2] 'Kovarnïy drug' was an outstanding favourite:

Ex. 214

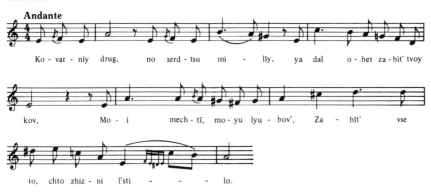

Ko - var - nïy drug, no serd - tsu mi - lïy, ya dal o - .bet za - bït' tvoy kov, Mo - i mech - tï, mo - yu lyu - bov', Za - bït' vse to, chto zhiz - ni l'sti - - - lo.

(Insidious friend, but dear to my heart, I vowed that I would forget thy wiles, my dreams, my love – forget all that gilds life.)

Alyabiev's earliest known solo song is a harmless little *romance*, 'Vizhu babochka letaet sred' fiyalok, roz, liley' (I see a butterfly among the violets, roses, and lilies) and he wrote his quota of French songs. It was only after his exile to Siberia in 1828 that he emerged, particularly with his Pushkin settings, as the first really outstanding Russian song-composer comparable with all but the greatest Western masters. Even before his exile his setting of Delvig's 'Solovey' (The Nightingale),[3] a mating of *romance* with 'Russian song' when it was published a few years later in 1831 quickly brought him celebrity:

[1] Ibid., p. 394.
[2] Ibid., pp. 381 and 383.
[3] Complete in Ginzburg, iii (Moscow and Leningrad, 1952), p. 230.

Ex. 215

(My nightingale, loud-voiced!)

Another composer whose main work, in his case opera, belongs to the
1830s was Aleksey Nikolaevich Verstovsky (1799–1862). As a song-
composer he specialized in what he called the 'cantata', the dramatic
narrative ballad and his setting of Pushkin's 'Chernaya shal' (The
black shawl)[1] was sung in Moscow in 1824 in costume and with scenic
background. Much of Verstovsky's declamation – and harmony – is
commonplace enough but here and there it underlines the text very
forcibly;

[1] Ibid., p. 27.

Ex. 216

Ya dal e - mu _____ zla - ta i pro - klyal e - vo, l ver - no - vo po - zval ra - ba mo - e - vo.

(I gave him gold and cursed him, and called him my slave.)

The piano here does little more than double the voice in octaves. The accompaniment was later orchestrated and there can be little doubt that the dramatic ballad as a genre was to encourage Russian song-composers to enrich the hitherto conventional and unimaginative harmony and figuration of their accompaniments.

(c) France

By GEORGES FAVRE

VOGUE OF THE *ROMANCE*

Before the Revolution French society, Parisian and provincial alike – and among professional musicians as well as amateurs – had developed a marked taste for a new type of vocal music. The numerous *brunettes, petits airs,* and *chansons tendres* popular during the earlier part of the century were gradually supplanted by a rather more compact, more developed, and much more varied genre, the *romance* with fully written-out keyboard accompaniment. During the period of transformations and profound changes in every sphere after 1789, every new tendency was to be reflected in the *romance*. The next four decades saw the publication of an unbelievable quantity, some separately, some in collections of three or six, some in such musical periodicals as *L'Ariette du Jour* (1789), the *Feuilles de Terpsichore* (1794), *La Muse du Jour* (1796), the *Journal d'Apollon* (1802), the *Souvenir des Ménestrels* (1825), *Le Chansonnier des Grâces*, the *Étrennes de Polymnie*, etc.

Every composer tried his hand in this genre, even amateur musicians who flooded the market with their mediocre productions. A theoretician of the day, Alexis de Garaudé, wrote in 1810: 'Twenty years ago one could count barely eight or ten composers in Paris; today five or six thousand individuals imagine they can compose. On every side you see *manufacturers* of *romances*'.[1] A little later, in 1828, Castil-Blaze noted similarly: 'Paris swarms with fabricators of *romances*, but their ephemeral productions are the laughing-stock of connoisseurs'.[2]

THE TEXTS

Few great names figure among the favourite poets of the *romance* composers. Marie-Joseph Chénier, Jean-Baptiste Rousseau, Jean-Pierre Florian, Charles-Hubert Millevoye are among the few. Then come some lesser authors, much appreciated at the time and who enjoyed a certain position in the literary world, such as La Harpe, Jean-François Marmontel, André-François de Coupigny, Colardeau. Others are known mainly as opera librettists: Jean-Nicolas Bouilly, Saint-Just, Alexandre Duval, Emmanuel Dupaty, Nicolas Lemercier, and Charles de Longchamp.

The poems are almost always in strophic form; three or four quatrains sufficed. Very rarely the strophes are separated by a short refrain. They express a simple impression, a direct emotion, devoid of ambiguity or complication. The text of a *romance*, observes the editor of the *Mercure*[3] 'demands what Nature alone gives, that is to say artlessness and sentiment. A *romance* should always speak to the heart and never reveal anything purely of the mind'. Round about 1790 the favourite eighteenth-century subjects were still in vogue; naïve pastoral scenes, *fêtes galantes*, would-be rustic subjects close to nature. But new tendencies began to make themselves felt. Fresh subjects began to appear and were very quickly taken up by the majority of the poets. Poems became more narrative and told a story; they became much more dramatic and, still more, lyrical. Pre-romantic traits are perceptible: the quest for a genuine feeling for nature, for sincere emotion less artificial than in the classic age. One finds new themes of inspiration – solitude, melancholy, love of ruins – and poets delight in singing the beauties of forest, night, sea, and mountain. They are attracted also by the Middle Ages, chivalry, the troubadours, and they begin to discover the exotic. Nor must we overlook one less important,

---

[1] *Tablettes de Polymnie*, March 1810, p. 8.
[2] *Dictionnaire de musique moderne*, article 'Romance'.
[3] 26 September 1789, p. 80.

much more limited and temporary aspect of the *romance*; during the most agitated period of the Revolution, between 1789 and 1800, it often reflected the patriotic sentiments then fashionable and endeavoured to celebrate in its way the great events of the time.

THE COMPOSERS

One category of composers, though admittedly not a very important one, must be mentioned first: the specialists, the *romance*-manufacturers who wrote nothing else but wrote a vast quantity of them. But their works are of little interest, often very mediocre technically and devoid of genuine personality of style. They flattered the public taste but enjoyed only very ephemeral success. One need mention only the names of Pierre-Jean Garat (1764–1828), a highly esteemed singer who performed his own *romances*, of Pierre-Martin d'Alvimar (1772–1839), who taught the Empress Josephine the harp, of Giuseppe Blangini (1781–1841), Italian in origin but settled in Paris, and of Charles Plantade (1764–1839), professor at the Paris Conservatoire and *maître de musique* of the Chapel Royal from 1816 to 1830.

Fortunately all the great composers of the day were also attracted by this minor genre and wrote excellent *romances*, inspired and sensitive as well as well written. Thus Grétry and Dalayrac have left us pleasant examples. But with Méhul (1763–1817) the *romance* took on much more musical substance, particularly in the six *Chants Anacréontiques* (1796), settings of translations from Anacreon made by the celebrated Hellenist Jean-Baptiste Gail. François Devienne (1759–1803) was another of the better composers, witness his collection of *Romances de Gonzalve de Cordou*, Op. 53, in 1795. Louis-Emmanuel Jadin (1768–1853) wrote in 1796 'La mort de Werther', then a very novel subject, with its dramatic end:

Ex. 217

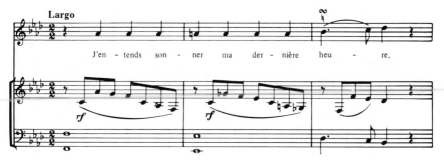

(I hear my last hour sound, Charlotte, farewell for ever.)

and also essayed the exotic in a 'Romance africaine' after Évariste de Parny. More attracted by opera than by domestic music, Henri-Montan Berton (1767–1844) composed a very remarkable 'Imitation libre de Métastase' in 1796 and went on to write 'Juliette au tombeau de sa mère' in the *Chansonnier des Grâces* of 1798 and the collection of seven pieces entitled *Romances d'Ismaël et Christine, nouvelle africaine*. In 1801 appeared his *Verselets à mon premier né* on poems by Clotilde de Surville and then in 1812 *Neuf Romances extraites de la Princesse de Nevers ou Mémoires du Sire de Tourailles*. The brilliant Parisian pianist and organist Jean-François Tapray (1738–1819) deserves to be remembered for his 'Oh! Galatée, oh! tendre amie' and for 'D'une amante abandonnée' (1793), with words by La Harpe, as well as two songs published in 1795, 'Le premier regard d' Aspasie' and 'Ton absence fait ma tristesse'. Another pianist and organist, like Tapray, Jacques-Marie Beauvarlet-Charpentier (1766–1834) published in the *Chansonnier des Grâces* of 1805 two novel pieces, the 'Chanson de Roland', with text by Alexandre Duval, and 'Romance de la belle Yseult'.

Another interesting figure was Honoré Langlé (1741–1807), Monegasque by origin, who lived in Paris from 1774 and subsequently became Librarian of the Conservatoire. His contemporaries particularly liked his collection of *Romances d'Alix et d'Alexis*, his six *romances* from the *Journal Anacréontique* with words by 'le citoyen Jardin', and above all his *Romance sur la liberté des hommes de couleur* inspired by the enthusiasm following the National Assembly's proclamation of the emancipation of all slaves (16 pluviôse, an II/4 February 1794). To the same category belong Langlé's patriotic songs composed during the great days of the Revolution: 'Hymne à Bara et Viala' (1794), 'Hymne à la Liberté', to words by Desorgues (1795), 'Hymne a l'Éternel' on a text by Lebrun, and the curious '*Déclarations des Droits de l'Homme et du Citoyen*, mises on 30 strophes pour être chantées par les hommes libres de tous les pays, par le citoyen Mantelle, de la section du Muséum . . . . dédié à tous les sans-culottes de la République'.

BOIELDIEU

In this gallery of song-composers we need merely mention the names of Catel, Cherubini, and Lesueur who wrote very few *romances*, but their colleague Adrien Boieldieu (1775–1834) demands more extended notice. Charming and sensitive, he was one of the indisputable masters of the genre. Though not as important as his dramatic works, his *romances* reveal a very attractive side of his personality. While still a child, at Rouen, it was into this narrow mould that he poured his first inspirations. Between 1793 and 1830 he composed fifteen collections of songs, to say nothing of numerous isolated ones published separately or in the musical periodicals of the day. 'He excels particularly in the genre of the *romance*', remarked one of his contemporaries in 1816.[1]

He scored a first and lasting success with 'S'il est vrai que d'être deux', published in his *Premier Recueil* in 1794. It is very short and extremely simple in style; under a new title 'Vivre loin de ses amours', it was frequently republished in France and abroad during the course of the nineteenth century. The next to last piece in his *Deuxième Recueil* is very dramatic, almost a genuine *scène lyrique*; it is entitled 'Romance avec Récitatif, sur la véritable Nina morte à Rouen en 1789'. There is another noteworthy song in the *Quatrième Recueil*, the 'Chant montagnard', full of poetry and mystery, which must be classed among Boieldieu's best things:

---

[1] *Biographie des Hommes vivants*, i, p. 468.

Ex. 218

(The sun that follows thee, too slow a harbinger)

Successive editions attest its lasting popularity.

Sometimes a common idea connects the various poems used in a collection, thus forming a genuine song-cycle. This is the case in the *Cinquième Recueil* (1795) and above all in the *Recueil*, Op. 11, published in 1798, which consists of a genuine suite of six *tableaux* commenting on the sufferings of an abandoned lover. Boieldieu places these different scenes in delicately indicated settings, exactly right and very evocative. The first two, 'Bois muet, sombre asile' and 'Adieu, bocage frais et sombre', are rural – the latter shot through with mysterious horn-like sonorities. The same quest for unity is apparent in the *Trois Romances* dedicated to the Duc de Vicence in 1811: 'Longtemps je crus à la tendresse', 'Quelque gloire, beaucoup d'amour', and 'Las d'espérer vainement le bonheur'. They form a single literary whole and comment on the same story.

One or two of the separate songs also deserve special mention: for instance 'Célestine' (1799), a poetic evocation of springtime marked by melodic freshness and a charming spontaneity that makes one think of Schubert, limpid and transparent. Again, in the 'Romance de Don Quichotte' (1807) to a poem by Florian, Boieldieu demonstrates a true feeling for nature in his evocation of the mysterious silence of a summer night:

Ex. 219

(O night, how beautiful thou seemest to me under thy thick veils)

During his last years he wrote no more *romances* for, as he explained, 'one has to say so many things in so few words; all that is more difficult than one would believe'.[1]

THE MUSIC OF THE *ROMANCES*

Although a theoretician wrote in 1813 that 'one kills the *romance* when one tries to subject it to severe analysis',[2] something may be usefully said about the structure of the *romances*. Composers adopted the strophic form, without refrain. The number of verses generally varies from two to four. They are usually very short and almost all the melodies are in binary form, the two parts – almost always separated by a rest or a modulation to the dominant (or relative major when the mode is minor) – are of nearly the same length and formed of homogeneous elements. Occasionally unobtrusive modulations to neighbouring keys occur at the end of the second part, lightly colouring the end of the piece. Much more rarely one comes across the *rondeau* form, in which case the three parts are often very short.

Almost all the *romances* are written for soprano. The tempo is, naturally, determined by the sense and expression of the words. But, as Thiébault remarks,[3] that 'most suited to *romances* is slow movement'. All the *romances* have accompaniments for piano or harp but the instrument plays only a supporting role and is heard alone only in very short preludes and postludes.

In this vast output of *romances*, hasty and unequal as it was, many suggest the dazzling improviser rather than the inspired and expert composer. All the same, if not many deserve to be rescued from the oblivion where they rest for ever, there remain a handful that do deserve to survive. For, when he took the trouble, Boieldieu knew how to supply even a feeble poem with an expressive and perfectly balanced musical commentary. He was a master of technique and lacked neither feeling nor refinement. And, without exaggerating their importance, such things as 'Dans ces affreux déserts', 'Vous qui loin d'une amante', the 'Romance de Don Quichotte', 'Dans mes ennuis, onde tranquille et pure', and some others, are among his most beautiful and personal inspirations – and also among the best contemporary songs. With Méhul, Berton and Cherubini, he easily outclasses all the lesser *romance* composers of the Revolution and Empire. These four remarkable musicians showed what inspiration, coupled with assured technique, could accomplish within such a limited frame. In the

[1] Letter of 27 April 1826.
[2] Baron Thiébault, *Du chant et particulièrement de la romance* (Paris, 1813), p. 67.
[3] Op. cit., p. 57.

evolution of the solo song with instrumental accompaniment, their works form a natural bridge between the naïve *brunettes* of the eighteenth century and the first modern *mélodies* of Berlioz and Gounod.

(*d*) England

By GERALD ABRAHAM

During the last decade of the eighteenth century English solo song began to break out of its long tradition of entertainment music for the playhouse or public garden and to exploit a more intimate genre: the piano-accompanied song for private performance, often styled canzonetta. Storace had led the way with his *Eight Canzonetts, with an Accompaniment for a Piano Forte or Harp* (1782).[1] Haydn on his visits to London supplied superb models with his two sets of *Original Canzonettas* (1794 and 1795),[2] and the theatre-composer William Shield followed immediately with *A Collection of Canzonetts and an Elegy* (1796). But the real pioneer of the English art-song was Mozart's pupil Thomas Attwood (1765–1838) with his settings of songs from *The Lady of the Lake* (1810) – the 'Boat Song', the 'Coronach',[3] Ellen's so-called 'Ave Maria' – and Moore's *Lalla Rookh* (1817).[4]

Another composer who set the 'Coronach', also in 1810, was John Clarke-Whitfeld (1770–1836); indeed he later told Scott he had set all the songs in *The Lady of the Lake*. He had already composed songs from *Marmion*, including 'Where shall the traitor rest', and in 1812 he went on to compose the songs in *Rokeby*.[5] Clarke-Whitfeld sometimes indulges in more elaborate accompaniments, as in 'Here's the vow she falsely swore' and 'What voice is this?', but in his canzonet 'To Thyrza' from Byron's *Childe Harold* he does little more than supply supporting harmony.[6]

[1] See Vol. VII, p. 341.

[2] Ibid., pp. 357–8.

[3] In *Musica Britannica*, xliii, *English Songs 1800–1860*, ed. Geoffrey Bush and Nicholas Temperley (London, 1979), no. 1.

[4] 'The cold wave my love lies under' in ibid., no. 2.

[5] Gerald W. Spink, 'Walter Scott's Musical Acquaintances', *Music and Letters*, li (1970), p. 61.

[6] All three songs in *Musica Britannica*, xliii, nos. 6, 8 and 7.

Two younger contemporaries of Clarke-Whitfeld, George Pinto (1785–1806) and Henry Bishop (1786–1835) developed on quite different lines. The young Pinto published *Six Canzonets, with an Accompaniment for the Piano Forte* (1804) and (posthumously) *Four Canzonets and a Sonata* (1808)[1] with a third set in 1846, true drawing-room songs of great promise, while Bishop – very much a man of the theatre – 'adapted and compressed from the Score for Voice and Piano Forte' – songs with orchestral accompaniment composed for productions of Shakespeare's plays *c.* 1816–19,[2] thus continuing the older tradition of 'entertainment' song. The impulse to song-composition given by the romantic verse of Scott, Moore, and Byron is significant; and Pinto discovered Burns – though the early and uncharacteristic Burns[3] who imitated English poets.

[1] Two songs from *Six Canzonets* and one from *Four Canzonets*, ibid., nos. 9–11.
[2] Three examples, ibid., nos. 12–14.
[3] Ibid., no. 10.

XIII

CHORAL MUSIC

By ANTHONY LEWIS

INTRODUCTION

IN a period primarily concerned with instrumental developments, choral music is liable to be neglected or at least subordinated. Those seeking evidence of such a situation in the years that saw the production of the piano sonatas, string quartets and symphonies of Beethoven might point on the one hand to the comparative dearth of unaccompanied choral music, and on the other detect signs of an alien yoke in the use of the voices in the Choral Symphony. But though it is true that *a cappella* writing languished save in the smaller forms, a dispassionate analysis of the relationship between choral and orchestral music at this critical epoch can only lead to the conclusion that during their advance into choral domains the orchestral forces conferred more benefits than they extracted tribute.

Having spent a great part of the preceding fifty years in the evolution of symphonic design and the consolidation of the orchestral ensemble, it was natural that composers should wish to use the experience and technique gained thereby in dealing with the problems of choral music. Thus the entry of the orchestra into the church, and its subsequent abduction of the choir from there into the concert room should not be regarded with disapproval but accepted as the natural course of events. Since the great choral masterpieces of Bach and Handel a profound change had come over the status of the orchestra, which was now an independent and standardized body, normally accustomed to a role of its own, and by no means content to be used at will as a convenient prop for a chorus that should be self-supporting, nor even to be treated solely as a *ripieno* to the *concertino* of the voices.

There was consequently a tendency for the chorus and orchestra to become progressively more intermingled, constituting one homogeneous texture rather than two distinct groups that are periodically associated to gain sonority. This movement away from antiphony and towards continuity was in line with the general trend of symphonic development, which was gradually turning aside from systematic patterns of construction to explore the prospects of organic growth. One would expect therefore to see a decline in the previously overwhelming Italian influence on choral music, since this had focused attention on the interplay of opposing masses of sound marshalled into a series of balanced designs, relying for their effect on the impressiveness of each statement and the nature of its disposition within the movement, and scarcely ever, except in fugue, making use of the cumulative force derived from the expansion of a number of basic ideas. Even in fugue the Italian school were more concerned in preserving the identity of the subject or in achieving an orderly fugal plan than in extracting any new significance from their material.

THE GERMAN STYLE

Thus although the Italian idiom was still widespread, and often predominant, strong new influences were apparent, striving to reconcile the demands of choral music with recent developments in other spheres. The subjective polyphony of J. S. Bach, which the succeeding generation of composers had disregarded in concentrating their gaze to the south, was now coming again into view. Mozart's close study of Bach's methods had borne splendid fruit in his Requiem, and Beethoven was to find similar stimulus when engaged on the Mass in D. But it was no doubt instrumental practice that was principally responsible for this different approach to vocal polyphony. The choral ensemble now ceased only to be regarded as one collective voice, but was frequently treated as an amalgam of individual voices, each contributing its own melodic testimony to the general statement. The section 'Et vitam venturi' in Beethoven's Mass in D represents not so much the communal acceptance of an article of the Creed as the sum of a myriad personal confessions of faith.

The intimacy inherent in what may for convenience be called the German style of choral polyphony had a harmonic counterpart based on the new strain of lyricism that was gradually emerging. The German *Romanze* had left its humble folk-song origins for more sophisticated surroundings, and had gained a firm hold on the operatic stage beside the long-established aria, into which it was steadily instilling much of its atmosphere. In choral terms the *Romanze* was essentially homophonic, introducing a type of simple, informal, contemplative movement that was a welcome addition to the hitherto rather narrow and standardized range open to the composer. The lyricism that sprang from the *Romanze* pervaded the whole musical scene, so that in the choral works of Schubert and others one finds over long passages with a perceptibly lyrical flavour. In such cases the chorus acts as the soloist in a *Lied*, the lower voices supporting in exact sympathy an upper melodic line that has all the contours of a solo cantilena and conveys the same character of emotion.

INFLUENCE FROM THE THEATRE

These fresh interpretative resources were further extended by an increased flexibility in choral technique gained through experience in operatic ensemble. The matchless skill of Mozart in this latter field had provided a model for the subtle interplay of soloists and chorus. The contrast of the solo vocal quartet with the full choir gave an added depth to the perspective, while the weaving together of the solo and choral strands tended to produce a seamless fabric well suited to the symphonic process. No longer were the vocal participants segregated musically as well as physically, the principals might mingle with the crowd instead of always leading an existence on a different plane. This was a further step towards unity of construction, particularly in a large work where a lengthy succession of separate arias and choruses can give a somewhat piecemeal effect if two of the chief elements in the score are not heard occasionally in combination.

From the theatre came also the growing inclination, on the part of composers of church music, to dramatize the liturgy. Even such a disciplinarian of the emotions as Cherubini rarely missed an opportunity of underlining a suggestive phrase in such a way as to make it stand out from its context with the vivid clarity and unsuspected force demanded by the stage. No doubt this was partly due as well to the progress of the Romantic movement with its impulse towards imaginative exuberance which could degenerate into mere naïve sensationalism, One has continually to beware of misjudging the sincerity of the early Romantic church composers in this respect, since in exploring their new language they sometimes chose terms ill-fitted to express what was in fact a depth of genuine feeling.

ROMANTICISM

The preoccupation of Romantic literature with Nature found its musical equivalent in similar leanings towards effects of atmosphere and colour. The initial researches were carried out in the instrumental field, but later one finds composers becoming more and more sensitive to the quality of choral sound for its own sake, and unusual experiments in the spacing and disposition of the voices are quite frequent. Some of the unfavourable reaction to the church music of this period may indeed be due to the element of sensuousness in its texture. Yet in this matter of timbre choral composers were to lag far behind the orchestral and keyboard virtuosi. Berlioz the orchestrator was generally far more resourceful than Berlioz the autocrat of massed choirs, while Weber would show a greater variety of hues in one page of his piano sonatas than were apparent throughout the whole of his choral writing. This was probably in some measure due to the widely differing capacity of the performers concerned. While orchestras and pianists had reached a high degree of proficiency, the technique of the average chorus member would have been decidedly lower, rendering inadvisable any of the more daring subtleties of scoring. The day was yet to come when the large highly trained chorus could master all lying within its true idiom that a composer could devise, and rival the orchestra in refinement of nuance.

In their choice of texts choral composers were naturally much guided by the course of contemporary thought, which was leading towards new horizons of intellectual and creative activity. The release of emotional and spiritual forces that accompanied the Romantic movement found some of its purest expression in music, and the choral ensemble was not only a wonderfully sensitive and plastic medium, but also symbolic of the social ideals that inspired western civilization. The enthusiastic viewed the chorus as an emblem of the brotherhood of mankind, rendering articulate the aspirations of those that were setting out to build a new structure of society. In the songs and cantatas of the French Revolution one gets a sense of this visionary fervour, while in such tremendous utterances as Beethoven's Choral Symphony, the multitude of protagonists seem to transcend the limits of human speech.

ORATORIO AND CANTATA

Although at the end of the eighteenth century the Church was still the leading patron of choral music, the rise and establishment of secular organizations, wholly or partly concerned with the development of choral societies, began to offer composers an alternative outlet. Handel's oratorios had shown that the form need by no means be confined to the church, while the spread of public concert-giving opened up new prospects for the secular choral cantata which had hitherto enjoyed little scope. The popularity of Italian opera, resulting in the extension of many of its features to other kinds of music, was also a powerful factor in promoting further expansion and greater freedom of style in this respect. Indeed, we shall find the oratorios of this epoch derived much more from the theatre than the church. The principles of J. S. Bach were certainly not entirely disregarded, in fact they secured a growing number of adherents, but his devotional approach in the church cantatas and Passions no longer persisted in the same manner in his successors. 'Never was I so pious as when composing *The Creation*', said Haydn, yet the work is singularly free from outward traces of piety. It presents with deep sincerity a solemn dramatic event, but abstains from anything in the nature of personal commentary. A religious text is treated with great reverence; at the same time it is expounded by an opera-lover rather than by a church-goer. This is symptomatic of the gradually relaxing influence of the Church on choral music, even when, as in oratorio, the subject matter might be deemed within its province. With outside choral bodies and other independent resources at their disposal, composers could afford to disregard the limitations, material and psychological, associated with the Church.

The newly reconstituted Tonkünstler-Societät of Vienna was an example of an organization that supplied a valuable stimulus through its benefit performances of large-scale choral works. That its role was an important one can be judged from the fact that Haydn's first oratorio *Il Ritorno di Tobia*,[1] which represents in many respects the culmination of the eighteenth-century Italian style in that form, was written for the Society in 1775, while over twenty years later his two masterpieces that set a new standard in choral music and so profoundly influenced its future course, *The Creation* and *The Seasons*, were also committed to its charge. The opportunity of exploiting a large and unusually accomplished chorus had stirred Haydn to produce some of the finest music in *Tobia*, that of the choral movements, whose brilliant and florid polyphony made greater demands on the executants than anything since Bach. The experience gained thereby gave him an exceptional ease and confidence in the handling of choral texture, which is one of the features of the great works of his maturity that sets them on such a high peak within their period and makes them dominate the scene so far beyond it.[2]

CHRISTUS AM ÖLBERGE

Two years after the completion of *The Seasons* in 1801 there appeared Beethoven's only essay in oratorio form, *Christus am Ölberge*. It is unfortunate that Beethoven unwittingly gave offence to some by the style of the music he assigned to the character of Jesus, since it is clear that this is an important work of his early period, which ill deserves the comparative neglect into which it has fallen. Although

[1] See Vol. VII, p. 327.
[2] Haydn's later oratorios are discussed in ibid., pp. 332–5.

termed an oratorio, it is scarcely more than a dramatic religious scene, being in length substantially shorter than the first part of *The Creation*. Yet it contains all the elements of oratorio as understood by those who looked to Italy rather than Germany for certain kinds of artistic guidance, and is in many respects the logical development of Haydn's initiative. As for the music itself, the style is hardly more operatic than in much of *The Creation*, while the sincerity of the composer is never in question. Indeed the Introduction should finally dispel all doubts on this latter point; the splendour of its sombre colouring and the tender poignancy of its inflection make it in some ways Beethoven's most impressive orchestral statement to the date. So much power and so much restraint is rarely found compressed into so short a space. One may note also that for the first time his own peculiar command of the orchestra is manifest in its maturity. This nobly tragic prelude proceeds with quiet dignity and deep reverence until it is hushed to a whisper before Jesus speaks. Following Haydn's example in *The Seasons*, Beethoven now most effectively carries over material from the Introduction to give added force to the recitative. The mood becomes more emphatic, and the full sonority of the trombones is exploited at the words: 'Ich höre deines Seraphs Donnerstimme'. In the succeeding *arioso* the accompaniment reacts very flexibly to every implication of the text, and, having once accepted its conventions, one cannot say less of the aria which is its natural culmination.

It is as well to recognize from the description of the music up to this point that Beethoven has quite unequivocally chosen to present the narrative in dramatic fashion according to the Viennese style of his day, rather than after the manner of German Passion music. Thus the florid coloratura aria of the Seraph (closely related in sprightly cheerfulness to Haydn's hierarchy), his highly expressive duet with Jesus and the strongly characterized trio, when both are joined by St. Peter, should cause no surprise to the student of the Viennese dramatic cantata.

In the choral movements the orchestra is handled with independence and never chained to the vocal line. The *fugato* sections are full of vigour and personality (though they do not yet show Haydn's mastery of development), and the final chorus has a majestic brilliance not unworthy of its counterpart in *The Creation*. There are also many things in the score for which Beethoven sought no precedent, but let his powerful and, at this time, impulsive imagination be his guide. The result is a work of vital, if variable, quality which occupies a significant place in its composer's career. Some of the technique of *Fidelio* is to be found in these pages (however inappropriate that may

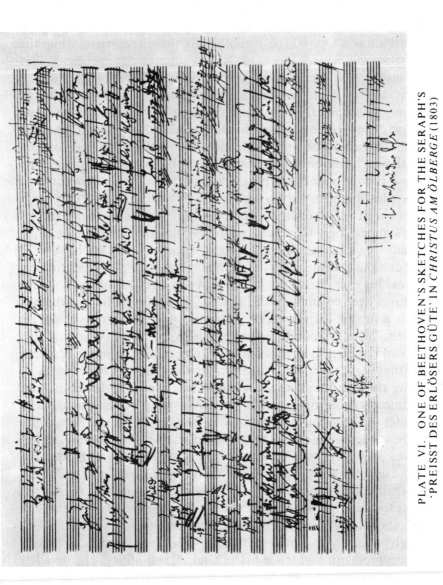

PLATE VI. ONE OF BEETHOVEN'S SKETCHES FOR THE SERAPH'S 'PREISST DES ERLÖSERS GÜTE' IN *CHRISTUS AM ÖLBERGE* (1803)

Reproduced in *Kniga eskizov Betkhovena za 1802–1803 godi. Issledovanie i rasshifrovka N. L. Fishmana* (Moscow, 1962).

seem), but in its own right *Christus am Ölberge* marks a notable stage in the history of dramatic oratorio.

BEETHOVEN'S OTHER CHORAL WORKS

Very different was Beethoven's next enterprise involving a chorus. In the Fantasia Op. 80 the pianoforte is the protagonist, while the orchestra and voices act chiefly as supporting agencies. This relationship, and indeed the unusual form of the work as a whole, springs largely from the original circumstances for which it was written – to round off a concert of the composer's music at which he was also to be the solo pianist. Thus the improvisatory opening Adagio is probably just a tranquil recollection in cold print of the emotional flourish which Beethoven extemporized in the heat of the moment. Its purpose is to arouse the expectation of the audience for what is to follow. But the little phrase which the orchestra then initiates soon proves abortive and ends in a series of question-marks that leave his hearers much where they were before. We find here a classic example of Beethoven's acute sense of stage management; only after two false starts does he consider that the dramatic tension is sufficient for him to reveal his true intentions. These prove to be based on an innocent little tune, derived from an earlier song called 'Gegenliebe', which is used as a subject for variations. After the original announcement on the piano he calls upon his resources progressively, first adding solo woodwind, then solo strings until the full orchestral tutti is reached. After that point the theme passes through a wide variety of disguises, ranging through many keys and showing unsuspected melodic and rhythmic potentialities, until an arpeggio sweep on the piano and a reminder of the earlier preparatory motive on the orchestra suggests that the composer has yet other forces in reserve. Here again they are released by degrees, solo voices entering first against a background of merry roulades from the piano, then full chorus and orchestra combined take up the refrain. In the coda all concerned pursue the subject to an enthusiastic conclusion on the sentiments of 'Wenn sich Lieb' und Kraft vermählen lohnt dem Menschen Götter-Gunst'. Though popularly known as the 'Choral' Fantasia, the chorus features even less predominantly than in the 'Choral' Symphony. The parallels with the latter are obvious, and this attractive work, intended primarily as a *pièce d'occasion*, may be regarded as a sketch for the vast canvas that was to follow years later.

Beethoven's remaining compositions in this category do not need lengthy consideration. The *Opferlied*, Op. 121b, is a strophic song with a noble melody treated antiphonally between soprano and chorus; the

Bundeslied, Op. 122, is a purely ephemeral affair, while the *Elegischer Gesang*, Op. 118, is a slight but moving threnody. Of more consequence is the setting of Goethe's 'Meeresstille und Glückliche Fahrt'. The contrasted moods of the two poems are conveyed in simple, telling fashion and the whole is as sensitive and shapely as a chorus from *The Seasons* and of about the same scale and weight. Would that an equally beneficial comparison could be made concerning *Der glorreiche Augenblick*, Op. 136, the cantata written for the Congress of Vienna in 1814. The prospect of the large and brilliant assembly, including several crowned heads, seems to have stiffened Beethoven into a pompous rigidity that is a dismal caricature of his real self. One turns the pages of this protracted work in the hope of finding some touch of the true master, but when one reaches the culmination, a fugue to the words 'Vindobona, Vindobona, Heil und Glück, Heil und Glück', one closes it in despair. It was, however, successful in its purpose of promoting an atmosphere of inter-allied congratulation, and thus made political, rather than musical, history.

WEBER'S *DER ERSTE TON*

It is with some curiosity that one turns to see how the founder of German romantic opera, who was to strike such an admirable vein in his vocal ensembles on the stage, would deal with the widening possibilities of choral music outside the theatre. Leaving out of account his routine productions for the Saxon Court, Weber's reactions were certainly not conventional. *Der erste Ton* (1808),[1] a setting of a poem by Friedrich Rochlitz, is an essay in the type of spoken declamation to music which he was to develop further in the incantation scene in *Der Freischütz*. Unlike the few earlier examples in this genre,[2] Weber goes far beyond the idea of 'spoken recitative'; in *Der erste Ton* all the resources of the early romantic equipment are brought into play to illustrate the speaker's narrative, and are developed to a point at which the words become a pretext for the music, thus reversing their relationship in the dramatic monologue with rhythmic punctuation that is the basis of *recitativo secco*. Weber's work is therefore the true forerunner of the melodramas of Liszt, Schumann, and others. The subject being the Creation, it is of some interest to compare the tone-painting with that of Haydn's maturity; Weber's music sprawls and he takes ten bars to say what Haydn could express in two beats; but in that he represents the outlook of a new generation, his score is valuable evidence of the nature of the change

[1] The first chorus was rewritten in 1810.
[2] See Vol. VII, pp. 76–9.

that had taken place in the interval, a change that is not always so easy
to exemplify in music as it is here. Space does not permit lengthy
quotations, but anyone who sets the relevant passages from both
works side by side will get a clearer insight into the distinction between
late eighteenth and early nineteenth-century style than might be
obtained from the most precise literary description. One very brief
extract will show how constant is the association of ideas with certain
melodic idioms.

Ex. 220

(The Prince of the earth unlocks a heart oppressed with longing)

Der erste Ton justifies its inclusion in the present context by the final
chorus which follows the declamation. This plan in itself is unusual
and would be very effective were the choral section more grateful and
characteristic. But although a good deal of energy is displayed and a
quantity of contrapuntal heat engendered, the voices are hindered
from achieving their true sonority, so angular and instrumental is
their line for the most part.

The scheme of the Hymn *In seiner Ordnung schafft der Herr* (1812)
also owes little to any previously established formula. In fact the
rather aimless poem, by Rochlitz again, would have gained from a
firmer outline and steadier sense of direction. The composer is forced
into a sequence of fragments of arioso, chorus, and recitative, few of
which last long enough to make an impression on the hearer but
sufficiently long to give a sense of frustration at the abortive hopes
they arouse.

In the finale Weber gets the opportunity he needs to build up a brilliant and substantial movement, and he launches a vigorous fugue that ranges forth boldly and resourcefully, gathering momentum, until it reaches a climax that may fairly be called irresistible. When the end is reached one realizes to what degree the poet has been a drag on his creative rein, emphasizing that persistent lack of literary discrimination that was to handicap Weber so grievously in his operas. Despite the exhilaration of its closing pages, *In seiner Ordnung* can hardly be considered an advance in choral technique over *Der erste Ton*. If anything the instrumental character of the vocal part-writing is accentuated and as Weber gets carried away by the rising excitement of the music, he tends to overlook the nature of the medium in which he is working and to think in terms of the orchestra, which was more instinctive to him. Thus in several passages the chorus is in the curious position of appearing to double the orchestral accompaniment, instead of taking the lead itself.

WEBER'S CANTATAS

Kampf und Sieg, described as a cantata 'to celebrate the defeat of the enemy in June 1815 at Belle Alliance and Waterloo', has at least the advantage of unity of purpose in its text. Whether the jejune realism demanded of compositions of this type was worthy of Weber is another matter. But these marches and countermarches and battles in sound, punctuated by choruses of the People and illumined by the joint comments of Faith (bass), Hope (tenor), and Charity (soprano), did afford him valuable experience in the organization of a dramatic scene at a time when his operatic style was rapidly maturing. That this aspect of the subject gripped his attention is evident from the seriousness with which he treated a project that from its very nature could only excite an ephemeral interest. The Introduction is a soundly constructed operatic overture in miniature, containing many striking touches that anticipate its more famous successors, and performing its function appropriately and with dignity. This creates exactly the right atmosphere for the opening chorus, giving added conviction to its sincere and moving statement. After this auspicious beginning, the entry of the three personifications and the various warring protagonists sets a strain on the quality of the composer's invention to which it is not always equal. Nevertheless the battle music retains its artistic self-respect throughout the clamour, and some of the soldiers' choruses have a force and gusto derived from something more substantial than mere factitious energy. In such a passage as the following Weber is clearly fashioning his tools for something more ambitious.

Ex. 221

(Swiftly as consuming fire or rushing mountain torrent his ranks are scattered.)

When the strains of 'God Save the King' have died down, and the final observations of the soloists have been recorded, the work is completed with a choral fugue on the now customary pattern. A majestic, and essentially vocal, subject persuades Weber to take a more accommodating view of the singers' role. This is rich, and indisputable, choral territory:

Ex. 222

(Lord God, we praise Thee, we thank Thee!)

Having reached such a promising stage, it is disappointing that Weber should have henceforward confined his choral music to works required for Court celebrations.

The most considerable work in this category is the *Jubel-Cantate*, written in 1818 to celebrate the fifty-year reign of the King of Saxony. At times Weber seems rather oppressed by the dignity of the occasion, but in general there is less sense of constraint than one might have expected in the circumstances. The opening, with its suggestion of distant organ tones and pealing bells, is full of poetry (largely absent from Friedrich Kind's text) and initiates a spacious choral design. The conventional obsequiousness of the tribute is marked by a welcome variety of phrasing and orchestration in the recitatives, while the arias often manage to achieve, within their narrow limits, a real eloquence. The outburst of choral rejoicing at the words 'Schmücket die Thore mit Blüthen und Zweigen' is no mere manufactured demonstration of loyal enthusiasm, but has a spontaneity and gusto that persuades one of its sincerity.

SCHUBERT'S QUASI-ORATORIOS

Weber's secular cantatas had many imitators amongst his contemporaries, but the great lyrical genius of the age was not amongst them. Outside liturgical music, Schubert's chief essays in the choral field were both of the oratorio type, and both, in different ways, incomplete. *Miriams Siegesgesang*, Op. 136 (1828), for soprano solo and chorus has survived with a pianoforte accompaniment only, though it is clear from its character and from Schubert's known intention, that it represents merely the sketch for an orchestral setting. This is undoubtedly a handicap in performance, but it does not fundamentally affect the nature of this short work, which has a curiously strong eighteenth-century flavour that amounts almost to conscious archaism in places. The opening pages pay obvious tribute to Handel, whose influence is, indeed, never far off throughout, but there is also an echo of French opera in the constant practice of following a solo air by a harmonized choral version. This device becomes too persistent in what is in any case a rather mannered score, making the scheme rigid and artificial and tending to give the chorus an unimpressively parrot-like role. When at last it escapes from the soloist's leading strings in the final fugue, it is a thankless path it has to tread, chosen by Schubert, one feels, more out of duty than inclination. Despite these drawbacks, there are many beautiful moments in this piece, but it cannot as a whole be considered characteristic of its composer.

While *Miriams Siegesgesang* is scarcely more than a dramatic religious scene, *Lazarus* (1820), of which only part is extant, was planned on a large scale. From what remains (one complete Act and part of a second, out of three), this 'religious drama' might well have been a work of considerable importance. From the outset it is evident that Schubert has been gripped by his subject and is minded to infuse his score with all the deep and tender poetry at his command:

Ex. 223

(Here let me pass my last hours, and yet once more enjoy the beauties of God's creation. In soft and gentle tones the voice of redemption addresses me.)

The pathos of the scene at Lazarus's death-bed is most movingly conveyed in terms that are simple yet impressive, arising from a sincere emotion that requires no over-emphasis to make its effect. The arias in the First Act are full of Schubert's most limpid melody, and the scoring is correspondingly delicate. The orchestra is used with great restraint, almost as if it were a chamber ensemble, which well befits the intimate atmosphere of the scene. Rarely in religious music since Bach does one find such a sensitive treatment of declamation, both in the voice line and in its accompaniment. The beginning of the Second Act, in which the scene is laid at Lazarus's grave, is set in darker mood. A sombre introduction, in which trombones have a commanding role, leads through some vivid recitative to an impassioned bass aria, which must rank as one of Schubert's most powerful achievements in this vein. The confidence with which bold strokes of harmonic and orchestral colouring are applied greatly increases the impact of this forceful passage, and it is indeed tantalizing that we cannot see how Schubert planned to continue this mood. We get an inkling of his intentions in the striking fragment of an aria which ends the surviving portion of this highly interesting work.

Although *Lazarus* is described as a 'religious drama' and contains a number of stage directions, it appears most unlikely that it was ever intended for the theatre. Not only is there very little action, but the whole score is permeated with the kind of spacious lyricism and breadth of line that is better suited to the concert room than the opera house. Indeed it would seem as if the qualities which denied Schubert operatic success should have been diverted towards oratorio, with its more deliberate pace and the scope it offers for meditative soliloquy.

SPOHR

Between Schubert's *Lazarus* and *Miriams Siegesgesang* appeared an oratorio quite different in character from either. This was *Die lezten Dinge* by Louis Spohr (1784–1859), first performed at Kassel in 1825. Here the overture gives the impression at the beginning of being an act of homage to Handel after the nature of *Miriams Siegesgesang*, but it is soon patent that the strength of the earlier style (which had at least been consistently maintained by Schubert) is to be weakened by an equivocal harmonic idiom quite alien to its spirit. The chromaticism that in *Lazarus* had been such a powerful expressive weapon is here rendered ineffective by persistent over-indulgence. Twenty bars of Spohr may cover as much harmonic ground as twenty pages of Schubert and yet not achieve half as much, since the ear is so dulled by continual evasions that little definite emerges from a relatively complex chromatic operation. The monumental dignity of Handel's choral writing, which Spohr often attempts to imitate, is sapped at its very foundations by instability in the part-writing. Had Spohr adapted his style to his harmonic language, the result might have been more successful.

Spohr is not the least overawed by his ambitious subject. Musically, he approaches the Last Judgement with complete assurance, singing of the destruction of Babylon and the glory of God with no undue disparity – the horror of the one and the brilliance of the other being equally tempered and qualified in his interpretation. When one recalls the remarkable intensity of the declamation in *Lazarus* or *Christus am Ölberg*, Spohr's flaccid calls to repentance seem as little impressive as his gushing choruses of praise. Despite the undeniable invention and constructive sense, there is an underlying insincerity which renders the work profoundly unconvincing.

Nor are the failings of *Die letzten Dinge* less prominent in *Des Heilands letzte Stunden* (1833), which once enjoyed an equally wide popularity. The overture is a good example of Spohr's fatal tendency to defeat his own ends. The main theme contains at least the seed from which might have grown a noble and tragic utterance:

Ex. 224

But the crucial second bar is allowed neither to stand in relief against a diatonic background nor to excite further stress in contrapuntal conflict. The chromatic steps of its gradual descent are paralleled by the counter-subject, thus rendering flat and insipid what might have been poignant and arresting. When at the end Spohr's creative power is put to the test to retrieve the situation by some unsuspected stroke, the most effective device he can think of is to double the speed:

Ex. 225

Again in the first chorus he has the opportunity to create a more impressive atmosphere; instead he produces an opening phrase which is a veritable masterpiece of indecisive banality.

Ex. 226

This harmonic vacillation infects all that comes into contact with it. The recitatives lack contrast and emphasis, since the orchestral background is equally irresolute, whatever the context. The confession and remorse of Judas fail to convince because the terms are much the same as those of John's preceding accusation, while Mary's declaration of faith is weakened in the very quality it needs most by hesitant cadences and ambiguous passing-notes. If further proof were wanted of the inadequacy of Spohr's expressive power in this work, one need only compare his setting of 'He is despised and rejected of men' with Handel's in *Messiah*.

ORATORIO IN FRANCE AND ENGLAND

France and England had little of consequence to offer in this field. Samuel Wesley never redeemed in his maturity the promise of the astonishingly precocious oratorios of his childhood, and William Crotch's *Palestine* (1811) is an indifferent substitute for the work Wesley might have written. In France the *Oratorio de Noël* (1786)[1] of François Le Sueur (1760–1837) exhibits most of the characteristics of that composer's highly individual personality, but is noteworthy rather for its intentions than for their execution. Carols are introduced liberally, and an attractive setting of the Shepherds' *Gloria* for two sopranos shows that when Le Sueur curbs his overflowing exuberance a little he can produce something that has polish, originality, and charm. This is the sort of music that would prove most stimulating to a young impressionable mind, and there is little doubt that it profoundly influenced Le Sueur's most celebrated pupil, Hector Berlioz, who was to break entirely new ground with his *Huit Scènes de Faust* (1834) with results clearly to be discerned in his *L'Enfance du Christ* (1850). But that story belongs to another place.

LITURGICAL MUSIC IN THE NEW CENTURY

Although choral music for the concert room had been steadily increasing in extent, liturgical music was still the most abundant field of choral composition in the early decades. For, despite rapid expansion, public concert giving did not yet offer conditions as favourable as those of larger religious establishments and the private chapels of the nobility. The Church and the great patrons that supported it offered not only a livelihood to those who provide music for its ritual, but could also put trained resources at their disposal in performance. The liturgical tradition still provided a solid basis on which the aspiring imagination of the nineteenth century could build. It also set a common standard by which the characteristics of the age can be judged more clearly than perhaps by any other means. This applies both to the period in general and to the idiosyncrasies of individual composers, for by a comparison of their settings of the Mass one can distinguish in an unmistakable manner the personalities of the three chief liturgical composers during this era: Beethoven, Schubert, and Cherubini.

CHERUBINI'S MASSES

Luigi Cherubini (1760–1842) did not start writing church music to any serious extent until comparatively late in his career, so that it forms a consistently mature section of his creative activity. It also

---

[1] The score published in 1826 is a drastically rewritten version. See Donald H. Foster, 'The Oratorio in Paris in the 18th Century', *Acta Musicologica*, xlvii (1975), pp. 119 ff.

represented a radical departure from his previous experience, for it was almost exclusively by his operas that Cherubini was known when, in his fiftieth year, he composed his Mass in F. It was then only by chance that he entered this new field; a holiday in the country and the importunity of a local choir combined to persuade him to explore the unfamiliar ground. What had been undertaken as hardly more than a gesture and diversion, was destined to have very important consequences. It turned the composer's mind towards religious music, a direction in which it was sustained by his subsequent appointment as Master of the Royal Choir in 1816, and led to what have since proved to be some of his most enduring achievements.

In keeping with the circumstances of its composition, the Mass in F (1809) wears a less premeditated air than most of Cherubini's productions. The beginning of the *Kyrie* has a natural ease and fluency that betokens an unusual degree of relaxation from the tight hold he normally maintained over his material. He disposes of the available orchestral resources – one flute, two clarinets, a bassoon, and two horns in addition to the strings – with a discrimination admirably matched to the intimate style of the work. In common with a large number of Masses of the period, it is scored for three voices only, soprano, tenor, and bass – male altos being scarce and the Catholic authorities having forbidden women to sing in church choirs in many parts of the Continent. The design, although agreeably less self-conscious than on other occasions, is none the less very astutely managed; the recapitulation and coda of the *Kyrie* is an example of inspired craftsmanship, giving no appearance of the mechanical repetition so frequently found elsewhere, but adding new significance to the initial statement by a slight, but telling, redistribution of emphasis. His expert technique is more often the servant than the master of his thought, and enables him to make the most of an incident of such tender charm as this:

Ex. 227

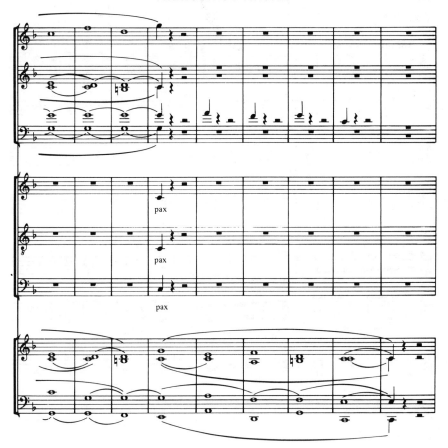

Later in the *Gloria*, in the opening phrase of the middle section, 'Laudamus te', Cherubini gains the reward of his comparative austerity in the use of chromaticism. In a predominantly diatonic context the passage has an emotional effect out of all proportion to its moderate harmonic complexity. In Spohr it might pass almost unnoticed.

Ex. 228

It is when the text seems to demand more formal expression of praise or faith that Cherubini is inclined to withdraw the quickening force of his personality, leaving only a cold official shell behind. On the other hand, the mystery of the Incarnation or the deep sense of personal tragedy implicit in the Crucifixion will produce a response that is strikingly human and sensitive.

Cherubini's Mass in D minor (1811), planned and carried out after his return to Paris, reflects the change from rural to metropolitan surroundings. Here there is no need to suit the scale to local exigencies, and full-size choral and orchestral resources are employed. Some of the intimacy of the earlier work is exchanged for breadth and dignity without, in most cases, sacrificing musical quality. This is exemplified in the orchestral introduction to the first movement which, while clearly marking from the outset the difference in character between the two Masses, yet does not achieve its spaciousness at the cost of intensity. In fact the Mass in D minor owes much of its distinction to the degree of reconciliation that Cherubini has managed to effect between the poetic and the architectural elements in his style.

It is perhaps in the fugue that concludes the *Kyrie* that this first becomes most clearly evident. The manner in which the exposition is presented, the voices *sempre piano* over a background of periodic quiet sustained chords on the strings and wind, is a sign that this is to be no mere academic product of the Conservatoire, while the beauty and eloquence of the counterpoint soon distract attention from the perfect finish of the technique. As the strands are gradually woven into a texture of serene loveliness, the fugal frame becomes less and less conspicuous until one almost ceases to be aware of it in admiration of the subtle colouring and rich expressive power of the design.

This expansiveness of spirit is continued into the *Gloria*, in which brilliance and conviction count for more than studied grace or ceremonial pomp. A real impetus sustains the triumphant cries of acclamation, and when the words 'Et in terra pax' are reached, they again form the substance of reflective interludes through which runs a note of genuine appeal. This would be the more impressive if Cherubini could have resisted the temptation, to which he often succumbed, of overworking a short phrase in imitative sequence. Moreover, this tendency underlines Cherubini's rather too prevalent weakness in thematic inventiveness.

There is more than a hint of opera in the lively ensembles of 'Laudamus te, glorificamus te' and in the suave cantilena of the 'Gratias', and this becomes more pronounced in the treatment of 'Qui tollis peccata mundi'. This section is dramatized into an effective contrast between the stern, reiterated flourishes that accompany 'Qui tollis peccata mundi' and the plaintive, drooping phrases of 'Miserere nobis'. One sees here, as again later in the 'Crucifixus', the emergence of that peculiarly Italian approach to the liturgy which was to reach its culmination in Verdi's Requiem. In the 'Quoniam' an interesting attempt is made to organize a choral movement on symphonic lines, after the manner of 'Nun schwanden vor dem heiligen Strahle' in *The Creation*. Cherubini cannot rival Haydn in keeping voices and orchestra independent and it is difficult to resist the conviction that the vocal line has been largely determined by instrumental considerations. For example, by omitting the contralto solo but without making any other alteration, the following passage would make an admirable starting point for a symphonic finale:

Ex. 229

Apart, however, from this fundamental incongruity, the movement is ingeniously developed, and, in addition to being delightful in itself, provides a refreshingly unconventional element in the general scheme of the Mass. It also enables the vigorous choral fugue of 'Cum sancto spiritu' to stand out in sharper contrast. For this is a straightforward fugal treatment of two subjects in which the orchestra is solely employed to support and reinforce the salient features of the choral line. The choice of themes, one broad and dignified, resembling an intonation, the other climbing the scale with irresistible impulse, seems to guarantee a brilliant outcome from the start. Cherubini's movement is sometimes liable to relapse as it progresses, but in this case he never checks the gathering momentum. The employment of operatic technique to obtain the utmost excitement in the coda is unquestionably justified in the result, which soars far above the theatrical.

After this peak the subsequent choral writing shows something of a recession. The 'Amen' chorus at the end of the *Credo* leads off at once with a brisk gait, but each stride covers only two short bars, and since this is never expanded, the prevailing impression is of bustling activity which expends much energy without a compensating return. The *Sanctus* and 'Hosanna' are appropriately festal in familiar terms, while the 'Benedictus' aspires to a quiet expressiveness which fails to convince owing to the inherent weakness of the musical substance. The *Agnus Dei* is more successful in this respect, but there is still an appreciable gap in spiritual quality between text and music. The fugal exposition of the 'Dona nobis pacem' is rather rigid and its rocking accompaniment figure is based on too short a rhythmic unit to impart either breadth or dynamic strength, yet despite these self-imposed handicaps, Cherubini manages to build up quite an imposing structure which he completes with a superb imaginative stroke that does much to redeem previous failings. The dramatic and moving final bars of this work restore it to its commanding position in Cherubini's achievement.

His other settings of the normal Mass do not add a great deal to our knowledge of Cherubini as a choral composer. In the Mass in C (1816) he is chiefly concerned with the possibilities of contrasting the solo voices, either singly or in ensemble, with the full choir. By this means he obtains many felicitous effects of tone-colour, but these are rarely supported by music of much intrinsic value.

The Mass in E minor (1818) presents a new approach to the artistic problem involved in setting the *Credo*. The long succession of separate clauses makes the composer's task of formal organization within a single movement a difficult one. Cherubini's method here is to use the orchestra as the unifying factor, by giving it a distinctive theme to develop throughout, over which the voices pronounce the text in stately, measured phrases. The character of the Creed as a personal confession of faith is retained more closely than usual by assigning a number of its constituent sections to each chorus part in unison or to individual solo voices, and reserving four-part harmony until 'Et resurrexit' is reached. For the 'Amen' the orchestral theme is used as a fugue subject, to which it is indifferently suited, and the chorus, by assuming a rather instrumental guise, join in its final apotheosis. Neither the original theme nor its subsequent treatment are particularly memorable, but the layout of the movement is a bold conception that creates a large measure of unity and generates considerable rhetorical force.

The intended coronation of Louis XVIII provided the occasion for which Cherubini's Mass in G (1819) was written. The spectacle of restored monarchy does not appear to have moved him very profoundly. His score wears its ceremonial robes with fitting solemnity in some places, rather easily in others. The *Kyrie* provokes a dramatic outburst that makes it sound more like a threat than a prayer. These last two Masses, together with the Short Mass in B flat (1821), a work of slight consequence, employ a four-part choir consisting of first and second sopranos (the latter in default of altos), tenors, and basses. The Mass in A (1825), written for the coronation of Charles X, reverts to the three-part scoring for voices (soprano, tenor, and bass) adopted in the Mass in F, but with the addition of a large-scale orchestra.

CHERUBINI'S REQUIEM MASSES

The two Requiem Masses are more important. That in C minor (1816) is for four-part mixed choir and orchestra, in which a special feature is the widespread use of the violas *divisi* (in three movements the violins are silent). The setting of the Introit 'Requiem aeternam' at once creates an atmosphere of sincerity and reverence in which one feels the influence of his long study of Palestrina and the other Italian polyphonic masters. The rather too obvious pages in which he uses his contrapuntal technique merely to keep the movement going are apt to make one overlook the more important occasions when the discreet use of discipline gives his style a strength and dignity in the highest traditions of Italian church music. In an epoch of increasing emotional extravagance Cherubini had a rare sense of poise.

Even the 'Dies Irae', although it naturally exploits the dramatic possibilities of the text, is kept well in hand and displays a vision of Judgement that is neither too lurid nor too plaintive. With the 'Pie Jesu' and *Agnus Dei* Cherubini regains the rapt, contemplative mood of the Introit. The first is a simple, touching appeal conveyed in the most intimate and subdued terms (this is one of the movements in which the lower strings only are used), and its meditative spirit is continued in the *Agnus*. Here the composer draws on his substantial creative reserve to provide a truly noble and thoughtful conclusion to an impressive work; the final strains of 'Et lux perpetua luceat eis' seem to lead the hearer away from earth and to vanish into some remote celestial perspective.

It is related that Cherubini's Requiem in C minor was chosen for the funeral of Boieldieu in 1834, but that owing to the ban on women singing in choirs, the ceremony had to take place in a chapel outside the jurisdiction of the Archbishop of Paris. Cherubini was so irritated by this display of intolerance that he declared he would write a Requiem for his own funeral to which no one could take exception. He was as good as his word; the Requiem in D minor (1836) needs male voices only. In the event it was by no means an ill chance that provoked this self-imposed limitation. The restriction of resources forced him to review the liturgical ground from a fresh angle, while the challenge to his technical virtuosity put him on his mettle.

Such is his command within this vocal compass that one is little aware of its comparatively narrow range. If he had banished the violins from parts of the C minor Requiem, here he will often exclude the violas as well, as in the *Kyrie*, but without appearing to lose his freedom of movement or constricting his expressive capacity. He is also more adventurous harmonically, and thereby underlines the drama of the Sequence, which he seems to have felt with something as near passion as he ever allowed himself to disclose. The note of personal entreaty at 'Oro supplex' is unmistakable and very moving. It is fervent, yet never abject:

Ex. 230

The darker colours of the men's voices allow the music to plumb great physical depths when in the Offertory, 'Ne absorbeat eas tartarus, nec cadant in obscurum' is reached, and in contrast the soaring phrase that emerges from the gloom seems to carry the hearer up to sublime heights for the vision of 'Signifer sanctus Michael'. Here again Cherubini invests the scene with special distinction by scoring of rare delicacy. The woodwind basis is so light that flute and violin can float above in serene detachment. The whole passage is truly luminous and impalpable; although the voices are confined to a low register, they are not permitted to cloud the transparency of the texture. One finds many other examples in this Requiem of Cherubini's skill in introducing freshness and buoyancy into a medium that might otherwise prove too consistently sombre. The rich, autumnal tones of the *Agnus Dei* epitomize the atmosphere of this noble work of old age, in which one detects many signs of an expansiveness of spirit.

Though perhaps neither of them would have admitted it, there was a place for both Berlioz and Cherubini in the artistic constitution of the Romantic movement. The young student represented the extremes of revolutionary impulsiveness and imaginative freedom; his hated Director, himself one of the earliest romantics, acted as a counterpoise in upholding a tradition based on sixteenth-century polyphony and eighteenth-century design, and demonstrating the essential continuity of musical thought.

SCHUBERT'S MASSES

With Schubert the case is very different. After the church music of Cherubini, the four quiet chords that open the early Mass in F (1814) by his young Viennese contemporary seem to usher in another world. Here all is warmth and tender lyricism. The supple, yielding phrases have an innocence and spontaneity that must touch the hearer even if they do not move him deeply; indeed every aspect of the *Kyrie*, from the scoring, which is skilful but discreet, to the design, which seems to enjoy instinctive freedom without becoming untidy, has an air of unstudied charm that is most refreshing. The doxology of *Gloria* is perforce more formal, though it has an invigorating youthful impulse, but when the 'Gratias' is reached, the vein of melody that is never far to seek in Schubert, comes to the surface again. Neither in the intimate quality of the cantilena nor in the eloquent flowing parts beneath it is there a hint of the aloof reticence of Cherubini – or, for that matter, much sign of the sentimentality that was to afflict Spohr. The line moves without constraint, as if guided by its own will and not according to some preconceived pattern. Where his generosity of spirit is curbed, as in the manifold clauses of the *Credo*, Schubert tends to lose interest, resuming his true inclination in the 'Benedictus' and *Agnus Dei*. His device of using the same material for the 'Dona nobis pacem' as in the *Kyrie* is entirely devoid of self-conscious artifice.

In none of his other youthful Masses does Schubert rise to the same level as in this first one, the most notable movement amongst them being the second 'Benedictus' of the Mass in C (1816), which was added in 1828. It is only when one reaches the Mass in A flat (1819) that he appears again to be fully in sympathy with his subject. Schubert was not a religious man, and it required more than a spirit of devotion to stir his creative energy, so it is fortunate that the opportunities for exploring choral texture afforded by the Mass evidently appealed to him strongly in certain moods, The *Kyrie* of the A flat Mass is a romantic idyll in which the delicate timbre of the voices (which scarcely rise above a mezzoforte throughout) is set against an almost impalpable orchestral background. The movement and spacing of the parts is contrived with such discrimination that sheer beauty of choral sound for its own sake is clearly one of Schubert's chief aims. This was a relatively new phenomenon in this type of music, but one that was destined to become more prominent as the Romantic movement developed. In settings of the liturgy, especially such short extracts as the *Kyrie*, where the same text could be repeated at will, composers could linger over a particularly colourful harmony or unusual effect of scoring without disturbing the balance of the design. It is in the reflective movements of his Masses, in which he could extend his lyrical genius and delight in newly forged harmonic progressions, unhampered by dramatic or symphonic exigencies, that Schubert is at his most characteristic. Thus, apart from the *Kyrie*, it is the 'Gratias' and the *Agnus Dei* of the A flat Mass that represent him best throughout their length. Elsewhere, notably in the poignant phrase associated with 'Crucifixus' and the vivid choral sequences of the *Sanctus*, there are lofty passages that could only spring from an exceptional imagination, but these are found amongst sections of a more pedestrian order. There are moments even when, contrary to his nature, he seems to follow Cherubini; the poetry of 'Domine Deus' is a little marred by the squareness of the rhythmic pattern and the formal exactitude of the repetitions. The monumental style of fugal chorus was not congenial to him. The contrapuntal conclusion of the *Gloria* is technically painstaking but is far too protracted in its attempt to manufacture vitality out of rather lifeless material. As for the scoring, the pointless bustling on the strings, maintained with dogged persistence throughout, and the doubling of the more florid voice parts on the trombones, are a relapse into antiquated methods. He makes an effort to secure artistic unity in the *Credo* by means of a recurring chordal motive, but can hardly be said to be successful; insistence on a musical statement at regular intervals will not serve the purpose if it is not equally appropriate in each context, and to treat the opening clause of the Creed and 'Confiteor meum baptisma' in the same way is to impose a misleading parallel on two different articles of faith.

The Mass in E flat (1828) shows much the same variation in quality according to the prevailing mood, but there is a more sensitive response to certain parts of the text that had hitherto failed to arouse any significant reaction. The *Gloria* opens in brilliant and sonorous style, after which the hushed reverence of 'Adoramus te' comes in impressive contrast, while the dramatic handling of 'Domine Deus' is forceful and compelling. The chronic stumbling block of 'cum sancto spiritu' does not prove much easier to negotiate, but the fugal setting is better constructed and more concise. The other fugal sections on 'Et vitam venturi' and 'Osanna in excelsis', show a further advance; in the former there is a welcome *a cappella* passage and the latter is based on a lively subject that produces a spirited sense of acclamation.

The sections to which Schubert was more temperamentally inclined produce, as one would expect, the richest yield. The *Kyrie* is more emphatic and less restricted in its dynamic range than that of the Mass in A flat; that it is also no less expressive may be judged from the following exquisite example of 'linked sweetness long drawn out':

Ex. 231

A comparison of the rich, yet controlled, use of new harmonic resource with the lavish and ineffectual chromaticism employed by Spohr under similar circumstances (Ex. 225) well illustrates the difference in calibre between the two composers. In many ways the most remarkable movement of all is the *Agnus Dei*. For this the main substance is derived from two themes, one in long sustained notes having the character of an intonation, the other with a flowing line that describes a smoothly graduated melodic curve. When these are woven together they form a rich choral texture of sombre beauty to which the orchestra adds a discreet embroidery. The whole design is splendidly dignified and is executed with unmistakable conviction. Unequal though it may be, Schubert's Mass in E flat is a noble tribute from one who was not primarily a choral, nor yet a religious, composer.

SCHUBERT'S OTHER SACRED MUSIC

Beside the Masses there are a number of shorter sacred works by Schubert, mostly dating from his early years. Amongst these must be mentioned two attractive settings of the 'Salve Regina' for solo soprano and orchestra. The first, in F (1815; wind parts added in 1823), is unashamedly operatic in style; the second, in A (1819) (which was left with accompaniment for strings only), is more restrained and contemplative, having a deeper basis for its cantilena. Within this category also are versions of the 'Stabat Mater' in the original (1815) and the vernacular (1816), the Latin words being set as one chorus movement while the German text by Klopstock is laid out on an elaborate scale in twelve separate sections. There is a delicate air of pathos about the former, but despite the slow tempo, its phrasing and idiom bring it perilously near a waltz rhythm. The latter has some pleasing moments, especially in the arias, but it cannot in general sustain so ambitious a plan. Other church music in German include a form of 'low Mass', a so-called *Deutsche Messe* (1827) for which Schubert supplied simple if not very distinguished music, and a touching version of Psalm 23 for four-part female chorus and pianoforte (1820). But the great bulk of his output is for the Latin ritual, and it was there that he made his most significant contribution, infusing into the formality of the ecclesiastical manner the warmth of Viennese lyricism.

BEETHOVEN'S C MAJOR MASS

Before both Cherubini's Mass in F and Schubert's first Mass in the same key came the first of Beethoven's two examples in this form, the Mass in C (1807). This fine work, once held in low esteem owing to largely irrelevant comparisons with the Mass in D, needs to be placed in its true perspective from the outset. Not only was it the first in point of time of the important settings of the Mass after Haydn's last masterpieces,[1] but it also remained unsurpassed in achievement by any of Beethoven's contemporaries. Thus whatever its relationship to the creative standard of the Mass in D, it occupies in its own right a very significant place in the particular sphere of liturgical music. With Beethoven's Mass in C the Viennese Mass reached its culmination; the Mass in D was to be universal in scope.

The qualities of the Mass in C are quick to reveal themselves. The simplicity of the material and the economy of its use in the *Kyrie* should not blind one to the unusual strength and cogency of its construction. There is a continuity of line and sense of purpose in this movement that at once set it apart from the routine productions of the time. Nor is its shape determined by the rigid frame Cherubini might have imposed; the music moves freely within its self-imposed limits and effects some distant modulations smoothly and without undue fuss. The rhythm, which might seem too square-cut when taken in small units, displays much pliancy if phrased broadly. As so often in Beethoven, the musical ideas must be read in complete sentences, not spelt out word by word.

Again, in the fugal sections, like 'Cum sancto spiritu' and 'Et vitam venturi', the development is never pretentious, as sometimes in Cherubini, or diffuse, as often in Schubert, but is continually governed by a clear feeling for direction. Beethoven treats choral fugue with much greater freedom than either Schubert or Cherubini, and is constantly searching for new expressive possibilities. The vigorous fugal writing of 'cum sancto spiritu' is surrounded by the majestic homophony of 'Quoniam tu solus sanctus' and eventually breaks through to the exaltation of 'Amen', alternately blazing with emphatic ardour and floating in ecstatic tranquillity. Fugue here is one of a number of resources combined to produce a visionary effect. The fugal treatment of 'Et vitam venturi' has equally unconventional features, reserving the full choral tutti until after the exposition has been completed and sealed off by the orchestra, and culminating in a coda whose serene diatonic passage-work for the soloists in turn, echoed by the instruments, anticipates the parallel section of the Mass in D. This is by no means the only instance of the later work being foreshadowed by the former – the contrast and combination of solo quartet and chorus in the 'Benedictus' being another – and one is continually

[1] See Vol. VII, pp. 319–23.

aware that Beethoven is building for the present and simultaneously
laying the foundations for the future. Indeed, so forward-looking is
the majority of the Mass in C, that on the rare occasions when it looks
back this comes as a surprise; the relatively stiff and short-winded
'Hosanna' passages seem to be an abrupt reversion to the Viennese
practice of thirty or forty years previously. In the course of the work
he makes several discoveries in choral texture as related to his own
style. One of the most notable for these is the rapid piling-up of
sonority by close successive entries; this is achieved with great
brilliance in the 'Quoniam' and with a noble lyricism towards the end
of the 'Dona nobis pacem'. Such moments as these belong to the Mass
in C alone, and yield to no comparison.

THE *MISSA SOLEMNIS*

With Beethoven's Mass in D (1819–23) the choral music of this
period reaches its summit. Its outlook is altogether loftier and broader
than any work previously considered; it is indeed one of the key points
from which one may survey man's achievement in music. Its spiritual
character is not confined to one creed although based on the Catholic
liturgy. Springing from Vienna, and based on Viennese culture, it
aspires far beyond such a limited scope. The grammar of its musical
language may be regional but its idiom is international.

For Beethoven the Mass in D was to be one of the major creative
ventures of his career. An imagination such as his could be fired by a
text, but it could not, in such a mood, be restricted by it. Haydn was
content to accept the general emotional temperature of the librettos of
his oratorios and let his inspiration blaze through it at frequent
intervals; Beethoven would admit no such limitation in the Mass in
D. He was not lacking in respect or reverence for the text, but in the
last analysis his artistic requirements were paramount. He was not
only concerned with providing the Mass with a great setting, but was,
perhaps principally, directing his full creative power towards
formulating one of the most important musical statements he had to
make, couched in terms specially fashioned for the purpose.

For side by side with the imaginative splendour of the Mass in D
stands the stylistic achievement. The intricate subjective polyphony
of Bach, in which each voice seems to be uttering a personal
commentary on the text, and the more homophonic textures and
clearer rhythms of Italian eighteenth-century choral music, which
found such magnificent expression in Handel and represented the
more collective attitude appeared destined to follow separate lines of
development. Sometimes the two styles may be seen in successive

movements, as in Mozart's Requiem and Haydn's *Creation*, but rarely is any serious attempt made to merge them together. Such inconsistency is not damaging when it is not at variance with the composer's main intention, but in case of the Mass in D it was central to Beethoven's purpose that there should be stylistic integration. He wanted the greatest available expressive range and the broadest front of communication, and for these he needed a consistent, universal language. The two styles which had hitherto been shown to contrast and interact, but not to blend, had to be fused so that their joint resources could be employed as a single technique, which would lend its unity to the conception of the work as a whole. Only a composer of Beethoven's stature would have attempted such a formidable task, or would have had the authority to carry it through against the accumulated weight of tradition. His success in this vital respect made the Mass in D an astonishing artistic phenomenon and a major historical landmark.

The dynamic energy of the work is implicit in its mighty upbeat opening and its vast scale is set by the slow harmonic rhythm with which first the orchestral introduction to the *Kyrie* and then the choral entries unfold. Phrase by phrase a monumental edifice of sound is built up on the Italian pattern; within this the soloists then meditate subjectively on the words 'Christe eleison', using Bach-like polyphony; and the structure is magnificently balanced about them by the return of the opening mood, extended and intensified. The union of the two styles has been impressively proclaimed and they have been brought together under a single span.

The *Gloria* shows the association at an even closer stage; it also repeats Beethoven's skilful use of the orchestra to assist in achieving formal unity. Since with his flexible technique the instruments can be entirely independent of the voices at will, problems of thematic repetition and development disappear. Whereas another composer might have tried to strain the opening melodic phrase, obviously conceived for 'Gloria in excelsis deo', to fit other lines of the text for the sake of formal balance, Beethoven assigns the theme to the orchestra in its later appearances, while the chorus either take an appropriate section of it, as at 'Laudamus te' or declaim quite independently, as at 'Domine Deus'. Thus one of the most obstructive technical problems facing composers of choral music at this period is solved. The distance that Beethoven has travelled beyond even the high imaginative level of the Mass in C appears in the Larghetto section 'Qui tollis'. The expressive woodwind introduction recalls the earlier work in movement and texture, as does the antiphonal writing for chorus and soloists later, but the deep religious significance of the words at this point leads Beethoven far further than before towards unexplored regions of emotional response. After the extraordinary tension of this passage the direct affirmation of 'Quoniam tu solus sanctus' comes as a relief – of short duration since the movement then plunges into a powerful and closely wrought fugal setting of 'In gloria Dei patris, Amen'. At first the subject, with its initial 'upbeat' semibreve and strongly accented sequential quavers, has a Handelian air but its countersubjects and continuations grow into a polyphonic density nearer to Bach. As with him, the sheer intellectual energy that is generated more than compensates for the loss of clarity. Where the orchestra had shown its value earlier in establishing a formal point, so now as the fugue approaches its final climax it is made to contribute discreetly to rhythmic momentum. Quiet detached chords on the woodwind and brass gently impel the vocal lines forward, in a situation where mere doubling would be both inappropriate and ineffective. The vocal and orchestral partners have achieved a very subtly integrated relationship. Their joint brilliance blazes forth in the coda, leaving the last bright ringing call to the chorus – a masterstroke.

The *Credo*, with its long succession of clauses, sets a notoriously difficult problem for the composer. Beethoven accepts the challenge with great confidence, and the tremendous affirmation of the opening bars of this setting provides a rock-like foundation on which the whole movement can be built. Each clause receives appropriate treatment without producing an episodic effect; the sharply characterized musical sections seem to flow logically into one another, following a continuous line of musical thought. An unusual device of verbal and musical punctuation is the repetition of the word 'et' to separate clauses or groups of clauses. The word 'non' from 'cujus regni non erit finis' is also repeated most emphatically before the principal return of the opening subject. This subject is now treated as a kind of ostinato, around which a number of clauses are declaimed freely in speech rhythm. This is a very apt structural device, but it does not sound in the least contrived; the insistent 'Credo, credo' from the *ostinato* voices strengthens the avowals of faith at a point in which musical settings are liable to flag and carries the movement irresistibly forward to the massive unison declaration 'Et expecto resurrectionem mortuorum'. What may be regarded as the central point in Beethoven's conception of the Mass in D is now reached. In contrast to the lengthy preceding text of the *Credo*, this great culminating section is confined to a setting of the words 'Et vitam venturi saeculi Amen'. Initially the texture is fugal, with growing intensity of detail, but the climaxes show how easily Beethoven, now in command of a fully integrated style, can make intricate and involved polyphony emerge into the spaciousness of monumental harmonies, into which the built-up tensions of the fiercely interacting counterpoint can be released. This is the conclusive demonstration of the synthesis to which the work aspired, both technically and emotionally convincing. For good measure, Beethoven shows in the superb coda that a decorative, almost operatic style is also capable of fusion with the other elements. The soloists' ornate coloratura seems to extend quite naturally into the orchestra, where it provides a graceful frieze above the closing scene of the movement – dramatic both in its expression and achievement.

In contrast the *Sanctus* is a solemn, almost sombre, vision of holiness; short but deeply felt. Brilliance does not return until the 'Pleni sunt coeli' and the triple time 'Osanna in excelsis' that follows. In these two sections Beethoven recalls similar brief contrapuntal movements in the earlier Viennese type Masses; but in these very different surroundings they take on a new significance. For their terseness of statement and strongly accented rhythmic vitality make the tranquil lyricism of the 'Benedictus' even more persuasive. The violin solo floats serenely above undertones of menace on the brass and awed mutterings from the chorus. Not even the outburst at the repetition of 'Osanna' can disturb the cantilena, which seems the very embodiment in sound of the concept of blessing.

The *Agnus Dei* opens with a threefold entreaty growing gradually but inexorably with cumulative power. There is very close liaison between voices and orchestra here; there is little doubling of the voices, yet the fabric is so closely interwoven that it is hardly possible to separate the strands. (This is a long way from the treatment of the orchestra as a ritornello group, so widely prevalent not many years previously.) The main subject, which consists of two dovetailing sections, is typical of this impression of two forces working as one; its first half is assigned to the orchestra, the second half belongs to the voices, both contributing to a single consistent statement. In the concluding pages of the work Beethoven presses on beyond his task of synthesis, so triumphantly accomplished, and enters a completely new area of expression. At the words 'Dona nobis pacem' he heads the score 'Bitte um innern und äussern Frieden', which may be rendered 'A prayer for spiritual and political peace'. As the music progresses the prayer begins to be so clamorous and insistent as to amount to a demand – Beethoven's keen sense of man's predicament will permit him no restraint here. He has ceased to be concerned with the liturgical aspect of the work, and is only in very general terms concerned with its religious function. But he is passionately involved in the human struggle fought in mind and body, and the music alternates, for much of the time, between warlike symbolism and fervent appeals for peace. Rarely can a 6/8 rhythm have been so restless and searching; only one serene phrase seems to promise reassurance, and that at length prevails and the prayer ends on a note of confidence.

BEETHOVEN'S CONTEMPORARIES

Since we have now reached the apotheosis of the settings of the Mass in this period, it may be appropriate to compare Beethoven's methods with those of the other principal exponents in this field. A brief extract from the beginning of the *Credo* of a Mass by each composer will give an idea of their respective style and relative stature. Cherubini presents us with a formal, dogmatic statement:

Ex. 232

Schubert's belief is expressed in warmer, more emotional terms:

Ex. 233

SCHUBERT: Mass in E flat

With Beethoven the declaration has an invincible strength that represents all mankind united by a mighty bond of faith:

Ex. 234

BEETHOVEN: Mass in D

To such a degree does Beethoven's Mass in D tower above its neighbours that it is difficult to retain the necessary sense of proportion when leaving it to consider works on a lower level. But despite this disparity, there is a certain amount of other liturgical music of which brief mention must be made in order to get a comprehensive view of the contemporary scene. Within this category one would certainly include the Masses of Michael Haydn (1737–1806), which provide a valuable link between baroque church music and the new tendencies of the early nineteenth century. His *Missa St. Francisci* (1803), for instance, is a sound piece of craftmanship, even if it contains little that is memorable. The pleasing impression it gives is slightly vitiated by the composer's irritating habit (which he shared with many others of his time) of keeping the accompanying strings in a state of continuous bustling activity that contributes nothing to the total effect except a certain specious animation. Also of the older generation was Luigi Boccherini (1743–1805), whose 'Stabat Mater' is the most distinguished of a not very numerous company. It has all the grace and charm (and rather more depth of feeling) that one would expect from so polished a chamber-music composer. The expert use of the string ensemble in support of the voice is its most remarkable feature, as the following extract indicates:

Ex. 235

(Most renowned virgin of virgins, please be not harsh to me, suffer me to weep with thee.)

Other composers who ventured occasionally from their normal medium into the realms of choral music include Giovanni Paisiello (1741–1816), Vincenzo Bellini (1801–35), J. N. Hummel (1778–1837), and Weber. The first of these made the most extensive but at the same time the most superficial contribution. Indeed there are passages that make one wonder at the circumstances that permitted such meaningless vapidity in ecclesiastical surroundings as the 'Oro supplex' of a Requiem Mass:

Ex. 236

Bellini had far more self-respect, and though his suave melodic style is ill-suited to express sincere religious conviction, he is never slovenly. His A minor Mass would not pass as church music even on the stage, but viewed apart from its context it has undeniable charm. On the other hand, the easy fluency of Hummel's pianoforte writing is transmuted into something more solid in his larger choral works. There is a seriousness of purpose here that demands respect, and some moments of real poetic imagination, notably in his Mass in D (1808):

Ex. 237

The sacred music of Weber does not alter appreciably the estimate
of his choral methods from his pieces for secular occasions. He is
palpably less at home in ecclesiastical surroundings, and never seems
quite sure what attitude to adopt towards his text, which leads to
strange inconsistencies. Some beautiful and arresting phrases give a
hint of great potentialities but the total result is disappointing. Even
his finest liturgical work, the E flat Mass of 1818, is partly pasticcio.

Though nominally a church composer, Le Sueur always give the
impression that he should properly have been cast in an operatic role
from the start. His Masses abound in 'stage directions', whose high-
flown terms the music sometimes finds it difficult to support. In the
Gloria of his First Mass in B flat (1786?) the second soprano is directed
to acquire 'le ton, les intentions, l'accent naif et cependant joyeux, qui
conviennent à l'Ange des célestes nouvelles, publiant les divers bien
faits du ciel répandus sur les hommes', and is then given this not very
elevated material to work upon:

Ex. 238

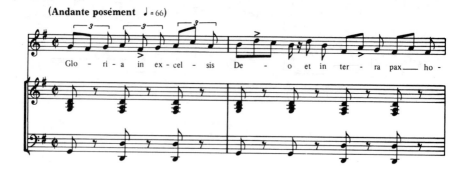

Elsewhere his passion for theatrical effect is indulged in the most unpredictable manner. One would have hardly expected an operatic finale at this point in the 'Qui sedes':

Ex. 239

Yet, despite these inequalities and incongruities, Le Sueur is an engaging figure, possessed of a lively and inventive mind. His music is at least more diverting than that of some of his contemporaries in other parts of Europe. There is little creative strength, for instance, in the output of most Spanish composers during this period. Mariano Rodriguez de Ledesma (1779–1847) in his motet 'Principes persecuti sunt' sometimes comes near to asserting a personality of his own, but in the main he is content to be a pale reflection of a Viennese original or even Weber whom he greatly admired. Francisco Cabo (1768–1832), eschewing the baroque style, follows in the earlier Spanish polyphonic tradition and earns a certain respect without, however, achieving anything very noteworthy. It was left to Juan Crisóstomo Arriaga (1806–26) in his setting of the *Stabat Mater* for male voices and orchestra to show signs of emerging individuality which his early death did not allow him to mature.

SAMUEL WESLEY

There is a welcome freshness and independence about the English contribution, which emanates chiefly from one man. Thomas Attwood (1765–1838) had a talent to be reckoned with, but it is Samuel Wesley (1766–1837) who above all dominates the scene. His firm handling of contrapuntal technique and keen sense of spacing and sonority in massive choral effects give his fine Latin motets real distinction. Wesley rarely fumbles, he knows what he wants to say and how to say it, and his idiom is by no means conventional. At his best his music has a rhythmic pliancy within the bar and the phrase that is in admirable contrast to the prevailing squareness of this period. In his motet 'Exultate Deo' this springs almost naturally from the dynamic vitality of the theme, which is treated with much resourcefulness and attended by great freedom and virtuosity in the part-writing. A particularly impressive passage is introduced by a quiet harmonization of the subject:

Ex. 240

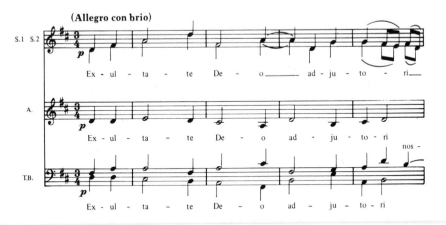

These motets show remarkably little Continental influence: Wesley follows his own course with complete integrity and undeviating purpose. Such allegiance as he owns is to the Elizabethan school, where he finds a great source of strength. Here is a cadence in 'Constitues eos principes' that Byrd would not have despised:

Ex. 241

(They will be mindful of thy name, Lord.)

Slender as is the significant part of his achievement – which must certainly include the large-scale 'Confitebor',[1] 'In exitu Israel' and 'Tu es sacerdos' in addition to the above – it shows enormous potential.

[1] Ed. John Marsh, *Musica Britannica*, xli (1978).

BORTNYANSKY

Russian church music differs from that of the West in several respects. The Orthodox liturgy in Church Slavonic has almost nothing in common with that of the Catholic rite and its music is restricted by an absolute veto on any kind of instrumental participation. Nevertheless a polyphonic style *sui generis* energed during the eighteenth century. A number of Russian musicians were sent to study in Italy and the most gifted of them, Dmitry Stepanovich Bortnyansky (1751–1825) became director of the Imperial Chapel in 1796 and wrote for it a great number of psalm-concertos and 'cherubic hymns'. Two excerpts from the first section of his Concerto, no. 21, on passages from Psalm 91, give some idea of his style:

Ex. 242

    (i) (He that dwelleth in the secret place of the most High shall abide under the shadow of the Almighty.)   (ii) (In him will I trust.)

SMALL SECULAR FORMS

The end of the eighteenth century saw a considerable revival of interest in secular choral music on a much smaller and more informal scale. Particularly was this so in respect of compositions for male voices, with or without accompaniment. It is a natural tendency for convivial assemblies to seek choral expression at some stage of their proceedings, especially when encouraged by certain kinds of stimulus. These appear to have been rarely lacking, at any rate amongst the English, since one meets frequent references to 'gin punch' and 'kettles of burnt champagne' in accounts of their musical gatherings, and there were few composers of this period who did not consider it, if not a musical, at least a social duty to provide suitably for such occasions. The nature of their offerings varied to a certain extent – Beethoven favoured canons, Schubert and Weber part-songs, Wesley the glee – but they were all of a simple and unpretentious character.

The canon is perhaps the least satisfying type from the point of view of the audience, however enjoyable it may be to the performer (for whom, after all, it is designed). But Beethoven's ingenuity is continual, and if the musical result is slight, the humour, ponderous at times, can also be lively and full of point – as in 'Ich bitt' dich'. The part-song of this epoch is less of a mere companionable diversion and more of an artistic species, though it too does not aspire to any great profundity. The several sets by Weber, for instance, consist of straightforward harmonizations of a few short strains, which are repeated for each verse of the lyric. Rarely does he attempt even the most elementary tone-painting, but the quiet, rippling effect in 'Schlummerlied' (*Sechs Gesänge*, Op. 68) produces a delicate, veiled atmosphere.

The examples by Schubert are far more substantial. In some a typically spontaneous melody will be carried over a lilting dance measure ('Die Nachtigall', Op. 11, no. 2, and 'Frühlingsgesang', Op. 16, no. 1), in others a more reflective, but no less lyrical vein will be pursued by means of richer harmonies, strong in romantic allusion ('Geist der Liebe', Op. 11, no. 3, and 'Mondenschein', Op. 102). There are some unusual additions to the rather restricted amount of colour possessed by the male voice ensemble; the delicious serenade 'Zögernd, leise' has an alto solo that gives a welcome extension to the combined vocal range as well as admirable contrast in tone through dialogue with the chorus (both these qualities lose their force in the arrangement for female voices), while the unique employment of a quartet of horns in the noble 'Nachtgesang im Walde' is a fine poetic stroke. In one outstanding case, the 'Gesang der Geister über den

Wassern', the original unaccompanied four-part male voice setting could not contain the text within such a narrow frame, and it had later to be expanded over a wider canvas. A comparison of the two versions is interesting in its indication of the points at which Schubert felt that his limited earlier resources were insufficient to evoke the conflicting images of Goethe's poem. By entirely recasting his material on the basis of further subdivision of the voices into eight parts with a background of violas, cellos, and basses, a rather inconsequential essay is transformed into a most impressive piece of creative interpretation.

The English glee has some claim to be considered an independent variant of the part-song type. It was strictly for unaccompanied male voices and a special feature was the regular use of the male alto register, which was not greatly cultivated on the Continent. The glees also sought to find a different way between the 'strophic' and the 'continuous' methods of setting the words in a part-song by suiting each separate self-contained musical section to the changing moods of the text. Glees became extremely popular, and great numbers of them were produced, mainly for the consumption of the glee clubs that were springing up everywhere. Amongst the most notable glee composers were Samuel Webbe (1740–1816), R. J. S. Stevens (1757–1837), Sir Henry Bishop (1786–1855), and Samuel Wesley who, even in this very different sphere, preserves the distinctive personality he displays in his motets.

THE MUSIC OF THE FRENCH REVOLUTION

In conclusion some account must be given of the music written for the festivals and ceremonies of the French Revolution, since a large proportion of this was choral. The Revolution coincided with a period when France was well supplied with musicians of high calibre. At its inception Gossec was conductor of the band of the Garde Nationale, and when the musical element of this latter institution was used as the nucleus on which was founded the Conservatoire National de Musique in 1795, personalities of the eminence of Cherubini, Méhul, and Le Sueur were available to join Gossec in the first inspectorate.

The new Republic demanded of its composers a resourceful and adaptable outlook. Trained to the fervent, even effusive, celebration of the Divine Right of Kings, they were now suddenly called upon to devote their talents to extolling the virtue of republican ideals, subjects hitherto hardly mentioned under the breath behind locked doors, let alone declaimed by massed choirs on the Champ de Mars. To shift one's artistic ground from the godlike properties of reigning monarchs to the yet more celestial qualities of official regicides demands a constitutional agility not possessed by all. There are signs that some found the strain upon their creative versatility to be too severe, and fell back upon a comfortable, non-committal idiom which served them equally for Hymns to Agriculture, Odes on the State of the Republic, and National Tributes to the Goddess of Reason.

The conditions for which the music in these different festivals was required to be adapted were also markedly different from anything that composers had previously encountered. Instead of the studied dignity of some coronation in a great cathedral, there was the uncontrolled improvisation of a vast popular concourse in the open air, and most of the methods employed for the one would have been hopelessly inappropriate to the other. This fundamental conflict is revealed with disarming frankness by Gossec in his *Te Deum* written for 14 July 1790 on the Champ de Mars. The work opens with a sprightly introduction, such as might have heralded the rise of the curtain on one of his light operas, then with the entry of the voices changes to a spacious ceremonial style suggesting elaborate ecclesiastical pageantry; but this is not maintained for long before it is deemed necessary to give the public, who might already be shuffling inattentively, a lively passepied to occupy their restless feet. When music ventures outside four walls, the resulting diffusion of sound and lack of cohesion amongst the audience materially increase the task of the composer in making and retaining contact. Simplicity of statement, clarity of outline, and incisiveness in orchestral colouring are invaluable qualities in such situations and since these were characteristic traits of their style it is not surprising that composers of the type of Gossec and Méhul achieved considerable success. Viewed in cold print, without the excitement of the occasion or the ardour of the participants, their odes and hymns seem rather empty and banal, but there are moments, such as the following from Gossec's *Hymne à la Liberté* (1792), when one gets a passing sensation of glowing fires of revolutionary zeal:

Ex. 243

(Let all France exclaim, 'Long live Liberty!')

It was also Gossec who arranged for chorus and orchestra the more famous *Hymne à la Liberté* known as the 'Marseillaise', written in 1792 by J. Rouget de Lisle. With the sureness of unguided instinct this fulfils exactly its necessary function, and springs confidently forward where learning and experience would fumble to seek a footing.

Gossec's pupil, Charles Simon Catel (1773–1830) followed his master in contributing substantially to this national fund of occasional music and, at rather wider intervals, gives a hint of a certain lyrical charm. This gently felicitous passage from his *Ode Patriotique* (1793) is prompted by the image of the river Seine:

Ex. 244

(Fair nymph, honour of Paris, guide your stream into the heart of Neptune, that thereby all rivers may acknowledge you their queen.)

But for significance of content the most consistently high standard in this connection is maintained by Cherubini whose impregnable technique was so firmly ingrained in his nature as to forbid a casual or perfunctory approach to his subject, whether it were *Chant républicain du 10 août* (1795), *Hymne Funèbre sur la mort du Général Hoche* (1797), or *Ode sur le 18 Fructidor* (1798). That he must sometimes have been sorely tried is evident from the character of the lines (wisely anonymous) entitled 'Le Salpètre Républicain', which he was given to set in 1798. The first verse ends thus:

Ex. 245

(To call on Pitt by ship, all we need is saltpetre.)

Elsewhere, however, he had more of a chance, and the results are usually worthy, if a trifle sententious, and are invariably delivered in orderly, deliberate fashion with every detail carefully finished. One suspects that it was this very conscientiousness of his that prevented him from really entering into the spirit of these popular demonstrations. For Cherubini never seems at ease amongst the revolutionaries; whatever his personal opinions, musically his place is in the tumbril rather than with the mobs that speeded it to the guillotine.

If it were only a question of temperament, then Le Sueur should have been almost ideally suited to this sort of task. In him there was no lack of iconoclastic, dramatic fervour or vaulting aspiration, no diffidence in handling large choral masses or in serving as the mouthpiece of popular emotions. The man who aimed at taking the theatre into the church would have had no hesitation in dramatising the Republican creed to obtain the maximum effect over the greatest number. Unfortunately his ambition exceeded his capacity, and he never quite succeeded in carrying off the fine abandon of his manner. His scores are almost as individual as those of his famous pupil, but the personality behind them is not nearly so rich. Le Sueur can manage a large canvas with assurance, as in the *Chant du 1er Vendémiaire An IX* with its orchestra, soloists, and four diversely situated choirs. But whereas Berlioz, using comparable forces in his Requiem, puts them to convincing musical ends, too often with Le Sueur the outcome is merely 'sound and fury', signifying but little. A good deal of theatrical excitement is generated during the course of the *Scène patriotique* (1794) and some rather questionable elation displayed in the *Chant dithyrambique pour l'entrée triomphale des objects de Science et d'Art recueillis* (sic) *en Italie,* but the artistic interest of both pieces is largely ephemeral. By this unexpectedness Le Sueur would have held the attention of his contemporary audience, but once curiosity was satisfied, there was little left to claim more profound consideration.

The importance of this music of the French Revolution lies not so much in its intrinsic value, as in the role it plays in a great social movement. Organized music, which had for so long served lords spiritual or temporal, now made articulate the will of the people. The united voices of the community spoke through the medium of choral song inspired by the same passionate faith and held firm by an inner bond of sympathy. Thus in these festal and ceremonial odes and hymns the musical function of the chorus is transcended by its symbolic representation of the brotherhood of man entering, full of hope, upon a new epoch and uplifted in the first, undimmed glow of idealism.

BIBLIOGRAPHY

The bibliographies for Chapters III and VI have been compiled by William Drabkin, and all others by Margaret Ross Griffel.

GENERAL

(i) Modern Anthologies

ABERT, ANNE AMALIE: *Die Oper: von den Anfängen bis zum Beginn des 19. Jahrhunderts* (*Das Musikwerk*, v) (Cologne, 1953, English edition 1962).

GINZBURG, SEMYON LVOVICH, ed.: *Istoriya russkoy muzïki v notnïkh obraztsakh*, ii and iii (Leningrad and Moscow, 1949 and 1952).

POHANKA, JAROSLAV: *Dějiny české hudby v příkladech* (Prague, 1958).

STEPHENSON, KURT: *Romantik in der Tonkunst* (*Das Musikwerk*, xxi) (Cologne, 1961, English edition 1961).

STRUMIŁŁO, TADEUSZ, ed.: *Źródła i początki romantyzmu w muzyce polskiej*, suppl. vol. of musical examples (Cracow, 1956).

WOLFF, HELLMUTH CHRISTIAN, ed.: *Die Oper III: 19. Jahrhundert* (*Das Musikwerk*, xl) (Cologne, 1972, English edition 1975).

(ii) Books and Articles

ABBIATI, FRANCO: *Storia della musica*, iv (2nd ed., Milan, 1945).

ABERT, ANNA AMALIE: 'Die Oper zwischen Barock und Romantik. Ein Bericht über die Forschung seit dem Zweiten Weltkrieg', *Acta musicologica*, xlix (1977), pp. 137–93.

ADLER, GUIDO, ed.: *Handbuch der Musikgeschichte*, ii (2nd ed., Berlin, 1930, repr. Tutzing, 1961).

BECKER, HEINZ, ed.: *Beiträge zur Geschichte der Oper* (*Studien zur Musikgeschichte des 19. Jahrunderts*, xv), (Regensburg, 1969).

—— *Die 'Couleur locale' in der Oper des 19. Jahrhunderts* (*Studien zur Musikgeschichte des 19. Jahrhunderts*, xlii) (Regensburg, 1976).

—— *Geschichte der Instrumentation* (*Das Musikwerk*, xxiv) (Cologne, 1964, English edition 1964).

BECKING, GUSTAV: 'Klassik und Romantik', *Bericht über den I. musikwissenschaftlichen Kongress der Deutschen Musikgesellschaft in Leipzig . . . 1925*, i (Leipzig, 1926), pp. 292–6.

BERNARD, ROBERT: *Histoire de la musique*, ii (Paris, 1961).

BLUME, FRIEDRICH: *Classic and Romantic Music, A Comprehensive Survey* (New York, 1970).

Bücken, Ernst: *Die Musik des 19. Jahrhunderts bis zur Moderne*, vol. v of *Handbuch der Musikwissenschaft* (Wildpark-Potsdam, 1929, repr. New York, 1949).

Carse, Adam: *The Orchestra from Beethoven to Berlioz* (Cambridge, 1948).

Cole, Malcolm S.: 'Sonata-Rondo, The Formulation of a Theoretical Concept in the 18th and 19th Centuries', *Musical Quarterly*, lv (1969), pp. 180–92.

Dahlhaus, Carl: *Die Musik des 19. Jahrhunderts*, vol. vi of *Neues Handbuch der Musikwissenschaft* (Wiesbaden, 1980).

Dalton, David: 'Goethe and the Composers of his Time', *Music Review*, xxxiv (1973), pp. 157–74.

Dent, Edward: *The Rise of Romantic Opera* (Cambridge, 1976).

—— 'The Romantic Spirit in Music', *Proceedings of the Royal Musical Association*, lix (1932–3), pp. 85–102.

Druskin, M. S. and Keldïsh, Y., edd.: *Ocherki po istorii russkoy muzïki,1790–1825* (Moscow, 1956).

Dumesnil, René: *La Musique romantique française* (Paris, 1944).

Einstein, Alfred: *Music in the Romantic Era* (New York, 1947).

Farinelli, A[rturo]: 'Il Romanticismo e la musica', *Rivista musicale italiana*, xxxiii (1926), pp. 161–80.

Fischer, Wilhelm: 'Instrumentalmusik von 1750–1828', *Handbuch der Musikgeschichte*, ed. Guido Adler, ii (2nd ed., Berlin, 1930, repr. Tutzing, 1961), pp. 795–833.

Forchert, Arno: '"Klassisch" und "romantisch" in der Musikliteratur des frühen 19. Jahrhunderts', *Die Musikforschung*, xxxi (1978), pp. 405–425.

Goldron, Romain: *Du Romantisme à l'expressionisme*, vol. ix of *Histoire de la musique*, (Lausanne, 1966).

—— *Les Débuts de romantisme*, vol. viii of *Histoire de la musique* (Lausanne, 1966).

Grout, Donald Jay: *A Short History of Opera* (2nd ed., New York, 1965).

Hanslick, Eduard: *Geschichte des Concertwesens in Wien* (Vienna, 1869–70, repr. Farnborough, 1971).

Istel, Edgar: *Die Blütezeit der musikalischen Romantik in Deutschland* (Leipzig, 1909).

Jachimecki, Zdzisław: *Muzyka polska w rozwoju historycznym*, i/2 (Cracow, 1951).

Keldïsh, Yury: *Istoriya russkoy muzïki*, i (Moscow and Leningrad, 1948).

Knepler, Georg: *Musikgeschichte des 19. Jahrhunderts*, 2 vols. (Berlin, 1960–1).

Lang, Paul Henry: *Music in Western Civilization* (New York, 1941).

Le Huray, Peter and Day, James, edd.: *Music and Aesthetics in the Eighteenth and Early-Nineteenth Centuries* (Cambridge, 1981).

Levasheva, O., Keldïsh, Y. and Kandinsky, A., edd.: *Istoriya russkoy muzïki*, i (Moscow, 1972).

Lissa, Zofia: 'Polish Romanticism and Neo-Romanticism', *Polish Music*, ed. Stefan Jarociński (Warsaw, 1965), pp. 104–27.

Loewenberg, Alfred: *Annals of Opera 1597–1940* (Cambridge, 1943; 3rd ed., Totowa, N.J., 1978).

Longyear, Rey M.: *Nineteenth-Century Romanticism in Music* (2nd ed., Englewoods Cliffs, N.J., 1973).

Newman, William S.: *The Sonata in the Classic Era* (2nd ed., Chapel Hill, N.C., 1972).

—— *The Sonata Since Beethoven* (2nd ed., Chapel Hill, N.C., 1972).

Nowak-Romanowicz, Alina, et al.: *Z dziejów polskiej kultury muzycznej*, ii (Cracow, 1965).

Riemann, Hugo: *Handbuch der Musikgeschichte*, ii/3 (Leipzig, 1922, repr. New York, 1972).

Ringer, Alexander L.: 'On the Question of "Exoticism" in 19th Century Music'. *Studia musicologica*, vii (1965), pp. 115–23.

RITZEL, FRED.: *Die Entwicklung der "Sonataform" im musiktheoretischen Schrifttum des 18. und 19. Jahrhunderts* (*Neue musikgeschichtlichen Forschungen*, i) (Wiesbaden, 1968).

ROSEN, CHARLES: *Sonata Forms* (New York, 1980).

SALMEN, WALTER, ed. *Beiträge zur Geschichte der Musikanschauung im 19. Jahrhundert* (*Studien zur Musikgeschichte des 19. Jahrhunderts*, i) (Regensburg, 1965).

SMITH, PATRICK J.: *The Tenth Muse. A Historical Study of the Libretto* (New York, 1970).

STRUMIŁŁO, TADEUSZ, ed.: *Źródła i początki romantyzmu w muzyce polskiej* (Cracow, 1956).

STRUNK, OLIVER, ed.: *Source Readings in Music History* (New York, 1950). Also available in separate volumes, including vol. iv: *The Classic Era* and vol. v: *The Romantic Era* (New York, 1965).

TIERSOT, JULIEN: *La Musique aux temps romantiques* (Paris, 1930).

TISCHLER, HANS: 'Classicism, Romanticism, and Music', *Music Review*, xiv (1953), pp. 205–8.

WAGNER, MANFRED: *Die Harmonielehren der ersten Hälfte des 19. Jahrhunderts* (*Studien zur Musikgeschichte des 19. Jahrhunderts*, xxxviii) (Regensburg, 1974).

WOLFF, HELLMUTH CHRISTIAN: *Oper: Szene und Darstellung von 1600 bis 1900*, vol. iv/1 of *Musikgeschichte in Bildern*, ed. Heinrich Besseler and Max Schneider (Leipzig, 1968).

CHAPTER I

GENERAL MUSICAL CONDITIONS

(i) Books and Articles

BLUME, FRIEDRICH: 'Bach in the Romantic Era', *Musical Quarterly*, 1 (1964), pp. 290–306.

BRION, MARCEL: *Daily Life in the Vienna of Mozart and Schubert* (New York, 1962).

DAHLHAUS, CARL: 'Romantik und Biedermeier. Zur musikgeschichtlichen Charakteristik der Restaurationszeit', *Archiv für Musikwissenschaft*, xxxi (1974), pp. 22–41.

DORIAN, FREDERICK: *The History of Music in Performance. The Art of Musical Interpretation from the Renaissance to our Day* (New York, 1942, repr. New York, 1966).

DUCKLES, VINCERT: 'Johann Nicolaus Forkel: the Beginning of Music Historiography', *Eighteenth-Century Studies*, i (Spring, 1968), pp. 277–90.

—— 'Patterns in the Historiography of 19th-Century Music', *Acta musicologica*, xlii (1970), pp. 75–82.

EHINGER, HANS: *E.T.A. Hoffmann als Musiker und Musikschriftsteller* (Olten and Cologne, 1954).

EINSTEIN, ALFRED: *Nationale und universale Musik* (Zurich, 1958).

ELKIN, ROBERT: *The Old Concert Rooms of London* (London, 1955).

ELVERS, RUDOLF: *Breitkopf & Härtel 1719–1969. Ein historischer Überblick zum Jubiläum* (Wiesbaden, 1968).

FELLINGER, IMOGEN: *Verzeichnis der Musikzeitschriften des 19. Jahrhunderts* (*Studien zur Musikgeschichte des 19. Jahrhunderts*, x) (Regensburg, 1968).

FORKEL, JOHANN NIKOLAUS: *Allgemeine Litteratur der Musik* (Leipzig, 1792, repr. Hildesheim, 1962).

[GARDETON, CÉSAR]: *Bibliographie musicale de la France et de l'étranger* (Paris, 1822), repr. as vol. vi of *Archives de l'Édition Musicale Française* (Geneva, 1978).

GEIRINGER, KARL: '"The Friends of Music" in Vienna (1812–1937)' *Musical Quarterly*, xxiv (1938), pp. 243–8.

GERBER, ERNST LUDWIG: *Neues historisch-biographisches Lexikon der Tonkünstler*, 4 vols. (Leipzig, 1812–14), repr. with suppl. of contemporary additions, corrections and reviews, ed. Othmar Wessely, 3 vols. (Graz, 1966–9).

GRAF, MAX: *Composer and Critic. Two Hundred Years of Music Criticism* (New York, 1946, repr. New York, 1971).

HARDING, ROSAMOND E. M.: *The Piano-Forte, Its History Traced to the Great Exhibition of 1851* (Cambridge, 1933, repr. New York, 1973).

HEUSSNER, HORST: 'Das Biedermeier in der Musik', *Die Musikforschung*, xii (1959), pp. 422–31.

HEYER, HERMANN, ed.: *Festschrift zum 175 jährigen Bestehen der Gewandhauskonzerte 1781–1956* (Leipzig, 1956).

HITCHCOCK, H. WILEY: *Music in the United States: A Historical Introduction* (2nd ed., Englewood Cliffs, N.J., 1974).

HUMPHRIES, CHARLES and SMITH, WILLIAM: *Music Publishing in the British Isles from the Beginning until the Middle of the Nineteenth Century* (2nd ed., with suppl., Oxford, 1970).

KING, ALEC HYATT: *Four Hundred Years of Music Printing* (2nd ed., London, 1968).

KIRCHMEYER, HELMUT: 'Ein Kapitel Adolf Bernhard Marx. Über Sendungsbewusstsein und Bildungsstand der Berliner Musikkritik zwischen 1824 und 1830', *Beiträge zur Geschichte der Musikanschauung im 19. Jahrhundert*, ed. Walter Salmen (Regensburg, 1965).

KÜMMEL, WILHELM FRIEDRICH: 'Die Anfänge der Musikgeschichte in der deutschsprachigen Universitäten', *Die Musikforschung*, xx (1967), pp. 262–80.

MACKERNESS, E. D.: *A Social History of English Music* (London, 1964).

MATTHÄUS, WOLFGANG: *Johann André Musikverlag zu Offenbach am Main. Verlagsgeschichte und Bibliographie 1772–1800*, i, completed Hans Schneider (Tutzing, 1973).

NETTEL, REGINALD: *The Orchestra in England, a Social History* (2nd ed., London, 1956).

PIERRE, CONSTANT: *Les Hymnes et chansons de la Révolution* (Paris, 1904).

—— *Le Magasin de musique à l'usage des fêtes nationales et du Conservatoire* (Paris, 1895; reprinted Geneva, 1973).

PROD'HOMME, J[ACQUES]-G[ABRIEL]: 'Napoleon, Music and Musicians', *Musical Quarterly*, vii (1921), pp. 579–605.

SALMEN, WALTER, ed.: *Der Sozialstatus des Berufsmusikers vom 17. bis 19. Jahrhundert* (Kassel, 1971).

SCHMITT-THOMAS, REINHOLD: *Die Entwicklung der deutschen Konzertkritik im Spiegel der Leipziger Allgemeinen Musikalischen Zeitung (1798–1848)* (Frankfurt/Main, 1969).

SCHÜNEMANN, GEORG: *Die Singakademie zu Berlin 1791–1941* (Regensburg, 1941).

WEINMANN, ALEXANDER: *Die Wiener Verlagswerke von Franz Anton Hoffmeister* (*Beiträge zur Geschichte des Alt-Wiener Musikverlages*, Reihe 2, Folge 8) (Vienna, 1964).

[WHISTLING, CARL FRIEDRICH]: *Handbuch der musikalischen Literatur* (Leipzig, 1817, and 10 suppl., 1818–27), repr. with new introd. Neil Ratcliff (New York and London, 1975).

WIORA, WALTER, ed.: *Die Ausbreitung des Historismus über die Musik, Aufsätze und Diskussionen* (*Studien zur Musikgeschichte des 19. Jahrhunderts*, xiv) (Regensburg, 1969).

CHAPTER II

FRENCH OPERA

(i) Modern Editions

(a) Anthologies

DIETZ, MAX: *Geschichte des musikalischen Dramas in Frankreich während der Revolution bis zum Direktorium (1787 bis 1795)*, appendix of musical examples (Leipzig, 1893, repr. Hildesheim and New York, 1970). (Includes excerpts by Cherubini, Grétry, Le Sueur, Méhul, and Steibelt.)

PIERRE, CONSTANT: *Musique des fêtes et cérémonies de la Révolution française. Oeuvres de Gossec, Cherubini, Le Sueur, Méhul, Catel, etc.* (Paris, 1899).

WOLFF, HELLMUTH CHRISTIAN: *Die Oper III: 19. Jahrhundert (Das Musikwerk, xl)* (Cologne, 1972, English edition 1975). (Includes excerpts by Auber, Méhul, Spohr and Spontini.)

(b) Works by Individual Composers

AUBER, D. F.-E. *Fra Diavolo*, vocal score ed. R. Kleinmichel (Leipzig, 1902); ed. N. Macfarren (London, *c*. 1870); ed. K. Gutheim (Mainz, 1966).
—— *La Muette de Portici*, facsimile ed. (printed orch. score, Paris, *c*. 1828), ed. C. Rosen, 2 vols. (*Early Romantic Opera*, xxx) (New York and London, 1980).

BOIELDIEU, A.: *La Dame blanche*, ed. G. F. Kogel (Leipzig, 191–); vocal score ed. P. Puget (Paris, 1932).
—— *Le Nouveau Seigneur du village*, vocal score (Paris, 196–).

CATEL, C.-S.: *Les Bayadères*, ed. V. d'Indy (*Les Chefs d'oeuvre classiques de l'opéra français*, vii) (Paris, 1881, repr. New York, 1971).

CHERUBINI, L.: *Les Abencérages*, vocal score ed. F. Brissler (Leipzig, 188–).
—— *Démophoön*, facsimile ed. (printed orch. score, Paris, 1788), ed. C. Rosen (*Early Romantic Opera*, xxxii) (New York and London, 1978).
—— *Les Deux Journées*, facsimile ed. (printed orch. score, Paris), ed. C. Rosen (*Early Romantic Opera*, xxxv) (New York and London, 1980).
—— *Eliza, ou Le Voyage aux glaciers du Mont S. Bernard*, facsimile ed. (printed orch. score, Paris), ed. C. Rosen (*Early Romantic Opera*, xxxiv) (New York and London, 1979).
—— *Lodoïska*, facsimile ed. (printed orch. score, Paris), ed. C. Rosen (*Early Romantic Opera*, xxxiii) (New York and London, 1978).
—— *Médée*, facsimile ed. (printed orch. score, Paris, 1797) (Farnborough, 1971).
—— *Pimmalione (Pigmalione)*, vocal score ed. D. Menichetti (Florence, 1970).

GRÉTRY, A. E. M.: *La Caravane du Caire; Guillaume Tell; Richard, Coeur de Lion, Collection complète des oeuvres de Grétry*, ed. F. A. Gevaert *et al.* (Leipzig and Brussels, 1883–1937).
—— *La Caravane du Caire*, vocal score ed. F. A. Gevaert (*Les Chefs-d'oeuvre classiques de l'opéra français*, xii) (Paris, 1881, repr. New York, 1971).

HÉROLD, F.: *Le Pré aux clercs*, vocal score (Mainz, 1879); ed. R. Kleinmichel (Leipzig, 1891).
—— *Les Rosières*, ed. L. Delibes (Paris, 186–).
—— *Zampa*, vocal score ed. J. Pittman (London, 187–); ed. C. Blum (Mainz and Antwerp, 1884).

ISOUARD, N.: *Cendrillon*, vocal score (Paris, *c*. 1870); ed. R. Kleinmichel (Vienna, 191–).

LE SUEUR, J.-F.: *Ossian ou Les Bardes*, facsimile ed. (printed orch. score, Paris), ed. C. Rosen (*Early Romantic Opera*, xxxvii) (New York and London, 1979); vocal score ed. T. Salomé (*Les Chefs-d'oeuvre classiques de l'opéra français*, xv) (Paris, 1886, repr. New York, 1971).

MÉHUL, E.-T.: *Ariodant*, facsimile ed. (printed orch. score, Paris), ed. C. Rosen (*Early Romantic Opera*, xxxix) (New York and London, 1978).

—— *Euphrosine ou Le Tyran corrigé*, facsimile ed. (printed orch. score, Paris, ms addits.), ed. C. Rosen (*Early Romantic Opera*, xxxviii) (New York and London, 1980).

—— *Joseph*, facsimile ed. (printed orch. score, Paris, *c.* 1807), ed. C. Rosen (*Early Romantic Opera*, xli) (New York and London, 1979).

—— *Uthal*, facsimile ed. (printed orch. score, Paris, *c.* 1806), ed. C. Rosen (*Early Romantic Opera*, xl) (New York and London, 1978).

ROSSINI, G.: *Le Comte Ory*, facsimile ed. (printed orch. score, Paris, 1828), ed. P. Gossett (*Early Romantic Opera*, xvi) (New York and London, 1978).

—— *Guillaume Tell*, facsimile ed. (printed orch. score, Paris, 1829–30), ed. P. Gossett, 2 vols. (*Early Romantic Opera*, xvii) (New York and London, 1980).

—— *Moïse*, facsimile ed. (printed orch. score, Paris, 1827), ed. P. Gossett (*Early Romantic Opera*, xv) (New York and London, 1980).

—— *Le Siège de Corinthe*, facsimile ed. (printed orch. score, Paris, 1826–27), ed. P. Gossett (*Early Romantic Opera*, xiv) (New York and London, 1980).

SALIERI, A.: *Les Danaïdes*, facsimile score (printed orch. score, Paris, 1784) (Bologna, 1969); vocal score ed. G. Lefèvre (*Les Chefs-d'oeuvre classiques de l'opéra français*, xxxix) (Paris, 1881, New York, 1971).

—— *Tarare*, ed. R. Angermüller, 2 vols. (*Die Oper*, ii) (Munich, 1978); vocal score ed. G. Lefèvre (*Les Chefs-d'oeuvre classiques de l'opéra français*, xl) (Paris, 1882, repr. New York, 1971).

SPONTINI, G.: *Fernand Cortez, ou, La Conquête du Mexique*, facsimile ed. (printed orch. score, Paris, 1809), 2 vols. (Bologna, 1969); facsimile ed. (printed orch. score, Paris, *c.* 1817), ed. C. Rosen (*Early Romantic Opera*, xliii) (New York and London, 1980).

—— *Olympie*, facsimile ed. (printed orch. score, Paris, *c.* 1826), ed. C. Rosen (*Early Romantic Opera*, xliv) (New York and London, 1980).

—— *La Vestale*, facsimile ed. (printed orch. score, Paris), ed. C. Rosen (*Early Romantic Opera*, xlii) (New York and London, 1979).

(ii) Books and Articles

(a) General

ARNOLDSON, LOUISE PARKINSON: *Sedaine et les musiciens de son temps* (Paris, 1934).

BORREL, EUGÈNE: 'L'Orchestre du Concert Spirituel et celui de l'Opéra de Paris, de 1751 à 1800, d'après "Les Spectacles de Paris"', *Mélanges d'histoire et d'esthétique musicales offerts à Paul-Marie Masson*, ii (Paris, 1955), pp. 9–15.

BÜCKEN, ERNST: *Der heroische Stil in der Oper* (Leipzig, 1924).

COOPER, MARTIN: *Opéra Comique* (London, New York, 1949).

DEAN, WINTON: 'Opera under the French Revolution', *Proceedings of the Royal Musical Association*, xciv (1967–8), pp. 77–96.

—— 'Shakespeare and Opera', *Shakespeare in Music*, ed. Phyllis Hartnoll (London 1964), pp. 89–175.

DEANE, BASIL: 'The French Operatic Overture from Grétry to Berlioz', *Proceedings of the Royal Musical Association*, xcix (1972–3), pp. 67–80.

DENT, EDWARD: *The Rise of Romantic Opera* (Cambridge, 1976).

DIETZ, MAX: *Geschichte des musikalischen Dramas in Frankreich während der Revolution bis zum Direktorium (1787 bis 1795)*, (Leipzig, 1893, repr. Hildesheim and New York, 1970).

FAVRE, GEORGES: 'L'Amitié de deux musiciens, Boieldieu et Cherubini', *La Revue musicale*, xxii (1946), no. 201, pp. 217–25.

GALLIVER, DAVID: 'Jean-Nicolas Bouilly (1763–1842), Successor of Sedaine', *Studies in Music*, xiii (1979), pp. 16–33.

GOURRET, JEAN: *Histoire de l'Opéra de Paris, 1669–1971* (Paris, 1977).

GREGOR, JOSEPH: 'Revolutionszeitalter und Romantik', *Kulturgeschichte der Oper: Ihre Verbindung mit dem Leben, den Werken des Geistes und der Politik* (2nd ed., Vienna and Zurich, 1950), pp. 263–339.

KNEPLER, GEORG: 'Die Technik der sinfonischen Durchführung in der französischen Revolutionsoper', *Beiträge zur Musikwissenschaft*, i (1959), pp. 4–22.

LABAT-POUSSIN, BRIGITTE: *Archives du Théâtre National de l'Opéra* (Paris, 1977).

LONGYEAR, REY: 'Notes on the Rescue Opera', *Musical Quarterly*, xlv (1959), pp. 49–66.

'L'Opéra-Comique au XIXe siècle', *La Revue musicale*, xiv/4 (1933), no. 140 (special issue), pp. 243–308.

PENDLE, KARIN: *Eugène Scribe and French Opera of the Nineteenth Century* (*Studies in Musicology*, vi) (Ann Arbor, Michigan, 1979).

PIERRE, CONSTANT: *L'École de chant de l'Opéra, 1672–1807* (Paris, 1895).

—— *Les Hymnes et chansons de la Révolution* (Paris, 1904).

POUGIN, ARTHUR: *L'Opéra-Comique pendant la Révolution de 1788 à 1801* (Paris, 1891, repr. Geneva, 1973).

PROD'HOMME, JACQUES-GABRIEL: *L'Opéra (1669–1925)* (Paris, 1925, repr. Geneva, 1972).

RADIGUER, HENRI: 'La Musique française de 1789 à 1815', *Encyclopédie de la musique et dictionnaire du Conservatoire*, ed. Lionel de la Laurencie and Albert Lavignac, i/3 (Paris, 1921), pp. 1562–1677.

RINGER, ALEXANDER: 'The Political Uses of Opera in Revolutionary France', *Bericht über den internationalen musikwissenschaftlichen Kongress Bonn* (1970), pp. 237–42.

Storia dell'Opera, ed. Alberto Basso, ii/1, pt. I: 'L'opera in Francia', Jacques Chailley, Claudio Casini, France-Yvonne Bril (Turin, 1977), pp. 3–204.

TENEO, MARTIAL: 'Napoleon as Operatic Director', *Fortnightly Review*, cxix, new series (January–June 1921), pp. 983–96.

WÖRNER, KARL: 'Beiträge zur Geschichte des Leitmotivs in der Oper', *Zeitschrift für Musikwissenschaft*, xiv (1931–2), pp. 151–72.

(b) Individual Composers

Auber

LONGYEAR, REY: 'La muette de Portici', *Music Review*, xix (1958), pp. 37–46.

TIERSOT, JULIEN: 'Auber', *La Revue Musicale*, xiv/4 (1933), no. 140, pp. 265–78.

Boieldieu

CURZON, HENRI DE: 'Les Opéras-Comiques de Boieldieu (1797–1829)', *La Revue musicale*, xiv/4 (1933), no. 140, pp. 248–63.

FAVRE, GEORGES: *Boieldieu: sa vie, son oeuvre*, 2 vols. (Paris, 1944–5).

ROBERT, PAUL-LOUIS: 'Lettres inédits d'Adrien Boieldieu', *La Revue musicale*, vii/4 (1926), pp. 111–30.

SCHAEFFNER, ANDRÉ: 'A propos de "La Dame blanche"', *La Revue musicale*, vii/4 (1926), pp. 97–101.

Cherubini

DEANE, BASIL: *Cherubini* (London, 1965).

KUNZE, STEFAN: 'Cherubini und der musikalische Klassizismus', *Analecta Musicologica*, ix (1974), no. 14, pp. 301–23.

RINGER, ALEXANDER: 'Cherubini's *Médée* and the Spirit of French Revolutionary Opera', *Essays in Musicology in Honor of Dragan Plamenac on his 70th Birthday*, ed. Gustave Reese and Robert J. Snow (Pittsburgh, 1969), pp. 281–99.

SELDEN, MARGERY STOMNE: 'Cherubini and Melodrama', *Journal of the American Musicological Society*, ix (1956), pp. 63–5.

—— 'Napoleon and Cherubini', *Journal of the American Musicological Society*, viii (1955), pp. 110–15.

Dalayrac

CHARLTON, DAVID: 'Motif and Recollection in Four Operas of Dalayrac', *Soundings*, vii (1978), pp. 38–61.

KLOPPENBURG, W. C. M.: 'Nicolas Dalayrac (1753–1809)', *Mens en melodie*, ix (1954), pp. 378–83.

Gossec

HELLOUIN, FRÉDÉRIC: *Gossec et la musique française à la fin du XVIIIe siècle* (Paris, 1903).

PROD'HOMME, JACQUES-GABRIEL: *François-Joseph Gossec (1734–1829)* (Paris, 1949).

THIBAUT, WALTER: *François-Joseph Gossec, chantre de la Révolution française* (Gilly, 1970).

Grétry

BRENET, MICHEL: *Grétry, sa vie et ses oeuvres* (Paris, 1884).

CLERCX, SUZANNE: *Grétry, 1741–1813* (Brussels, 1944, repr. New York, 1978).

Hérold

DUHAMEL, RAOUL: 'Ferdinand Hérold (1791–1883)', *La Revue musicale*, xiv/4 (1933), no. 140, pp. 279–90.

POUGIN, ARTHUR: *Hérold* (Paris, 1908).

Kreutzer, R.

FRIEBE, FREIMAT: 'Rodolphe Kreutzer als Opernkomponist', *Chigiana. Rassegna annuale di studi musicologici*, xxiii, new series 3 (1966), pp. 149–62.

Le Sueur

CHARLTON, DAVID: 'Ossian, Le Sueur and Opera', *Studies in Music*, xi (1977), pp. 37–48.

MONGRÉDIEN, JEAN: *Jean-François Le Sueur (1760–1837). Catalogue thématique de l'oeuvre complète* (New York, 1980).

Méhul

BRANCOUR, RENÉ: *Méhul* (Paris, 1912).

GODFREY, CAROL: 'Gros and Méhul', *Burlington Magazine*, cxiv (1972), no. 836, pp. 769–75.

POUGIN, ARTHUR: *Méhul: sa vie, son génie, son caractère* (Paris, 1889, repr. Geneva, 1973).

STROBEL, HEINRICH: 'Die Opern von E. N. Méhul', *Zeitschrift für Musikwissenschaft*, vi (1923–4), pp. 362–402.

Rossini

PROD'HOMME, J.-G.: 'Rossini and his Works in France', *Musical Quarterly*, xvii (1931), pp. 110–37.

Salieri

ANGERMÜLLER, RUDOLPH: *Antonio Salieri. Sein Leben und seine weltlichen Werke unter besonderer Berücksichtigung seiner 'grossen' Opern*, ii/i (*Publikationen des Instituts für Musikwissenschaft der Universität Salzburg*, xvii) (Munich, 1974).

RUSHTON, JULIAN: 'Salieri's *Les Horaces*: A Study of an Operatic Failure', *Music Review*, xxxvii (1976), pp. 266–82.

Spontini

ABRAHAM, GERALD: 'The Best of Spontini', *Music and Letters*, xxiii (1942), pp. 163–71; also in *Slavonic and Romantic Music* (London and New York, 1968), pp. 23–7.

BOUVET, CHARLES: *Spontini* (Paris, 1930).

GHISLANZONI, ALBERTO: *Gasparo Spontini: Studio storico-critico* (Rome, 1951).

LIBBY, DENNIS: 'Spontini's Early French Operas', *Musical Times*, cxvii (1976), pp. 23–4.

CHAPTER III

BEETHOVEN'S ORCHESTRAL MUSIC

(i) Modern Editions

BEETHOVEN, LUDWIG VAN: *Ludwig van Beethoven's Werke: vollständige kritisch durchgesehene überall berechtige Ausgabe* (Leipzig, 1864–7, 1888–90), i, 'Symphonien für Orchester', ii, 'Verschiedene Orchesterwerke', iii, 'Ouvertüren für Orchester'.

—— *Supplemente zur Gesamtausgabe* 4, 'Werke für Orchester', ed. W. Hess (Wiesbaden, 1961).

—— *Werke*, ii/1, 'Ouvertüren und Wellingtons Sieg', ed. H.-W. Küthen (Munich, 1974), ii/2, 'Ballettmusik', ed. K. Kropfinger (Munich, 1970).

—— *Symphony No. 5 in C Minor*, ed. E. Forbes (New York, 1971). (Includes historical and analytical commentary.)

—— *Sinfonie Nr. 5 C-moll Opus 67*, ed. P. Gülke (Leipzig, 1977). (Restores the repeat of bars 4-239 of the third movement, originally planned but subsequently rejected by Beethoven.)

(ii) Facsimile Editions of Autograph Manuscripts

BEETHOVEN LUDWIG VAN: *Fünfte Symphonie*, ed. G. Schünemann (Berlin, 1941).

—— *Sinfonie mit Schlusschor über Schillers Ode 'An die Freude'* (Leipzig, 1924; reprinted 1975).

(iii) Sketchbooks in Complete Facsimile or Transcription; General Sketchbook Studies

BEETHOVEN, LUDWIG VAN: *Autograph Miscellany from circa 1786 to 1799 ... (The 'Kafka Sketchbook')*, facsimile and transcription, ed. J. Kerman, 2 vols. (London, 1970).

—— *Ein Skizzenbuch zur Pastoralsymphonie op. 68 und zu den Trios op. 70, 1 und 2*, transcription, ed. D. Weise, 2 vols. (Bonn, 1961).

—— *Beethovens eigenhändiges Skizzenbuch zur 9, Symphonie*, facsimile, ed. W. Engelmann (Leipzig, 1913).

BRANDENBURG, SIEGHARD: 'Ein Skizzenbuch Beethovens aus dem Jahr 1812: zur Chronologie des Petterschen Skizzenbuches', *Zu Beethoven*, ed. H. Goldschmidt (Berlin, 1979), pp. 117–48. (Includes transcriptions of early sketches for the Eighth Symphony.)

KERMAN, JOSEPH: 'Beethoven's Early Sketches', *The Musical Quarterly*, lvi (1970), pp. 515–38.
—— 'Beethoven Sketches in the British Museum', *Proceedings of the Royal Musical Association*, xciii (1966–7), pp. 77–96.
MIES, PAUL: *Die Bedeutung der Skizzen Beethovens zur Erkenntnis seines Stiles* (Leipzig, 1925; reprinted 1969). Eng. trans. by D. L. MacKinnon as *Beethoven's Sketches* (London, 1929, repr. 1969).
NOTTEBOHM, GUSTAV: *Beethoveniana* (Leipzig and Winterthur, 1872, 2nd ed., 1925; 1925 ed. repr. Hackensack, N.J., 1970). Collection of essays, most of which first appeared in the *Allegemeine musikalische Zeitung*, 1869–71.
—— *Ein Skizzenbuch von Beethoven* (Leipzig, 1865, 2nd ed. 1924); 1924 ed. repr. Hackensack, N.J., 1970). English translation by J. Katz in *Two Beethoven Sketchbooks: a Description with Musical Extracts* (London, 1979). (Includes substantial transcriptions of sketches for the Second Symphony.)
—— *Ein Skizzenbuch von Beethoven aus dem Jahre 1803* (Leipzig, 1880, 2nd ed. 1924; 1924 ed. repr. Hackensack, N.J., 1970). English translation by J. Katz in *Two Beethoven Sketchbooks* (London, 1979). (Includes substantial transcriptions of sketches for the Third and Fifth Symphonies.)
—— *Zweite Beethoveniana*, ed. E. Mandyczewski (Leipzig, 1887, 2nd ed. 1925; 1925 ed. repr. Hackensack, N.J., 1970). Collection of essays, most of which first appeared in the *Musikalisches Wochenblatt*, 1875–9.
TYSON, ALAN: 'A Reconstruction of the Pastoral Symphony Sketchbook', *Beethoven Studies* (New York, 1973, London, 1974), pp. 67–96.
WADE, RACHEL W.: 'Beethoven's Eroica Sketchbook', *Fontes artis musicae*, xxiv (1977), pp. 254–89.

(iv) General Surveys

BERLIOZ, HECTOR: *À travers chants* (Paris, 1862). English translation of material relating to Beethoven by E. Evans Snr., as *A Critical Study of Beethoven's Nine Symphonies* (London, 1913, repr. 1958).
D'AMICO, FEDELE: *Sulle sinfonie di Beethoven* (Rome, 1973).
DEANE, BASIL: 'The Symphonies and Overtures', *The Beethoven Companion*, ed. D. Arnold and N. Fortune (London, 1971), pp. 281-317.
EVANS, EDWIN Snr.: *Beethoven's Nine Symphonies Fully Described and Annotated*, 2 vols. (London, 1923–4).
FISKE, ROGER: *Beethoven Concertos and Overtures* (London, 1970).
GROVE, GEORGE: *Beethoven and His Nine Symphonies* (London, 1896, 3rd ed. 1898; 3rd ed. repr. New York, 1962).
HOPKINS, ANTONY: *The Nine Symphonies of Beethoven* (London and Seattle, 1980).
LAM, BASIL: (Ludwig van Beethoven (1770–1827)', *The Symphony, Volume One: Haydn to Dvořák*, ed. R. Simpson (London, 1966), pp. 104–74.
NEF, KARL: *Die neun Sinfonien Beethovens* (Leipzig, 1928).
PIKE, LIONEL: *Beethoven, Sibelius and the 'Profound Logic': Studies in Symphonic Analysis* (London, 1978).
PROD'HOMME, JACQUES-GABRIEL: *Les symphonies de Beethoven (1800–1827)* (Paris, 1906, 5th ed. 1947).
SIMPSON, ROBERT: *Beethoven Symphonies* (London, 1970).
TOVEY, DONALD F.: *Essays in Musical Analysis*, i, ii, and iv (London, 1935–6).
WEINGARTNER, FELIX: *Ratschläge für die Aufführung der Symphonien Beethovens* (Leipzig, 1906). Eng. trans. J. Crosland (London, 1907; repr. in *Weingartner on Music and Conducting*, New York, 1969).

(v) Symphonies

Symphony no. 1

LEVARIE, SIEGMUND: 'Once More: the Slow Introduction to Beethoven's First Symphony', *The Music Review*, xl (1979), pp. 168–75.

MISCH, LUDWIG: 'Der persönliche Stil in Beethovens erster Symphonie', *Beethoven-Jahrbuch, Zweite Reihe*, ii (1955-6), pp. 55–107.

SCHENK, ERICH: 'Beethovens "Erste" – eine B-A-C-H-Symphonie', *Neues Beethoven-Jahrbuch*, viii (1938), pp. 162–72.

Symphony no. 2

COREN, DANIEL: 'Structural Relations between Op. 28 and Op. 36', *Beethoven Studies 2*, ed. A. Tyson (London, 1977), pp. 66–83.

WESTPHAL, KURT: *Vom Einfall zur Symphonie: Einblick in Beethovens Schaffensweise* (Berlin, 1965).

Symphony no. 3 ('Eroica')

ANTONICEK, THEOPHIL: 'Humanitätssymbolik im Eroica-Finale', *De ratione in musica: Festschrift Erich Schenk* (Kassel, 1975), pp. 144–55.

DOWNS, PHILIP G.: 'Beethoven's "New Way" and the *Eroica*', *Musical Quarterly* lvi (1970), pp. 585–604.

HALM, AUGUST: 'Über den Wert musikalischer Analysen, i: Der Fremdkörper im ersten Satz der Eroica', *Die Musik*, xxi (1929), pp. 48–9.

LOCKWOOD, LEWIS: 'Eroica Perspectives': Strategy and Design in the First Movement', *Beethoven Studies 3*, ed. A. Tyson (London, 1982).

RIEZLER, WALTER: *Beethoven* (Berlin and Zürich, 1936, 9th ed. 1966). English translation by G. D. H. Pidcock (London, 1938). (Includes substantial analysis of the first movement of the 'Eroica'.)

SCHENKER, HEINRICH: 'Beethovens dritte Sinfonie zum erstenmal in ihrem wahren Inhalt dargestellt', *Das Meisterwerk in der Musik*, iii (1930), pp. 29–101.

Symphony no. 4

MISCH, LUDWIG: *Die Factoren der Einheit in der Mehrsätzigkeit der Werke Beethovens* (Bonn and Munich, 1958). (Includes an analysis of the Fourth Symphony.)

Symphony no. 5

CARSE, ADAM: 'The Sources of Beethoven's Fifth Symphony', *Music and Letters*, xxix (1948), pp. 249–62.

GÜLKE, PETER: *Zur Neuausgabe der Sinfonie Nr. 5 von Ludwig van Beethoven: Werk und Edition* (Leipzig, 1978).

HOFFMANN, E. T. A.: Review of Beethoven's Fifth Symphony, *Allgemeine musikalische Zeitung*, xii (1809–10), columns 630–42 and 652–9. Eng. trans. F. J. Adams Jr. in *Beethoven; Symphony No. 5 in C Minor*, ed. E. Forbes (New York, 1971), pp. 150–63.

IMBRIE, ANDREW: '"Extra" Measures and Metrical Ambiguity in Beethoven', *Beethoven Studies*, ed. A. Tyson (New York, 1973, pp. 45–66).

SCHENKER, HEINRICH: *Beethoven: Fünfte Sinfonie* (Vienna, 1925; repr. 1969). Originally published in instalments in *Der Tonwille* (1921–4). (Partial Eng. trans. by E. Forbes in *Ludwig van Beethoven: Symphony No. 5 in C minor*, ed. E. Forbes (New York, 1971), pp. 164–82).

Symphony no. 6 ('Pastoral')

GOSSETT, PHILIP: 'Beethoven's Sixth Symphony: Sketches for the First Movement', *Journal of the American Musicological Society*, xxvii (1974), pp. 248–84.

KAHL, WILLI: 'Zu Beethovens Naturauffassung', *Beethoven und die Gegenwart: Festschrift Ludwig Schiedermair zum 60. Geburtstag* (Berlin and Bonn, 1937), pp. 220–65.

KOJIMA, S. A.: 'Probleme im Notentext der Pastoralsymphonie op. 68 von Beethoven', *Beethoven-Jahrbuch, Zweite Reihe*, ix (1973–7), pp. 217–61.

KIRBY, F. E.: 'Beethoven's Pastoral Symphony as a *sinfonia caracteristica*', *Musical Quarterly*, lvi (1970), pp. 605–23.

SANDBERGER, ADOLF: 'Zu den geschichtlichen Voraussetzungen der Pastoralsinfonie', *Ausgewählte Aufsätze zur Musikgeschichte*, ii (Munich, 1924), pp. 154–200.

Symphony no. 7

BELOW, ROBERT: 'Some Aspects of Tonal Relationships in Beethoven's Seventh Symphony', *The Music Review*, xxxvii (1976), pp. 1–4.

OSTHOFF, WOLFGANG: 'Zum Vorstellungsgehalt des Allegretto in Beethovens 7. Symphonie', *Archiv für Musikwissenschaft*, xxxiv (1977), pp. 159–79.

SILLIMAN, A. CUTLER: 'Familiar Music and the a Priori: Beethoven's Seventh Symphony', *Journal of Music Theory*, xx (1977), pp. 215–26.

Symphony no. 8

HESS, WILLY: 'Zum ursprünglichen Schluss des 1. Satzes von Beethovens achter Symphonie', *Beethoven-Studien* (Munich, 1972), pp. 158–62. Originally published in the *Schweizerische Musikzeitung*, ci (1961).

JONAS, OSWALD: 'The Autograph of Beethoven's Eighth Symphony', *Music and Letters*, xx (1939), pp. 177–82.

OREL, ALFRED: 'Der ursprüngliche Schluss des ersten Satzes in Beethovens achter Symphonie', *Schweizerische Musikzeitung*, xc (1950), pp. 50–53.

Symphony no. 9 ('Choral')

BAENSCH, OTTO: *Aufbau und Sinn des Chorfinales in Beethovens neunter Symphonie* (Berlin and Leipzig, 1930).

FORBES, ELLIOT: '"Stürzet nieder, Millionen"', *Studies in Music History: Essays for Oliver Strunk*, ed. H. S. Powers (Princeton, 1968), pp. 449–57.

MILA, MASSIMO: *Lettura della Nona Sinfonia* (Turin, 1977).

MÜLLER-BLATTAU, JOSEPH: 'Das Finale der Neunten Sinfonie', *Von der Vielfalt der Musik* (Freiburg im Breisgau, 1966), pp. 269–84.

RETI, RUDOLPH: *The Thematic Process in Music* (New York, 1951), chapter 1.

SANDERS, ERNEST: 'Form and Content in the Finale of Beethoven's Ninth Symphony, *Musical Quarterly*, l (1964), pp. 59–76.

SCHENKER, HEINRICH: *Beethovens Neunte Sinfonie* (Vienna, 1912; repr. 1969).

SYCHRA, ANTONÍN: 'Ludwig van Beethovens Skizzen zur IX, Sinfonie', *Beethoven-Jahrbuch, Zweite Reihe*, iv (1959–60), pp. 85–101.

TOVEY, DONALD F.: *Beethoven's Ninth Symphony* (London, 1928).

TREITLER, LEO: 'History, Criticism, and Beethoven's Ninth Symphony', *19th-Century Music*, iii/3 (1980), pp. 193–210.

VAUGHAN WILLIAMS, RALPH: *Some Thoughts on Beethoven's Choral Symphony, with Other Musical Subjects* (London, 1953).

WINTER, ROBERT: 'The Sketches for the "Ode to Joy"', *Beethoven, Performers, and Critics*, ed. R. Winter and B. Carr (Detroit, 1980), pp. 176–214.

(vi) The 'Leonore' Overtures

BRAUNSTEIN, JOSEF: *Beethovens Leonore-Ouvertüren; eine historisch-stilkritische Untersuchung* (Leipzig, 1927).

HESS, WILLY: 'Zur Quellenfrage und Textrevision der zweiten Leonoren-Ouvertüre', *Beethoven-Studien* (Munich, 1972), pp. 152–7. Originally published in *Schweizerische Musikzeitung*, cvi (1966).

TYSON, ALAN: 'The Problem of Beethoven's "First" *Leonore* Overture', *Journal of the American Musicological Society*, xxviii (1975), pp. 325–31.

—— 'Yet Another "Leonore" Overture?', *Music and Letters*, lviii (1977), pp. 192–203.

(vii) Other Orchestral Works

KÜTHEN, HANS-WERNER: 'Neue Aspekte zur Entstehung von *Wellingtons Sieg*', *Beethoven-Jahrbuch, Zweite Reihe*, viii (1971–2), pp. 73–92.

MIES, PAUL: 'Ludwig van Beethovens Werke über seinen Kontretanz in Es-Dur', *Beethoven-Jahrbuch, Zweite Reihe*, i (1953–4), pp. 80–102.

—— 'Zur Coriolan Overtüre op. 62', *Beethoven-Jahrbuch, Zweite Reihe*, vi (1965–8), pp. 260–8. Originally published as 'Beethoven – Collin – Shakespeare' in *Zeitschrift für Musik*, cx (1938), pp. 156 ff.

MISCH, LUDWIG: 'Wo sind Beethovens Skizzen zur X. Symphonie?', *Neue Beethoven-Studien und andere Themem* (Bonn and Munich, 1967), pp. 80–84.

WINTER, ROBERT: 'Noch eii..nal: Wo sind Beethovens Skizzen zur Zehnten Symphonie?', *Beethoven-Jahrbuch, Zweite Reihe*, ix (1973–7), pp. 531–52. In English.

(viii) Related Studies

BECKING, GUSTAV: *Studies zu Beethovens Personalstil: das Scherzothema* (Leipzig, 1921). Reprinted in *Gustav Becking zum Gedächtnis*, ed. W. Kramolisch (Tutzing, 1975).

BIBA, OTTO: 'Beethoven und die "Liebhaber Concerte" in Wien im Winter 1807/08', *Beethoven-Kolloquium 1977: Dokumentation und Aufführungspraxis*, ed. R. Klein (Kassel, 1978), pp. 82–93.

GÁL, HANS: 'Die Stil-Eigentümlichkeiten des jungen Beethoven', *Studien zur Musikwissenschaft*, iv (1916), pp. 58–115.

JOHNSON, DOUGLAS: 'Music for Prague and Berlin: Beethoven's Concert tour of 1796', *Beethoven, Performers, and Critics*, ed. R. Winter and B. Carr (Detroit, 1980), pp. 24–40.

KERMAN, JOSEPH: 'Beethoven's Early Sketches', *Musical Quarterly*, lvi (1970), pp. 515–38.

KERMAN, JOSEPH: 'Notes on Beethoven's Codas', *Beethoven Studies 3*, ed. A. Tyson (London, 1982).

LEVIEN, J. MEWBURN: *Beethoven and the Philharmonic Society* (London, 1927).

MERTON, JOSEF: 'Zur Klangbalance im symphonischen Werk Beethoven's, *Beethoven-Kolloquium 1977: Dokumentation und Aufführungspraxis*, ed. R. Klein (Kassel, 1978), pp. 52–6.

MIES, PAUL: 'Die Bedeutung der Pauke in den Werken Ludwig van Beethovens', *Beethoven-Jahrbuch, Zweite Reihe*, viii (1971–2), pp. 49–71.

ROLLAND, ROMAIN: *Beethoven: les grandes époques créatrices*, 6 vols. (Paris, 1928–45). Eng. trans. of vol. 1 by E. Newman as *Beethoven the Creator, I: from the Eroica to the Appassionata* (London, 1929).

ROSEN, CHARLES: *Sonata Forms* (New York, 1980).

—— *The Classical Style: Haydn, Mozart, Beethoven* (New York, 1971).

SCHERING, ARNOLD: *Beethoven und die Dichtung* (Berlin, 1936; repr. 1973). (Includes programmatic interpretations of various symphonies.)

SOLOMON, MAYNARD: 'Beethoven and Schiller', *Beethoven, Performers, and Critics*, ed. R. Winter and B. Carr (Detroit, 1980), pp. 162–75.

TOVEY, DONALD F.: *Beethoven* (London, 1944).

TYSON, ALAN: 'Beethoven's Heroic Phase', *Musical Times*, cx (1969), pp. 139–41.

WADE, RACHEL W.: 'Beethoven's Eroica Sketchbook', *Fontes artis musicae*, xxiv (1977), pp. 254–89.

WAGNER, RICHARD: *Gesammelte Schriften und Dichtungen* (Leipzig, 1871–83); Eng. trans. of 2nd (1887) ed. W. A. Ellis (London, 1892–9). (Includes essays on the Third and Ninth Symphonies and the *Coriolan* Overture, and a monograph on Beethoven (first published Leipzig, 1870).)

CHAPTER IV

THE ORCHESTRAL MUSIC OF BEETHOVEN'S CONTEMPORARIES

(i) Modern Editions

(a) Anthology

HOFFMANN-ERBRECHT, LOTHAR, ed.: *Die Sinfonie* (*Das Musikwerk*, xxix) (Cologne, 1967, English edition 1967).

(b) Works by Individual Composers

BOMTEMPO, J. D.: Symphony No. 1 in E flat, Op. 11, ed. F. de Sousa, *Portugaliae Musica*, series B, viii (Lisbon, 1963).

CHERUBINI, L.: Symphony in D, ed. J. S. Winter (Leipzig and Vienna, 1935).

CLEMENTI M.: Symphony No. 1 in B flat, Op. 18, ed. R. Fasano (Milan, 1961).

—— Symphony No. 2 in D major, Op. 18, ed. R. Fasano (Milan, 1959).

—— Symphony No. 1 in C, WO 32, completed and ed. A. Casella (Milan, 1938).

—— Symphony in D (mvt i: WO 35, mvt ii, iv: WO 33, mvt iii: WO 36), ed. A. Casella (Milan, 1938).

—— Symphony No. 3 in G ('The Great National Symphony'), WO 34, ed. P. Spada (Milan, 1977).

DITTERSDORF, K.: Symphony in A, Krebs 93, ed. H. Kretzschmar (Leipzig, 1895).

—— Symphony in A minor, Krebs 95, ed. V. Luithlen (*Denkmäler der Tonkunst in Österreich*, lxxxi Jg. 43 (2) (Vienna, 1936).

KOŽELUH, L.: Symphonies in D, F, and G minor, ed. M. Poštolka (*Musica Antiqua Bohemica*, lxxii) (Prague, 1969).

NEEFE, C. G.: Partita in E flat, ed. L. Schiedermair, *Sinfonien um Beethoven* (*Denkmäler rheinischer Musik*, i) (Düsseldorf, 1951).

PLEYEL, I.: Symphony in C, ed. A Carse (London, 1949).

—— *Four Symphonies and One Symphonie Concertante*, ed. R. Smith and D. Townsend (*The Symphony 1720–1840*, series D, vi) (New York and London, 1981).

REICHA, A.: Symphony in E flat, Op. 41 (*Musica Antiqua Bohemica*, lxxvi) (Prague, 1973).

RÖSSLER (ROSETTI), A.: *Ausgewählte Sinfonien*, ed. O. Kaul (*Denkmäler der Tonkunst in Bayern*, xii/1) (Leipzig, 1912).

—— Symphony in G minor, ed F. Kneusslin (Basel, *c.* 1965).

SCHUBERT, F.: *Drei Symphonie-Fragmente* (D 615, D 708A, D 936A), facsimile ed. of the autographs, ed. E. Hilmar (*Documenta Musicologica*, 2nd series, vi) (Kassel, 1978).

—— *Ouvertüren und andere Orchesterwerke*, ed. J. N. Fuchs, *Franz Schubert's Werke. Kritisch durchgesehene Gesammtausgabe*, series II (Leipzig, 1886, repr. New York, 1965).

—— *Sinfonien 1–3*, ed. A. Feil and C. Landon, *Franz Schubert. Neue Ausgabe sämtlicher Werke*, series V, i (Kassel, 1967).

—— *Symphonien für Orchester*, ed. J. Brahms, *Franz Schubert's Werke. Kritisch durchgesehene Gesammtausgabe*, series I, i–ii (Leipzig, 1884–5, repr. New York, 1965).

—— Symphony in E, D 729, completed and ed. F. Weingartner (Vienna, 1934).

—— Symphony in B minor ('Unfinished'), D 759, ed. M. Chusid (New York, 1971); facsimile ed. (*Publikationen der Sammlung der Gesellschaft der Musikfreunde in Wien*, iii) (Munich–Salzburg, 1978).

SPOHR, LUDWIG: Symphony No. 3 in C minor, Op. 78, ed. H. Heussner (Kassel, 1957).

VAŇHAL (WANHAL), J. B.: Symphony in F, ed. P. Bryan (*Diletto musicale*, cccxxix) (Vienna, *c.* 1978).

VOŘÍŠEK, J. H.: Symphony in D, ed. J. Racek and F. Bartoš (*Musica Antiqua Bohemica*, xxxiv) (Prague, *c.* 1957).

WALDSTEIN, F.: Symphony in D, ed. L. Schiedermair, *Sinfonien um Beethoven* (*Denkmäler rheinischer Musik*, i) (Düsseldorf, 1951).

WEBER, C. M. von: Symphony No. 1 in C, Op. 19, ed. F. Oeser (London, *c.* 1948).

—— Symphony No. 2 in C, ed. H. Schönzeler (London, New York, *c.* 1970).

WESLEY, S.: Symphony No. 2 in D, ed. R. Platt (London, *c.* 1976).

—— Symphony No. 5 in A, ed. R. Platt (London, 1974).

WITT, F.: Symphony in C ('Jena' Symphony), ed. F. Stein (incorrectly ascribed to Beethoven) (Leipzig, 1911).

WRANITZKY (VRANICKÝ), P.: Symphony in C, Op. 2, ed. B. Ferenc (Budapest, *c.* 1978).

(ii) Books and Articles

(a) General

BROOK, BARRY S.: *La Symphonie française dans la seconde moitié du XVIIIe siècle*, 3 vols. (Paris, 1962).

FISCHER, HANS: 'Instrumentalmusik von 1750–1828', *Handbuch der Musikgeschichte*, ii, ed. Guido Adler (2nd ed., Berlin, 1930, repr. Tutzing, 1961), pp. 795–833.

HINTERMAIER, ERNST: 'Michael Haydns Salzburger Schülerkreis', *Österreichische Musikzeitschrift*, xxvii (1972), pp. 14–24.

HOFFMANN-ERBRECHT, LOTHAR, ed.: *Die Sinfonie* (*Das Musikwerk*, xxix) (Cologne, 1967, English edition 1967), introduction, pp. 5–48.

KLOIBER, RUDOLF: *Handbuch der klassischen und romantischen Symphonie* (2nd ed., Wiesbaden, 1976).

KRETZSCHMAR, HERMANN: *Sinfonien und Suite von Gabrieli bis Schumann* (*Führer durch den Konzertsaal*, I/1), ed. and exp. Friedrich Noack (Leipzig, 1932).

LANG, PAUL HENRY: *The Symphony 1800–1900*, preface (New York, 1969), pp. vii–xxxvii.

LA RUE, JAN: 'Major and Minor Mysteries of Identification in the 18th Century Symphony', *Journal of the American Musicological Society*, xiii (1960), pp. 181–96.

—— 'A Union Thematic Catalogue of Eighteenth-Century Symphonies', *Fontes Artis Musicae*, vi (1959), pp. 18–20.

NEF, KARL: *Geschichte der Sinfonie und Suite* (Leipzig, 1921, repr. Wiesbaden, 1970).

SCHIEDERMAIR, LUDWIG: 'Die Blütezeit der Öttingen-Wallerstein'schen Hofkapelle', *Sammelbände der internationalen Musikgesellschaft*, ix (1907–8), pp. 83–130.

SCHWARZ, BORIS: *French Instrumental Music Between the Revolutions* (New York, 1982).

SIMPSON, ROBERT, ed.: *The Symphony*, i (Harmondsworth, 1966).

Tiersot, Julien: 'La Symphonie en France', *Zeitschrift der internationalen Musikgesellschaft*, iii (1901–2), pp. 391–402.
Walin, Stig: *Beiträge zur Geschichte der schwedischen Sinfonik. Studien aus dem Musikleben des 18. und des beginnenden 19. Jahrhunderts* (Stockholm, 1941).
Wohlfahrt, Frank: *Geschichte der Sinfonie* (Hamburg, 1966).

(b) Individual Composers

Cherubini

Deane, Basil: *Cherubini* (London, 1965).
Rinaldi, Mario: 'La musica sinfonica, da camera e d'occasione di Luigi Cherubini', *Luigi Cherubini nel II centenario della nascità*, ed. Adelino Damerini (Florence, 1962), pp. 57–69.

Clementi

Bennet, Clive: 'Clementi as Symphonist', *Musical Times*, cxx (1979), pp. 207–10.
Casella, Alfredo: 'Muzio Clementi et ses symphonies', *La Revue musicale*, xvii (1936), no. 164, pp. 161–70.
—— 'Le sinfonie di Muzio Clementi', *Musica d'oggi*, xvii (1935), pp. 413–19.
Plantinga, Leon: *Clementi: His Life and Music* (London, 1977).
Saint-Foix, Georges De: 'Muzio Clementi', *Musical Quarterly*, ix (1923), pp. 350–82.
—— 'Les Symphonies de Clementi', *Rivista musicale italiana*, xxxi (1921), pp. 1–22.
Tyson, Alan: *Thematic Catalogue of the Works of Muzio Clementi* (Tutzing, 1967).

Dittersdorf

Krebs, Carl: *Dittersdorfiana* (Berlin, 1900, repr. New York, 1972).

Eberl

Ewens, Franz Josef: *Anton Eberl: Ein Beitrag zur Musikgeschichte in Wien um 1800* (Dresden, 1927). With thematic catalogue.
Haas, Robert: 'Anton Eberl', *Mozart-Jahrbuch 1951* (Salzburg, 1953), pp. 123–30.
Landon, H. C. Robbins: 'Two Orchestral Works Wrongly Attributed to Mozart', *Music Review*, xvii (1956), pp. 29–34. Refers to Witt's Symphony in C, 1785.

Elsner

Nowak-Romanowicz, Alina: *Józef Elsner* (Cracow, 1957).

Gossec

Hellouin, Frédéric: *Gossec et la musique française à la fin du dix-huitième siècle* (Paris, 1903).

Gyrowetz

Doernberg, Erwin: 'Gyrowetz', *Music and Letters*, xliv (1963), pp. 21–30.

L. Kozeluch (Koželuh)

Poštolka, Milan: *Leopold Koželuh, Život a dílo* (Prague, 1964). With thematic catalogue.
Weinmann, Alexander: *Verzeichnis der Verlagswerke des Musikalischen Magazins in Wien, 1784–1802, 'Leopold Koželuch'* (Vienna, 1950).

Méhul

Ringer, Alexander L.: 'A French Symphonist at the Time of Beethoven: Etienne Nicolas Méhul', *Musical Quarterly*, xxxvii (1951), pp. 543–56.

Neukomm

Angermüller, Rudolph: *Sigismund Neukomm. Werkverzeichnis, Autobiographie, Bezeichnungen zu seinen Zeitgenossen* (Munich, 1977).

Pleyel
BENTON, RITA: À la recherche de Pleyel perdu', *Fontes Artis Musicae*, xvii (1970), pp. 9–15.
—— *Ignace Pleyel: A Thematic Catalogue of his Compositions* (New York, 1977).
CARSE, ADAM: 'A Symphony by Pleyel', *Monthly Musical Record*, lxxix (1949), pp. 231–6.

Reicha
BÜCKEN, ERNST: *Anton Reicha, sein Leben und seine Kompositionen* (Munich, 1912).
EMMANUEL, MAURICE: *Antonin Reicha* (Paris, 1937).
ŠOTOLOVÁ, OLGA: *Antonin Rejcha* (Prague, 1977). With thematic catalogue.

Ries
HILL, CECIL: *The Music of Ferdinand Ries: A Thematic Catalogue* (Armidale, New South Wales, 1977).
SEITZ, REINHOLD: 'Ries, Ferdinand', *Rheinische Musiker*, ii, ed. Karl Gustav Fellerer (*Beiträge zur rheinischen Musikgeschichte*, liii) (Cologne, 1962), pp. 82–5.

A. J. and B. H. Romberg
WULF, ELMAR: 'Romberg, Andreas Jacob', 'Romberg, Bernhard Heinrich', *Rheinische Musiker*, i, ed. Karl Fellerer (*Beiträge zur rheinischen Musikgeschichte*, xliii) (Cologne, 1960), pp. 210–18, 219–24.

Rössler (Rosetti)
FITZPATRICK, HORACE: 'Antonio Rosetti', *Music and Letters*, xliii (1962), pp. 234–47.
KAUL, OSCAR: 'Einleitung', 'Thematisches Verzeichnis der Instrumentalwerke', *Anton Rosetti. Ausgewählte Sinfonien* (*Denkmäler der Tonkunst in Bayern*, xii/1) (Leipzig, 1912); pp. ix–lxvi; 'Thematisches Verzeichnis' repr. Wiesbaden, 1968, ed. Hans Schmid.
MURRAY, STERLING ELLIS: 'The Rösler-Rosetti Problem; A Confusion of Pseudonym and Mistaken Identity', *Music and Letters*, lvii (1976), pp. 130–43.

Schubert
ABRAHAM, GERALD: 'Finishing the Unfinished', *Musical Times*, cxii (1971), pp. 547–8.
BIBA, OTTO: 'Schubert's Position in Viennese Musical Life', *19th Century Music*, iii (1979), pp. 106–13.
BROWN, MAURICE J. E.: 'The Genesis of the Great C Major Symphony', *Essays on Schubert* (London, 1966), pp. 29–58.
—— *Schubert Symphonies* (London, 1970).
CARNER, MOSCO: 'The Orchestral Music', *The Music of Schubert*, ed. Gerald Abraham (London and New York, 1947, repr. Port Washington, New York, 1969, pp. 17–87.
CHUSID, MARTIN, ed. *Franz Schubert: Symphony in B Minor ('Unfinished'). An Authoritative Score. Schubert's Sketches. Commentary. Essays in History and Analysis* (rev. ed., New York, 1971).
DEUTSCH, OTTO ERICH: 'The Riddle of Schubert's Unfinished Symphony', *Music Review*, i (1940), pp. 36–53.
DEUTSCH, OTTO ERICH and WAKELING, DONALD: *Schubert. Thematic Catalogue of All his Works in Chronological Order* (London, 1951), rev. and exp. as *Franz Schubert. Thematisches Verzeichnis seiner Werke in chronologischer Folge*, ed. Editorial Board of the New Schubert Edition and Werner Aderhold (Kassel, 1978).
GRIFFEL, L. MICHAEL: 'A Reappraisal of Schubert's Methods of Composition', *Musical Quarterly*, lxiii (1977), pp. 186–210.

LAAFF, ERNST: 'Schuberts grosse C-dur Symphonie', *Festschrift Friedrich Blume, zum 70. Geburtstag*, ed. Anna Amalie Abert and Wilhelm Pfannkuch (Kassel, 1963), pp. 204–13.

—— 'Schuberts h-moll-Sinfonie', *Gedenkschrift für Hermann Abert von seinen Schülern*, ed. Friedrich Blume (Halle, 1928), pp. 93–115.

—— *Schuberts Sinfonien* (Wiesbaden, 1933).

LANDON, CHRISTA: 'New Schubert Finds', *Music Review*, xxxi (1970), pp. 215–31.

NEWBOULD, BRIAN: 'Schubert's Other "Unfinished"', *Musical Times*, cxix (1978), pp. 587–9.

PRITCHARD, T. C. L.: 'The Unfinished Symphony', *Music Review*, iii (1942), pp. 10–32.

REED, JOHN: 'How the "Great" C Major was Written', *Music and Letters*, lvi (1975), pp. 18–25.

THERSTAPPEN, HANS JOACHIM: *Die Entwicklung der Form bei Schubert dargestellt an den ersten Sätzen seiner Sinfonien* (Leipzig, 1931).

WICKENHAUSER, RICHARD: *Franz Schuberts Symphonien. Analytische Einführung* (Leipzig, 1928).

Spohr

GÖTHEL, FOLKER, ed.: *Louis Spohr: Lebenserinnerungen* (Tutzing, 1968).

HEUSSNER, HORST: 'Spohr als Symphoniker', *Musica*, xiii (1959), pp. 297–9.

Waldstein

HEER, JOSEF: *Der Graf von Waldstein und sein Verhältnis zu Beethoven* (Leipzig, 1933).

Weber

JÄHNS, FRIEDRICH WILHELM: *Carl Maria von Weber in seinen Werken. Chronologisch-thematisches Verzeichnis seiner sämmtlichen Compositionen* (Berlin, 1871, repr. Berlin-Lichterfelde, 1967).

TENSCHERT, ROLAND: 'Die Sinfonien Webers', *Neue Musik-Zeitung*, xlviii (1927), pp. 481–5.

WARRACK, JOHN: *Carl Maria von Weber* (London and New York, 1968).

Wesley, S.

SCHWARZ, JOHN I., JR.: 'Samuel and Samuel Sebastian Wesley, the English Doppelmeister', *Musical Quarterly*, lix (1973), pp. 190–206.

Witt

LANDON, H. C. ROBBINS: 'The "Jena" Symphony', *Music Review*, xviii (1957), pp. 109–13.

LEAVIS, RALPH: 'Die "Beethovenianismen" der Jenaer Symphonie', *Die Musikforschung*, xxiii (1970), pp. 297–302.

Wranitzky (Vranický)

POŠTOLKA, MILAN: 'Thematisches Verzeichnis der Sinfonien Pavel Vranickýs', *Miscellanea Musicologica*, xx (Prague, 1967), pp. 101–28.

CHAPTER V

THE CONCERTO

(i) Modern Editions

(a) Anthology

LANG, PAUL HENRY, ed.: *The Concerto 1800–1900* (New York, 1969). (Includes excerpts from works by Beethoven, Chopin, Mendelssohn, and Weber.)

(b) *Works by Individual Composers*

BEETHOVEN, L. van: Piano Concerto in E flat, WoO 4, completed W. Hess (rev. ed., Kassel, 1961, London, 1969).
—— Piano Concertos nos. 1–5, Opp. 15, 19, 37, 58 and 73; Concerto in C, Op. 56, for piano, violin and violoncello; Choral Fantasia in C minor, Op. 80; *Ludwig van Beethoven. Werke. Vollständige kritisch durchgesehene überall berechtigte Ausgabe*, series ix/1–2 (Leipzig, *c.* 1865).
—— Concerto in C, Op. 56, for piano, violin and violoncello, ed. B. van der Linde, *Ludwig van Beethoven. Werke. Neue Ausgabe sämtlicher Werke*, series iii/1 (Munich–Duisburg, 1968).
—— Violin Concerto in D, Op. 61; Romance no. 1 in G, Op. 40, for violin and orchestra; Romance no. 2 in F, Op. 50, for violin and orchestra; *Ludwig van Beethoven. Werke. Vollständige kritisch durchgesehene überall berechtigte Ausgabe*, series iv (Leipzig, *c.* 1865).
—— Violin Concerto, Op. 61; Romances nos. 1–2, Opp. 40, 50, ed. S. A. Kojima, *Ludwig van Beethoven. Werke. Neue Ausgabe sämtlicher Werke*, series iii/4 (Munich, 1973).
—— Violin Concerto in D, Op. 61, ed. W. Hess, *Ludwig van Beethoven. Werke. Supplemente zur Gesamtausgabe*, series x/2 (Wiesbaden, 1969).
—— Violin Concerto, Op. 61, facsimile ed. ed. F. Grasberger (*Auftrag des Instituts für Österreichische Musikdokumentation* i) (Graz, 1979).
BELLINI, V.: Oboe Concerto in E flat, ed. R. Meylan (Munich, 1969).
CHOPIN, F.: Piano Concerto no. 1 in E minor, Op. 11, ed. K. Sikorski, *Fryderyk Chopin. Complete Works*, xix (Warsaw, 1949).
—— Piano Concerto no. 2 in F minor, Op. 21, ed. K. Sikorski, *Fryderyk Chopin. Complete Works*, xx (Warsaw, 1949).
DONIZETTI, G.: English Horn Concerto (Concertino) in G, piano score ed. R. Meylan (Frankfurt, New York, *c.* 1966).
FIELD, J.: Piano Concertos nos. 1–3, ed. F. Merrick (*Musica Britannica*, xvii) (London, 1961).
HUMMEL, J.: Piano Concerto in A minor, Op. 85, piano score (New York, 1966).
—— Piano Concerto in B minor, Op. 89, piano score (New York, 1969).
—— Trumpet Concerto in E [flat], ed. E. Tarr (*Accademia Musicale*, xxx) (Mainz, 1972); piano ed. F. Stein (Leipzig, 1957).
KOŽELUH, L.: Piano Concerto in D major, op. 30, piano score ed. R. Meylan (Wiesbaden, 1963).
KROMMER, F.: Clarinet Concerto in E flat, Op. 36, ed. M. Berlász (Budapest, *c.* 1975), piano score ed. J. Kratochvíl and L. Simon (*Musica Antiqua Bohemica*, xiii) (Prague, 1953).
—— Oboe Concerto in F, Op. 52, piano score ed. F. Suchý (*Musica Antiqua Bohemica*, xxvii) (Prague, 1956); ed. J. Ledward (London, *c.* 1976).
LIPIŃSKI, K.: Violin Concerto in D, Op. 21, piano ed. F. Hermann (Leipzig, *c.* 1934).
MENDELSSOHN, F.: Piano Concerto no. 1 in G minor, Op. 25; Piano Concerto no. 2 in D minor, Op. 40, ed. J. Rietz, *Felix Mendelssohn–Bartholdy's Werke. Kritisch durchgesehene Ausgabe*, viii (Leipzig, *c.* 1874).
—— Concerto in D minor for violin, piano, and strings, ed. R. Unger, *Leipziger Ausgabe der Werke Felix Mendelssohn Bartholdys*, series II/6 (Leipzig 1973).
—— Double Piano Concerto in E, ed. K.-H. Köhler, *Leipziger Ausgabe der Werke Felix Mendelssohn Bartholdys*, series ii/4 (Leipzig, 1960).
—— Double Piano Concerto in A flat, ed. K.-H. Köhler, *Leipziger Ausgabe der Werke Felix Mendelssohn Bartholdys*, series ii/5 (Leipzig, 1961).
—— Violin Concerto in E minor, Op. 64, ed. J. Rietz, *Felix Mendelssohn-Bartholdy's*

Werke. Kritisch durchgesehene Ausgabe, iv (Leipzig, *c.* 1874; repr. Farnborough 1968).

MOSCHELES, I.: Piano Concerto no. 3 in G minor, Op. 58, piano score ed. C. Schultze (New York, 1971).

PAGANINI, N.: Violin Concerto no. 1 in E flat, Op. 6, (New York, *c.* 1968); piano score ed. W. Stross (Leipzig, 1943).

—— Violin Concerto no. 5 in A minor, orchestrated F. Mompellio (Genoa, 1973).

—— Violin Concerto no. 6, in E minor, orchestrated F. Mompellio (Genoa, 1973).

RODE, P.: Violin Concerto no. 7 in A minor, Op. 9, piano ed. A. A. Sarvas (Bucharest, 1956), ed. S. M. Kuszewski (Cracow, 1966).

ROMBERG, B.: Flute Concerto in B minor, Op. 30, ed. D. H. Förster (Zürich and New York, *c.* 1978).

SPOHR, L.: Violin Concerto no. 7 in E minor, Op. 38, ed. F. Göthel (Frankfurt and New York, 1964).

—— Violin Concerto no. 12 in A, Op. 79, piano ed. O. Seeger (Leipzig, 1904), ed. F. Göthel (Kassel, 1955).

Numerous editions of the other concertos by Auer, Hellmesberger, Joachim, *et al.*

VIOTTI, G. B.: Violin Concertos nos. 7, 13, 18 and 27, *Four Violin Concertos*, ed. C. White (*Recent Researches in the Music of the Pre-Classical, Classical and Romantic eras*, iv–v) (Madison, Wisconsin, 1976).

—— Violin Concerto no. 22 in A minor, ed. A. Einstein (Leipzig, 1929).

WEBER, K. M. von: Piano Concerto no. 1 in C, Op 11, ed. H. H. Schönzeler (London, 1959).

—— Piano Concerto no. 2 in E flat, Op. 32, ed. H. H. Schönzeler (London, 1959).

—— Konzertstück in F minor, Op. 79 (Leipzig, 1926, repr. Leipzig, 1962; London and New York, 1943).

—— Clarinet Concertino in E flat, Op. 26, ed. G. Hausswald (Leipzig, 1953).

(ii) Books and Articles

(a) General

AMSTER, ISABELLA: *Das Virtuosenkonzert in der ersten Hälfte des 19. Jahrhunderts: ein Beitrag zur Geschichte des deutschen Klavier-Konzerts* (Wolfenbüttel, 1931).

BLEES, GISELA: *Das Cello um 1800. Eine Untersuchung der Cello-Konzerte zwischen Haydns op. 101 und Schumanns op. 129* (Regensburg, 1973).

ENGEL, HANS: *Die Entwicklung des deutschen Klavierkonzerts von Mozart bis Liszt* (Leipzig, 1927, repr. Hildesheim and New York, 1970).

—— *Das Instrumentalkonzert, Führer durch den Konzertsaal*, iii (Leipzig, 1932), revised and expanded as *Das Instrumentalkonzert. Eine musikgeschichtliche Darstellung*, 2 vols. (Wiesbaden, 1971, 1974).

—— *Das Solokonzert* (*Das Musikwerk*, xxv) (Cologne, 1964, English edition 1964), introduction, pp. 33–92.

ERLEBACH, RUPERT: 'Style in Pianoforte Concerto Writing', *Music and Letters*, xvii (1936), pp. 131–9.

FISCHER, WILHELM: 'Instrumentalmusik von 1750–1828', *Handbuch der Musikgeschichte*, ii, ed. G. Adler (2nd ed., Berlin, 1932, repr. Tutzing, 1961), pp. 795–833.

HILL, RALPH (ed.): *The Concerto* (London, 1952, repr. Westport, Connecticut, 1978).

HOFFMANN-ERBRECHT, LOTHAR: 'Das Klavierkonzert', *Gattungen der Musik in Einzeldarstellungen. Gedenkschrift Leo Schrade*, i, ed. Wulf Arlt (Bern, 1973), pp. 743–84.

KLOIBER, RUDOLF: *Handbuch des Instrumentalkonzerts*, 2 vols. (Wiesbaden, 1972–3).

KNÖDT, HEINRICH: 'Zur Entwicklungsgeschichte der Kadenzen im Instrumentalkonzert', *Sammelbände der internationalen Musikgesellschaft*, xv (1913–14), pp. 375–419.

LA LAURENCIE, LIONEL DE: *L'École française du violon de Lully à Viotti*, ii–iii (Paris, 1923–4, repr. Paris, 1971).

LA RUE, JAN: 'Union Thematic Catalogues for 18th Century Chamber Music and Concertos' [*c*. 1740–*c*. 1810], *Fontes artis musicae*, vii (1960), pp. 64–6.

LANG, PAUL HENRY: 'The Concerto in the Nineteenth Century', *The Concerto 1800–1900* (New York, 1969), pp. vii–xxxvi.

McCREDIE, ANDREW W.: 'Symphonie Concertante and Multiple Concerto in Germany (1780–1850). Some Problems and Perspectives for a Source–Repertory Study', *Miscellanea Musicologica* (Adelaide), viii (1975), pp. 115–47.

MEYER, JOHN ARTHUR: 'The Idea of Conflict in the Concerto', *Studies in Music* (Perth, Australia), viii (1974), pp. 38–52.

MIES, PAUL: *Das Konzert im 19. Jahrhundert. Studien zu Formen und Kadenzen* (Bonn, 1972).

PAPE, WINFRIED: 'Das Violoncello in Solokonzerten, Kammermusik-und Orchesterwerken unter besonderer Berücksichtigung des 19. Jahrhunderts', *Schweizerische Musikzeitung*, cix/4 (1969), pp. 208–13.

RINGER, ALEXANDER L.: 'Beethoven and the London Pianoforte School', *Musical Quarterly*, lvi (1970), pp. 742–58.

SCHERING, ARNOLD: *Geschichte des Instrumentalkonzerts bis auf die Gegenwart* (2nd ed., Leipzig, 1927, repr. Hildesheim, 1965).

SCHWARZ, BORIS: 'Beethoven and the French Violin School', *Musical Quarterly*, xliv (1958), pp. 441–7.

—— *French Instrumental Music between the Revolutions* (New York, 1982).

STEVENS, JANE R.: 'An 18th-Century Description of Concerto First-Movement Form', *Journal of the American Musicological Society*, xxiv (1971), pp. 85–95.

—— 'Theme, Harmony and Texture in Classic-Romantic Descriptions of Concerto First-Movement Form', *Journal of the American Musicological Society*, xxvii (1974), pp. 25–60.

SWALIN, BENJAMIN FRANKLIN: *The Violin Concerto; a Study in German Romanticism* (Chapel Hill, North Carolina, 1941, repr. New York, 1973).

TOVEY, DONALD F.: 'Concertos', *Essays in Musical Analysis*, iii (London, 1936).

VEINUS, ABRAHAM: *The Concerto* (Garden City, New York, 1944, 2nd ed., New York, 1964).

WERNER, ERIC: 'Instrumental Music Outside the Pale of Classicism and Romanticism', *Instrumental Music*, ed. David Hughes (Cambridge, Mass., 1959, repr. New York, 1972), pp. 57–69.

(b) Individual Composers

Beethoven

BENARY, PETER: 'Zur Wiedergabe des Violinkonzerts von L. van Beethoven', *Neue Zeitschrift für Musik*, cxxix (1968), pp. 447–8.

DEANE, BASIL: 'The Concertos', *The Beethoven Reader*, ed. Denis Arnold and Nigel Fortune (London and New York, 1971), pp. 318–28.

FISKE, ROGER: *Beethoven Concertos and Overtures* (London, 1971).

GRASBERGER, FRANZ: 'Die beiden ersten Klavierkonzerte von Ludwig van Beethoven', *Österreichische Musikzeitschrift*, xxiii (1968), pp. 18–23.

HESS, WILLY, ed.: *Beethoven-Studien* (*Veröffentlichungen des Beethovenhauses in Bonn*, series iv/7) (Bonn, 1972).

—— 'Das Klavierkonzert des vierzehnjährigen Beethoven', *Musica*, xxii (1968), p. 362.

—— 'Die Originalkadenzen zu Beethovens Klavierkonzerten', *Revue musicale suisse*, cxii (1972), pp. 270–5.

—— 'Die verschiedenen Fassungen von Beethovens Violinkonzert', *Schweizerische Musikzeitung*, cix (1969), pp. 197–201.

KOJIMA, SHIN AUGUSTINUS: 'Die Solovioline-Fassungen und -Varianten von Beethovens Violinkonzert op. 61 – ihre Entstehung und Bedeutung', *Beethoven Jahrbuch, Zweite Reihe*, viii (1971–2), pp. 97–145.

KÖRNER, KLAUS: 'Formen musikalischer Aussage im zweiten Satz des G-dur Klavierkonzerts von Beethoven', *Beethoven Jahrbuch, Zweite Reihe*, ix (1973), pp. 201–16.

KROSS, SIEGFRIED: 'Improvisation und Konzertform bei Beethoven', *Beethoven-Kolloquium 1977. Dokumentation und Aufführungspraxis*, ed. Rudolf Klein (Kassel, 1978), pp. 132–9.

KÜTHEN, HANS-WERNER: 'Probleme der Chronologie in den Skizzen und Autographen zu Beethovens Klavierkonzert op. 19), *Beethoven Jahrbuch, Zweite Reihe*, ix (1973), pp. 263–92.

LOCKWOOD, LEWIS: 'Beethoven's Unfinished Piano Concerto of 1815: Sources and Problems', *Musical Quarterly*, lvi (1970), pp. 624–46; also in *The Creative World of Beethoven*, ed. Paul Henry Lang (New York, 1971), pp. 122–44.

MIES, PAUL: *Die Krise der Konzertkadenz bei Beethoven* (Bonn, 1970).

MOHR, WILHELM: 'Beethovens Klavierfassung seines Violinkonzerts Op. 61', *Bericht über den internationalen musikwissenschaftlichen Kongress Bonn 1970*, ed. Carl Dahlhaus *et al.* (Kassel, 1971), pp. 509–11.

OSTHOFF, WOLFGANG: *Ludwig van Beethoven. Klavierkonzert Nr. 4 c-moll, op. 37* (Munich, 1965).

TYSON, ALAN: 'Beethoven's Choral Fantasia', *Music and Letters*, xlviii (1967), pp. 412–13.

—— 'Textual Problems of Beethoven's Violin Concerto', *Musical Quarterly*, liii (1967), pp. 482–502.

Chopin

ABRAHAM, GERALD: 'Chopin and the Orchestra', *The Book of the First International Musicological Congress Devoted to the Works of Frederick Chopin, Warszawa, 16th–22nd February 1960*, ed. Zofia Lissa (Warsaw, 1963), pp. 85–7; also in *Slavonic and Romantic Music* (London and New York, 1968), pp. 23–7.

FRĄCZKIEWICZ, ALEKSANDER: 'Faktura fortepianowa Koncertów Fryderyka Chopina', *Annales Chopin*, iii (Warsaw, 1958), pp. 133–55. 'Koncerty fortepianowe Chopina jako typ koncertu romantycznego', *The Book of the First International Musicological Congress Devoted to the Works of Frederick Chopin, Warszawa, 1960*, ed. Zofia Lissa (Warsaw, 1963), pp. 293–6.

GOULD, PETER: 'Concertos and Sonatas', *Frédéric Chopin*, ed. Alan Walker (London, 1966), pp. 144–58.

HOESICK, FERDYNAND: *Chopin. Życie i twórczość*, 4 vols. (2nd ed., Warsaw, 1967–8).

Dussek

SCHIFFER, LEO: *Johann Ladislaus Dussek, seine Sonaten und seine Konzerte* (Munich, 1914, repr. New York, 1972).

TRUSCOTT, HAROLD: 'Dussek and the Concerto', *Music Review*, xvi (1955), pp. 29–53.

Field

BRANSON, DAVID: *John Field and Chopin* (London, 1972).

HOPKINSON, CECIL: *A Bibliographical Thematic Catalogue of the Works of John Field* (London, 1961).

PIGGOTT, PATRICK: *The Life & Music of John Field, 1782–1837, Creator of the Nocturne* (London, 1973).

TEMPERLEY, NICHOLAS: 'John Field's Life and Music', *Musical Times*, cxv (1974), pp. 386–8.

Hummel

BENYOVSZKY, KARL: *J. N. Hummel. Der Mensch und Künstler* (Bratislava/Pressburg, 1934).

DAVIS, RICHARD: 'The Music of J. N. Hummel, its Derivation and Development', *Music Review*, xxvi (1965), pp. 169–91.

SACHS, JOEL: 'A Checklist of the Works of Johann Nepomuk Hummel', *Music Library Association Notes*, xxx (1973–4), pp. 732–54.

ZIMMERSCHIED, DIETER: *Thematisches Verzeichnis der Werke von Johann Nepomuk Hummel* (Hofheim, 1971).

Koželuh, L.

POŠTOLKA, MILAN: *Leopold Koželuh: Život a dílo* (Prague, 1964). With thematic catalogue.

Mendelssohn

THOMAS, MATHIAS: *Das Instrumentalwerk Felix Mendelssohn-Bartholdys. Eine systematisch-theoretische Untersuchung unter besonderer Berücksichtigung der zeitgenössischen Musiktheorie* (Göttinger Musikwissenschaftliche Arbeiten, iv) (Göttingen, 1972).

WERNER, ERIC: *Mendelssohn. A New Image of the Composer and his Age* (London and New York, 1963).

—— 'Two Unpublished Mendelssohn Concertos', *Music and Letters*, xxxvi (1955), pp. 126–38. (Refers to the Double Piano Concertos in E and A flat major.)

Moscheles

HEUSSNER, INGEBORG: 'Formale Gestaltungsprinzipe bei Ignaz Moscheles', *Festschrift Hans Engel*, ed. Horst Heussner (Kassel, 1964), pp. 155–65.

Paganini

AUDIBERT, HENRI: *Paganini Concerto Style* (Narbonne, 1974).

PULVER, JEFFREY: *Paganini, the Romantic Virtuoso* (London, 1936, repr. New York, 1970).

Spohr

GÖTHEL, FOLKER: Louis Spohr–Heute', *Musica*, xiii (1959), pp. 293–300.

JUNG, HANS RUDOLF: 'Louis Spohr – der Geiger und seine Violin-konzerte', *Louis Spohr: Festschrift 1959*, ed. Günther Kraft *et al.* (Weimar, 1959), pp. 78–87.

Viotti

GIAZOTTO, REMO: *Giovanni Battista Viotti* (Milan, 1956). With thematic catalogue.

WALTER, MARTA: 'Ein Klavier-Konzert von J. B. Viotti', *Schweizerische Musikzeitung*, xciii (1955), pp. 99–103.

WHITE, CHAPPELL: 'Did Viotti Write any Original Piano Concertos', *Journal of the American Musicological Society*, xxii (1969), pp. 275–84.

—— 'Toward a More Accurate Chronology of Viotti's Violin Concertos', *Fontes artis musicae*, xx (1973), pp. 111–24.

Weber

JÄHNS, FRIEDRICH WILHELM: *Carl Maria von Weber in seinen Werken. Chronologisch-thematisches Verzeichnis seiner sämmtlichen Compositionen* (Berlin, 1871, repr. Berlin–Lichterfelde, 1967).

WARRACK, JOHN: *Carl Maria von Weber* (London and New York, 1968).

CHAPTER VI

BEETHOVEN'S CHAMBER MUSIC

(i) Modern Editions

BEETHOVEN, LUDWIG VAN: *Ludwig van Beethoven's Werke: vollständige kritisch durchgesehene überall berechtigte Ausgabe* (Leipzig, 1864–7, 1888–90), vi, 'Streichquartette', vii, 'Streichtrios', viii, 'Für Blasinstrumente', x, 'Pianoforte-Quintett und Quartette', xi, 'Pianoforte Trios', xii, 'Für Pianoforte und Violine', xiii, 'Für Pianoforte und Violoncell', xiv, 'Für Pianoforte und Blasinstrumente'.
—— *Supplemente zur Gesamtausgabe*, ed. W. Hess (Wiesbaden), 6, 'Kammermusik für Streichinstrumente' (1963), 7, 'Kammermusik für Blasinstrumente, Kammermusik für Bläser und Streicher' (1963), 9, 'Kammermusik mit Klavier' (1965).
—— *Werke* (Munich), 'Klavierquintett und Klavierquartette', ed. S. Kross (1964), 3, 'Klaviertrios II', ed. F. Klugmann (1965), 1–2, 'Werke für Klavier und Violine', ed. S. Brandenburg (1974), 3, 'Werke für Violoncello und Klavier', ed. B. van der Linde (1971), 2, 'Streichquintette', ed. J. Herzog (1968), 3, 'Streichquartette I', ed. P. Mies (1962), 4, 'Streichquartette II', ed. P. Mies (1968), 6, 'Streichtrios und Streichduos', ed. E. Platen (1965).

(ii) Facsimile Editions of Autograph Manuscripts

BEETHOVEN, LUDWIG VAN: *Violin Sonata in G Major*, Op. 30 no. 3, ed. A. Tyson (London, 1981).
—— *String Quartets Opus 59 nos. 1–3*, 3 vols., ed. A. Tyson (London, 1980–81).
—— *Sonata for Violoncello and Pianoforte, Opus 69, First Movement*, ed. L. Lockwood (New York, 1970). Also published in *The Music Forum*, II (1970).
—— *Sonate für Klavier und Violine G-dur, Op. 96*, ed. M. Staehelin (Munich, 1977).

(iii) Sketchbooks

(a) In facsimile

BEETHOVEN, LUDWIG VAN: *Autograph Miscellany from circa 1786 to 1799 . . . (The 'Kafka Sketchbook')*, facsimile and transcription, ed. J. Kerman, 2 vols. (London, 1970).
—— *Ein Skizzenbuch zu Streichquartetten aus Op. 18*, facsimile and transcription, ed. W. Virneisel, 2 vols. (Bonn, 1972–4).
—— *Ein Notierungsbuch von Beethoven aus dem Besitz der Preussischen Staatsbibliothek zu Berlin*, transcription, ed. K. L. Mikulicz (Leipzig, 1927). (Includes amongst other material sketches for the violin sonatas Opp. 23–4).
—— *Kesslersches Skizzenbuch*, facsimile and transcription, ed. S. Brandenburg, 2 vols. (Bonn, 1976–8). (Includes amongst other material sketches for the violin sonatas Opp. 30 and 47.)
—— *Kniga eskizov Beethovena za 1802–3 gody*, facsimile and transcription, ed. N. Fishman, 3 vols. (Moscow, 1962). (Includes sketches for the Violin Sonata Op. 47.)
—— *Ein Skizzenbuch zur Pastoralsymphonie op. 68 und zu den Trios op. 70, 1 und 2*, transcription, ed. D. Weise, 2 vols (Bonn, 1961).
—— *Ein Moskauer Skizzenbuch von Beethoven*, facsimile and commentary, ed. M. Ivanov-Boretsky, *Muzïkal'noe obrazovanie*, nos. 1–2 (Moscow, 1927), pp. 9–58, 75–91; (republished Vienna, 1927). (Sketches for the quartets opp. 130 and 132).

(b) *Studies of the Sketches*

HOLSCHNEIDER, ANDREAS: 'Unbekannte Beethoven-Skizzen in Bergamo', *Analecta musicologica*, ix (Cologne and Vienna, 1977), pp. 130–34. (On op. 5.)

JOHNSON, DOUGLAS: 'Beethoven's Sketches for the Scherzo of the Quartet Op. 18, no. 6', *Journal of the American Musicological Society*, (1970), pp. 385–404.

KERMAN, JOSEPH: 'Beethoven's Early Sketches', *The Musical Quarterly*, lvi (1970), pp. 515–38.

—— 'Beethoven Sketches in the British Museum, *Proceedings of the Royal Musical Association*, xciii (1966–7), pp. 77–96.

KRAMER, RICHARD: 'Ambiguities in *La Malinconia*: What the Sketches Say', *Beethoven Studies 3*, ed. A. Tyson (Cambridge, 1982).

MIES, PAUL: *Die Bedeutung der Skizzen Beethovens zur Erkenntnis seines Stiles* (Leipzig, 1925, repr. 1969). Eng. trans. by D. L. Mackinnon as *Beethoven's Sketches* (London, 1929, repr. Cambridge, 1969).

NOTTEBOHM, GUSTAV: *Beethoveniana* (Leipzig and Winterthur, 1872, 2nd ed. 1925; 2nd ed. repr. Hackensack, N.J., 1970). Collection of essays, most of which first appeared in the *Allgemeine musikalische Zeitung*, 1869–71.

—— *Ein Skizzenbuch von Beethoven* (Leipzig, 1865, 2nd ed. 1924; 2nd ed. repr. Hackensack, N.J., 1970). Eng. trans. J. Katz in *Two Beethoven Sketchbooks: a Description with Musical Extracts* (London, 1979). (Includes substantial transcriptions of sketches for the violin sonatas Opp. 30 and 47.)

—— *Zweite Beethoveniana*, ed. E. Mandyczewski (Leipzig, 1887, 2nd ed. 1925; 2nd ed. repr. Hackensack, N.J., 1970). Collection of articles, most of which first appeared in the *Musikalisches Wochenblatt*, 1875–9.

RODA, CECILIO DE: 'Un quaderno di autografi di Beethoven del 1825', *Rivista musicale italiana*, xii (1905), pp. 63–108, 592–622, 734–67. Also published separately (Turin, 1907). (Transcriptions, with commentary, of sketches for Opp. 130, 132 and 133.)

TYSON, ALAN: 'A Reconstruction of the Pastoral Symphony Sketchbook', *Beethoven Studies* (New York, 1973 and London, 1974), pp. 67–96.

VIRNEISEL, WILHELM: 'Aus Beethovens Skizzenbuch zum Streichquintett op. 29', *Zeitschrift für Musik*, cxiii (1952), pp. 142–6.

(iv) The Works

(a) *The String Quartets*

ABRAHAM, GERALD: Beethoven's Second-Period Quartets (London, 1942).

BRANDENBURG, SIEGHARD: 'The Autograph of Beethoven's String Quartet in A minor, Opus 132', *The Quartets of Haydn, Mozart and Beethoven*, ed. C. Wolff (Cambridge, Mass., 1981), pp. 278–300.

—— 'The First Version of Beethoven's G Major String Quartet, Op. 18 No. 2', *Music and Letters*, lviii (1977), pp. 127–52.

—— 'The Historical Background to the "Heiliger Dankgesang" in Beethoven's A minor Quartet, Op. 132', *Beethoven Studies 3*, ed. A. Tyson (London, 1982).

BROYLES, MICHAEL E. 'Beethoven's Sonata Op. 14, No. 1 – Originally for Strings?', *Journal of the American Musicological Society*, xxiii (1970), pp. 405–19.

COOKE, DERYCK: 'The Unity of Beethoven's Late Quartets', *The Music Review*, xxiv (1963), pp. 30–49.

D'INDY, VINCENT: 'Beethoven', *Cobbett's Cyclopedic Survey of Chamber Music*, ed. W. W. Cobbett (London, 1929, 2nd ed. 1963).

EBERT, ALFRED: 'Die ersten Aufführungen von Beethovens Es-dur Quartet (Opus 127) im Frühling 1825', *Die Musik*, ix (1910), pp. 42–63, 90–106.

FINSCHER, LUDWIG: 'Beethovens Streichquartett Op. 59, 3', *Zur musikalischen Analyse*, ed. G. Schuhmacher (Darmstadt, 1974), pp. 122–60.

FISCHER, KURT VON: '"Never to be performed in public": zu Beethovens Streichquartett Op. 95', *Beethoven-Jahrbuch, Zweite Reihe*, ix (1973–7), pp. 87–96.

FISKE, ROGER: *Beethoven's Last Quartets* (London, 1940).

GLAUERT, AMANDA: 'The Double Perspective in Beethoven's Opus 131', *19th-Century Music*, iv/2 (1981), pp. 113–20.

HELM, THEODOR: *Beethovens Streichquartette: Versuch einer technischen Analyse* (Leipzig, 1885, 3rd ed. 1921; 3rd ed. repr. Wiesbaden, 1971).

JONAS, OSWALD: 'A Lesson with Beethoven by Correspondence', *Musical Quarterly*, xxxviii (1952), pp. 215–21. On Op. 127.

KERMAN, JOSEPH: 'Beethoven: the Single Journey', *Hudson Review*, V (1952–3), pp. 32–55. On Op. 132.

—— *The Beethoven Quartets* (New York, 1967).

KIRKENDALE, WARREN: 'The "Great Fugue" Op. 133: Beethoven's "Art of Fugue"', *Acta musicologica*, xxxv (1963), pp. 14–24.

KRAMER, JONATHAN D.: 'Multiple and Non-linear Time in Beethoven's Opus 135', *Perspectives of New Music*, xi/2 (spring–summer 1973), pp. 122–45.

KREFFT, EKKEHARD: *Die späten Quartette Beethovens: Substanz und Substanzverarbeitung* (Bonn, 1969).

LAM, BASIL: *Beethoven String Quartets*, 2 vols. (London, 1975).

LOCHHEAD, JUDY: 'The Temporal in Beethoven's Opus 135', in *Theory Only*, iv (January 1979), pp. 3–30.

MAHAIM, IVAN: *Beethoven: naissance et renaissance des derniers quatuors* (Paris, 1964).

MARLIAVE, JOSEPH DE: *Les quatuors de Beethoven* (Paris, 1925). Eng. trans. by H. Andrews (London, 1928, repr. 1961).

MASON, DANIEL GREGORY: *The Quartets of Beethoven* (New York, 1947).

MILA, MASSIMO: 'Lettura della "Grande Fuga" op. 133', *Scritti in onore di Luigi Ronga* (Milan and Naples, 1973), pp. 345–66.

MISCH, LUDWIG: *Beethoven-Studien* (Berlin, 1950). English translation by G. I. C. de Courcy (Norman, Okla., 1953). Includes short essays on Op. 59 no. 3, Op. 130 and Op. 133.

MITCHELL, WILLIAM J.: 'Beethoven's La Malinconia from the String Quartet Op. 18, no. 6: Technique and Structure', *The Music Forum*, iii (1973), pp. 269–80.

OREL, ALFRED: 'Das Autograph des Scherzos aus Beethovens Streichquartett op. 127', *Festschrift Hans Engel zum siebzigsten Geburtstag*, ed. H. Heussner (Kassel, 1964), pp. 274–80.

PLATEN, EMIL: 'Ein Notierungsproblem in Beethovens späten Streichquartetten', *Beethoven-Jahrbuch, Zweite Reihe*, viii (1971–2), pp. 147–56.

—— '"Das Organische der Fuge": On the Autograph of Beethoven's String Quartet in F Major, Opus 59, No. 1', *The String Quartets of Haydn, Mozart, and Beethoven: Studies of the Autographs* ed. C. Wolff (Cambridge Mass., 1980), pp. 223–265. Response by Robert Winter, *ibid.*, pp. 260–272.

—— 'Zeitgenössische Hinweise zur Aufführungspraxis der letzten Streichquartette Beethovens', *Beethoven-Kolloquium 1977: Dokumentation und Aufführungspraxis*, ed. R. Klein (Kassel, 1978), pp. 100–7.

RADCLIFFE, PHILIP: *Beethoven's String Quartets* (London, 1965).

RATZ, ERWIN: *Einführung in die musikalische Formenlehre* (Vienna, 1951, 3rd edn. 1973), chapter 6: 'Beispiele aus den Streichquartetten Beethovens'.

RIEMANN, HUGO, *Beethovens Streichquartette* (Berlin, 1903).

SALMEN, WALTER: 'Zur Gestaltung der "Thèmes russes" in Beethovens opus 59', *Festschrift für Walter Wiora*, ed. L. Finscher and C.-H. Mahling (Kassel, 1967), pp. 397–404.

SIMPSON, ROBERT: 'The Chamber Music for Strings', *The Beethoven Companion*, ed. D. Arnold and N. Fortune (London, 1971), pp. 241–80.

STEPHAN, RUDOLF: 'Zu Beethovens letzten Quartetten', *Die Musikforschung, xxiii* (1970), pp. 245–56.

TOVEY, DONALD F.: 'Some Aspects of Beethoven's Art-Forms', *Music and Letters*, viii (1927), pp. 131–55. repr. in *Essays and Lectures on Music* (London, 1949), pp. 271–97. (Includes discussion of Op. 131.)

TRUSCOTT, HAROLD: *Beethoven's Late String Quartets* (London, 1968).

TYSON, ALAN: 'The "Razumovsky" Quartets: Some Aspects of the Sources', *Beethoven Studies 3* (London, 1982).

WEBSTER, JAMES: 'Traditional elements in Beethoven's Middle-Period String Quartets', *Beethoven, Performers, and Critics*, ed. R. Winter and B. Carr (Detroit, 1980), pp. 94–133.

WEDIG, H. J.: *Beethovens Streichquartett op. 18, Nr. 1 und seine erste Fassung* (Bonn, 1922). (Includes score of the first version.)

WINTER, ROBERT: 'Plans for the Structure of the String Quartet in C Sharp Minor, Op. 131', *Beethoven Studies 2*, ed. A. Tyson (London, 1977), pp. 106–37.

ZUCKERKANDL, VICTOR: *Man the Musician* (Princeton, 1973), chapter 17: 'Musical Thought', pp. 292–331. (Includes discussion of the sketches for Op. 127.)

(b) The Violin Sonatas

BRANDENBURG, SIEGHARD: 'Bemerkungen zu Beethovens Op. 96', *Beethoven-Jahrbuch, Zweite Reihe*, ix (1973–7), pp. 11–25.

EIBNER, FRANZ: 'Einige Kriterien für die Apperzeption und Interpretation von Beethovens Werk', *Beethoven-Kolloquium 1977: Dokumentation und Aufführungspraxis*, ed. R. Klein (Kassel, 1978), pp. 20–36. Analysis of Op. 24.

ENGELSMANN, WALTER: *Beethovens Kompositionspläne, dargestellt in den Sonaten für Klavier und Violine* (Augsburg, 1931).

HERWEGH, MARCEL *Technique et interprétation sous forme d'essai d'analyse psychologique expérimentale appliquée aux sonates pour piano et violon de Beethoven* (Paris, 1926, 2nd ed. 1937).

JONAS, OSWALD: 'Beethovens Skizzen und ihre Gestaltung zum Werk', *Zeitschrift für Musikwissenschaft*, xvi (1934), pp. 449–59. Includes discussion of op. 96.

OBELKEVICH, MARY ROWEN: 'The Growth of a Musical Idea – Beethoven's Opus 96', *Current Musicology*, xi (1971), pp. 91–114.

SZIGETI, JOSEPH: *The Ten Beethoven Sonatas for Piano and Violin* (Urbana, Ill., 1965).

(c) The Cello Sonatas

BORINGHIERI, GUSTAVO: 'Le due sonate di Beethoven, Op. 102, n. 1 e 2, per pianoforte e violoncello', *Nuova rivista musicale italiana*, ix (1977), pp. 537–72.

DAHLHAUS, CARL: '"Von zwei Kulturen in der Musik": die Schlussfuge aus Beethovens Cellosonate opus 102, 2', *Die Musikforschung*, xxxi (1978), pp. 397–405.

LOCKWOOD, LEWIS: 'Beethoven's Early Works for Violoncello and Contemporary Violoncello Technique', *Beethoven-Kolloquium 1977: Dokumentation und Aufführungspraxis*, ed. R. Klein (Kassel, 1978), pp. 174–82). (Mainly on Op. 5.)

—— 'The Autograph of the First Movement of Beethoven's sonata for Violoncello and Pianoforte, opus 69, *Music Forum*, ii (1970), pp. 1–109.

(d) Other Chamber Works

FORTUNE, NIGEL: 'The Chamber Music with Piano', The Beethoven Companion, ed.
D. Arnold and N. Fortune (London, 1971), pp. 197–240.

ENGEL, CARL: 'Beethoven's Opus 3: an "Envoi de Vienne"?', Musical Quarterly, xiii
(1927), pp. 261–79.

MIES, PAUL: 'Ein Menuett von L. van Beethoven für Streichquartett', Beethoven–
Jahrbuch, Zweite Reihe, v (1961–4), pp. 85–6.

MISCH, LUDWIG: 'Beethovens "Variierte Themen", op. 105 und op. 107', Beethoven–
Jahrbuch, Zweite Reihe, iv (1959–60), pp. 102–42.

PLATEN, EMIL: 'Beethovens Streichtrio D-dur Opus 9 Nr. 2', Colloquium amicorum,
ed. S. Kross and H. Schmidt (Bonn, 1967), pp. 260–83.

SCHWAGER, MYRON: 'A Fresh Look at Beethoven's Arrangements', Music and
Letters, liv (1973), pp. 142–60.

STAEHELIN, MARTIN: 'Another Approach to Beethoven's Last String Quartet Oeuvre'.
The Unfinished String Quintet of 1826/27', The String Quartets of Haydn,
Mozart, and Beethoven: Studies of the Autograph Manuscripts, ed. C. Wolff
(Cambridge, Mass., 1980), pp. 302–23.

TYSON, ALAN: 'Beethoven's "Kakadu" Variations and Their English History',
Musical Times, civ (1963), pp. 108–110. See also Musical Times, cxi (1970) p.
1001.

——— 'Stages in the Composition of Beethoven's Piano Trio Op. 70, No. 1', Proceedings
of the Royal Musical Assocation, xcvii (1970–71), pp. 1–19.

——— 'The Authors of the Op. 104 String Quintet', Beethoven Studies (New York,
1973), pp. 158–73.

CHAPTER VII

THE CHAMBER MUSIC OF BEETHOVEN'S CONTEMPORARIES

(i) Modern Editions

(a) Anthology

KRAMARZ, JOACHIM, comp.; Von Haydn bis Hindemith: das Streichquartett in Beispielen
(Wolfenbüttel, 1961).

(b) Works by Individual Composers

CHERUBINI, L.: String Quintet no. 1 in E minor, ed. E. Bonelli (Padua, 1968).
——— String Quartet no. 2 in C, ed. W. Höckner (Locarno and New York, 1963).
——— String Quartet no. 4 in E, ed. B. Päuler (Wilhelmshaven and New York, 1967).
——— String Quartet no. 6 in A minor, ed. B Päuler (Zürich, 1973).

DITTERSDORF, K.: String Quartet no. 1 in D, ed. W. Altmann (London, 1938, repr.
1968), ed. W. Höckner (Wilhelmshaven, 1963).
——— String Quartet no. 2 in B flat, ed. W. Altmann (London, 1937, repr. 1968).
——— String Quintet in C, ed. W. Höckner (Leipzig, 1949).

DUSSEK, J. L.: Notturno Concertante for piano, violin and horn (viola) or piano and
violin in E flat, Op. 68, ed. C. D. S. Field (Kassel, 1972).
——— Sonata in B flat, Op. 69, no. 1, Sonata in G, Op. 69, no. 2 for violin and piano,
ed. J. and B. Štědroň (Musica Antiqua Bohemica, xli) (Prague, 1959).
——— Trio (Grand Sonata) in F, Op. 65, for flute, violoncello and piano, ed. D.
Lasocki (London, 1975), ed. N. Delius (Zürich and New York, 1977).

FÖRSTER, E. A.: *E. A. Förster: 2 Quartetten, 3 Quintetten* (Op. 16, nos. 4, 5; Op. 19, 20, 26), ed. K. Weigl (*Denkmäler der Tonkunst in Österreich*, lxvii, Jg. 35 (1) (Vienna, 1928). With thematic catalogue of chamber music.
—— String Quartet in C, Op. 21, no. 1, ed. P. Angerer (*Diletto musicale*, ii) (Vienna, 1957).
LOUIS FERDINAND: *Louis Ferdinand, Prinz von Preussen, Musikalische Werke*, ed. H. Kretzschmar (Leipzig, 1915–17, 1926). (Includes Opp. 1–6, 9–10).
—— Octet in F minor, Op. 10 (12) (London, 1971).
—— Piano Quartet in E flat, op. 5 (Wiesbaden, 1969).
MENDELSSOHN, F.: *Felix Mendelssohn-Bartholdy's Werke. Kritisch durchgesehene Ausgabe*, ed. J. Rietz (Leipzig, 1874–77, repr. Farnborough, 1967–78): String Quintet no. 1 in A, Op. 18; String Octet in E flat, Op. 20, series v (repr. New York, 1978); String Quartet no. 1 in E flat, Op. 12; String Quartet no. 2 in A minor, Op. 13; String Quartets nos. 3–5, Op. 44, nos. 1–3, series vi (repr. New York, 1978); Piano Quartet no. 1 in C minor, Op. 1; Piano Quartet no. 2 in F minor, Op. 2; Piano Quartet no. 3 in B minor, Op. 3, series ix.
—— *Leipziger Ausgabe der Werke Felix Mendelssohn Bartholdys*: String Quartet no. 1 in E flat, Op. 12; String Quartet no. 2 in A, Op. 13, series iii/1, ed. G. Schumacher (Leipzig, 1976); String Quartets nos. 3–5, Op. 44, nos. 1–3, series iii/2, ed. G. Schumacher (Leipzig, 1977).
ONSLOW, G.: Wind Quintet in F, Op. 81, no. 3, ed. K. Redel (Munich, 1956).
—— Sextet in A minor, Op. 77b, for wind and piano, ed. J. S. Schmidt (*Le Pupitre*, xliii) (Paris, 1972).
PLEYEL, I.: Flute Quartets Op. 20, nos. 1–3 (Benton 384–6), ed. H. Albrecht (*Organum*, series iii, nos. 39, 44, 47) (Lippstadt, 1951).
—— Quartet in E flat (Benton 395) for flute, 2 clarinets, and bassoon, ed. G. Meerwein (London, 1970).
—— Quartet in F, Op. 17, no. 2 (Benton 382) for flute and string trio (London, 1972).
—— String Quartet in E flat (Benton 352), ed. U. Drüner (Zürich, 1976).
—— Quintet in E flat, Op. 10, no. 3 (Benton 282) for flute, oboe, violin, viola and violoncello, ed. H. Steinbeck (*Diletto musicale*, cxcviii) (Vienna, 1968).
REICHA, A.: Wind Quintet in A minor, Op. 91, no. 2, ed. F. Kneusslin (Basel, 1970).
—— Wind Quintet in A, Op. 91, no. 5, ed. F. Kneusslin (Basel, 1961).
—— Wind Quintet in C minor, Op. 91, no. 6, ed. F. Kneusslin (Basel, 1975).
—— Wind Quintet in E minor, Op. 100, no. 4, ed. F. Kneusslin (Basel, 1957).
—— *Tre Quintetti per stromenti da fiato*, Op. 88, no. 3 in G, Op. 91, no. 9 in D, Op. 91, no. 11 in A, ed. R. Hertl and V. Smetáček (*Musica Antiqua Bohemica*, xxxiii) (Prague, 1957).
—— Quintet in F, op. 107, for clarinet and strings, ed. I. Měrka (Padua, 1971); arr. for oboe and strings, ed. J. Degen (London, 1969).
SCHUBERT, F.: *Franz Schubert's Werke. Kritisch durchgesehene Gesammtausgabe* (Leipzig, 1884–97, repr. New York, 1965): series iii: *Oktette*, ed. E. Mandyczewski (Leipzig, 1889); series iv: *Quintett für Streichinstrumente*, ed. E. Mandyczewski (Leipzig, 1890, repr. New York, 1973); series v: *Quartette für Streichinstrumente*, ed. J. Hellmesberger and E. Mandyczewski (Leipzig, 1890, repr. New York, 1973); series vi: *Trio für Streichinstrumente*, ed. E. Mandyczewski (Leipzig, 1890, repr. New York, 1973); series vii: *Pianoforte-Quintett, -Quartett und -Trios*, 2 vols., ed. I. Brüll (Leipzig, 1886, repr. New York, 1973); series viii: *Für Pianoforte und ein Instrument*, ed. I. Brüll (Leipzig, 1886); Trio in B flat, D 581, *Supplement*, ed. E. Mandyczewski (Leipzig, 1887, repr. New York, 1973).
—— *Neue Schubert-Ausgabe*, series vi/1: *Oktette und Nonett*, ed. A. Feil (Kassel, 1969); series vi/2: *Streichquintette*, ed. M. Chusid (Kassel, 1971); series vi/3: *Streichquartette*, ed. M. Chusid (Kassel, 1979); series vi/7: *Werke für Klavier und*

mehrere Instrumente, ed. A. Feil (Kassel, 1975); series vi/8: *Werke für Klavier und ein Instrument*, ed. H. Wirth (Kassel, 1970).

SPOHR, L.: Nonet in F, Op. 31, ed. E. Schmitz (Kassel, 1959).

—— Octet in E, Op. 32, ed. F. Uhlendorff (Kassel, 1958).

—— Double String Quartet no. 1 in D minor, Op. 65, ed. E. Schmitz (Kassel, 1951).

—— String Quartet in E flat, Op. 15, no. 1; String Quartet in D, Op. 15, no. 2, ed. O. Leinert (Kassel, 1954).

—— String Quartet in E flat, Op. 29, no. 1, ed. O. Leinert (Kassel, 1955).

—— Piano Quintet in C minor, Op. 52, ed. E. Schmitz (Kassel, 1956).

WEBER, C. M. von: Adagio and rondo in E flat for 2 clarinets, 2 horns and 2 bassoons, ed. G. Dobrée (London, 1971), ed. W. Sandner (Mainz and New York, 1973).

—— Clarinet Quintet in B flat, Op. 34, ed. G. Hausswald (Leipzig, 1954).

—— *Sechs Sonaten für Klavier und Violine*, Op. 10 (b), ed. E. Zimmermann, H.-M. Theopold and K. Rohrig (Munich–Duisburg, 1965).

—— Trio in G minor, Op. 63, for piano, flute, and violoncello, ed. P. Wackernagel (Berlin, 1953), ed. R. Fiske (London and New York, 1977).

(ii) Books and Articles

(a) General

ALTMANN, WILHELM: *Kammermusik-Katalog* (6th ed., Leipzig, 1945, repr. Hofheim, 1967).

BRUUN, KAI AAGE: *Kammermusik*, ii (Copenhagen, 1962).

COBBETT, WALTER WILLSON, ed.: *Cobbett's Cyclopedic Survey of Chamber Music*, 2 vols. (London, 1929), with supplement by Colin Mason (2nd ed., London, 1963).

DUNHILL, THOMAS F.: *Chamber Music: A Treatise for Students* (London, 1925).

FERGUSON, DONALD N.: *Image and Structure in Chamber Music* (Minneapolis, 1964).

FINSCHER, LUDWIG: *Studien zur Geschichte des Streichquartetts*, i (Kassel, 1974).

FISCHER, WILHELM: 'Instrumentalmusik von 1740–1828', *Handbuch der Musikgeschichte*, ii, ed. G. Adler (2nd ed., Berlin, 1932, repr. Tutzing, 1961), pp. 795–833.

HINSON, MAURICE: *The Piano in Chamber Ensemble: An Annotated Guide* (Bloomington, Indiana, and London, 1978).

KING, A. HYATT: *Chamber Music* (London and New York, 1948, repr. Westport, Connecticut, 1972).

KIRKENDALE, WARREN: *Fugue and Fugato in Rococo and Classical Chamber Music* (2nd ed., Durham, North Carolina, 1979).

LA LAURENCIE, LIONEL DE: 'Les débuts de la musique de chambre en France', *Revue de Musicologie*, xv (1934), pp. 25–33, 86–96, 159–67, 204–31.

LOFT, ABRAM: *Violin and Keyboard: The Duo Repertoire*, 2 vols. (New York, 1973).

MERSMANN, HANS: *Die Kammermusik*, 4 vols. (Leipzig, 1930–3).

RICHTER, JOHANNES FRIEDRICH: *Kammermusik-Katalog, Verzeichnis der von 1944 bis 1958 veröffentlichten Werke für Kammermusik und für Klavier vier- und sechshändig sowie für zwei und mehr Klaviere* (Leipzig, 1960).

ROBERTSON, ALEC. ed.: *Chamber Music* (London, 1957).

SAAM, JOSEPH: *Zur Geschichte des Klavierquartetts bis in die Romantik* (Strasbourg, 1933).

SALMEN, WALTER: *Haus- und Kammermusik. Privates Musizieren in gesellschaftlichen Wandel zwischen 1600 und 1900* (*Musikgeschichte in Bildern*, iv) (Leipzig, 1969).

SCHWARZ, BORIS: *French Instrumental Music Between the Revolutions* (Columbia, 1950, rev. ed. New York, 1982).

SIRKER, UDO: *Die Entwicklung des Bläserquintetts in der ersten Hälfte des 19. Jahrhunderts* (Regensburg, 1968).

SÝKORA, VÁCLAV JAN: 'Tschechische Musik der Beethovenzeit', *Report of the Tenth Congress, Ljubljana, 1967* (Kassel, 1970), pp. 209–15.

TEMPERLEY, NICHOLAS: 'Domestic Music in England, 1800–1860', *Proceedings of the Royal Musical Association*, lxxxv (1958–9), pp. 31–47.

ULRICH, HOMER: *Chamber Music* (2nd ed., New York, and London, 1966).

UNVERRICHT, HUBERT: *Geschichte des Streichtrios* (*Mainzer Studien zur Musikwissenschaft*, ii) (Tutzing, 1969).

WERNER, ERIC: 'Instrumental Music Outside the Pale of Classicism and Romanticism', *Instrumental Music*, ed. David Hughes (Cambridge, Mass., 1959, repr. New York, 1972), pp. 57–69.

(b) Individual Composers

Cherubini

DEANE, BASIL: *Cherubini* (London, 1965).

RINALDI, MARIO: 'La musica sinfonica, da camera e d'occasione di Luigi Cherubini', *Luigi Cherubini nel II centenario della nascitá*, ed. Adelino Damerini (Florence, 1962), pp. 57–69.

SAAK, SIEGFRIED: *Studien zur Instrumentalmusik Luigi Cherubinis* (Göttingen, 1979).

—— 'Ein unbekannter Streichquartettsatz Luigi Cherubinis', *Die Musikforschung*, xxxi (1978), pp. 46–51.

Dittersdorf

KREBS, CARL: *Dittersdorfiana* (Berlin, 1900, repr. New York, 1972).

RIGLER, GERTRUDE: 'Die Kammermusik Dittersdorfs', *Studien zur Musikwissenschaft*, xiv (1927), pp. 179–212.

Field

HOPKINSON, CECIL: *A Bibliographical Thematic Catalogue of the Works of John Field, 1782–1837* (London, 1961).

PIGGOTT, PATRICK: *The Life and Music of John Field* (London, Berkeley, and Los Angeles, 1973).

E. A. Förster

LONGYEAR, REY: 'Echte und unterschobene Försteriana', *Die Musikforschung*, xxviii (1975), pp. 297–9.

SALTSCHEFF, NESCHO: *Emanuel Aloys Förster* (Munich, 1914).

WEIGL, KARL: 'Emanuel Aloys Förster', *Sammelbände der internationalen Musikgesellschaft*, vi (1904–5), pp. 274–314.

Louis Ferdinand

HAHN, ROBERT: *Louis Ferdinand von Preussen als Musiker. Ein Beitrag zur Geschichte der musikalischen Frühromantik* (Breslau, 1935).

Mendelssohn

GODWIN, JOSCELYN: 'Early Mendelssohn and Late Beethoven', *Music and Letters*, lv (1974), pp. 272–85.

HORTON, JOHN: *Mendelssohn Chamber Music* (London, 1972).

KRUMMACHER, FRIEDHELM: *Mendelssohn der Komponist. Studien zur Kammermusik für Streicher* (Munich, 1978).

—— 'Zur Kompositionsart Mendelssohns. Thesen am Beispiel der Streichquartette', *Das Problem Mendelssohn*, ed. Carl Dahlhaus (*Studien zur Musikgeschichte des 19. Jahrhunderts*, xli) (Regensburg, 1974).

THOMAS, MATHIAS: *Das Instrumentalwerk Felix Mendelssohn-Bartholdys. Eine syste-matisch-theoretische Untersuchung unter besonderer Berücksichtigung der zeitge-nössischen Musiktheorie* (*Göttinger Musikwissenschaftliche Arbeiten*, iv) (Göttin-gen, 1972).

Pleyel

BENTON, RITA: *Ignace Pleyel: A Thematic Catalogue of his Compositions* (New York, 1977).

KLINGENBECK, JOSEF: 'Ignaz Pleyel, sein Streichquartett im Rahmen der Wiener Klassik', *Studien zur Musikwissenschaft*, xxv (1962), pp. 276–97.

Reicha

BÜCKEN, ERNST: *Anton Reicha, sein Leben und seine Kompositionen* (Munich, 1912).

EMMANUEL, MAURICE: *Antonin Reicha* (Paris, 1937).

ŠOTOLOVÁ, OLGA: *Antonin Rejcha* (Prague, 1977). With thematic catalogue.

Schubert

ABERT, ANNA AMALIE: 'Rhythmus und Klang in Schuberts Streichquintett', *Festschrift Karl Gustav Fellerer*, ed. Heinrich Hüschen (Regensburg, 1962), pp. 1–11.

BROWN, MAURICE J. E.: 'Schubert's Trio Op. 99', *Music and Letters*, xxxiv (1953), pp. 181–2.

COOLIDGE, RICHARD A.: 'Form in the String Quartets of Franz Schubert', *Music Review*, xxxii (1971), pp. 309–25.

DAHLHAUS, CARL: 'Die Sonatenform bei Schubert. Der erste Satz des G-dur-Quartetts D 887', *Musica*, xxxii (1978), pp. 125–30.

GEIRINGER, KARL: 'Schubert's *Arpeggione Sonata* and the "super arpeggio"', *Musical Quarterly*, lxv (1979), pp. 513–23.

GILLETT, JUDY: 'The Problem of Schubert's G Major String Quartet (D. 887)', *Music Review*, xxxv (1974), pp. 281–92.

HOLLANDER, HANS: 'Stil und poetische Idee in Schuberts d-Moll-Streichquartett', *Neue Zeitschrift für Musik*, cxxxi (1970), pp. 239–41.

HOORICKX, REINHARD van: 'Old and New Schubert Problems', *Music Review*, xxxv (1974), pp. 76–89.

MARX, KARL: 'Einige Anmerkungen zu Schuberts Forellenquintett und Oktett', *Neue Zeitschrift für Musik*, cxxxii (1971), pp. 588–92.

NEWMAN, WILLIAM S.: 'Freedom of Tempo in Schubert's Instrumental Music', *Musical Quarterly*, lxi (1975), pp. 528–45.

OREL, ALFRED: 'Franz Schuberts "Sonate" für Klavier, Violine und Violoncell aus dem Jahre 1812', *Zeitschrift für Musikwissenschaft*, v (1922–3), pp. 209–18.

RIEZLER, WALTER: *Schuberts Instrumentalmusik, Werkanalysen* (Zürich, 1967).

SACHSE, HANS-MARTIN: *Franz Schuberts Streichquartette* (Münster, 1959).

TRUSCOTT, HAROLD: 'Schubert's D Minor String Quartet', *Music Review*, xix (1958), pp. 27–36.

—— 'Schubert's String Quartet in G Major', *Music Review*, xx (1959), pp. 119–45.

WESTRUP, JACK A.: 'The Chamber Music', *Schubert: a Symposium*, ed. Gerald Abraham (London, 1946, New York, 1947, as *The Music of Schubert*, repr. Port Washington, N.Y., 1969), pp. 88–110.

—— *Schubert Chamber Music* (London, 1969).

WILLFORT, MANFRED: 'Das Urbild des Andantes aus Schuberts Klaviertrio Es-Dur, D 929', *Österreichische Musikzeitschrift*, xxxiii (1978), pp. 277–83.

Spohr

GÖTHEL, FOLKER: 'Louis Spohr. Heute', *Musica*, xiii (1959), pp. 293–300.

Weber

JÄHNS, FRIEDRICH WILHELM: *Carl Maria von Weber in seinen Werken. Chronologisch-thematisches Verzeichnis seiner sämmtlichen Compositionen* (Berlin, 1871, repr. Berlin-Lichterfelde, 1967).

WARRACK, JOHN: *Carl Maria von Weber* (London and New York, 1968).

CHAPTER VIII

PIANO MUSIC

(i) Modern Editions

(a) Anthologies

FARRENC, ARISTIDE and LOUISE, comp. and ed.: *Le Trésor des pianistes*, vols. 16, 18, 19, 20, 21, 22, 23 (Paris, 1861–72, repr. New York, 1978). (Includes works by Chopin, Clementi, Cramer, Dussek, Hummel, Mendelssohn, Steibelt and Weber.)

FERGUSON, HOWARD: *Style and Interpretation. An Anthology of Keyboard Music*, iii: *Classical Piano Music*, iv: *Romantic Piano Music* (London, 2nd ed., 1972). (Includes excerpts from works by Beethoven, Clementi, Field, Mendelssohn and Schubert.)

——— *Style and Interpretation*, v/1: *Keyboard Duets* (London and New York, 1971). (Includes works by Beethoven, Clementi and Weber.)

GEORGII, WALTER, ed.: *400 Jahre europäischer Klaviermusik (Das Musikwerk*, i) (Cologne, 1950; English edition 1959). (Includes works by Beethoven, Clementi, Mendelssohn and Schubert.)

GILLESPIE, JOHN, ed.: *Nineteenth-Century European Piano Music* (New York, 1977). (Includes works by Clementi, Czerny, Dussek, Field, Hummel, Moscheles, Tomášek and Voříšek.)

KAHL, WILLI: *Lyrische Klavierstücke der Romantik* (Stuttgart, 1926). (Includes works by Berger, Cramer, Tomášek and Voříšek.)

POHANKA, JAROSLAV: *Dějiny české hudby v příkladech* (Prague, 1958). (Includes works by Dussek, Tomášek and Voříšek.)

RACEK, JAN, EMINGEROVÁ, K. and KREDBA, O., ed.: *České Sonatiny (Musica Antiqua Bohemica*, xvii) (Prague, 1954). (Includes works by Dussek and Voříšek.)

RACEK, JAN and SÝKORA, VÁCLAV JAN, ed.: *Classici boemici*, 2 vols. (*Musica Antiqua Bohemica*, xiv, xx) (Prague, 1954, 1953). (Includes excerpts from works by Dussek, Tomášek and Voříšek.)

SCHLEUNING, PETER: *Die Fantasie*, ii (*Das Musikwerk*, xliii) (Cologne, 1971; English edition, 1971). (Includes excerpts from works by Czerny and Kalkbrenner.)

STEPHENSON, KURT, ed.: *Romantik in der Tonkunst (Das Musikwerk*, xxi) (Cologne, 1961; English edition 1961). (Includes excerpts from works by Berger, Clementi, Cramer, Field, Schubert, Voříšek.)

(b) Works by Individual Composers

BEETHOVEN, L. van: *L. van Beethoven's Werke. Vollständige kritisch durchgesehene überall berechtigte Ausgabe* (Leipzig, 1862–5); series xvi: *Sonaten für das Pianoforte*, 2 vols.; series xvii: *Variationen für das Pianoforte*; series xviii: *Kleinere Stücke für das Pianoforte*.

——— *Supplemente zur Gesamtausgabe*, ed. W. Hess: ix: *Klavierwerke, Kammermusikwerke mit Klavier* (Wiesbaden, 1965).

—— *L. van Beethoven: Werke, neue Ausgabe sämtlicher Werke*, series vii/1: *Werke für Klavier zu vier Händen*, ed. H. Schmidt (Munich–Duisburg, 1966); series vii/2–3: *Klaviersonaten*, ed. H. Schmidt (Munich–Duisburg, 1971; Munich, 1976); series vii/5: *Variationen für Klavier*, ed. J. Schmidt-Görg (Munich–Duisburg, 1961).

—— *Klavierstücke*, ed. O. von Irmer (Munich–Duisburg, 1950).

—— *Die letzten fünf Sonaten von Beethoven: kritische Ausgabe mit Einführung und Erläuterung*, ed. H. Schenker (Vienna, 1913–27), rev. O. Jonas, 5 vols. (Vienna, 1971–2).

—— *Klaviersonaten nach den Autographen und Erstdrucken*, 4 vols., ed. H. Schenker and E. Ratz (Vienna, 1946–7).

—— *Variationen für Klavier*, i, ed. E. Ratz, ii, ed. M. Holl (Vienna, 1958, 1960).

CLEMENTI, M.: *Oeuvres complettes de Muzio Clementi*, 13 vols. (Leipzig, 1804–19; repr. New York, 1973).

—— Sonatas, Opp. 28/1; 10/3; 7/3; 14/3; 14/1; 40/2, ed. H. Albrecht (*Organum*, series v/1, 4, 15, 16, 18 and 20) (Lippstadt, 1950–54).

—— *Muzio Clementi: Works for Pianoforte*, 4 vols., ed. F. Dawes (London, 1958).

—— *Clementi: 18 Sonate per il pianoforte*, 3 vols., ed. G. Piccioli (Milan, 1949).

—— *Clementi: Klaviersonaten: Auswahl*, ed. S. Gerlach and A. Tyson (Munich, 1978).

DUSSEK, J. L.: *Oeuvres complètes pour le pianoforte*, 12 vols. (Leipzig, 1813–17; repr. New York, 1978).

—— *Selected Piano Works*, 2 vols., ed. H. A. Craw (*Recent Researches in the Music of the Nineteenth and Early Twentieth Centuries*, i) (Madison, Wisconsin, 1979).

—— *Sonate per il clavicembalo*, ed. M. Knotková, A. Němec (*Musica Antiqua Bohemica*, viii) (Prague, 1951).

—— *Sonate*, 4 vols., ed. J. Racek, rev. V. J. Sýkora (*Musica Antiqua Bohemica*, xlvi, liii, lix, lxiii) (Prague, 1960–3).

—— Sonata in G minor, Op. 10, no. 2, Sonata in E flat, Op. 44, ed. H. Albrecht (*Organum* series, v/3, 6) (Lippstadt, 1950, 1951).

FIELD, J.: *Nocturnes* (complete), ed. L. Köhler (Leipzig, *c*. 1880). Nocturne in A, no. 8, *Norton Anthology of Western Music*, ii (New York, 1980) ed. C. Palisca, reprinted from Köhler's edition.

—— *Nokturny wybrany*, ed. S. Szpinalski (Cracow, 1969).

—— *Selected Piano Works*, ed. D. Branson (New York, 1979).

HUMMEL, J. N.: *Complete Piano Sonatas*, ed. H. Truscott (London, 1975).

—— *Zehn Variationen über ein Thema aus Glucks Armida*, ed. H. Albrecht (*Organum*, series vi/8) (Lippstadt, 1951).

MENDELSSOHN, F.: *Felix Mendelssohn Bartholdy's Werke. Kritisch durchgesehene Ausgabe*, ed. J. Rietz (Leipzig, 1874–7): series xi: *Für Pianoforte allein*, 4 vols. (repr. New York, 1975).

MOSCHELES, I.: *Sonate mélancolique in F sharp minor*, Op. 49, first movement, *Thirteen Keyboard Sonatas of the 18th and 19th Centuries*, ed. W. S. Newman (Chapel Hill, 1947).

SCHUBERT, F.: *Franz Schuberts Werke. Kritisch durchgesehene Gesammtausgabe* (Leipzig, 1884–97, repr. New York, 1965): series ix: *Für Pianoforte zu vier Händen*, 3 vols., ed. A. Door (Leipzig, 1888, 15 works repr. New York, 1977); series x: *Sonaten für Pianoforte*, ed. J. Epstein (Leipzig, 1888, repr. New York, 1970); series xi: *Phantasie, Impromptus und andere Stücke für Pianoforte*, ed. J. Epstein (Leipzig, 1889); series xii: *Tänze für Pianoforte*, ed. J. Epstein (Leipzig, 1889).

—— *Franz Schubert. Neue Ausgabe sämtlicher Werke*, series vii/2: *Werke für Klavier zu vier Hände*, ed. C. Landon (Kassel, 1978); vii/4: *Märsche und Tänze*, ed. C. Landon (Kassel, 1972).

—— *Franz Schubert. Klaviersonaten*, 2 vols. ed. P. Mies (Munich–Duisburg, 1961).

——— *Franz Schubert. Klaviersonaten nach den Autographen und Erstdrucken*, 2 vols., ed. E. Ratz (Vienna, 1953).

Tomášek, J. V.: *Ausgewählte Klavierwerke*, ed. D. Zahn and A. Weinmann (Munich–Duisburg, 1971).

——— Sonata, Op. 21, first movement, *Die Solosonate*, ed. F. Giegling (*Das Musikwerk*, xv) (Cologne, 1959, English edition, London and New York, 1960).

——— Tre Dittirambi, Op. 65, ed. J. Pohanka (*Musica Antiqua Bohemica*, xxix) (2nd ed., Prague, 1972).

Voříšek, J. H.: *Ausgewählte Klavierwerke*, ed. D. Zahn and A. Weinmann (Munich–Duisburg, 1971).

——— *Klavírní skladby* (*Musica Antiqua Bohemica*, lii) (Prague, 1961).

——— Impromptus, Op. 7 (*Musica Antiqua Bohemica*, i) (Prague, c. 1957).

——— Sonata, Op. 20, ed. L. Kundera (*Musica Antiqua Bohemica*, iv) (Prague, 1949).

Weber, C. M. von: Grande Sonate no. 3 in D minor, Op. 49, ed. W. Georgii (Munich, 1920).

——— Piano Sonatas, Opp. 24, 49, 70, 139, ed. L. Köhler and A. Ruthardt (Leipzig, rev. ed. 1954).

——— *Klavierstücke zu zwei Händen*, ed. L. Köhler and A. Ruthardt (Frankfurt and New York, rev. ed. 1967).

Wölfl, J.: *Sonate précédée d'une introduction et fugue*, Op. 25, *Thirteen Keyboard Sonatas of the 18th and 19th Centuries*, ed. W. S. Newman (Chapel Hill, 1947).

(ii) Books and Articles

(a) General

Dale, Kathleen: *Nineteenth-Century Piano Music* (London, New York, 1954, repr. New York, 1972).

Demuth, Norman: *French Piano Music. A Survey with Notes on Its Performance* (London, 1959).

Egert, Paul: *Das Klaviersonate im Zeitalter der Romantik. Beiträge zur Geschichte der Klaviermusik* (Berlin, 1934).

Favre, Georges: *La Musique française de piano avant 1830* (Paris, 1953).

Fischer, Wilhelm: 'Instrumentalmusik von 1750–1828', *Handbuch der Musikgeschichte*, ii, ed. Guido Adler (2nd ed., Berlin, 1932, repr. Tutzing, 1961), pp. 795–833.

Georgii, Walter: *Klaviermusik* (3rd ed., Zürich, 1956).

Golos, George S.: 'Some Slavic Predecessors of Chopin', *Musical Quarterly*, xlvi (1960), pp. 437–47.

Harding, Rosamond E. M.: *The Pianoforte. Its History Traced to the Great Exhibition of 1851* (London, 1933, repr. New York, 1973).

Hering, Hans: 'Das spielerische Element in der klassisch-romantischen Klaviersonate', *Neue Zeitschrift für Musik*, cxxxv (1974), pp. 227–32.

Kahl, Willi: 'Das lyrische Klavierstück Schuberts und seiner Vorgänger seit 1810', *Archiv für Musikwissenschaft*, iii (1921), pp. 54–82, 99–122.

Krueger, Wolfgang: *Das Nachtstück. Ein Beitrag zur Entwicklung des einsätzigen Pianofortestückes im 19. Jahrhundert* (*Schriften zur Musik*, ix) (Munich, 1971).

Matthews, Denis, ed.: *Keyboard Music* (New York and London, 1972).

Newman, William S.: 'The Pianos of Haydn, Mozart, Beethoven, and Schubert Compared' *Piano Quarterly*, xxvii (1979), pp. 14–16.

——— *The Sonata in the Classic Era* (Chapel Hill, 1963).

——— *The Sonata since Beethoven* (Chapel Hill, 1969).

Pilková, Zdeňka: 'Charakteristische Züge im Klavierschaffen der tschechischen Komponisten an der Wende des 18. zum 19. Jahrhundert', *Bericht über den internationalen musikwissenschaftlichen Kongress Bonn 1970*, ed. Carl Dahlhaus *et al.* (Kassel, 1971), pp. 531–3.

RINGER, ALEXANDER: 'Beethoven and the London Pianoforte School', *Musical Quarterly*, lvi (1970), pp. 742–57.

SCHÜNEMANN, GEORG: *Geschichte der Klaviermusik*, rev. Herbert Gerigk (2nd ed., Münchberg, 1953).

SIMPSON, ADRIENNE: 'Piano Music by Bohemian Composers of Beethoven's Time', *Musical Times*, cxiii (1972), pp. 666–7.

TEMPERLEY, NICHOLAS: 'Domestic Music in England, 1800–1860', *Proceedings of the Royal Musical Association*, lxxxv (1958–9), pp. 31–47.

VOGEL, JOHANN PETER: 'Die böhmischen Klassiker. Einige Bemerkungen zu ihrer Klaviermusik', *Musica*, xxvii (1973), pp. 124–9.

WORBS, HANS: '*Le tribut à la mode*. Die Anfänge der Salonmusik', *Neue Zeitschrift für Musik*, cxxxii (1971), pp. 128–33.

(b) Individual Composers

Beethoven

BADURA-SKODA, PAUL and DEMUS, JÖRG: *Die Klaviersonaten von Ludwig van Beethoven* (Wiesbaden, 1970).

BARBAG-DREXLER, IRENA: 'Beethoven and Chopin', *Beethoven Almanach 1970*, ed. Hans Sittner (Vienna, 1970), pp. 74–9.

BARFORD, PHILIP: 'The Piano Music–II', *The Beethoven Companion (Reader)*, ed. Denis Arnold and Nigel Fortune (London and New York, 1971), pp. 126–93.

Beethoven-Kolloquium 1977, ed. Rudolf Klein (Kassel, 1978).

COCKSHOOT, JOHN V.: *The Fugue in Beethoven's Piano Music* (London, 1959).

COLE, MALCOLM S.: 'Techniques of Surprise in the Sonata-Rondos of Beethoven', *Studia Musicologica*, xii (1970), pp. 233–62.

CONE, EDWARD T.: 'Beethoven's Experiments in Composition: The Late Bagatelles', *Beethoven Studies*, ii, ed. Alan Tyson (London and New York, 1977), pp. 84–105.

COOPER, MARTIN: *Beethoven. The Last Decade, 1817–1827* (London and New York, 1970).

COREN, DANIEL: 'Structural Relationships between Op. 28 and Op. 36', *Beethoven Studies*, ii, ed. Alan Tyson (London and New York, 1977), pp. 66–83.

CZERNY, CARL: *Über den richtigen Vortrag der sämtlichen Beethoven'schen Klavierwerke*, ed. Paul Badura-Skoda (Vienna, 1963, Eng. trans. 1970).

FISCHER, EDWIN: *Beethoven's Pianoforte Sonatas*, trans. Stanley Goodman and Paul Hamburger (London, 1959).

FÖDERMAYR, FRANZ: 'Klangliche Ausdrucksgestalten in Beethovens Klaviersonaten', *Beethoven-Studien. Festgabe* (Vienna, 1970), pp. 327–40.

GRUNDMANN, HERBERT and MIES, PAUL: *Studien zum Klavierspiel Beethovens und seiner Zeitgenossen* (Bonn, 1966).

HESS, WILLY, ed.: *Beethoven-Studien* (Munich–Duisburg, 1972).

KAISER, JOACHIM: *Beethovens 32 Klaviersonaten und ihre Interpretation* (Frankfurt, 1975).

KAMIEN, ROGER: 'Aspects of the Recapitulation in Beethoven Piano Sonatas', *Music Forum*, iv (1976), pp. 195–235.

LANG, PAUL HENRY, ed.: *The Creative World of Beethoven* (New York, 1971).

LEICHNER, ANNELIESE: *Untersuchungen zur Originalausgaben Beethovenscher Klavierwerke* (Wiesbaden, 1976).

MISCH, LUDWIG: 'Fuge und Fugato in Beethovens Variationenform', *Neue Beethoven-Studien und andere Themen* (Munich–Duisburg, 1967), pp. 59–73.

MÜLLER-BLATTAU, JOSEPH: 'Beethoven und die Variation', *Neues Beethoven-Jahrbuch*, v (1933), pp. 101–36.

NAGEL, WILLIBALD: *Beethoven und seine Klaviersonaten* (rev. ed., Langensalza, 1924).

NEWMAN, WILLIAM S.: *Performance Practices in Beethoven's Piano Sonatas: An Introduction* (New York, 1971).

OPPEN, JÜRGEN von: 'Beethoven's Klavierfantasie Op. 77 in neuer Sicht', *Bericht über den internationalen musikwissenschaftlichen Kongress Bonn 1970*, ed. Carl Dahlhaus *et al.* (Kassel, 1971), pp. 528–31.

RATZ, ERWIN: 'Beethoven's Grösse dargestellt an Beispielen aus seinen Klaviersonaten', *Beethoven im Mittelpunkt. Beiträge und Anmerkungen. Festschrift Internationales Beethovenfest in Bonn 1970*, ed. Gert Schroers (Bonn, 1970), pp. 41–57.

RÉTI, RUDOLPH: *Thematic Patterns in Sonatas of Beethoven* (New York and London, 1967).

ROSEN, CHARLES: *The Classical Style: Haydn, Mozart, Beethoven* (New York, 1972).

ROSENBERG, RICHARD: *Die Klaviersonaten Ludwig van Beethovens*, 2 vols. (Olten, 1957).

TRUSCOTT, HAROLD: 'The Piano Music–I', *The Beethoven Companion (Reader)*, ed. Denis Arnold and Nigel Fortune (London and New York, 1971), pp. 68–125.

TYSON, ALAN: 'The First Editions of Beethoven's Op. 119 Bagatelles', *Musical Quarterly*, xlix (1963), pp. 331–8.

UHDE, JÜRGEN: *Beethovens Klaviermusik*, 3 vols. (Stuttgart, 1968–74).

L. Berger

SIEBENKÄS, DIETER: *Ludwig Berger: Sein Leben und seine Werke (Berliner Studien zur Musikwissenschaft*, vi) (Berlin, 1963).

Clementi

ALLORTO, RICCARDO: *Le Sonate per pianoforte di Muzio Clementi. Studio critico e catalogo tematico* (Florence, 1959).

BARFORD, PHILIP: 'Formalism in Clementi's Pianoforte Sonatas', *Monthly Musical Record*, lxxxii (1952), pp. 205–8, 238–41.

PLANTINGA, LEON: *Clementi: His Life and Music* (London, 1977).

—— 'Clementi, Virtuosity, and the "German Manner"', *Journal of the American Musicological Society*, xxv (1972), pp. 303–30.

RINGER, ALEXANDER: 'Clementi and the "Eroica"', *Musical Quarterly*, xlvii (1961), pp. 454–68.

STAUCH, ADOLF: *Muzio Clementis Klavier-Sonaten im Verhältnis zu den Sonaten von Haydn, Mozart und Beethoven* (Bonn, 1930).

TYSON, ALAN: *Thematic Catalogue of the Works of Muzio Clementi* (Tutzing, 1967).

Cramer

GANZ, P. FELIX: 'Johann Baptist Cramer and his Celebrated Etudes', *Clavier*, vi (1967), pp. 14–17, 22–8.

SCHLESINGER, THEA: *Johann Baptist Cramer und seine Klaviersonaten* (Munich, 1928).

Czerny

DALE, KATHLEEN: 'The Three C's: Pioneers of Pianoforte Playing', *Music Review*, vi (1945), pp. 138–48 (Clementi, Cramer, Czerny).

Dussek

BLOM, ERIC: 'The Prophecies of Dussek', *Classics Major and Minor* (London, 1958), pp. 88–117.

SCHIFFER, LEO: *Johann Ladislaus Dussek, seine Sonaten und seine Konzerte* (Munich, 1914, repr. New York, 1972).

Elsner

NOWAK-ROMANOWICZ, ALINA: *Józef Elsner* (Cracow, 1957).

Field

BRANSON, DAVID: *John Field and Chopin* (London, 1972).

DESSAUER, HEINRICH: *John Field, sein Leben und seine Werke* (Langensalza, 1912).

HIBBARD, TREVOR DAVIES: 'The Slow Movements of the Sonatas of John Field', *Music Review*, xxii (1961), pp. 89–93.

PIGGOTT, PATRICK: *The Life & Music of John Field 1782–1837, Creator of the Nocturne* (London, Berkeley and Los Angeles, 1973).

TEMPERLEY, NICHOLAS: 'John Field and the First Nocturne', *Music and Letters*, lvi (1975), pp. 335–40.

TYSON, ALAN: 'John Field's Earliest Compositions', *Music and Letters*, xlvii (1966), pp. 239–48.

Hummel

DAVIS, RICHARD: 'The Music of J. N. Hummel. Its Derivation and Development', *Music Review*, xxvi (1965), pp. 169–91.

Mendelssohn

FELLERER, KARL GUSTAV: 'Mendelssohn in der Klaviermusik seiner Zeit', *Das Problem Mendelssohn*, ed. Carl Dahlhaus (*Studien zur Musikgeschichte des 19. Jahrhunderts*, xli) (Regensburg, 1974), pp. 195–200.

GODWIN, JOSCELYN: 'Early Mendelssohn and Late Beethoven', *Music and Letters*, lv (1974), pp. 272–85.

THOMAS, MATHIAS: *Das Instrumentalwerk Felix Mendelssohn-Bartholdys. Eine systematisch-theoretische Untersuchung unter besonderer Berücksichtigung der zeitgenössischen Musiktheorie* (*Göttinger Musikwissenschaftliche Arbeiten*, iv) (Göttingen, 1972).

Moscheles

HEUSSNER, INGEBORG: 'Formale Gestaltungsprinzipe bei Ignaz Moscheles', *Festschrift Hans Engel*, ed. Horst Heussner (Kassel, 1964), pp. 155–65.

ROCHE, JEROME: 'Ignaz Moscheles: 1794–1870', *Musical Times*, cxi (1970), pp. 264–6.

Ogiński

BELZA, IGOR: *Michał Kleofas Ogiński* (Cracow, 1967).

Schubert

BILSON, MALCOLM: 'Schubert's Piano Music and the Pianos of his Time', *Piano Quarterly*, xxvii (1978–9), pp. 56–61.

BISOGNI, FABIO: 'Rilievi filologici sulle sonate giovanili di Franz Schubert (1815–1817)', *Nuova Rivista italiana di musicologia*, ii (1968), pp. 453–72.

—— 'Rilievi filologici sulle sonate della maturità di Franz Schubert (1817–1828)', *Rivista italiana di musicologia*, xi (1976), pp. 71–105.

BROWN, MAURICE J. E.: 'An Introduction to Schubert's Sonatas of 1817', *Music Review*, xii (1951), pp. 35–44.

—— 'Schubert's Piano Sonatas', *Musical Times*, cxvi (1975), pp. 873–5.

—— 'Schubert's "Wanderer" Fantasy', *Musical Times*, xcii (1951), pp. 540–2.

CHUSID, MARTIN: 'Cyclicism in Schubert's Piano Sonata in A major (D. 959)', *Piano Quarterly*, xxvii (1978–9), pp. 38–40.

—— 'A Suggested Reading for Schubert's Piano Sonata in E flat, Op. 122', *Schubert-Kongress Wien 1978*, ed. Otto Brusatti (Graz, 1979), pp. 37–44.

DALE, KATHLEEN: 'The Piano Music', *Schubert: A Symposium*, ed. Gerald Abraham (London, 1946; New York, 1947, as *The Music of Schubert*, repr. Port Washington, N.Y., 1969), pp. 111–48.

DICHLER, JOSEF: 'Interpretationsprobleme bei Schuberts Klaviermusik', *Oesterreichische Musikzeitschrift*, xxvii (1972), pp. 200–7.

HOORICKX, REINHARD van: 'Fugue and Counterpoint in Schubert's Piano Music', *Piano Quarterly*, xxvii (1979), pp. 48–52.

KOMMA, KARL MICHAEL: 'Franz Schuberts Klaviersonate a-moll op. posth. 164 (D 537): zur Wandlung des klassischen Formbegriffs'. *Zeitschrift für Musiktheorie*, iii (1972), pp. 2–15.

MIES, PAUL: 'Die Entwürfe Franz Schuberts zu den letzten drei Klaviersonaten von 1828', *Beiträge zur Musikwissenschaft*, ii (1960), pp. 52–68.

—— 'Der zyklische Charakter der Klaviertänze bei Franz Schubert', *Kongressbericht über den internationalen musikwissenschaftlichen Kongress Wien Mozartjahr 1956* (Graz-Cologne, 1958), pp. 408–11.

RADCLIFFE, PHILIP: *Schubert Piano Sonatas* (London, 1967).

SAMS, ERIC: 'Schubert's Piano Duets', *Musical Times*, cxvii (1976), pp. 120–1.

TRUSCOTT, HAROLD: 'Organic Unity in Schubert's Early Sonata Music', *Monthly Musical Record*, lxxxix (1959), pp. 62–6.

—— 'Schubert's Unfinished Piano Sonata in C major (1825)', *Music Review*, xviii (1957), pp. 114–37.

—— 'The Two Versions of Schubert's Op. 122', *Music Review*, xiv (1953), pp. 89–106.

UHDE, JÜRGEN: 'Zur Interpretation des 1. Satzes des Schubert-Sonate Op. posth. B-dur D 960', *Musica*, xxxii (1978), pp. 174–8.

WHAPLES, MIRIAM K.: 'Style in Schubert's Piano Music from 1817 to 1818', *Music Review*, xxxv (1974), pp. 260–80.

Steibelt

MÜLLER, GOTTFRIED: *Daniel Steibelt, sein Leben und seine Klavierwerke* (*Etüden und Sonaten*) (Strasbourg, 1933).

Szymanowska

MIRSCY, JÓZEF and MARIA, ed.: *Maria Szymanowska: Album* (Cracow, 1953).

Tomášek

POKORA, MILOŠ: 'Vaclav Jan Tomášek—Skladatel na rozhrani dvou stylových epoch', *Hudebni Rozhledy*, xxviii (1974), pp. 233–6.

TOMÁSEK, V. J.: *Vlastní Životopis* (Prague, 1941).

Voříšek

SIMPSON, ADRIENNE: 'A Profile of Jan Václav Voříšek', *Proceedings of the Royal Musical Association*, xcvii (1970–1), pp. 125–32.

Weber

BERGE, G.: 'Der Klavierkomponist Weber', *Musik und Gesellschaft*, xi (1961), pp. 668–9.

GEORGII, WALTER: *Karl Maria von Weber als Klavierkomponist* (Leipzig, 1914).

HUSCHKE, KONRAD: 'Webers *Aufforderung zum Tanz*', *Neue Musik-Zeitung*, xlii (1921), pp. 201–4.

RIEHL, WILHELM HEINRICH: 'Weber als Klavierkomponist', *Musikalische Charakterköpfe*, ii (6th ed., Stuttgart, 1886), pp. 260–301.

WARRACK, JOHN: *Carl Maria von Weber* (London and New York, 1968).

Wölfl

BAUM, RICHARD: *Joseph Wölfl, sein Leben und seine Klavierwerke* (Kassel, 1928).

CHAPTER IX

ITALIAN OPERA

(i) Modern Editions

(a) Anthologies

CORTE, ANDREA DELLA, ed.: *Piccola antologia settecentesca* (Milan, 1925). (Includes examples by Cimarosa, Paisiello, and Salieri.)

WOLFF, HELLMUTH CHRISTIAN, ed.: *Die Oper III: 19. Jahrhundert* (*Das Musikwerk*, xl) (Cologne, 1972; English edition 1975). (Includes examples by Bellini and Rossini.)

(b) Works by Individual Composers

BELLINI, V.: *Beatrice di Tenda*, facsimile ed. (orch. score, Rome, *c*. 1833), ed. P. Gossett (*Early Romantic Opera*, v) (New York, 1980).

—— *I Capuleti e i Montecchi*, facsimile ed. of autograph, ed. P. Gossett (*Early Romantic Opera*, iii) (New York, 1981).

—— *La Sonnambula*, vocal score ed. M. Parenti (Milan, 1960).

CIMAROSA, D.: *Il matrimonio segreto*, vocal score ed. F. Donatoni (Milan, 1976).

—— *I traci amanti*, ed. R. Blanchard and A. Seay, 2 vols. (Paris, 1974).

DONIZETTI, G.: *Le convenienze ed inconvenienze teatrali*, vocal score ed. E. R. Orecchia (2nd ed., Florence, 1971).

MAYR, J. S.: *L'amor coniugale*, ed. A. Gazzaniga (*Monumenta Bergomensia*, xxii) (Bergamo, 1967).

MEYERBEER, G.: *Il Crociato in Egitto*, facsimile of original autograph version, ed. P. Gossett, 2 vols. (*Early Romantic Opera*, xviii) (New York, 1979).

PAISIELLO, G.: *Il barbiere di Siviglia*, vocal score ed. M. Parenti (Milan, 1961).

—— *La molinara, ossia L'amor contrastato*, ed. A. Rocchi (Florence, 1962).

—— *Nina*, vocal score, ed. C. Gatti (Milan, 1940).

ROSSINI, G.: *Il barbiere di Siviglia*, ed. A. Zedda (Milan, 1969).

—— *La Cenerentola*, facsimile of autograph, ed. P. Gossett, 2 vols. (Bologna, 1969).

—— *Elisabetta, regina d'Inghilterra*, facsimile of autograph, ed. P. Gossett, 2 vols. (*Early Romantic Opera*, vii) (New York, 1979).

—— *L'italiana in Algeri*, vocal score ed. M. Parenti (Milan, 1960).

—— *Maometto II*, ed. P. Gossett (*Early Romantic Opera*, xi) (New York, 1981).

—— *Mosé in Egitto*, facsimile of autograph, ed. P. Gossett (*Early Romantic Opera*, ix) (New York, 1979).

—— *Otello*, facsimile of autograph, ed. P. Gossett (*Early Romantic Opera*, viii) (New York, 1979).

—— *Ricciardo e Zoraide*, facsimile of printed orch. score, Rome, *c*. 1828), ed. P. Gossett (*Early Romantic Opera*, x) (New York, 1980).

—— *Semiramide*, facsimile of autograph, ed. P. Gossett, 2 vols. (*Early Romantic Opera*, xiii) (New York, 1978).

—— *Zelmira*, facsimile of autograph, ed. P. Gossett (*Early Romantic Opera*, xii) (New York, 1979).

SALIERI, A.: *Falstaff*, vocal score ed. E. R. Orecchia (Florence, 1969).

(ii) Books and Articles

(a) General

BÜCKEN, ERNST: 'Die Musik in Italien und Frankreich vor 1830', *Die Musik des 19. Jahrhunderts bis zur Moderne* (Wildpark-Postsdam, 1929, repr. New York, 1949), pp. 135–76.

CELLETTI, RODOLFO: 'Il vocalismo italiano da Rossini a Donizetti', *Studien zur italienisch-deutschen Musikgeschichte*, v (*Analecta musicologica*, v) (1968), pp. 267–94, vi (vii) (1969), pp. 214–47.

DENT, EDWARD: *The Rise of Romantic Opera*, ed. Winton Dean (Cambridge, 1976).

EINAUDI, GINO, ed.: *Il melodramma italiano dell'Ottocento. Studi e ricerche per Massimo Mila* (Turin, 1977).

Enciclopedia della spettacolo, 9 vols., appendix, supplement (Rome, 1954–68).

KIRSCH, WINFRIED: 'Zur musikalischen Konzeption und dramaturgischen Stellung des Opernquartetts im 18. und 19. Jahrhundert', *Die Musikforschung*, xxvii (1974), pp. 186–99.

LIPPMANN, FRIEDRICH: 'Der italienische Vers und der musikalische Rhythmus: zum Verhältnis von Libretto und Musik in der italienischen Oper des 19. Jahrhunderts, mit einem Rückblick auf die 2. Hälfte des 18. Jahrhunderts', *Studien zur italienisch-deutschen Musikgeschichte*, viii (*Analecta Musicologica*, xii) (1973), pp. 253–369, ix (xiv) (1974), pp. 324–410, x (xv) (1975), pp. 298–333.

—— 'Zur *italianità* der italienischen Oper im 19. Jahrhundert', *Die 'Couleur locale' in der Oper des 19. Jahrhunderts* (Studien zur Musikgeschichte des 19. Jahrhunderts, xlii) (Regensburg, 1976), ed. Heinz Becker (Regensburg, 1976), pp. 229–56.

MEDICUS, LOTTE: *Die Koloratur in der italienischen Oper des 19. Jahrhunderts* (Zürich, 1939).

MIRAGOLI, LIVIA: *Il melodramma italiano nell'Ottocento* (Rome, 1924).

PANNAIN, GUIDO: *Ottocento musicale italiano. Saggi e note* (Milan, 1952).

PIZZETTI, ILDEBRANDO: *La musica italiana dell'Ottocento* (Turin, 1947).

RINALDI, MARIO: *Felice Romani* (Rome, 1965).

RUHNKE, MARTIN: 'Das einlage-Lied in der Oper der Zeit von 1800 bis 1840', *Die 'Couleur locale' in der Oper des 19. Jahrhunderts* (*Studien zur Musikgeschichte des 19. Jahrhunderts*, xlii), ed. Heinz Becker (Regensburg, 1976), pp. 75–97.

SCHLITZER, FRANCO: *Mondo teatrale dell'Ottocento* (Naples, 1954).

—— *Storia dell'opera*, ed. Alberto Basso, i: *L'opera in Italia* (Turin, 1977).

(b) *Individual Composers*

Bellini

BOROMÉ, JOSEPH A.: 'Bellini and *Beatrice di Tenda*', *Music and Letters*, xlii (1961), pp. 319–35.

BRAUNER, CHARLES SAMUEL: 'Textual Problems in Bellini's *Norma* and *Beatrice di Tenda*', *Journal of the American Musicological Society*, xxix (1976), pp. 99–118.

LIPPMANN, FRIEDRICH: 'Su "La Straniera" di Bellini', *Nuova rivista musicale italiana*, v (1971), pp. 565–605.

—— 'Verdi e Bellini', *Atti del I. congresso internazionale di studi verdiani, Venezia 1966* (Parma, 1969), pp. 184–96; in German, *Beiträge zur Geschichte der Oper*, ed. Heinz Becker (Regensburg, 1969), pp. 77–88.

—— *Vincenzo Bellini und die italienische Opera seria seiner Zeit* (*Analecta Musicologica*, vi) (Cologne-Vienna, 1969).

OEHLMANN, WERNER: *Vincenzo Bellini* (Zürich, 1974).

ORREY, LESLEY: *Bellini* (London, 1969).

—— 'The Literary Sources of Bellini's First Opera', *Music and Letters*, lv (1974), pp. 24–9.

PASTURA, FRANCESCO: *Bellini secondo la storia* (Parma, 1959).

PETROBELLI, PIERLUIGI: 'Bellini e Paisiello. Altri documenti sulla nascita dei Puritani', *Il melodramma italiano dell' Ottocento, Studi e ricerche per Massimo Mila*, ed. Guilio Einaudi (Turin, 1977), pp. 351–63.

—— 'Note sulla poetica di Bellini: a proposito di *I puritani*', *Muzikološki Zbornik*, viii (1972), pp. 70–85.

PIZZETTI, ILDEBRANDO, ed.: *Vincenzo Bellini. L'uomo, le sue opere, la sua fama* (Milan, 1936).
WEINSTOCK, HERBERT: *Bellini. His Life and Works* (New York, 1971).

Cimarosa
CHIESA, MARIA TIBALDI: *Cimarosa e il suo tempo* (Milan, 1939).
DEAN, WINTON: 'The Libretto of "The Secret Marriage"', *Music Survey*, iii (1950), pp. 33–8.
ENGEL, CARL: 'A Note on Domenico Cimarosa's *Il matrimonio segreto', Musical Quarterly*, xxxiii (1947), pp. 201–6.
FILIPPIS, FELICE DE, ed.: *Per il Bicentenario della nascità di Domenico Cimarosa 1749–1949* (Aversa, 1949).
SCHLITZER, FRANCO: *Cimarosa* (Milan, 1950).
—— *Goethe e Cimarosa* (Siena, 1950).

Donizetti
ASHBROOK, WILLIAM: *Donizetti* (London, 1965).
COMMONS, JEREMY: 'Emilia di Liverpool', *Music and Letters*, xl (1959), pp. 207–28.
LIPPMANN, FRIEDRICH: 'Donizetti' in *Vincenzo Bellini und die italienische Opera seria seiner Zeit* (*Analecta Musicologica*, vi) (Cologne-Vienna, 1969), pp. 304–17.
—— 'Die Melodien Donizettis', *Studien zur italienisch-deutschen Musikgeschichte*, iii (*Analecta musicologica*, iii) (1966), pp. 80–113.
—— 'Verdi und Donizetti', *Opernstudien. Anna Amalie Abert zum 65. Geburtstag*, ed. Klaus Hortschansky (Tutzing, 1975), pp. 153–73. Also on Bellini.
SCHAPP, JAN: 'Donizetti and his Il Borgomastro di Saardam', *Donizetti Society*, i (1974), pp. 51–7.
WEINSTOCK, HERBERT: *Donizetti and the World of Opera in Italy, Paris and Vienna in the First Half of the Nineteenth Century* (New York, 1963; London, 1964).

Mayr
ALLITT, JOHN S.: 'Mayr's L'amor coniugale', *Donizetti Society*, i (1974), pp. 59–79.
CARNER, MOSCO: 'Simone Mayr and his "L'amor coniugale"', *Music and Letters*, lii (1971), pp. 239–58.
FREEMAN, JAMES: 'Johann Simon Mayr and his *Ifigenia in Aulide', Musical Quarterly*, lvii (1971), pp. 187–210.
GAZZANIGA, ARRIGO: 'Su L'amor coniugale di Giovanni Simone Mayr', *Nuova rivista musicale italiana*, v (1971), pp. 799–826.
JENKINS, NEWELL: 'Giovanni Simone Mayr's "Medea in Corinto"', *Donizetti Society*, i (1974), pp. 81–90.
KRETZSCHMAR, HERMANN: 'Die musikgeschichtliche Bedeutung Simon Mayr', *Gesammelte Aufsätze*, ii (Leipzig, 1911, repr. Leipzig, 1973), pp. 226–41.
SCHIEDERMAIR, LUDWIG: *Beiträge zur Geschichte der Oper um die Wende des 18. und 19. Jahrhunderts: Simon Mayr*, 2 vols. (Leipzig, 1907, 1910; reprint Walluf bei Wiesbaden, 1973).

Mercadante
CARLI BALLOLA, GIOVANNI: 'Incontro con Mercadante, *Chigiana*, xxvi-xxvii (1969–70), pp. 465–500.
LIPPMANN, FRIEDRICH: 'Mercadante' in *Vincenzo Bellini und die italienische Opera seria seiner Zeit* (*Analecta Musicologica*, vi) (Cologne-Vienna, 1969), pp. 328–40.
SCHMID, PATRIC: 'Rediscovering Mercadante', *Opera*, xxvi (1975), pp. 332–7.
RONCAGLIA, GINO: 'Il giuramento', *La Scala*, lxi (1954), pp. 81–4, 131–4.

Meyerbeer
BECKER, HEINZ, ed.: *Giacomo Meyerbeer. Briefwechsel und Tagebücher*, i–ii (Berlin, 1960, 1970).

ISTEL, EDGAR: 'Meyerbeer's Way to Mastership', *Musical Quarterly*, xii (1926), pp. 72–109.

KAPP, JULIUS: *Meyerbeer* (Berlin and Leipzig, 1920).

KRUSE, GEORG: 'Meyerbeers Jugendopern', *Zeitschrift für Musikwissenschaft*, i (1918–19), pp. 399–413.

Paer

CELLETTI, RODOLFO: 'La "Leonora" e lo stile vocale di Paër', *Rivista italiana di musicologica*, vii (1972), pp. 214–29.

ENGLÄNDER, RICHARD: 'Paërs "Leonora" und Beethovens "Fidelio"', *Neues Beethoven-Jahrbuch*, iv (1930), pp. 118–32.

Paisiello

GHISLANZONI, ALBERTO: *Giovanni Paisiello. Valutazioni critiche retificate* (Rome, 1969).

LOEWENBERG, ALFRED: 'Paisiello's and Rossini's "Barbiere di Siviglia"', *Music and Letters*, xx (1939), pp. 157–67.

SAMSON, INGRID: 'Paisiello—*La bella molinara', Neue Zeitschrift für Musik*, cxx (1959), pp. 368–71.

TARTAK, MARVIN: 'The Two "Barbieri"', *Music and Letters*, l (1969), pp. 453–69.

Rossini

BONACORSI, ALFREDO, ed.: *Gioacchino Rossini* (Florence, 1968).

CAGI, BRUNO: 'Fonti letterarie dei libretti di Rossini: Maometto II', *Bolletino del centro rossiniano di studi*, i (1972), pp. 10–32.

CELLETTI, RODOLFO: 'Origine e sviluppi della coloratura rossiniana', *Nuova rivista musicale italiana*, ii (1968), pp. 872–919.

FALLER, H.: *Die Gesangskoloratur in Rossinis Opern und ihre Ausführung* (Berlin, 1935).

GALLARATI, PAOLO: 'Dramma e *ludus* dall'*Italiana* al *Barbiere', Il melodramma italiano dell'Ottocento. Studi e ricerche per Massimo Mila*, ed. Giulio Einaudi (Turin, 1977), pp. 237–80.

GOSSETT, PHILIP: 'The Candeur virginale of *Tancredi', Musical Times*, cxii (1971), pp. 326–9.

—— 'Le fonti autografe delle opere teatrali di Rossini', *Nuova rivista musicale italiana*, ii (1968), pp. 936–60.

—— 'Gioacchino Rossini and the Conventions of Composition', *Acta Musicologica*, xlii (1970), pp. 48–58.

—— 'The Overtures of Rossini', *19th Century Music*, iii (1979), pp. 3–31.

—— 'Rossini in Naples: Some Major Works Recovered', *Musical Quarterly*, liv (1968), pp. 316–40.

—— *The Tragic Finale of 'Tancredi'* (Pesaro, 1977).

KLEIN, JOHN W.: 'Verdi's "Otello" and Rossini's', *Music and Letters*, xlv (1964), pp. 130–40.

LIPPMANN, FRIEDRICH: 'Gioacchino Rossini' in *Vincenzo Bellini und die italienische Opera seria seiner Zeit* (*Analecta Musicologica*, vi) (Cologne-Vienna, 1969), pp. 152–206.

—— 'Per un' esegesi dello stile rossiniano', *Nuova rivista musicale italiana*, ii (1968), pp. 813–56.

LOEWENBERG, ALFRED: 'Paisiello's and Rossini's "Barbiere di Siviglia"', *Music and Letters*, xx (1939), pp. 157–67.

PORTER, ANDREW: 'A Lost Opera by Rossini', *Music and Letters*, xlv (1964), pp. 39–44 (about *Ugo*).

RADICIOTTI, G.: *Gioacchino Rossini: vita documentata, opere ed influenza su l'arte* (three vols.) (Tivoli, 1927–29).

ROGNONI, LUIGI: *Rossini* (2nd ed., Bologna, 1968).

TAMMARO, FERRUCCIO: 'Ambivalenza dell'*Otello* rossiniano', *Il melodramma italiano dell'Ottocento. Studi e ricerche per Massimo Mila*, ed. Giulio Einaudi (Turin, 1977), pp. 187–236.

TARTAK, MARVIN: 'The Two "Barbieri"', *Music and Letters*, l (1969), pp. 453–69.

WEINSTOCK, HERBERT: *Rossini, a Biography* (New York, 1968).

Salieri

ANGERMÜLLER, RUDOLPH: *Antonio Salieri. Sein Leben und seine weltlichen Werke unter besonderer Berücksichtigung seiner "grossen" Opern*, ii/1 (*Publikationen des Instituts für Musikwissenschaft der Universität Salzburg*, xvii) (Munich, 1974).

BOLLERT, WERNER: 'Antonio Salieri und die italienische Oper. Eine Studie zur Geschichte der italienischen Oper im 18. Jahrhundert', *Aufsätze zur Musikgeschichte* (Bottrop, 1938), pp. 43–93.

CHAPTER X

GERMAN OPERA

(i) Modern Editions

(a) Anthologies

ABERT, ANNA AMALIE: *Die Oper von den Anfängen bis zum Beginn des 19. Jahrhunderts* (*Das Musikwerk*, v) (Cologne, 1953, English edition 1962). (Includes examples by Dittersdorf and Spohr.)

BRODY, ELAINE: *Music in Opera. A Historical Anthology* (Englewood Cliffs, New Jersey, 1970). (Includes examples by Beethoven and Weber.)

WOLFF, HELLMUTH CHRISTIAN, ed.: *Die Oper III: 19. Jahrhundert* (*Das Musikwerk*, xl) (Cologne, 1972, English edition 1975). (Includes examples by Hoffmann, Spohr, and Weber).

(b) Works by Individual Composers

BEETHOVEN, L. van: *Fidelio, L. van Beethoven's Werke. Vollständige kritisch durchgesehene überall berechtigte Ausgabe*, series xx, no. 206 (Leipzig, 1865).

—— *Supplemente zur Gesamtausgabe*, ed. W. Hess: xi-xii: *Leonore* (1805 version); xiii: *Leonore* (1806 version) (Wiesbaden, 1967, 1970).

DITTERSDORF, K.: *Doktor und Apotheker*, vocal score ed. H. Burkhard (Vienna, 1935, repr. Vienna, 1961).

—— *Hieronymous Knicker*, vocal score ed. R. Kleinmichel (Leipzig, 1890).

HOFFMANN, E. T. A.: *Ausgewählte musikalische Werke*, i-iii: *Undine*, ed. J. Kindermann (Mainz, 1971–2); iv-v: *Die lustigen Musikanten*, ed. G. Allroggen (Mainz, 1975–6).

MARSCHNER, H.: *Hans Heiling*, ed. G. F. Kogel (Leipzig, c. 1893).

—— *Der Templer und die Jüdin*, vocal score ed. R. Kleinmichel (Vienna, 1912).

—— *Der Vampyr*, vocal score ed. G. F. Kogel (Leipzig, 1902).

MENDELSSOHN, F.: *Die beiden Pädagogen*, ed. K.-H. Köhler, *Leipziger Ausgabe der Werke Felix Mendelssohn Bartholdys*, series v/1 (Leipzig, 1966).

—— *Die Heimkehr aus der Fremde*, series xv/8, *Felix Mendelssohn Bartholdy's Werke. Kritisch durchgesehene Ausgabe*, ed. J. Rietz (Leipzig, 1874–7).

SCHENK, J.: *Der Dorfbarbier*, ed. R. Haas (*Denkmäler der Tonkunst in Österreich*, xxxiv (vol. 66) (Vienna, 1927).

SCHUBERT, F.: *Franz Schubert's Werke. Kritisch durchgesehene Gesammtausgabe* (Leipzig, 1884–97, repr. New York, 1965): series xv: *Dramatische Werke*, ed. J. N. Fuchs: xv/1: *Des Teufels Lustschloss* (1888); xv/2: *Der vierjährige Posten*,

Fernando, Die Freunde von Salamanka (1888); xv/3: *Die Zwillingsbrüder, Die Verschworenen* (1889); xv/4: *Die Zauberharfe, Rosamunde* (1891); xv/5: *Alfonso und Estrella* (1892); xv/6: *Fierrabras* (1886); xv/7: *Claudine von Villa Bella, Der Spiegelritter, Die Bürgschaft, Adrast* (1893).

—— *Franz Schubert. Neue Ausgabe sämtlicher Werke*, series ii/4: *Die Zauberharfe*, ed. R. Dalmonte (Kassel, 1975).

SPOHR, L.: *Faust*, vocal score ed. P. Pixis (Leipzig, *c.* 1876).

—— *Jessonda*, ed. G. F. Kogel (Leipzig, *c.* 1881); overture ed. A. de Almeida (Paris, 1962).

WEBER, C. M. von: *Carl Maria von Weber. Musikalische Werke. Erste kritische Gesamtausgabe* (Augsburg, 1926–32, repr. New York, 1977), series ii/1: *Das stumme Waldmädchen, Peter Schmoll und seine Nachbarn*, ed. A. Lorenz (1926); ii/2: *Rübezahl, Silvana*, ed. W. Kaehler (1928); ii/3: *Preciosa*, ed. L.K. Mayer (*c.* 1932).

—— *Abu Hassan*, full score ed. W. W. Göttig (Offenbach, 1925, repr. Farnborough, 1968).

—— *Euryanthe*, full score ed. E. Rudorff (Berlin, 1866, repr. Farnborough, 1969).

—— *Der Freischütz*, full score (Berlin, 1843, repr. Farnborough, 1969); ed. K. Soldan (Leipzig, 1926); ed. J. Freyer (Leipzig, 1976).

—— *Oberon*, full score (Berlin, *c.* 1881, repr. Farnborough, 1969).

WEIGL, K.: *Die Schweizerfamilie*, vocal score ed. R. Kleinmichel (Leipzig, *c.* 1889).

(ii) Books and Articles

(a) General

BAUER, ANTON: *Opern und Operetten in Wien. Verzeichnis ihrer Erstaufführung in der Zeit von 1629 bis zur Gegenwart* (Graz-Cologne, 1955).

DENT, EDWARD: *The Rise of Romantic Opera*, ed. Winton Dean (Cambridge, 1976).

FARGIA, FRANZ: *Die Wiener Oper von ihren Anfängen bis 1938* (Vienna, 1947).

FLAHERTY, MARIA GLORIA: 'Opera and Incipient Romantic Aesthetics in Germany', *Studies in Eighteenth-Century Culture*, iii (1973), pp. 205–17.

—— *Opera in the Development of German Cultural Thought* (Princeton, 1978).

GARLINGTON, AUBREY S., Jr.: 'August Wilhelm von Schlegel and the Creation of German Romantic Opera, *Journal of the American Musicological Society*, xxx (1977), pp. 500–6.

—— 'German Romantic Opera and the Problem of Origins', *Musical Quarterly*, lxiii (1977), pp. 247–63.

GÖPFERT, BERND: *Stimmtypen und Rollencharaktere in der deutschen Oper von 1815–1848* (Wiesbaden, 1977).

GOSLICH, SIEGFRIED: *Beiträge zur Geschichte der deutschen romantischen Oper* (Leipzig, 1937).

—— *Die deutsche romantische Oper* (Tutzing, 1975).

HORTSCHANSKY, KLAUS: 'Der *Deus ex machina* im Opernlibretto der ersten Hälfte des 19. Jahrhunderts', *Beiträge zur Geschichte der Oper* (*Studien zur Musikgeschichte des 19. Jahrhunderts*, xv), ed. Heinz Becker (Regensburg, 1965), pp. 45–76.

ISTEL, EDGAR: *Die komische Oper* (Stuttgart, 1906).

JARNOWITZ, OTTO: 'Goethe als Librettist', *German Life and Letters*, new series, ix (1955–6), pp. 110–17, 265–76.

KLOB, KARL MARIA: *Beiträge zur Geschichte der deutschen komischen Oper* (Berlin, 1903).

LÜTHGE, KURT: *Die deutsche Spieloper* (Braunschweig, 1924).

OTT, ALFONS: 'Von der frühdeutschen Oper zum deutschen Singspiel' [1644–1870], *Musik in Bayern*, i, ed. Robert Münster and Hans Schmidt (Tutzing, 1972), pp. 165–77.

SCHIEDERMAIR, LUDWIG: *Die deutsche Oper* (2nd ed., Bonn and Berlin, 1940).

WARRACK, JOHN: 'German Operatic Ambitions at the Beginning of the 19th Century', *Proceedings of the Royal Musical Association*, civ (1977–8), pp. 79–88.

WOLFF, HELLMUTH and HAUSSWALD, GÜNTER: 'L'opera in Germania e in Austria', *Storia dell'opera*, ii/1, ed. Alberto Basso (Turin, 1977), pp. 207–343.

WÖRNER, KARL: 'Beiträge zur Geschichte des Leitmotivs in der Oper', *Zeitschrift für Musikwissenschaft*, xiv (1931–2), pp. 151–72: excerpts from his dissertation (Berlin, 1931).

ZIMMERMANN, CHRISTOPH: 'Die Geisterinseldarstellung in der Oper des 19. Jahrhunderts', *Die 'Couleur locale' in der Oper des 19. Jahrhunderts* (*Studien zur Musikgeschichte des 19. Jahrhunderts*, xlii), ed. Heinz Becker (Regensburg, 1976), pp. 213–28.

(*b*) *Individual Composers*

Beethoven

BLAUKOPF, KURT: 'Die Funktion der 3. Leonoren-Ouvertüre im "Fidelio"', *Beethoven-Almanach 1970* (Vienna, 1970), pp. 35–9.

BRINCKER, JENS: 'Leonore and Fidelio', *Festskrift Jens Peter Larsen*, ed. Nils Schiø rring, Nils Glahn and Carsten Hatting (Copenhagen, 1972), pp. 351–68.

DEAN, WINTON: 'Beethoven and Opera', *The Beethoven Companion* (*Reader*) (London, 1971, New York, 1971), pp. 331–86.

GRAF, WALTER: 'Zum klanglichen Ausdruck in Beethovens "Fidelio"', *Beethoven-Studien, Festgabe* (Vienna, 1970), pp. 253–70.

HADAMOWSKY, FRANZ: 'Beethovens *Fidelio* in Wien', *Österreichische Musikzeitschrift*, xxv (1970), pp. 276–81.

HESS, WILLY: *Beethovens Bühnenwerke* (Göttingen, 1962).

—— *Beethovens Oper Fidelio und ihre drei Fassungen* (Zürich, 1966).

—— 'Eine unbekannte Frühfassung zweier Nummern der Oper *Leonore*', *Colloquium amicorum. Joseph Schmidt-Görg zum 70. Geburtstag*, ed. Siegfried Kross and Hans Schmidt (Bonn, 1967), pp. 118–31.

ISTEL, EDGAR: 'Beethoven's *Leonora* and *Fidelio*', *Musical Quarterly*, vii (1921), pp. 226–51.

MISCH, LUDWIG: '*Fidelio* als ethisches Bekenntnis', *Beethoven-Studien* (Berlin, 1950), pp. 143–9.

OSTHOFF, WOLFGANG: 'Beethovens "Leonoren"-Arien', *Bericht über den internationalen musikwissenchaftlichen Kongress Bonn 1970*, ed. Carl Dahlhaus *et al.* (Kassel, 1971), pp. 191–9.

RUHNKE, MARTIN: 'Die Librettisten des *Fidelio*', *Anna Amalie Abert zum 65. Geburtstag. Opernstudien*, ed. Klaus Hortschansky (Tutzing, 1975), pp. 121–40.

SCHENK, ERICH: 'Über Tonsymbolik in Beethovens "Fidelio"', *Beethoven-Studien, Festgabe* (Vienna, 1970), pp. 223–52.

STEGLICH, RUDOLF: 'Das melodische Hauptmotiv in Beethovens *Fidelio*', *Archiv für Musikwissenschaft*, ix (1952), pp. 51–67.

TYSON, ALAN: 'The Problem of Beethoven's "First" *Leonore* Overture', *Journal of the American Musicological Society*, xxviii (1975), pp. 292–334.

Hoffmann

ALLROGGEN, GERHARD: *E.T.A. Hoffmanns Kompositionen: ein chronologisch-thematisches Verzeichnis seiner musikalischen Werke mit einer Einführung* (*Studien zur Musikgeschichte des 19. Jahrhunderts*, xvi) (Regensburg, 1970).

—— 'Die Opern-Asthetik E.T.A. Hoffmanns', *Beiträge zur Geschichte der Oper* (*Studien zur Musikgeschichte des 19. Jahrhunderts*, xv), ed. Heinz Becker (Regensburg, 1969), pp. 25–34.

EHINGER, HANS: *E.T.A. Hoffmann als Musiker und Musikschriftsteller* (Olten and Cologne, 1954).

GARLINGTON, AUBREY S., JR.: 'E.T.A. Hoffmann's "Der Dichter und der Komponist" and the Creation of German Romantic Opera', *Musical Quarterly*, lxv (1979), pp. 22–47.

—— 'Notes on Dramatic Motives in Opera: Hoffmann's *Undine*', *Music and Letters*, xxxii (1971), pp. 136–45.

KINDERMANN, JÜRGEN: 'Romantische Aspekte in E.T.A. Hoffmanns Musikanschauung', *Beiträge zur Geschichte der Musikanschauung im 19. Jahrhundert* (*Studien zur Musikgeschichte des 19. Jahrhunderts*, i), ed. Walter Salmen (Regensburg, 1965), pp. 51–9.

SCHAFER, R. MURRAY: *E.T.A. Hoffmann and Music* (Toronto, 1975).

SCHLÄDER, JÜRGEN: '"Undine" von E.T.A. Hoffmann', *Undine auf dem Musiktheater. Zur Entwicklungsgeschichte der deutschen Spieloper* (Bonn-Bad Godesberg, 1979), pp. 232–357.

Kauer

SCHLÄDER, JÜRGEN: '"Das Donauweibchen" von Ferdinand Kauer', *Undine auf dem Musiktheater. Zur Entwicklungsgeschichte der deutschen Spieloper* (Bonn-Bad Godesberg, 1979), pp. 99–227.

Marschner

KÖHLER, VOLKMAR: 'Rezitativ, Szene und Melodram in Heinrich Marschners Opern', *Bericht über den internationalen musikwissenschaftlichen Kongress Bonn, 1970*, ed. Carl Dahlhaus et al. (Kassel, 1971), pp. 461–4.

MÜNZER, GEORG: *Heinrich Marschner* (Berlin, 1901).

PALMER, A. DEAN: *Heinrich August Marschner 1795–1861. His Life and Stage Works* (Ann Arbor, 1980).

Mendelssohn

SCHÜNEMANN, GEORG: 'Mendelssohns Jugendopern', *Zeitschrift für Musikwissenschaft*, v (1922–3), pp. 506–45.

Meyerbeer

BECKER, HEINZ, ed.: *Giacomo Meyerbeer. Briefwechsel und Tagebücher*, i–ii (Berlin, 1960, 1970).

—— 'Meyerbeers Beziehungen zu Louis Spohr', *Die Musikforschung*, x (1957), pp. 479–86.

ISTEL, EDGAR: 'Meyerbeer's Way to Mastership', *Musical Quarterly*, xii (1926), pp. 72–109.

KRUSE, GEORG: 'Meyerbeers Jugendopern', *Zeitschrift für Musikwissenschaft*, i (1918–19), pp. 399–413.

Reichardt

PRÖPPER, ROLF: *Die Bühnenwerke Johann Friedrich Reichardts (1752–1814). Ein Beitrag zur Geschichte der Oper in der Zeit des Stilwandels* (*Abhandlungen zur Kunst-, Musik-, und Literaturwissenschaft*, xxv) (Bonn, 1965).

Schubert

BISOGNI, FABIO: 'Rossini e Schubert', *Nuova rivista musicale italiana*, ii (1968), pp. 920–35.

BRANSCOMBE, PETER: 'Schubert and his Librettists—1', *Musical Times*, cix (1978), pp. 943–7.

BROWN, MAURICE J. E.: 'Schubert's Two Major Operas. A Consideration of the Possibility of Actual Stage Production', *Music Review*, xx (1959), pp. 104–18. (On *Alfonso und Estrella* and *Fierrabras*.)

—— 'Schubert's "Fierrabras"', *Musical Times*, cxii (1971), pp. 338–9.

DALMONTE, ROSSANA: 'Die Bedeutung der Skizzen der "Zauberharfe", D. 644, zur Erkenntnis der Schubertschen Schaffensweise', *Schubert-Kongress Wien 1978, Bericht*, ed. Otto Brusatti (Graz, 1979), pp. 141–52.

HOORICKX, REINHARD VAN: 'Les Opéras de Schubert', *Revue belge de musicologie*, xxviii–xxx (1974–6), pp. 238–59.

KING, A. HYATT: 'Music for the Stage', *Schubert: a Symposium*, ed. Gerald Abraham (London, 1946; as *The Music of Schubert*, New York, 1947, repr. Port Washington, N.Y., 1969), pp. 198–216.

LEICHTENTRITT, HUGO: 'Schubert's Early Operas', *Musical Quarterly*, xiv (1928), pp. 620–38.

MCKAY, ELIZABETH NORMAN: 'Schubert's Music for the Theatre', *Proceedings of the Royal Musical Association*, xciii (1966–7), pp. 51–66.

RACEK, FRITZ: 'Franz Schuberts Singspiel Der häusliche Krieg und seine jetzt aufgefundene Ouvertüre', *Biblos*, xii (1963), pp. 136–43.

SZMOLYAN, WALTER: 'Schubert als Opernkomponist', *Österreichische Musikzeitschrift*, xxvi (1971), pp. 282–9.

Spohr

ABERT, ANNA AMALIE: 'Webers "Euryanthe" und Spohrs "Jessonda" als grosse Opern', *Festschrift für Walter Wiora*, ed. Ludwig Finscher and Christoph-Hellmut Mahling (Kassel, 1967), pp. 435–40.

BROWN, CLIVE: 'Spohr's "Jessonda"', *Musical Times*, cxxi (1980), pp. 94–7.

SCHMITZ, EUGEN: 'Louis Spohrs Jugendoper "Alruna"', *Zeitschrift der internationalen Musikgesellschaft*, xiii (1911–12), pp. 293–9.

—— 'Louis Spohrs erster Opernversuch', *Archiv für Musikforschung*, vii (1942), pp. 45–52.

WASSERMANN, RUDOLF: 'Ludwig Spohr als Opernkomponist', *Die Musik*, ix/2 (1909–10), no. 33, pp. 76–88.

Süssmayr

LEHNER, WALTER: 'Franz Xaver Süssmayr als Opernkomponist', *Studien zur Musikwissenschaft*, xviii (1931), pp. 66–96.

Weber

ABERT, ANNA AMALIE: 'Webers "Euryanthe" und Spohrs "Jessonda" als grosse Opern', *Festschrift für Walter Wiora*, ed. Ludwig Finscher and Christoph-Hellmut Mahling (Kassel, 1967), pp. 435–40.

BLAUKOPF, HERTA: 'Eine Oper "Aus Weber"', *Österreichische Muzikzeitschrift*, xxxiii (1978), pp. 204–8. (On *Die drei Pintos*.)

ENGLÄNDER, RICHARD: 'The Struggle between German and Italian Opera at the Time of Weber', *Musical Quarterly*, xxxi (1945), pp. 479–91.

HAUSSWALD, GÜNTER, ed.: *Carl Maria von Weber: ein Gedenkschrift* (Dresden, 1951).

HSU, DOLORES MENSTELL: 'Carl Maria von Weber's *Preciosa*. Incidental Music on a Spanish Theme', *Music Review*, xxvi (1965), pp. 97–103.

—— 'Weber on Opera: A Challenge to Eighteenth-Century Tradition', *Studies in Eighteenth-Century Music. A Tribute to Karl Geiringer on his 70th Birthday*, ed. H.C. Robbins Landon and Roger E. Chapman (London and New York, 1970), pp. 297–309.

KÖHLER, SIEGFRIED: 'Progressive Klangstrukturen in den Opern Carl Maria von Webers', *Musik und Gesellschaft*, xxvi (1976), pp. 328–32.

KOMORZYNSKI, EGON: '"Zauberflöte" und "Oberon"', *Mozart-Jahrbuch 1953* (1954), pp. 150–61.

KROLL, ERWIN: *Carl Maria von Weber* (Potsdam, 1934).

LAUX, KARL: 'In Erinnerung gebracht "Die drei Pintos". Zum 150. Todestag Carl Maria von Webers', *Musikbühne 76: Probleme und Informationen* (1976), pp. 89–111.

RADICE, MARK A.: 'Carl Maria von Weber: Forefather of Wagner', *Music Review*, xxxvii (1976), pp. 165–70.

SANDERS, ERNEST: '*Oberon* and *Zar und Zimmermann*', *Musical Quarterly*, xl (1954), pp. 521–32.

SEEGER, HORST: 'Das "Original-Libretto" zum "Oberon"', *Musikbühne 76: Probleme und Informationen* (1976), pp. 33–87.

WALTERSHAUSEN, HERMANN VON: *Der Freischütz, Ein Versuch über die musikalische Romantik* (Munich, 1920).

WARRACK, JOHN: *Carl Maria von Weber* (London and New York, 1968).

—— '"Oberon" und der englische Geschmack. Zum 150. Todestag Carl Maria von Webers', *Musikbühne 76: Probleme und Informationen* (1976), pp. 15–31.

WIRTH, HELMUT: 'Natur und Märchen in Webers *Oberon*, Mendelssohns *Ein Sommernachtstraum* und Nicolais *Die lustigen Weiber von Windsor*', *Festschrift Friedrich Blume*, ed. Anna Amalie Abert and Walter Pfannkuch (Kassel, 1963), pp. 389–97.

Weigl

BOLLERT, WERNER: 'Joseph Weigl und das deutsche Singspiel', *Aufsätze zur Musikgeschichte* (Bottrop, 1938), pp. 95–114.

CHAPTER XI

OPERA IN OTHER COUNTRIES

Denmark and England

Books and Articles

BEHREND, WILHELM: 'Weyse und Kuhlau: Studien zur Geschichte der dänischen Musik', *Die Musik*, iii, 2 (1904), no. 22, pp. 272–86.

CORDER, FREDERICK: 'The Works of Sir Henry Bishop', *Musical Quarterly*, iv (1918), pp. 78–97.

FOG, DAN: *Kompositionen von C.E.F. Weyse. Thematisch-bibliographischer Katalog* (Copenhagen, 1979).

—— *Kompositionen von Fridr. Kuhlau: Thematisch-bibliographischer Katalog* (Copenhagen, 1977).

HOLMES, WILLIAM C.: 'L'opera in Inghilterra', *Storia dell'opera*, ii/1, ed. Alberto Basso (Turin, 1977), pp. 423–86.

HORTON, JOHN: *Scandinavian Music: A Short History* (London, 1963).

KROGH, TORBEN: *Zur Geschichte des dänischen Singspiels im 18. Jahrhundert* (Copenhagen, 1924).

WHITE, ERIC WALTER: *The Rise of English Opera* (London, 1951, repr. New York, 1972).

Poland

(i) Modern Editions

(a) Anthology

PROSNAK, JAN: *Kultura muzyczna Warszawy xviii wieku* (Cracow, 1955). (Includes examples by Kamieński.)

(b) Works by Individual Composers

ELSNER, J.: *Amazonki*, aria; *Król Łokietek*, overture, Alina Nowak-Romanowicz, *Józef Elsner* (Cracow, 1957), supplement.
—— *Leszek*, overture, ed. G. Fitelberg (Cracow, 1950).
KURPIŃSKI, K.: *Jadwiga, królowa polska*, (full score) ed. A. Nowak-Romanowicz (*Opery polskie*, v) (Cracow, 1980).
—— *Marcinowa w seraju*, overture, Tadeusz Strumiłło, *Źródła i początki romantyzmu w muzyce polskiej* (Cracow, 1956), supplement.
—— *Zamek na Czorstynie, czyli Bojomir i Wanda* (*Opery polskie*, i), ed. A. Papierzowa and W. Poźniak (Cracow, 1968).
STEFANI, J.: *Cud mniemany czyli Krakowiaki i Gorale*, ed. E. Kucharski (Warsaw, 1923); ed. W. Raczkowski (Cracow, 1956); overture ed. G. Fitelberg (Cracow, 1951).

(ii) Books and Articles

(a) General

ABRAHAM, GERALD: 'The Early Development of Opera in Poland', *Essays on Opera and English Music. In Honour of Sir Jack Westrup*, ed. Frederick Sternfeld *et al.* (Oxford, 1975), pp. 148–65.
BEŁZA, IGOR: *Między Oświeceniem i Romantyzmem* (Cracow, 1961).
GLOWACKI, JOHN M.: 'Early Polish Opera', *Paul A. Pisk. Essays in his Honor*, ed. J. Glowacki (Austin, Texas, 1966), pp. 131–40.
JACHIMECKI, ZDZISŁAW: *Muzyka polska w rozwoju historycznym*, i, 2 (Cracow, 1951).
KARASOWSKI, MAURYCY: *Rys historyczny opery polskiej* (Warsaw, 1859).
LISSA, ZOFIA: 'Polish Romanticism and Neo-Romanticism', *Polish Music*, ed. Stefan Jarociński (Warsaw, 1965), pp. 104–27.
MICHAŁOWSKI, KORNEL: *Opery polskie* [1778–1953] (Cracow, 1954).
MUSIOŁ, KAROL: 'Mozart und die polnische Komponisten des XVIII. und der ersten Hälfte des XIX. Jahrhunderts', *Mozart-Jahrbuch*, xv (1967), pp. 286–311.
NOWAK-ROMANOWICZ, ALINA: 'Muzyka polskiego Oświecenia i wczesnego romantyzmu', *Z dziejów polskiej kultury muzycnej*, ii, ed. Zygmunt M. Szweykowski *et al.* (Cracow, 1966), particularly pp. 108–122.
—— 'Niektóre problemy opery polskiej między oświeceniem a romantyzmem', *Studia Hieronymo Feicht septuagenario dedicata*, ed. Zofia Lissa (Cracow, 1967), pp. 328–36.
PAPIERZOWA, ANNA: *Libretta oper polskich z lat 1800–1830* (Cracow, 1959).
PROSNAK, JAN: *Kultura muzyczna Warsawy XVIII wieku* (Cracow, 1955).
STRUMIŁŁO, TADEUSZ, ed.: *Źródła i początki romantyzmu w muzyce polskiej* (Cracow, 1956).
SZABOLCSI, BENCE: 'Die Anfänge der nationalen Oper im 19. Jahrhundert', *International Musicological Society Congress Report*, ix (Salzburg, 1964), pp. 57–62.
WIERZBICKA, KARYNA: *Źródła do historii teatru warszawskiego od roku 1762 do roku 1833* (Wrocław, 1951).

(*b*) *Individual Composers*

Elsner

HERMANN, JOACHIM: *Josef Elsner und die polnische Musik* (Munich, 1969).
JACHIMECKI, ZDZISŁAW: 'Deux opéras polonais sur Napoléon', *La revue musicale*, v, 3 (1924), pp. 132–42. (On Elsner's *Andromeda*.)
NOWAK-ROMANOWICZ, ALINA: *Józef Elsner* (Cracow, 1957).

Kurpiński

POMORSKA, HANNA: *Karol Kurpiński* (Warsaw, 1948).
PRZYBYLSKI, TADEUSZ: *Karol Kurpiński* (Warsaw, 1975).
STRUMIŁŁO, TADEUSZ: *Uwertury Kurpińskiego* (Cracow, 1954).

Russia

(i) Modern Editions

(*a*) *Anthology*

GINZBURG, S. L., ed.: *Istoriya russkoy muzïki v notnïkh obraztsakh*, ii-iii (Leningrad and Moscow, 1949 and 1952). (Includes examples by Cavos, Davïdov, Titov and Verstovsky.)

(*b*) *Works by Individual Composers*

CAVOS, C.: *Dneprovskaya rusalka*, excerpts, M. S. Pekelis, *Istoriya russkoy muzïki*, i (Moscow-Leningrad, 1940, repr. Ann Arbor, 1963).

(ii) Books and Articles

(*a*) *General*

DRUSKIN M.S. and KELDÏSH, Y.: ed.: *Ocherki po istorii russkoy muzïki 1790–1825* (Leningrad, 1956).
FINDEISEN, NIKOLAY: 'The Earliest Russian Operas', *Musical Quarterly*, xix (1933), pp. 331–40.
GINZBURG, S. L., ed.: *Russkiy muzïkal'nïy teatr 1700–1835* (Moscow, 1941).
GOZENPUD, ABRAM: *Muzïkal'nïy teatr v Rossii ot istokovo do Glinki: ocherk* (Leningrad, 1959).
—— *Russkiy opernïy teatr XIX veka*, i (Leningrad, 1969).
KELDÏSH, YURY: *Istorïya russkoy muzïki*, i (Moscow, 1948).
LEVASHEVA, O., KELDÏSH, Y. and KANDINSKY, A., ed.: *Istoriya russkoy muzïki*, i (Moscow, 1972).
LIVANOVA, TAMARA: *Opernaya kritika v Rossii*, i (Moscow, 1966).
MOOSER, R.-ALOYS: *L'Opéra-comique française en Russie aux XVIIIe siècle* (2nd ed., Geneva, 1954).
ODOEVSKY, VLADIMIR E.: *Muzïkal'no-literaturnoe nasledie*, ed. G. B. Bernandt (Moscow, 1956).
PEKELIS, M S.: *Istoriya russkoy muzïki*, i (Moscow-Leningrad, 1940, repr. Ann Arbor, 1963).
RABINOVICH, ALEKSANDR S.: *Russkaya opera do Glinka* (Moscow, 1948).

(*b*) *Individual Composers*

Cavos

MOOSER, R.-ALOYS: 'Un musicista veneziano in Russia: Catterino Cavos', *Nuova rivista musicale italiana*, iii/1 (1969), pp. 13–23.

Verstovsky
DOBROKHOTOV, BORIS: *A. N. Verstovsky* (Moscow, 1949).

CHAPTER XII

SOLO SONG

Germany and Italy

(i) Modern Editions

(a) Anthologies

BÖHME, F. M., ed.: *Volkstümliche Lieder der Deutschen im 18 u. 19 Jh.* (Leipzig, 1895).
FRIEDLAENDER, MAX: *Das deutsche Lied im 18. Jahrhundert*, i/2 (Stuttgart, 1902, repr.
    Hildesheim, 1970). Includes songs by Naumann, Neefe, Reichardt and
    Zumsteeg.
MANICKE, DIETRICH, ed.: *Balladen von Gottfried August Bürger in Musik gesetzt* (*Das
    Erbe deutscher Musik*, xlv–xlvi (Mainz, 1970). Includes songs by Reichardt and
    Zumsteeg.
MASCHEK, HERMANN and KRAUS, HEDWIG, ed.: *Das Wiener Lied von 1792 bis 1815*
    (*Denkmäler der Tonkunst in Österreich*, Jg. xlii (2) vol. 79) (Vienna, repr. 1960).
    Includes songs by Dietrichstein, Eberl, Fuss, Jacquin, C. Kreutzer, Krufft,
    Neukomm and Teyber.
MOSER, HANS JOACHIM, ed.: *Das deutsche Sololied und die Ballade* (*Das Musikwerk*,
    xiv) (Cologne, 1957, English edition 1958). Includes songs by Beethoven, Loewe,
    Schubert and Weber.
REIMANN, HERMANN, ed.: *Das deutsche Lied*, 4 vols. (Berlin, 1892–3). Includes
    examples by Himmel, Kreutzer, Nägeli, Neefe, Reichardt, Schulz and Zumsteeg.
STEPHENSON, KURT: *Romantik in der Tonkunst* (*Das Musikwerk*, xxi) (Cologne, 1961,
    English edition 1961). Includes songs by Reichardt, Schubert and Weber.

(b) Works by Individual Composers

BEETHOVEN, L. van: *Ludwig van Beethoven's Werke. Vollständige kritisch durchgesehene
    überall berechtigte Ausgabe* (Leipzig, 1864–90); series xxii *Gesänge mit Orchester*:
    incl. 'Ah! Perfido!'; series xxiii: *Lieder und Gesänge*; series xxiv: *Lieder mit
    Pianoforte, Violin und Violoncello*, series xxv: *Supplement: Gesang-Musik*.
—— *Supplemente zur Gesamtausgabe*, ed. W. Hess, ii: *Gesänge mit Orchester*
    (Wiesbaden, 1962); v: *Lieder und Gesänge mit Klavierbegleitung* (Wiesbaden,
    1962).
—— *An die ferne Geliebte*, Op. 98, facsimile ed. (autograph) (Munich-Duisburg, 1970).
BELLINI, V.: *15 composizioni da camera* (Milan, 1935, repr. 1966).
—— 'Vanne, o rosa fortunata', ed., Frits Noske, *Das ausserdeutsche Sololied 1500–
    1900* (*Das Musikwerk*, xvi) (Cologne, 1958, English edition 1958).
LOEWE, C.: *Carl Loewes Werke: Gesamtausgabe der Balladen, Legenden, Lieder und
    Gesänge*, ed. M. Runze, 17 vols. (Leipzig, 1899–1904, facsimile ed. Farnborough,
    1970).
REICHARDT, J. F.: *Goethes Lieder, Oden, Balladen und Romanzen mit Musik*, ed. W.
    Salmen, 2 vols. (*Das Erbe deutscher Musik*, lviii–lix) (Munich, 1964–70).
—— *Goethes Lieder, Oden, Balladen und Romanzen. Dritte Abteilung: Balladen und
    Romanzen*, ed. F. Zschoch (repr. Leipzig, 1969).
SCHUBERT, F.: *Franz Schuberts Werke. Kritisch durchgesehene Gesammtausgabe*
    (Leipzig, 1884–97, repr. New York, 1965): series xx: *Sämtliche einstimmige
    Lieder und Gesänge*, ed. E. Mandyczewski (Leipzig, 1894–5), selections repr. as

Franz Schubert. Complete Song Cycles. Die schöne Müllerin—Die Winterreise—Schwanengesang (New York, 1970), and *Schubert's Songs to Texts by Goethe* (New York, 1979).

—— *Franz Schubert. Neue Ausgabe sämtlicher Werke*, series iv/1, iv/2, iv/4, iv/6, iv/7, ed. W. Dürr (Kassel, 1970, 1975, 1979, 1969, 1968).

—— *Ausgewählte Lieder nach Gedichten von Matthisson [et al]*, ed. W. Dürr and R. van Hoorickx (Kassel, 1969).

—— *Goethe Lieder*, ed. W. Dürr (Kassel, 1970, 1978).

—— *Die schöne Müllerin, Schwanengesang*, ed. D. Fischer-Dieskau and E. Budde (Frankfurt, New York, 1976).

—— *Die Winterreise*, Op. 89, ed. W. Dürr (Kassel, 1979).

SPOHR, L.: *Sechs deutsche Lieder*, Op. 103, ed. F. O. Leinert (Kassel, 1959, 1971).

—— *Sechs Lieder*, Op. 25, ed. F. O. Leinert (Kassel, 1949).

WEBER, C. M. von: *100 Lieder und Gesänge* (two vols.), ed. F. W. Jähns (Berlin, 1869); *Ausgewählte Lieder* (Leipzig, *c.* 1887).

ZUMSTEEG, J. R.: *Drei Lieder mit Klavier-Begleitung von J. R. Zumsteeg. Als Muster zu Franz Schuberts gleichnamigen Gesänge*, ed. E. Mandyczewski (Leipzig, 1885).

—— *Kleine Balladen und Lieder* (Leipzig, 1800–5, facsimile ed. Farnborough, 1969).

—— *Kleine Balladen und Lieder in Auswahl*, ed. F. Jöde, Nagels Musik-Archiv, no. 82 (Hanover, 1932).

(ii) Books and Articles

(a) General

ALBERTI-RADANOWICZ, EDITHA: 'Das Wiener Lied von 1789–1815', *Studien zur Musikwissenschaft*, v (1918), pp. 37–78.

BÜCKEN, ERNST: *Das deutsche Lied. Probleme und Gestalten* (Hamburg, 1939).

DALTON, DAVID: 'Goethe and the Composers of his Time', *Music Review*, xxxiv (1973), pp. 157–74.

DÜRING, WERNER-JOACHIM: *Erlkönig-Vertonungen, Eine historische und systematische Untersuchung* [1782–1957] (*Kölner Beiträge zur Musikwissenschaft*, lxix) (Regensburg, 1972).

FRIEDLAENDER, MAX: *Das deutsche Lied im 18. Jahrhundert*, 3 vols. (Stuttgart, 1902, repr. Hildesheim, 1970).

GERSTENBERG, WALTER: 'Goethes Dichtung und die Musik', *Bericht über der internationalen musikwissenschaftlichen Kongress, Leipzig 1966*, ed. Carl Dahlhaus *et al.* (Kassel, Leipzig, 1970), pp. 3–11.

GRASBERGER, FRANZ: *Das Lied, Kostbarkeiten der Musik*, i (Tutzing, 1968).

GUDEWILL, KURT: 'Über einige "Töne" von volkstümlichen Liedern, Singspiel- und Opernliedern des ausgehenden 18. und 19. Jahrhunderts', *Anna Amalie Abert zum 65. Geburtstag. Opernstudien*, ed. Klaus Hortschansky (Tutzing, 1975), pp. 103–19.

KRABBE, WILHELM: 'Das deutsche Lied im 17. und 18. Jahrhundert', *Handbuch der Musikgeschichte*, ii, ed. Guido Adler (2nd ed., Berlin, 1930, repr. Tutzing, 1961), pp. 691–703.

KRETZSCHMAR, HERMANN: *Geschichte des neuen deutschen Liedes* (Leipzig, 1911, repr. Hildesheim, Wiesbaden 1966).

MOSER, HANS JOACHIM: *Das deutsche Lied seit Mozart* (Zürich, 1937, 2nd ed. Tutzing, 1968).

MÜLLER, GÜNTHER: *Geschichte des deutschen Liedes vom Zeitalter des Barocks bis zur Gegenwart* (Munich, 1925, repr. Darmstadt, 1959).

MÜLLER-BLATTAU, JOSEPH: *Das Verhältnis von Wort und Ton in der Geschichte der Musik* (Stuttgart, 1952).

PAMER, FRITZ EGON: 'Deutsches Lied im 19. Jahrhundert', *Handbuch der Musikges-chichte*, ii, ed. Guido Adler (2nd ed., Berlin, 1930, repr. Tutzing, 1961), pp. 939–55.

RADCLIFFE, PHILIP: 'Germany and Austria', *A History of Song*, ed. Denis Stevens (London, 1960; New York, 1970), pp. 228–64.

RAUHE, HERMANN: 'Zum volkstümlichen Lied des 19. Jahrhunderts', *Studien zur Trivialmusik des 19. Jahrhunderts*, ed. Carl Dahlhaus (*Studien zur Musikgeschichte des 19. Jahrhunderts*, viii) (Regensburg, 1967), pp. 159–98.

SCHWAB, HEINRICH WILHELM: *Sangbarkeit, Popularität und Kunstlied. Studien zu Lied und Liedästhetik der mittleren Goethezeit 1770–1814* (*Studien zur Musikgeschichte des 19. Jahrhunderts*, iii) (Regensburg, 1965).

STEIN, FRANZ A.: *Verzeichnis der Lieder seit Haydn* (Bern and Munich, 1967).

STEIN, JACK: *Poem and Music in the German Lied from Gluck to Hugo Wolf* (Cambridge, Mass., 1971).

WIORA, WALTER: *Das deutsche Lied: zur Geschichte und Ästhetik einer musikal-ischen Gattung* (Wolfenbüttel and Zürich, 1971).

—— 'Die "Gattung" Lied', *Festschrift für Ernst Hermann Meyer*, ed. Georg Knepler (Leipzig, 1973), pp. 141–50.

(b) Individual Composers

Beethoven

BOETTCHER, HANS: *Beethoven als Liederkomponist* (Augsburg, 1928, repr. Walluf, 1974).

CURZON, HENRI DE: *Les Lieder et airs détachés de Beethoven* (Paris, 1905).

KERMAN, JOSEPH: '"An die ferne Geliebte"', *Beethoven Studies*, i, ed. Alan Tyson (New York and London, 1973), pp. 123–57.

MIES, PAUL: '"Sehnsucht" von Göthe und Beethoven', *Beethoven-Jahrbuch, Zweite Reihe*, ii (1955–6), pp. 112–19.

ORREY, LESLIE: 'The Songs', *The Beethoven Companion* (*Reader*), ed. Denis Arnold and Nigel Fortune (London and New York, 1971), pp. 411–39.

ORTNER, ROMAN: 'Das Liedschaffen Beethovens im Rahmen seines Gesamtwerkes', *Beethoven-Almanach 1970* (Vienna, 1970), pp. 53–9.

POSER, MARTIN: 'Beethoven und das Volksliedgut der Britischen Inseln', *Bericht über den internationalen Beethoven-Kongress 20. bis 23. März 1977 in Berlin*, ed. Harry Goldschmidt *et al.* (Leipzig, 1978), pp. 405–9.

SCHERING, ARNOLD: *Beethoven und die Dichtung* (Berlin, 1936, repr. Hildesheim, New York, 1973).

SCHNEIDER, ANNELIESE: 'Bemerkungen zur Konzeption des Liederkreis, Op. 98, *An die ferne Geliebte*', *Bericht über den internationalen Beethoven-Kongress 10–12 Dezember 1970 in Berlin*, ed. Heinz Brockhaus and Konrad Niemann (Berlin, 1971), pp. 327–32.

Bellini

OEHLMANN, WERNER: *Vincenzo Bellini* (Zürich, 1974).

C. Kreutzer

LANDAU, ANNELIESE: *Das einstimmige Kunstlied Conradin Kreutzers und seine Stellung zum zeitgenössischen Lied in Schwaben* (Leipzig, 1930; repr. Niederwalluf bei Wiesbaden, 1972).

PEAKE, LUISE EITEL: 'Kreutzer's *Wanderlieder*: The Other Winterreise', *Musical Quarterly*, lxv (1979), pp. 88–102.

Loewe

BROWN, MAURICE J. E.: 'Carl Loewe 1796–1869', *Musical Times*, cx (1969), pp. 357–9.

ENGEL, HANS: *Karl Loewe: Überblick und Würdigung seines Schaffens* (Greifswald, 1934).

KLEEMANN, HANS: *Beiträge zur Ästhetik und Geschichte der Loeweschen Ballade* (Halle, 1913).

Reichardt

PAULI, WALTHER: *J. F. Reichardt: sein Leben und seine Stellung in der Geschichte des deutschen Liedes* (Berlin, 1903).

SALMEN, WALTER: *Johann Friedrich Reichardt* (Zürich, 1963).

Schubert

ARMITAGE-SMITH, JULIAN: 'Schubert's *Winterreise*, part I: The Sources of the Musical Text', *Musical Quarterly*, lx (1974), pp. 20–36.

BAUM, GÜNTHER: 'Schubert-Müllers *Winterreise*—neu gesehen', *Neue Zeitschrift für Musik*, cxxviii (1967), pp. 78–80.

BROWN, MAURICE J. E.: *Schubert Songs*, (London, 1969).

CAPELL, RICHARD: *Schubert's Songs* (3rd ed., ed. Martin Cooper, London, 1973).

CHAILLEY, JACQUES: *Le Voyage d'hiver de Schubert* (Paris, 1975).

—— 'Le *Winterreise* de Schubert—est-il une oeuvre ésotérique?', *Revue d'esthétique* (1965), pp. 113–24.

—— 'Le "Winterreise" et l'énigme de Schubert', *Studia musicologica*, xi (1969), pp. 107–12.

DAMIAN, FRANZ VALENTIN: *Franz Schuberts Liederkreis Die schöne Müllerin* (Leipzig, 1928).

DÜRING, WERNER JOACHIM: *Erlkönig-Vertonungen* (*Kölner Beiträge zur Musikforschung*, lxix) (Regensburg, 1972).

EGGEBRECHT, HANS HEINRICH: 'Prinzipien des Schubert-Liedes', *Archiv für Musikwissenschaft*, xxvii (1970), pp. 89–109.

FEIL, ARNOLD: *Franz Schubert: Die schöne Müllerin, Winterreise* (Stuttgart, 1975).

—— 'Zur Genesis der Gattung Lied wie sie Franz Schubert definiert hat', *Muzikološki Zbornik*, xi (1975), pp. 40–53.

FISCHER-DIESKAU, DIETRICH: *Auf den Spuren der Schubert-Lied. Werden, Wesen, Wirkung* (Wiesbaden, 1971), trans. and ed. Kenneth S. Whitton as *Schubert: A Biographical Study of his Songs* (London, 1976).

GEORGIADES, THRASYBULOS G.: *Schubert—Musik und Lyrik* (Göttingen, 1967).

GERSTENBERG, WALTER: 'Der Rahmen der Tonalität im Liede Schuberts', *Musicae Scientiae Collectanea. Festschrift Karl G. Fellerer*, ed. Heinrich Hüschen (Cologne, 1973), pp. 147–55.

GRAY, WALTER: 'The Classical Nature of Schubert's Lieder', *Musical Quarterly*, lvii (1971), pp. 62–72.

HAAS, HERMANN: *Über die Bedeutung der Harmonik in den Liedern Franz Schuberts* (Bonn, 1957).

HOORICKX, REINHOLD van: 'Notes on a Collection of Schubert Songs Copied from Early Manuscripts around 1821–25', *Revue belge de musicologie*, xxii (1968), pp. 86–101.

KINSEY, BARBARA: 'Schubert and the Poems of Ossian', *Music Review*, xxiv (1973), pp. 22–9.

KRAMARZ, JOACHIM: *Das Rezitativ im Liedschaffen Franz Schuberts* (Berlin, 1959).

KRETZSCHMAR, HERMANN: 'Franz Schuberts Müllerlieder', *Gesammelte Aufsätze, i* (Leipzig, 1910, repr. Leipzig, 1973), pp. 36–44.

MARSHALL, H. LOWEN: 'Symbolism in Schubert's "Winterreise"', *Studies in Romanticism*, xii (1973), no. 3, pp. 607–32.

McKAY, ELIZABETH NORMAN: 'Schubert's *Winterreise* Reconsidered', *Music Review*, xxxviii (1977), pp. 94–100.

MIES, PAUL: *Schubert, der Meister des Liedes* (Berlin, 1928).

Moore, Gerald: *The Schubert Song Cycles* (London, 1975).

Neumann, Friedrich: *Musikalische Syntax und Form im Liederzyklus Die schöne Müllerin von Franz Schubert, eine morphologische Studie* (Tutzing, 1978).

Reed, John: '"Die schöne Müllerin" Reconsidered', *Music and Letters*, lix (1978), pp. 411–19.

Sams, Eric: 'Notes on a Magic Flute. The Origins of the Schubertian Lied', *Musical Times*, cix (1978), pp. 947–9.

Schaeffer, Erwin: 'Schubert's "Winterreise"', *Musical Quarterly*, xxiv (1938), pp. 39–57.

Schochow, Maximilian and Lilly, edd.: *Franz Schubert; die Texte seiner einstimmig komponierten Lieder und ihre Dichter*, 2 vols. (Hildesheim and New York, 1974).

Seidel, Elmar: 'Ein chromatisches Harmonisierungsmodell in Schuberts "Winterreise"', *Bericht über den internationalen musikwissenschaftlichen Kongress Leipzig, 1966* ed. Carl Dahlhaus *et al.* (Leipzig and Kassel, 1970), pp. 437–51; slightly alt. in *Archiv für Musikwissenschaft*, xxvi (1969), pp. 285–96.

Steglich, Rudolf: 'Das romantische Wanderlied und Franz Schubert', *Musa— Mens—Musici. Im Gedenken an Walter Vetter*, ed. Heinz Wegener (Leipzig, 1969), pp. 267–76.

Thomas, J. H.: 'Schubert's Modified Strophic Songs with Particular Reference to Schwanengesang', *Music Review*, xxxiv (1973), pp. 83–99.

Thomas, Werner: 'Der "Doppelgänger" von Franz Schubert', *Zur musikalischen Analyse*, ed. Gerhard Schumacher (Darmstadt, 1974), pp. 363–83.

Werba, Erik: 'Historisches und aktuelles zur Interpretation des Schubertliedes', *Österreichische Musikzeitschrift*, xxvii (1972), pp. 194–200.

Spohr

Gorrell, Lorraine: 'The Songs of Louis Spohr', *Music and Letters*, xxxix (1978), pp. 31–8.

Weber

Degen, Max: *Die Lieder von C.M. von Weber* (Basel, 1923).

Zumsteeg

Landshoff, Ludwig: *Johann Rudolf Zumsteeg, ein Beitrag zur Geschichte des Liedes und der Ballade* (Berlin, 1902).

Maier, Gunter: *Die Lieder Johann Rudolf Zumsteegs und ihr Verhältnis zu Schubert* (Göpping, 1971).

Szymichowski, Franz: *Zumsteeg als Komponist von Balladen und Monodien* (Frankfurt, 1932).

The Slav Lands

Bohemia

(i) Modern Editions

(a) *Anthology*

Pohanka, Jaroslav: *Dějiny české hudby v příkladech* (Prague, 1958). (Includes examples by Doležálek, Ryba and Tomášek.)

(b) *Works by Individual Composers*

Tomášek, V. J.: 'Leonore', *Balladen von Gottfried August Bürger in Musik gesetzt*, ed. D. Manicke (*Das Erbe deutscher Musik*, xlvi) (Mainz, 1970).

(ii) Books and Articles

(a) General

ABRAHAM, GERALD: 'Czechoslovakia', *A History of Song*, ed. Denis Stevens (London, 1960; New York, 1970), pp. 181–93.
NETTL, PAUL: 'Schubert's Czech Predecessors', *Music and Letters*, xxiii (1942), pp. 61–8.

(b) Individual Composers

Ryba
NĚMEČEK JAN: *Jakub Jan Ryba: Život a dilo* (Prague, 1963). With thematic catalogue.

Tomášek
TARANTOVÁ, MARIE: *Václav Jan Tomášek* (Prague, 1946).

POLAND

(i) Modern Editions

Works by Individual Composers

CHOPIN, F.: *Fryderyk Chopin. Complete Works*, xvii; *Songs*, ed. I. J. Paderewski *et al.* (Warsaw, 1949).
ELSNER, J.: 'Duma Luidgardy', 'Wieśniaczka', 'Pasterka', in *Józef Elsner*, Alina Nowak-Romanowicz (Cracow, 1957), supplement.
—— 'Życzenia w samotności', in *Z diejów polskiej pieśni solowej*, Jerzy Gabryś and Janina Cybulska (Cracow, 1960), p. 152.

(ii) Books and Articles

(a) General

ABRAHAM, GERALD: 'Poland', *A History of Song*, ed. Denis Stevens (London, 1960; New York, 1970), pp. 323–37.
BARBAG, SEWERYN: 'Polska pieśń artystyczna', *Muzyka polska*, ed. Mateusz Gliński (Warsaw, 1927), pp. 91–107.
BELZA, IGOR: *Istoriya Polskoy Muzïkalnoy Kultury*, ii (Moscow, 1957).
GABRYŚ, JERZY and CYBULSKA, JANINA: *Z diejów polskiej pieśni solowej* (1800-1830) (Cracow, 1960).
JACHIMECKI, ZDZISŁAW: *Muzyka polska w rozwoju historycznym*, i/2 (Cracow, 1951).
NOWAK-ROMANOWICZ, ALINA: 'Muzyka polskiego Oświecenia i wczesnego romantyzmu', *Z dziejów polskiej kultury muzycnej*, ii, ed. Zygmunt M. Szweykowski *et al.* (Cracow, 1966), especially pp. 122–7.
SIMON, ALICJA: *The Polish Songwriters* (Warsaw, 1936).

(b) Individual Composers

Chopin
BARBAG, SEWERYN: *Studium o pieśniach Chopina* (Lvov, 1927).
PRILISAUER, RICHARD: 'Frédéric Chopins "Polnische Lieder"', *Chopin Jahrbuch*, ii (1963), pp. 117–32.
STOOKES, SACHA: 'Chopin the Song-writer', *Monthly Musical Record*, lxxx (1950), pp. 96–9.

Elsner

HERMANN, JOACHIM: *Josef Elsner und die polnische Musik* (Munich, 1969).
NOWAK-ROMANOWICZ, ALINA: *Józef Elsner* (Cracow, 1957).

Kurpiński

POMORSKA, HANNA: *Karol Kurpiński* (Warsaw, 1948).
PRZYBYLSKI, TADEUSZ: *Karol Kurpiński (1785–1857)* (Warsaw, 1975).

Lessel

KRUSZEWSKA-RUDNICKA, HANNA: *Wincenty Lessel* (Cracow, 1968).

RUSSIA

(i) Modern Editions

(a) Anthologies

GINZBURG, S. L., ed.: *Istoriya russkoy muzïki v notnïkh obraztsakh* i (Moscow and
    Leningrad, 1940; 2nd ed. 1968). (Includes songs by Teplov, Trutovsky, Prach,
    Dubyansky, and Kozłowski.) Vol. ii (Moscow and Leningrad, 1949). (Includes
    examples by Kashin, Kozłowski, N. A. and N. S. Titov, Shaposhnikov, and
    Zhilin.) Vol. iii (Moscow and Leningrad, 1952). (Includes examples by Alyabiev
    and Verstovsky.)
LEVASHEVA, OLGA: *Pamyatniki russkovo muzïkal'novo iskusstva*, i, ed. Yury Keldïsh
    (Moscow, 1972). (Includes settings of French poems.)

(b) Works by Individual Composers

ALYABIEV, S. A.: *Izbrannïe romansy i pesni* (Moscow, 1951).
PRACH, I.: *Sobranie narodnïkh russkikh pesen*, ed. V. M. Belyaev (Moscow, 1955).
TEPLOV, G. N.: *Mezhdu delom bezdel'e ili Sobranie pesen s prilozhennïmi tonami na tri
    golosa*, complete in Tamara Livanova, *Russkaya muzïkal'naya kultura XVIII
    veka*, i (Leningrad and Moscow, 1952), pp. 189–245.
TRUTOVSKY, V.: *Sobranie russkikh prostïkh pesen s notami*, ed. V. M. Belyaev (Moscow,
    1953).

(ii) Books and Articles

(a) General

ABRAHAM, GERALD: 'Russia', *A History of Song*, ed. Denis Stevens (London, 1960;
    New York, 1970), pp. 338–75.
KELDÏSH, YURY: 'Das russische Lied vor Glinka', *Report of the 10th Congress of the
    International Musicological Society Ljubljana 1967* (Kassel, 1970), pp. 202–9.
—— *Istoriya russkoy muzïki*, i (Moscow, 1948).
—— *Russkaya muzïka XVIII veka* (Moscow, 1965).
LEVASHEVA, O., KELDÏSH, Y. and KANDINSKY, A., ed.: *Istoriya russkoy muzïki*, i
    (Moscow, 1972).
LIVANOVA, TAMARA: *Russkaya muzïkal'naya kul'tura XVIII veka*, 2 vols. (Leningrad
    and Moscow, 1952–3).
PEKELIS, M. S.: *Istoriya russkoy muzïki*, i (Moscow-Leningrad, 1940; repr. Ann Arbor,
    Mich., 1963).
VASINA-GROSSMAN, V. A.: *Russky klassichesky romans XIX veka* (Moscow, 1956).

(b) Individual Composers

Alyabiev

DOBROKHOTOV, BORIS V.: *Aleksandr Alyab'ev* (Moscow, 1966).
SHTEYNPRESS, B.: *Strantsï iz zhizni A. A. Alyab'eva* (Moscow, 1956).
—— *A. A. Alab'ev v izgnanii* (Moscow, 1959).
TIMOFEEV, GRIGORIY: *A. A. Alyab'ev: ocherk zhizni i tvorchestva* (Moscow, 1912).

Kashin and Zhilin

LEVASHEVA, O. E.: 'Romans i pesnya. A. D. Zhilin, D. N. Kashin', in *Ocherki po Istorii Russkoy Muzïki, 1790–1825*, ed. M. S. Druskin and Yu. V. Keldïsh (Leningrad, 1956), pp. 98–142.

Kozłowski

GRACHEV, P. V.: 'O. A. Kozlovsky', in *Ocherki po Istorii Russkoy Muzïki, 1790–1825*, pp. 168–216.
LEVASHEVA, OLGA: 'Kozlovsky i russky klassitsizm', *Musica antiqua Europae orientalis III: Bydgoszcz 1972*, pp. 825–46.

Verstovsky

DOBROKHOTOV, BORIS V.: *A. N. Verstovsky* (Moscow, 1949).
FINDEIZEN, N. F.: 'Aleksey Nikolaevich Verstovsky', in *Ezhegodnik Imperatorskikh Teatrov* (1896–7), supp. 2, pp. 86–134.

France

Books and Articles

(a) General

COY, ADELHEID: *Die Musik der französischen Revolution. Zur Funktionsbestimmung von Lied und Hymne* (*Musikwissenschaftliche Schriften*, xiii) (Munich-Salzburg, 1978).
GOUGELOT, HENRI: *La Romance française sous la Révolution et l'Empire*, 2 vols. (Melun, 1938 and 1943).
NAUDIN, MARIE: *Évolution parallèle de la poésie et de la musique en France: Rôle unificateur de la chanson* (Paris, 1968).
PIERRE, CONSTANT: *Les Hymnes et chansons de la Révolution* (Paris, 1904).
TIERSOT, JULIEN: *Histoire de la chanson populaire en France* (Paris, 1889, repr. Geneva, 1978).

(b) Individual Composers

Boieldieu

FAVRE, GEORGES: *Boieldieu: sa vie, son oeuvre*, ii (Paris, 1945).

Méhul

POUGIN, ARTHUR: *Méhul: sa vie, son génie, son caractère* (Paris, 1889, repr. Geneva, 1973).

CHAPTER XIII

CHORAL MUSIC

(i) Modern Editions

(a) Anthologies

MASSENKEIL, GÜNTHER, comp.: *Das Oratorium* (*Das Musikwerk*, xxxvii) (Cologne, 1970; English edition 1970). (Includes examples by Beethoven, Gossec, Le Sueur, and Fr. Schneider.)

OSTHOFF, HELMUTH: *Das deutsche Chorlied vom 16. Jahrhundert bis zur Gegenwart* (*Das Musikwerk*, x) (Cologne, n.d., English edition 1955). (Includes examples by Reichardt, Schubert, and Zelter.)

PIERRE, CONSTANT: *Musique des fêtes et cérémonies de la Révolution française* (Paris, 1899).

RADIGUER, HENRI: 'La musique française de 1789 à 1815', *Encyclopédie de la musique et dictionnaire du Conservatoire*, ed. Lionel de La Laurencie and Albert Lavignac, i/3 (Paris, 1921), pp. 1562–1660. (Includes hymns by Catel, Cherubini, Gossec, and Le Sueur.)

STEPHENSON, KURT, ed.: *Romantik in der Tonkunst* (Cologne, 1961, English edition 1961). (Includes examples by Loewe, Nägeli, and Schubert.)

WARREN, EDMUND THOMAS: *A Collection of Catches, Canons and Glees*, 4 vols., introd. Emanuel Rubin, Malcolm A. Nelson (London, 1762–93; facsimile ed. Wilmington, Delaware, 1970).

(b) Works by Individual Composers

BEETHOVEN, L. van: *L. van Beethovens Werke: Vollständige kritisch durchgesehene überall berechtigte Ausgabe* (Leipzig, 1862–5), series xix/1–3: *Kirchenmusik*; series xxi: *Cantaten*; series xxii: *Gesänge mit Orchester*: incl. Opp. 116, 121b, 122, 118; series xxv: *Supplement. Gesang-Musik*, nos. 264–85.

—— *Supplemente zur Gesamtausgabe*, ed. W. Hess: v: *Lieder und Gesänge mit Klavierbegleitung, Kanons und musikalische Scherze* (Wiesbaden, 1962).

—— *Bundeslied*, Op. 122, ed. K. Etti (*Diletto musicale*, cccliiviii) (Vienna, 1970).

—— *Drei Skizzenbücher zur Missa Solemnis*, ed. J. Schmidt-Görg (Bonn, 1952).

—— *Kniga eskizov Beethovens za 1802–3 gody*, facsimile and transcriptions ed. N. Fishman, 3 vols (Moscow, 1962). (Includes sketches for *Christus am Ölberg*.)

—— *Missa solemnis, Kyrie*, facsimile ed. (holograph), ed. W. Virneisel (Tutzing, 1965).

CHERUBINI, L.: Mass no. 2 in D minor, vocal score (London, c. 1870)

—— Mass no. 3 (Coronation Mass) in A, full score (Paris, 1825).

—— Mass no. 4 in C, vocal score (London, c. 1870)

—— Requiem in C minor, ed. R. Lück (Frankfurt and New York, 1964); vocal score ed. G. Confalonieri (Milan, 1946).

—— Requiem in D minor, ed. R. Lück (London and New York, 1962).

GOSSEC, F.-J.: Various hymns and choruses, in Adelheid Coy, *Die Musik der französischen Revolution. Zur Funktionsbestimmung von Lied und Hymne* (*Musikwissenschaftliche Schriften*, xiii) (Munich and Salzburg, 1978).

SCHUBERT, F.: *Franz Schuberts Werke: Kritisch durchgesehene Gesammtausgabe* (Leipzig, 1884–97, repr. New York, 1965): series xiii: *Messen*, ed. E. Mandyczewski (1887); series xiv: *Kleinere Kirchenmusikwerke*, ed. E. Mandyczewski (1888); series xvi: *Für Männerchor*, ed. E. Mandyczewski (1891); series xvii: *Für gemischten Chor*, ed. J. Gänsbacher and E. Mandyczewski (1892); series xviii: *Für Frauenchor*, ed. J. Gänsbacher and E. Mandyczewski (1891);

series xix: *Kleinere drei- und zweistimmige Gesangwerke*, ed. J. Gänsbacher and
    E. Mandyczewski (1892); series xxi: *Supplement. Gesang-Musik*, nos. 32–44, ed.
    E. Manyczewski (1897).
—— *Franz Schubert. Neue Ausgabe sämtlicher Werke*, series iii/4: *Mehrstimmige
    Gesänge für gleiche Stimmen ohne Begleitung*, ed. D. Berke (Kassel, 1974).
—— *Deutsche Messe*, D. 872, ed. F. Burkhardt (Vienna, 1977).
—— *Lazarus*, compl. and ed. P. White, vocal score (New York, 1978).
—— Magnificat in C, D. 486, ed. O. Biba (*Musica sacra des 19. Jahrhunderts*, i)
    (Altötting, 1977).
—— Mass in A flat, D. 678, ed. D. Finke-Hecklinger, 2 vols. (Kassel, 1980)
—— Mass in C, D. 452, vocal score ed. U. Haverkampf (Wiesbaden, 1972).
SPOHR, L. Mass in C, Op. 54, ed. O. Biba (*Musica sacra des 19. Jahrhunderts*, ii)
    (Altötting, 1977).
—— *Die letzten Dinge* (*The Last Judgment*), (London, *c.* 1881).
WEBER, C. M. von: Mass in E flat (London, *c.* 1870).
—— Mass in A flat (London, *c.* 1870)
—— *Jubilee Cantata* (English text from the second libretto, *Ernte Cantate*, by
    Amadeus Wendt) (London, *c.* 1870).
WESLEY, S.: *Confitebor tibi, Domine*, ed. J. Marsh (*Musica Britannica*, xli) (London,
    1978).
—— 'Sing Aloud with Gladness'; *A Treasury of English Church Music*, iv: 1760–1900,
    ed. G. H. Knight and W. L. Reed (London, 1965).

(ii) Books and Articles

(a) General

BLUME, FRIEDRICH, ed.: *Geschichte der evangelischen Kirchenmusik* (2nd ed., Kassel,
    1965); trans. and expanded as *Protestant Church Music: A History* (New York,
    1974).
BURBACH, HERMANN-JOSEPH: 'Das "triviale" in der katholischen Kirchenmusik des
    19. Jahrhunderts', *Studien zur Trivialmusik*, ed. Carl Dahlhaus (*Studien zur
    Musikgeschichte im 19. Jahrhundert*, viii), pp. 71–82.
COY, ADELHEID: *Die Musik der französischen Revolution. Zur Funktionsbestimmung
    von Lied und Hymne* (*Musikwissenschaftliche Schriften*, xiii) (Munich and
    Salzburg, 1978).
DONAKOWSKI, CONRAD L.: *A Muse for the Masses: Ritual and Music in an Age of
    Dramatic Revolution, 1770–1870* (Chicago, 1977).
FELLERER, KARL: 'Das deutsche Chorlied im 19. Jahrhundert', *Gattungen der Musik
    in Einzeldarstellungen: Gedenkschrift für Leo Schrade*, ed. Wulf Arlt *et al.* (Bern
    and Munich, 1973), pp. 785–812.
—— *Geschichte der katholischen Kirchenmusik* (2nd ed., Düsseldorf, 1949), trans.
    Francis A. Brunner as *The History of Catholic Church Music* (Baltimore, 1961).
FOSTER, DONALD H.: 'The Oratorio in Paris in the 18th Century', *Acta musicologica*,
    xlvii (1975), pp. 119–33.
GECK, MARTIN: *Deutsche Oratorien, 1800 bis 1840, Verzeichnis der Quellen und
    Aufführungen* (*Quellen-Kataloge zur Musikgeschichte*, iv) (Wilhelmshaven, 1971).
—— *Die Wiederentdeckung der Matthäus Passion im 19. Jahrhundert. Die zeitgenös-
    sischen Dokumente und ihre Ideengeschichtliche Deutung* (*Studien zur Musikges-
    chichte des 19. Jahrhunderts*, ix) (Regensburg, 1967).
KRABBE, WILHELM: 'Chormusik (Lied und kleinere Chorwerke)', *Handbuch der
    Musikgeschichte*, ii, ed. Guido Adler (2nd ed., Berlin, 1930, repr. Tutzing, 1961),
    pp. 955–63.

KRUMMACHER, FRIEDHELM: 'Kunstreligion und religiöse Musik. Zur ästhetischen Problematick geistlicher Musik im 19. Jahrhundert', *Die Musikforschung*, xxxii (1979), pp. 365–93.

MONGRÉDIEN, JEAN: 'La musique du sacre de Napoléon Ier', *Revue de musicologie*, liii (1967), pp. 137–74.

MOSER, HANS-JOACHIM: *Die evangelische Kirchenmusik in Deutschland* (Berlin-Darmstadt, 1954).

PIERRE, CONSTANT: *Les Hymnes et chansons de la Révolution* (Paris, 1904).

RADIGUER, HENRI: 'La musique française de 1789 à 1815', *Encyclopédie de la musique et dictionnaire du Conservatoire*, ed. Lionel de La Laurencie and Albert Lavignac, i/3 (Paris, 1921), pp. 1562–1660.

ROBERTSON, ALEC: *Requiem: Music of Mourning and Consolation* (London, 1967; New York, 1968).

SCHERING, ARNOLD: *Geschichte des Oratoriums* (Leipzig, 1911, repr. Wiesbaden, 1966).

SCHNOOR, HANS: 'Das Oratorium vom Ende des 18. Jahrhunderts bis 1800', *Handbuch der Musikgeschichte*, ii, ed. Guido Adler (2nd ed., Berlin, 1930, repr. Tutzing, 1961), pp. 927–39.

URSPRUNG, OTTO: *Die katholische Kirchenmusik* (*Handbuch der Musikwissenschaft*, ix) (Wildpark-Potsdam, 1931, repr. New York, 1949).

VALENTIN, ERICH, ed.: *Handbuch der Chormusik*, 2 vols. (Regensburg, 1953–8).

WIORA, WALTER, ed.: *Religiöse Musik in nichtliturgischen Werken von Beethoven bis Reger* (*Studien zur Musikgeschichte des 19. Jahrhunderts*, li) (Regensburg, 1978).

(*b*) *Individual Composers*

Beethoven

ETTI, KARL: 'Beethoven und der Männerchor', *Beethoven-Almanach 1970* (Vienna, 1970), pp. 49–52.

GEORGIADES, THRASYBULOS G.: 'Zu den Satzschlüssen der Missa solemnis', *Bericht über den musikwissenschaftlichen Kongress Bonn 1970* (Kassel, 1971), pp. 37–42.

FELLERER, KARL: 'Beethoven und die liturgische Musik seiner Zeit', *Beethoven-Symposium Wien 1970*, ed. Erich Schenk (Vienna, 1971), pp. 61–76.

FORBES, ELLIOT: 'Beethoven as a Choral Composer', *Proceedings of the Royal Musical Association*, xcvii (1970–1), pp. 69–82.

GERSON-KIWI, EDITH: 'Beethoven's Sacred Drama—a Re-evaluation', *Bericht über den internationalen musikwissenschaftlichen Kongress Bonn 1970* (Kassel, 1971), pp. 402–5.

HESS, WILLY: *Beethoven Studien* (Vienna, 1972), pp. 169–75, 176–8, 232–62. (On Choral Fantasia, Missa solemnis.)

KIRKENDALE, WARREN: 'New Roads to Old Ideas in Beethoven's *Missa solemnis*', *Musical Quarterly*, lvi (1970), pp. 665–701; slightly emended as 'Beethovens *Missa solemnis* und die rhetorische Tradition', *Beethoven-Symposium Wien 1970*, ed. Erich Schenk (Vienna, 1971), pp. 121–58.

KLEIN, RUDOLPH: 'Die Struktur von Beethovens Missa Solemnis', *Erich Valentin zum 70. Geburtstag*, ed. Günther Weiss (Regensburg, 1976), pp. 89–107.

LARSEN, JENS PETER: 'Beethovens C-dur Messe und die Spätmessen Joseph Haydns', *Beethoven-Kolloquium 1977, Beiträge '76–78*, ed. Rudolf Klein (Kassel, 1978), pp. 12–19.

LESTER, JOEL: 'Revisions in the Autograph of the *Missa solemnis* Kyrie', *Journal of the American Musicological Society*, xxiii (1970), pp. 420–38.

SCHMIDT-GÖRG, JOSEPH: 'Missa solemnis. Beethoven in seinem Werk', *Bericht über den internationalen musikwissenschaftlichen Kongress Bonn 1970* (Kassel, 1971), pp. 13–25.

SPARBER, MARGARETE: 'Stimmtechnik am Beispiel von Beethovens Messe in C-dur op. 86', *Beethoven-Almanach 1970* (Vienna, 1970), pp. 183–7.
TYSON, ALAN: 'The 1803 Version of Beethoven's *Christus am Oelberge*', *Musical Quarterly*, lvi (1970), pp. 551–84.

Cherubini
ALBERTI, LUCIANO: 'I tempi e i modi della produzione sacra di Luigi Cherubini', *Luigi Cherubini nel II centenario della nascita*, ed. Adelmo Damerini (Florence, 1962), pp. 70–92.
CONFALONIERI, GIULIO: 'Il "Credo" a otto voci di Cherubini', *Chigiana*, xxiii (1966), new series, iii, pp. 265–82.
DEANE, BASIL: *Cherubini* (London, 1965).
HOHENEMSER, R. H.: *Luigi Cherubini, sein Leben und seine Werke* (Leipzig, 1913).

Grétry
QUINTIN, JOSÉ: 'Les compositions de musique religieuse d'André Modeste Grétry', *Revue belge de musicologie*, xviii (1964), pp. 57–69.

Le Sueur
HERMAN, MARTIN M.: 'The Turbulent Career of Jean-François Le Sueur, maître de chapelle, I', *Recherches sur la musique française classique*, ix (1969), pp. 187–215.
SEVIÈRES, GEORGES: *Les Oratorios de J.-F. Le Sueur* (Paris, 1914).

F. Schneider
LOMNITZER, HELMUT: *Das musikalische Werk Friedrich Schneiders (1786–1853), insbesondere die Oratorien*, 2 vols. (Marburg, 1961).

Schubert
BROWN, MAURICE J. E.: 'Lazarus or the Feast of Resurrection', *Essays on Schubert* (London and New York, 1966, repr. New York, 1978), pp. 101–24.
BURKHART, FRANZ: 'Franz Schuberts "Deutsche Messe"', *Österreichische Musikzeitschrift*, xxxi (1976), pp. 565–73.
KELDORFER, VIKTOR: 'Schuberts Chorschaffen', *Österreichische Musikzeitschrift*, xiii (1958), pp. 257–61.
NIEMEYER, ANNEMARIE: 'Franz Schuberts "Lazarus"-Fragment und seine Beziehung zur Textdichtung', *Bericht über den internationalen musikwissenschaftlichen Kongress Leipzig 1966*, ed. Carl Dahlhaus *et al.* (Kassel, Leipzig, 1970), pp. 300–5.
ROSENTHAL, C. A. and LOFT, ABRAM: 'Church and Choral Music', *The Music of Schubert*, ed. Gerald Abraham (New York, 1947).

Spontini
FELLERER, KARL: 'Gasparo Spontini und die Kirchenmusikreform', *Festschrift für Walter Wiora zum 30. Dezember 1966*, ed. Ludwig Finscher and Christoph-Hellmut Mahling (Kassel, 1967), pp. 427–34.

Weber
WARRACK, JOHN: *Carl Maria von Weber* (London and New York, 1968).

S. Wesley
SCHWARZ, JOHN I., JR.: 'Samuel and Samuel Sebastian Wesley, the English Doppelmeister', *Musical Quarterly*, lix (1973), pp. 190–206.
TEMPERLEY, NICHOLAS: 'Samuel Wesley', *Musical Times*, cvii (1966), pp. 108–10.

INDEX

compiled by Frederick Smyth

Page numbers in **bold** type indicate the more important references; *italic* figures denote illustrations or their captions.
Operas and other stage works are indexed under composers and librettists, the latter being identified as such.